Jamestown Colony

Jamestown Colony

A Political, Social, and Cultural History

Frank E. Grizzard, Jr.
D. Boyd Smith

ABC-CLIO

Santa Barbara, California • Denver, Colorado • Oxford, England

Library of Congress Cataloging-in-Publication Data
Grizzard, Frank E.
Jamestown Colony : a political, social, and cultural history / Frank E. Grizzard, Jr., D. Boyd Smith.
p. cm.
Includes bibliographical references and index.
ISBN-10: 1-85109-637-X (hardcover : alk. paper)
ISBN-10: 1-85109-642-6 (e-book)
ISBN-13: 978-1-85109-637-4 (hardcover : alk. paper)
ISBN-13: 978-1-85109-642-8 (e-book)
1. Jamestown (Va.)—History—17th Century—Encyclopedias. 2. Virginia—History—Colonial period, ca. 1600–1775—Encyclopedias. I. Smith, D. Boyd. II. Title.

F234.J3G75 2007
973.2'1—dc22 2006037359

11 10 09 08 07 10 9 8 7 6 5 4 3 2 1

This book is also available on the World Wide Web as an eBook. Visit abc-clio.com for details.

ABC-CLIO, Inc.
130 Cremona Drive, P.O. Box 1911
Santa Barbara, California 93116-1911

Production Editor	Vicki Moran
Editorial Assistant	Alisha Martinez
Production Manager	Don Schmidt
Media Editor	Julie Dunbar
Image Coordinator	Ellen Dougherty
Media Manager	Caroline Price
File Manager	Paula Gerard

This book is printed on acid-free paper. ♾
Manufactured in the United States of America

To the memory of my parents, Boyd and Gladys Smith,
Always loved, never forgotten,

and

To the long-forgotten Grizzards,
who settled near Jamestown in the seventeenth century

Contents

Sidebars

Acknowledgments

THE AUTHORS WOULD LIKE to thank D. Alan Williams, Professor Emeritus of History at the University of Virginia, for his valuable history of Jamestown in its formative years, which serves as the introduction to this volume. Thanks are also due to Rick Britton, author and cartographer, for his essay on the Monacan Indians, adapted herein as an entry on the same subject; to Rob Bolling, Park Historian at the Fort Raleigh National Historic Site on Roanoke Island, North Carolina, for clarifying certain aspects of what is known about the early English attempts at settlement there; to Dr. Alex Mikaberidze, submissions editor; Vicki Moran, senior production editor; April Wells-Hayes, copy editor; Julie Dunbar, senior media editor; and Bill Nelson, cartographer, for their assistance, patience, and professionalism in seeing this volume through the editorial process; and to Alicia Merritt, former senior acquisitions editor at ABC-CLIO, who first expressed an interest in this project. Thank you to Ivor Noël Hume for providing the nautical woodcut used on section opening pages of the book. Of inestimable value also was Mr. Smith's attendance at the Jamestown Archaeological Field School, led by William M. Kelso, Director of Archaeology at the Jamestown Rediscovery project. Working at the fort site—arguably the most important archaeological dig in America—proved a truly memorable and valuable learning experience, largely because of Mr. Kelso's vision, energy, and direction. The opportunity to walk and work on the same ground, and to be the first to see and touch artifacts last handled by the original Jamestown colonists, produces emotions that defy description. In addition to appreciation for the privilege of Mr. Smith's attending the Field School and the benefit derived therefrom by the authors, thanks are also in order to Mr. Kelso for the subsequent award of an internship in archaeology to Mr. Smith.

In addition, Mr. Smith thanks the Elizabethan Inn in Manteo on Roanoke Island and the Woodlands Hotels and Suites in Colonial Williamsburg, which provided comfortable and quiet accommodations for researching and writing at those locations, and Donny Smith, his brother, for the use of his farm near Jamestown during writing and archaeological work at the fort site. He also expresses appreciation to his friends and mentors at the Papers of George

Washington, W. W. Abbot, Dorothy Twohig, and Philander D. Chase, all former editors in chief, and co-author Frank Grizzard, former senior associate editor, who provided the opportunity to participate in this exciting project. Mr. Abbot, who wrote for the 350th Anniversary Celebration of Jamestown *A Virginia Chronology 1585–1783* (Williamsburg, 1957), has been particularly inspiring. Finally, Mr. Smith expresses his deep, heartfelt appreciation to his parents, who provided a happy, loving, and safe home environment about one mile (as the crow flies) from Jamestown Island. No place could have been better to instill and nourish in a child an appreciation for our nation's rich heritage.

A Note about Sources

THE AUTHORS OF THIS BOOK gratefully acknowledge having stood on the shoulders of many fine writers, editors, and historians who in their turn have sifted through the rich documentary history related to the founding of Jamestown and Virginia. Although many have long since ceased their labors, their scholarship lives on, and their names appear numerous times in the Suggested Readings and in the Bibliography of this volume. Because the primary source material surrounding the Jamestown colony has been published so many times, in so many versions, across such a span of time, the authors have not scrupled to provide citations for the many quotations given in the texts of the entries, when those quotations are in the public domain or have been transcribed by the authors from manuscript. Of particular use in this regard are the following titles: Charles M. Andrews, ed., *Narratives of the Insurrections, 1675–1690* (New York, 1915); Edward Arber, ed., *Travels and Works of Captain John Smith* (Edinburgh, Scotland, 1910); Robert Beverley, *The History of Virginia, in Four Parts* (Richmond, Virginia, 1855); Alexander Brown, *The Genesis of the United States* (Boston, 1890); William Waller Hening, *The Statutes at Large, being a Collection of All the Laws of Virginia from the First Session of the Legislature, in the Year 1619* (New York and Philadelphia, 1823); Susan Myra Kingsbury, ed., *The Records of The Virginia Company of London* (Washington, D.C., 1933, 1935); and Edward D. Neill, *History of the Virginia Company of London, with Letters to and from the First Colony Never Before Printed* (Albany, New York, 1869). In most instances, a close reading of the entry will lead a so-inclined reader to the particular source quoted. Finally, the sixteenth- and seventeenth-century usage of *u* and *v* and *i* and *j* has been modernized, and square brackets within quotation marks represent editorial insertions.

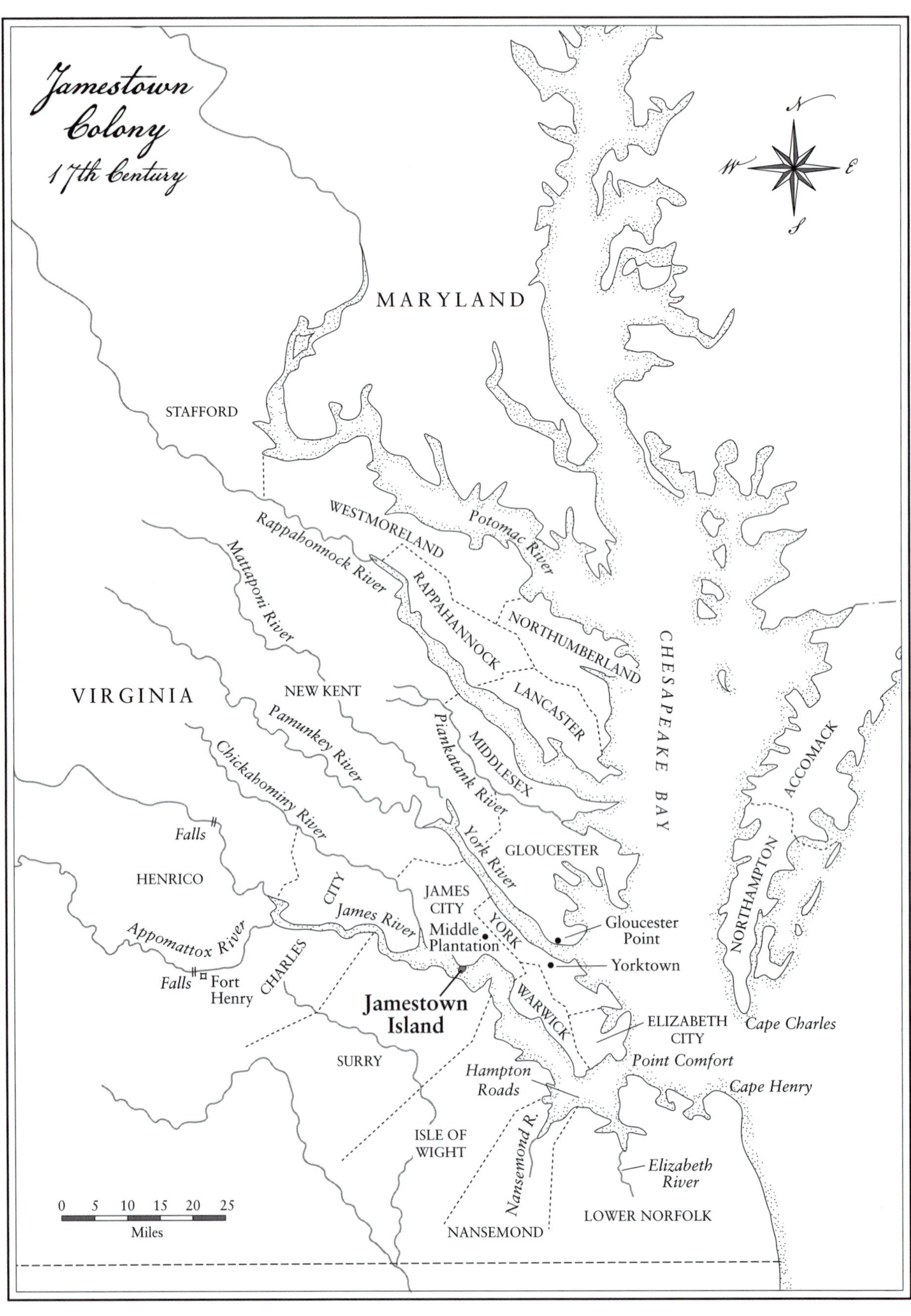

Jamestown Colony 17th Century
N
W
E
S
MARYLAND
STAFFORD
WESTMORELAND
Potomac River
Rappahonnock River
RAPPAHANNOCK
Mattaponi River
NORTHUMBERLAND
CHESAPEAKE BAY
LANCASTER
VIRGINIA
NEW KENT
Pamunkey River
Piankatank River
MIDDLESEX
ACCOMACK
Chickahominy River
York River
GLOUCESTER
Falls
HENRICO
NORTHAMPTON
JAMES CITY
CITY
James River
Middle Plantation
YORK
Gloucester Point
Appomattox River
Yorktown
Falls
Fort Henry
CHARLES
WARWICK
Jamestown Island
ELIZABETH CITY
Cape Charles
Point Comfort
SURRY
Hampton Roads
Cape Henry
ISLE OF WIGHT
Nansemond R.
Elizabeth River
0 5 10 15 20 25
Miles
LOWER NORFOLK
NANSEMOND

Introduction

D. Alan Williams

I. The Founding of Virginia

In April 1606, Englishmen once again took up their quest to plant an English society in the New World. It was an auspicious time. Peace with Spain ended a generation of wars, armadas, insurrections, and privateering. A succession of crop failures, storms, plagues, and domestic riots gave way to prosperity. And the political uncertainty aroused by the death of Elizabeth Tudor abated as the Scotsman James VI thwarted his rivals and consolidated power as the first Stuart. Although James I had no grand economic scheme, or even an abiding interest in trade and commerce, he did have the good sense to follow those so inclined—the great merchants of London, the national-minded nobles, and the gentry adventurers, the men who together planted Virginia.

It was not ordained, or even desired, by Englishmen that the first colony should be along the Chesapeake Bay. That region came to them almost by default. Spanish and Portuguese colonizers and traders had captured the preferred lands and islands of the Caribbean and South America, finding there advanced Indian civilizations, hoards of wealth, and a tropical climate capable of producing goods deemed necessary to national economic independence. Other Europeans already had abandoned the North American coast before the first feeble English probes. Thousands of Spaniards died following Ponce de León, Hernando de Soto, and Pedro Menendez into the Florida and Carolina wildernesses; in 1570, Jesuit missionaries perished farther north, perhaps inside the Chesapeake capes; only the isolated posts at St. Elena and St. Augustine remained. By 1580, the Spanish could confirm the warning of Peter Martyr—"To the South: . . . they that seek riches must not go into the cold and frozen North." The French tried both: to the North with Jacques Cartier along the St. Lawrence in the 1530s and 1540s, and to the South with Huguenots Jean Ribault and Rene Laudonniere at Port Royal in South Carolina and Fort Caroline in Florida in the 1560s. They, too, failed.

Certainly Martyr's stricture seemed correct to the English after Sir Humphrey Gilbert and most of his Bristol associates drowned returning from

Sir Francis Drake (c. 1540–1596)

Navigator, privateer, ship captain, and eventually vice admiral, Sir Francis Drake of Otterton spent his life at sea. His pirating voyages took him to all parts of the world, and between 1577 and 1580 he became the first captain to completely circumnavigate the globe, claiming the Pacific coast of North America for England along the way.

After a five-week harbor in present-day Washington or Oregon to make repairs to his ship, the *Golden Hind,* Drake sailed due west into the vast uncharted Pacific. After 68 days he reached Indonesia, and from there he crossed the Indian Ocean and rounded the Cape of Good Hope. By the time his three-year voyage ended with his arrival back in England in the fall of 1580, Drake had sailed some 36,000 miles.

Queen Elizabeth knighted him for the exploit. His raids against Spanish vessels earned Drake the title of *El Draque* (The Dragon), and in 1588 he was second in command of the English naval fleet that defeated the Spanish Armada. In 1586, Drake took back to England the perishing colonists of Roanoke Island, who had tried to establish the first permanent English presence in the New World. He died near Porto Bello while commanding a voyage and was buried at sea in the Gulf of Mexico.

Sir Francis Drake, an English privateer, naval commander, and explorer of the Elizabethan era. He was the first Englishman to circumnavigate the globe and was second in command of the English fleet that defeated the Spanish Armada in 1588. (Ellyson, J. Taylor. The London Company of Virginia, *1908)*

Newfoundland in 1583. Even the South became suspect when Sir Walter Raleigh, Ralph Lane, and John White failed on the Carolina Outer Banks a few years later.

Elizabethan merchants and adventurers shied away from colonizing America. They were more intrigued with the successes enjoyed by the Muscovy Company in northern Europe and the Levant Company in the Near East, with establishing regular trade with Spain and the Low Countries, or by Martin Frobisher's quest for an arctic passage to the Far East. Ambitious gentry saw greater opportunities closer to home through suppressing recalcitrant Irish tribal lords and sequestering their lands. Those Englishmen who did envision New World opportunities ignored the North American coast for the Caribbean Sea. There,

John Hawkins, Francis Drake, and other would-be traders tried to penetrate the mercantilist cordon Spain threw around her Caribbean trade. Rebuffed, they settled instead for spectacular freebooting ventures as Sea Dog privateers on the Spanish Main in the 1570s and 1580s.

Piracy and privateering for the glory of England, the destruction of Catholic Spain, and personal wealth were the principal attractions to early English overseas investors. In fact, they were necessary ingredients in all early stock company ventures. Privateering offered hope for quick infusions of capital and a hedge against personal failures. Of the estimated £8,000,000 invested in overseas joint-stock companies between 1575 and 1630, almost £4,000,000 went into privateering syndicates, much of it between 1575 and 1605. Several colonizing ventures, including Raleigh's Roanoke, may have been lost because ship captains went after Spanish treasure ships rather than supplies. Still, it is with Raleigh and Roanoke that Virginia began.

Sir Walter Raleigh combined the experience and character that recur among backers of the Virginia ventures: the daring of West Country sea captains like John Hawkins, Francis Drake, John Davis, and Richard Grenville; a harshness derived from planting English society by the sword in Ireland shared with Ferdinando Gorges, Ralph Lane, Sir John Popham, the Earl of Southampton, and Lord De La Warr; and the unpredictable but potentially rewarding life of a courtier. Born about 1552 into an impecunious Devon gentry family, Raleigh early was aware of Plymouth and Bristol fishing voyages into the North Atlantic, the value of a military career in Ireland, and the fortunes to be made harassing the Spaniards. His half brother, Humphrey Gilbert, had done them all, although none well. However, the handsome, intelligent, ambitious, confidently arrogant, and "damnable proud" Raleigh opted to live by his wits as a courtier. After brief stints studying at Oxford and soldiering in France, he joined Gilbert in 1578 for a sortie along the New England–Newfoundland coast (Gilbert was always vague about the final destination of his voyages). Instead, Raleigh and his crew ended up in the West Indies futilely looking for stragglers from the Spanish treasure fleet. In 1580, he turned to Ireland and won public notice when his troops slaughtered an Irish garrison at Smerwick. Back in London, he gained the attention first of court officials and then of Elizabeth herself. Marks of the queen's favor soon followed—preferments, trade licenses, a seat in Parliament, pensions, knighthood, aid for Gilbert's abortive voyage in 1583, and the acquisition of Gilbert's claim to settlement rights in America. The years of the Roanoke voyages were the years of Raleigh's ascendance at Court. Only connections with London merchants were missing from his experience.

The times were ripe for challenging the Spanish along the southern coast. English nationalism swelled in response to the covert, treasonous, and inept Spanish efforts to replace Elizabeth with Mary Queen of Scots. Popular demands for Mary's head and for driving the Spanish from the Dutch Netherlands raised anti-Catholic and anti-Spanish feeling to a feverish pitch. An English colony in America would be a direct challenge to Spanish territorial claims and a base for attacking the Spanish New World treasures.

Raleigh carefully planned a three-stage settlement: exploration for a site, then a military expedition to gain a foothold, and finally the establishment of English town society, including traders, craftsmen, priests, husbandmen, soldiers, women, and children.

Sir Walter Raleigh orders the standard of Queen Elizabeth I to be erected on the Virginia coastline in 1585. (Library of Congress)

In early 1584, he dispatched Plymouth sea captains Philip Amadas, Arthur Barlowe, and Portuguese pilot Simon Fernandez, a veteran of the Gilbert voyages, on a reconnaissance mission. They chose Roanoke Island inside the Carolina Outer Banks for the settlement site. Overcome by the summer warmth and the lushness of the land, Barlowe exclaimed, "I think in all the world the like abundance is not to be found." Beguiled by friendly Indians, Amadas and Barlowe took several back to England with them, not knowing that these Indians represented a weak tribe decimated by disease. They ignored the absence of a good harbor and were unaware of the vicious hurricanes and treacherous currents that track the Hatteras coast in other seasons. Raleigh then commissioned Richard Hakluyt to draw up a plan for a full colony and submitted it to the queen. She approved Hakluyt's *Discourse of Western Planting* (1584); Parliament confirmed Raleigh's right to the land; Elizabeth knighted Sir Walter; and he, or she, or both together, named the land Virginia.

In April 1585, Sir Richard Grenville departed with a fleet of 7 ships carrying perhaps 100 men, mostly veteran soldiers. This was a military expedition commanded by Captain Ralph Lane, another veteran of the Irish wars. Not until late July did Lane and Grenville agree where they ought to build their fort on Roanoke Island. Grenville left the colonizers, sailed into the West Indies, captured a Spanish merchant ship, and reached Plymouth in September with enough booty to pay off the investors.

Lane was less successful. The season was too far advanced for planting, and his supplies quickly ran low. His soldiers, who proved adept at building strong forts and exploring rivers and bays, including the Chesapeake, knew only the soldiers' way to secure food—by confiscation and foraging. The Roanoke Indians, an Algonquin tribe, retaliated and attacked Lane's contingent on numerous occasions. In the autumn, Lane sent a squad of men northward to winter along the Chesapeake Bay. Learning that they had fared well, Lane determined to move the whole colony to the Chesapeake once Sir Richard Grenville delivered the spring supplies. But Grenville was delayed. In the meantime, Sir Francis Drake, racing up the Florida coast after sacking several Spanish West Indian ports, stopped by the colony. He offered a ship, men, and supplies for the Chesapeake removal. Lane hesitated. Then a terrifying June storm swept over the Outer Banks, sank the ship, and forced Lane to return home with Drake, missing Grenville by only days. Grenville, uncertain of Lane's fate, immediately sailed off to try his luck on the Spanish Main. Unaccountably, he left fifteen men, expecting them to hold the fort until another expedition arrived. None of them was ever found again.

Far from discouraged, Raleigh looked upon the Lane–Grenville voyages as extensions of the Amadas–Barlowe explorations. He had lost few men and no money. In fact, Grenville's privateering probably turned him a profit. The positive experience of Lane's men convinced everyone that the future lay not along the Outer Banks but inside the Chesapeake capes. John White's magnificent drawings of Virginia flora, fauna, and Indians, the preliminary reports by the scientist Thomas Hariot, the public display in London of the gentle Indian chief Manteo, and the riches seized by Grenville's freebooting operations all elicited enthusiastic responses. Raleigh had no difficulty mounting a new expedition for 1587.

In marked contrast to the 1586 military expedition, Raleigh's third venture included men, women, and children. The time was at hand to found a true colony of Englishmen, "the Citie of Raleigh in Virginia." Raleigh, at the behest of Hakluyt, ordered John White and the colonists to stop by Roanoke Island, pick up Grenville's men, and then proceed to the Chesapeake. Instead, Simon Fernandez deposited the whole company at Roanoke and went off privateering. Desperate for supplies, Governor White sailed off to England in a tiny pinnace, leaving behind his daughter and her baby, Virginia Dare, the first America-born English child.

Raleigh tried valiantly throughout 1588 to resupply his colony. He could not. Short of funds, he divided his grant into three shares: one for himself, one for White and the Virginia settlers, and one for a new set of investors, London merchants led by Thomas Smythe. Translated into gentry–merchants–colonists, this same combination in 1609 was to underwrite the long-term refinancing, resettlement, and salvation of Jamestown. However, in 1589 Raleigh's backers were willing to underwrite only a single voyage. This was not enough. Bad luck, leaky ships, and the aftermath of the Spanish Armada prevented Raleigh from sending out White until August 1590. The governor found no reliable traces of his colonists. They were the Lost Colony. Speculation on the colonists' fate now centers on a removal into Virginia proper, or at least to a site along the present North Carolina–Virginia border, rather than a southward move.

The decade of the 1590s was a dismal time for exponents of English colonization. As the Spanish wars grew more intense, attention focused on the Iberian Peninsula, the Netherlands, France, and a new Spanish armada. London merchants still preferred investing in privateering, not colonizing. The heroic figures of the sea-venturing era were gone: Hawkins and Drake died leading expeditions into the West Indies in 1595–1596. Raleigh, banished from the court for seducing Elizabeth Throckmorton, the Queen's lady-in-waiting, fell completely from grace after 1593 and became consumed with recapturing his lost glory by finding El Dorado in Guiana. Eventually, his fascination with Guiana gold would cost him his head after a disastrous voyage in 1617–1618. Keeping Virginia alive became a task not for adventurers but for Richard Hakluyt, an English clergyman who never went to sea.

Richard Hakluyt the younger (c.1552–1616), son of a London merchant and grandson of Hereford gentry, carried on the work of his cousin and guardian, Richard Hakluyt the elder. This Hakluyt was a lawyer whose mercantile and seafaring clients led him into a study of geography and commerce. The younger Hakluyt became a clergyman not to minister to a parish but to acquire clerical and teaching stipends, which would free him to collect and edit his vast compendium, *The Principal Navigations, Voyages, Traffiques, and Discoveries of the English Nation* (1589 and 1598–1600) and to draw up a prospectus for overseas ventures as he had done for Raleigh with the *Discourse of Western Planting* (1584). Between the first edition of the *Principal Navigations* in 1589 and the second in 1598, he shifted his emphasis from English opportunities in northern Europe and Asia to the New World.

Hakluyt's greatest contribution was his rationale for overseas colonies. He fastened the possibilities for commercial profits to an English colony in the New World and surrounded the whole project with a sense of national purpose. America, with its vital raw materials and markets, could make England self-sufficient and free from the insecurities of Dutch middlemen and the threats of European wars, could provide every commodity England bought from European traders—wine, salt, tar, pitch, resin, timber, silk, spices, and dyestuffs—and could augment the mother country's fishing, fur, and skin trades. Of course, there was always the possibility of discovering gold, silver, copper, and precious stones (although these remained secondary to a diversified economy that would complement England's products.) From American colonies, Englishmen could easily raid the Spanish in the Caribbean or drive French fishermen from the Newfoundland banks. Once settlements were made, major missionary efforts among the Indians could be undertaken. Hakluyt's goal was a commercially viable colony of Englishmen set down among a native population that would be anglicized. It was to be not an outpost but an entrepôt for a continuous influx of England's honest poor, who desired employment they could not find, and the lazy poor and criminals, whose presence threatened the social stability of a supposedly overpopulated Elizabethan England.

To attract investors and settlers, Hakluyt had to demonstrate that colonies could be settled profitably and in a short time. Therefore, his emphasis was on a wilderness Canaan overflowing with natural resources, land awaiting industrious gentry and yeomen farmers, a healthful climate, seas teeming with fish, and an easier, more certain life for all. Yet Hakluyt was no reckless land jobber, a sixteenth-century public relations man. He believed what he wrote. So did those who had seen Virginia. It is significant that no matter how much they suffered, no matter how many friends they saw die, all who went to Virginia—whether Ralph Lane, John White, Thomas Hariot, Bartholomew Gosnold, or ordinary seamen—remained wildly optimistic about Virginia. It was an Eden, needing only righteous, industrious men to cultivate its gardens.

For Englishmen, Virginia and America were one and the same. That part of Virginia they now fixed upon was the Chesapeake Bay and its magnificent tributaries flowing out of the Blue Ridge and southern Appalachian mountains. The English occupied Virginia in an east–west movement from the bay, up the rivers, across the Piedmont, over the Blue Ridge mountains, down the seven valleys of the Valley of Virginia, then over the mountains once more and into the valleys of the Ohio, Kentucky, and Tennessee rivers. The land they occupied actually had evolved in reverse order, emerging west-to-east during 200 million years of upheavals in the Earth's crust, violent erosion by winds and storms, and constant invasions and retreats by the seas. Exactly how this happened is a matter for dispute among geologists.

One scenario goes like this. In the most distant past, much of the present Piedmont and all of Virginia west of the Blue Ridge lay submerged by vast seas. Sedimentary erosion had left extensive limestone beds and coal swamps in the western regions. Subsequent upheavals converted these beds and swamps into great folded ridges, locked the coal into the folds, and expelled the inland seas. The next series of upward thrusts formed the present Appalachian Mountains. Erosion flattened the western mountaintops and covered the eastern plains with rich sands and clays. Another series of uplifts raised the whole western area several thousand feet above the eastern seas. River erosion cut deep valleys between the long, parallel ridges of the Blue Ridge and the Appalachians running northeast to southwest. In the meantime, the eastward-retreating seas left the Susquehanna an extended river running north-to-south, with numerous long tributaries cutting into a plain sloping gradually from the first set of western mountains—the Blue Ridge. Then, in the last stage of formation, the sea once more invaded the Susquehanna and its tributaries, scooped out the Chesapeake Bay, and widened the tributaries, creeks, and estuaries, often as far as 150 miles inland. There, the invading tides met shrinking glaciers. At those points, rock formations left falls in the rivers. This line of falls became a clear demarcation between two regions. Thus, by the time the Indians appeared some 12,000 years ago (or perhaps 20,000 years ago—anthropologists are not certain), three distinct geographical divisions existed: the coastal plains of the Tidewater and Eastern Shore, the gently rolling hills the English named the Piedmont, and the mountains of the Blue Ridge and Appalachians with their numerous valleys between.

Regardless of how this came to pass, the land possessed the finest system of interior waterways along the Atlantic coast. That these river basins were settled by an agrarian people from an island kingdom just emerging into a period of vigorous commercial expansion proved to be crucial. Geography and seventeenth-century English commercial and agricultural interests combined to form a riverine society around the Chesapeake Bay. A century and a half later, farmers from the hills, coves, and glens of Scotland, Ireland, and Germany were to occupy the valleys, coves, hills, and mountains of western Virginia. That, too, would prove crucial for Virginia's history beyond the colonial period.

North American settlement commanded new attention after 1600. James I made peace with Spain, ending the fitful wars of the past thirty years. Peace also ended the official sanction for English privateers to prey on treasure ships in the Spanish Main. Tacitly, at least, the Spanish had to accept the possibility of English colonies in North America. Some merchants and gentry never accepted this coexistence with Catholic Spain as in either their personal interests or those of the nation. Other merchants, encouraged by the success of the East India Company (founded by Sir Thomas Smythe in 1600), saw brighter vistas in overseas trade. Between 1602 and 1605, West Country ship captains, noblemen like the Earl of Southampton and Lord Arundel, gentry-soldiers like Chief Justice John Popham, Ferdinando Gorges, and even the out-of-favor Raleigh sent off at least six unrelated voyages to explore the North American coasts. Two of these voyages, commanded by Bartholomew Gilbert and Samuel Mace, sailed into the Chesapeake. One brought Indians back to England in 1603. Such grandiose talk abounded about the wonders of the New World that Ben Jonson in *Eastward Ho* (1605) satirically portrayed Virginia "as pleasant a country as ever the sun shined on . . . [where] all their dripping-pans and their chamberpots are pure gould . . . [and] all their prisoners they take are fettered in gould."

In late 1605, the competing English interests set aside their differences and petitioned James for a joint charter to settle Virginia. On 10 April 1606, James granted the request and issued a charter to the Virginia Company of London and Plymouth. In these same years, Frenchmen sent out Samuel Champlain, first to the West Indies and then to the St. Lawrence valley; Dutch merchants hired Henry Hudson to explore the region that soon became New Amsterdam. Far to the west, Spanish missionaries settled Santa Fe. The European race for North America was on.

The Virginia that James granted to the company lay between the 34th parallel (the Cape Fear River) and the 45th parallel (Maine). The London investors could settle no farther north than the 41st parallel (New York City), the Plymouth adventurers no further south than the 38th (the mouth of the Potomac River), and neither closer than 100 miles to each other. Neither company could settle land already occupied by a "Christian prince." Actually, James only granted permission to settle within these lines, not the whole territory itself. The true grant was for the land 50 miles north and south and 100 miles east and west of the initial settlement. Only after a successful planting would he enlarge the boundaries. Still, from any Englishman's viewpoint, a tract of 20,000 miles was a handsome domain. (By comparison, the total area of England with Wales is 58,350 square miles; England proper is 50,033 square miles.) In fact, the king's limitation was well founded, for by February 1608 the Plymouth promoters had explored, built, and failed to sustain a settlement at Sagadahoc (Massachusetts). With investor confidence lost, the Plymouth contingent forfeited its charter claims. Thus, Virginia was to be a southern colony.

The charter James signed carefully balanced corporate ends with national needs. The company held a trading monopoly so long as that trade was in English ships and to and through English ports. The company had full control over the colony, providing it made no law contrary to the laws of England or engaged in foreign adventures without royal approval. All colonists must take the oaths of allegiance to the Crown and the Church. These same colonists were to enjoy all the "liberties, franchises, and immunities" they would have had in

England. As Charles M. Andrews noted, these concessions had "nothing to do with civil liberty, self-government, or democracy; they were strictly legal, tenurial, and financial in their applications." This was an era, says English historian Charles Wilson, when "'Freedom' in legal language meant special exemption from a general rule of compulsion; 'Liberty' still implied a special privilege to do something forbidden to others." Only as later Englishmen expanded their "liberties, franchises, and immunities" and as eighteenth-century Virginians developed their own customary law did these words acquire the breadth and significance of meaning so forthrightly proclaimed in 1776. Nevertheless, James assured the would-be Virginians that being beyond the seas did not place them beyond protection of the law. He reaffirmed Elizabeth's assurance to the Roanoke colonists that non-Englishmen in Virginia would be treated as if they were English-born. And he made clear that a private corporation granted a public monopoly must operate in the public interest.

James appointed a royal council to provide central company administration and liaison with the Crown. Directing the colony was a resident council of thirteen appointed by the royal council. That James should have named a royal council to supervise the company is hardly surprising. More surprising would have been a decision to allow the company to function independently of the Crown. In this respect, James was moved less by any absolutist tendencies than by a desire to identify Virginia as a national enterprise to which he had committed himself and the nation. Although James often told the Spanish ambassador Baltassare Zuniga that "he was not informed as to the details of what was going on, so far as the voyages to Virginia were concerned," the Spaniard knew better. James was deeply involved. To be sure, by making peace with Spain, by prohibiting the privateering so tempting to his subjects, and by barring settlement within areas already occupied by Spain and France, James hoped to limit the possibilities for war. Still, he was willing to defend the colony if necessary. And that guarantee represented the ultimate and potentially most costly royal investment in overseas expansion.

The political problem with the 1606 charter was not the royal council in London but the absence of an effective executive in Virginia. There was no executive. The president of the colony, elected annually for a one-year term by his fellow councilors, had all the responsibility but little more authority than the other councilors; the president had two votes, the others one each. Government in Virginia was to be by committee, and as events were to prove, it did not work.

The royal council appointed in November 1606 was a composite group of investors, London and West Country merchants, and politicians interested in overseas expansion. The most prominent councilors were Sir Thomas Smythe, Sir Ferdinando Gorges, Sir Francis Popham, and Thomas De La Warr (later governor in Virginia), all long involved in overseas enterprises, and three Crown officeholders, John Dodderidge, the Solicitor General and sometime supporter of privateers, Sir Henry Montague, Recorder of London and later the Earl of Manchester, and Sir William Wade, Lieutenant of the Tower. Lord Salisbury was the principal secretary of state responsible for Spanish affairs and could hardly appear publicly as a councilor; he was thus represented by his close associate, Sir William Cope. Sir Edwin Sandys, son of the Archbishop of York, joined the London Council in March 1607. No wonder Zuniga was incredulous when James called the company a "private affaire."

The importance of London to the Virginia enterprise cannot be overestimated. London represented more than just access to the great merchants, the gentry-nobles, and the Crown. The city was the center of the country, the heart of a vibrant new nationalism and mercantilism. London funneled thousands of settlers and tens of thousands of pounds sterling into Virginia before the company collapsed. Without the patriotism and economic nationalism emanating from London, Virginia in 1609 and again in 1619 would have gone the way of Sagadahoc and Roanoke.

With little fanfare, a Virginia-bound expedition of three ships, 105 settlers, and 55 crewmen dropped down the Thames on 20 December 1606. Commanded by veteran sea captains Christopher Newport, Bartholomew Gosnold, and John Ratcliffe, the 100-ton *Susan Constant,* the smaller *Godspeed* or *Goodspeed* (actually the same word), and the tiny pinnace *Discovery* endured a miserable six weeks setting off the English coast amidst storms and contrary winds. The belowdecks were crammed with supplies and ships' gear. Most passengers spent their days and nights on the open decks sharing space with the animals. Sailing ships were notoriously filthy, the odors foul, privacy nonexistent, and diseases rampant. These ships were incubators for nearly every English sickness. The non-gentry, coming from the poorer classes in England and already suffering from the effects of lifelong dietary deficiencies, became ready prey for every germ that passed their way. As fate would have it, the Reverend Robert Hunt, their devoted pastor with whom they were so long cooped up, was a typhoid carrier.

The ships finally cleared the channel for the Canary Islands in February, almost certainly too late to make the planting season in Virginia. They took the traditional southern route from the Canaries out past the Azores to the outer West Indian islands. These were familiar waters to Newport, veteran of more than thirteen privateering ventures, for here in 1591 he had lost his right arm attacking a Spanish merchantman. Newport and his men spent three weeks island-hopping northward, replenishing their water casks, revictualing the ships, and revitalizing themselves. On 10 April, they turned northward into stormy seas and entered the Chesapeake on 26 April 1607. They disembarked at Cape Henry, planted their flags, and gave thanks to God for their safe passage to a land whose beauty and plenty "almost ravished us at the first sight thereof." Their idyll was rudely interrupted by an Indian attack that severely wounded two Englishmen. Not until 13 May did they agree on a site for James Town. By then, the spring planting season was past.

The first official governmental act was the opening by Newport of a sealed box containing the names of the seven Virginia councilors. Probably nominated by the larger investors, the councilors were Captain Newport; Edward-Maria Wingfield, a major investor and the only colonist named in the 1606 charter; Bartholomew Gosnold, who had sailed into the area in 1602; Captain John Martin, the irascible son of Richard Martin, the wealthy goldsmith and onetime Lord Mayor of London; Captain George Kendall, a Sandys family relation and political agent for Sir Robert Cecil, Earl of Salisbury; and two men of lesser rank—Captain John Smith, a soldier of fortune and small investor associated with Gosnold, and Captain John Ratcliffe, sometimes named John Sicklemore, a sea captain of whom little is known except that his ambition exceeded the reach of his abilities. Wingfield, quite logically, was chosen first president.

Colonists arrive on the shores of Virginia at the mouth of the James River in 1607. (Library of Congress)

Smith, under arrest since the ships left the Canaries, probably for challenging Wingfield's authority, was not admitted to the council until June.

The settlement site these councilors chose was destined to be as controversial as the councilors themselves. Instructed to select an easily defendable place on high ground, inland along a large river flowing from the northwest, they put down on a neck of land jutting out into a sweeping bend in the river thirty miles upstream from the bay. Quite politically conscious, they named the river the James and the place James Fort. Their choice has been roundly criticized, for the isle was a low-lying swampland, surrounded by marshes and tar bogs, easily cut off by the Indians, and devoid of an unpolluted water supply. The isle was one of the New World's "worst gastro-intestinal death traps."

However, in view of previous experience and anticipated problems, the choice for James Fort is understandable and even defensible. The land was high enough and the channel deep enough for the largest ships to tie up directly at the shoreline. The fort easily commanded the river, protecting the isle and any upriver sites from the Spanish, deemed the greatest threat. Much of the land itself had been cleared of first growth by the Paspahegh Indians and was lying fallow with a light second growth coming on. The tar bogs augured well for naval stores production. And no one really expected Englishmen to depend upon water for their drinking supply. Many years later, Governor Francis Wyatt lamented, "to plant a colony by water drinkers was an inexcusable error." Under any circumstances, James Fort was not meant to be the only settlement site. It was to be a port of entry and protection for the whole colony. What went wrong here and elsewhere in early Virginia was that Englishmen relied on what little experience they had to predict what actions they should take.

In a desultory fashion, Wingfield organized his men. He built a fort of sorts, although not until after an Indian attack in late May did he order log palisades constructed around the area; and not until a friendly Indian suggested it did he cut down the tall grass in which the natives lurked. No houses were erected. The gentlemen slept in rude tents, the lesser folk on the ground. A small garden was planted. Newport, Smith, George Percy, and Gabriel Archer explored the James, meeting friendly receptions from the Indians along the way. However, their hopes for the northwest waterway were dashed on the massive rocks at the falls of the James (Richmond). When Newport departed in June, he carried a load of clapboard as cargo. His enterprising crew had stashed more than a ton of wild sassafras into their ship's hold, knowing the roots commanded a high price on the London market as a cure for syphilis.

The summer of 1607 was a series of disasters. Scorching heat, high humidity, improper diet, a fouled water supply, and no beer all prepared the way for diseases of improper diet and pestilence—scurvy, pellagra, dysentery, typhoid, and beriberi. Accompanying death were "fluxes, fevers, and bellyaches" and "wild vomits into the black night." By September, forty-eight had died. In the winter, pneumonia, influenza, and pleurisy took their toll, and by January, twenty-eight more had departed. Only a handful died at the hands of Indians. The rest fell victim to "seasoning," the adaptation of Englishmen to the diseases and climate of Virginia. Seasoning took a heavy toll of every migrant group arriving until the 1670s. European diseases, especially smallpox and measles, had an equally devastating effect on the Indians, decimating whole tribes upon first contact with Europeans.

Unprepared for such staggering losses, the councilors quarreled continuously. Their two stabilizing influences were gone, Christopher Newport to England and Bartholomew Gosnold to the grave. Bickering abounded. Scapegoats were soon found. The councilors removed Kendall in August. In September, Smith, Martin, and Ratcliffe voted out Wingfield as president on trivial grounds. In November, these three tried and executed Kendall for an alleged Spanish connection. In December, while leading a scouting party into the Chickahominy region, Smith was ambushed. Several men were killed, and Smith was taken prisoner and carried to the great Indian chief, Powhatan. There took place an event so encrusted with myth that the truth may never come through—the rescue of Smith by Powhatan's young daughter Matoaka—Pocahontas. The evidence now supports Smith's perception that Pocahontas rescued him, possibly while he was undergoing an Indian initiation and adoption rite in which the chief's daughter acts as the "protector" for the initiate.

The Pocahontas story obscures the fact that Smith did narrowly escape execution—at the hands of his fellow councilors. Released by Powhatan, Smith made his way back to Jamestown in January 1608. Immediately, the other councilors arrested him at the behest of Captain Gabriel Archer and charged him with the loss of the men under his command, a crime under the ancient Levitical code. Tried before President Ratcliffe, he was condemned to death. On the very eve of the execution, Captain Newport arrived from London and saved Smith.

For a time, Newport calmed the turbulent spirits. He brought with him additional settlers, food, and materials, the First Supply. Another disaster struck. Fire destroyed the few shelters built during the fall, forcing the colonists to set aside differences in order to survive. Peaceful Indians brought in food and taught the colonists how to fish. That spring, the colonists cleared fields, planted Indian corn, and seemed well on their way to stability. John Smith explored the upper Chesapeake Bay and the Potomac, Susquehanna, and Rappahannock rivers.

Governmental confusion continued, stemming directly from factionalism on the Virginia council, a weak presidency, and the absence of vital elements of the English social structure. From what little is known about how settlers were recruited, it appears likely that the principal investors recruited their own colonists and placed their clients on the council. This ensured factionalism.

Equally important, the stabilizing influences of English society were missing. There were no families, no women, no true church parish, no continuity, and no sense of community, none of the normal leadership found in an English village or town. Later, in New England, the Pilgrims and Puritans brought English society with them. In Virginia, a half-century passed before a cohesive social structure emerged and nearly a century before a stable leadership gained control.

In a rank-conscious society, there were five men on the first council who by previous position would have provided leadership in an English town. Of these five, Bartholomew Gosnold died, Christopher Newport was necessarily absent, Wingfield proved ineffectual, Martin kept to himself when not ill, and Kendall was executed. A sixth man, George Percy, the brother of the Earl of Northumberland, was content to avoid government and was not named to the council, probably because of the Northumberland family involvement in the Gunpowder Plot of 1605. The minister, Reverend Mr. Robert Hunt, succumbed in 1608. The early loss of the usual community leaders thrust management upon Ratcliffe and Smith, those two younger men of distinctively lower status. Ratcliffe proved adept at making cabals with his cohort, Gabriel Archer, and inept at managing government when his cabals succeeded. Smith, when finally able to assert his natural organizing talents in 1608, undoubtedly saved the colony.

The social problem rested not only with the leaders and their leadership but also with the social composition of all the first settlers. Smith later declared Virginia to be a land in which "heaven & earth never agreed better to frame a place for man's inhabition, being of our constitutions, were it fully manured and inhabited by industrious people." In a very real sense, Jamestown lacked enough "industrious people." In the original company and in the two relief complements, the First and Second Supply of 1608, there were 294 persons, of whom 239 have been identified as to occupation. There were 119 gentlemen and councilors, 49 laborers, 6 boys, 1 drummer, 1 minister, 4 surgeons, 7 tailors, 1 barber, 1 perfumer, and 2 women, Mrs. Thomas Forrest and her maid, Anne Burros, later Anne Burrus Leyden, both arriving in October 1608. Smith notes that the "laborers" were actually footmen and retainers to the gentlemen and not laborers in the conventional sense.

There were also 5 goldsmith-refiners, 2 apothecaries, 1 jeweler, 1 tobacco pipe maker, and 8 "Dutchmen and Poles," who were makers of glass, iron, and pottery. These men were to set up small industries that would free England from dependence on European suppliers. Finally, there were 14 undifferentiated artisans, 4 carpenters, 2 blacksmiths, 3 bricklayers, 1 gunsmith, 1 cooper, and 1 fisherman. The remaining men had no trade or skill and presumably were day laborers, soldiers, and a few tenant farmers. This is the stuff of which privateering ventures, the occupation of Ireland, and the Spanish conquests were made. Clearly, it bespeaks a people who expected to find a native population ready to trade and capable of being set to work and a countryside that was full of natural resources easy to exploit.

Misreading the environment's hostility, the company sent men untrained, wrongly trained, or unneeded to a wilderness colony. Only the craftsmen and artisans brought with them skills of immediate use and an understanding of productivity related to individual efforts. One can sympathize with Smith's bitter comment to London after the Second Supply came in: "I entreat you rather send but thirty carpenters, husbandmen, gardeners, fishermen, blacksmiths, masons, and diggers up of tree roots well provided; than a thousand such as we have." Equally, one can empathize with those gentlemen and their retainers, the perfumer or the jeweler unneeded in a subsistence economy, the tradesmen sent out in numbers too few to practice specialized trades too sophisticated for a wilderness, or even the workers who had been led to believe they would find a new Eden where labor would nearly cease.

Much abuse has been heaped upon these early settlers, the gentry because they knew not how to work, and the workers because they would not work. Yet, in England the role of the "gentleman" was to fight, to command, to govern. To expect such people to be "gainfully employed" is to misread what they did in England. By the same token, the subsistence laboring groups, farmers and townsmen alike in England, had little reason to work hard, and they did not. They lacked a "work ethic," hardly surprising in a premarket economy. Constantly told by social critics that they were "lazy scum," "worthless vagabonds," "idle," "slothful," and "dissolute," they came to believe that they were. Not surprisingly, they had little hope of improving themselves, for they knew "by long experience, that by their labors they can make no profits to themselves." Thus the attraction of a new Eden where, even when John Smith and later Marshal Thomas Dale instituted a work-or-else policy, a full workday meant only a six-hour day.

When all of this is said and their backgrounds explained, it is still not clear what the mindset was of so many who, when faced with the realities of the New World, did not adjust, did not work, became dependent and passive, lay down in large numbers, and died. The debilitating effects of dysentery and other diseases, many related to an imbalanced diet, alone do not explain what happened. In sum, this was an inverted society, wrongly selected for tasks that did not exist, and which relied for food on the local labor force—the Indians.

The Virginia Indians were unique among coastal Indians encountered by English colonizers. They were the only eastern coastal tribes capable of driving the English off their lands and the only ones to undertake all-out war to exterminate the English. Along the Chesapeake Bay, up its many rivers, and across the bay on the Eastern Shore lived more than thirty Algonquian-speaking tribes. Related to other Algonquin tribes northward into Canada and southward into coastal Carolina, they numbered more than 10,000 people and could arm perhaps 2,500 warriors. There probably had been thousands more Indians in the 1570s who died of European diseases spreading up the coast from Spanish settlements and exploratory expeditions. The Algonquin were a sedentary people who lived in more than 160 villages, built Quonset-type houses, tilled gardens and cornfields, cleared large tracts of forestland, and possessed a real sense of tribal territory. The English fastened Algonquin tribal names on nearly all the major waterways—the Patawomeke (Potomac), the Rappahannock, the Pamunkey, the Mattaponi, the Chickahominy, the Appomattox, the Nansemond, and the Chesapeake.

To the west on the Piedmont were 7,000 to 10,000 Siouan Indians who had moved eastward from the Ohio Valley, up the Kanawha and New rivers, into the

A late sixteenth-century Indian village is depicted in this illustration by explorer and artist John White, engraved by Theodor de Bry. (Library of Congress)

Valley of Virginia, and then onto the Piedmont. These tribes were less stable, more nomadic, and lived in six large tribal units—the Manahoac on the northern Piedmont; the Monacan at and west of the falls of the James; the Saponi in Albemarle County and the central Piedmont; the Tutelo (sometimes, the Saponi Tutelo) on the southern Piedmont; and the Mohetan, mountain Indians along the New River in present-day West Virginia. Each of these tribes had numerous smaller tribal units. In the swampy areas south of the James lived the Nottoway and Meherrin, poor relations of the powerful northern Iroquois. And in the far southwestern region lived a portion of the equally powerful Cherokee.

The Algonquin were the greatest single obstacle facing the English during their first half-century in Virginia. They also made the greatest cultural impact on the English. The Sioux influence was indirect. Because they constantly challenged the Algonquin for the lands along the fall line, the Sioux often diverted Algonquin attentions from the English. The Iroquois and Cherokee tribes had little influence on seventeenth-century Virginians, English or Indian.

The strength of the Powhatan Confederacy was in the remarkable organizational abilities of its chief ruler, or Powhatan, Wahunsonacock. Smith describes Powhatan as a "tall, well proportioned man, with a sower looke, his head somewhat gray, his beard so thinne, that it seemeth none at all, his age neare sixtie, of a very able and hardy body to endure any labour." Sometime before 1580, Powhatan through his mother inherited six tribes—the Arrohattoc, Appomatuck, Mattaponi, Pamunkey, Powhatan, and Youghtanund. Utilizing a small force of well-disciplined warriors, he extended his influence until by 1600 he had brought nearly all the Tidewater Indians, from the fall line to the Eastern Shore and from the James to the Rappahannock, under his suzerainty. Thomas Jefferson called it a confederacy, but that term is misleading, implying a collective decision-making process among equal tribal units. John Smith was closer to the mark when he called it a "monarchical government, one as an emperor ruleth over many kings or governors." The authority of Powhatan and his werowances (or chieftains) was absolute. He coerced some tribes into fealty; others he defeated in quick, decisive battles. Occasionally he executed tribal leaders. Usually he removed the defeated chieftains to his own villages and appointed his brothers, sons, and trusted lieutenants as the new werowrances. Those who challenged his authority, as did the Chesapeake tribe in 1607, suffered horrible and brutal consequences. It is less certain whether Powhatan's authority extended to positive actions such as unified attacks against enemies—the Sioux tribes or the English.

Fortunately for the colonists, the heart of Powhatan's strength was along the upper James toward the falls and along the York, Pamunkey, and Mattaponi rivers. Jamestown sat on an abandoned village site in Paspahegh territory adjacent to the Chickahominy. The Chickahominy, perhaps 950 people, was the one tribe Powhatan could never bring under full control. In the early years, despite occasionally collaborating with Powhatan, that tribe feared that a liaison between Powhatan and the English would squeeze them off their lands. Therefore, they tended to offend the colonists as little as possible and traded extensively with them.

The magnitude of Indian warfare and hostility toward the English in the first years has been overemphasized. Stories of scattered attacks, beginning with the first night at Cape Henry, mysterious appearances of painted warriors, ambushes of scouting parties, or an Indian maid saving a white captain are dramatic. More characteristic are tales of Indian hospitality, gifts of goods, trade, starving white men fleeing to the Indians for help, and generally friendly relations. Certainly, relations were more harmonious than invaders usually enjoy. Colonists' writings in 1607 and 1608 are filled with such comments: " . . . We are at peace with all the inhabitants of the surrounding country"; " . . . our mortal enemies . . . relieve us with victuals . . . otherwise we had all perished"; "The Emperor . . . and all his vassals deal peacefully with the English"; " . . . the Indians bring us Corne . . . when we rather expected they would destroy us." Without the Indians, the colonists would have perished during the first years, certainly during the first fall.

The obvious question is, why did Powhatan not destroy the Jamestown settlement? Even with their fear of guns and cannon, the Indians appear to have had enough warriors to undertake the task in the early days. The most obvious answer is that the Indians never were organized well enough to mount a sustained attack. Powhatan, even if he had commanded it, could not have called out all his warriors into the field at one time, for his power was not all-encompassing in matters of "foreign policy." Although the Virginia Indians were masters of infiltration and hit-and-run tactics, they were not able to carry out the long-term siege necessary to reduce a fortified town to ruins. Moreover, intertribal warfare, especially around the falls of the James and the Rappahannock with the Monacan and Manahoac tribes, did not allow Powhatan the luxury of concentrating his forces in one place.

Perhaps Powhatan thought he could ally himself with the Englishmen and utilize their guns against his two Sioux foes. There can be no doubt that he wanted the English to invade Monacan territory above the falls. Repeatedly, he plied Newport with stories of copper pits near the mountains in Monacan lands. Upon releasing John Smith in January 1608, he so openly urged Smith to seek the water passage through the mountains that the usually aggressive captain drew back, wary of Powhatan's motives.

Powhatan may not have seen his power threatened by this sickly, bickering "tribe" at Jamestown. The white men would soon disappear. They always had in the past. Earlier Virginia–Carolina Indian contacts with Spanish and English explorers, the Jesuit missionaries of the 1570s, the Vasquez de Ayllon expedition of 1526, and Raleigh's various forays suggested such an end. The white men never seemed to survive long in one place. Thus, Powhatan's initial instinct would be to expect Jamestown to wither away.

Such a supposition coincided with his basic military strategy of avoiding direct confrontations where possible and pursuing a policy of watchful waiting. This was the procedure by which he seems to have brought most tribes under his control. Ironically, King Philip of Spain arrived at the same conclusion about these English invaders of "Spanish lands." His spies at Jamestown told him the colony would collapse, that no attack was necessary. Both kings were to rue their failure to subdue the English settlement at the outset.

Whatever the reasons for his early restraint, Powhatan changed his tactics in late 1608 from coexistence to war. He halted all food exchange with the colonists, threatening reprisals against noncompliant tribes, and applied steady pressure against colonists venturing away from Jamestown. The bellicose John Smith, relying on his experience gained fighting "infidels" in Eastern Europe, responded with attacks against Indians living in isolated villages. At the same time, the company also changed its initial policy and ordered the Virginia council to make all tribes render tribute to the king. Steady conflict began in 1609, continuing until a peace treaty was signed in 1614 and sealed with the marriage of Pocahontas to John Rolfe, the colony secretary.

Thus, after two years the company had little more than a beachhead in Virginia, and the stockholders had no dividends. The company's original scheme had been "to send people little by little" until the population reached 2,000. Economic plans, while including Indian trade and discovery of mineral resources, always stressed local industries and crafts, a diversified economy, and eventually a self-sufficient food production. To that end, each additional resupply had included a relatively larger number of craftsmen than farmers. Still, nothing had gone right. All the "gilded dirte" ship captains carried home turned out to be Virginia feldspar (fool's gold). Newport had brought orders in January 1608 with the First Supply that touched off a gold rush. There was "no talke, no hope, nor worke, but dig gold, wash gold, refine gold, load gold." For two crucial months this went on. Yet, when Newport departed in April, he had only more "gilded dirte" and a cargo of wood.

Increasingly worried about investor uneasiness, the company in 1608 gave Newport and President Smith three specific goals to attain as quickly as possible: either search for the Roanoke settlers or locate a northwest passage through the mountains; find gold and send back a cargo worth £2,000 to cover costs of the Second Supply; and crown Powhatan emperor after extracting from him an oath of fealty to the king. The unreality of all these infuriated both Smith and Newport. Newport and his men tried unsuccessfully to drag an ingeniously contrived collapsible barge over the rocky falls. Two men went off on a half-hearted trip toward Carolina to find the Lost Colony. Meanwhile, Smith, in a comic-opera coronation scene, managed to force a copper crown on the head of a justifiably suspicious Powhatan. This time, the colonists ignored the gold search, concentrating instead on a promising iron ore dig. Still, a £2,000 cargo could not be produced. Newport went off in December 1608 with yet another load of wood and a stinging letter from Smith rebuking the London council for expecting a struggling colony to produce in months what England herself had never produced.

From September 1608 to August 1609, John Smith commanded Virginia as president of the council, unchallenged by his rivals, all of whom had either died or returned to England. Taking forceful military action, he confiscated large food caches from weaker Indian tribes. At Jamestown he ordered his men to "work or not eat." In a short time, he rebuilt the town, established new outposts up and down the James, and started glass, soap, iron, and naval stores production. Still, a full workday was only six hours, and Smith had to confess he never attained real labor from more than 50 of the 200 survivors at any one time.

Then, just as it appeared they would make it through the winter without starving, the Virginians found their food reserves infested by ship rats, an unexpected blow, for rats were not native to America. President Smith had no choice other than to disperse the colonists to outposts at the falls and Point Comfort, close the fledgling factories, and wait. Help arrived in July, when Samuel Argall, cousin to Sir Thomas Smith, brought his ship in. Argall also carried news of a massive Third Supply following him with 600 settlers, food, animals, a new charter, and a new government.

Smith cogently described the alternatives facing the investors and colonists in February 1609: "[W]e chanced in a land even as God made it, where we found only an idle, improvident, scattered people, ignorant of the knowledge of gold and silver or any commodities and careless of anything but from hand to mouth except baubles of no worth. [Before] we could bring [anything] to recompense our pains, defray our charges, and satisfy our Adventurers, [either] we were to discover the country, subdue the people, bring them to be tractable, civil, and industrious, and teach them trades, that the fruits of their labors might make us some recompense; or plant such colonies of our own that must first make provision how to live ourselves." Despite the factionalism, mutinies, and disease, Smith was surprisingly sanguine, seeing these events as typical of all New World colonies. Even the Spanish and Portuguese, those symbols of colonial success, had had to endure hardships before their victories.

Although Smith and Newport found no Northwest Passage, no mountain pass, no El Dorado, and no Aztec or Inca civilization, they had discovered something of equal importance—the Chesapeake Bay region. They had stumbled upon the James, York, Rappahannock, Potomac, Patuxent, and Severn rivers, deep waterways navigable as much as 150 miles into the interior. They had happened upon thick forests, meadows, marshes, orchards, fish, and game, "strawberries, four times bigger and better than ours in England," and a climate in which "summer is hot as in Spaine; the winter colde as in France or England . . . [with] no extreame long continueth." That Virginians in 1608 also told of savage Indians and terrible deaths did not stem the flow of colonists to Virginia. Dying held no terror, for death and pestilence threatened seventeenth-century men and women everywhere.

During the winter of 1608–1609, while the rats ate the colonists' food, the London council reappraised its future, abandoned its "little by little" approach, and launched a bold new scheme "to establish ourselves all at once." There remained only a residue of Hakluyt's hope for an Anglo–Indian society. For the time being, the thrust would be on Smith's alternative—"to plant such colonies of our own that must first make provision to live ourselves."

II. The Rise and Fall of Corporate Colonization, 1609–1624

By the winter of 1608–1609, deeply disturbed London investors reached the inescapable conclusion that survival of the Virginia enterprise depended upon completely restructuring and refinancing operations in London and Virginia. There was the obvious ineptness of the Virginia council, a need for more efficient corporate management in London, the diplomatic necessity for James to officially separate the London Company from the Crown to appease Spanish protests, and a desire to increase the colony's area. A new charter, drafted by Sir Edwin Sandys, vested "full and absolute" power in the company. The royal council was dissolved, replaced by a new council elected by the stockholders and headed by a treasurer. In Virginia, there would be a resident governor with absolute authority, with the councilors reduced to being the governor's advisors. James accepted the colony as having been "founded" and enlarged its bounds to cover an area 200 miles north and south of Point Comfort, running west and northwest from sea to sea. Although abrogated by the charter's suspension in 1624, this grant in the 1609 charter became Virginia's later claim to western Virginia, Kentucky, the forks of the Ohio, and the Northwest Territory.

The second London Company was a full joint-stock company, not an investor partnership as in 1606. Through this corporate device, England united her merchants, who knew that Virginia's needs exceeded their financial resources, with the gentry, who always possessed a great patriotic fervor for the colony but who lacked the managerial skills to bring off the enterprise. The London Company became the largest of all early English stock companies, attracting nearly 1,700 investors between 1609 and 1624, among which were 333 members of Parliament. Merchant interest was greatest in 1609–1610, gentry interest most pronounced between 1610–1613 and 1619–1621. Profits and national glory attracted the merchants. The chances for both seemed real in 1609, spurred no doubt by the sensational dividends paid by the East Indies Company in 1608. Although not averse to gold, land, and profits, the gentry were far more apt to listen to the siren calls of national destiny, "the love of God, and true religion." While it has been conventional wisdom to set merchants and gentry at odds with each other almost from the beginning, it must be noted that nearly 90 percent of the private stockholders, large and small, merchants and gentry, were related to another investor. London Company investors were as closely related as the sea dogs and privateers of the 1580s and 1590s had been and as the eighteenth-century Virginia planters were to become.

The 1609 charter transformed Virginia into a corporate, capitalistic community. The new company joined not just the monies of the gentry to those of the merchants but also the English stockholders (called adventurers) to Virginia colonists (planters). Each planter received one share for venturing to the Virginia plantation. It was hoped that, with a share in the company, planters would not revert to the nonproductive days of 1607–1608. For the same reason, all colonists were to work for the common, corporate good, and at the end of seven years they were to share in the company dividends, even those who had indentured themselves to go to Virginia. Thus, the London Company became a shared investment, the stockholder offering his money, the planter his labor and perhaps his life.

Exploiting an unfathomable outpouring of nationalism and optimism, promoters attracted the great merchants, the landed nobility, the gentry, the London guilds, and the old Plymouth interests. In three months, 650 persons and 50 guilds subscribed more than £10,000 at a minimum of £12 10s per share, the estimated cost of maintaining one settler in Virginia for a year. By the spring of 1609, a gigantic new migration was under way. Responding to Robert Johnson's clever propaganda pamphlet, *Nova Britannica,* 600 men and women clamored to go with the first fleet; hundreds more eagerly awaited later passage.

The new esteem in which Virginia was held in London is apparent in the leadership going out with the Third Supply: Thomas West, Lord De La Warr, one-time commander of Irish expeditionary forces and a member of the original royal council, was governor; Sir Thomas Gates was made lieutenant governor; and Sir George Somers, the fleet admiral; William Strachey, secretary to the English ambassador to Constantinople, was named colonial secretary. The redoubtable Christopher Newport was reduced to vice admiral. In recognition of "the great confidence and trust we have in his care and diligence," the Londoners raised John Smith to second-ranking member of the new Virginia council and appointed him head of the Virginia defenses. However, his enemies Archer, Ratcliffe, and Martin also were named to the council.

A different breed of settler constituted the Third Supply. Forthrightly admitting that they had allowed too many "parents to disburden themselves of lascivious sons, masters of bad servants, and wives of ill husbands . . . an idle crue . . . that will rather starve for hunger, than lay their hands for labor," company promoters advertised for those "sufficient, honest and good artificers" who knew how to work and would work.

But what began on an optimistic note in May 1609 had turned into an almost unbelievable nightmare twelve months later. Somers, Gates, and Newport, taking the *Sea Venture* along the West Indian route to Virginia, ran into a summer hurricane and shipwrecked on the coast of Bermuda. Meanwhile, the Third Supply, carrying some 450 inexperienced and undisciplined settlers, managed to evade the storms by sailing directly across the Atlantic, straggling into Jamestown from August into mid-October. Many settlers were near death from sunstroke, dysentery, scurvy, and the plague. Their supplies were gone, and their leaders, they thought, were lost at sea. Ratcliffe, Archer, and Martin wasted little time exploiting the political confusion. They tried to depose John Smith as president. Failing in that, they undermined his authority by declaring the old

Illustration of Captain John Smith's capture in Romania. (Smith, John. The True Travels, Adventures, and Observations of Captaine John Smith, *1630)*

charter void and Smith powerless. Wounded in a gunpowder explosion and harassed by his opponents, Smith yielded his presidency to George Percy.

John Smith left Jamestown in October 1609, ending the Virginia phase of a flamboyant career. He had begun life around 1580, the son of poor Lincolnshire farmers. Apprenticed to a merchant, he quit to become a soldier. He fought Catholics in the Netherlands and Ottoman Turks in Austria and Hungary. Captured in battle in Hungary, Smith was sold into slavery in Turkey. Escaping, he fled into Russia and returned to his patron in Transylvania. Discharged with the rank of captain and given a sizeable reward, the short, stocky, red-bearded soldier of fortune made his way back to England, where he invested in the Virginia voyage. Smith's *History of Virginia* caused historians to brand him a braggart and a liar. His pre-Virginia adventures seemed the figment of a fertile imagination and the Pocahontas story incurably romantic. If he had an obvious penchant to place himself at center stage and if "at times he exercised the prerogative of a veteran in recounting his conquests of war and love," the egocentric Smith has emerged more right than wrong. His Turkish and Hungarian tales have been verified, and his Virginia judgments on balance were correct. He was a man uncommonly able both to adapt and to survive in any environment into which he was thrust. And he lived long enough to write his own history.

The following winter of 1609–1610 became known as the Starving Time. As many as 430 of the 500 settlers may have died. Famine and disease were rampant. Renewed Indian hostilities were the most serious problem. Alarmed by the appearance of another horde of Englishmen, Powhatan forced the abandonment of the forts below the falls and at Point Comfort where the James River joins the bay, and penned most of the remaining colonists on Jamestown isle. Capturing Ratcliffe, who was foraging for food in Indian villages, Powhatan executed him by scraping off his skin with oyster shells.

Those who survived were desperate men and women in a desperate way. Haunted by hunger and hunted by the Indians, they subsisted on roots, rats, snakes, seeds, the breeding stock, dogs, cats, and their dead. One wretch murdered his shrewish wife, "powdered her up," and avoided starvation. Upon being found out, he was burned at the stake for his villainy. The survivors tore down nearly all of their sixty houses for firewood and left the fort a shambles. Many have blamed George Percy for lacking the will to lead; it is questionable whether even John Smith or Thomas Dale could have prevented such losses. There were too many people, too few supplies, too many Indians, and too much disease.

In contrast, Somers, Gates, and Newport were living on an island paradise. In Bermuda, they found fertile soil, fresh water, wild hogs, and no Indians, nor any diseases except ship fever, which soon dissipated in the salubrious climate. Of the 150 crewmen and planters, only a handful died over the winter. The whole adventure lives on in Shakespeare's *The Tempest.*

Reluctantly, Gates and his contingent sailed from Bermuda in two pinnaces they had built, expecting to find a substantial colony at Jamestown. Instead, desolation and despair greeted them. Gates, Somers, and Percy quickly concluded that they must all abandon Virginia and sail north to the Newfoundland coast, where they might find English fishermen who would take them home. On 7 June 1610, as they boarded ship and dropped down the James, they miraculously met an English party coming upriver. Governor De La Warr had arrived. With a mixture of fear and relief, they turned back—fear at having to suffer further deprivations, relief that what they already had endured would not be for naught. Jamestown nearly went the way of Roanoke. Yet, to an age that believed in divine guidance, the Bermuda deliverance and De La Warr's timely arrival were signs of God's providence writ large.

If the primary achievement of the first three years at Jamestown had been survival, the main achievements of the immediately succeeding years were ensuring stability and discipline among the colonists, driving back the Indians from the James River basin, producing an adequate food supply, and "discovering" tobacco. The men who achieved these goals were Governor De La Warr, Lieutenant Governor Sir Thomas Gates, Marshal Sir Thomas Dale, and Secretary John Rolfe, together with several hundred men and women scattered along the James River.

An aloof man, vain and a trifle pompous, Thomas, Lord De La Warr was not a popular governor. Certainly, his manner and bearing did not endear him to the older settlers. He was not in Virginia to be popular; he equated popularity with weakness. He was there to govern fairly and firmly. De la Warr fit precisely the requirements of Sir Edwin Sandys that there must be in Virginia one man who had "full and absolute power and authority to correct, punish, pardon, governe, and rule all . . . and who would act more as a chancelor than as a judge," relying discreetly upon a "summary and arbitrary way of justice" rather than on "niceness and the lettre of the laws." Rigor and discipline would prevail.

Nonetheless, the governor never was happy in Virginia. Disease took a heavy toll on his men and his servants. He himself fell violently ill. In less than a year, he was on his way back to London; he never returned.

Dispirited stockholders and councilors in London came close to abandoning the colony in late 1610. Each returning ship brought news of another disaster or disappointment, the return of De La Warr being the final blow. Company officers seriously considered cutting their losses. Gates protested. Virginia was still the glorious land of promise. What was needed, he said, were experienced soldiers to drive out the Indians, more artisans, breeding stock for an indigenous food supply, fruit to halt scurvy, and a governor in "absolute command." Virginia must not be abandoned to the Spanish.

The company officers, their flagging spirits bolstered, raised another £18,000 in stock subscriptions, principally from national-minded gentry. Incredibly, another 600 Englishmen volunteered as settlers. In March 1611, Sir Thomas Dale sailed from London with 300 well-equipped colonists, soldiers, and skilled craftsmen. Unfortunately, many were the usual motley sorts of earlier years. In May, Gates sailed with another 300 plus three ships full of livestock, fowl, and seed grain. Starvation was to be met by producing their own foodstuffs in Virginia and ending reliance on the Indians. Killing any breeding stock without permission would be a capital offense. A planter who placed his personal well-being above the colony's commonweal would be eliminated from the community in much the same fashion as the horse thief on the Great Plains in the nineteenth century. He was a threat to everyone's survival.

The arrival of Gates in August inaugurated a new era. Virginians faced hunger and difficult times into the 1630s, and often one-half to three-fourths of every shipload failed to survive the "seasoning" period. But no one ever again advocated abandoning the colony. After five years and 1,600 colonists, two-thirds of them already in their graves, the "Plantation of Virginia in America" was firmly settled.

To maintain discipline and order, Gates carried with him new instructions for the colonists. These instructions were a potpourri of religious, civil, and military rules. All colonists were expected to frequently and fervently worship the Lord. Perpetrators of the universally abhorred crimes of blasphemy, murder, sodomy, rape, bestiality, trespass and robbery, slander, conspiracy, and embezzlement were to be "impartially" awarded severe penalties, generally branding, disfigurement, or execution. Unsparing punishment awaited those who traded illegally with the Indians, killed breeding stock, violated sanitary codes, or refused to work. John Smith's "work or not eat" edict was now law.

These instructions, to which Sir Thomas Dale later appended rules of military conduct, were edited by Secretary William Strachey and published in 1611 as the *Lawes Divine, Morall, and Martiall.* Misnamed "Dale's Laws," the *Lawes* were intended as much for reading in London as for enforcement in Virginia, for there had been much criticism in England about administrative permissiveness. There is clear evidence that the promoters, despite public claims to the contrary, again had sent out too many "old soldiers," "lascivious sons," and "debauched hands" from "riotious, lousy, and infected places," men who responded only to stern rules and arbitrary justice. There is no doubt that for Englishmen the chief end of the law was to maintain order and to "terrify the evildoer." The heavy emphasis upon terrifying the evildoers suggests just how limited the freedoms of Englishmen were in 1610, for the *Lawes* were not in conflict with English rights.

Governor De La Warr had already restored a measure of discipline and order among the survivors. Immediately upon arrival in June 1610, he chastised the colonists for their "sluggish idleness" and ordered the church rebuilt and flags hung on the battlements. To later generations, these actions seem to have a ring of pomposity and hypocrisy, but De La Warr was well aware that Englishmen of that era responded to the signs and symbols of nationalism and religious unity. He divided the colonists into labor bands. Quickly, the old settlers and the new recruits rebuilt Jamestown and Point Comfort, cleared the fields, planted crops, and tended the livestock Gates brought in. Gates and Percy forced back the Indians from the forts, exacting ruthless revenge on the Kecoughtan and Paspahegh tribes, destroying the latter in a particularly brutal manner. The crisis passed.

There arrived in 1611 Captain Thomas Dale, Marshal for Virginia and commander of military forces. A veteran soldier of obscure origins, Dale had entered into the service of the United Netherlands as a captain in 1603 along with Gates. He was there in 1611 when the London Company secured his release from the Netherlands for five years to rejoin Gates in Virginia. Although he originally expected to serve only as marshal, circumstances between 1611 and 1616 often left him as the chief authority and acting governor in Virginia. Dale and "Dale's Laws" have become so synonymous that it is often forgotten that to him must go the credit for placing the colony on a permanent footing.

Quickly, Dale deduced that he must build new settlements, drive out the Indians from the peninsula between the James and the York, open up land for farmers, and place craftsmen and artisans to work behind secure palisades. These goals required a disciplined work force. Following De La Warr's example, Dale placed settlers into units under military officers with a published work schedule: work from 6 a.m. to 10 a.m., morning prayers, midday meals, rest, work again from 2 p.m. to 4 or 5 p.m., evening prayers, and evening meals. Sundays, in theory, were devoted to church services. At other times, the colonists could tend their own gardens. Still, both Dale and Gates had to drive their workers hard to exact even a six- or seven-hour workday. This lends credence to the view that the labor problem in early Jamestown rested not so much with the corporate community system of labor as it did with the expectations of Englishmen who migrated to Virginia believing that they could live with less effort than they had exerted in England. Why else would one migrate to a wilderness? Unfortunately, the tasks at which many labored in England demanded little consistent work. Or, perhaps more important, the tasks at which they labored rewarded them so poorly that they had had little incentive to exert themselves beyond what was absolutely necessary. In Virginia, old habits were hard to break, even when survival depended on it.

To the De La Warr–Gates instructions, the tall, gaunt marshal added his military orders. A new concept in Virginia, the instructions were fairly conventional military orders to those Englishmen who had served in Ireland or the Netherlands, "that University of War." All males were expected to stand watch or march against the Indians. For them, the *Lawes Divine* proved to be short courses in military science, courses they frequently refused to pass. Dale and his officers enforced the code with uniform sternness. Both Dale's methods and the *Lawes* remind us that Virginia was the first American frontier outpost. And, as in many frontier outposts, arbitrary justice, necessary to restrain the irresponsible and the criminal, injured the innocent in the process, though far fewer than tradition would have it.

Having organized the militia, Dale turned his attention to expansion. The colony had to escape the confines of the ill-starred and diseased Jamestown site. The best sites were on the upper James, where, as it drops down from the falls, the river meanders back and forth, leaving numerous necks and curls jutting out into the water. Dale selected the largest of these (Farrar's Island), "a convenient, strong, healthie, and sweet seate . . . about fifteen miles below the falls" to be the new main post. There, in September 1611, he moved 300 planters and built at Henrico forts, homes, a large church, storehouses, and a palisade across the two-mile neck of land, fronting the palisade with a moat after the Dutch manner. Then, he repeated this process at other sites down the river. The most successful enclosure was Bermuda City at the confluence of the James and Appomattox rivers. This large area, some twenty miles around, gradually became the new population center. Jamestown, with perhaps fifty residents, remained as the administrative center. By 1616, from the falls to the bay the James was dotted with enclosed farm communities at Henrico, Bermuda, West and Shirley Hundreds, Jamestown, and Kecoughtan. Across the bay at Cape Charles, on the tip of the peaceful Eastern Shore, the colonists erected Dale's Gift plantation.

Dale knew that Virginia could not flourish if the planters permanently hid behind palisades. Peace with the Indians was a necessity. Peace to Dale meant not coexistence between Indians and whites, but Indian removal from the James River basin. Steadily he, Gates, and Argall mounted attacks against isolated tribal villages and divided Powhatan's Confederacy. Then, in April 1613, Argall captured Pocahontas, who was visiting relatives along the Potomac, by bribing her hosts. With Powhatan's supposedly favorite daughter as a pawn, Dale played his own waiting game for nearly a year. Finally, he took several hundred men into the heart of Powhatan's territory. This show of blunt force, together with the conversion and marriage in April 1614 of Pocahontas to her tutor, Secretary John Rolfe, ended hostilities. A treaty was agreed upon. The Chickahominy tribe also capitulated and vacated their James River lands. The Pocahontas Peace survived eight years, outlasting both Pocahontas, who died of smallpox in 1617 during a triumphal visit to England with Rolfe, and the aged Powhatan, who died the following year.

For all his military successes, Dale's greatest achievement was stability. The infusion of new planters raised the population to 700 in 1611. Deaths reduced the numbers to 350 by 1613. Although there were few immigrants for the next three years, there were few deaths as well. In 1616, there were still 350 planters. For the first time—and the only time until the 1660s—births may have exceeded deaths. Among the 350 were 65 women and children. The keys to survival were ample food, peace, a tough sanitary code (including such simple changes as moving latrines and garbage pits outside the forts), and a respite from new waves of immigrants. The administrations of Gates and Dale provided the former; the latter was the inadvertent by-product of declining company revenues.

In one sense, the whole history of the London Company is a simple one: The company was never able to work its London and Virginia operations in tandem. When enthusiasm mounted in London, fortunes waned in Virginia; and news of these Virginia misfortunes caused "a great damp of coldness" among English investors, often just as conditions in the colony improved.

So it was after 1611. London faltered, financially drained, unable to attract new investors. In a revised charter in 1612, James granted permission for public lotteries. These raised little cash, often failed to pay off public ticket holders, and became such a scandal that Parliament eventually ended them. Ironically, the inability to raise monies meant that the company did not pour new shiploads of colonists into Virginia—giving the "ancient planters" relief from annual rounds of epidemics and raids on their carefully hoarded food caches.

Offsetting flagging interest in Virginia were the rising hopes for Bermuda. These semitropical isles just 700 miles east of Cape Hatteras might have provided the profits that Jamestown did not. James issued a third charter in 1612, extending Virginia's boundaries far enough to sea to encompass the Bermudas. The charter also radically changed the function of stockholder meetings. It shifted power from the company council to weekly and quarterly meetings at which stockholders openly debated corporate decisions. The treasurer and the council became administrators of this policy. Initially, little changed. Sir Thomas Smythe continued as treasurer, and most councilors remained in office. Later, this change had momentous effects and led to corporate factionalism and divisiveness within the London meetings. Although the stockholder meetings ended with the company's dissolution in 1624, the 1612 charter was the prototype of the Massachusetts Bay Company structure in 1629 and enabled the New England-bound stockholders to gain control of their own government by moving the stockholder meetings to New England.

The London Company promptly sold Bermuda to a subsidiary association of company investors, who in turn founded the Somers Island (Bermuda) Company under a separate royal charter in 1615. One could hardly tell the difference between the Virginia and Somers companies. Smythe was the treasurer of one and governor of the other. Both held their meetings in his London townhouse. The pleasant climate, the absence of Indians on the isles, and quick farming profits made Bermuda a flourishing colony. Eventually, the Somers Island Company came to an unprofitable end. With only 11,000 acres of land, the Bermuda islands could not sustain a commercially viable agricultural economy. Unfortunately, before this became apparent, the scramble for Bermuda profits created conflicts among the Virginia investors that proved fatal to the London Company.

Ironically, while England focused its attention on Bermuda, the colonists in Virginia stumbled onto their economic salvation—they became tobacco farmers. A corollary to aggressive expansion into Indian lands was agricultural self-sufficiency. Since the irate Indians would sell no more food, the planters had to feed themselves. The quest for food turned the Virginians from planters of a colony into planters of the soil. Freed from Indian attacks, inured to local diseases, and hardened by a tough work regimen, many colonists were ready to support themselves. Dale knew that few planters would remain in Virginia once their seven-year contracts were up unless they held land of their own. Therefore, in 1613 he offered to each "ancient Planter" whose indenture (contract) had expired three acres of land at Bermuda Hundred to work as his own, relieving these men of all obligations to the company except one month's service and an annual contribution of corn. Conversely, these men and their families no longer could call at the company magazine for food supplies.

The scheme succeeded. Both on company lands and at Bermuda Hundred, men and women became productive farmers. By 1616, the London Council proclaimed joyously and with only a modicum of hyperbole, "they sow and reape their Corne in sufficient proportion . . . their Kine [cattle] multiple to some

Cover of King James's tract attacking tobacco. (James I, A Counter-Blaste to Tobacco, *R.B.: London, 1604)*

hundreds; their Swine to many thousands." The colonists even sold food to the Indians whose crops had failed. In a very telling comment the Londoners added, "[E]very man hath house and ground to his own use . . . [and is] prepared and ready . . . to plant and sow such severall kindes of Seeds and Fruits, as may best befit the Soyle and Climate." After nine years, the company finally was willing to accept what Virginia could produce. What the adventurers did not say was that among the seeds to be planted was tobacco.

Tobacco first appeared in England in the 1580s, brought back by Drake and by the Roanoke settlers, who were fascinated by its Indian ceremonial uses. Through Raleigh, the "fragrant weed" gained rapid acceptance in fashionable Elizabethan circles. Smoking evoked mixed responses. Some physicians, ever alert to miracle cures, prescribed it as a most singular and sudden remedy against the migraine, the toothache, the fits of the mother, the falling-sickness, the dropsy, the gout, etc. Others called it the "noxious weed." King James, in his famous and anonymously published *A Counter-Blaste to Tobacco* (1604), branded smoking "a custome lothsome to the eye, hatefull to the Nose, harmefull to the braine, daungerous to the Lungs," and imposed a steep 12d-per-pound import duty on it. (The king acknowledged the pamphlet in 1616, just as Virginia tobacco entered the London market.)

King James and the Bible

Most people associate the name of James I of England with the authorized version of the English Bible. "Could never yet see a Bible well translated in English," he wrote, "I wish some special pains were taken for an uniform translation, which should be done by the best learned men in both Universities, then reviewed by the Bishops, presented to the Privy Council, lastly ratified by the Royal authority, to be read in the whole Church, and none other." When the translation committee named by James (fifty-four scholars, of whom forty-seven took part) issued the translation in 1611, with a dedicatory epistle to the king, it eclipsed all previous versions of the Bible.

Over time its majestic language, greatly influenced by the flowering of English literature under Elizabeth's long reign, became commonplace as worshippers heard it read at church services throughout Britain. In turn, the Authorized Version (as it became known in Britain) itself greatly impacted subsequent English literature. Even today, with many other English versions of the Bible readily available, the King James Version (as it is known in America) remains perhaps the one still most widely read.

The first king of Great Britain (England and Scotland) and Ireland, King James I founded the ill-fated Stuart dynasty in the early seventeenth century. (Ellyson, J. Taylor. The London Company of Virginia, *1908)*

James did not act out of personal prejudice alone. Tobacco cultivation and importation ran counter to prevailing economic thought. The prime purpose of colonies was the production of essential raw materials. Tobacco was a costly, nonessential luxury, a "dirty, filthy habit" that yearly drained off £200,000 into Spanish and Dutch mercantile coffers. Moreover, in the public mind its users were dilettantes who sat in idleness "drinking tobacco" in London's 7,000 coffee and tobacco houses. Tobacco might bring individual profits, but it did not fit Hakluyt's national economic goals even if it was produced in Virginia. Repeatedly, Englishmen from James I and Edwin Sandys to Charles I, Charles II, and the commissioners of trade and plantation in the 1670s urged diversification of the Virginia economy to produce useful and necessary staples, not tobacco. Only in the late 1680s did English policy makers accept the fact that a prosperous economy could be built on smoke and turn a nice profit for the English treasury as well.

John Rolfe, secretary of the colony, seeking tobacco for his own use, produced the first English tobacco in 1611. Finding the Indian variety, *Nicotiana rustica,* not to his taste, he covertly imported seeds of the milder West Indian crop, *Nicotiana tabacum.* In 1613, he shipped a small amount to Sir Thomas Smythe for private appraisal. After additional cultivation at his Varina farm, Rolfe sent off the first commercial crop of 2,300 pounds in 1615. That crop sold for 3s per pound (£345), the greatest single payload yet sent to London. The response was immediate: 20,000 pounds went out in 1617, earning 5s per pound, and 49,000 pounds in 1618. Virginians exported 330,000 pounds in 1626 and nearly 500,000 in 1630. After 1630, prices dropped below a shilling per pound and fell quickly thereafter toward the standard seventeenth- and eighteenth-century price of 1 to 3d per pound. Tobacco became the new gold. Colonists gave up cultivating company lands, filling their own small plots and the Jamestown streets with plants. The rush to tobacco came so quickly that many ignored their food crops, a few nearly starving in the midst of their tobacco boom. Just before leaving Virginia in 1616, Dale had to compel tobacco planters to till at least two acres of crops. His temporary successor, Captain George Yeardley, could not enforce the order, and by 1618 a food shortage loomed. When Rolfe returned to Virginia following the death of Pocahontas in 1617, he found Jamestown in disrepair, the "colony dispersed all about, a shambles," and all Indian defenses abandoned. Yet the colonists seemed contented.

The new deputy governor, the aggressive and corrupt Captain Samuel Argall, faced a difficult disciplinary problem. A new wave of epidemics and a brutal winter killed colonists, Indians, and animals alike in 1617–1618. Argall reinstituted the *Lawes Divine,* which Dale had removed at his departure. While he managed to avoid further catastrophe, Argall did not administer the colony with equanimity. Unlike Dale but very much like Yeardley, he frequently placed personal aggrandizement before the common good, especially in the use of his redoubtable ship, *The Treasurer,* outfitted by Sir Robert Rich, a principal Bermuda investor, which went privateering among the Spanish islands. Most of the accusations against De La Warr, Gates, and Dale for their maladministration of the *Lawes Divine, Morall, and Martiall* were actually chargeable against Argall.

By 1616, the company had come to a clear turning point. The end of the first seven-year stock period was at hand, and a dividend was due to stockholders and planters alike. But there were no cash dividends to be had. Instead, the company offered its only resource—land. Even then, it offered only 100 acres per share to paid-up stockholders who would buy an additional share. Virginia planters arriving before 1617 ("ancient planters") earned fifty acres for their efforts. That same year, the company established the famous headright system, offering fifty acres for each person paying his or another's passage into Virginia. The headright grants survived as the principal means of acquiring land for the remainder of the seventeenth century. At the outset, few new stockholders or settlers responded to the offer. However, the grants to the "ancient planters" were enough to squelch "the general desire in the best sort of return to England."

Lacking resources to transport additional colonists, the company devised a new form of settlement—the particular plantation. This was a private plantation formed by a voluntary association of stockholders who pooled their dividends and concentrated their efforts in a specific settlement along the James. The associates financed the full costs of their plantation, including transporting and maintaining settlers, most of whom came as indentured servants with allegiance to that particular plantation, not to the company. The first particular plantation was Smythe's Hundred (renamed Southampton Hundred in 1620), formed by Thomas Smythe, Sandys, and the Earl of Southampton in 1617. It encompassed nearly 80,000 acres in abandoned tribal lands along the Chickahominy River. Smythe's Hundred, Martin's Hundred, Berkeley Hundred, Flowerdew Hundred, Martin's Brandon, and Christopher Lawne's Plantation soon followed. Martin's Brandon was truly unique, for John Martin, an original councilor, had somehow wangled (probably through his father, a former Lord Mayor of London) a particular plantation totally independent of any company control. (The most famous of all particular plantations was one never settled in Virginia. In 1620, the company awarded a grant to the Pilgrims of Plymouth, England, who settled on Cape Cod, just beyond the 41st parallel limits of the 1606 grant.) Excavations at Martin's Hundred and at Flowerdew Hundred reveal that these plantations were relatively tightly settled villages reminiscent of the English village countryside. They were administered separately from company lands, often by men like Governor George Yeardley, Lieutenant William Peirce, and Abraham Peirsey, company officers, soldiers, and officials whose first obligation was supposedly to the company.

Invigorated by the first tobacco sales, stockholder enthusiasm revived in 1618. Governor De La Warr, having recovered his health, once again sailed forth "to make good the Plantation." He took with him instructions for completely reordering the land system and the government. En route, the luckless governor fell ill and died. Additional disturbing news reached London about Argall's administration and possible privateering escapades by *The Treasurer* against the Spanish. Smythe ordered Argall brought home to account for his stewardship. Others seized the occasion to charge Argall with misgovernment.

The company designated Captain George Yeardley governor. Yeardley was the son of a small London merchant, apprenticed into the army under Gates in the Netherlands in 1601 and commissioned in 1608. A survivor of the Bermuda wreck, he had been in Virginia since 1610, serving as acting governor in 1616–1617. Determined to make his fortune in Virginia, he had gone to London in 1617, married Temperance Flowerdieu, and was about to return to Virginia as manager of Smythe's Hundred when De La Warr died. Thomas Smythe and Edwin Sandys chose Yeardley to be governor, speedily procured a knighthood from the king, and sent Sir George Yeardley off to Virginia, the first Virginia governor to come from the rank and file of colonists.

Yeardley took with him a thoroughly revised set of orders and instructions, popularly called "the Great Charter." A major reform of the Virginia enterprise, these instructions are among the most important documents in Virginia history. Drawn by Treasurer Thomas Smythe and Assistant Treasurer Edwin Sandys, they contained two basic sections: the first and longest outlined a comprehensive land system for the colony; the brief second section extended the London Company government to the colony. From the second grew the Virginia General Assembly, hailed by later generations as the cornerstone of American representative government. To the colonists and stockholders, the most significant portion was the reformed land system. The colonists called this section "the Charter of Orders, Lawes, and Privileges." The governmental changes followed naturally upon this changed relationship of private landowners to the company.

The new land system was a carefully integrated plan to reward investors and planters, encourage immigrants, pay the cost of company management in Virginia, and finance a diversified economy. First, a dividend with no strings attached gave each shareholder 100 acres per share, with 100 acres more to be granted later; each "ancient planter" (pre-1616) paying his own way received the same dividend; each company tenant sent before 1616 received 100 acres but had to pay an annual quitrent fee of 2s per 100 acres to the company; and each person arriving after 1616 and paying his or another's way received the 50-acre headright and paid the quitrent fee.

Second, the company permitted stockholders to join with nonstockholders to purchase rights for particular plantations and even allowed nonstockholders to receive particular plantations by buying into the company.

Third, the company restructured its own Virginia operations. It divided the James River area into four corporate boroughs straddling the river, beginning with Henrico at the falls, then Charles City, James City, and Kecoughtan at the bay (renamed Elizabeth City by the General Assembly in 1619). In each borough, the company reserved 3,000 acres for its own enterprises, run by half-share tenants sent at company expense. To pay the cost of local government, it set aside 1,500 acres in each borough for the use of borough officials. The governor occupied a 3,000-acre tract near Jamestown in lieu of salary. Each parish minister would have a 100-acre farm (called a glebe) and an assurance that he could earn additional income equal to his annual salary of £200.

Finally, the company undertook to meet its initial promise to educate and Christianize the Indians. It established an Indian "college" at Henrico on Farrar's Island, to be supported by income from 10,000 acres of College Lands worked by half-share tenants.

The company expected to produce revenue from company enterprises, the sale of land rights for particular plantations, quitrents on private lands, and its own trade monopoly controlled through a resident agent, the cape merchant. Because the company now had to bear the cost only of maintaining settlers on its own lands, most of its income would go directly into stockholder dividends.

The results were immediate. The population jumped from 400 in 1618 to 1,000 in 1619. Hundreds of other settlers followed. Quickly, plantation villages sprang up along the James.

Smythe and Sandys knew that by establishing particular and private plantations they also had changed the lines of political authority. No longer did the governor have direct control over the colony's labor force. Each association ran its particular plantation, and the private planters controlled their own land. Furthermore, the Londoners deliberately blurred distinctions between company officials and private planters by employing men who had personal stakes in Virginia rather than men who intended to make their fortunes and return home. For instance, Yeardley as governor was responsible for supervising company lands and the cape merchant, but he also managed Smythe's Hundred and Weyanoke, developed the governor's lands for his salary, and established a large personal plantation, Flowerdew Hundred, as a long-term investment. Not surprisingly, these officers had a tendency to look out for their personal interests before meeting their obligations to the company.

Direct corporate government from Jamestown was no longer possible; cooperative government became essential. Yeardley was not governor with the "full and absolute power" of De La Warr, Gates, and Dale. He governed with the advice of an appointed council. For orders binding the whole colony, including the particular plantations, he must call representatives from the boroughs and plantations into an annual general assembly.

The Virginia General Assembly was a lineal descendent of the London Company stockholders' meeting. In Yeardley's instructions, the Londoners explicitly stated that they were establishing "a laudable form of Government . . . like as we have already done for the well ordering of our courts here." The planters' right to vote derived from the 1609 and 1612 charters, wherein a planter was considered to have earned a share by venturing to Virginia. The London stockholders voted their shares in the London meetings; the Virginia planters voted their shares through elected burgesses in the General Assembly. This concept of shared stockholder government carried over into a promise to allow the Virginia Assembly to accept or reject orders from the London council just as the London council could veto laws passed in Virginia. One also suspects that Company officials created the General Assembly to relieve themselves of burdensome administrative details.

Initially the General Assembly had only limited powers. The governor and the council, the main agents of administration, were appointed from London; the governor possessed an absolute veto; and the London council could exercise an additional veto over the governor. Although the assembly met again in 1621, 1624, and 1625, almost twenty years elapsed before the assembly became a fixed institution sanctioned by royal approval. At first, there was no two-house legislature. Seated at the first meeting on 30 July 1619 in the Jamestown church were Governor Yeardley, his 6 councilors, and 22 burgesses from the 4 boroughs and 7 plantations. John Pory, colony secretary and one-time member of Parliament, sat as speaker. Although then and later the two groups met separately in executive sessions, not until the 1640s did a bicameral assembly appear. Limited as its powers might be, the assembly established two important precedents at this session: Its members represented directly the boroughs and plantations from which they were chosen; and the members claimed the right to determine their own membership by excluding the burgesses from Martin's Brandon, on the grounds that under John Martin's grant his plantation was outside the company charter, an exemption rectified in 1622.

With no ringing declarations or recorded rhetoric, 27 sweltering and often sick men worked hard on day-to-day matters. With "general assent" and applause, they accepted as law the company's "charter of orders, lawes, and privileges," asking only greater protection for those "ancient planters" who had arrived before 1616. Melding together the governors' instructions with their own experiences, they passed a series of laws touching affairs peculiar to Virginia—a simple tax, tobacco price regulation, profit limits on prices charged by the cape merchant, acts concerning Indian trade, rules governing servants and masters, and prohibitions against drunkenness, gambling, swearing, and the wearing of "excessive apparell." To promote economic diversification, they ordered certain farmers to plant corn, mulberry trees, grape vines, hemp, and flax. They also required all religious services to be by "order of the church of

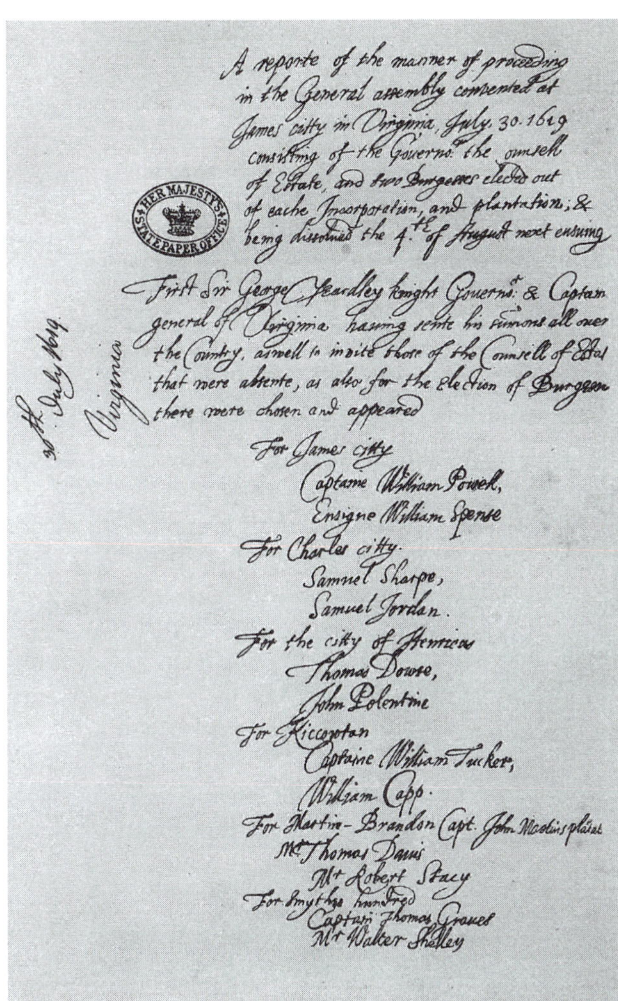

A reporte of the manner of proceeding in the Generall assembly convented at James citty in Virginia, July 30. 1619 consisting of the Gouernor the Counsell of Estate, and two Burgesses elected out of eache Incorporation, and plantation; & being dissolued the 4th of August next ensuing

HER MAJESTY'S STATE PAPER OFFICE

30th July 1619 Virginia

First Sir George Yeardley knight Gouernor & Captaine generall of Virginia hauing sente his summons all ouer the Country, aswell to invite those of the Counsell of Estat that were absente, as also for the election of Burgesses there were chosen and appeared

For James citty
Captaine William Powell,
Ensigne William Spense
For Charles citty
Samuel Sharpe,
Samuel Jordan.
For the citty of Henricus
Thomas Dowse,
John Polentine
For Kiccowtan
Captaine William Tucker,
William Capp.
For Martin-Brandon Capt. John Martins plantation
Mr Thomas Davis
Mr Robert Stacy
For Smythes hundred
Captain Thomas Graues
Mr Walter Shelley

Report from the Virginia General Assembly, the first representative legislative assembly in the colony, July 30–August 4, 1619. (Library of Congress)

England" and established a registry for marriages, births, baptisms, burials, and land grants.

Unfortunately, concurrent company affairs in London had not followed as smooth a course. Fundamental disagreement between Sir Thomas Smythe and Sir Edwin Sandys and their followers over economic goals for Virginia led to the ouster of Smythe as the treasurer, the elevation of Sandys to the post, then to bitter factional fighting at stockholders' meetings, and finally the dissolution of the company.

Sandys desired a return to Hakluyt's broad program of economic self-sufficiency. Along with many gentry, he had invested in Virginia out of patriotism as well as personal gain. The merchant leadership, including Smythe, were no less patriotic and strongly supported silk, iron, glass, wine, and naval stores production, but once tobacco and the carrying trade developed, they were willing to direct their attentions to those profitable ends. Tobacco, however, tended to benefit merchants more than it did the rank-and-file stockholders, who were willing to believe stories that the merchants profited from subcompanies such as

Robert Rich, Earl of Warwick (1587–1658)

Member of Parliament, proponent of English piracy against the Spanish, and holder of the English trade monopoly in Guinea and Binney, Robert Rich, second Earl of Warwick, became a member of the King's Council for the Virginia Company in 1619, the same year he succeeded to the title that his father had held. He was a strong ally of the Sandys faction as it attempted to control the Virginia Company and, through it, the Jamestown colony. When the king dissolved the company in 1624, Warwick was named to the Council in England for Virginia affairs. In his capacity as colonial administrator Warwick played instrumental roles in the procuring of patents for English colonies in Massachusetts, Connecticut, and Rhode Island. His Puritan leanings and advocacy of religious toleration eventually alienated him from the Crown, however, and led him to side with Cromwell during the English Revolution. Warwick River in Virginia was named in his honor, as was the town of Warwick in Rhode Island.

Sir Robert Rich, Second Earl of Warwick, was a colonial administrator and admiral. (Ellyson, J. Taylor. The London Company of Virginia, *1908)*

the Bermuda and cape merchant operations, which they were told drained potential dividends away from the parent company. Sandys, a full partner with Smythe in several tobacco enterprises, worried along with the king that Virginia was abandoning national goals for the "vile weed." Actually, the very success of tobacco may have rekindled interest in diversification. Many believed that if tobacco could succeed in Virginia, so could other, more useful staples.

A third and uncontrollable faction was led by Sir Robert Rich (now the Earl of Warwick) and the Rich family. Intensely nationalistic, the Puritan Riches had a fatal attraction to piracy against Spanish shipping and would not accept James's peace policy with Spain or his prohibitions against the use of both Bermuda and Virginia as bases for privateering.

In any event stockholders grew restless, the Sandys and Warwick factions united and forced Smythe to resign his office. Sandys became treasurer, and his associate, John Ferrar, became deputy treasurer. The king gave his assent to the changes.

Sandys entered upon his task full of the enthusiasm that had marked his progress from the favored son of the Archbishop of York to a leading member of Parliament. Long an advocate of aggressive colonization, he believed the key to economic diversification and self-sufficiency in Virginia was a large population. Devoting himself full-time to the company, Sandys somehow reversed the dismal popular image of Virginia. Between 1619 and 1623, the company awarded more than forty new patents for particular plantations, started several factories, settled the college lands at Henrico, persuaded 4,000 Englishmen to migrate, and found new investors for the project. Grape vines for wine and mulberry trees for silkworms were planted in every settlement. Yet Sandys's very success would lead to his failure.

The Sandys economic program placed special emphasis upon production of naval store, iron, silk, wine, pottery, and glass on company lands. To that end, the company invested thousands of pounds and sent out hundreds of colonists. A bold plan, it failed because it overdiversified, spread company resources too thinly, and relied for implementation on Virginia officials who devoted their attention to private plantations. Lacking capital reserves, Sandys had to secure quick returns from the iron, glass, and pottery factories. He could not. Nor could he overcome the colonists' devotion to growing tobacco. The sudden influx of thousands of ill-equipped, unseasoned new inhabitants stretched to the breaking point Virginia's ability to absorb new colonists.

Among the new settlers there was a noticeable decline in gentry and unskilled workers, a noticeable increase in farmers and tradesmen, and a sprinkling of German, Italian, and Polish artisans to start the new factories. With them, the company sent "an extraordinary choice lot" of 90 young women willing to go out as wives to settled Virginians. In 1620, 100 "maids, young and uncorrupt" sailed over. Following spirited bidding at the wharves in Jamestown, they were quickly spoken for. Several hundred boys and some girls, drawn mainly from the London streets, were sent out as apprentices and servants, their passage paid by charitable organizations. From London and Middlesex almshouses and jails came vagrants and criminals, but a decidedly lower percentage of the total than in the past. Most newcomers responded to the pamphleteers' radiant promises of a "new world," where the vexations of English life would be forever overcome. These were people who had hope. They were from among the "honest and industrious" poor, those who sought employment and believed they could improve their lots. From among these men, women, and children the English promoters hoped would come a stable family society in Virginia.

There also arrived in Jamestown one group of migrants for whom Sandys had made no plans. Late in August 1619, a Dutch privateer, battered while raiding the Spanish West Indies with Argall and *The Treasurer,* limped into the James River and traded "20 and odd Negroes" to Cape Merchant Abraham Peirsey for supplies. Several days later, Argall brought in the equally battered *Treasurer* with fourteen more Africans. Suddenly, Governor Yeardley and his councilors became aware of their predicament. To allow Argall with his illegally acquired cargo of Spanish slaves into Virginia would outrage the king by violating the Spanish peace. They drove off the *Treasurer* with its cargo to Bermuda. The Dutchman's black passengers were allowed to remain and were distributed among private plantations of Peirsey and Yeardley. Nothing was said about their presence to London. Four more Africans arrived between 1621 and 1623, and two black children were born in Virginia. The total number listed in the 1625 census was twenty-three. Their high survival rate suggests that these were either born in the Spanish West Indies or already "seasoned" against New World diseases. The status of these first Virginia black men and women remains unclear. Apparently, they were Spanish slaves when captured. Legally, they were treated as indentured servants; socially, they were identified from the beginning as a people apart.

The early 1620s saw misfortune piled upon misfortune. Simultaneously in 1621, the company lost its lottery license, the mainstay of its income; was deprived of its privilege to import tobacco tariff free into England; and negotiated a most unfavorable tobacco contract with the Crown. That same year, Yeardley resigned as governor to tend his private plantations. The company replaced him with the very popular and able Sir Francis Wyatt and sent over George Sandys, Sir Edwin's younger brother, to be resident treasurer.

Terrible weather ruined crops in both 1622 and 1623, and a plague decimated the livestock in 1623. Epidemic after epidemic ravaged the "unseasoned" new Virginians at an appalling rate. In 1619, there were nearly 1,000 inhabitants; in March 1620 only 887; and in March 1621, just 843, although 1,051 Englishmen sailed to Virginia the previous year. Nearly 1,000 new immigrants a year entered the James from 1619 to 1623. Yet Virginia had only 1,193 white persons alive in 1625. The cruelest blow was the great Indian uprising of 1622.

The peace with Powhatan had been a major factor in the colony's expansion after 1614. Freed from constant guard duty, planters worked their fields at ease. New lands were added by treaty with neighboring tribes, and trade flourished between colonists and the Indians. With reorganization, the country could turn to its stated purpose of converting the Indians to Christianity. As the son of an archbishop and himself a writer of religious papers, Edwin Sandys was an ardent proponent of missionary activities. Aided by John Ferrar and his brother, Nicholas Ferrar, Sandys dispatched George Thorpe, another former M.P. and a member of the London council, to Virginia to open the long-planned "college" to educate and catechize Indian boys. The "college" opened on the Henrico lands in 1621. Other youths were taken into colonists' homes, and even a few English boys went off to live in Indian villages. An integrated society of English and anglicized Indians appeared in the making.

The rapid expansion of occupied lands frightened the Indians. Many of the new villages were on traditional tribal farming lands, which were never replaced. The yearly influx of thousands of immigrants was equally distressing, not just because of the numbers but because the "epidemics" often killed as many Indians as colonists. After 1617, the Indians frequently had to purchase food from the Virginians. Nor was the rapprochement offered by Thorpe any consolation, for the Indian priests quickly recognized the "college" for what it was—an undermining of Indian culture and religion through the capture of the minds and souls of Indian youths. Aroused, the often-divided Powhatan tribes united behind Opechancanough. A charismatic leader who assumed direction of the confederacy in 1619, Opechancanough brilliantly organized an attack to drive the English from Virginia.

On Good Friday morning, 22 March 1622, Indians living in settlements and tribes adjacent to each plantation launched coordinated assaults. The extent of the attack and the relatively few security breaches confirm the magnitude of Indian fears about coexisting with the English on their land. Nearly 350 colonists died, among them 6 councilors, and most tragically, the gentle George Thorpe, a target for a particularly hideous execution. Jamestown was saved by an Indian youth, Chanco, who alerted his master of the impending strike. Hardest hit were the dispersed, isolated, and unprotected settlements along the upper James and Appomattox Rivers. The colonists abandoned many plantations, including Martin's Brandon, Henrico, Weyanoke, the College Lands, and the Iron Works. Planters moved downriver and onto the Eastern Shore. Not surprisingly, plague, scurvy, dysentery, and typhoid fever came with them into the overcrowded, unsanitary posts, killing more than the uprising itself had.

The massacre marked an irreversible turning point in Indian–white relations. The hopes of Thorpe, Sandys, and Wyatt for a compatible Christian Indian–English society in Virginia disintegrated in the face of Opechancanough's war of extermination. Embittered by "the treacherous violence of the Savages" in response to their own policy of "gentleness and fair usage," nearly all in the colony agreed with Edward Waterhouse, who wrote that we "may now by right of Warre, and law of Nations invade the Country, and destroy them who sought to destroy us . . . turning the laborious Mattocke into the victorious Sword." Serious intent to educate the Indians disappeared and did not reappear until the founding of the College of William and Mary in 1693. Virginian Indian policy now was directed toward driving out hostile Indians and forcing surviving tribes to submit to Crown authority in a tributary status.

Retribution by the "victorious sword" was decisive and cruel. Led by Yeardley, among the most outspoken exponents of an aggressive Indian policy, the colonists wreaked havoc on Indian villages, killing hundreds of tribesmen and their families, spreading smallpox among villages, seizing food caches, and burning fields. Although the Indians managed an occasional victory, only new epidemics and a shortage of munitions kept the planters from completely destroying all Tidewater Virginia Indians. By the time the seasonal attacks ended in 1626, the Virginians had broken the confederacy and driven Opechancanough north of the York River, where he remained on the defensive until he made one last sortie in 1644.

The Indian Massacre of 1622 was the beginning of the end for the London Company. Although more settlers died from disease in 1622 than died at the hands of the native warriors, news of Indian wars had a psychologically disruptive effect on English investors and populace alike. At first, the company suppressed word of the disasters and ignored the colonists' plaintive pleas for arms and men. Then the London Council blamed the disaster on the planters, whose "sinful transgressions" brought down the "heavie hand of Allmightie God" in judgment. Food, arms, and soldiers were not forthcoming. Instead, the company ordered Wyatt to stay at Jamestown, reoccupy the major plantations, and collect all customs and fees owed the company. The council turned to the king for aid. He offered only a few decrepit cannons from the tower. Incredibly, several hundred scantily supplied migrants sailed out to the plantations in 1622 and 1623, where they arrived disease wracked, unleashing another wave of pestilence upon the colony. In all ways, the company response to the disaster revealed the bankruptcy of leadership and finances that were to destroy the company within months.

Had Sandys devoted his full attention to reforming the Virginia economy and closing wounds opened by his election as treasurer, he might have averted the internal problems that ruined the company. As historian Charles M. Andrews observed long ago, Sandys was "high spirited, something of a visionary, a tolerationist, and a liberal by temperament. When convinced of the rightness of his course, he could become intolerant and obstinate in seeking his ends." This intractableness converted debates over general policy into petty and personal disagreements.

In 1620, the Sandys–Warwick alliance had fallen apart. The issue: the old Rich interest in piracy, privateering, and the Spanish. In 1617 and 1618, Sandys had pushed the company to inquire into Argall's governorship and into the operation of *The Treasurer.* The result of the inquiry convinced him that the Riches intended to use Bermuda and Virginia as privateering bases for raids on Spanish shipping. As detente with Spain was the cornerstone of James's foreign policy, to condone such raids would endanger the company. Rightly, Sandys stopped all nonofficial voyages from Bermuda. Then he carried the matter one extra step and reported the voyages to the Privy Council, unnecessarily exposing Warwick before the king. Tenuous at best, the Sandys–Warwick ties were sundered.

Sometime before April 1620, Sir Thomas Smythe sent to James word that Sandys's maneuvers and lack of business acumen were undermining mercantile support and confidence in the company. James informed the company council that he would not approve Sandys's reelection and suggested they turn to a merchant again. Shocked by the king's intervention, the council inquired further and found that the king's suggestion was not an order, only an observation. With that, the stockholders elected as treasurer the Earl of Southampton, Shakespeare's patron and Sandys's closest ally. The change was only cosmetic. Sandys continued to lead the company until the Jones Commission took control in 1623.

Whereas the Indian Massacre of 1622 exposed the company's weaknesses, the tobacco contract brought down the Southampton–Sandys leadership. All along, Sandys had been determined to restrain tobacco planting. For one thing, the cape merchant, forced by the General Assembly to buy tobacco in Virginia for 3s per pound, lost money when reselling it on the European market, where Virginia tobacco could not compete with superior Spanish varieties. For another, the whole Sandys economic program presupposed weaning Virginia away from tobacco to useful staples. To that end, the company in 1620 limited the number of tobacco plants a planter could tend and in 1621 limited production to 100 pounds of tobacco per planter. Neither measure was successful. The planters were not about to be weaned from a product that Secretary John Pory reported in 1619 returned £200 to one man, "another by the means of sixe servants hath cleared at one crop a thousand pound English," or allowed the local cowherd to go about on Sundays "in freshe flaming silkes" and the wife of a one-time coalminer to dress in "a silken suite" and a beaver hat with a "faire perle hattband." Few achieved such success, but the possibilities seemed there. In any case, a myth that is believed is more significant than a truth unaccepted. All colonists, whatever their trade, quickly became tobacco planters, forsaking their crafts and undermining the company factories.

James refused to renew the company's exemption from tobacco duties and levied the standard 12d duty on Virginia tobacco. When smuggling immediately appeared, James established a tobacco trade monopoly and sold it to Lon-

Henry Wriothesley, Third Earl of Southampton (1573–1624)

Cambridge graduate, friend, and patron of Shakespeare (who dedicated to Henry his poems "Venus and Adonis" and "The Rape of Lucrece"), and conspirator in the Essex Rebellion, Henry Wriothesley became interested in the colonization of Virginia in 1602. A strong financial backer of many voyages of exploration and discovery, he was named to the Royal Council for Virginia in the Charter of 1609. In 1620, he was elected treasurer of the Virginia Company, an office he held until the king dissolved the company in 1624. Southampton was a supporter of the Sandys faction that led the colony for many years; he was often embroiled in controversy and various intrigues.

Southampton also had a penchant for military service, which he engaged in as early as 1596 and 1597 when he joined the naval expeditions led by his friend Robert Devereux, second earl of Essex. He accompanied Essex to Ireland in 1599 as General of the Horse but was recalled after Queen Elizabeth learned that he had secretly married one of her ladies in waiting. In 1614 Southampton served as a Protestant volunteer in Germany, and in 1624 he raised a troop of volunteers to fight in the Netherlands against Spain. He had hardly landed in the Netherlands when he caught fever and died, as did his companion, his son James.

Portrait of Henry Wriothesley, patron of William Shakespeare and proponent of the settlement of Virginia. (Ellyson, J. Taylor. The London Company of Virginia, *1908)*

don merchant Sir Thomas Roe. As a sop, he halted all tobacco planting in England. In 1621, the Privy Council ended the Roe monopoly and further restrained Spanish imports. However, the council required all Virginia and Bermuda tobacco to pass through England and pay English customs before being resold in Europe. Finally, in 1622, Sandys concluded that the Virginia and Bermuda companies would have to take over the tobacco monopoly themselves. Unhappily, by the time the tobacco contract was negotiated, the Indian uprising had taken place. Aware that Sandys's economic program was in collapse and with no bargaining leverage, the Sandys–Southampton leadership accepted a most unfavorable contract. Among stockholders, the contract brought dismay and distress and a violent hue and cry about the high administrative salaries, even from Sandys–Southampton men. Warwick was outraged by what he perceived was a cost distribution deliberately weighted against his Bermuda interests. Nevertheless, Sandys gained company approval of the contract by packing the company meetings. Warwick determined to get better terms and to bring the Sandys–Southampton leadership down.

Sir Nathaniel Rich, in a brilliant and persuasive presentation before the Privy Council, demonstrated that the contract, with its monopolistic features, was counterproductive to the financial interests of colonists and Crown alike. In March 1623, the Privy Council revoked the tobacco contract and in its stead substituted a plan whereby any Englishman could import all the tobacco he wished, providing he paid customs duties and shipped all his tobacco to England for transshipment to the Continent.

Revocation of the tobacco contract had major consequences. Politically, it was a major defeat for the Sandys–Southampton faction; economically, it allowed any English merchant and Virginia planter to bypass the cape merchant, thus completely undermining any profits the company could make from its only profit-making staple. Finally, it signified a reluctant recognition in England that tobacco could not be eliminated as a crop. Yet James's hope for other staples did not diminish. In 1622, he wrote endorsements for a book on vine growing and silk production and ordered copies sent to every Virginia plantation.

By late 1622, company quarterly stockholder meetings became contentious, often tumultuous affairs. Because voting was by head, not by shares owned, numbers became advantageous. As the numbers grew, order became almost impossible. Speakers were shouted down. Members stopped attending. In its dying days, the company could not maintain common courtesies. The nadir came when Lord Cavendish, a Sandys man, challenged Warwick to a duel; it never came off.

It was these company stockholder meetings in London that aroused protests against the "democratical" character of the company and caused James to question "popularness" in corporate government. Nowhere are there Crown complaints about the existence or conduct of the Virginia General Assembly. The source for the abhorrence of "democratical tendencies" was the reaction to events in London, not in Virginia.

Encouraged by their success in the tobacco negotiations, the Warwick and Smythe factions pressed upon the king in council the unbusinesslike character of the Southampton–Sandys management. James, whose inclination always had been that the merchant adventurers, not gentry, should manage overseas enterprises, was disposed to listen. In April 1623, Captain Nathaniel Butler, the ousted governor of Bermuda, laid before the Privy Council a copy of his "The Unmasked Face of Our Colony in Virginia as it was in the Winter of the Year 1622" (actually 1622–1623). A highly partisan tract, the "Unmasked Face" revealed in dramatic fashion for the first time what the company desperately had tried to hide and never effectively allayed—that all the glorious efforts of the past three years had come to naught. Virginia was in a shambles and thousands of Englishmen in their graves. Butler's observations were confirmed by dozens of letters sent from Jamestown in 1623. In bitter and unguarded words never

William Cavendish, Earl of Devonshire (c. 1550–1626)

Born to prominent parents, William Cavendish, member of Parliament for Newport and sheriff of Derbyshire, was an early supporter of the effort to colonize Virginia and the prime mover in the incorporation of the Bermudas into the territory of Virginia, which took place in 1612. After being created the first Earl of Devonshire in 1618, he became a strong supporter of the Sandys faction in its bid to maintain control of the London Company—so much so that he challenged the Earl of Warwick to a duel during a meeting of company stockholders. Fortunately for both, the duel never came off.

Devonshire was supported at court by his niece, Arbella Stewart (1575–1615), an English noblewoman who for a while was being groomed as a potential successor to Queen Elizabeth. Devonshire himself was for almost two decades the patron of Thomas Hobbes (1588–1679), the English philosopher, political theorist, and author of *Leviathan* (1651), who served as tutor and traveling companion to Cavendish's namesake and heir.

Portrait of William Cavendish, Earl of Devonshire. Cavendish was an English politician and supporter of colonizing Virginia. (Ellyson, J. Taylor. The London Company of Virginia, *1908)*

meant for public eyes, Virginia Secretary George Sandys castigated the London leadership for poor management and its pathetic response to the Indian uprising. Governor Wyatt curtly wished "little Mr. Deputy" Ferrar would visit the colony, where he could meet face to face those whom he was chastising as indolent high-livers and sinners.

In April 1623, the king appointed a commission headed by Sir William Jones, justice of the Court of Common Pleas, to fully investigate the operations of both the Smythe and the Sandys–Southampton regimes. All factions were ordered to restrain themselves in public and in company courts. Unfortunately, the Sandys faction, enraged by Butler's "Unmasked Face," issued "A Declaration made by the Council for Virginia," a vicious and unnecessary diatribe against Warwick. They had overreached themselves.

After lengthy hearings throughout the summer, the king, the Privy Council, and the Jones Commission agreed that the company had to be reconstituted if it were to be more responsive to national and investor needs. To that end, the Privy Council proposed that both the treasurer and council in London and the governor and his council in Virginia would be selected with concurrence of the king. This would be a return to the 1606 form of government. No mention was made of a General Assembly in Virginia, probably because it was the London management that was at issue. In October, the Sandys faction refused to accept the revised charter. Neither would Smythe or Warwick.

In November 1623, James went into court. Not surprisingly, in view of the total disarray of Company affairs and the inability of the Jones Commission to find hope for leadership in any faction, the King's Bench handed down a decision on 24 May 1624 favoring the king and dissolving the company. In June, James appointed the Mandeville Commission to recommend a new government for Virginia affairs. In effect, Virginia affairs were placed in royal receivership.

In Virginia, another commission, established by the Jones Commission, was investigating conditions in the colony. Composed of John Harvey, a ship captain trading into Virginia; John Pory, the former secretary; Abraham Peirsey, the onetime cape merchant; Samuel Mathews, a planter; and John Jefferson, who had been a member of the first House of Burgesses; the commission arrived in Virginia in February 1624. Its very positive report on conditions in Virginia did not reach England until after the court rescinded the charter.

And so the London Company came to an inglorious end, bankrupt, strife torn, and devoid of its charter. In the process of giving birth to a colony in the New World, a colony and a country that eventually became all and more than the Smythes, Sandyses, and Hakluyts predicted it would be, the company had killed itself. It was an act of unintended self-sacrifice that consumed both the stockholders and all but 1,200 of the 6,700 colonists who had gone out to the Chesapeake. In a way, they had founded not one colony, but two, for without Virginia, a lone proprietor, Lord Baltimore, could never have planted Maryland, an occurrence that took place within a decade of the company's demise.

A

Accohannock Indians

The Native Americans occupying the northern area of the Eastern Shore of the Chesapeake Bay at the time of the English settlement of Jamestown were an ancient Algonquian-speaking people allied with the so-called Accomac Confederacy. Subsisting on small crops of corn and squash and the abundance of wild game on the large peninsula, the tribe's principle village was on the Annemessex River near present-day Crisfield, Maryland. Other villages were scattered along the Annemessex and along Accohannock Creek (in present-day Virginia) as well as on some of the nearby islands in the bay. With the bay as a barrier, the Accohannock (sometimes spelled Occohannock) were able to exercise considerable autonomy compared to other tribes in Powhatan's empire. Because the colonists had been directed to position their settlement far enough inland from the Atlantic Ocean to stay out of sight of the Spanish, the Eastern Shore was off limits for immediate settlement by the English, and hence the Accohannock perceived no threat to their way of life. The European arrivals found the Accohannock peaceful, friendly, and willing to furnish them with foodstuffs, which were always in short supply during the colonists' early years. Captain John Smith thought generally that the native peoples inhabiting the rivers of the Eastern Shore were "of little stature, of another language from the rest, and very rude"—by contrast, the Accohannock "doth equalize any of the Territories of *Powhatan* and speak his language."

After the death of Chief Powhatan, the Accohannock became even more alienated from their sister tribes on the Virginia mainland. Powhatan's successor, his half brother Opechancanough, tried to entice the Accohannock to join his efforts to rid the land of the English; but this they rejected, causing Opechancanough in turn to renounce the Accohannock. In the 1640s, the Accohannock began to lose their lands to the English as the latter began to see the advantages of having their own outposts on the Eastern Shore. The tribe soon was forced to formally surrender its ancestral lands to the English; some of its members retreated toward Maryland, and others adopted the ways of the white settlers. Intermarriage between the Accohannock and the English became a common practice, and some present-day tribal families can trace their history back to that time. Tradition has it that the Clan Mothers of the tribe "prayed for peace and survival and received a vision to follow Pocahontas, to marry their daughters to the white colonists in order to hide *in plain sight,* survive and preserve the tribal bloodlines until in the fullness of time the tribe could be reborn." By the time Governor Sir William Berkeley needed to seek refuge on the Eastern Shore (during Bacon's Rebellion), the Accohannock settlements had almost completely

Sixteenth-century Native Americans cultivate a field near Fort Caroline at the mouth of the St. John's River, as portrayed in a woodcut by French artist, cartographer, and explorer, Jacques Le Moyne de Morgues (c.1533–1588). (de Morgues, Jacques Le Moyne. Brevis narratio eorum quae in Florida Americai provincia Gallis acciderunt, *Frankfurt, Germany, 1591)*

given way to the colonists. In 1659, the Maryland Accohannock began calling themselves a different name, Annemessex, reflecting the name of the river along which they lived.

The Accohannock are among those Native American peoples of the eastern United States who have petitioned the federal government for official recognition. The tribal office and museum are located north of Crisfield in Marion, and the tribe has plans to establish nearby a Native American Living Village to interpret early Algonquin life and culture. The Accohannock also hold annual summer and fall powwows, both of which are open to the public.

Related entries: Accomac Indians; Berkeley, Sir William; Chesapeake Indians; Chickahominy Indians; Kecoughtan Indians; Manahoac Indians; Mattaponi Indians; Monacan Indians; Nansemond Indians; Opechancanough; Pamunkey Indians; Paspahegh Indians; Warraskoyak Indians

Suggestions for further reading

Helen C. Rountree. 1989. *The Powhatan Indians of Virginia: Their Traditional Culture.* Norman, OK, and London: University of Oklahoma Press.

C. A. Weslager. 1959. *The Accomac and Accohannock Indians from Early Relations.* Onancock, VA: Eastern Shore of Virginia Historical Society.

Accomac Indians

"On-the-other-side-of-the-water place" or, more simply, "across the water," was the meaning of the name of the Native American people who occupied the Chesapeake Bay's Eastern Shore at the time of the English colonization of Virginia. Captain John Smith was the first settler to meet the Accomac (Accawmacke), an event that took place while Smith was making his first expedition up the Chesapeake Bay. According to Smith, the natives at Cape Charles gave him directions for finding the principal town of the Accomac, which lay on the peninsula at the head of Kings Creek, near Cheriton in present-day Northampton County. At the Accomac village, Smith and his fellow explorers "were kindly intreated" by the tribe's chief, whom Smith in his *Map of Virginia* (1612) described as the most civil native he had yet met in the New World (Smith changed his mind after running across the Massawomeke). Smith differentiated between the two tribes that he encountered, the Accomac proper, with about eighty warriors, and its sister tribe to the north, the Accohannock, of about forty warriors.

Smith's account of the Accomac, the longest written one from the period, is a somewhat odd story that perhaps recounts a quick-acting infectious disease that had recently struck the tribe. "This king," wrote Smith,

> was the comliest proper civill Salvage wee incountred: his country is a pleasant fertill clay-soile. Hee told us of a straunge accident lately happened him, and it was? Two deade children by the extreme passions of their parents, or some dreaming visions, phantasie, or affection moved them againe to revisit their dead carkases, whose benummed bodies reflected to the eies of the beholders such pleasant delightfull countenances, as though they had regained their vital spirits. This as a miracle drew many to behold them, all which, (being a great part of his people) not long after died, and not any one escaped. They spake the language of Powhatan wherein they made such descriptions of the bay, Iles, and rivers that often did us exceeding pleasure.

The Accomac chief, known variously as Esmy Shichans, Debedeavon, and, to the English, the Laughing King, commanded the southern part of the peninsula, whereas his younger, more charismatic brother Kiptopeke commanded the people in the upper territory, the Accohannock. Later, Okiawampe became king of the Accomac, and after him, in the 1650s, his daughter became queen.

The two sister tribes of the Eastern Shore got along well with one another but paid only grudging tribute to the powerful chief on the mainland, Powhatan. After the arrival and settlement of the English, the Accomac were even less amiable to Powhatan's successor, Opechancanough. Not only did living on the fringe of Powhatan's empire give the Accomac relative autonomy from their more dominant and warlike neighbors, it also gave rise to significant social and cultural differences. The Eastern Shore Indians, for instance, practiced different rituals and befriended Europeans more easily, providing food and trading beaver skins without compulsion, and refraining from joining in the Indian attacks on the settlers in 1622 and 1644. The Accomac also subsisted more on fishing and crops than on hunting (although they did partake of the abundant fowl along the coast). Smith said the Accomac did not fish with hook and line or arrows like other Powhatan Indians but "use staves like unto Javelins headed with bone. With these they dart fish swimming in the water. They have also many artificiall weares in which they get abundance of fish."

Although the Accomac were friendly with the English, most of the tribe's lands ultimately passed out of its hands, and its people were either displaced or acculturated into English society—despite the facts that the Virginia General Assembly had passed laws prohibiting the colonists from settling on Accomac lands in 1660 and that the tribe had assisted Governor Sir William Berkeley in 1676 when he fled to the Eastern Shore to escape the army led by the insurrectionist Nathaniel Bacon. A century later, Thomas Jefferson observed in his *Notes on the State of Virginia* that the Accomac and the Pamunkey were the only tribes still living on their ancestral lands. Even so, it was only a handful of Accomac men and women, and even fewer remained in the area in the nineteenth century.

The colonists adopted the name Accomac in 1634 when creating the shire that encompassed the whole Eastern Shore; in 1642, the name was changed to Northampton, the name also given to the original county. In 1663, however, the county was divided and the northern part renamed Accomac County. The Virginia General Assembly changed the name to Accomack in 1940. Still largely rural, Accomack County today has a population of about 39,000 people, of whom only about .03 percent can trace their ancestry back to their Accomac forebears.

Related entries: Accohannock Indians; Berkeley, Sir William; Chesapeake Indians; Chickahominy Indians; Kecoughtan Indians; Monacan Indians; Manahoac Indians; Mattaponi Indians; Nansemond Indians; Opechancanough; Pamunkey Indians; Paspahegh Indians; Warraskoyak Indians

Suggestions for further reading

Helen C. Rountree. 1989. *The Powhatan Indians of Virginia: Their Traditional Culture.* Norman and London: University of Oklahoma Press.

Captain John Smith. 1612. *Map of Virginia.* London: S.I.

C. A. Weslager. 1959. *The Accomac and Accohannock Indians from Early Relations.* Onancock, VA: Eastern Shore of Virginia Historical Society.

Algernon, Fort

Located at Cape Comfort (now Old Point Comfort) on the northern bank of the mouth of the James River at present-day Fort Monroe, Virginia, Fort Algernon was part of the earliest English defenses established on the Chesapeake Bay. Planned as a defense against the Spanish, orders for its construction were given to Captain John Ratcliffe by George Percy, president of the Council in Virginia, shortly after John Smith left the colony for the last time on 4 October 1609. First called Algernon's Fort and variously spelled as Algernown, Algernourne, Algarnoone, Algernoone, and Algernoune, it was named after an ancestor of Percy, William Algernourne de Percy, who came to England with William the Conqueror. It was from there that any ships wishing to travel up the James would be challenged by cannon fire if friendly contact were not established first. It was also from here on 8 June 1610, that representatives of the recently arrived Thomas West, Lord Governor De La Warr, intercepted and turned back the departing colonists who had abandoned Jamestown on the preceding day, following the tragic period that came to be known as the Starving Time. Fort Algernon appears to have been destined to ensure the permanence of the English in North America and could have played a larger and earlier role than it did. While it was used as a point of defense on the James River and served as the launching point for returning the colonists to Jamestown, it possibly could have prevented, or at least reduced, the number of deaths related to the Starving Time at James Fort. Traveling to Fort Algernon just days before the arrival of Lord De La Warr, President Percy was astonished to find that the inhabitants were so well provisioned that they were feeding their abundance of crabs to their hogs. Scores of people had starved to death in the preceding months, although less than forty miles downriver their countrymen were living in relative abundance.

Following Percy's return to England in April 1612, the battlements became known as Point Comfort Fort. At times falling into disrepair and ravaged by hurricanes and Dutch marauders, the fort and its successors intermittently continued to be part of the defense of the entrance to the James River until 1667, when it was completely destroyed by a "great storm." In 1727, it was decided to rebuild the defenses and name it Fort George; a more substantial fortification stood there until 1749, when another powerful hurricane arrived, and the fort that had contributed so much apparently lost its last battle.

Related entries: Percy, George; West, Thomas, Lord De La Warr

Suggestions for further reading

Edward Wright Haile, ed. 2001. *Jamestown Narratives: Eyewitness Accounts of the Virginia Colony: The First Decade: 1607–1617.* Champlain, VA: Round House.

David Beers Quinn. 1977. *North America from Earliest Discovery to First Settlements: The Norse Voyages to 1612.* New York: Harper & Row.

Conway Whittle Sams. 1929. *The Conquest of Virginia: The Second Attempt: An Account, Based on Original Documents, of the Attempt, Under the King's Form of Government, to Found Virginia at Jamestown, 1606–1610.* Norfolk, VA: Keyser-Doherty.

Lyon Gardiner Tyler, ed. 1906. *The Cradle of the Republic: Jamestown and James River.* Richmond, VA: Hermitage Press.

——. 1907. *Narratives of Early Virginia: 1606–1625.* New York: Scribner's.

A Silly Sort of a Fort

James Town Island is rather a *Peninsula,* being joyned to the Continent by a small Neck of Land, not past twenty or thirty Yards over, and which at Spring-tides is overflowed and is then an absolute Island. Now they have built a silly sort of a Fort, that is, a brick Wall in the shape of a Half-Moon, at the beginning of the Swamp, because the Channel of the River lies very nigh the Shoar; but it is the same as if a Fort were built at *Chelsea* to secure *London* from being taken by Shipping. Besides Ships passing up the River are secured from the Guns of the Fort, till they come directly over-against the Fort, by reason the Fort stands in a Vale, and all the Guns directed down the River, that should play on the Ships, as they are coming up the River, will lodge their Shot within ten, twenty, or forty Yards in the rising Bank, which is much above the Level of the Fort; so that if a Ship gave but a good Broad-side, just when she comes to bear upon the Fort, she might put the Fort into that confusion, as to have free Passage enough. There was indeed an old Fort of Earth in the Town, being a sort of *Tetragone,* with something like Bastions at the four Corners, as I remember; but the Channel lying further off to the middle of the River there, they let it be demolished, and built that new one spoke of, of Brick, which seems little better than a blind Wall, to shoot wild Ducks or Geese.

If they would build a Fort for the Security of the Town and Country, I conceive it should be on *Archer's Hope Point,* for that would stop the Ships from passing up the River, before they come to the Town, and would secure the Town from being blocked up by Sea. The Channel at *Archer's Hope Point* lies close by the Shoar, and makes such an Angle there by reason of *Hog Island,* that going up or down the River, let the Wind be where it will, they must there bring the contrary Tack on Board, and generally when they about the Ship as they call it, they are so near the Shoar, that a Man may almost fling a Finger-stone on Board. How much this hinders the Motion of a Ship, and what Confusion it must be to them to bring a contrary Tack on Board, whilst they have all the Guns of a Fort playing so nigh upon them, may readily be conceived. *Archer's Hope* is a neck of Land, that runs down three Miles long, not much past half a Mile broad betwixt the main River and *Archer's Hope Creek,* which has large Marshes and Swamps; so that a Citadel built upon the Point, would almost be impregnable, being it could be attack'd no way but one, which is so narrow a slender Neck of Land, that it would be difficult to take it that way: And it would secure *James Town* from being blocked, being it would not be past a Mile by Water, to the Point of *James Town Island.* The Island is so surrounded with Water and marshy Land, that the Town could never be bomb'd by Land.

—The Reverend John Clayton to the Royal Society, 17 August 1688

Annemessex Indians

See Accohannock Indians

Archaeology

Archaeology at Jamestown has had a relatively short, sometimes controversial history. Perhaps the earliest archaeological excavations recorded at Jamestown, although amateur by today's standards, were those conducted by Mary Jeffrey Galt, one of the founding forces of the Association for the Preservation of Virginia Antiquities (APVA). In 1897, four years after the APVA acquired the site, Galt claimed to have dug "quite deep inside of the south wall of the church" at the original settlement site. The APVA had acquired about 22 ½ acres of Jamestown Island from the previous owners, Mr. and Mrs. Edward E. Barney. Fortuitously, their acquisition included the original fort site and the only standing, above-ground, seventeenth-century structure on the island—"the lonely ruins of the old church tower." In 1901, the Barneys began digging for artifacts on their remaining part of the island, and

Jamestown archaeological site. Archaeologists have been exploring the Jamestown site since the late nineteenth century. The Jamestown Rediscovery project was initiated in 1994 to find evidence of the 1607 James Fort. To date, the project has recovered 200,000 artifacts and the remnants of fort structures. (Photo by Frank E. Grizzard, Jr.)

in the same year, the APVA began its excavations of the church. The church site and many accompanying graves were explored, with the loss of much archaeological evidence. Many artifacts ended up in boxes with only minimal identification. Nonetheless, evidence was found to indicate that much would be gained by a proper excavation of the site.

At the turn of the twentieth century, Colonel Samuel H. Yonge conducted a series of excavations in conjunction with his work with the "United States Engineer Department" to construct a seawall along the banks of Jamestown Island as a preservation measure. He concluded that the fort—although in the general vicinity of where it was found during the most recent excavations, beginning in 1994—had been washed away many years before his work in the area by the erosive actions of wind and the waters of the James River. He made a very detailed map of his findings and conjectures, and the fort site is shown as having its easternmost bulwark in nearly the same location as the actual fort's westernmost bulwark. It was a very good approximation, other than the fact that most of the fort as described by Yonge already had been washed away by the time he began his investigations. As Yonge described it,

> A natural site for the fort would have been just east of the "little vale" at the upper extremity of the fourth ridge [at the western end of Jamestown

> Island]. Thus situated, the guns of its north bastion would have swept the branch of the swamp below and of the vale above, while those of its east and west bastions would have commanded the river front and the channel approaching from below, as did the guns of its successor, the Confederate fort of 1861. In the above described position the part of the branch of the swamp between the second and fourth ridges would have afforded additional protection against the Indians. The third ridge was possibly strategically as favorable as the fourth, but its crest is two feet lower and its area above the level of great tides much smaller. It was, therefore, not as well adapted to the needs of the first settlers.

Yonge added that, while the Confederate forces were excavating the soil to make their fortifications, "pieces of armor and weapons of the early 'James Towne' period were found, a good indication that the fort of 1607 was located about as above described." One cringes at the thought of what was lost during the building of those fortifications.

Yonge cannot be faulted for his conclusions, however. American archaeology at the time of his work was in its infancy, and the sources that describe the location of the fort site were unclear and, in some cases, still unknown. As he wrote in 1903,

> No ancient charts of the island and town of the Jamestown period (1607–1698) have been discovered. "The Draughte by Roberte Tindall, of Virginia, Anno 1608," and "Chart of Virginia," sent to Philip III of Spain in the same year by Zuñiga to accompany the report of Francisco Maguel . . . "the Irishman," a spy in the service of Spain . . . although possessing some merit as reconnoisance sketches, prove to be inaccurate on comparison with modern maps, and furnish information of but little value as to the shape of the island and the site of the town.

Considering that the channel of the James River was quite far from shore during Yonge's excavations, and the writings of George Percy, who reported that "our shippes doe lie so neere the shoare that they are moored to the Trees in six fathom water," it was natural for Yonge to assume that the original fort site had been lost to the river for centuries. For reasons known mainly to him, he concluded:

> It seems probable that the island was not attacked by the river before 1700. Under this assumption, therefore, the whole period of the island's abrasion to the time of its protection in 1901, would be two hundred and one years. Observation of the bank in recent years shows that its annual rate of recession has been about four feet. Prior to the extensive use of side wheel steamers on James River, probably about 1860, and when occasional strong winds between west and north were the sole destroying agents, the rate probably did not exceed two feet. Applying the above rates for forty years and one hundred and sixty-one years respectively, the total width of the prism of abrasion would amount to about 482 feet.

Allowing for the questionable assumption that the island suffered no erosion for nearly the first century of the settlement, the calculated 200 years of erosion, coupled with Percy's statement about how close deep water had been to the fort site, would certainly lend credence to the belief that most of the fort had long since disappeared before Yonge's time. According to Yonge's estimate, "the hydrographic contours off the western shore of the island [where the fort was thought to have been] show the channel gradually nearing that shore from above until it approaches to within about one hundred and seventy-five yards of it, at about three hundred yards above the tower ruin." Deep water that far from shore would not have allowed for mooring of the ships to trees onshore at the fort site as Percy described. The reasonable conclusion that Yonge drew from that understanding was that too much of the settlement-era shoreline had disappeared for remains of the fort to be extant.

A contemporary of Yonge who was much involved in discovering what remained of "Old James Towne" was the president of the College of William and Mary, Lyon Gardiner Tyler. His writings about the findings on Jamestown Island provide more insight into the thinking followed by Yonge and others when reaching their conclusions about the location and fate of the original fort site. Tyler quoted French professor L. H. Girardin from his monthly magazine, *Amoenitates Graphicae* (1805), who wrote,

> This place of original settlement (Jamestown) has undergone a very considerable alteration by

James Fort

The accent left no doubt they were British. "What are you doing?"

I was lost in the act of scraping loose dirt from a dark streak in Jamestown's yellow clay.

"Archaeology," I answered, hoping that would end the dialogue so I could get on with the digging.

No luck. "So have you found anything?" he said earnestly enough that I felt compelled to give a serious answer.

"Absolutely. See this black stain in the clay?"

"Yes."

"Well, that's what's left of a 1607 fort wall . . . James Fort."

"Really? Hmmmmm."

Silence for a moment, then she said, "You mean that's it? That's all there is? America, the last of the world's superpowers, began as . . . just dirt?"

"I never thought about it quite like that . . . but, yes, I guess it was . . . just dirt."

"But," she continued, "shouldn't there be a ruined castle or . . . some marble columns . . . or something real?"

"No. . . . There was indeed . . . just dirt. . . . but you know what else? I guess plenty of . . . well . . . just hope."

"Oh . . . BRILLIANT," they said in unison. "Yes. . . . brilliant indeed."

—William M. Kelso, *Jamestown Rediscovery*

Reconstruction of defensive palisade with 1606 de Gheyne musketeer shown above excavated palisade. (Courtesy of APVA Preservation Virginia)

the elementary war which the waters and the winds have unceasingly waged against it. Its diminution both on the southern and western side may be easily traced. Many yards of the palisades erected by the first settlers are still to be seen at low tide standing at least 150 to 200 paces from the present shore. The pieces of timber which were fixed perpendicularly in the ground, have decayed, until they have become entirely submerged by the gradual advancement of the river upon the land, where the fort originally stood. This fact shows that the land has sustained a great loss on its southern side; on the western the attrition is perhaps still more consid-

> erable. This conjecture acquires a high degree of probability for what we see every day still taking place, and from the very narrow slip of land (even this is inundated at the time of high water) now remaining on that side as the only obstacle to the force of the water, which threatens soon unless counteracted by labor, to form a new channel through the island, *a denomination which Jamestown may shortly assume.*

Tyler related that he was

> told by a person who lived on the island as a youth that a cypress tree that now stands two hundred and ninety feet in the water from the shore near the old magazine, was, in 1846, on the shore where the water at high tide would scarcely flood. . . . Probably, then, fifty or sixty acres at the upper part of the island [where the fort was assumed to have been placed] have been worn away in the course of two hundred and ninety-three years.

The work of Yonge and Tyler, although valuable and informative, and their conclusions, although reasonable but ultimately proven incorrect, left the fate of the original fort site still shrouded in mystery.

The next major archaeological inquiries began on 11 July 1934, after the National Park Service, which had recently acquired the part of Jamestown Island not already owned by the APVA, sent John Zaharov and a crew of the Civilian Conservation Corps to the site. As renown archaeologist Ivor Noël Hume describes it, the archaeologists included individuals who had spent time on both the Colonial Williamsburg and the Yorktown excavations. The 100 Civilian Conservation Corps crew members arrived "commanded by foremen reportedly experienced in archaeological work." As Hume tellingly relates, "Even when the supervisors *are* fully trained, the prospect of launching fifty untrained diggers onto a fragile and complex archaeological site is enough to chill the blood. In this instance the supervisors were not and could not have been trained to do justice to the remains of a hitherto unstudied archaeological period." The result was, said Hume, "a totally inappropriate means" of conducting archaeological research. As the months passed, frictions developed between the architects and the crews of archaeologists, until, during the summer of 1936, it got to the point that, as Hume puts it, "legend has it, the dispute extended to the troops in the trenches. Across one of [the] . . . arbitrary three-foot frontiers [established between the two crews], pickaxes and shovels were wielded in malice as invaders and defenders faced off." Excavations were temporarily suspended until better arrangements could be made. As Hume describes it, the two groups were involved in what may be termed almost a culture war. The architects were interested mainly in the structures that could be found, analyzed, and recorded. The archaeologists, on the other hand, understood the larger picture and what the purpose and scope of historical excavations meant. As Hume points out, however, the contemporary understanding of proper archaeological techniques still hindered the effectiveness of the relatively enlightened views of the archaeologists working on the site at the time. Then, in 1936, "the Harrington Era in the history of Jamestown" began.

J. C. Harrington arrived in Jamestown late in 1936 to continue the excavations, but, unlike his predecessors, he had the advantage of having been trained in both architecture *and* anthropology. Harrington brought both of those backgrounds to bear with positive results. His work, according to Hume, resulted in "first-rate field drawings (the product of his architectural training) and . . . improved digging and recording techniques designed to address the kinds of concerns expressed in 1935 by the beleaguered and frustrated anthropologists."

In the summer of 1937, archaeologist Carl F. Miller was given the task of investigating an area of the island that some earlier researchers had suggested might be the site of the original fort site. This area, known as the Elay-Swann site, was east of the true fort site and had yielded some intriguing evidence of early occupation. But after excavations revealed too few artifacts of the right age, Harrington concluded that the site did not contain enough seventeenth-century remains to warrant further investigation as a possible original fort site.

The 1930s excavations, bedeviled by squabbling between the two major classifications of professionals assigned to the task—architects and archaeologists—lasted only a few years and left a legacy of unanswered questions and controversies. Although Harrington's approach yielded better science than had previous attempts, the original fort site remained undiscovered.

In the mid-1950s, as the 350th anniversary of the founding of Jamestown approached, another attempt to discover the James Fort site was made, this time under the leadership of John L. Cotter, who assigned assistant archaeologist Joel Shiner to the task of conducting test excavations to determine the best digging site. The method with the greatest promise of finding the desired site, at least if one is looking for signs of a fort palisade, was not employed in the 1950s or at any previous time, for that matter. In order to find a length of wall, large areas must be excavated so that any continuous lines of post molds can be discovered. Most of the excavations conducted through the 1950s had consisted of small trenches and pits dug at various locations in search of artifacts. Large-scale patterns are not easily revealed when such disjointed searches are conducted. Nonetheless, Shiner's work did at least help rule out that further time needed to be spent on the Elay-Swann site. While the fort site remained as mysterious as ever, successive generations of archaeologists were being afforded the luxury of narrowing their search for its remains—if there were any to be found.

Because of the general state of archaeological technique at the times of the earlier excavations, along with the destruction inflicted on the site during the erection of Confederate earthen fortifications in 1861, a protective seawall in 1901, and decades of plowing while the land was in use for farming, some information about the site of America's beginnings was uncovered—and much of it was lost. Many theories about the fort's exact location were put forth, and various locations around Jamestown Island were excavated and investigated to determine exactly where the original fort site might have been. Some, such as Colonel Yonge, had come close in their estimation of its location, but none had demonstrated indisputable proof. In the last decade of the twentieth century, however, the elusive fort's secret hiding place was to be uncovered at last.

As already discussed, the early attempts at uncovering Jamestown's past were sometimes more harmful than useful. Certain techniques and rules must be understood and followed if the maximum amount of information is to be extracted from an archaeological site without losing crucial evidence in the process. If these methods are not followed, more can be lost than gained. These techniques were well understood by the team that began excavations on Jamestown Island in the mid-1990s under the leadership of William M. Kelso. This was a new breed of archaeologists, with years of experience unearthing some of the most important history in the United States, and they were formally trained in the latest archaeological techniques. A new approach arrived with Kelso, and it was to have dramatic and long-sought effects. James Fort would be found and with it a new and better understanding of the birthplace of America.

Prior to coming to Jamestown as director of archaeology, Kelso had already had a long and prestigious career in the field. He had been director of archaeology at Colonial Williamsburg's Carter's Grove, as well as at Thomas Jefferson's two homes, Monticello and Poplar Forest. Additionally, he served as commissioner of archaeology for the Virginia Historic Landmarks Commission. He had spent more than thirty years acquiring knowledge of historic archaeology and its techniques, and he was well prepared for what could be considered the most important archaeological undertaking in the history of the United States: uncovering and interpreting the genesis of the nation.

Kelso conducted extensive research before beginning to excavate at Jamestown, including an exhaustive examination of the work done at the site by his predecessors. Layers of soil uncovered by the earlier efforts were labeled and could be seen under glass at the site, and there was a written record of much of the previous work. As Kelso writes, he and his colleagues studied the descriptions of the excavations conducted before he arrived and concluded that this site required further investigation, and he knew he was the man to do the job.

As Kelso points out, there are very few known, seventeenth-century written records on which to

Jaquelin-Ambler House

Ruins of the Jaquelin-Ambler House, located in the "New Towne" section of Jamestown. The house was built, c.1710. (iStockphoto.com/Joshua Leigh)

The ruined walls of the Jaquelin-Ambler House stand as a testimony of the late colonial period (eighteenth century), when Jamestown Island was no longer the seat of government and when, as the town declined, the island became the private estate of two families, Ambler and Travis. The present walls of the Jaquelin-Ambler House constitute the center portion of a rather impressive residence that was flanked by two wings. It was begun about 1710, and when fully established, it had formal gardens, the brick walks of which have been partly uncovered during archaeological work on the town site.

—Charles E. Hatch, Jr., *Jamestown, Virginia: The Town Site and Its Story* (Washington, D.C., 1952) rely when attempting to locate and define the fort site. Mentions are made of the fort and its environs, and scant few contemporaneous representations of the fort's location and shape have been uncovered. And (as discussed previously) most researchers had concluded that the original settlement site had been lost to the river forever. But along with all the previous excavations and limited first-hand accounts of the colony, as Kelso relates, when it came to his approach to the project, there was also "plenty of . . . well . . . just hope." To supplement this hope, Kelso employed exceptional scientific and archaeological skill combined with extensive historical research and knowledge. As he writes, definitive archaeological proof had to be discovered before he could claim that the original fort site had been found. Discovering this proof required a "deliberate, ever-expanding excavation going from one excavated area to an adjoining area where the apparent pattern of fort period fragments led." This was problematic due to the history of Jamestown Island following the establishment of the colony.

With the basic technique determined for searching for the fort's remains, it was then necessary to decide where to start looking. Kelso had three basic theories for finding the best locations to begin the search. First, Kelso reasoned that, as churches seldom move from their original sites without leaving a record of the move, it was probable that the church at Jamestown was at or very close to its original location. Second, a most likely place to look would be wherever artifacts associated with the correct time period already had been found. As the third theory—and possibly the most useful in the end because it was supported by firsthand, contemporaneous accounts of the location of the site—written descriptions of the first colonists and visitors to the settlement, coupled with a map from around 1608, provided enough detail to compare the data with the present-day terrain and make an educated guess. This was done, and "ongoing archaeological discoveries corrected and re-corrected the hypothetical fort model until it finally fit precisely onto the modern landscape."

After determining the method and location, work began in earnest. Then, in 1994, an exciting discovery was made. A section of palisade trench running near the river's edge was found, along with a parallel line of postholes. This was interpreted as possibly the southern wall of the fort, as predicted from the documented evidence. By September 1996, the evidence uncovered led to the conclusion that part of the original fort site still remained on land. Over the next few seasons, more evidence of the fort's exact extent was revealed. But "it was not until the last possible projected segment of the east wall and extensive area within the Civil War earthwork were opened up that the model and the ground could be brought together with precision (2002–2003). The hypothetical model and the actual site became a perfect fit at last." But still, as Kelso also writes, the "mere 'claims' to finding something as important as ground zero of the 'genesis' of the United States of America needs detailed proof." More than a decade of careful excavation, preservation, and research have provided just such evidence.

The Jamestown Rediscovery project, as Kelso's excavations and research are known, has uncovered hundreds of thousands of artifacts, nearly half of which date to the 1607–1610 time period. Hundreds of feet of palisade wall stains have been revealed, as well as evidence of numerous buildings, cellars, and wells. To the east of the fort, another palisade wall stain and the remains of a large building were found attached to the fort's remains. Among the artifacts recovered is the whole gamut of items used in the everyday life of the first settlers: coins, ceramics, cloth, seals, tobacco pipes, pieces of armor and weapons, ammunition, eating utensils, medical instruments, copper beads and ornaments used for trade with the Native Americans, jewelry, tools, toys, glass, pieces of musical instruments, dice, parts of household furnishings—essentially everything that would have been part of the settlers' lives. Most important, many of these items can be and have been determined to have been in use during the first years of the settlement, and inside the confines of the now clearly defined fort walls.

The various episodes of archaeological excavation at Jamestown have been, at times, somewhat questionable, even tumultuous affairs. The first attempts were relatively crude and destructive compared to today's efforts. But the century of excavations has at last produced the desired results.

Because of the efforts of all the dedicated individuals who have contributed to the excavation and interpretation of the archaeological remains at Jamestown, the location of the birthplace of the first permanent English settlement in the New World is now known with assurance. With scientists and researchers of the caliber of Kelso and his colleagues continuing to apply their skills and expertise to the endeavor, that birthplace can now be understood and properly appreciated as well.

Related entries: James Fort; Jamestown Church Tower; Kelso, William M.; Smith's Fort

Suggestions for further reading

"APVA Preservation Virginia Fact Sheet." 2003. Richmond, VA: Association for the Preservation of Virginia Antiquities.

John L. Cotter. 1958. *Archaeological Excavations at Jamestown, Virginia.* Washington, DC: National Park Service.

William M. Kelso. 1984. *Kingsmill Plantations: Archaeology of Country Life in Colonial Virginia.* San Diego, CA: Academic Press.

William M. Kelso, et al. 1995–2001. *Jamestown Rediscovery.* 7 vols. Richmond, VA: Association for the Preservation of Virginia Antiquities.

—— with Beverly Straube. 2004. *Jamestown Rediscovery 1994–2004.* Richmond, VA: Association for the Preservation of Virginia Antiquities.

Ivor Noël Hume. 1994. *The Virginia Adventure: Roanoke to James Towne: An Archaeological and Historical Odyssey.* New York: Alfred A. Knopf.

Lyon Gardiner Tyler. 1906. *The Cradle of the Republic: Jamestown and James River.* Richmond, VA: Hermitage Press.

Samuel H. Yonge. 1904. *The Site of Old "James Towne" 1607–1698.* Richmond, VA: Hermitage Press.

Archer, Gabriel (c.1575–c.1610)

Captain Gabriel Archer, one of the original colonists who landed at Jamestown, had the distinction, with Mathew Morton (after whom Morton's Bay was named because of the serious wounds he received there), of being among the first Jamestown settlers to encounter and be wounded by "the Savages creeping on all foure, from the Hills like Beares, with their Bowes in their mouthes," during the First Landing at Cape Henry. Educated at Cambridge and Gray's Inn, Archer took part in Bartholomew Gosnold's expedition to New England in 1602, which he wrote about and is credited with having written some of the best surviving firsthand accounts of the early Jamestown expedition and settlement.

Archer's first stay in Virginia lasted a year, from April 1607 to April 1608, when he and Edward-Maria Wingfield, a member of the original Jamestown Council with Archer, left for England with Christopher Newport on the *John and Francis.* In the summer of 1609, Archer returned to Jamestown as an avowed member of the anti-Smith faction and remained there until his death during the Starving Time that winter.

In addition to being remembered for his writings, Archer is remembered as the namesake of Archer's Hope Creek and Archer's Hope, the point of land just east of Jamestown on the James River, explored first on 12 May 1607, when it was considered for settlement—before Jamestown. Archer's Hope so impressed the colonists with its resources and the fact that it "was sufficient with a little labour to defend our selves against any Enemy" that "if it had not beene disliked, because the ship could not ride neere the shoare, we had setled there to all the Collonies contentment."

A man of learning and adventure, Gabriel Archer can be appreciated for contributing much to what we now know about the earliest days at Jamestown.

Related entries: Archer's Hope; Gosnold, Bartholomew; Wingfield, Edward-Maria

Suggestions for further reading

Philip L. Barbour, ed. 1986. *The Complete Works of Captain John Smith (1580–1631)* (vol. 1). Chapel Hill and London: University of North Carolina Press.

George Percy. 1922. "'A Trewe Relacyon'—Virginia from 1609 to 1612" (*Tyler's Quarterly Historical and Genealogical Magazine,* vol. 4).

Lyon Gardiner Tyler, ed. 1907. *Narratives of Early Virginia: 1606–1625.* New York: Scribner's.

Archer's Hope

On 12 May 1607, while searching the banks of the James River for the best location for their settlement, the Jamestown colonists discovered a promising point of land at the mouth of College Creek, five or six miles northeast of their eventual choice. According to George Percy, it

> was sufficient with a little labour to defend our selves against any Enemy. The soile was good and fruitfull, with excellent good Timber. There are also great store of Vines, in bignesse of a mans thigh, running up to the tops of the Trees in great abundance. We also did see many Squirels, Conies, Black Birds with crimson wings, and divers other Fowles and Birds of divers and sundrie collours of crimson, Watchet [light blue], Yellow, Greene, Murry [reddish brown], and of divers other hewes naturally without any art using. We found store of Turkie nests and many Egges. If it had not beene disliked because the ship could not ride neere the shoare, we had setled there to all the Collonies contentment.

This site was named for Captain Gabriel Archer, who may have been the first to spot it, and who, along with Bartholomew Gosnold and others, appears to have preferred it as the location for their settlement. Archer's Hope may have been the name given this spot because of Gabriel Archer's discovery and preference for the site, but the word *hope* was still applied to a small bay or river mouth. Whether it was merely Archer's desire to settle there or just common usage of the word *hope* at the time, Captain Wingfield and others won out, and the following day they moored their ships to the trees at Jamestown Island, at the time still connected to the mainland by a now washed-away land bridge. The next day, 14 May 1607, they began the work of unloading their ships and building the first fortifications of James Fort.

Related entries: Archer, Gabriel; Gosnold, Bartholomew; Wingfield, Edward-Maria

Suggestions for further reading

Edward Arber, ed. 1910. *Travels and Works of Captain John Smith* (part 1). Edinburgh, Scotland: J. Grant.

Philip L. Barbour, ed. 1986. *The Complete Works of Captain John Smith (1580–1631)* (vol. 3). Chapel Hill and London: University of North Carolina Press.

Charles E. Hatch, Jr. 1957. "Archer's Hope and the Glebe" (*Virginia Magazine of History and Biography*, vol. 65).

Conway Whittle Sams. 1929. *The Conquest of Virginia: The Second Attempt: An Account, Based on Original Documents, of the Attempt, Under the King's Form of Government, to Found Virginia at Jamestown, 1606–1610.* Norfolk, VA: Keyser-Doherty.

Argall, Sir Samuel (1580–1626)

Although not one of the original colonists, Sir Samuel Argall played an integral role in the English settlement and advancement of the Virginia colony, taking on the role of enforcer for the Virginia Company at Jamestown.

Born in 1580, he was cousin by marriage to Sir Thomas Smythe, treasurer of the Virginia Company during its early years, and was chosen by the company to find a shorter route to its interests in Virginia, which he did from May to October 1609. Argall briefly succeeded Christopher Newport as the company's pilot for Virginia and spent some months during 1610–1611 surveying and trading around Chesapeake Bay and the east coast, opening trade with the chief of the Potomac Indians, described at the time as "a King as great as Powhatan, who still remaines our enemie, though not able to doe us hurt." In 1613, Argall's deeds took on a bit of an ominous nature, at least to the rivals of the English, when he kidnapped Pocahontas and held her hostage for the return of English prisoners, weapons, and tools taken by members of her father Powhatan's tribe. That deed was done in the "heate of our home furies & disagreements," an atmosphere created by five years of constant warfare between the English and the "revengefull implacable Indians," as colonist Ralph Hamor phrased it when describing Argall's exploits. Argall's strategy was psychological, buttressed by brute force; he "partly by gentle usage & partly by the composi-

Sir Samuel Argall meets with Virginia natives. Argall is remembered for opening trade with the Potomac Indians, kidnapping Pocahontas for the return of English prisoners taken by Powhatan, and serving for a short term as governor of Virginia. (Library of Congress)

tion & mixture of threats hath ever kept faire & friendly quarter with our neighbours bordering on other rivers of affinity."

A few months after taking Pocahontas, in 1614, Argall, "flourishing thus under the blessings of peace and plenty, and having no occasion of fear or disturbance from the Indians," decided to explore further northward. When he reached Cape Cod, the natives gave him the surprising news that white people had settled in the area. Suspecting non-English inhabitants and "being very zealous for the honor and benefit of England," he went out looking for the settlement, which he soon found: a French fortification, complete with a ship, at Mt. Desert Island (Maine). Argall's sudden and unexpected appearance caught the French completely off guard, and what followed was quite dramatic:

> His unexpected arrival so confounded the French, that they could make no preparation for resistance on board their ship; which Captain Argall drew so close to, that with his small arms he beat all the men from the deck, so that they could not use their guns, their ship having only a single deck. Among others, there were two Jesuits on board, one of which being more bold

Sir Samuel Argall

Governor Argall made the colony flourish and increase wonderfully, and kept them in great plenty and quiet.

—Robert Beverley, *The History and Present State of Virginia* (1705)

than wise, with all that disadvantage, endeavored to fire one of their cannon, and was shot dead for his pains. Captain Argall having taken the ship, landed and went before the fort, summoning it to surrender. The garrison asked time to advise; but that being denied them, they stole privately away, and fled into the woods. Upon this, Captain Argall entered the fort, and lodged there that night; and the next day the French came to him, and surrendered themselves.

From his Jesuit prisoners, Argall learned of another French settlement at Port Royal (Annapolis Royal, Canada) as well as remnants of another on the Isle de Ste. Croix on the Ste. Croix River. Argall rather effectively destroyed these settlements also, although he left standing at Port Royal the "barns, mills, and other conveniences" that the French had constructed. He then returned to Virginia with a cargo of plunder and French prisoners.

Argall served as acting governor of Virginia beginning in 1617 but was replaced by Sir George Yeardley in 1619 after falling out of favor with the Virginia Company. In 1617, he established the short-lived Argall's Town, or Gift, about a mile north of Jamestown in the "old fields" where the seat of the Paspaheghs had stood before the arrival of the English. He returned to England in May 1619 and was knighted in 1622. Described by contemporaries as a "Gentleman of good service" and "a good Mariner, and a very civil Gentleman," Argall died suddenly following a military expedition to Spain in 1625–1626.

Related entries: London Company; Pocahontas; Smythe, Sir Thomas

Suggestions for further reading

Philip L. Barbour, ed. 1986. *The Complete Works of Captain John Smith (1580–1631)* (vol. 1). Chapel Hill and London: University of North Carolina Press.

Alexander Brown. 1890. *The Genesis of the United States* (vol. 2). Boston: Houghton Mifflin.

Edward Wright Haile, ed. 2001. *Jamestown Narratives: Eyewitness Accounts of the Virginia Colony: The First Decade: 1607–1617.* Champlain, VA: Round House.

Edward D. Neill. 1871. *The English Colonization of America: During the Seventeenth Century.* London: Strahan.

Ivor Noël Hume. 1994. *The Virginia Adventure: Roanoke to James Towne: An Archaeological and Historical Odyssey.* New York: Alfred A. Knopf.

David Beers Quinn, ed. 1979. *New American World: A Documentary History of North America to 1612* (vol. 5). New York: Arno Press and Hector Bye.

Lyon Gardiner Tyler, ed. 1907. *Narratives of Early Virginia: 1606–1625.* New York: Scribner's.

Association for the Preservation of Virginia Antiquities

In its 118th year and the nation's oldest statewide preservation organization, the Association for the Preservation of Virginia Antiquities (APVA) is largely responsible for the recovery of most of the extant physical evidence of the original fort at colonial Jamestown, as well as the evidence of its first and subsequent inhabitants and history. Founded in 1889 under the guidance of Mary Jeffrey Galt, its "originating spirit," in 1893 the APVA acquired 22 ½ acres of Jamestown Island from the previous owners, Mr. and Mrs. Edward E. Barney. According to its mission statement,

> The Association for the Preservation of Virginia Antiquities preserves, interprets, and promotes real and personal property relating to the history and people of Virginia.
>
> It serves as an educational and cultural resource for its membership, the general public, and special audiences.

> The Association is dedicated to upholding the public's trust by adhering to current standards of accepted preservation and museum practices.

The association manages or owns thirty-three properties throughout Virginia, including the aforementioned James Fort site, located on the 1,500-acre Jamestown Island, the remainder of which is owned by the National Park Service. The APVA also is associated with Bacon's Castle, Virginia's "oldest datable brick residence;" the Old Cape Henry Lighthouse, which sits in sight of the original Jamestown settlers' first landing site in Virginia; and Smith's Fort Plantation, which includes the site of a fort begun by John Smith in 1608 or early 1609 (presumably as a refuge in case the original fort site came under attack) on Grays Creek in Surry County, just across the James River from Jamestown.

Shortly after acquiring the acreage on Jamestown Island, the APVA, in association with an engineer named John Tyler, Jr., began excavating the interior of the old church site adjacent to what is now known to be the location of the original fort. It is here that the old brick church tower still stands. Dating back to just after 1647, this tower is the oldest above-ground structure still standing on Jamestown Island. The excavations were part of a project undertaken in preparation for the 1907 tercentennial celebration of the founding of Jamestown. Fifty years later, more excavations were carried out in anticipation of the 350th anniversary of the establishment of the first permanent English settlement in the New World. In all of those and other excavations at the site, many artifacts were found and much was learned, but because of the archaeological understanding and techniques at the time, much was destroyed. To its great credit, however, the APVA severely restricted archaeological investigations at Jamestown during most of the twentieth century. In 1994, under the auspices of the APVA, the most extensive, careful, and productive excavation of the James Fort site began in earnest.

In its own words,

> In 1994 the APVA launched Jamestown Rediscovery, an ongoing archaeological research, interpretation, and education program to identify and interpret the remains of the original 1607 James Fort. Led by Dr. William Kelso this work is considered to be one of the most important archaeological programs in America. Besides the dramatic finding of the remains of the original fort in 1996, archaeologists have unearthed more than 500,000 artifacts that are revealing much new information about the settlers.

Indeed, the findings at Jamestown are astounding, considering that for at least 200 years it was thought that the site had been washed away by the James River. In addition to the everyday artifacts to be expected at such a site, also found were "over 250 feet of two palisade wall lines, the east cannon projection (bulwark), three filled-in cellars, and a building, all part of the triangular James Fort. Also a palisade wall line and a large building were found attached to the main fort to the east."

Wells have provided a treasure trove of artifacts that includes everything from drinking mugs to pieces of armor and weapons used by the original inhabitants. Inside the palisade wall of Jamestown fort was made one of the most intriguing discoveries. On 5 September 1996, archaeologists uncovered "the buried skeletal remains of one of Virginia's first colonists. Nicknamed 'JR' after the cataloguing designation JR102C, this settler was a European male who stood five feet six inches tall and was between the ages of 19 and 22. The lead bullet and shot fragments lodged in his lower right leg contained enough force to fracture his tibia and fibula bones, rupturing a major artery below the knee. JR would have bled to death within minutes."

Such efforts to identify and preserve sites as those described above have led the APVA to be considered one of the premiere preservation organizations in America. Through its programs and branches, the organization purports to serve more than 625,000 interested individuals annually, with millions more accessing its online resources. Because of its stewardship of its portion of Jamestown Island, the Association for the Preservation of Virginia Antiquities has preserved and is helping to interpret one of the most important historical and archaeological sites yet found: Jamestown, the birthplace of America.

Related entries: Archaeology; James Fort; Jamestown Church Tower; Kelso, William M.; Smith's Fort

Suggestions for further reading

William M. Kelso. 1984. *Kingsmill Plantations: Archaeology of Country: Life in Colonial Virginia.* San Diego, CA: Academic Press.

—— et al. 1995–2001. *Jamestown Rediscovery.* 7 vols. Richmond, VA: Association for the Preservation of Virginia Antiquities.

—— with Beverly Straube. 2004. *Jamestown Rediscovery 1994–2004.* Richmond, VA: Association for the Preservation of Virginia Antiquities.

Ivor Noël Hume. 1994. *The Virginia Adventure: Roanoke to James Towne: An Archaeological and Historical Odyssey.* New York: Alfred A. Knopf.

B

Bacon, Nathaniel the Elder (1620–1692)

Colonel Nathaniel Bacon the elder was a cousin of Nathaniel Bacon the younger of Bacon's Rebellion fame. Colonel Bacon came to Jamestown in 1650. At the time of Bacon's Rebellion, the elder Bacon was (wrote a contemporary) "Long Standing in the Council a very rich Politick Man," and "a most steadfast, Loyall subject to his Majestie, maugne all the malice and severe treatment of the Rebells."

Commander in chief of York County, and a member of the Council of State from 1656 to 1658 and again from 1661 to 1692, Bacon is counted among the governors of the Virginia colony, for the duties of the governor's office fell upon him as president of the Council of State when the governor left the colony, briefly in 1684 and from October 1688 to October 1690. Bacon also served on the colonial courts.

Bacon was one of nine members of the Council of State who petitioned Governor Berkeley in June 1676 to pardon Nathaniel Bacon the younger, despite the fact that the rebels had occupied his house on King's Creek as a rendezvous and had taken Mrs. Bacon hostage during the seige of Jamestown. Bacon later claimed that the insurrectionists had cost him £1,000 sterling.

Bacon was related to Sir Francis Bacon (1561–1626), the essayist, scientist, and Parliament member. Bacon died childless, and the daughter of his sister, Martha, and her husband, Anthony Smith, became his heir. The young Miss Smith married Lewis Burwell II, the builder of Fairfield.

Related entries: Bacon's Rebellion; Berkeley, Sir William; General Assembly

Suggestion for further reading

Charles M. Andrews, ed. 1915. *Narratives of the Insurrections, 1675–1690.* New York: Charles Scribner's Sons.

Bacon, Nathaniel the Younger (1647–1676)

See Bacon's Rebellion

Bacon's Rebellion

Although the 1660s were a period of unparalleled growth for the Jamestown colony, prosperity did not come to everyone. King Tobacco still reigned, but the glitter of its royalty was tarnished by overproduction and declining prices, the inevitable

In 1676, English colonist Nathaniel Bacon led a popular revolt of colonial Virginia's frontier settlers, known as Bacon's Rebellion, against Virginia governor William Berkeley and his allies. (Library of Congress)

result of a one-crop economy. Like tobacco, the "high-spirited Old Cavalier" governor of the colony, Sir William Berkeley, still headed the government, but his sway, too, was not what it once had been, as his age and diminishing abilities began to show. In 1662, Berkeley had discovered that the legislature was made up of men almost entirely allied with his own interests and inclined to let him have his way; thereafter, he prohibited new elections. Nothing stood in the way of the governor levying new taxes except his good sense, and that Sir William did not seem to exercise as well as he once had. The poor, especially, felt the brunt of taxation. Colony-wide land reform was needed, but not only was it not forthcoming, problems stemming from it were greatly exacerbated by the difficulty of laying claim to any of the land north of Jamestown in the large, unsettled region known as the Northern Neck. Hostilities with some of the native peoples aggravated the situation, as Indians that had never been a part of Powhatan's empire felt squeezed by spreading white settlement on the one side and more Native Americans on the other. Many colonists viewed the government as hell-bent on keeping the lucrative fur trade open at all costs, even if it meant looking the other way when Indians committed atrocities against the settlers. The atmosphere in Virginia was volatile, and Berkeley either did not know it or, if he had an inkling, ignored it. Many thought he was preoccupied with indulgence in the revelries occasioned by his marriage to Lady Frances, a vivacious widow almost thirty years his junior. Onto this stage stepped Nathaniel Bacon the younger, a cousin of Lady Frances.

Nathaniel Bacon was born in 1647 and educated at Cambridge University. In 1674, he married Elizabeth Duke and took his bride to the New World colony at Jamestown, settling at Curles Neck, an upriver site on the James about twenty miles below the falls. (Bacon's Quarter, his second seat, was near the falls.) With the help of his cousin Lady Frances and her governor husband, Bacon soon found himself a member of the Council, universally respected across the colony. Described by contemporaries as tall, slender, and black haired, he was a natural leader, confident, courageous, and clearheaded, but with an "ominous, pensive, melancholy aspect"; when animated, he became both eloquent and impetuous. The subject on everyone's mind more than any other was Indian affairs, and Bacon was not bashful about where he stood on the subject, declaring publicly that he would take revenge on any Indians who dared "meddle with me." When Doeg Indians killed Robert Hen on his outlying plantation in Stafford County, the militia sent to punish the attackers retaliated against friendly natives as well, resulting in a general escalation in border hostilities. When the group of settlers who coalesced in Charles City County to launch an expedition against the natives clamored for Bacon to ride at their head, he accepted. His reason was as much personal as public, for his own overseer at Bacon's Quarter had been killed around the same time.

Upon taking charge of the armed settlers, who numbered about 500, Bacon asked Governor Berkeley to issue an official commission for him

Bacon's Declaration to the People

The Declaration of the People, against Sr: Wm: Berkeley, and Present Governors of Virginia

For having upon specious Pretences of publick Works raised unjust Taxes, upon the Commonaltie, For advancing of Private Favourites. And other sinister Ends, but noe visible Effect, in any Measure adequate.

For not having during the Long time of his Government, In any Measure advanced, this hopefull Colonie, either by Fortifications, Towns, or Trade.

For having abused, and rendered Contemptable, his Maties: Justice, by advancing to Places of Judicature, Scandalous and ignorant Favourites.

For having wronged his Maties: Prorogative, and Interest, by assuming the Monopolie of the Bever Trade.

For having in that unjust Gaine, betrayed and sold, His Matie: Countrie, and the Liberties of his Loyall Subjects to the Barbarous Heathen.

For having, Protected, favoured, and Emboldned, the Indians against his Maties: most Loyall Subjects; never Contriving, requiring, or appointing any due or proper Meanes of Satisfaction; for theire many Incursions, Murthers, and Robberies, Committed, upon Us.

For having when the Armie of the English, was upon the Tract of the Indians, which now in all Places, burne spoile, and Murder, And when Wee might with ease, have destroyed them, Who were in open hostilitie.

For having expresslie, countermanded, and sent back, our Armie, by Passing his word, for the Peaceable demeanours of the said Indians, Who Immediatly prosecuted theire Evill Intentions—Committing horrid Murders and Robberies, in all Places, being Protected by the said Engagement, and Word passed by Him the said Sr: Wm: Berkeley having Ruined and made Desolate, a greate Part of his Maties: Countrie, having now drawn themselfes into such obscure and remote places, and are by theire success soe Emboldned, and Confirmed, and by theire Confederates strengthned. That the Cryes of Blood, are in all Places, and the Terror, and Consternation of the People soe greate, That They are not only become difficult, but a very formidable Enemie Who might with Ease have bin destroyed.

When upon the loud outcries of Blood, the Assemblie had with all Care, raised and framed an Armie, for the Prevention of future Mischeifs, and safeguard of his Maties: Colonie.

For having only with the Privacie of a fewe favourites, without the Acquainting of the People, only by Alteration of a Figure forged a Commission, by I Know not what hand, not only without, but against the Consent of the People, for the Raising and Effecting of Civill Warr, and Destruction, which being happilie and without Bloodshed prevented.

For having the second time attempted the same, thereby calling down our forces from the Defence of the frontiers, and most weakened and Exposed Places, for the prevention of Civill Mischeife, and Ruine amongst our selves; whilest the Barborous Enemie in all places did Invade Murder and spoile us, his Maties: Loyall Subjects.

(*continued on next page*)

Bacon's Declaration to the People, continued

Of these the aforesaid Articles Wee accuse Sr. Wm: Berkeley as guiltie of Each and Everie of the same. As one who hath Traiterouslie attempted, Violated and Injured his Maties: Interest here, by the Loss of a greate Part of his Maties: Colonie, and many of his faithfull and Loyall Subjects, by Him betrayed in a Barbarous and shamefull Manner Exposed to the Incursion, and murder of the Heathen. And We farther declare the Ensuing Persons in this List to have bin his wicked and Pernicious Councellours and Confederates, Aiders, and Assistants against the Commonaltie in these our Civill Commotions.

Sr: Henrie Chicekly	Wm: Cole	
Coll: Chritopr: Wormly	Rich: Whitecar	Jon: Page: Clerke
Phillip Ludwell	Rich: Spencer	Jon: Cuffe: Clerk
Robert Beverlie	Joseph Bridges	Hub: Farrill
Richard Lee	Wm: Claybourne	John: West
Thomas Ballard	Thom: Hawkins	Tho: Readmuch
Wm: Sherwood	Math: Kemp	

And we farther Command that the said Sr: Wm: Berkeley, with all the Persons in this List bee forthwith delivered upp, or Surrender Themselves, within foure dayes after the notice hereof, or otherwise Wee declare as followeth.

That in whatsoever place, House, or Shipp, any of the said Persons shall Reside, bee hid, or protected, Wee doe declare the Owners, Masters and Inhabitants of the said Parties, to bee Confederates, Traytors to the People and ye Estates, of them; as alsoe of all the aforesaid Persons, to be Confiscated, this Wee the Commons of Virginia doe declare.

Desiring a firme union amongst our Selves, that Wee may Joyntly and with one accord defend our selves against the Common Enimie, and lett not the faults of the Guiltie, bee the Reproach of the Innocent, or the faults and Crimes of the Oppressors, devide and sepperate Us Who have suffered, by theire oppressions.

These are therefore in his Maties: Name to Command you: forthwith to seize the Persons abovementioned, as Traytors to the King, and Countrie, and Them to bring to the Middle Plantations, and there to secure them till further Order and in Case of opposition, if yu: want any farther Assistance, you are forthwith to demand It. In the Name of the People, in all the Counties of Virginia.

—Nathaniell Bacon Generall, by Consent of the People.
[30 July 1676]

and his band to march, but Berkeley failed to act. Making matters worse, the governor soon afterward issued a proclamation declaring the army illegal; all but about 60 men immediately returned home. Bacon and his much-reduced force disbanded after making assaults on natives from the region of Bacon's Quarter all the way down into Carolina. As for his part, Governor Berkeley put his own force in the field to apprehend his rogue councilor. Meanwhile, the governor felt compelled to allow elections for a new General Assembly—the first since 1660—and the people of Henrico County elected Bacon as one of their burgesses. En route to Jamestown, Bacon was arrested, paroled, and then taken to the Assembly, where he did

> most readily, freely and most humbly acknowledge that I am and have been guilty of diverse late unlawfull, mutinous and rebellious practices, contrary to my duty to his most sacred majesties governour and this country, by beating up of drums, raiseing of men in armes, marching with them into severall parts of this his most sacred majesties colony, not only without order

> and commission, but contrary to the express orders and comands of the R[igh]t Hon[orable] Sir William Berkeley, Kn[igh]t his majesties most worthy governour, and captain general of Virginia.

Bacon asked for pardon and promised to give a bond of £2,000 for security for "my good and quiett bahaviour." Pardon was granted, Bacon took his seat on the Council, and the matter seemed to rest. Berkeley even promised Bacon a commission to gather a small army to fight the natives.

As it turned out, however, all was not well. The June Assembly had ended its work except for the issuance of the commission to Bacon. Rumors circulated that Berkeley planned to have Bacon assassinated despite the pardon, and Bacon fled Jamestown. Once the upriver inhabitants discovered that Berkeley was still hesitating to take war to the Indians, men rallied around the fugitive Bacon, and the rebel suddenly returned to Jamestown at the head of 600 armed settlers, including 120 horsemen. The governor was unable to muster a defense of the capital, and in the end he and the Assembly succumbed to Bacon's demands for commissions for himself and some 30 officers to serve with him. While this little drama was being acted out, news came to Jamestown that the natives had struck two settlements on the York River, killing 8 settlers. In short order, Bacon and his army set out in search of the raiders. Berkeley also raised an armed force, as much to rout Bacon's force as to subdue the Indians, but, being unequal to the rebel's, it was forced to seek refuge on the Eastern Shore in Accomac County, where the population was among the colony's most loyal supporters of the governor. Several weeks of confusion and violence ensued in the colony, during which colonists and Indians alike were slain. As the toil of war and summer wore on, the number of insurrectionists dwindled to fewer than 140 men. General Bacon (as he was now addressed) returned to Jamestown, only to discover that the Governor had got there before him. The rebels besieged the town, and, after a few days, entered it and, according to the governor, "burned five houses of mine and twenty of other gentlemen's, and a very commodious church. They say he set to with his own sacrilegious hand." From Jamestown, Bacon took his men a few miles away to Berkeley's estate, Green Spring, where he issued a "Declaration of the People" accusing Berkeley and 20 of his supporters of treason.

Bacon and his followers next went to Tindall's Point in Gloucester County, where they commandeered for their headquarters the home of the speaker of the House of Burgesses, Colonel Augustine Warner. The county's inhabitants had not been among the strongest of Bacon's supporters, despite the fact that the rebels tended to rendezvous in the region, so Bacon demanded that that the residents sign loyalty oaths. Rather than risk the ire of the rebels, hundreds of men took the oath. At Gloucester, however, the rebellion ended much more quickly than it had started: Bacon suddenly fell ill and died. He was buried in secret, and his followers then dispersed. Governor Berkeley sent Major Robert Beverley to capture the ringleaders, more than twenty of whom were tried and executed. Despite the insurrection's sudden halt, however, Bacon achieved one major success: His attacks on Virginia's Native Americans were so merciless and demoralizing that never again would any Indians east of the Blue Ridge Mountains rise up against white settlers.

About the time the insurrection came to its inglorious end, there arrived at Jamestown three commissioners sent by King Charles II to look into the colony's affairs and confer with Governor Berkeley. The royal commissioners, Herbert Jeffreys, John Berry, and Francis Moryson, offered pardons to the rebels; that should have ended the whole business, except that Berkeley still held grudges and sufficient power to thwart the commissioner's purposes. A few months passed, and Governor Berkeley was recalled to England; Jeffreys, as lieutenant governor, was named his successor. Berkeley died shortly after arriving in London, before he could present a defense of his governorship to the king. Bacon left a wife, Elizabeth Duke, who married two more times, and a daughter, Mary, whose own daughter, Anna Maria, married Edward Hopkins, a member of Parliament and secretary of state for Ireland. As for Bacon's Rebellion, for a period of time, historians tended to think of it as a prototype of the American Revolution exactly a century later, with its ideals of freedom and revolt against taxation and royal tyranny. In recent decades, however, the consensus has been to downplay comparisons with the Revolution and to describe the insurrection in terms of strong-willed personalities, grabs for power, Anglo-Indian relations, and the socioeconomic complexities of the era.

Related entries: Berkeley, Sir William; Berkeley, Lady Frances Culpeper; Cole, William; General Assembly; List of Those Executed for Bacon's Rebellion, 1676 (Selected Writings); Tindall's Point

Suggestions for further reading

Charles M. Andrews, ed. 1915. *Narratives of the Insurrections, 1675–1690.* New York: Charles Scribner's Sons.

Edmund S. Morgan. 1975. *American Slavery, American Freedom: The Ordeal of Colonial Virginia.* New York: W. W. Norton.

Mary Newton Standard. 1907. *The Story of Bacon's Rebellion.* New York: Neale.

Wilcomb E. Washburn. 1957. *The Governor and the Rebel.* Chapel Hill: University of North Carolina Press for the Institute of Early American Culture.

Thomas Jefferson Wertenbaker. 1914. *Virginia Under the Stuarts: 1607–1688.* Princeton, NJ: Princeton University Press.

Banister, John (1650–1692)

John Banister, the first English botanist of the New World, was born in Twigworth, Gloucestershire. Although his family was of humble origin, he matriculated at Oxford University's Magdalen College in 1667, becoming a chorister the following year and earning bachelor and master of arts degrees in 1671 and 1674, respectively; he served as a clerk and chaplain at Magdalen College after taking his second degree. At Oxford, Banister studied under Robert Morison (1620–1683), Charles II's physician and custodian of the royal gardens, who was appointed professor of botany at Oxford in 1669. Banister began collecting and cataloging plant specimens in the botanical garden near Magdalen College known as Oxford Physick Garden; his findings were published in Robert Plot's *Natural History of Oxford-shire* in 1677. Banister left Oxford for Virginia in 1678, apparently at the request of the Bishop of London, Henry Compton (whose diocese included Virginia), who was in the habit of sending missionaries and others to the colony and who had exceptional gardens at Fulham Palace in west London.

Of the sciences encompassed by natural history in the seventeenth century, botany was the most conspicuous. In contrast to animals, the other great subject of natural history science, plants could be more easily acquired and studied and were routinely shipped across the Atlantic between the Old and New Worlds. The discovery of tobacco and potatoes by Europeans in the sixteenth century fueled the quest for more medicinal and food plants as well as more exotic ornamental plants; the English settlers as well as their benefactors were enthusiastic about what might be found in Virginia. Upon his arrival at Jamestown, Banister immediately set about cataloging plants and collecting specimens to be sent back to England. He traveled as far as the falls of the James River in quest of exotic or unusual plants (in addition to animals and fish), carefully listing what he found. In 1680, he sent to fellow botanist John Ray (1627–1705) in England a catalog of plants that he had observed in Virginia, which Ray later included in volume two of his *Historiæ Plantarum* (London, 1688). Ray counted Banister's colonial contributions a "great addition" to the *Historiæ*'s 18,600 specimens.

Banister recorded the rich plant life of Virginia for fourteen years. He was the first to collect American ginseng, for instance, and he published essays on Virginia's insects and mollusks in the Royal Society's *Philosophical Transactions.* He sent to England species of American plants that had not yet been introduced to Europe, and he also attempted to learn which European crops could be grown in the colony. Banister became an Anglican minister by the late 1680s, baptizing some of the colony's inhabitants. He also found a friend and a patron in William Byrd I, the wealthy and influential trader and landowner who lived near the falls of the James River and later at Westover. In 1690, he became, with Byrd, one of the founders of the College of William and Mary; by 1690, he also had purchased property and a few slaves and indentured servants.

Banister planned to write a natural history of the Virginia colony, but before he could, he was killed by Jacob Colson in the spring of 1692 in an accidental shooting during a botanical trip up the Roanoke River in Henrico County. His colleagues in England were stunned, and attempts to send a replacement of Banister's caliber to Jamestown proved futile. After Banister's untimely death, some of his unfinished manuscipt material eventually fell into the hands of Robert Beverley, who drew heavily upon it when writing his *History and Present State of Virginia* (London, 1705). By the time of his death, Banister had sent to England an impressive 340 species of plants in addition to insects, mollusks, fossils, and rocks. Joseph and Nesta Ewan, in their definitive *John Banister and His Natural History of Virginia, 1678–1692* (Urbana, Illinois, 1970), painstakingly identify many of Banister's materials (in the botany department of the British Museum), and trace their eventual use by other botanists. In addition to his prodigious contributions to the natural history sciences in colonial Jamestown, Banister also left behind a detailed description of the Appomattox Indians.

Banister had married a widow, Mary (whose maiden and former married names are lost to history), who was married a third time, to Stephen Cocke in 1694. Banister's grandson and namesake served in the American Revolutionary War. The Virginia Natural History Society honored Banister in 1992 with the inauguration of a semiannual journal devoted to the natural history of Virginia, *Banisteria.*

Related entry: Byrd, William I

Suggestion for further reading

Joseph and Nesta Ewan. 1970. *John Banister and His Natural History of Virginia, 1678–1696.* Urbana: Illinois University Press.

Berkeley, Lady Frances Culpeper (b. 1634)

No woman in colonial America rivaled the preeminence of Lady Frances Berkeley, the wife of the longest-serving governor in Virginia history. By the time she married Berkeley in 1669, Frances already had been a widow for one to six months, having married Samuel Stephens, the governor of Albemarle, North Carolina, in 1652, when she was eighteen years old. Stephens had been a wealthy man, but Albemarle was nearly uninhabited, and the headstrong young lady refused to leave the Virginia frontier for the even more isolated country to the south. (Perhaps the story of Sir Walter Raleigh's Lost Colony frightened her, as Stephens owned the colony's settlement site, Roanoke Island.) Instead, she lived at Boldrup, Stephens's 1,350-acre plantation on the Warwick River, until her remarriage took her to Green Spring, Berkeley's estate a few miles outside Jamestown. (She and Berkeley sold Boldrup to William Cole in 1671.)

Lady Berkeley's father, Lieutenant Colonel Thomas Culpeper, had been a staunch Royalist who lost everything in his service of Charles I. The Crown rewarded Culpeper by naming him one of the original seven grantees of the 5-million-acre Virginia land grant known as the Northern Neck Proprietary, and Culpeper had come to the New World seeking to rebuild his fortune. He lived in Virginia for a short time only, however, dying in 1652, after which his family, save Lady Stephens, returned to England. Later, with the assistance of Governor and Lady Berkeley, Culpeper's interest in the Northern Neck was sold to his cousin, Lord Thomas Culpeper, Second Baron of Thoresway, who at Berkeley's death succeeded him as governor of Virginia. Lady Berkeley's mother was Katherine, the daughter of Sir Warham St. Leger of Ulcombe (d. 1631), an investor and ship commander in Sir Walter Raleigh's disastrous final expedition to the New World.

A pretty, blue-eyed blonde, Lady Frances gave neither Stephens nor Berkeley children, but she was very much the matriarch of Virginia's social and political elite. It was a commanding role, one for which she was born, and she enjoyed playing it. An unrepentant aristocrat, she was assertive, domineering, obstinate, and fussy; she could also be high-handed, but she was not a snob. Always attentive to the rise and fall of the fortunes of the monarch in both Europe and in the New World, she was a militant royalist. She was even more intransigent when it came to defending the actions of her husbands. In each case, she brought to her marriages a companionship that was soon eclipsed by a partnership in government, sharing in the successes and failures of her husbands. For example, when her cousin Nathaniel Bacon the younger arrived in Virginia in 1674, it was she who made possible his immediate acceptance into the governor's circle; with her assistance, Bacon became the recipient of a lucrative grant of land. No wonder that later, in 1676, when Bacon led the revolt that bears his name, Lady Berkeley denounced him bitterly as a scheming and ungrateful malcontent. Her bitterness turned to hatred when she and Sir William were driven from Green Spring. Upon their return, the Berkeleys found their rebel-occupied home in shambles, and, although the rebels did not destroy the mansion as they did Jamestown, Lady Berkeley estimated that £300 worth of repairs would be necessary before they could move back in. When Berkeley was recalled to England in the aftermath of Bacon's insurrection, she kept him apprised of happenings in the colony.

Lady Berkeley could be merciless. When intercession was made on behalf of one of Bacon's rebels, Robert Jones, Lady Berkeley wrote, "If I am at all acquainted with my heart, I should with more easinesse of mind have worne the Canvas Lynnen the Rebells said they would make me be glad off, than have had this fatal occasion of interceding for mercy." Her husband, however, did give Jones a reprieve long enough for him to appeal to the Crown for amnesty, which was eventually granted by Charles II.

Lady Berkeley also could give affront. When three commissioners from the Crown took leave after a visit to the governor at Green Spring in April 1677, she ordered her coach to carry them down to the river landing, seemingly a gesture of generosity. Unknown to the commissioners until later, however, was the fact that she had replaced the family's regular postillion with another—the colony's "Common Hangman"—all the while peering at the scene from her chamber window. When the commissioners finally learned of the insult, they complained to the governor about being escorted by the man responsible for placing the "Halters about the Prisoner's Necks in Court when they were to make their submission"—a slave or free black, no less—but the governor denied any knowledge or participation. One of the offended saw clearly, however, noting that it appeared "more like a woman's, than a Man's malice."

Governor Berkeley died in London in 1677, leaving Green Spring and his vast fortune to Lady Berkeley. She described Green Spring about that time as "the finest seat in America & the only tollerable place for a Govenour." She also ran her own business affairs, which included the management of a large force of slaves. Sir Berkeley's estate, coupled with her interests in lands in Virginia and North Carolina, made Lady Frances the wealthiest person in Virginia, if not all of English America. By family or economic interests she was related to most of the Virginia elite, and she became as much a force to be contended with as Governor Berkeley had been. The late governor's supporters, loath to relinquish the power they had hitherto enjoyed, welcomed Lady Berkeley's influence. To the great embarrassment of Berkeley's successor, Lieutenant Governor Herbert Jeffreys, she and the gentry of northeast Virginia ran the Council and the House of Burgesses for the next three years—until her cousin Governor Lord Culpeper came to Virginia himself. One burgess, William Sherwood, observed during that time that the "colony would be as peaceful as could be wished except for the malice of some discontented persons of the late Governor's party, who endeavour by all ye cunning contrivances that by their artifice can be brought about, to bring a Contempt of Colonel Jeffreys, our present good Governor." Lady Berkeley headed Sherwood's list of those troubling the peace, followed by her soon-to-be new husband, Philip Ludwell, the colony's secretary of state, with whom she was already well acquainted. Ludwell lived at Rich Neck, an estate near Middle Plantation (later Williamsburg) in James City County, and was part of a well-connected family. Politically, the marriage was a wise move on the parts of both, for Lady Berkeley was able to help Ludwell secure the office of governor of Albemarle, the same office formerly held by her first husband, Samuel Stephens, from whom Lady Berkeley had inherited Roanoke Island. Mindful of her status in Virginia society, however, Lady Frances retained the name of Lady Berkeley for the rest of her life. She outlived Ludwell, too, and was buried at Green Spring. Her remains were later moved to the Jamestown Church Tower, where her tombstone can still be seen.

Related entries: Cole, William; Culpeper, Lord Thomas, Second Baron of Thoresway; Green Spring; Northern Neck

Suggestions for further reading

Jane Carson. 1951. "Sir William Berkeley, Governor of Virginia: A Study in Colonial Policy" (Ph.D. thesis., University of Virginia). Charlottesville, VA.

Thomas Jefferson Wertenbaker. 1914. *Virginia Under the Stuarts: 1607–1688.* Princeton, NJ: Princeton University Press.

Susan Westbury. 2004. "Theatre and Power in Bacon's Rebellion: Virginia, 1676–77." In *The Seventeenth Century* (vol. 19). Manchester, England.

Berkeley, Sir William (1605–1677)

William Berkeley was born near London into a family of distinguished ancestry. Little is known about his early life other than that he entered Oxford University at age 17 and took degrees in 1625 and 1629. Three years later, the Crown took him into the privy-chamber extraordinary, where he joined a popular group of courtier-playwrights, "The Wits." His first play, a tragicomedy entitled *The Lost Lady, A Tragi-Comedy* (London, 1638), debuted for Queen Henrietta Maria at Blackfriars around Christmas 1637 and was performed subsequently over the next several decades. With its complex plot and serious tone, *The Lost Lady* typified its genre, but its fluency of language, reflecting Berkeley's own refinement and grace, made it somewhat better than the typical run-of-the-mill dramas of the period. Another tragicomedy, *Four True Tragicomicall Histories of Late Tymes by the Names of the Lady Cornelia. The Farce of Blood. The Two Damsells. and the Spanish Lady Don Diego Puedesser* (London, 1638), described as "too witty for the vulgar sort," was less popular. Although not rising to the level of Jonson or Shakespeare, Berkeley's literary efforts were warmly received and may have played a part in the Crown's rewarding him with knighthood in July 1639, about three months after he joined Charles I in Scotland to take part in the First Bishop's War.

Berkeley was named governor of Virginia on the last day of July 1641. Why he was chosen over other candidates is not known, for his only affiliation with the colony at Jamestown was a few dormant shares in the Virginia Company purchased in 1607 by his father, Sir Maurice Berkeley (d. 1617) and mother, Elizabeth, née Killigrew. He had been offered a diplomatic post in Constantinople the previous spring but apparently had declined it, possibly in anticipation of an appointment in the New World. He arrived at Jamestown in the spring of 1642 with instructions from the Crown aimed at promoting stability and patriotism and stimulating economic growth. Specifically charged to cooperate with the Virginia General Assembly, Berkeley's first seven years at Jamestown can be characterized as a period during which both the legislature and the executive worked together in increasing harmony. Early in his administration, Berkeley took pains to bring various factions together, to lessen the tax burden in the colony, and to find common ground with the colony's planters. The Assembly was so pleased with the new governor's performance in the first year that it presented Berkeley with a reward: the former brick residence and orchard of Governor Harvey in Jamestown.

Two years into Berkeley's governorship, disaster struck the colony in the form of a Native American insurrection known as the Indian Massacre of 1644, led by Pamunkey Chief Opechancanough on Good Friday (18 April). Berkeley personally took command of the armed forces that gathered to retaliate against the adversaries, and squelched the rebellion within six weeks. Because he had acted with courage and spirit, Berkeley's popularity increased across the colony. That June he returned to England, where he hoped to discuss the colony's affairs and future with the Crown, only to discover that Charles I was faring badly in his own war with parliamentary forces. Returning to Jamestown the following summer with little, if anything, to show for his year in England, the governor found the colony had fared well except for a resurgence of violence between

> ### Sir William Berkeley to Charles II
>
> I always in all conditions had more fears of your Majesties Frownes than the Swords or Tortues of your Enemies.
>
> —Sir William Berkeley to Charles II upon the latter's ascendency to the British throne, 1660

the settlers and the Indians. Berkeley took to Indian fighting again and this time captured Opechancanough. A treaty in October 1646 between Berkeley and Opechancanough's successor, Necotowance, established land boundaries and promised safety to the natives in exchange for their recognition of the supremacy of the English Crown and their promise to pay an annual tribute to the governor—a time-honored tradition that still takes place every fall.

For the next four years or so, the colony prospered beyond the wildest expectations of either the governor or the legislature, despite the fact that the mother country was in the throes of a war that would bring death to Charles I and usher in a period in which the monarchy itself was unwelcome in England. Berkeley was fiercely loyal to the Crown, as were most persons in Virginia, and he invited fellow Royalists fleeing England to make their way to Jamestown, where he promised them refuge. Although many did reach the New World, including a few key supporters of Charles, parliamentary commissioners arrived at Jamestown in the spring of 1652 and took control of the colony's government. Berkeley quietly retired to Green Spring, his estate less than a half dozen miles from Jamestown, where he lived out the Interregnum entirely unmolested, prospering as a Virginia planter. The General Assembly reinstated Berkeley as governor pro tempore in March 1660, on the eve of the Restoration; Berkeley promised to give up the office if required by a new protectorate or to resubmit the government to Charles II if the monarchy were reestablished. When the monarchy was restored and Charles II was placed on the throne, the Virginia General Assembly, in a gesture of allegiance, appropriated 200,000 pounds of tobacco for Berkeley to carry to England to spread around as "gifts" in an effort to court favor with the Crown. Fortunately for the Jamestown colony, so it was thought, Charles II's closest courtiers included several of Berkeley's relatives. Reminiscent of his attempt fifteen years earlier to take counsel of Charles I, this errand lasted a year and ended with mixed success at court. Berkeley returned to Virginia with new instructions, however, largely aimed at enforcing Parliament's unpopular Navigation Acts.

The 1660s were years of increasing distress for Virginia's chief executive. Major changes in the way land was distributed threw into question the validity of land titles in the colony; a spirit of noncooperation caused many disagreements with the neighbors to the north in Maryland; violence from the Anglo–Dutch wars spilled over into the New World, interrupting trade with Holland. What was more, the Crown insisted on limiting the production of tobacco, but attempts to diversify crops in the colony failed dismally. (Berkeley's own example of exporting a variety of crops grown at Green Spring was not followed.) As the decade wore on, Berkeley became more and more alienated from Charles II and his advisors in England and, what was worse, isolated from members of the General Assembly. Signs of aging and declining health took their toll, and Dame Berkeley, whom he had married in the spring of 1650, died. To top it all off, on the horizon it looked like hostilities might break out at any moment between the settlers and the Indians they had displaced. All told, the governor experienced a general loosening of his grip on authority.

The new decade began with the sixty-five-year-old Berkeley's second marriage, to Frances Culpeper Stephens, whose first husband, Samuel Stephens, governor of Albemarle, had just died. Almost thirty years his junior, Lady Frances was a very wealthy woman: Her father had been one of the original seven grantees of the 5-million-acre

Northern Neck Proprietary (her cousin would soon become sole owner); with her first husband and a handful of others, she had been proprietor of a large grant in North Carolina; and she inherited the whole estate of Governor Stephens, including Roanoke Island, the site of the Lost Colony. Like her new husband, Lady Berkeley was haughty, aristocratic, and a resolute Royalist firmly committed to Charles II; unlike Sir William, she was in the prime of her life, with energy to spare for supporters as well as perceived enemies of her husband. She also was first cousin of the man who would cause a great disruption to Virginia society, resulting in the recall of Governor Berkeley to England—Nathaniel Bacon.

Nathaniel Bacon the younger came to the Jamestown colony in 1674, and with the patronage of Lady Frances and Sir William, established himself as a member of the political and economic elite of Virginia. As previously noted, lurking in the background of seventeenth-century Virginia society—especially on its frontier—was the ever-present danger of the eruption of violence between the colony's European settlers and its native inhabitants. In July 1675, Doeg Indians assaulted whites at a plantation in Stafford County, a raid not dissimilar to others that had occurred ever since Berkeley had been in the colony. Berkeley's responsibilities as governor included protecting the king's subjects and, to the degree possible, preventing outbreaks of violence between those subjects and those of other sovereign nations, including Indian ones. Although he showed diligence in prosecuting the earlier wars against the Indians, the governor's attitude was to interpret isolated outbreaks as no threat to the general peace—this despite the fact that a few years earlier he had predicted that the English would need to wipe out the Doeg: "I think it necessary to Destroy all those Northern Indians. . . . Twill be a great Terror and example and Instruction to all other Indians." What Berkeley apparently failed to grasp about his own people, however, was that a sizeable segment of the colony's white population was not faring too well economically and, anxious to find scapegoats for their plight, cast blame on the Indians. All that was needed for them to rally around Bacon was for him to step forth. Bacon did, and in short order more than 1,000 men were exacting retribution from Indians throughout the colony. None of the natives were exempt—not even the tribes living peacefully on reservation lands.

Governor Berkeley declared Bacon's army of Indian fighters illegal and attempted to halt its indiscriminate attacks on the Native Americans. Bacon himself was formally designated a rebel and expelled from the Council, although with 1,000 armed men at his side he was as much in power as the governor. Berkeley prorogued the General Assembly—without election since the early 1660s—and set a date for new elections. Bacon, reelected by the voters in Henrico County, was in the meantime detained, interrogated, and pardoned. The assembly took up the issue of frontier defense, resolving to handle Indian incursions itself, but before it could act, Bacon returned to Jamestown with another army, demanding and receiving authority from the legislature to wage a new war against the natives. Berkeley then recognized how desperate his own situation had become. He once again denounced Lady Frances's cousin as a rebel, formed his own army, and went in search of the insurrectionists. About the same time, Bacon issued his own proclamations denouncing the governor and accusing about 20 others of crimes against the colony. Over the course of the summer of 1676, Bacon and his followers occupied Green Spring and Jamestown, burning the latter on 19 September. After Bacon's unexpected sudden death of the "Bloodie Flux" in October, the insurrection dissipated as quickly as it had begun, leaving Berkeley once again in control of the colony's reigns of power. The Crown, however, having learned of the insurrection, had sent 1,000 soldiers to put down the rebellion. That the royal army was not needed was of little consolation or consequence to anyone, and Governor Berkeley was recalled to England.

Berkeley left Virginia in May 1677, never to return. Broken in body and spirit, the six-week voyage finished him off. Not even a promised audience with King Charles II, in which he was to make a defense of his thirty-five years as governor, could revive him. Dying at his brother's home on 9 July, Sir Berkeley was buried at Twickenham in Middlesex. Faithful to the Crown, to the Church, and to Virginia, his effect on the

Jamestown colony cannot be overstated, even though his legacy seems a mixed one; contemporaries credited him with being the sole author of most of the laws passed during his governorship, while at the same time they criticized him for all the woes that befell the colony. In any case, the period of his governorship proved to be the era of the colony's greatest growth in population, size, and prosperity and paved the way for the golden era of Virginia history that would soon follow.

In addition to his literary efforts, Sir William Berkeley lent his pen to a description of his adopted land, *A Discourse and View of Virginia* (London, 1663).

Related entries: Berkeley, Lady Frances Culpeper; General Assembly; Green Spring; Massacre of 1644; Pamunkey Indians

Suggestions for further reading

William Berkeley. 1663. *A Discourse and View of Virginia.* London.

Warren M. Billings. 2004. *Sir William Berkeley and the Forging of Colonial Virginia.* Baton Rouge: Louisiana State University Press.

Jane Dennison Carson. 1951. "Sir William Berkeley, Governor of Virginia: A Study in Colonial Policy" (Ph.D. thesis, University of Virginia). Charlottesville, VA.

Thomas Jefferson Wertenbaker. 1914. *Virginia Under the Stuarts: 1607–1688.* Princeton, NJ: Princeton University Press.

Bermuda City

See City Point

Black Point

When the three English ships sailed up the James River in search of a harbor in 1607, the first land spotted by the ships' sailors was Black Point, the easternmost of several ridges rising on Jamestown Island. Although it could not and did not serve as either a landing or settlement site, Black Point provided a sweeping, panoramic view of the James River, which lay to its east and south, and of the Thorofare, to its north, into which the Back River empties.

Surprisingly, given its prominence as the place first sighted by the colonists and its proximity to Jamestown, Black Point did not play much of a role in the colony's history other than to provide a convenient location at which to occasionally station lookouts interested in the sea. Archaeological excavations in the 1990s found evidence of occupation during the Middle Woodland period but revealed little from the early English colonial era. The excavations also revealed that the settlers did not use the area for either habitation or farmland, and that significant erosion has taken place near the marshy river edge over the ensuing centuries. Confederate forces built defensive works at Black Point during the American Civil War, but otherwise the land has remained relatively unscathed. Today, Black Point is covered by pine trees and wax myrtle shrub and is owned by the U.S. National Park Service. It is accessible by auto via the Island Road.

Related entry: Three Ships

Suggestions for further reading

Stevan C. Pullins and Dennis B. Blanton. 2000. "Prehistoric Settlement on Jamestown Island: Archaeological Data Recovery at Site 44JC895 on Black Point, Jamestown Island, James City County, Virginia." Yorktown, VA: National Park Service.

Captain John Smith. 1630. *The True Travels, Adventures and Observations of Captain John Smith in Europe, Asia, Africa and America* (vol. 1). London: John Haviland for Thomas Slater.

Blaney, Edward (Blayney; born c.1595)

Sent by the London Company to serve as its factor in the Virginia colony in 1620, Edward Blaney arrived at Jamestown in June of that year after a six-week voyage on board the *Francis Bonaventure,* a 240-ton vessel laden with 153 passengers and a store of goods charged to the new factor's care. Although relatively little is known about his background, the young Blaney, born in England and only about twenty-five years old, may have been the son of Edward Blaney and

Mr. Edward Blaney's "Men Over ye Watter"

The Jamestown colony's musters of 1624/25 listed Edward Blaney as having two indentured servants living and working for him at Jamestown: Robert Bew, age 20, who came to the colony in the *Duty* in 1620, and John Russell, age 19, who was on board the *Bona Nova* in 1621 when Blaney made his second trip to Virginia. Another fifteen men were listed as living at Blaney's "plantacon Over ye Watter," one of whom had accompanied Blaney on his first voyage to the New World in 1621. In the coming decades, some of these seventeen men, for whom Blaney was entitled a headright of fifty acres of land each, earned their freedom, married and had families, and became quite prosperous in the colony.

—1624/25 Muster Rolls, Public Record Office, London, England

his wife Margaret, who, after her husband died married Captain Francis West sometime before 1607. If so, prominent connections aided by natural talent must have helped the young Blaney ease his way into the circle of London Company investors, who recruited him to directly represent their economic interests in the New World. Blaney immediately set to work disposing of the ship's cargo, trading it, according to instructions, to the colonists for tobacco. How he went about conducting his business dealings was not recorded, but within a year he had earned the trust and goodwill of the settlers as well as London Company officials and had made plans to sail back to London to assist in outfitting another cargo—to the great delight of the company. By May 1621, when he left Jamestown for London, he had been so enormously successful that only one outstanding debt was owed the company.

When Blaney sailed from London for Virginia the second time, in September 1621 on board the pinnace *Tyger,* the London Company's ten-member council placed upon him the added responsibility of collecting 150 pounds of the "best leafe tobacco" for each of the more than 50 "maids & young woemen" who were also going to the colony to live permanently. Blaney's success as an intermediary between the London Company and the settlers earned him seats in the Virginia House of Burgesses in 1623 and 1625, which in turn led to a seat on the Council of State in 1626. Blaney kept a store on the east end of Jamestown (one of only three in the colony), and his efforts on behalf of the company paid off sufficiently for him to establish a plantation on the south side of the James River at Grays Creek, which came to be known as Blaney's Point. By February 1624, Blaney's Point boasted 15 servants as well as Blaney and his wife Margaret, whose first husband, Captain William Powell, had been killed by Indians in January 1623. When Blaney married the widow Powell, the estate of Captain Nathaniel Powell (later known as Merchant's Hope), which William Powell had claimed after Nathaniel and his family were killed in the Massacre of 1622, came under Blaney's control. Under his management, the Powell plantation prospered—but suddenly the King's Privy Council in London declared that William Powell had no claim to the property; the estate was sold and the proceeds given to Nathaniel Powell's legitimate heirs. In addition to the 15 indentured servants who worked for Blaney at his plantation, 2 more lived in Jamestown, bringing the total to 17 persons whom he had imported into the colony, each of which entitled him to 50 acres of land. Before Blaney disappeared from the Jamestown records in 1627, the muster rolls credited him with owning 3 dwelling houses, 3 tobacco barns, 2 boats, 12 swords, 3 pistols, 7 pounds of powder,

The Muster of Mr. Edward Blaney at Jamestown

Mr. Edward Blaney came in the *Francis Bonaventure*

Servants

Robert Bew, age 20, came in the *Duty*

John Russell, age 19, came in the *Bona Nova*

At Mr. Blaney's Plantation, Over the Waters

Servants

Rice Watkins, age 30, came in the *Francis Bonaventure*

Nathaniel Floid, age 24, came in the *Bona Nova*

George Rogers, age 23, came in the *Bona Nova*

John Shelley, age 23, came in the *Bona Nova*

Thomas Ottowell, age 40, came in the *Bona Nova*

Thomas Crouch, age 40, came in the *Bona Nova*

Robert Shepherd, age 20, came in the *Hopewell*

William Sawyer, age 18, came in the *Hopewell*

Robert Chauntrie, age 19, came in the *George*

William Hartley, age 23, came in the *Charles*

Lawly Damport, age 29, came in the *Duty*

William Ward, age 20, came in the *Jonathan*

Jeremy White, age 20, came in the *Tyger*

John Hacker, age 17, came in the *Hopewell*

Robert Whitmore, age 22, came in the *Duty*

12 pounds of shot, 1 murderer (a small ordnance piece), 7 pieces of armor (including 2 coats of mail), and 1 jack (probably a leather coat worn for defense). Additionally, he owned 20 neat cattle, 10 goats, 21 swine, 8 pigs, and a variety of foodstuffs. That was a pretty impressive accomplishment for less than 5 years work in Virginia, given that the entire colony's population of more than 1,230 people held fewer than 50 houses (22 in Jamestown), 9 boats, 60 swords, 209 swine, and 121 goats.

Related entries: London Company; Martin's Hundred

Suggestion for further reading

James Taylor Ellyson. 1908. *The London Company of Virginia: A Brief Account of its Transactions in Colonizing Virginia with Photogravures of the More Prominent Leaders* . . . New York and London: De Vinne Press.

Buck, Richard (1582–1624)

Richard Buck of Wymondham in Norfolk, England, is said to have studied at both Oxford University and at Cambridge University's Caius College. Buck was recruited to serve as a minister at the Jamestown settlement after the successor of the Reverend Robert Hunt, Jamestown's first minister who died in 1608, proved incapable of winning the settlers' respect. Buck and his wife and two daughters sailed to Virginia in 1609 on board the *Sea Venture,* which wrecked and stranded its passengers in Bermuda for nine months. By the time Buck and the others arrived at Jamestown in May 1610, the colony was on the verge of total collapse from the effects of the winter known as the Starving Time, and Buck's first officiation was to lead the people in a "zealous and sorrowful" prayer, an act that apparently brought to mind the pious Hunt and instantly won Buck the hearts of the colonists.

William Crashaw, a minister and prime promoter of the colony, described Buck as

> an able and painfull Preacher . . . of whom I have heard Sir *Thomas Gates* give a good and worthie testimonie, and he came to the Counsell, and to this imployment, with the commendation of a right reverend Prelate [Thomas Ravis, Lord Bishop of London, one of the translators of the King James Bible] . . . he will shortly give notice to the world what he is, and what the countrey of *Virginia* is, and what hope there is of that Plantation; for the service whereof he hazarded his dearest life, and the rather do I expect it from him because he is a man now of long experience, having been there so long a time, and was himselfe in person in the danger and deliverance at the *Barmudaes.*

John Rolfe, who befriended Buck in Virginia, agreed that Buck was a "veerie good preacher," a description echoed by other colonists. (Speculation has it that Buck conducted the wedding ceremony of Pocahontas and John Rolfe.) Buck's ecclesiastical duties included leading the colonists in prayers twice a day and preaching sermons on Thursdays and Sundays. In addition, Buck often officiated at other public events in Jamestown; for instance, he opened the first session of the Virginia General Assembly in 1619 with a prayer "that it would please God to guide and sanctifie all our proceedings to his owne glory and the good of this Plantation."

Buck apparently resided in the Jamestown fort, where the church was, rather than on the 100-acre tract that the London Company had set aside for glebe lands. In 1619, Buck patented 750 acres of land in an area known as Neck-of-Land, the land separated by water from the north side of Jamestown Island. Buck apparently relied on indentured servants to improve the land, including a caretaker, Richard Kingsmill, who later owned some of the property. The plantation's proximity to Jamestown Island made it a natural area for expansion, especially after the Indian Massacre of 1619, when settlers wanted to stay close to the fort. Between the time that Buck acquired his land and 1650, 145 people settled at Neck-of-Land, raising livestock and building more than 30 dwellings and 6 storehouses.

In 1620, Buck purchased from William Fairfax a house and an outbuilding situated on a dozen acres of land in Jamestown, for his home. The Bucks raised a large family at Jamestown, including six children who survived into adulthood. (At least two of the children were dimwitted; the first recorded "idiot" in the colony, Benoni Buck, apparently was born with Down syndrome, and his sister Mara was described as "very dull.") When Buck and his wife died within a few months of one another, their four minor children (aged 13 and under) were raised by other families of colonists.

Extensive archaeological excavations at Buck's Neck-of-Land plantation conducted by the Association for the Preservation of Virginia Antiquities (APVA) in 1996 and 1997 yielded a rich treasure of artifacts and a number of graves from the period beginning with Buck's ownership.

Related entries: Hunt, Robert; Jamestown Church Tower; Rolfe, John

Suggestions for further reading

E. Clowes Chorley. 1930. "The Planting of the Church in Virginia" (*William and Mary Quarterly,* 2d ser., vol. 10).

Seth W. Mallios. 1999. *Archaeological Excavations at 44JC568, The Reverend Richard Buck Site.* Richmond, VA: Association for the Preservation of Virginia Antiquities.

Byrd, William I (1652–1704)

William Byrd I was born to London goldsmith John Byrd and his wife Grace Stegge, the second of their six children. He came to Virginia in the late 1660s to live with his mother's brother, Thomas Stegge, Jr., a prominent Indian trader and the auditor general of the colony who lived at the falls of the James River. Stegge passed on his knowledge about the Virginia countryside and its native inhabitants before dying in 1671, when he left to Byrd the bulk of his business and landed estate (by then situated on both sides of the James) as well as a handful of slaves. Two years after his uncle's death, Byrd married Mary Horsemanden Filmer (b. 1652), the widow of Samuel Filmer and the daughter of Warham and Susannah Horsemanden of Essex County, England, who lived in Virginia beginning in

William Byrd I of Westover

According to your desire I have herewith sent you an Indian habitt for your boy, the best I could procure amongst our neighbor Indians. There is a flap or belly clout 1 pair stockings & 1 pair mocosins or Indian shoes also some shells to put about his necke & a cap of wampum. I could not get any dyed hair, which would have been better & cheaper. These things are put up in an Indian basket, directed as you desired, there are a bow & arrows tyed to itt. I hope they will come safe, & find you at your desired porte in health. I am sorry I was not so fortunate to see you ere your departure. You formerly advised mee to some books & promised you would procure them. I therefore inttreat you to send mee a treatise or two or minerals & stones the fittest you find for my purpose either of Mr. [Robert] Boyles [*An Essay about the Origin and Virtues of Gems,* 1672] or any other English author, also [William] Salmons Polygraphice [*The Art of Drawing, Engraving, Etching, Limning, Painting, Washing, Varnishing, Colouring, and Dyeing,* 1672] the last edition, & if you can conveniently, I pray you send mee some samples of oare, especially of lead tin or silver, for our ignorance therein hath made us neglect, some things which I conceive might bee of value. Sir I beg your pardon for imposing this trouble, & assure you if I can any way serve you here, you may freely command Sir your reall friend & servant. If you send pray send by some of the (first) James River ships.

—Letter to John Clayton, Rector of Crofton at Wakefield in Yorkshire, England, 25 May 1686

the mid-1650s. William and Mary had five children, William Byrd II (1674–1744), Susan (1676–1710), Ursula (1681–1698), Mary (b. 1683), and Warham (1685–c.1689). Mary's cousin married Sir William Berkeley, the governor of the colony.

Byrd's inheritance of his uncle's lucrative business brought with it responsibilities for the colony's defense; despite his young age, he soon was commissioned a captain of the Henrico County militia, charged with defending the colony's frontier. His standing also brought him into the colony's first circle, and he became a friend and business acquaintance of Governor William Berkeley, who had married a cousin of Byrd's wife, and of Nathaniel Bacon, Jr., a cousin of the governor himself. Byrd and Bacon entered into a business agreement with the governor, aimed at gaining control of the Indian trade in Virginia, but an act passed by the General Assembly in March 1676 thwarted their intentions. Byrd initially supported Bacon's strikes on Indian settlements and the subsequent disorder that menaced the colony later that spring, but soon he distanced himself from the insurrection and realigned with the governor. The next year, the citizens of Henrico County rewarded his stance by sending him to the House of Burgesses. In 1679, he was promoted to colonel of the militia and placed in command of the falls; it was Byrd's responsibility to secure peace between the English and the natives in the area. He was appointed to the Governor's Council in 1682.

In the 1680s, Byrd's popularity was still on the rise. His eagerness to extend his trade with the Indians had taken him into the Virginia wilderness as far as the upper Roanoke River as early as 1671, and over the next two decades he occasionally attempted to travel into the mountains. His successes included treating with the Indians not only in Virginia but in New York, where he met that colony's leading citizens, including its governor, and traveling to England, where he secured his uncle's office as deputy auditor and receiver general of the revenues. He used his influence to assist in the creation of the College of William and Mary (of which he served as rector) and the establishment of a French Huguenot settlement

Nicholas Ferrar the Younger (1592–1637)

Son of wealthy merchant Nicholas Ferrar the elder and a Cambridge graduate, the younger Nicholas became a member of the Council for the Virginia Company in 1619. He served as deputy treasurer of the company from 1622 to its dissolution in 1624, during which time he made copies of the company records. The copies passed into the hands of the Earl of Southampton and descended in his family until William Byrd I purchased them. The Byrd family conveyed the papers to William Stith, president of William and Mary College, and later they went to Peyton Randolph and then to Thomas Jefferson, who sold them with his personal library to the Library of Congress after the British burned the Capitol in Washington, D.C., during the War of 1812. As it turned out, many of the documents of the company survived only in Ferrar copies.

About 1626 Ferrar was ordained a deacon and with his mother and a brother established a communal religious community dedicated to prayer, fasting, and almsgiving at Little Gidding Manor in Huntingdonshire, England. Charles I made three visits, including a secret community in 1646, and Little Gidding became the subject of T. S. Eliot's poem *Four Quartets* in 1942.

Portrait of Nicholas Ferrar, the younger, member of the council of the Virginia Company (1592–1637). (Ellyson, J. Taylor. The London Company of Virginia, *1908)*

in Virginia, at Manakin Town above the falls of the James, which conveniently served as a buffer between the Indians and the English. He eventually became the senior member of the Governor's Council, acting as the colony's chief executive when the governor was away. Meanwhile, he enlarged his land holdings and increased his tobacco cultivation, purchasing in 1688 a 1,200-acre plantation in Charles City County, Westover, closer to Jamestown and near the confluence of the Appomattox and the James Rivers, in his words, "about two miles above where the great ships ride." Byrd built a small wooden house on the property, which his son and namesake, William Byrd II, replaced in about 1730 with an elaborate Georgian brick mansion, complete with formal gardens and secret passages to escape from the Indians. (Byrd's landholdings eventually numbered more than 25,000 acres.) Byrd took an interest in mining, purchasing the Falling Creek Iron Mine, which was situated about 66 miles from Jamestown, in 1687, although the venture proved unsuccessful. Byrd also was a patron of John Banister, the English botanist who was accidentally shot and killed while working on a natural history of Virginia; Byrd's son-in-law, Robert

Beverley, later relied on Banister's work when writing his *History and Present State of Virginia* (London, 1705).

William Byrd I left a literary legacy of unparalleled importance to colonial Virginia. While on a trip to England in 1678, apparently following the death of his father, he purchased a manuscript copy of the records of the Virginia Company from the estate of the Earl of Southampton. The two-volume manuscript, now in the Library of Congress, somehow became the only surviving copy of the Virginia Company's records. A letterbook containing Byrd's correspondence has also survived, recorded by Byrd on the blank pages of an auditor's account ledger kept by his uncle.

Byrd died one of the wealthiest men in the colony, and he and his wife Mary are buried at Westover Plantation, which is open to the public.

Related entries: Bacon's Rebellion; French Huguenots; London Company

Suggestions for further reading

Joseph and Nesta Ewan. 1970. *John Banister and His Natural History of Virginia, 1678–1692.* Urbana: Illinois University Press.

Pierre Marambaud. 1973. "William Byrd I: A Young Virginia Planter in the 1670s" (*Virginia Magazine of History and Biography,* vol. 81).

Marion Tinling, ed. 1977. *The Correspondence of the Three William Byrds of Westover, Virginia, 1684–1776* (vol. 1). Charlottesville: University Press of Virginia.

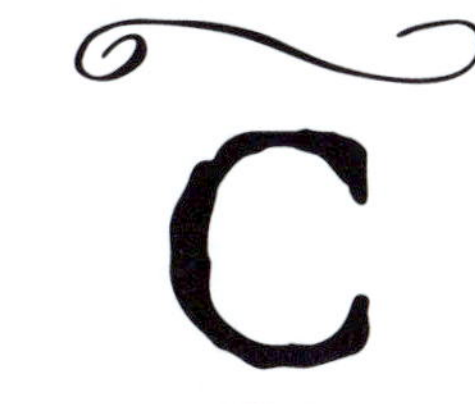

C

Cannibalism

Although there had been reports of cannibalism during other attempts to establish settlements in the New World, the ones stemming from the Starving Time in the winter of 1609–1610, whether or not entirely true, reflect the hardships and horrors that the first settlers endured during their struggle for survival in the first years of the colony.

George Percy wrote of a Spanish settlement "in the River of Plate and the Straits of Magellan" that suffered from hunger so much that "mutinies did arise and grow amongst them for the which the general, Diego Mendosa, caused some of them to be executed, extremity of hunger enforcing others secretly in the night to cut down their dead fellows from off the gallows and bury them in their hungry bowels." An earlier report of an expedition to Newfoundland in 1536 led by Robert Hore recalls how at one time men began disappearing after famine set in. The officers could not understand what was happening to the men, thinking the disappearances were the result of animal or Indian attack, until one day a man was discovered feasting in a field. When challenged he "burst out into these wordes: If thou wouldest needes know, the broiled meate that I had was a piece of such a mans buttocke." It had apparently become the practice of at least one, and possibly more, of the men to kill another of the crew "and cutting out pieces of his bodie whom he had murthered, broiled the same on the coles and greedily devoured them."

By far the most gruesome accounts, however, come from sources at Jamestown referring to the Starving Time. Food had become so scarce during the winter of 1609–1610 that the colonists had been "constrained to eat dogs, cats, rats, snakes, toadstools, horsehides, and whatnot. One man out of the misery he endured, killing his wife, powdered [salted] her up to eat her, for which he was burned. Many besides fed on the corpse' of dead men." The hunger became so terrible that none were considered safe from the practices. "Nay, so great was our famine, that a Salvage we slew, and buried, the poorer sort tooke him up againe and eat him, and so did divers one another boyled and stewed with roots and herbs." But Percy provided the most horrific example when he wrote,

> now famine beginning to look ghastly and pale in every face that nothing was spared to maintain life and to do those things which seem incredible, as to dig up dead corpse out of graves and to eat them, and some have licked up the blood which hath fallen from their weak fellows. And amongst the rest, this was most lamentable that one of our[s], Collines, murdered his wife, ripped the child out of her womb and threw it into the river, and after chopped the mother in pieces and salted her for his food. The same not being discovered before he had eaten part thereof, for the which cruel and unhuman fact I

> adjudged him to be executed [burned alive], the acknowledgment of the deed being enforced from him by torture, having hung by the thumbs with weights at his feet a quarter of an hour, before he would confess the same.

In an attempt to reassure potential investors of the soundness of the colony, instead of reporting the crime as due to hunger, Thomas Gates reported that the man had killed his wife because he "mortally hated" her, apparently implying that the murder and subsequent cannibalism took place out of anger instead of hunger.

No matter how much truth is actually in the reports, and whatever the cause of the alleged cannibalism at Jamestown, its being reported by various sources further demonstrates the hardships and complexities faced by those attempting to establish England's first permanent presence in the New World.

Related entry: Percy, George

Suggestions for further reading

Philip L. Barbour, ed. 1986. *The Complete Works of Captain John Smith (1580–1631)* (vol. 3). Chapel Hill and London: University of North Carolina Press.

Henry S. Burrage, ed. 1932. *Early English and French Voyages: Chiefly from Hakluyt: 1534–1608.* New York: Charles Scribner's Sons.

Edward Wright Haile, ed. 2001. *Jamestown Narratives: Eyewitness Accounts of the Virginia Colony: The First Decade: 1607–1617.* Champlain, VA: Round House.

Giles Milton. 2000. *Big Chief Elizabeth: How England's Adventurers Gambled and Won the New World.* London: Hodder and Stoughton.

Ivor Noël Hume. 1994. *The Virginia Adventure: Roanoke to James Towne: An Archaeological and Historical Odyssey.* New York: Alfred A. Knopf.

Chesapeake Bay

The entrance into Virginia for shipping is by the mouth of Chesapeake bay, which is indeed more like a river than a bay; for it runs up into the land about two hundred miles, being everywhere near as wide as it is at the mouth, and in many places much wider. The mouth thereof is about seven leagues over, through which all ships pass to go to Maryland.

—Robert Beverley, *The History and Present State of Virginia* (1705)

Cape Accowmack

See Cape Charles

Cape Charles

Known as Accowmack by the native peoples and sometimes referred to as the North Cape by the English, Cape Charles lies at the southern tip of the Eastern Shore of Virginia. Along with Cape Henry about twelve miles to its south, it forms the mouth and, at the time of first settlement in the area, the only entrance by ship to the Chesapeake Bay. (The Chesapeake and Delaware Canal now connects the Chesapeake Bay to the Delaware Bay.)

Named after the younger son of King James I, Cape Charles was first explored in depth in June 1608 by John Smith, who was probably responsible for giving the point its name. Unlike many other expeditions in the region, this one held some promise of peaceful and mutually beneficial associations between the Europeans and native populations. As described by members of Captain Smith's expedition to the area, the first people seen "were 2 grimme and stout Salvages upon Cape-Charles with long poles like Javelings, headed with bone, they boldly demanded what we were, and what we would, but after many circumstances, they in time seemed very kinde, and directed us to Acawmacke the habitation of the Werowans [leader] where we were kindly intreated." Indeed, the native Accomacs and Accohannocks did prove to be more amiable in comparison to many other tribes in the region.

Cape Charles was also the site of Dale's Gift, the first English settlement on the western side of the Chesapeake Bay. Established in June 1614, this colony began as a company of eighteen men who extracted salt from seawater at nearby Smith's Isle and harvested and salt-cured fish for the other colonists during the spring and fall seasons. While experiencing varying levels of occupation and success, this colony became the basis for the permanent English presence on the Eastern Shore of Virginia.

Related entry: Cape Henry

Suggestions for further reading

Edward Arber, ed. 1910. *Travels and Works of Captain John Smith* (part 1). Edinburgh, Scotland: J. Grant.

Charles E. Hatch, Jr. 1995. *The First Seventeen Years: Virginia, 1607–1624.* Charlottesville: University Press of Virginia.

Edward Wright Haile, ed. 2001. *Jamestown Narratives: Eyewitness Accounts of the Virginia Colony: The First Decade: 1607–1617.* Champlain, VA: Round House.

Ivor Noël Hume. 1994. *The Virginia Adventure: Roanoke to James Towne: An Archaeological and Historical Odyssey.* New York: Alfred A. Knopf.

David Beers Quinn, ed. 1979. *New American World: A Documentary History of North America to 1612* (vol. 5). New York: Arno Press and Hector Bye.

Helen C. Rountree. 1990. *Pocahontas's People: The Powhatan Indians of Virginia Through Four Centuries.* Norman: University of Oklahoma Press.

Conway Whittle Sams. 1929. *The Conquest of Virginia: The Second Attempt: An Account, Based on Original Documents, of the Attempt, Under the King's Form of Government, to Found Virginia at Jamestown, 1606–1610.* Norfolk, VA: Keyser-Doherty.

Cape Henry

Named after the eldest son of England's King James I and known as the original Jamestown colonists' first landing site, Cape Henry is a point of land on the southern end of the mouth of the Chesapeake Bay in Virginia. It was here on 26 April 1607 (old style calendar) that Master Edward-Maria Wingfield, Captains Bartholomew Gosnold, Christopher Newport, Gabriel Archer, and George Percy, along with twenty-eight others set foot on North American soil, thus ending a voyage of more than four months that had seen six weeks of delay before leaving sight of England, storms at sea, and intrigues and suspected mutinous intentions among the passengers and crew of the three ships in the expedition. That there was great relief felt by the crews at the sight of the land sometimes referred to as Cape San Nicolas, Cape Saint Nicholas, and Cape Henrick, was evidenced by the words of George Percy, who wrote that they found "faire meddowes and goodly tall Trees, with such Fresh-waters running through the woods, as I was almost ravished at the first sight thereof." Their relief was to be tempered by the greeting they received from what may have been five members of the Chesapeake tribe from their nearby village on the Lynnhaven River. After spending their first day exploring inland, Percy wrote,

> when wee were going aboard [ship], there came the Sauages creeping vpon all foure, from the Hills like Beares, with their Bowes in their mouthes, charged vs very desperately in the faces, hurt Captaine Gabrill Archer in both his hands, and a sayler [Mathew Morton] in two places of the body very dangerous. After they had spent their Arrowes, and felt the sharpnesse of our shot, they retired into the Woods with a great noise, and so left vs.

That night, the box with the sealed orders from the King was opened to reveal the names for the governing council. Wingfield, Newport, Gosnold, John Smith, George Kendall, John Ratcliffe, and John Martin were named to the council, with Wingfield later elected its president. After placing a wooden cross at the site to mark their landing and thanksgiving, the colonists made further explorations of the land, bay, and rivers until the site of present-day Jamestown was finally selected.

Cape Henry was the site of other important events in the history of what became the United States. In the 5 September 1781 Battle of the Capes, French Admiral Comte François Joseph Paul de Grasse defeated British Admiral Thomas Graves in a sea battle within sight of Cape Henry, thereby preventing Graves from providing relief to or evacuation of British Major General Lord

35
36
37 Occi-dens
38
The Sea of China
and the Indies.
Sr Francis Drake
was on this sea and landed
An.o 1577 in 37 deg. where hee tooke
Possession in the name of Q:
Eliza: Calling it new Albion.
Whose happy shoers, (in ten dayes march with 50 foote and 30 hors-men from the head of Ieames River, ouer those hills
and through the rich adiacent Vallyes beautyfied with as proffitable rivers, which necessarily must run into ye peacefull
Indian sea, may be discoverd. to the exceeding benefit of Great Brittain, and joye of all true English.
Mangoatke C.
Manikes C.
Ould
VIRGINIA, &
RAWLIANA
Meridies
Carolana
The falls
Sassafras tree
Ca. Feare
Nansamon
James River
The Bay of
Chicepiac
Cape Henry
Cape Charles
Smiths Ile
C. Hatturas
MARE
AT
LAN
TI
Fots Iland
Cingoto Ile
Cape James
John Goddard sculp:
Domina Virginia Farrer Collegit. Are sold by John Overton without Newgate at the corner of little old
35
36
37 Ori ens
38

Map of the Virginia Colony, c.1667, depicting Cape Charles, Cape Henry, Jamestown, Henrico City, and the Chesapeake Bay area. (Library of Congress)

Charles Cornwallis, who was then under siege at Yorktown by American and French forces commanded by American General George Washington. Without reinforcements or means of escape by sea, Cornwallis was forced to surrender on 19 October 1781.

Another milestone for Cape Henry was its selection as the site of the first lighthouse to be built under the direction of the United States of America. The first Congress of the United States, during its first session, passed an act with the intention of establishing a lighthouse at the mouth of the Chesapeake Bay. On 7 August 1791, President Washington signed the act into law. On 15 December 1881, the old lighthouse was taken out of service and its replacement ignited about 350 feet southeast in the nation's first, and still tallest, cast iron tower.

Cape Henry today, along with both lighthouses, a statue honoring Admiral de Grasse, and a concrete replica of the original wooden cross planted by the first colonists, sits within the boundaries of Fort Story, Virginia.

Related entries: Cape Charles; Gosnold, Bartholomew; Three Ships

Suggestions for further reading

Philip L. Barbour. 1969. *The Jamestown Voyages Under the First Charter: 1606–1609* (vol. 1). Cambridge, England: Cambridge University Press.

Edward Wright Haile, ed. 2001. *Jamestown Narratives: Eyewitness Accounts of the Virginia Colony: The First Decade: 1607–1617.* Champlain, VA: Round House.

Norma Elizabeth and Bruce Roberts. 2001. *Cape Henry: First Landing, First United States Lighthouse.* Morehead City, NC: Outer Banks Lighthouse Society.

Conway Whittle Sams. 1929. *The Conquest of Virginia: The Second Attempt: An Account, Based on Original Documents, of the Attempt, Under the King's Form of Government, to Found Virginia at Jamestown, 1606–1610.* Norfolk, VA: Keyser-Doherty.

Carter's Grove

See Martin's Hundred

Chanco

On the night of 21 March 1622, a young man known as "Perries Indian" was staying at the plantation of Richard Pace just across the James River from Jamestown. The Indian had just been visited by another man, possibly his brother, who told him "to kill Pace (so commanded by their King as he declared) as hee would kill [William] Perry: telling further that by such an houre in the morning a number would come from divers places to finish the Execution." This apparently caused great distress to the young Indian in that he was being told to kill a man with whom he had such good relations that Pace "used him as a Sonne." No doubt distraught at the prospect of betraying either his own people or a man who treated him as one of his own children,

> Perries Indian rose out of his bed and reveales it to Pace . . . [who] upon this discovery, securing his house, before day rowed over the River to James-City (in that place neere three miles in bredth) and gave notice thereof to the Governor, by which meanes they were prevented [from successful attack] there, and at such other Plantations as was possible for a timely intelligence to be given.
>
> . . . Such was (God bee thanked for it) the good fruit of an Infidell converted to Christianity; for though three hundred and more of ours died by many of these Pagan Infidels, yet thousands of ours were saved by the means of one of them alone which was made a Christian.

Thus was born the legend of Chanco, whose decision to help his friend and benefactor helped save Jamestown's, and many other, inhabitants on the morning of 22 March 1622, when English settlements all along the James River were attacked, and many destroyed, by the forces of Powhatan's successor, Opechancanough. But according to Helen C. Rountree, a leading scholar on the Indians of Powhatan's empire, Chanco the man never existed. Rather, later writers combined two men into one to create the hero who helped save England's first permanent colony in the New World.

According to Rountree, there was a young baptized Indian whose name has not been found recorded who worked for William Perry but often stayed with Richard Pace just across the James River, as he was doing the night of 21 March 1622. He was indeed visited by another Indian that night and told of the plans, later warning Pace, as related in the official account of the attack written by Edward Waterhouse, the secretary of the Virginia Company in London at the time. But this young Indian's identity was recorded only as "Perries Indian," not "Chanco." There was, however, another man from the Pamunkey River area, whose name was written as "Chauco" in an English document identifying him as being remembered by the English as one who had "spent much time" with them and who, when he visited the English in 1623 as a messenger for Opechancanough, was welcomed as a friend who had warned them of the impending attack the year before. Rountree's research and careful study of the surviving documents have convinced her that the recorded name for at least one Indian man who warned the English colonists of the impending attack is "Chauco." There are apparently no contemporaneous references to an Indian man known as Chanco.

Although his name has been honored and perpetuated in American history—for instance, he is recognized by a plaque on the wall inside the reconstructed church at Jamestown and by a historical marker on Route 10, the Colonial Trail, near the site of Richard Pace's former plantation in present-day Surry County, Virginia; a summer youth camp near the same locations is administered by the Episcopal Diocese of Southern Virginia, and a now-defunct Order of the Arrow Lodge of the Boy Scouts of America bears his name—Chanco may not have existed. But the actions on which the legend is based did; many English lives, and possibly even the very existence of the first permanent English settlement in North America, are owed to the kindness and affection between at least a few participants of what otherwise had become a clash of empires.

Related entries: Massacre of 1622; Massacre of 1644; Thorpe, George

Suggestions for further reading

Susan Myra Kingsbury, ed. 1933. *The Records of The Virginia Company of London* (vol. 3). Washington, DC: Government Printing Office.

Helen C. Rountree. 1990. *Pocahontas's People: The Powhatan Indians of Virginia Through Four Centuries.* Norman: University of Oklahoma Press.

Charles City

See City Point

Chesapeake Indians

Perhaps as early as 1546, Indians who later became known to the Jamestown colonists as the Chessepians, or Chesapeake Indians, had been trading with Europeans near the mouth of the Chesapeake Bay around Cape Henry. After encountering bad weather, a French ship that had been sent out to capture Spanish treasure or merchant ships found a safe harbor around 37 degrees north latitude, near the mouth of the Chesapeake Bay. Thirty canoes filled with men carrying bows and arrows came out to greet the ship and, in groups of two, the Indians were allowed to come aboard the ship to trade marten skins for fishhooks, shirts, and knives. The ship carried a young English boy named John who, because of this encounter, may have been the first Englishman to come in contact with Indians of the Chesapeake Bay (although John Rut may have had some contact with them on his voyage along the east coast of North America in 1527).

The next significant recorded encounter between the English and what was thought to be the Chesapeake Indians, whose name means "big salt bay," was in 1585, when a party from Ralph Lane's Roanoke colony was dispatched to explore further northward, where it spent time among a friendly tribe they found in the Chesapeakes' area of influence—present-day Chesapeake, Norfolk, Virginia Beach, and Portsmouth. The English expedition included Thomas Hariot and John White, and they spent the winter of 1585–1586 with the tribe there, recording in words and drawings an account of a pleasant place with friendly inhabitants. The agreeability of the area must have been remarkable, as evidenced by Ralph Lane when he wrote that "this teritory

Native Americans fish in colonial Virginia in this sixteenth-century illustration by John White, engraved by Theodor de Bry. (Library of Congress)

being 15. myle from the shoare, for pleasantnest of seate, for temporature of climate, fertility of soyle and comoditie of the Sea, besides beares, good woods, *Saxefras, Walnuts, &c.* is not to be excelled by any other whatsoeuer."

As well as being some of the first to come in contact with the English adventurers and colonists, the Chesapeake Indians are associated with one of the greatest mysteries in North American history. It is thought that some of the "Lost Colonists" from the abandoned attempts at settlement on Roanoke Island may have wandered north in 1587 to live among the Chesapeakes after the English relief ships failed to return in time with essential supplies. Although it is controversial whether or not any of the Roanoke colonists did travel northward and stay with the Chesapeakes for any substantial length of time, William Strachey, secretary to the Jamestown colony, may have believed they had when he wrote that the English for "20 and odd years had peaceably lived and intermix'd with those savages." So far, however, all attempts to verify any long-term English presence before the 1630s in the Chesapeakes' former territory have come up lacking. Solid evidence of English colonists living among the Chesapeakes may never be found, in fact, because sometime around the arrival of the first Jamestown colonists the entire Chesapeake chiefdom was wiped out by Powhatan.

When the Chesapeakes were exterminated is not known, except that it was before September 1608, around which time John Smith reported seeing almost no signs of people while on an expedition there. Sometime before the arrival of the Jamestown colonists, Powhatan's priests prophesied that his empire would be threatened by enemies from the east. It is thought that he interpreted this to mean the Chesapeakes, for they had never been assimilated into Powhatan's chiefdom (although it is interesting to note that the English, who eventually did destroy his empire, came from England, east across the Atlantic, and through the mouth of the Chesapeake Bay—just east of Powhatan's domain). There has been speculation that Powhatan wiped out the Chesapeakes just before, at the time of, or even a year or so after the arrival of, the Jamestown colonists. John Smith wrote that upon the colonists' first landing at Cape Henry (within the bounds of the Chesapeake chiefdom) in April 1607, a group of what may have been Nansemond Indians attacked the English shore party while they were returning to their ships. If that had been the case, then the Chesapeake Indians likely would have been destroyed before the arrival of the colonists because the Nansemond territory was west of Cape Henry and the attacking party would have had to cross miles of Chesapeake territory to reach the colonists. There is some written evidence suggesting that the Chesapeakes were being destroyed at the time of the arrival of the colonists. One account reported smoke from a great fire in part of the region where the Chesapeakes had lived. But as yet, it has not been possible to determine exactly when Powhatan's main native rivals to the east were destroyed. It appears clear only that it was near the time of arrival of the first Jamestown colonists, but that the Chesapeakes were not the real threat from the east that Powhatan's priests had predicted.

Related entries: Accohannock Indians; Accomac Indians; Chickahominy Indians; Kecoughtan Indians; Manahoac Indians; Mattaponi Indians; Monacan Indians; Nansemond Indians; Pamunkey Indians; Paspahegh Indians; Powhatan; Warraskoyak Indians

Suggestions for further reading

Edward Arber, ed. 1910. *Travels and Works of Captain John Smith* (part 1). Edinburgh, Scotland: J. Grant.

Edward Wright Haile, ed. 2001. *Jamestown Narratives: Eyewitness Accounts of the Virginia Colony: The First Decade: 1607–1617.* Champlain, VA: Round House.

David Beers Quinn. 1974. *England and the Discovery of America, 1481–1620.* New York: Alfred A. Knopf.

———. 1985. *Set Faire for Roanoke: Voyages and Colonies, 1584–1606.* Chapel Hill and London: University of North Carolina Press.

Helen C. Rountree. 1989. *The Powhatan Indians of Virginia: Their Traditional Culture.* Norman and London: University of Oklahoma Press.

———. 1990. *Pocahontas's People: The Powhatan Indians of Virginia Through Four Centuries.* Norman: University of Oklahoma Press.

Native Americans sit around a fire in this sixteenth-century illustration by explorer and artist, John White, engraved by Theodor de Bry. (Library of Congress)

Chickahominy Indians

One of the tribes not subordinate to the powerful Algonquin chief Powhatan at the time of the English colonization of Jamestown was the Chickahominy, a group of Native Americans living in a series of villages strung out along the Chickahominy River between the Jamestown settlement and central present-day New Kent County. Numbering 800 or 900 people (including about 250 warriors) in 1608, when the tribe first encountered the English, the Chickahominy initially were neither hostile to the colonists nor eager to antagonize their native neighbors, with whom they were loosely allied and who surrounded them on all sides. Farming played an important role in the life of the Chickahominy, a largely agricultural people who annually raised an abundant crop of corn in the rich, marshy lands adjacent to the river that bore the tribe's name. Indeed, translated roughly, Chickahominy means "coarse pounded corn people," and even before the English began to explore the region inhabited by the Chickahominy, they learned that these native people could be called on routinely to provide a supply of foodstuffs.

By late 1607, the Chickahominy had become wary of the colonists' incursions into the region and did not scruple to take captive Captain John Smith when they discovered him deep in their territory. Unaware of exactly who Smith was and unwilling to release him without finding out, they triumphantly delivered him to Chief Powhatan, who, according to Smith after he had permanently left the colony, would have executed him but for the intervention of his daughter, Pocahontas. Captain Edward-Maria Wingfield, the

Treaty Negotiations with the Chickahominy, 1614

The Governours and people of Checkahomanics, who are five hundred bow-men, and better, a stout and warlike Nation have made meanes to have us come unto them, and conclude a peace, where all the Governours would meete me. They having thus three or foure times importuned mee, I resolved to go, so taking Captain Argall, with fifty men in my frigot, and barge I went thither: Captain Argall with forty men landed, I kept aboord for some reasons. Upon the meeting they tould Captain Argall they had longed to be friends, that they had no King, but eight great men, who governed them. He tould them that we came to be friends, asked them if they would have King James *to be their* King, & whether they would be his men? They after som conference between themselves seemed willing of both, demaunding if we would fight against their enemies, he tould them that if any did them injury, they should send me word, and I would agree them, or if their adversaries would not, then I would let them have as many men as they would to help them: they liked well of that, and tould him that all their men should helpe us. All this being agreed upon, C. Argall *gave every* Councellor *a* Tamahawk, and a peece of copper, which was kindly taken; they requested further, that if their boats should happen to meet with our boats, and that they said they were the Chikahominy Englishmen, *and* King James his men, we would let them passe: we agreed unto it, so that they pronounced them selves English men, and King James and his men, promising within fifteen daies to come unto James town to see me, and conclude theese conditions; every bowman being to give me as a Tribute *to* King James two measures of Corne every harvest, the two measures containing two bushells and a halfe, and I to give every bowman a small Tamahawke, and to every Counseller a suit of red cloath, which did much please them. This people never acknowledged any King, before; no nor ever would acknowledge Powhatan for their King, a stout people they be, and a delicate seat they have.

—Ralph Hamor, *A True Discourse of the Present State of Virginia (London, 1615)*

colony's first president, gave an account of Smith's capture to the colony's investors in England, and like Smith's first relation of his experience among the Chickahominy, Wingfield made no mention of Smith's rescue by Chief Powhatan's daughter, Pocahontas.

> Decem.—The 10th of December, Mr Smyth went up the ryver of the Chechohomynies to trade for corne. He was desirous to see the heade of that river; and, when it was not passible wth the shallop, he hired a cannow and an Indian to carry him up further. The river the higher grew worse and worse. Then hee went on shoare wth his guide, and left Robinson & Emmery, twoe of our Men, in the cannow; wch were presently slayne by the Indians, Pamaonke's men and hee himself taken prysoner, and, by the means of his guide, his lief was saved; and Pamaonché, haveing him prisoner, carryed him to his neybors wyroances to see if any of them knew him for one of those wch had bene, some twoe or three yeeres before us, in a river amongst them Northward, and taken awaie some Indians from them by force. At last he brought him to the great Powaton (of whome before wee had no knowledg), who sent him home to our towne the viii of January.

Smith's capture by the Chickahominy inadvertently had introduced the colonists to the most powerful Indian chief in Virginia, of whom they had not even heard before.

Subsequent interaction between the Chickahominy and the English revolved around trade, as the settlers constantly depended on the natives for food. The colonists forced the Chickahominy into an alliance in 1613, and the following year Captain Samuel Argall negotiated a written treaty by which the tribe agreed to provide two and one-half bushels of corn per warrior per year and warriors to fight the Spanish, if needed. In return, the colonists agreed to give each warrior a tomahawk and a suit of red clothes to the tribal elders, and to let the Indians govern their own affairs. Thereafter, relations were friendly until 1616, when the Indians grew tired of the settlers' repeated demands for corn. An English attack on the Chickahominy, led by the colony's governor, Sir George Yeardley in May 1616, resulted in the death of about two dozen Indians and pushed the tribe into the welcoming arms of Powhatan. The colonists lost an important source of trade and a strong ally and had to contend with the tribe from then until 1646, when a new treaty relegated the tribe to a reservation in the Pamunkey Neck area (present-day King William County). By 1669, the tribe had declined to a little more than 200 people, including about 60 warriors, and when the Treaty of Middle Plantation was negotiated in 1677 after Bacon's Rebellion, the Chickahominy was not even allowed to send their own delegate—the Queen of Pamunkey represented the tribe. After the turn of the century, the tribe even lost its reservation, although by 1750 remnants of the tribe had begun to migrate back to their ancestral lands.

The Chickahominy people managed to survive the onslaught and expansion of the English in Virginia, and today the tribe, with more than 1,000 members, is by far the largest in Virginia. Many tribal members still live on lands inhabited by their ancestors, without benefit of reservation, although the tribe itself also owns some ancestral property where it erected a tribal center in 1976. The tribe's church, the Samaria Baptist Church, is located near the center, as is a baseball field. (Although a Chickahominy child was one of the first Indians to be educated at Brafferton College, a grammar school for Indians established at the College of William and Mary in 1723, the Chickahominy conversion to Christianity did not take off until the 1790s, when a Christian missionary went to live among the tribe, married an Indian woman, and had a family.) Currently, the Chickahominy is one of six Virginia tribes seeking recognition from the federal government, having been granted official recognition by the state in 1983. Tribal officials, including the chief, two assistant chiefs, and ten-member council (evenly divided between male and female), are elected democratically every four years and serve on a volunteer basis.

Piney Grove, built around 1790 and said to be the best-preserved example of early log architecture in Tidewater Virginia, is on lands occupied by the Chickahominy before the settlement of Jamestown.

Related entries: Accohannock Indians; Accomac Indians; Chesapeake Indians; Chickahominy River; Kecoughtan Indians; Manahoac Indians; Mattaponi Indians; Monacan Indians; Nansemond Indians; Pamunkey Indians; Paspahegh Indians; Pocahontas; Smith, Captain John; Warraskoyak Indians; Wingfield, Edward-Maria

Suggestions for further reading

Charles Deane, ed. 1860. *"A Discourse of Virginia," by Edward-Maria Wingfield . . . now First Printed from the Original Manuscripts in the Lambeth Library.* Boston: J. Wilson and Son.

Charles Dudley Warner. 1881. *Captain John Smith.* New York: Henry Holt.

Chickahominy River

The Chickahominy, deriving its name from the ancient Indian tribe that lived in numerous villages along its shores, is, along with the Appomattox, Pagan, Nansemond, and Elizabeth Rivers, one of the chief coastal tributaries of Virginia's mightiest river, the James. Robert Beverley, in his *History and Present State of Virginia* (London, 1705), included the Chickahominy among the "abundance of lesser rivers" that were "capable of receiving the biggest merchant ships," i.e., the Elizabeth, Nansemond, Pamunkey, Mattaponi, and many others. Flowing southeast from about twenty miles above Richmond in western Henrico County, the river runs about ninety miles before emptying into the north side of the James River about seven miles from Jamestown.

The Chickahominy was navigable from its mouth to about a mile below Providence Forge (about halfway between Richmond and Williamsburg), where it is three to four and one-half feet deep. About six miles southeast of Providence Forge, the Chickahominy becomes an estuary and takes a turn to the south. Thomas

Jefferson, in his *Notes on the State of Virginia* (1781), observed that the "Chickahominy has at its mouth a bar, on which is only 12 feet water at common flood tide. Vessels passing that, may go 8 miles up the river; those of 10 feet draught may go four miles further, and those of six tons burthen, 20 miles further." Above Providence Forge, the Chickahominy narrows considerably, becoming what Confederate General Richard Taylor described as "a sluggish stream and subject to floods." From then on, the river is too shallow for navigation except by canoe or bateau, although at various times the river floods its banks, leaving one to three feet of water and mud in its wake.

In December 1607, after sailing the Chickahominy the distance described by Jefferson, Captain John Smith and two soldiers, desirous of discovering the headwaters of the river, abandoned the shallop that had carried them thus far. When the river could no longer support their barge, Smith hired a native to take them farther upstream in a canoe, and when the "river the higher grew worse and worse" Smith eventually had to go ashore and walk, leaving his companions behind. Smith was captured by members of the Chickahominy tribe, who then turned him over to Chief Powhatan. That great chief, according to Smith, spared his life at the request of his princess daughter, Pocahontas. Within a decade, the English had driven the Chickahominy Indians away from their lands in the river basin, although some of their descendents would return to the area in the eighteenth century.

Despite being a "lesser river," the Chickahominy proved to have an interesting history over the centuries. Thomas Rolfe, the son of Pocahontas and John Rolfe, established the seat of his 1,200-acre manor plantation, The Fort, on the Chickahominy in James City County. During the Revolutionary War, in 1776, the Virginia General Assembly erected a shipyard on the Chickahominy near Toano in James City County, about sixteen miles west of Williamsburg. Burned by the British army when it invaded Virginia, remnants of the shipyard can still be seen along the marshy waterfront. A canal connected the river to the forge that gave Providence Forge its name until British Colonel Banastre Tarleton destroyed it, too, in the campaigns of 1780 or 1781. Later in the eighteenth century, an elaborate system of drainage ditches was set up in the Chickahominy Swamp in an attempt to reclaim some of the rich, waterlogged land for agricultural cultivation. During the American Civil War, several sites along the Chickahominy became critical staging areas for both the Union and Confederate armies because of the river's proximity to Richmond, and major campaigns and battles were conducted near its banks in 1862 and 1864. In 1943, the state created a shallow but scenic 1,230-acre reservoir, Chick Lake, near Lenexa (a small town about halfway between Richmond and Williamsburg), which became an important drinking water impoundment for the Newport News area.

The Chickahominy River watershed area covers about 470 square miles, or about 300,000 acres, and is one of Virginia's most valuable wildlife habitats. The Chickahominy has been called one of the cleaner tributaries of the Chesapeake Bay; the river and its open marshes are home to an assortment of wildlife, including wood ducks, black ducks, mallards, bald eagles, red-shouldered hawks, blue herons, and ospreys; rare amphibians and reptiles like the nonpoisonous glossy crayfish snake; an abundance of largemouth and striped bass, crappie, blue catfish, and herring; beavers that have been known to alter the water flow patterns and cause flooding; and a thick growth of cypress trees and rare plant species.

Related entries: Chickahominy Indians; Elizabeth River; James River; Mattaponi River; Nansemond River; Pamunkey River; Rappahannock River; York River

Suggestion for further reading

Michael J. Focazio and Robert E. Cooper. 1995. *Selected Characteristics of Stormflow and Base Flow Affected by Land Use and Cover in the Chickahominy River Basin, Virginia, 1989–91.* Richmond, VA: U. S. Department of the Interior, U. S. Geological Survey.

City Point

The eight day of May we discovered up the River. We landed in the Countrey of Apamatica. At our landing, there came many stout and able Savages

> to resist us with their Bowes and Arrowes, in a most warlike manner, with the swords at their backes beset with sharpe stones, and pieces of yron able to cleave a man in sunder. Amongst the rest one of the chiefest, standing before them cross-legged, with his Arrow readie in his Bow in one hand, and taking a Pipe of Tobacco in the other, with a bold uttering of his speech, demanded of us our being there, willing us to bee gone. Wee made signes of peace, which they perceived in the end, and let us land in quietnesse.

Thus reads George Percy's description of the English colonists' first visit to the region later called City Point, in the spring of 1607. Five years later, in 1612, the year after the English settled Henrico and Bermuda Hundred, the colonists came back to City Point to settle a plantation, which became known as Bermuda City (later Charles City, in honor of Prince Charles).

Ralph Hamor, in his *A True Discourse of the Present State of Virginia* (London, 1615), described the "undertaking of the Bermuda City, a businesse of greatest hope," its "great fields and woods abounding with Strawberies much fairer and more sweete then ours, Mulberries of great bignesse . . . great store thereof, Maricocks of the fashion of a Lemmon whose blossome may admit comparison with our most delightsome and bewtifull flowers, and the fruite exceeding pleasant and tastfull." The town of City Point proper, complete with defensive works, was built between 1614 and 1616. Bermuda City had been renamed Charles City by the time of the Virginia census of 1619, at which time there were thirty-seven residents (twenty-seven men, seven women, and three children). It is unclear how successful the City Point plantation was in relation to its goals, either as a plantation venture or as a fortification.

The sudden and violent Massacre of 1622 left five men dead at City Point and gave rise to severe criticism by the governor of Bermuda, Captain Nathaniel Butler, who, after visiting the outpost following the attack, described what he had seen:

> I found the Antient Planters of Henrico and Charles Citty wholly quitted and lefte to the spoile of the Indians, who not onely burned the houses saide to be once the best of all others, but fell uppon the Poultry, Hoggs, Cowes, Goates and Horses wherof they killed great numbers to the greate griefe as well as ruine of the Olde Inhabitants, whoe stick not to affirme that these were not onely the best and healthiest parts of all others, but might allsoe by their naturall strength of scituacion have been the most easefully preserved of all the rest.

Planters of the region censured Butler's description, however. According to their response,

> *Henrico* was quitted in Sir Thomas Smith's time, only the Church and one House remaining. *Charles City,* so much spoken of never had but six Houses. The Soil of both is barren, worn out, and not fit for Culture. The loss of our stocks the Informer hath less Reason to urge. For he joined with the Indians in killing our Cattle, and carried the Beef aboard his Ship.

Regardless of who was more correct, the first effort to settle City Point ended in failure, and no immediate resettlement took place following the Indian uprising.

In 1635, settler Francis Eppes patented 1,700 acres at City Point and established a family plantation. For more than three and a half centuries, some of Eppes's original acreage remained in the possession of his descendants, including the mansion house built by the family in the mid-eighteenth century, Appomattox Manor. (The National Park Service acquired Appomattox Manor in 1979. Archeological digs by the Park Service in the 1980s discovered an earlier house, possibly built by Eppes as early as 1620.) Eventually, City Point and the Eppes plantation became the site of a small port that enabled tobacco farmers in the region to more easily get their crops to market, and a few other buildings sprung up at City Point. During the Revolutionary War, defensive works at City Point fired on British vessels in the river under the command of the American traitor, General Benedict Arnold. City Point took on a more important economic role in 1797, when the collector of customs established his office in the town. City Point received another boost in 1826, when the town was officially founded, and again in the late 1830s, when the second railroad in the state connected the port at City Point with the nearby city of Petersburg. General Ulysses S. Grant headquartered at City Point during the seige of Petersburg in 1864, building earthworks and setting up an important supply post for the Union army, and eventually seven hospitals. President Lincoln made his way to City Point on board the *River Queen* on 25 March 1865 to meet with Grant; Lincoln and his wife stayed at City Point for two weeks. Still, City Point remained a small hamlet with a population of about 300 people until the twentieth century, when the DuPont Company opened a dynamite factory there. City Point's population, along with that of neighboring Hopewell, quickly grew to the greatest in its history, but DuPont left City Point after World War I, and Hopewell annexed City Point in 1923; until its annexation, it was in Prince George County (after 1703).

City Point is situated on the bluffs above the Appomattox (to the west) and James rivers (to the northeast); the area is a natural harbor for the deep navigational waters it overlooks. Described as standing "upon high ground the Cliffes being steepe, but of a clay mould," it is across the river from both Bermuda Hundred and West and Shirley Hundred, two other important landmarks from the early Jamestown settlement period. Archeological excavations in the City Point section of Hopewell in 2002 by the William and Mary Center for Archaeological Research found evidence of occupation as far back as 5,000 years. Artifacts from the English settlement period were sparse, however—an indication that City Point never became more than a sparsely settled community during the era of Jamestown's ascendancy. At the same time, the archaeologists determined that City Point is "one of the nation's premier Civil War archaeological sites." City Point was added to the National Register of Historic Places in 1979.

Related entries: Martin's Hundred; Percy, George; Shirley Hundred

Suggestions for further reading

A. J. Foster. 1965. *Early James River History in and Around Hopewell, Virginia.* Falls Church, VA: Falcon.

David W. Lewes, et al. 2003. *Windows into the Past: Archaeological Assessment of Three City Point Lots, City of Hopewell, Virginia.* Williamsburg, VA: William and Mary Center for Archaeological Research.

Claiborne, William (1600–1677)

His biographer called him the "foremost genius of early Virginia," yet the name William Claiborne is remembered now, if at all, only in connection with the unhappy hostilities that existed between the early settlers of Virginia and Maryland. He was born in Crayford in Kent, England, the second son of Thomas and Sara Smith James Clayborne, and he entered Cambridge University's Pembroke College in 1617. Claiborne decided to seek his fortune in the New World after finishing his studies at Cambridge, and when the London Company reorganized the Jamestown colony in 1621, it appointed Claiborne royal surveyor of the plantations of Virginia. (A contemporary described Claiborne as a "gentleman, recommended unto us as very fit in the art of surveying.") He sailed for Virginia with the newly appointed governor of the colony, Sir Francis Wyatt, and several members of the new council on board the *George,* one of the nine ships bringing more settlers to Jamestown. Claiborne was listed among the new colonists as a gentleman, without occupation, but his surveying commission provided him ample opportunities for personal advancement, and he eventually registered more than 45,000 acres of land in his own name. King Charles I named Claiborne to the Governor's Council in 1625, with an appointment of secretary of state for the colony, and the following year he applied to the Privy Council for permission to explore some of Virginia's unstaked regions and open trade with the Indians.

One of the regions in which Claiborne received permission to explore and trade was the head of the Chesapeake Bay, an area later claimed by Lord Baltimore, the founder of Maryland. As Claiborne described it, in 1631 he "entered upon the Isle of Kent, unplanted by any man, but possessed of the natives of that country, with about one hundred men and there contracted with the natives and bought their right, to hold of the Crown of England." He "stocked and planted" the island, which is in the Chesapeake Bay opposite the site of the future Maryland capital, Annapolis, and sent a burgess to the Virginia

General Assembly in 1632. With friendly Susquehannock Indians, Claiborne established a lucrative trade for high-quality furs, which were shipped on to England. That same year, in June, a charter was issued to Cecilius Calvert, the second Lord Baltimore, for the settling of a colony to the north of Jamestown, known as Maryland, and not long afterwards Claiborne's ownership and possession of Kent Island was called into question. The governor at Jamestown, Thomas Harvey, not only sided with Baltimore in the controversy but went so far as to dismiss Claiborne from his post as secretary of state in 1634, replacing him with a Richard Kemp, who was later elected governor during the Interregnum. Although Charles I was a strong supporter of Lord Baltimore, he asked Baltimore not to interfere with his subjects or their improvements on Kent Island—after all, Claiborne's own claims to the territory derived from Charles. Baltimore nevertheless seized Claiborne's trading vessel, the *Long Tail,* for illegally sailing in Maryland waters and attempted to capture Claiborne, but without success. The incident prompted Claiborne to arm his merchant sloop, the *Cockatrice,* but that vessel, too, was soon taken. A second armed ship outfitted by Claiborne was more successful and allowed Claiborne to keep control of the island.

Portrait of William Claiborne, original Jamestown colonist and royal surveyor of the plantations of Virginia (1587–1677). (Courtesy Virginia Historical Society)

Back at Jamestown, Claiborne's supporters were furious at Lord Baltimore's effrontery and took it out on Governor Harvey, forcing him to step aside in 1635. Matters stood still until 1637, when Baltimore succeeded in winning to his side George Evelin, the agent for Claiborne's chief trading partner in London, Cloberry & Company. With Evelin's help, Lord Baltimore's Maryland representatives—led by his brother Leonard Calvert—took control of Kent Island by force, an act eventually sanctioned by the Board of Commissioners for the Plantations in the spring of 1638. At the same time, the Maryland General Assembly charged Claiborne with piracy and murder and confiscated all his property, but they still could not lay hands on Claiborne himself, who had returned to Jamestown. Although the ruling had gone against Claiborne by the Crown's commissioners, in 1642 Claiborne was appointed treasurer for life of the Virginia colony by Charles, who perhaps wanted to placate Claiborne for his loss of Kent Island. Nevertheless, Claiborne attempted to regain possession by force in 1644 through an alignment with Richard Ingle (1609–1653), a wealthy Protestant trader allied with the anti-Crown forces in Parliament. Together they captured Kent Island and St. Mary's and drove Leonard Calvert out of Maryland and into Virginia. (Around the same period, after the Massacre of 1644, Claiborne, as commander in general of the forces recruited to wage war on the Indians, was instrumental in driving the Mattaponi Indians away from Pamunkey Neck to a site near the Rappahannock River.) In 1646, Calvert retook Maryland with assistance from Virginia's governor, William Berkeley. The controversy continued with neither side winning for another decade, and finally, in November 1657, a compromise was reached. Claiborne lost the six-square-mile Kent Island but was granted more than 20,000 acres of land elsewhere in Virginia.

Claiborne, always a loyal supporter of the Crown and of most of the royal governors, including William Berkeley, somehow found favor with the Commonwealth as well, and served as the Jamestown colony's secretary of state during the Interregnum. Claiborne continued in that capacity after Berkeley was restored to power in Virginia and after the Restoration of Charles II as well.

Much of the land Claiborne held was along the Pamunkey River in old New Kent County and present-day King William County, and included a plantation later operated by George Washington as part of his wife's estate (often referred to simply as Claiborne's) adjacent to Romancoke, where Claiborne spent his last years. Claiborne was married about 1635, in Virginia, to Elizabeth Butler (Boteler), a daughter of John Butler of Litell Burch Hall in Essex, England; together they raised at least six children. Claiborne's descendants remained on his lands and became perhaps the most prominent family in the region; in addition to Romancoke, their estates included Sweet Hall, Tuckacommon, Cohoke, and Windsor.

Related entry: Berkeley, Sir William

Suggestions for further reading

John Herbert Claiborne. 1917. *William Claiborne of Virginia, with Some Account of His Pedigree.* New York and London: G. P. Putnam's Sons.

Nathaniel C. Hale. 1951. *Virginia Venturer: A Historical Biography of William Claiborne, 1600–1677.* Richmond, VA: Dietz Press.

Malcolm H. Harris. 1977. *Old New Kent County: Some Account of the Planters, Plantations, and Places in King William County, St. John's Parish.* West Point, VA: M. H. Harris.

George Southall Vest. 1947. "William Claiborne" (M.A. thesis, University of Virginia). Charlottesville.

Cole, William (1638–1694)

William Cole of Warwick County, Virginia, a member of the Governor's Council during the period of Bacon's Rebellion, was the eldest son and namesake of William Cole (Coale; 1598–1664), an immigrant from Tillinham in Essex, England, who had come to the Jamestown colony aboard the *Neptune* in 1618 and settled in Elizabeth City County (later Warwick) by 1623. The elder Cole became a member of the House of Burgesses in 1629, representing the settlement at Nutmeg Quarter, and with his wife Francis (Frances; b. 1597), who came to Virginia in the *Susan* in 1616), Cole had three sons, William, John, and Richard. The younger William purchased Boldrup (Balthrope), a 1,350-acre tract on the Warwick River northwest of Nutmeg Quarter not far from Denbigh, from Governor William Berkeley in 1671. (Berkeley's wife, Lady Frances, had received the property from her first husband, Samuel Stephens, governor of Albemarle.) Three years later, Cole was named to the Governor's Council, where his associates singled him out as "an active member of the councill."

With one other councilor, Cole was appointed to negotiate with Nathaniel Bacon and his followers when the latter besieged Jamestown in 1676. Although he was a strong ally of Governor Berkeley, Cole thought that some of the grievances of the insurrectionists were just and ought to be addressed; the governor was not as flexible, however, and the negotiations came to naught. When Bacon drafted his "Declaration of the People, against Sr: Wm: Berkeley, and Present Governors of Virginia," he named Cole among the nineteen associates of the governor that "have bin his wicked and Pernicious Councellours and Confederates, Aiders, and Assistants against the Commonaltie in these our Civill Commotions." Bacon apparently had taken offense at Cole's defense of the legal rights of Native Americans (Cole was an attorney), for at his trial Bacon was accused of arraigning Cole "*for saying* that the English are bound to protect the Indians at the haserd of their blood." Furthermore, Cole, as a colonel of the militia, had represented the citizens of Gloucester to Bacon and several hundred of his followers at a public meeting, giving the troublemakers the "sence of all the Gloster men there present: which was sumed up in their desires, not to have the oath imposed upon them, but to be indulged the benefitt of Neutralitie." Bacon's response was to declare that neutrality was not an option, "that in this their request they appeared like the worst of sinners, who had a desire to be saved with the righteous, and yet would do nothing whereby they might obtaine there salvation." Cole's more judicious approach was not heeded by Bacon, nor did it win from Governor Berkeley anything but ire, albeit only temporarily. (Berkeley, in fact, engaged Cole to attest to the authenticity of his last will and testament the following year.) When Berkeley fled to Maryland to escape the reaches of Bacon's grasp, Cole was among the group that accompanied the governor.

Cole received a royal appointment as Virginia's secretary of state in the fall of 1689 and served in that capacity for almost three years, tendering his resignation because he was "lately much decayed in body" and suffering from "deepe Melancholly." At the same time, Cole gave up his office as collector of the Lower District of the James River. Cole was among the colonists who petitioned the Crown for the establishment of a college in the colony, and when the College of William and Mary was formed in 1692, Cole was named one of its first trustees.

Cole married at least three times, first in 1674 (wife unknown), again in 1680, to Ann Diggs (c.1657–1686), and after Ann's death, to Martha Lear (1668–1704), the daughter of fellow Councilor John Lear, by whom Cole had a son, William Cole, III (d. 1729), a burgess in the eighteenth century. Boldrup was the home of Cole and his descendents for about a century, but all that remains of the estate now are some brick foundations, archaeological remains, and a gravesite. The cemetery contains the graves of Cole and two of his wives; his tombstone, inscribed with the family coat of arms, reads in part, "Of him this may be loudly sounded far He was unspotted on ye bench untaynted at ye bar." A dig conducted by the James River Institute for Archaeology in the late 1980s revealed earlier English occupation of Boldrup from about 1636 to 1650. Cole patented a tract of 618 acres in York County in 1683, and two years later he purchased another 1,433 acres lying in both Warwick and Elizabeth City Counties, the site of the original settlement of Newport News.

Related entries: Berkeley, Sir William; Claiborne, William; Newport News

Suggestions for further reading

Donald A. D'Amato. 1992. *Warwick's 350-Year Heritage: A Pictorial History.* Virginia Beach, VA: Donning.

Edward M. Riley and Charles E. Hatch, Jr., eds. 1946. *James Towne In the Words of Contemporaries.* Washington, DC: National Park Service.

College at Henricus

With the attempt to shift the base of operations from Jamestown to Henricus (Henrico), the Virginia Company of London began planning to establish a college just north of the new base on a 10,000-acre land grant set aside for that purpose. The grant was known as College Land, and the intended college was to have an affiliated school, the East India School, named after some of the first contributors to the effort. The London Company's goals of the college were defined in its charter, issued on 18 November 1618:

East India School

Shortly after the College at Henricus was chartered in 1618, members of the East India Company sailing back to England from the New World aboard the ship *Royal James* began collecting money to establish a "collegiate or free school" at Charles City (present-day City Point), to be associated with the new college. The purpose of the school was twofold: to prepare English students for eventual attendance at the College at Henricus and to introduce young Indian boys—kidnapped and enslaved—to English culture and to Christianity. Appropriately named the East India School in honor of its early benefactors, the school was assigned 1,000 acres for the support of its master and usher. The school actually opened, but most of its occupants were killed in the Indian Massacre of 1622. Renewed efforts to establish the school failed.

Nicholas Ferrar the Elder (1546–1620)

This merchant adventurer made for himself a fortune moving goods between the East and West Indies and London. A supporter of the Sandys faction that controlled the colony, Ferrar at his death left the huge sum of £300 to establish a college in the Jamestown colony for the purpose of educating at least "ten of the Infidels children placed in it." His endowment was to support "three discreete and godly men in the Colonie, which shall honestly bring up three of the Infidels children in Christian Religion, and some good course to live by." The school opened at Henrico in 1621.

As Ferrar's bequest indicated, his chief interest in the London Company and in the Jamestown colony lay in the spreading of the Christian faith in the New World. A later historian characterized Ferrar as "one of the largest selfish men that ever lived. . . . proved himself able and indefatigable in business, devoted to his country and its Church, at once a Royalist and a wise and firm upholder of English liberties."

Portrait of Nicholas Ferrar, English merchant and benefactor of the first college in Jamestown (1546–1620). (Ellyson, J. Taylor. The London Company of Virginia, *1908)*

Whereas, by a special grant and licence from his Majesty, a general contribution over the Realm hath been made for the building and planting of a college for the training up of the children of those Infidels in true Religion, moral virtue, and civility, and for other godlyness, We do therefore, according to a former Grant and order, hereby ratifie, confirm and ordain that a convenient place be chosen and set out for the planting of a University at the said Henrico in time to come, and that in the mean time preparation be there made for the building of the said College for the Children of the Infidels, according to such instructions as we shall deliver. And we will and ordain that ten thousand acres, partly of the lands they impaled [settled; or impaled, as in setting up palisades], and partly of the land within the territory of the said Henrico, be allotted and set out for the endowing of the said University and College with convenient possessions.

The Reverend Patrick Copeland was to be the first rector, with George Thorpe intended as superintendent of the plantation and buildings.

Progress was made on the college and school, and by 1619, £2043.2.11½ had been donated for the endeavor. Collection of volumes for the library had begun as well, including "many excellent good religious bookes, worth ten pound," which apparently had among them "a treatise of St. Augustine of the *City of God,* translated into English." A workforce sent from England to begin the construction and setup of the facilities included the school's master and usher, and a manager and tenants for the college lands. In fact, all necessary crew and staff eventually arrived except Reverend Copeland. As with so many other endeavors along the James at that time, however, the massacre in March 1622 halted work on the college and effectively ended plans for such an institution in Virginia for many years to come. In 1923, the citizens of Hopewell, Virginia, not far from the original site of the college, honored the college's rector, Reverend Patrick Copeland, by naming a public school in his honor.

Related entries: Henricus; Thorpe, George

Suggestions for further reading

Robert Hunt Land. 1938. "Henrico and Its College" (*William and Mary Quarterly,* 2d ser., vol. 18).

Edward D. Neill. 1869. *History of the Virginia Company of London, with Letters to and from the First Colony Never Before Printed.* Albany, New York: Joel Munsell.

——. 1871. *The English Colonization of America: During the Seventeenth Century.* London: Strahan.

Lyon Gardiner Tyler. 1906. *The Cradle of the Republic: Jamestown and James River.* Richmond, VA: Hermitage Press.

——, ed. 1907. *Narratives of Early Virginia: 1606–1625.* New York: Charles Scribner's Sons.

A Counter-Blaste to Tobacco

Appearing anonymously in 1604, King James I's *A Counter-Blaste to Tobacco* was perhaps the earliest published attack on tobacco. James's reason for writing the pamphlet was to "discover the abuses thereof," and he did so admirably, in a light, even humorous, but detesting tone. "And surely in my opinion," he says in his introduction, "there cannot be a more base, and yet hurtfull corruption in a Countrey, then is the vile use (or other abuse) of taking *Tobacco* in this Kingdome." England, said James, was a peaceful and wealthy land; its people were loving and obedient to their sovereign, but their very fortune had given rise to a "generall sluggishnesse," an opportunity to wallow in all sorts of idle delights and soft delicacies—the first seeds of the subversion of all monarchies. "Our Cleargie are become negligent and lazie, our Nobilitie and Gentrie prodigall, and solde to their private delights, Our Lawyers covetous, our Common-people prodigall and curious; and generally all sorts of people more carefull for their private ends, then for their mother the Commonwealth." The widespread use of tobacco was as base and hurtful as any corruption in the country, and a reformation was called for.

Tobacco Vicious and Ruinous

The vicious ruinous plant of Tobacco I would not name, but that it brings more money to the Crown, then all the Islands in *America* besides.

—Sir William Berkeley, *A Discourse and View of Virginia* (1663)

According to James I, customs were introduced to a land in either of two ways. First, on a godly, necessary, and honorable ground, brought in by worthy and virtuous persons, and once accepted esteemed by all wise and temperate people. Or, on the other hand, a custom originated from "base corruption and barbarity" by "inconsiderate and childish affectation of Noveltie." Tobacco, a common herb, was carried to the English from the "barbarous *Indians*" as an antidote to the pox, a filthy disease rampant among primitive people because of their uncleanliness. To imitate the "beastly" manners of the "wilde, godlesse, and slavish *Indians,*" especially in so "vile and stinking a custome," was foolish and hurtful to individuals and to the commonwealth. The English, said James, might as well follow the Indians also by "walking naked" and "preferring glasses, feathers, and such toyes," to gold and precious stones.

Besides, experience taught that tobacco was unnatural and hurtful to the health of the body. It contained a "certaine venomous facultie," made apparent by its "hatefull smell," and contrary to received wisdom, could not purge the body of illness or pain. Every "foolish boy," "sillie wench," "olde doting wife," and "ignorant countrey clowne" played the physician when it came to toothaches, the colic, the gout, and many common diseases, but, said the King, "I hope no man is so foolish as to beleve them." In fact, James correctly reasoned, "what greater absurditie can there bee, then to say that one cure shall serve for divers, nay, contrarious sortes of diseases?" The "smoakie vapours" of tobacco was said to make one drunk, another sober; it might refresh a weary man yet make a man hungry. It could make a man sleep soundly when he went to bed, and to awake his brain and quicken his understanding if he was tired. "Omnipotent power of *Tobacco*!" he exclaimed. He was surprised that both the "superstitious Priests [Roman Catholics], and the insolent Puritanes" were not using it to cast out demons. If a large number of the people had discovered the smoking of tobacco to be to their "good liking" rather than the error that is was, it was because of their propensity to be drawn to the "foolish affectation" of novelty and fashion. Selfishness and envy in people led them to act "like Apes, counterfeiting the manner of others, to our owne destruction." If a man smoke himself to death with tobacco, "and many have done," then some other disease must bear the blame for it other than the real culprit, "stinking smoake." Like a drunkard who cannot abide being sober, who is never satisfied but with the next, and stronger drink, so must the smokers of tobacco be taken in by its "bewitching qualities." To those addicted, it made a kitchen of the inward parts of men, "soiling and infecting them" with an "oily kinde of Soote."

The tract concludes with an appeal to the reader to forbear following a custom so "lothsome to the eye, hateful to the Nose, harmefull to the braine, dangerous to the Lungs, and the blacke stinking fume thereof, nearest resembling the horrible Stigian smoke of the pit that is bottomlesse." Alas, however, the appeal fell on deaf ears, and James eventually chose to subject imported tobacco to a heavy tax rather than attempt to stamp out smoking by making it illegal. James's authorship of the *Counter-Blaste* was made known twelve years after its publication.

Related entries: Bacon's Rebellion; Banister, John; Berkeley, Sir William; Lee, Richard; Raleigh, Sir Walter; Slavery; Tobacco

Suggestions for further reading

William Berkeley. 1663. *A Discourse and View of Virginia.* London.

Robert Beverley. 1855. *The History of Virginia, in Four Parts.* Richmond, VA.

James I. 1604. *A Counter-Blaste to Tobacco.* London.

Crashaw, Reverend William (d. 1626)

If anyone was the central coordinator of promotion of the Virginia colony in England, it was William Crashaw, a Puritan churchman and scholar reputed to have officiated at the execution of Mary, Queen of Scots. Characterized as a learned and "argumentative but eloquent" defender of Protestantism, Crashaw had been born at Yorkshire and educated at St. John's College, Cambridge, where he was ordained in 1597. He served first as rector of Barton Agnes in Yorkshire and then from 1605–1613 at the renowed Temple Church in London, where he delivered a celebrated sermon favoring English colonization of the New World. The sermon, preached on 21 February 1609 and published the same year under the title *A Sermon Preached before the right honourable the Lord Lawarre,* was distributed widely in England and was influential among the supporters of Virginia. Preaching to an audience that included Lord De La Warr and those "who make the greatest ventures and bear the greatest burdens—who leave your ease and honour at home, and commend yourselves to the seas and winds for the good of the enterprise"—Crashaw encouraged and admonished his listeners. As a Christian mission, Crashaw said, the colonization of Virginia compared with the Israelites going down into Egypt, or with the poor, mean, and despised beginning of Rome, which went on to become mighty in the world after a few hundred years. "You go to commend it to the heathen, then practise it yourselves." As national policy, colonization offered the chance to "rectifie and reform" many social disorders in England, especially by providing an outlet for excess population. It offered England the potential to enrich itself through the discovery of new reserves of natural resources and commodities and thereby allow the country to wean itself from foreign dependence. And the increased demand for sea vessels and mariners would be a boon to the country's economy and defense. Many of the English supporters of the colony, especially Lord De La Warr, looked upon the subjects of Crashaw's sermon as a roadmap to colonization. In the long run, the themes of Crashaw's sermon proved prophetic, including the central one: "I say, many greater States than this is likely to prove hath as little or less beginning."

Related entries: Buck, Richard; Gosnold, Bartholomew; Hunt, Robert; London Company; West, Thomas, Lord De La Warr

Suggestions for further reading

Philip Alexander Bruce. 1896. *Economic History of Virginia in the Sevententh Century: An Inquiry into the Material Condition of the People, Based on Original and Contemporaneous Records.* New York: Macmillan.

Edward D. Neill. 1869. *History of the Virginia Company of London, with Letters to and from the First Colony Never Before Printed.* Albany, New York: Joel Munsell.

——. 1871. *The English Colonization of America: During the Seventeenth Century.* London: Strahan.

Culpeper, Lord Thomas, Second Baron of Thoresway (1635–1689)

Thomas, Lord Culpeper, Second Baron of Thoresway and eventual sole proprietor of the Northern Neck and governor of Virginia, was a grandson and the namesake of Thomas Culpeper (d. 1617) of Wigsell in Sussex, England, an original stockholder in the Virginia Company. His father, the elder Thomas's second son, John (1600–1660), inherited the interest in the company in 1617, shortly before matriculating at Oxford's Middle Temple. Knighted by King James I in 1621, John sold his stake in the Company and his ancestral estate, Wigsell, a couple of years later, settling after his marriage in 1628 at Hollingbourne, where he entered politics. Service to the king as a member of the Privy Council and as Chancellor of the Exchequer and as Master of the Rolls, along with military service on behalf of the Crown, culminated in Sir John's elevation to the peerage by Charles I in 1644 as first Baron of Thoresway. For John's loyalty to Charles and to his son when he went into exile in France, he was rewarded (with six others) all the previously unsettled land in Tidewater Virginia, a grant of 5 million acres known as the Northern Neck Proprietary. It was this land grant that brought the younger Thomas to Virginia and for which he is known to history.

Thomas accompanied his parents into exile during the Interregnum, marrying a Dutch woman from The Hague on the eve of the Restoration. When his father died, Thomas succeeded him as second Baron of Thoresway, and one of his first deeds was to successfully petition the Crown for restoration of the family's property. Charles II appointed the new Lord Culpeper to the lucrative office of Captain of the Isle of Wight in 1661. Living at Carisbrooke Castle, Culpeper held office for seven years, pleasing the Crown sufficiently to win an additional appointment as governor of the island. His effectiveness at administration won some allies, but his taking a mistress offended the island's social elite, and they attempted without success to have him recalled, although Culpeper tendered his resignation in 1668. In March 1671, he was appointed to the Council of Foreign Plantations. When the Crown reorganized and greatly expanded the powers of the council about a year and a half later, renaming it the Council for All Affairs Relating to Trade and Foreign Colonies and Plantations, Culpeper was named vice president, a position in which he served with more energy than he previously had exhibited. He held that office until the Council was abolished three years later, his competency in administrative affairs particularly apparent in his successful negotiation of a treaty of commerce with the Dutch. More important, for his personal affairs at least, Culpeper learned directly about the state of economic affairs of the New World, and he began to think about the potential use of Virginia's system of quit rents to secure from the Crown the yet-to-be satisfied promise to his father of

Portrait of Thomas Culpeper, Second Baron of Thoresway (1635–1689). (Library of Congress)

£12,000. King Charles granted him the rights to the rents for thirty-one years beginning in March 1672.

At the same time, Culpeper began to take an interest in Virginia's Northern Neck, a vast, unimproved wilderness with potentially unlimited resources, about one-third of which was now held, at least on paper, by him and a cousin (also named Thomas Culpeper). Culpeper began to purchase the other proprietors' interests in the Northern Neck, a process completed in 1681, making him the sole proprietor. In 1675, the Crown appointed him lieutenant and governor of the Virginia colony, effective at the death or abdication of Governor Sir William Berkeley; he took office in 1677 when Berkeley died. Under his stewardship, Jamestown was rebuilt, although after an accidental fire a few years later, the town was abandoned for the more healthful inland area at Middle Plantation, later known as Williamsburg. He traveled to Virginia twice, staying in the colony from May to August 1680 and from December 1682 to May 1683. On his first visit to Virginia, Culpeper was greeted enthusiastically by colony officials, and he had one major success, the General's Assembly's passage in June of *An Act for Cohabitation and Encouragement of Trade and Manufacture.* Culpeper believed that the colony needed market centers to realize its economic potential, and the aim of the act was to create and encourage the settlement and growth of a town in each of Virginia's twenty counties. Provisions of the act directed each county to set aside 10,000 pounds of tobacco for the purchase of fifty acres of land near an existing settlement within its borders to establish a town and to build a warehouse to handle the shipments of tobacco and other merchandise.

Culpeper's new villages gave the expected success for the most part but at the same time created among the people much resentment and dissatisfaction. Thus, his second stay in Virginia was not as congenial as his first. The rents collected in the Northern Neck had been much less than Culpeper had projected, and being in the colony in person did not bring much of an increase. In addition, he alienated his few admirers by using force to quell the opposition that had arisen to his establishment of towns—a number of leaders were hanged and Major Robert Beverley, clerk of the House of Burgesses, was imprisoned along with several others. Culpeper soon determined that he might stand a better chance of achieving his financial goals back in England. He left Virginia in 1683, never to return, forfeiting his post as governor. Back in England, Culpeper again entered into the political fray, and, despite the advantages he and his father had received from Charles I and II, he eventually cast his lot with those in the House of Lords looking to replace James II with the Prince of Orange.

Lord Culpeper died shortly after the Glorious Revolution. He left no sons, and two of his three daughters were illegitimate, the children of his long-time mistress, Susanna Wills, with whom he had lived since his days as captain of Isle of Wight. In fact, the affair between Culpeper and Wills had been the motive behind the citizens' attempt to have the Crown recall Culpeper. To the mistress and her girls, Culpeper left his estate, conveying it before he died. Culpeper's widow, Lady Margaret (Marguerite

Van Hesse), lived at Leeds Castle with her daughter Catherine; when she learned of her husband's will, she immediately filed suit, which was of course countered by Wills. Lady Margaret then appealed to the House of Lords, where a bill setting out her and Catherine's grievances and seeking a return of the property was narrowly defeated. After that, the two sides negotiated a settlement that gave Lady Margaret control of the Northern Neck. Upon her death, the grant went to Catherine, who married Thomas, Lord Fairfax, fifth Baron of Cameron. Catherine's son, Thomas, sixth Baron of Cameron, inherited the Northern Neck at her death and eventually settled in Virginia, relying on his relatives to manage the Proprietary. Lord Fairfax died during the American Revolutionary War, and the Proprietary was dissolved by the Virginia legislature at war's end in 1783.

Lord Culpeper has not fared very well with historians, as he had not with some contemporaries—a seventeenth-century connection described him as "one of the most cunning and covetous men in England." Writing with less invective, Robert Beverley, in his *History and Present State of Virginia* (London, 1705), said that Culpeper "had the art of mixing the good of the Country with his own particular Interest." Another concurred, writing that Culpeper was "a Man of Sound judgment . . . not wholly negligent of his own Interest." Yet another found him "A vicious and corrupt man" but one who "made a figure in the debates." Historian and diplomat George Bancroft gave the general consensus as far back as 1837:

> He had no high-minded regard for Virginia: he valued his office and his patents only as property. . . . yet Culpeper was not singularly avaricious. His conduct was in harmony with the principles which prevailed in England. As the British merchant claimed the monopoly of colonial commerce, as the British manufacturer valued Virginia only as a market for his goods, so the British Courtiers looked to appointments in America as a means of enlarging their own revenues or providing for their dependants. Nothing but Lord Culpeper's avarice gives him a place in American history.

Henry Cabot Lodge, usually a judicious writer, was even less charitable, characterizing Culpeper's administration as an "extensive swindle" of "simple greed and violent exaction" and wrote that, as governor, "Culpeper's sole object was extortion, which he freely practised." Even those seeking to say something positive about Culpeper seldom refrained from remarking on the negative side of his nature. The foremost early historian of colonial Virginia, Thomas Jefferson Wertenbaker, seems to have summed it up succinctly: "Few British colonial Governors are less deserving of respect than Thomas, Lord Culpeper." In fact, the Crown itself must have reconsidered its own appointment of Culpeper, for no other colonial governor ever received a lifetime appointment. Despite the hyperbole, however, there is no evidence that Culpeper ever sought to gain anything beyond the £12,000 that was owed to him as a result of the King's grant to his father. It seems Culpeper's methods, rather than his motives, combined with censure of his private life, provoked the ire of his contemporaries.

Related entries: Berkeley, Sir William; Northern Neck; Rappahannock River

Suggestions for further reading

Fairfax Harrison. 1926. *The Proprietors of the Northern Neck: Chapters of Culpeper Genealogy.* Richmond, VA: Old Dominion Press.

Mary R. Miller. 1983. *Place-Names of the Northern Neck of Virginia: From John Smith's 1606 Map to the Present.* Richmond: Virginia State Library.

D

Dale, Sir Thomas (d. 1619)

Knighted in 1606 at Richmond, England, by King James I, Sir Thomas Dale had served as a soldier and mercenary for the Dutch since 1588. But it was for his service in Jamestown as marshal, deputy governor, and governor that he is best remembered. Dale's first act after arriving in the colony on Sunday, 29 May 1611, was to convene a council to consider how to best use the carpenters, bricklayers, and other artisans who had accompanied him from England.

Shortly after his arrival at Jamestown, Dale implemented the *Lawes Divine, Morall and Martiall,* which he, Governor Thomas Gates, and Sir Thomas Smythe had developed for the colony. Although these laws were severe, even harsh by modern standards, they helped bring order and productivity to the colony following a period of drastic deterioration. As can be seen from Dale's letter to the Council of Virginia of 25 May 1611, there was much to be done. After landing at Jamestown on 29 May, wrote Dale,

> The next day, I called into consultation such whom I found here made of the council by his Lordship, where were proposed many businesses necessary, and almost every one essential, which indeed required much labor and many hands as, namely, the reparation of the falling church, and so of the storehouse, a stable for our horses, a munition house, a powder house, a new well for the amending of the most unwholesome waters which the old afforded, brick to be made, a sturgeon house—which the late curer you sent by the *Hercules* much complaineth of, his work otherwise impossible to come to good, and indeed he dresseth the same sturgeon perfect and well—a blockhouse to be raised on the north side of our back river to prevent the Indians from killing our cattle, a house to be set up to lodge our cattle in the winter, and hay to be appointed in his due time to be made, a smith's forge to be perfected, cask for our sturgeon to be made, and besides private gardens for each man, common gardens for hemp and flax and such and other seeds, and lastly a bridge to land our goods dry and safe upon, for most of which I took present order.

In addition to the improvements Dale was implementing at Jamestown, he was also attempting to establish a replacement settlement for Jamestown farther up the James River, which would be safer from the always-expected Spanish attacks and where the land and water were better suited for habitation. This he did just below present-day Richmond, Virginia, at a settlement he named Henricus after Prince Henry. In September 1611, Dale took about 300 men and began to establish the settlement, which was somewhat successful for a number of years. It was there that he most harshly implemented the *Lawes Divine, Morall and Martiall,* under which, as George Percy wrote, the worst offenders were "appointed to be hanged, some burned, some to be broken upon wheels, others to be staked, and some to be shot to death. All these extreme and cruel tortures he used and inflicted upon them to terrify the rest for attempting the like; and some which robbed the store, he caused them to be bound fast unto trees and so starved them to death." But Dale also established there what is thought to be the first English hospital, Mount Malado, as well as the first private ownership of land in the Virginia colony.

Dale's harsh rule and his solutions to the most pressing problems were not confined to the colonists alone, however. Shortly after his arrival, he began to attack the neighboring Indian population and was instrumental in the abduction and holding of Pocahontas hostage in exchange for the return of English captives, tools, and weapons taken by some of Powhatan's people. Indeed, after attacking and wiping out the settlement of Queen Opposunoquonuske, near the mouth of the Appomattox River, Dale's men occupied the area and began building another settlement, which he named Bermuda City.

Although Dale's service in the New World was considered cruel and harsh by some, he became a major figure in the establishment of the permanent English presence in North America. Dale ended his time in Jamestown by returning to England in 1616 on board the same ship that carried John Rolfe and Pocahontas to London, where they were wed.

In April 1618, Sir Thomas Dale was sent by the East India Company as commander of six ships to challenge Dutch actions around modern-day Jakarta, Indonesia. While succeeding in his military actions, he contracted an illness that apparently led to his death there the following year.

Related entries: Bermuda City; Henricus; Percy, George; Pocahontas; Rolfe, John; Smythe, Sir Thomas; Strachey, William

Suggestions for further reading

Ralph Hamor. 1615. *A True Discourse of the Present State of Virginia.* London.

David A. Price. 2003. *Love and Hate in Jamestown: John Smith, Pocahontas, and the Heart of a New Nation.* New York: Alfred A. Knopf.

D. Dewey Scarboro. 2005. *The Establisher: The Story of Sir Thomas Dale.* Fayetteville, NC: Old Mountain Press.

Discovery

See Three Ships

Drummond, William (d. 1677)

Scotsman William Drummond, often credited as the first governor of North Carolina, came to Virginia in 1637 as a servant indentured to Jamestown planter Theodore Moyes. His service with Moyes was brief, however, for Moyes soon sold him to another planter characterized as an "abusive master." After running away with a group of similarly treated servants, Drummond was apprehended, tried, and found guilty. After a public whipping, he served the remainder of his indenture (which was extended) without getting into any more trouble. After earning his freedom, Drummond engaged in planting, trade, and land speculation, living on the Governor's Land as a tenant of Sir William Berkeley. Drummond and his wife, Sarah, married off their daughter, also named Sarah, to Samuel Swann, the son of a prominent member of the Council of State.

Through the Swann family, Drummond won lucrative appointments, including a seat on the James City County bench, sheriff of James City, bailiff of the Quarter Court, sergeant-at-arms at the Virginia General Assembly, and governor of Albemarle, the one populated county out of the three existing in North Carolina at that time—in effect becoming the first governor of North Carolina. While serving in the latter capacity from 1664 to 1667, he criticized Governor Berkeley's policies toward the settlers of North Carolina and ultimately alienated the governor to the point where Berkeley had no choice but to dismiss him and appoint Samuel Stephens in his stead. Drummond returned to Virginia and once again settled on Berkeley's land, but their rupture proved to be irreversible, and Drummond sided with Nathaniel Bacon against Berkeley during the insurrection that bore Bacon's name.

In 1665, as governor of Albemarle, Drummond presided over the first meeting of what would become the North Carolina legislature, on the banks of Hall's Creek, a tributary of the Little River, in present-day Pasquotank County. Reputedly, the only surviving record from the minutes of that meeting reads, "[M]embers should wear shoes, if not stockings, during the session, and they must not throw their chicken bones under the oak tree where the assembly is being held." During Drummond's term as governor, he and several other men became lost after venturing into the Great Dismal Swamp while on a hunting trip; after several days, Drummond emerged, the only survivor. The water source for the Dismal Swamp, Lake Drummond, which lies at the center of the swamp, was discovered by Drummond in 1665 and still bears his name.

Drummond's governorship was generally successful, especially for the settlers in Albemarle, even though Drummond did not represent the motives of Sir Berkeley. Drummond, in fact, had been one of the first settlers to visit the area, as early as 1653; a nineteenth-century historian, John W. Moore, characterized Drummond as "a man who deserved the respect and confidence of the people whom he governed. He was plain and prudent in his style of life, and seems to have given satisfaction to the people who had been previously uncontrolled by law or magistrate." Drummond's success in North Carolina led him to a misplaced confidence when it came to insurrection in Virginia, however; he persuaded Nathaniel Bacon to "hope and half expect" that the Albemarle citizens would align with them against Governor Berkeley and his supporters. Drummond and Bacon were wrong, however, for, as Moore observed, the North Carolinians "took little thought for Virginia; and they could not have helped Mr. Bacon to succeed had they wished to help him."

Drummond's own alignment with Bacon was complete; in fact, Berkeley put out an offer of "free and ample pardon to all that would decline Bacons intress, and owne his"—excepting Drummond and Richard Lawrence, whom the governor described as the most "active promoters of Bacons designes" in the colony. A secret nighttime meeting of Bacon, Drummond, and Lawrence ended with Bacon's capture as he was departing. Drummond and Lawrence attempted to lead the rebels afterward, but neither had Bacon's charisma or military leadership abilities, and the insurrectionist forces quickly dwindled and faded away. Labeled as the "cheife Incendiarys, and promoters" of the rebellion, both Drummond and Lawrence were eagerly sought throughout the colony. Drummond burned his own house at Jamestown and fled into the Dismal Swamp, perhaps thinking he might live in North Carolina, but he was captured and sent to Berkeley's home, Green Spring. On the day of his capture, 14 January 1677, Drummond was tried, convicted, and hanged by Berkeley, who acted, says a recent biographer, "with unbecoming glee." Berkeley included Drummond in the "List of Those That Have Been Executed for the Late Rebellion in Virginia" that he sent to England: "AT THE MIDDLE PLANTATION. One Drummond, a Scotchman that we all suppose was the originall cause of the whole rebellion, with a common Frenchman, that had been very bloody. CONDEMNED AT MY HOUSE, AND EXECUTED WHEN BACON LAY BEFORE JAMESTOWN." Surviving papers relating to Bacon's Rebellion in the deeds and wills section of the general court appear a little more dispassionate when mentioning Drummond: "Wm. Drummond. Wm. Drummond being accused of treason and rebellion against his majestie, which appearing by divers oaths, and his own confession, sentance of death therefore past against the said Drummond to be hanged by the neck untill he be dead." It was Drummond's fate, as some had anticipated, to "dye without marcy."

Drummond's wife, Sarah, has been described as a firebrand and either celebrated as "zealous a patriot as himself," or "denounced as a wicked and notorious rebel." The story goes that she and her children were driven away from their home after her husband's death and lived off the goodwill of former supporters of the insurrection. After Berkeley died, she sued his estate for her losses and won. Drummond's Field, the site of the Drummond family homestead, a "multi-phase domestic quarter" near Jamestown, was excavated in the 1970s.

A surviving contemporary account of Bacon's Rebellion was written by Ann Dunbar Cotton, the wife of John Cotton of Queen's Creek in York County. Ironically, Drummond paid for the headrights that enabled them to come to the New World. Ann Cotton may have also written an elegiac poem honoring Bacon.

Related entries: Bacon's Rebellion; Berkeley, Sir William

Suggestions for further reading

An Account of Our Late Troubles in Virginia, 1676 (Selected Writings)

Warren M. Billings. 2004. *Sir William Berkeley and the Forging of Colonial Virginia.* Baton Rouge: Louisiana State University Press.

Eulogy of the Dead Rebel, 1676 (Selected Writings)

John W. Moore. 1879. *School History of North Carolina, from 1584 to the Present Time.* Raleigh, NC: Alfred Williams.

E

Early European Exploration of North America

Although there are claims promoting a wide range of visitors and explorers to North America before Christopher Columbus, including Chinese, Africans, Celts, Irish, Welsh, and Phoenicians, among others, there is not much evidence to support more than a few of the many suggested. Aside from the peoples who may have migrated across the land and ice bridge that apparently existed across the Bering Strait in prehistoric times, and who were the ancestors of the Native Americans living in North America when the Jamestown colonists arrived, one of the first probable "discoveries" of the New World was around 985 or 986 A.D. The *Greenland Saga,* first written down centuries after the voyage, records that a Norse merchant and navigator named Bjarni Herjolfsson (Herjulfson) set sail during this time in search of Eric the Red's Greenland settlement. His ship was blown off course, and he sailed too far west, where he apparently saw the coast of a large landmass, possibly Labrador. Sailing farther, he sighted another coast before turning back to find Greenland.

Leif Ericsson, son of Eric the Red, was the next somewhat reliably recorded European voyager to North America and the first thought to actually set foot on land considered part of North America. During his voyage of discovery around 1000 A.D., he encountered new landmasses, three of which he recorded as Helluland, a Norse term for the flat stones seen there and possibly referring to Baffin Island; Markland, possibly present-day Labrador and named for an abundance of trees; and Vinland, apparently named for the grapes growing plentifully there. It is at the latter site, Vinland, that archaeological evidence supports the existence of a Norse settlement, most likely from around the time that Leif Ericsson was supposed to have established a presence in the area. This settlement, on the northern peninsula of Newfoundland and known as L'Anse aux Meadows, has remnants of stone structures and has yielded a number of artifacts that have been associated with the Norse culture of the time. Those relics include, among other things, iron nails, a spindle whorl, and a bronze pin. The Norse apparently made contact with the local native people and associated with them for a number of years. The settlement was abandoned after a few years and, except for visits from Ericsson's brothers Thorvald and Thorstein and an Icelandic trader named Thorfinn Karlsefni (who may have taken Leif's daughter Freydis with him on one voyage to the New World), little is known of any European presence in North America for the next few centuries.

Some scholars have speculated that the next Europeans to approach the North American region after the Norse explorations and temporary settlements were fifteenth-century Portuguese mariners, who perhaps documented seeing Newfoundland, before Columbus's Spanish-funded expeditions. But the man most credited—and documented—with the discovery (or rediscovery) of the Americas, was Christopher Columbus, who made four voyages to the region, the first beginning in 1492 and the last in 1502. Although he explored the Caribbean and Central and South America, which he believed were Asian lands, his reports and maps would prove invaluable to those who would follow and colonize North America.

After the first two voyages of Columbus to the Americas, John Cabot was the next explorer of note to sail for the New World, this time in the name of England. He was granted a patent by King Henry VII to seek a northwest passage to Asia, and he set out on his first voyage for that purpose in May 1497. This voyage took him to the coast of Newfoundland, which he claimed for the Crown, and possibly as far south as Maine before he set return sail for England later in the same year. The next May, the same month Columbus began his third voyage to the region, Cabot again set sail for the New World, but after a few weeks at sea his ships encountered a storm. All ships but one, including Cabot's, were never heard from again and probably lost at sea.

Building upon these early attempts at discovery and exploration, the voyages to the Americas became increasingly frequent over the next century. In 1499, Amerigo Vespucci, for whom it is commonly believed the Americas were named, sailed with Alonso de Hajeda (Ojeda) to South America for Spain. He sailed there again in 1501, this time for Portugal, a country that already had sent some explorers to the Americas. Those earlier voyages had been made to the Newfoundland area in 1499 and 1500 and again in 1502, the year of Columbus's fourth and final voyage to the New World. Although there were many voyages and explorers during this first century of major European focus on the New World, some of the better-known names not in the employ of England included Juan Ponce de León, who began exploring Florida for Spain in 1513; Hernán Cortés, who in 1519 was instrumental in securing Mexico for Spain by helping to defeat the Aztec empire; Giovanni da Verrazano, who explored the east coast from the Carolinas to Nova Scotia or Newfoundland for France in 1524; Francisco Pizarro, who is credited for precipitating the downfall of the Incan empire in Peru while in the service of Spain in the early 1530s; Jacques Cartier, whose explorations in the 1530s and 1540s were instrumental in France's claims in Canada; and, of much importance because of its claim as the first permanent European settlement in the area that later became known as the United States, Pedro Menendez de Aviles, who established St. Augustine in Florida for Spain in 1565. There were other attempts by the Spanish, French, and Portuguese to establish a presence in the Americas during this time; of particular interest because of its proximity to the future site of

Portrait of Pedro Menendez de Aviles, Spanish explorer who established the St. Augustine settlement in present-day Florida. (Library of Congress)

Sir Humphrey Gilbert (1539–1583)

The older half brother of Sir Walter Raleigh was educated at Eton and Oxford before studying navigation and the art of war. He was knighted for bravery in 1570 for his service in the wars in Ireland, and the following year was elected to Parliament from Plymouth. In 1578, Queen Elizabeth granted his petitions for letters patent to establish a colony in the New World, but the venture failed. Another attempt in 1583 was also unsuccessful, but he did manage to reach Newfoundland and explore the Atlantic coast down to Florida. Later that year, he was lost at sea, and his estate passed to his more famous half brother. Gilbert's purported last words, said to men aboard a nearby vessel, were immortalized by Henry Wadsworth Longfellow (1807–1882) in his poem *Sir Humphrey Gilbert* (1849):

Alas! the land-wind failed,
  And ice-cold grew the night;
And nevermore, on sea or shore,
  Should Sir Humphrey see the light.

He sat upon the deck,
  The Book was in his hand;
"Do not fear! Heaven is as near,"
  He said, "by water as by land!"

Sir Humphrey Gilbert, English politician and explorer and half brother of Sir Walter Raleigh. (Ellyson, J. Taylor. The London Company of Virginia, *1908)*

the Jamestown colony was the settlement planted on the York River only a few miles overland from Jamestown. Spanish Jesuits began a mission there in the early 1570s, but the project was short lived. They became increasingly dependent on—and thus a nuisance and irritant to—the local Native Americans, who finally destroyed the mission and all but one of its inhabitants, thereby ending English colonization attempts in the region until the establishment of Jamestown in 1607.

Although England lagged far behind the other European powers active in the Americas during the first three quarters of the sixteenth century, the quest for a northwest passage to Asia, as well as the commodities and lands claimed by the other seafaring nations, finally led to more active and aggressive efforts by England to gain for itself a share of the wealth and opportunities the New World afforded. In 1576, Martin Frobisher embarked on the first of his voyages to the New World, followed by his second and third in the following two years. Like so many others, Frobisher was sent to find a northwest passage to the East; he, too, failed in the attempt. During his three voyages to America, he explored the regions around Baffin Island and made contact with native inhabitants. He carried back cargoes of a metal ore that were thought to be gold but which turned out to be pyrite. Frobisher's exploratory trips to the New World were followed by voyages of another explorer who sailed for England in 1585–1587, Captain John Davis. Davis made

Sir Richard Grenville (1542—1591)

Honored for his military service in the Hungarian army against the Turks, Sir Richard Grenville became a Member of Parliament in 1571. He became deeply interested in the discoveries resulting from the exploration of the New World and lent his assistance to the expeditions of Amadas and Barlowe in 1584. In 1585, he personally conducted the ill-fated first colony to Virginia, which settled on Roanoke Island in present-day North Carolina, and returned to England for help the following year. Grenville took part in England's successful fight against the Spanish Armada in 1588 but was killed two years later in the battle against the Spanish Plate fleet.

Portrait of Sir Richard Grenville, English colonizer of Roanoke Island. (Ellyson, J. Taylor. The London Company of Virginia, *1908)*

Greenville's final battle, conducted from his old flagship, *The Revenge,* was commemorated in verse by Alfred, Lord Tennyson, in his *The Revenge: A Ballad of the Fleet* (1880):

> "Shall we fight or shall we fly?
> Good Sir Richard, tell us now,
> For to fight is but to die!
> There'll be little of us left by the time this sun be set."
> And Sir Richard said again: "We be all good English men.
> Let us bang these dogs of Seville, the children of the devil,
> For I hever turned my back upon Don or devil yet."
>
> Sir Richard spoke and he laughed, and we roared a hurrah, and so
> The little *Revenge* ran on sheer into the heart of the foe.

three voyages to the same area in search of the passage, but his attempts to sail to Asia also were without success. Like Frobisher, though, he provided valuable information about the region that would be used later by others sailing to the west from Europe.

Although most English explorers traveling to America thus far had been concerned principally with finding a northwest passage to Asia, Sir Humphrey Gilbert, while anxious as any to find the passage, was involved with another endeavor that would soon come to dominate England's interest in the New World. In 1578, he sailed from England to establish a colony in North America, this one in Newfoundland. That voyage did not reach its destination, but in 1583 he made another attempt, and this time he established a colony there. After only a short time, however, the colony was abandoned, and Gilbert set sail for England. But before reaching home, he encountered an intense storm and was lost at sea. Gilbert's attempts to establish an English presence in the New World would be followed by his more famous half brother, Sir Walter Raleigh.

After Sir Gilbert's death, Raleigh inherited his half brother's patent from the English Crown

Landfall and First Contact

The six and twentieth day of Aprill, about foure a clocke in the morning, wee descried the Land of Virginia. The same day wee entred into the Bay of Chesupioc directly, without any let or hinderance. There wee landed and discovered a little way, but wee could find nothing worth the speaking of, but faire meddowes and goodly tall Trees, with such Fresh-waters running through the woods, as I was almost ravished at the first sight thereof.

At night, when wee were going aboard, there came the Savages creeping upon all foure, from the Hills, like Beares, with their Bowes in their mouthes, charged us very desperately in the faces, hurt Captaine Gabrill Archer in both his hands, and a sayler in two places of the body very dangerous. After they had spent their Arrowes, and felt the sharpnesse of our shot, they retired into the Woods with a great noise, and so left us.

The seven and twentieth day we began to build up our Shallop. The Gentlemen and Souldiers marched eight miles up into the land. We could not see a Savage in all that march. We came to a place where they had made a great fire, and had beene newly a rosting Oysters. When they perceived our comming, they fled away to the mountaines, and left many of the Oysters in the fire. We eat some of the Oysters, which were very large and delicate in taste.

—George Percy, *Observations Gathered Out of a Discourse of the Plantation of the Southerne Colonie in Virginia by the English, 1606*

to explore and colonize the Americas. In 1584, Raleigh sent Philip Amadas and Arthur Barlowe to scout for a suitable site for a colony in the New World. Once back in England, Amadas and Barlowe's report convinced Raleigh of a location in the Outer Banks of present-day North Carolina. The first group of settlers, under the command of Richard Grenville and Ralph Lane, left England in the spring of 1585; after sailing through the Caribbean, they reached Roanoke Island, where they began to establish the colony. Grenville returned to England for supplies, leaving Lane to build the settlement. But the settlers soon became desperate when food became scarce and relations with the indigenous peoples deteriorated, and when Sir Francis Drake arrived, not long after nearly destroying the Spanish settlement in St. Augustine, Florida, the settlers were ready to return home. Shortly after they left with Drake in June 1586, Grenville returned to find the settlement abandoned. Determined to keep an English presence in Virginia (which the country was now called in honor of Queen Elizabeth I, the Virgin Queen) Grenville left a number of men with supplies and once again set sail for England. When Raleigh's second group of colonists arrived in July 1587, this time under the leadership of John White, none of the men left behind by Grenville were to be found, but the new colonists—men, women, and children—went ashore and began to build again. In November, White returned to England for supplies, but his return voyage to the colony was delayed until the spring of 1588 by hostilities between England and Spain. When White finally did set sail, French ships attacked his vessel, and he was forced to return to England. It was not until August 1590 that Raleigh's relief ships finally arrived at Roanoke Island, again under the leadership of John White. All they found was an abandoned colony and the word *Croatoan* carved on a nearby tree. Thus were born the mystery and legend of what became known to history as the Lost Colony.

It took a number of years before the English made another attempt to establish a presence in the New World. Expeditions were sent to present-day Massachusetts under Captain Bartholomew Gosnold in 1602, to Maine under George Weymouth in 1605, and two more voyages intended to explore the northern reaches of Virginia in August and October of 1606, which at that time extended to what is now considered New England. But it was not until a group of settlers left for Virginia in December of the same year that a permanent English presence was finally established in the New World. These colonists reached their destination in May 1607, and the fates of nations on both sides of the Atlantic were altered forever.

Related entries: Gosnold, Bartholomew; James Fort; Lost Colony; Newport, Sir Christopher; Raleigh, Sir Walter; Smith, Captain John; White, John

Suggestions for further reading

Edward Arber, ed. 1910. *Travels and Works of Captain John Smith* (part 1). Edinburgh, Scotland: J. Grant.

Philip L. Barbour. 1964. *The Three Worlds of Captain John Smith.* Boston: Houghton Mifflin.

——, ed. 1986. *The Complete Works of Captain John Smith (1580–1631)* (vol. 1). Chapel Hill and London: University of North Carolina Press.

Michael Golay and John S. Bowman. 2003. *North American Exploration.* Hoboken, NJ: John Wiley.

Samuel Eliot Morison. 1971. *The European Discovery of America: The Northern Voyages A.D. 500–1600.* New York: Oxford University Press.

David Beers Quinn. 1971. *North American Discovery: Circa 1000–1612.* Columbia: University of South Carolina Press.

——. 1974. *England and the Discovery of America, 1481–1620.* New York: Alfred A. Knopf.

Arthur M. Schlesinger, Jr., ed. 1993. *The Almanac of American History.* New York: Charles Scribner's Sons.

Elizabeth River

Named in honor of King James I's daughter, Princess Elizabeth Stuart (1596–1662), later Queen of Bohemia, the Elizabeth River is one of the principal rivers draining into the Chesapeake Bay watershed area. The river was first explored by Englishmen in July 1608, when Captain John Smith and a dozen colonists made an exploratory expedition down the James River into the Chesapeake Bay region, the "second Voyage in discovering the Bay," in Captain Smith's words. (The first voyage had taken place earlier that summer, during which Smith almost died from a stingray wound.) After being entertained for two or three days by friendly Indians at Kecoughtan (present-day Hampton, Virginia), Smith and his entourage spent nearly two months exploring the coastline of the bay. On the return trip to Jamestown in late August, the explorers sailed to the area of present-day Norfolk in search of a safe harbor during a violent thunderstorm. A vivid description of the night and of the party's discovery of the Elizabeth River appeared in volume 1 of the *Travels of Captain John Smith* (London, 1630), although it apparently was taken from an account drafted not by Smith but by three of the men accompanying him, Anthony Bagnall, Nathaniel Powell, and Anas Todkill:

> In a fayre calme, rowing towards poynt Comfort, we anchored in Gosnolls Bay, but such a suddaine gust surprised us in the night with thunder and rayne, that we never thought more to have seene James Towne. Yet running before the wind, we sometimes saw the Land by the flashes of fire from heaven by which light onely we kept from the splitting shore, until it pleased God in that blacke darknesse to preserve us by that light to finde poynt Comfort: there refreshing our selves, because we had onely but heard of the Chisapeacks & Nandsamunds, we thought it as fit to know all our neighbours neare home, as so many Nations abroad.
>
> So setting sayle for the Southerne shore, we sayled up a narrow river [the Elizabeth] up the country of Chisapeack; it hath a good channell, but many shoules about the entrance. By that we had sayled six or seaven myles, we saw two or three little garden plots with their houses, the shore overgrowne with the greatest Pyne and Firre trees we ever saw in the Country. But nott seeing nor hearing any people, and the river very narrow, we returned to the great river [the James], to see if we could finde any of them.

The expedition arrived back at the Jamestown fort about a week later (7 September), where the

Queen Elizabeth (1533–1603)

The daughter of Henry VIII and Anne Boleyn, Elizabeth I was placed in direct line for succession to the throne after Edward and Mary by an act of Parliment in 1544. After Mary died in 1558 and Elizabeth ascended the throne as a Protestant queen, she proved a capable and wily monarch, adept at maneuvering through the complicated and dangerous foreign relations of Europe. England thrived during her reign, in great part because of the blind eye she turned toward the privateers returning home with spoils taken at sea. Half brothers Humphrey Gilbert and Walter Raleigh made their historic voyages in her name, and gave to the lands they sought to colonize a name in Elizabeth's honor: Virginia, for the Virgin Queen. During Elizabeth's forty-years reign, England came into its own as a power to be reckoned with in Europe; its military ascendance was matched by successes in exploration and discovery across the seas, and by prosperity and a cultural renaissance at home.

Since Elizabeth never married she produced no heir to her throne, nor was there an obvious successor standing in the wings. The defeat of the Spanish Armada in 1588 put to rest any fears Elizabeth had about external enemies, while a cadre of loyal and brilliant advisors protected her from within. She outlived most of her family and her closest friends; loneliness characterized the last decades of her reign, and she turned to religion for comfort.

Elizabeth I, queen of England from 1558 until her death in 1603, was the fifth and final monarch of the Tudor dynasty. Elizabeth's reign, referred to as the Elizabethan era, was notable for the expansion of English power and influence throughout the world. (Ellyson, J. Taylor. The London Company of Virginia, *1908)*

explorers found their fellow settlers very ill and completely demoralized.

Other English writers mentioned the Elizabeth River in the seventeenth century, mainly in conjunction with Virginia's other rivers—the Elizabeth was named first among the "abundance of lesser rivers, many of which are capable of receiving the biggest merchant ships"—or in relation to some of the English landowners who settled along its banks: Captain Thomas Willoughby, who patented a 200-acre plantation on the river's eastern branch (in present-day Norfolk) in 1626 and established his home there ten years later; Henry Sewell, who in the late 1620s settled a 150-acre tract at what came to be known as Sewells Point; Lieutenant Colonel Thomas Lambert (d. 1671), whose 100 acres on the river became known as Lamberts Point; or the half-dozen settlers who established the town of Norfolk in June 1680. The House of Burgesses's June 1680 *Act for Cohabitation and Encouragement of Trade and Manufacture* provided for the establishment of a tobacco warehouse on 50 acres of land near the confluence of the eastern and main branches of the Elizabeth River flow and thus ensured Norfolk's commercial success. An *Act for Establishing Ports and Towns* in 1705 further strengthened Norfolk's future by setting aside Tuesdays and Saturdays for market days. In the eighteenth century, Norfolk's growing importance as a mercantile center and its role in the American Revolution paved the way for the industrializtion of the entire Elizabeth River watershed area. The Dismal Swamp Canal, connecting the Elizabeth with the Pasquotank in northeastern North Carolina, was begun by George Washington and a company of investors who began draining the Great Dismal Swamp before the Revolution; it is the oldest continually operating canal in the United States. In the 1850s, the Elizabeth River was connected to the upper North Landing River in southern Chesapeake by the Albemarle and Chesapeake Canal, fueling even greater development. Early commerce soon spread outward to include Portsmouth, Hampton Roads, and Chesapeake.

The Elizabeth River has a long, rich history. Before white settlers took control of the land in the river's watershed area, the Chesapeake Indians occupied a settlement on the Elizabeth's southern branch near present-day Hampton Roads (Norfolk, once thought to be the site of Skicoak, apparently was Indian cropland or still forest). The Elizabeth came to be important primarily after the initial settlement period, however. The river is the site of the oldest naval shipyard in the United States, the Norfolk Naval Shipyard, which dates to the eighteenth century. During the American Revolutionary War, the British bombardment of Norfolk destroyed the city's wharves (1775), and the patriots supposedly scuttled as many as 100 ships in the Elizabeth to keep the British from capturing them (1779). The USS *Chesapeake* was built on the river at Gosport (opposite Norfolk on the river's west bank) in 1799; since then, warships have been built at what is now the site of the Norfolk shipyard. During the American Civil War, more important history was made on the Elizabeth River. In April 1861, Federal troops burned the Norfolk shipyard and the vessels in it before fleeing from Southern secessionist soldiers; the following year, the USS *Merrimack* was converted into an ironclad and renamed the CSS *Virginia*—the world-famous first battle of the ironclads took place in the Elizabeth River in March 1862 between the *Merrimack* and the USS *Monitor.* (The *Virginia* has been the subject of underwater excavations for a number of years.) In addition to the naval shipyard at Norfolk, the banks of the Elizabeth River are home to the oldest U.S. Navy hospital, Portsmouth's Naval Medical Center. Originally constructed in 1827 from bricks salvaged from the patriot garrison Fort Nelson (erected in 1776), the Naval Medical Center is on the register of National Historic Landmarks. Lighthouses on the Elizabeth at Lamberts Point and Craney Island served mariners from 1820 to 1936.

Since the first English settlers arrived, the Elizabeth River has changed dramatically. The Elizabeth River consists of three branches and a main branch that, with its watershed, cover about 200 square miles. The eastern and western branches flow toward Hampton Roads, the area of confluence of the Elizabeth and James Rivers that forms one of the world's most important harbors; the southern branch runs to Albemarle Sound in North Carolina. The eastern branch is approximately 25 miles long and as deep as 25 feet and runs from Norfolk to Chesapeake and Virginia Beach; the western branch flows between the cities of Portsmouth and Chesapeake, about 20 miles, and is as deep as 18 feet; the southern branch is about 40 miles long, as deep as 40 feet, and located in northern and central Chesapeake. The three branches form the main branch, which is about 5 miles long and 2 miles wide at its mouth—only two thirds as wide as it was in the English settlement period but twice as deep. Although some of its headwaters are fed by the lush and still largely unpolluted Dismal Swamp, the Elizabeth itself has been labeled one of the "more seriously degraded urban rivers in the country" and one of the "most polluted tributaries on the bay." The Elizabeth River Project was formed in 1992 for the purpose of cleaning and restoring the river and reviving its wetlands, of which 50 percent have disappeared since World War II.

Related entries: Chesapeake Indians; James River; Mattaponi River; Nansemond River; Pamunkey River; Rappahannock River; York River

Suggestions for further reading

Michael R. Bauer. 2001. "Collaborative Environmental Decisionmaking: A Power

Sharing Process that Achieves Results through Dialogue" (Ph.D. thesis, Virginia Polytechnic Institute and State University), Blacksburg.

Elizabeth River Project's Watershed Action Team and Stakeholder Review Team. 2002. *Elizabeth River Restoration and Conservation: A Watershed Action Plan,* rev. 2nd ed. Portsmouth, VA: Elizabeth River Project.

Captain John Smith. 1630. *The True Travels, Adventures and Observations of Captain John Smith in Europe, Asia, Africa and America* (vol. 1). London: John Haviland for Thomas Slater.

F

Falling Creek Ironworks

In 1619, the Virginia Company sent 150 men to build and man the first English ironworks in North America at Falling Creek, about five miles above their settlement at Henricus. It was to be headed by a Captain Bluett, but he died shortly after arriving, and John Berkeley (son of Sir John Berkeley) assumed control of the operation. (Berkeley, already long experienced in the iron business, was named to the Virginia Council after his arrival at Jamestown.)

Iron was "of most necessary use for the Colony," and the Virginia Company was anxious to establish the industry. (Mining for iron ore had occurred in Virginia as early as 1608, and a blacksmith, James Read, had been among the first arrivals in 1607; a second blacksmith, Richard Dole, soon followed, arriving in January 1608.) As described in the 25 July 1621 letter to the governor and council in Virginia,

> The advancement of the Iron Workes wee esteeme to be most necessarie, by p[er]servinge whereof we esteeme the Plantation is gained: Wee therefore require all possible assistance be given to mr Berkley, now sent, and all furtherance to his G[o]ing, espially good enterteinment at theire Landinge, that they may be well lodged and cherished wth such comfortable helpe as yor place will afford, wch we will thankfully requite to any that shall advance this or so much desired Worke.

By then, the recent General Assembly had labeled the ironworks the "greatest hope and expectation" of the colony. The furnace employed twenty workmen in addition to Berkeley, his son Maurice, and his family's three private servants.

Apparently, Berkeley and others were pleased with the location chosen for the ironworks, as evidenced in the paraphrasing by a secretary of the Virginia Company of one of Berkeley's letters, in which he states that "a more fit place for Iron-workes . . . th[a]n in Virginia, both for woods, water, mynes, and stone, was not to be found." The secretary continues that a Mr. George Sandis [Sandys] corroborated the belief:

> the place (called *The Falling Creeke*) to be so fitted for that purpose, as if Nature had applyed herselfe to the wish and direction of the workeman; where also were great stones hardly seene else-where in Virginia, lying on the place, as though they had beene brought thither to advance the erection of those Workes.

The industry appeared to have had much promise in that it was thought "no better iron existed in the world." As with so many other early efforts in the colony, however, the Indian massacre in March 1622 ended the enterprise at that location. Berkeley and most of his workers, a total of twenty-seven in all, were killed (son Maurice and two young children survived) and the ironworks destroyed and dumped in the river. Maurice

Berkeley was willing to rebuild the operation, but the Virginia Company failed to send the necessary tools, supplies, and workmen, and the effort was abandoned. Plans to restablish ironworks at Falling Creek were floated every few years in the seventeenth century, but nothing materialized until after William Byrd I acquired the land in the 1680s. Eventually, however, in the eighteenth and nineteenth centuries the original Falling Creek site did become home to a thriving iron manufacture industry.

Related entries: Glassmaking; London Company; Massacre of 1622

Suggestions for further reading

Charles E. Hatch, Jr., and Thurlow Gates Gregory. 1962. "The First American Blast Furnace, 1619–1622: The Birth of a Mighty Industry on Falling Creek in Virginia" (*Virginia Magazine of History and Biography*, vol. 70).

Susan Myra Kingsbury, ed. 1933. *The Records of The Virginia Company of London* (vol. 3). Washington, DC: Government Printing Office.

Edward D. Neill. 1869. *History of the Virginia Company of London, with Letters to and from the First Colony Never Before Printed.* Albany, New York: Joel Munsell.

Ivor Noël Hume. 1994. *The Virginia Adventure: Roanoke to James Towne: An Archaeological and Historical Odyssey.* New York: Alfred A. Knopf.

Lyon Gardiner Tyler. 1906. *The Cradle of the Republic: Jamestown and James River.* Richmond, VA: Hermitage Press.

French Huguenots

The earliest French settlers to come to Jamestown were artisans skilled in cultivating silk, apparently Protestants recruited from the thriving silk industry in France. Governor De La Warr was aware of their presence even before his arrival at the settlement in June 1610, for at his first disembarkation in Virginia, which took place downriver from the Jamestown fort, he was so taken with the vegetative richness of the region that he immediately resolved "to set a Frenchman heere awork to plant Vines, which grew naturally in great plenty." The French, however, like their English counterparts, soon abandoned their trade for the more lucrative profits to be gained from the growing of tobacco. They renewed their efforts to cultivate silk near the end of the decade at the order of the colony's treasurer, Sir Edwin Sandys, who boasted that the "divers skillful Vinerons" sent to cultivate the vines would bring them "to excellent perfection." The French vine dressers assured Sandys that "no Countrie in the World" was more properly suited for vines than Virginia. Nevertheless, the high price of tobacco ensured the continual neglect of the cultivation of any other crops. When Sir Francis Wyatt was sent to govern the colony in 1621, his instructions from the Virginia Company included a new set of directions to "plant Mulberry trees and make silk, and take care of the Frenchmen sent about that work." Whether these French settlers survived the Indian Massacre of 1622 or the disease epidemic of 1622–1623 is not known, but no silk to speak of was ever sent back to England.

A new attempt to cultivate silk came about at the end of the 1620s when the initial wave of French Huguenots was recruited to settle in Virginia. The plan was a colonization scheme hatched by the Baron De Sauce, a Frenchman who had fled to England after the fall of the French Protestant city La Rochelle. La Rochelle had long been one of Europe's major producers of silk and salt, and De Sauce wanted to capitalize on the abilities of tradesmen from the area. (A similar proposal to transport fifty to sixty Reformed Protestant families to Virginia from Walloon and France had been made in 1621 and had received tentative approval by the Virginia Company, but nothing ever came of the idea.) After getting permission from both French and English authorities, De Sauce sailed his group to Virginia and settled at Southampton Hundred (formerly Smythe's Hundred) on the south side of the James River near the Chickahominy River, on lands formerly occupied by Paspahegh Indians. Unfortunately, the area chosen for settlement was about as unhealthy as that chosen for Jamestown. It was "for the most part low Swampy ground," wrote Colonel William Byrd in 1698, "unfit for planting and Improvement, and ye air of it very moist and unhealthy, so that to send Frenchmen thither that came from a dry and Serene Clymate were to send them to their Graves." Although the fate of these French settlers, like that of their earlier brethren, has been lost to history, Huguenot emigration to Virginia had begun and was to continue for the rest of the seventeenth century. The Huguenot Relief Committee in London sponsored individuals, families, and groups as large as fifty or sixty people who wanted to begin life anew in the New World. Ministers of the gospel trickled in and began to occupy conspicuous positions among the colonial clergy. By mid-century, French Huguenots were thriving in Virginia; by the century's end, several hundred had immigrated to the colony. Another 700 came in 1700, soon after the capital of the colony was moved from Jamestown to Williamsburg, establishing a settlement on the James about twenty miles above Richmond and, eventually, on the Rappahannock River.

According to Robert Beverley in his *History and Present State of Virginia* (London, 1705), the French were self-sufficient, raising cattle and buffalo, making their own clothes, and manufacturing wine from wild grapes gathered in the woods. Although relatively poor, they were content and healthy. No wonder they were valued by the Governor and the General Assembly, which in 1700 granted them their own parish and freed them from taxation for the following seven years. Eventually, they spread into surrounding counties of central and southside Virginia.

Related entries: Glassmaking; Polish Workers

Suggestion for further reading

Lucian F. Fosdick. 1906. *The French Blood in America.* New York: F. H. Revell.

Fur Trade

The *French* possessing themselves of these Lakes, no doubt will in short time be absolute Masters of the beaver Trade, the greatest number of Beavers being catch'd there.

—The Reverend John Clayton to the Royal Society, 17 August 1688

The lucrative fur trade that grew up in the New World is usually associated with the myriad French trappers and traders who were able to operate in the vast regions of the American Midwest thanks to France's control of the Mississippi River. In the decades immediately following the founding of the Jamestown colony, however, the English supplanted the French as the principal players in the fur trade. The visionaries of English colonization held as a principal goal of New World settlement the establishment of friendly relations with natives skilled in hunting and obtaining hides. Once the Jamestown colony appeared to be solid, that goal was reached, at least for about a quarter of a century. As the English began to settle the lands along the rivers that fed into the Chesapeake Bay, and to dominate the Indians traditionally associated with those river valleys, it became increasingly easy to find and move furs and to send them back to Europe. Commerce really began to flourish when the trade monopoly enjoyed by the Virginia Company ended with the company's dissolution in 1624. For the next forty years, until the French wrestled the trade away at the end of the seventeenth century, the Jamestown colony was unrivaled in the New World as the center of fur trade. And only the growing of tobacco was more lucrative within the colony itself.

A variety of animal hides were in demand in England, but the fashions of the day leaned toward beaver, popular for use in making felt hats since the mid-sixteenth century—so popular, in fact, that the beaver had become extinct in Western Europe. Beaver skin was easy to process, would hold its shape for years, and could be used even after serving as an Indian's winter coat for a season. Beaver pelts could be acquired easily in Virginia, however, and sold or traded favorably

Musk Rats

Musk-Rats, in all things shaped like our Water-Rats, only something larger, and is an absolute Species of Water-Rats, only having a curious musky Scent: I kept one for a certain time in a wooden Chest; two Days before it died it was extraordinary odoriferous, and scented the Room very much; but the Day that it died, and a Day after the Scent was very small, yet afterwards the Skin was very fragrant; the Stones also smelt very well. They build Houses as Beavers do, in the Marshes and Swamps (as they there call them), by the Water-sides, with two or three ways into them, and they are finely daubed within. I pulled one in pieces purposely to see the Contrivance: There were three different Lodging-Rooms, very neat, one higher than another, as I conceive purposely made for Retirement when the Water rises higher than ordinary; they are considerably large, having much Trash and Lumber to make their Houses withal; I suppose they live mostly on Fish.

—The Reverend John Clayton to the Royal Society, 17 August 1688

for goods like tools, cloth, and personal items not easily made at Jamestown. Furthermore, both Native Americans and Europeans were familiar with the uses of beaver and the process of turning pelts into wearable goods. When beaver skin prices peaked in the 1640s, the Jamestown colony was sufficiently spread out and stable enough to capitalize on the European demand. Over time, beaver pelts became a major cash crop in the colony and in effect—quite literally—acceptable currency.

Virginia's dominance of the fur trade did not last long, however. By the early 1660s, Maryland had become a major player in the trade, the natives had been marginalized or pushed further west (although they compensated somewhat by developing the birch canoe to transfer the furs), and the colony's supply of skins was becoming exhausted from overtrapping. The Hudson Bay Company, chartered in 1670, soon entered the trade and further eroded Virginia's prominence; once the French began to dominate after 1700, the English forever after lagged far behind. As the country's population increased to the north and west, the center of the fur trade moved in those directions. Nevertheless, the Jamestown colony can justly claim to having been, at least for a brief time, at the center of the North American fur trade.

Related entries: Bacon's Rebellion; Glassmaking; Tobacco; Trades and Artisans

Suggestions for further reading

Nathaniel C. Hale. 1959. *Pelts and Palisades: The Story of Fur and the Rivalry for Pelts in Early America.* Richmond, VA: Dietz Press.

Milan Novak, Martyn E. Obbard, James G. Jones, Robert Newman, Annie Booth, Andrew J. Satterthwaite, and Greg Linscombe. 1987. *Furbearer Harvests in North America, 1600–1984.* Ontario, Canada: Ministry of Natural Resources.

G

General Assembly

The first decade of the Jamestown colony was characterized by false starts, instability, and failure. Martial law had brought about survival for the colony, but not much more, and by 1618 the investors of the Virginia Company were ready to reorganize the basis upon which the colony stood. Treasurer Sir Thomas Smith was replaced by his rival, Sir Edwin Sandys, whose "Great Charter" called for dismantling the existing system that relied on workers employed by the company, and replacing it with one that encouraged settlers to own land and to participate in the administration of the colony's affairs. Sandys assumed that the colony would have a much greater chance of succeeding if its settlers, like citizens in England, had a vested interest in Virginia. One provision of the reorganization called for the governor to convene a general assembly empowered to discern and advance the "pupliqe weale" of the colony. Who could be better attuned to the needs of the Virginia settlement than the colonists, who constantly observed conditions firsthand, and who could better devise and administer policy than those who had to obey it? A structured local control could simultaneously assist the governor in his duties, curb the tendency of the office to amass power, make the settlers more content, and ultimately enhance the interests of the Virginia Company.

Thus, the first General Assembly met in July 1619. The colony then had a new governor, Sir George Yeardley, who had served previously as deputy governor and who had made his first trip to Virginia in 1609. Knighted in November 1618 and married shortly thereafter to Temperance Flowerdieu, a cousin of the new secretary of the colony, John Pory, Yeardley sailed for the New World in early 1619 but was delayed in arriving at Jamestown until that April. After settling into his new role as governor, Yeardley in late June ordered the colony's freemen and tenants to elect "sufficient men" to meet with him and the six-member Council of State. Twenty-two burgesses (so named because of their status as freemen) were chosen, two from "eache Incorporation, & Plantation," and from 30 July to 4 August the representatives met with the governor and the council at Jamestown. The assembly's agenda included seating its members (which did not go smoothly), reading the Great Charter, determining how much authority the assembly itself had to conduct its own business, and ruling on a number of subjects most important to the colony at that time in its history—including land patents; tobacco and corn crops and mulberry groves; indentures and tenants; trade issues; Indian relations; outlawing idlers, "gaming at Dice & Cardes," drunkenness, and "excesse of apparel"; and regulating marriage and the functions of the church. The assembly also ruled on some criminal

First General Assembly, 1619

The first legislative assembly in America, which took place at Jamestown from 30 July to 4 August, 1619. The colony of Jamestown, Virginia, begun in 1607, was the first permanent English settlement in America. (Library of Congress)

The most convenient place we could finde to fitt in was the Quire of the Churche, Where Sir *George Yeardley* the Governour being sett downe in his accustomed place, those of the Counsel of Estate sate nexte him on both handes excepte onely the Secretary then appointed Speaker, who sate right before him; *John Twine* clerke of the General Assembly being placed nexte the Speaker and *Thomas Pierse* the Sergeant standing at the barre, to be ready for any service the Aseembly shold comand him. But for as muche as mens affaires doe little prosper wehre Gods service is neglected; all the Burgesses took their places in the Quire, till

First General Assembly, 1619, continued

a Prayer was said by Mr *Bucke,* the Minister, that it would please God to guide us & sanctifie all our proceedings to his owne glory, and the good of this Plantation, Prayer being ended, to the intente that as wee had begun at God Almighty soe wee might proceed wth awful and due respecte towards his Lieutenant, our most gratious & dread Soveraigne, all the Burgesses were intereated to retyre themselves into the body of the Churche; wch being done, before they were fully admitted, they were called in order & by name, & so every man (none staggering at it) tooke the oathe of Supremacy, & then entered the Assembly, At Captaine *Warde* the Speaker tooke exception, as at one that without any Comission or authority, had seated himselfe either upon the Companies, and then his Plantation could not be lawfull, or on Captaine *Martins* Lande, and so he was but a limbe or member of him, & so there could be but two Burgesses for all. So Captaine *Warde* was commanded to absente himselfe, till such time as the Assembly had agreed what was fitt for him to doe.

—First paragraph of John Pory's *A Report of the Manner of Proceeding in the General Assembly Convented at James Citty in Virginia, July 30, 1619*

cases and petty squabbles before sickness forced them to adjourn until the next March. (Indeed, Walter Shelley, one of the burgesses representing Smythes Hundred, died on Sunday, 1 August, and the governor and several other burgesses also fell ill.)

That first General Assembly set precedents for what was to follow. Disagreements about the eligibility and seating of its members were resolved when the assembly decided to imitate Parliament by determining for itself who would be allowed to sit in its chambers. The assembly also decided what matters could come under its jurisdiction. It passed regulations on trade and set constraints on personal behavior as it affected the public good. It established its primacy over church and state matters such as observance of the Sabbath. It tried criminal cases. The great attention paid to legislation and adjudication during the five days (no work was done on 1 August, the Sabbath) it met in 1619 foreshadowed what became the General Assembly's primary functions. The burgesses, working together in an orderly and apparently collegial fashion, aimed for consensus where possible but in the end relied on a simple majority vote. By interpreting its own authority as wide ranging—although with proper lip service to the colony's backers in the Virginia Company—the burgesses established conventions that would be emulated for the next 400 years. Ever afterward, elected representatives would meet annually to consider appeals from the courts, to levy taxes, to draft and enact laws, and to set public policy for the colonists and their descendants.

Neither the Virginia Company nor the Crown originally had planned to establish a legislative and adjudicative body like the General Assembly. Rather, the assembly evolved on its own from necessity, largely unaided and unhampered by company and royal neglect. The General Assembly's first five years fell during the period when the Virginia Company itself was on the verge of dissolution. The Indian Massacre of 1622 and its aftermath not only left the colony in shambles but effectively bankrupted the company and led James I to consider revoking its charter. When the Virginia Company was finally dissolved in 1624, questions arose about the General Assembly's legitimacy, but before the Crown could establish control over the colony, James I died and Charles I succeeded to the throne. Charles's interests extended to many things, but Virginia was not one of them, and during the unstable period from 1624 through 1638, when the Crown exercised only nominal oversight over the colony, Charles failed to provide any direction either to his own representatives in the colony or to the General Assembly. Thus, the assembly was left to its own devices in its march toward becoming the supreme rule of law in Virginia. It was aided by a series of royal governors and acting governors, all of whom continued to convene the assembly on a yearly basis. At each session, the assembly passed numerous new laws and enlarged the powers and privileges within its own sphere. Charles I subsequently confirmed the assembly's legitimacy in 1639, ushering in a new period for the legislators.

Charles's endorsement, coming shortly after the General Assembly's unseating, for a second time, of Governor John Harvey, reinforced the burgesses' sense of the primacy of their own authority. This took place at a critical juncture, for Charles was about to become entangled with his own Parliament, which was unwilling to support the king in conducting the Bishops' Wars in Scotland of 1639 and 1640, the prelude to the English Civil War, which ended with Charles's death a decade later. The 1640s proved to be a decade of growth for the colony and consolidation of power for the governor, the Council of State, and the General Assembly. The continuance of the General Assembly's relative autonomy from England and its fusion with the moneyed interest in the colony was buttressed by the colony's most important royal governor, Sir William Berkeley, who came to Virginia in 1642 and immediately allied himself with the planter elite. (Berkeley's service, though alloyed with the Indian Massacre of 1644, the English Civil War, and the Interregnum, coincided with unprecedented growth and prosperity in Virginia.) From the time of Berkeley's arrival until 1676, when Bacon's Rebellion forced the governor to return to England, the General Assembly wielded power through an ever-expanding system of self-governance. The move toward a bicameral system, in which the House of Burgesses met separately from the Governor and Council of State, was proposed by Berkeley before the 1643 session of the General Assembly and approved by the burgesses. The replacement of the unicameral system gave the institution more formality and credibility and allowed it to become intertwined with the great planter elite that itself was only beginning to emerge as the main holder of wealth and power in Virginia society.

During the English Civil War and the Interregnum, the General Assembly was allowed even more independence. Governor Berkeley remained loyal to the Crown during the Civil War and, for the most part, was successful in his attempt to keep armed conflicts from spilling over into Virginia. Eventually, after the regicide of Charles I, Berkeley was replaced by men representing Cromwell, but the Virginia governors of the Interregnum were as ineffectual as they were temporary. By that time, the General Assembly's bicameral nature was thoroughly established, and the House of Burgesses governed as it saw fit, forcing the governors and Council of State to compromise (and even acquiesce) in favor of the assembly. The colony's constitution was rewritten to reflect the current state of affairs, although it had to be rewritten yet again following the restoration of the monarchy in 1660. During the Restoration, Berkeley was called out of retirement to serve as governor again, and although he was a strong personality, neither he nor the governor's office ever regained the leverage exercised over the General Assembly in the pre-Civil War period. In 1675, the colony was hit with a wave of Indian attacks, counterattacks by settlers, and insurgencies led by Nathaniel Bacon. Jamestown was lost to the insurgents, recaptured, and lost again before being burned in September 1676 by Bacon and his followers. The result was swift and determined royal intervention—Berkeley was recalled to England, 1,000 troops were sent to Virginia to ensure stability in the countryside, and the General Assembly entered a period of forced retrenchment that lasted almost to the end of the next decade. By that time, the General Assembly had become such an integral part of Virginia colonial society that it could never be displaced, although the Jamestown settlement was about to be eclipsed by its neighboring child, Middle Plantation, soon to be known as Williamsburg. There the General Assembly would meet for over a century and would come into its own.

Related entries: Berkeley, Sir William; London Company; Pory, John

Suggestions for further reading

Warren M. Billings. 2004. *A Little Parliament: The Virginia General Assembly in the Seventeenth Century.* Richmond: Library of Virginia.

John Pory. 1915. *A Report of the Manner of Proceeding in the General Assembly Convented at*

James City in Virginia, July 30, 1619. (H. R. McIlwaine, ed. *Journals of the House of Burgesses of Virginia, 1619–1658/59,* vol. 6.) Richmond: Virginia State Library.

William J. Van Schreeven and George H. Reese. 1969. *Proceedings of the General Assembly of Virginia, July 30–August 4, 1619. Written & Sent from Virginia to England by Mr. John Pory.* Jamestown, VA: Jamestown Foundation.

Glassmaking

Often touted as America's first industry, glassmaking at Jamestown began in October 1608 when "eight Dutchmen [Germans] and Poles" arrived as part of the Second Supply on board the *Mary and Margaret.* Skilled in making pitch and tar, potash and soap ashes, and glass, the artisans immediately set to work firing test samples of glass for Captain Christopher Newport to carry back to England as a specimen of a New World commodity. Those first experimental firings took place within the Jamestown fort, where archaeologists have excavated Hessian crucibles with adhering glass, but the glass shop itself was set up away from the confines of the fort.

To establish an ongoing, working glass manufactory, the workmen needed large quantities of sand, in which the James River was abundant, and wood for fuel and potash, which could be harvested from the plentiful forests on the mainland. The area also contained an endless supply of oyster shells, which could be crushed and burned to make lime. The glassworkers thus chose an inland site not far from the Jamestown peninsula, in the words of Captain John Smith, "in the woods neare a myle" from the fort, as a convenient place to construct a sizeable workshop in which to practice their craft. The area selected, an ancient Indian camping ground, became known as Glass House Point. At the point, all the roads on the mainland converged and became known to

Obstacles to Glass Manufacture

The ill successe of ye glasse workes is allmost equall unto this: first the coveringe of ye house, ere fully finished, was blowne downe by a tempest, noe sooner repared but ye Indians came uppon us, which for awhile defered ye proceedinges. Then they built up ye furnace, which after one forthnight that ye fire was put in it, flew in peeces: yet ye wife of one of ye Italians (whom I have now sent home, haveinge receaved many wounds from her husband at severall times, & murder not otherwise to be prevented, for a more damned crew hell never vomited) revealed in her passion that Vincentio crackt it [the furnace] with a crow of iron; yet dare wee not punish theise desperat fellowes, least ye whole dessigne through theire stubbornesse should perish. The summer cominge on, Capt. Norton dyed with all saveinge one of his servants, & hee nothinge worth. The Italians fell extremely sicke, yet recoveringe in ye beginninge of ye winter, I hyred some men for that service, assisted them with mine owne, rebuilt the furnace, engaged my selfe for provisions for them & was in a manner a servant unto them. The fire hath now beene six weeks in ye furnace, and yett nothinge effected. They complaine that the sand will not run (though themselves made choise thereof, and likt it then well enough) & now I am sending up ye river to provide them with better, if it bee to bee had. But I conceave that they would gladly make the [glassmaking] worke appeare unfeasable, that it might by that meanes be dismissed for England. Much hath beene my trouble herein, and not a little my patience (haveinge beene called rascall to my face for reprovinge them of theire riot, negligence & dissension) but, for the debt which I am in, for their sustentation I hope the adventurers will see it discharged.

—Treasurer George Sandys, March 1623

Costumed artisan at Jamestown makes glass using seventeenth-century methods. The first glass factory in America was established in 1608 at the settlement. (Photo by Frank E. Grizzard, Jr.)

the settlers as the Greate Road, a natural path formerly used by Indians as a hunting trail that led from the fort to the mainland. Its distant location, although rich in resources and necessary in terms of the intended operation, made the workmen vulnerable to sneak attacks by Indians long familiar with the region.

The glassmaking operation required three furnaces of different sizes—a large main working furnace for melting glass, a smaller furnace for annealing (or cooling) the finished glass, and an even smaller fritting furnace for preheating the ingredients necessary to make glass—as well as lime and potash in addition to sand. A fourth, even smaller furnace was erected for firing the clay pots needed in the glassmaking process. The furnaces were constructed of boulders dragged from the river's edge and bonded together with mud. A rectangular wood-frame building was constructed to protect the furnaces and the workers from the weather. Overall, the Glass House was about thirty-seven feet wide by fifty feet long, and probably had a high thatched roof and partially open sides. William Strachey, secretary of the colony, described the building in 1610 as "a goodly howse . . . with all offices and furnaces thereto belonging."

According to archaeologist Jean Carl Harrington, who excavated the foundation of the furnaces and the pot-firing kiln in 1948–1949, the workmen produced large quantities of "common green" glass, a "workable glass comparable to that made in English glass houses." Fragments of window panes, bottles, and drinking vessels turned up during the excavation. The glass manufactory was built and operated exclusively by the Polish glassmakers. The Dutchmen, on 29 December 1608, went to Werowocomoco, an Indian village on the York River about fifteen miles from Jamestown, to build a house for Chief Powhatan. While living with Powhatan, they conspired to steal arms and powder from the settlers and, with about forty men, to "lie in Ambuscadoe" for Captain John Smith, whom they failed to kill. Sometime over the winter of 1609–1610, Powhatan decided the Dutchmen were too devious to be trusted and "caused his men to beat out their braines." The Poles apparently died during the Starving Time.

Glass production in the colony was discontinued in 1609, probably as a result of the Starving Time, and did not resume until the fall of 1621, when Captain William Norton and six Italian glassworkers (with their families) arrived at Jamestown with a charge from the Virginia Company to "sett up a Glass furnace and make all manner of Beads and Glasse." It is not clear whether the workers restored the abandoned Glass House or built a new one, but the new workers' structure lost its roof during a severe windstorm even before they began their operation. Shortly after repairs to the building were completed, the Indian raids of 22 March 1622 forced the glassworkers (who were not attacked) to abandon the works for a short time. The manufactory was beset by even more trouble, however. One of the craftsmen, Vincentio, apparently in a fit of drunken rage, demolished the main working furnace with a crowbar. As soon as the furnace was rebuilt but before operations could begin, several workers took sick, and Captain Norton died. It was not until late 1622 that glassmaking at the site finally resumed under the supervision of the colony's treasurer, George Sandys. By then, however, the cumulative effect of disasters and illnesses had taken its toll, and very little glass was actually manufactured; Sandys shut down the manufactory in the spring of 1624.

In the last analysis, both of the glassmaking ventures at Jamestown failed to achieve the Virginia Company's object of establishing glassmaking as a profitable manufacturing enterprise. No exports of notice were shipped to England, nor did the glass that was manufactured have any consequence within the colony. But the colonists and their backers did learn valuable lessons about the limits of commercial ventures in the New World.

The National Park Service exhibits the ruins of the furnaces of the original glass manufactory, and adjacent to the ruins is a working replica of the Glass House, erected and maintained by the Glass Packaging Institute, complete with costumed artisans who blow and shape glass in the seventeenth-century manner.

Related entries: Falling Creek Ironworks; French Huguenots; Polish Workers

Suggestions for further reading

Gary C. Grassl. 1997. *First Germans at Jamestown.* Washington, DC: German Heritage Society of Greater Washington.

Jean Carl Harrington. 1952. *Glassmaking at Jamestown, America's First Industry.* Richmond, VA: Dietz Press.

Charles E. Hatch, Jr. 1941. "Glassmaking in Virginia, 1607–1625" (*William and Mary Quarterly,* 2d ser., vol. 21).

J. Paul Hudson. 1962. *Glassmaking at Jamestown, 1608–09 and 1621–24: One of the First English Industries in the New World.* Jamestown, VA: Jamestown Foundation.

Godspeed

See Three Ships

Gosnold, Bartholomew (1572–1607)

Characterized by Captain John Smith as the "first mover" of the Virginia colony, the name of Bartholomew Gosnold is all but unrecognized today, and he has been largely ignored by history. Gosnold was born in Suffolk, England, where his prominent ancestors built its moated family seat, Otley Hall, around the year 1400. (Located about eight miles north of Ipswich and rich in architectural detail, Otley Hall has survived to the present time.) He received a classical education at Cambridge and legal training at New Inn, which was attached to Middle Temple. Coming of age during England's golden age of exploration, however, it is no wonder that the lure of excitement surrounding the exploration of the New World overshadowed for Gosnold any appeal that the practice of law might have exerted. His marriage to Mary Golding, the granddaughter of Sir Andrew Judd, the Lord Mayor of London, enabled him to move in circles from which he otherwise might have been excluded, circles that included geographer, minister, writer, and New World promoter Richard Hakluyt, influential and wealthy merchant Sir Thomas Smythe (Mary Golding's first cousin), Henry Wriothesley, third Earl of Southampton, and even Sir Walter Raleigh.

Gosnold was barely thirty years old in 1602, when he commanded his first voyage to the New World. He was already a veteran of the sea, having led a privateering expedition in 1599 that managed to pluck £1,625 from a Spanish galley. He and his small crew (eight seamen total) and twenty colonists aboard the *Concord,* an aging thirty-ton vessel of about seventy feet, sailed out of the beautiful natural harbor at Falmouth on the southwest coast of Cornwall in late March 1602 on a voyage of exploration, discovery, and trade. They reached St. Mary's in the Azores in mid-April, and from there they sailed directly across the Atlantic to "Northern Virginia"—meaning the area of Cape Neddick, Maine—thus making the first transatlantic crossing to New England. After treating with friendly Indians, who drew the Englishmen a map of the coastal region, they navigated the coast to Narragansett Bay, plotting the shoreline along the way and giving names to several islands, Cape Cod, and Martha's Vineyard (which he named after his first child, a daughter, Martha Gosnold, who had been named after her maternal grandmother, Martha Golding). Gosnold was impressed with the fertile New England landscape and "as healthful a climate as any can be" and chose Cuttyhunk Island (at the mouth of Buzzard's Bay in the Elizabeth Islands) as the place to erect a trading fort and settle his little trading colony. (Gosnold hoped to find and settle at the "great bay"—Narragansett Bay—visited by Florentine explorer Giovanni da Verrazano near the end of the first quarter of the sixteenth century.) The colony lasted only a few weeks, however, for by the middle of June, eight of the twenty colonists had become so discouraged that they declared their intention to return to England. Loaded with a cargo consisting mainly of a ton of sassafras root and twenty-six great cedar logs, the *Concord* returned to England, arriving in late July.

Gosnold's seventeen-week expedition of 1602 may not have ended with the spectacular settling of an English colony in the New World—that would have to wait until Jamestown five years later—but otherwise the undertaking was a complete success. Gosnold's unusual crossing of the ocean shaved more than 1,000 miles off the typical route; an uncharted coastline had been explored; contact had been made with the natives; a fort had been erected; a lucrative cargo had been delivered to England safely; and the entire mission had been completed with no loss of life. Two of the gentlemen accompanying Gosnold to New England, John Brereton and Gabriel Archer, left a record of the voyage. Archer's manuscript journal was not published until 1625, but a narrative account by Brereton appeared in print about three months after the *Concord* sailed back into English waters, a fitting supplement to Richard Hakluyt's published collection of geographical works devoted to exploration of the New World. Gosnold himself, however, all but disappears from the surviving records until 1605, when he begins to discuss his ideas about the New World with a newcomer on the exploration and colonization scene—Captain John Smith.

Both Gosnold and Smith apparently had given a lot of thought to New World colonization, and the two men worked for more than a year with a coalition of merchants, noblemen, and speculators to get the Crown's approval for settlement of a colony in Virginia. On 10 April 1606, King James granted a charter authorizing not one but two colonies—one each in "Northern" and "Southern" Virginia (i.e., present-day New England and Virginia)—and although Gosnold's name was not mentioned, it was he who was Captain Christopher Newport's vice admiral when the *Susan Constant,* the *Godspeed,* and the *Discovery* set sail for America in December 1606. Gosnold commanded the *Godspeed.* Undertaking the journey to Virginia with Gosnold was his brother Anthony Gosnold, another Anthony Gosnold (the young son of Bartholomew's first cousin Robert), a half-dozen men related to Gosnold's and his wife's families, and his friend Gabriel Archer, who had been on the 1602 voyage to New England. When the three English ships arrived in the Chesapeake Bay in late April 1607, the *Instructions* of the London Council were opened, and it was discovered that Gosnold's name was included among those appointed to serve as the local governing council for Virginia. (The others named were Captains Smith, Newport, and John Ratcliffe—commander of the *Discovery*—Master Edward-Maria Wingfield, and Captains John Martin and George Kendall.) Gosnold, it turned out, was the only person in the colony who could keep some semblance of peace between Wingfield, who was elected the colony's president, and Smith, who was ostracized by Wingfield because of his less-than-aristocratic background.

Gosnold himself, in fact, had his own run-ins with Wingfield. To begin with, Gosnold adamantly opposed Wingfield's selection of the location for the Jamestown fort—making an uncanny prediction that the site would be difficult to protect and was too unhealthful. Wingfield hesitated in fortifying Jamestown, resulting in an Indian attack and the first death of a colonizer. Smith's supporters, led by Gabriel Archer, began to agitate for a more prominent role for Smith in governing the colony. Wingfield felt his position as leader threatened, declaring Archer to be ambitious and Gosnold, who was Wingfield's cousin, "strong with friends and followers," although no evidence suggests that Gosnold ever thought of overthrowing Wingfield. Gosnold attempted to align himself with both Wingfield and Smith, an impossible tactic.

The settlers were unprepared for summer in the Virginia countryside. The brutality of the heat and humidity was exacerbated by the divisions among the leaders, the lack of food and deficient sources of drinking water, and the constant threats of ambush by the natives. What was worse, Gosnold's judgment regarding the unhealthfulness of the region proved accurate. In July, almost all the Englishmen fell sick, and by summer's end more than fifty people had died, most the casualties of scurvy and dysentery apparently brought on by typhoid. Gosnold fell ill along with the rest, and about 1 August his condition became serious. He lingered for three weeks, watching other men die almost daily and the colony sink into further demoralization. Knowing his own time was short, he made a deathbed attempt to reconcile Wingfield and Smith but to no avail. On 22 August, with the colony's future uncertain, Gosnold died. His compatriots gave him an honorable burial, complete with a salvo of small arms and artillery. Recently, the ongoing archaeological digs of the Jamestown Rediscovery project made the exciting discovery of Gosnold's remains—a well-preserved skeleton resting in the shadow of his coffin, accompanied by the decorative iron shaft of a ceremonial captain's leading staff (or half pike).

Bartholomew Gosnold was neither England's first promoter of New World colonization nor the first Englishman to attempt to colonize America. Captain John Smith thought him the prime mover of the Virginia colony, and another settler who knew Gosnold described him as "a brave soldier and very ingenious," an adventurer willing to spend much of his own money to explore the American Atlantic seaboard and bring over settlers. According to his biographers, Gosnold was one of the "unsung heroes of England's early expansion" and was likely the only Englishman of his time, aside from Sir Walter Raleigh, who "combined the vision, the practicality, and the persistence, to make colonization possible."

Related entries: London Company; Newport, Sir Christopher; Raleigh, Sir Walter; Sagadahoc (Popham) Colony; Three Ships

Suggestions for further reading

Warner F. Gookin and Philip L. Barbour. 1963. *Bartholomew Gosnold: Discoverer and Planter, New England—1602, Virginia—1607.* Hamden, CT, and London: Archon Books.

William M. Kelso with Beverly Straube. 2004. *Jamestown Rediscovery, 1994–2004.* Richmond, VA: Association for the Preservation of Virginia Antiquities.

Green Spring

Of the many estates that sprang up near Jamestown in the seventeenth century, none could rival Green Spring, the plantation and English manor home of Sir William Berkeley, the colony's governor from 1641 to 1652 and 1660 to 1677. Situated on the road running from Jamestown fort to Middle Plantation (Williamsburg), it was about three and one-half miles north and west of the Jamestown settlement, at a former Paspahegh Indian village. Berkeley acquired the first part of what eventually became an estate of more than 2,000 acres in June 1643, and between 1646 and 1650 he built a two-story house, the first of several to occupy the site. The name of the plantation was derived from a spring on the property that had provided (and still does) fresh water from time immemorial. John Clayton, the rector of Crofton at Wakefield in Yorkshire, England, described Green Spring in a letter to the Royal Society in May 1688 after he visited Virginia: "There's a Spring at my Lady Berkley's, called *Green-Spring,* whereof I have been often told, so very cold, that 'tis dangerous drinking thereof in Summer-time, it having proved of fatal Consequence to several. I never tried any thing of what Nature it is of."

Green Spring plantation became the center of Governor Berkeley's attentions when he was not concerned with the executive business of the colony at Jamestown. At Green Spring, his extensive agricultural pursuits included the cultivation of sweet tobacco in addition to experiments in growing hemp, flax, cotton, rice, barley, oats, wheat, hops, and nuts. He also grew a great variety of vegetables and fruits—his fruit orchard numbered 1,500 trees—and he was able to produce silk of sufficient quality to present to the King. Livestock and poultry were also raised in abundance. Not far from the manor house, Berkeley planted formal English gardens enclosed by serpentine brick walls, and nearby he erected a large, mostly glass greenhouse (about sixteen feet by forty-five feet). Other outbuildings included a large detached kitchen, a smith's shop, a pottery kiln, servants' quarters, a stable, a windmill, and a jail, some built, perhaps, after the original dwelling house (about sixty-eight feet wide by seventy feet deep) burned and was greatly enlarged in the 1660s or early 1670s. To oversee the day-to-day management of activities at Green Spring, Berkeley relied on overseers.

Governor Berkeley was at the center of the political, social, and cultural life of the Jamestown colony, but unfortunately the rich history associated with Green Spring has largely disappeared. Both indentured and slave labor seem to have been introduced at the plantation fairly early, perhaps as much as twenty years before Berkeley purchased the property, but little is known about how the labor system evolved on any of the lands owned by Berkeley. The aforementioned experiments in agriculture and the grand architectural works at the plantation set an example for Berkeley's peers, but the extent of their actual influence remains unknown. Nathaniel Bacon and his supporters camped at Green Spring in 1676, occupying the manor house before and after their attack on Jamestown, earning them the ire of Sir William's wife, Lady Frances. The rioting rebels treated Green Spring better than they did Jamestown, which they burned to the ground, but still they left the house in such a state, wrote Lady Berkeley, that it cost "almost as much to repair as if it had beene new to build, & noe signe that ever there had beene a fence about it, in soe much that it had cost about £300 to make it habitable." The Virginia General Assembly met at Green Spring after the attack on Jamestown, as the malcontents' destruction had included leveling the State House, but, again, little is known about the sessions other than what is recorded in the proceedings.

After Berkeley's death, Green Spring eventually fell under the control of his widow's new husband, Colonel Philip Ludwell of Rich Neck, who had been a staunch political ally of Berkeley and who later served as the governor of North and South Carolina. From Ludwell, Green Spring in the eighteenth century passed into the hands of the descendants of Berkeley's secretary, Richard Lee, the immigrant founder of the prominent Lee family of Virginia, and shortly before the siege of Yorktown an important Revolutionary War battle was fought there between Lord Cornwallis and Anthony Wayne (on 6 July 1781). The manor house erected by Berkeley was the oldest inhabited house in English America when the Lees

Green Spring, as portrayed by surveyor John Soane, c.1683, was built by Sir William Berkeley, colonial governor of Jamestown, 1641–1652 and 1660–1677. (Courtesy of Colonial National Historical Park)

demolished it following their construction nearby of a new mansion. Fortunately, the architect Benjamin Henry Latrobe had made a watercolor drawing of the older house before it was demolished, showing a steeply pitched roof with dormer windows. The new structure was burned by Federal troops during the American Civil War. Archaeological excavations at Green Spring in 1928 and 1929 and again in 1954 and 1955 revealed stunning ruins of an architectural and construction nature but little in the way of cultural artifacts. The National Park Service currently owns Green Spring ruins and about 200 acres; elsewhere on the site are a hotel and golf course.

Related entries: Bacon, Nathaniel; Berkeley, Lady Frances Culpeper; Berkeley, Sir William; Lee, Richard

Suggestions for further reading

Warren M. Billings. 1994. "Imagining Green Spring House" (*Virginia Cavalcade*, vol. 44).

Louis R. Caywood. 1957. "Green Spring Plantation" (*Virginia Magazine of History and Biography*, vol. 65).

Jesse Dimmick. 1929. "Green Spring" (*William and Mary Quarterly*, 2d ser., vol. 9).

J. Paul Hudson. 1970. *Plantation, Refuge, Prison, Statehouse: This Was Green Spring.* Jamestown, VA: Jamestown Foundation.

H

Harwood, William

See Martin's Hundred

Henricus

Intended to succeed Jamestown as the main base for English operations in the region, Henricus (Henerico, Henrico) was established by Sir Thomas Dale, then marshal and deputy governor of Jamestown, in September 1611 as the second substantial English settlement of the Jamestown colonists. Dale took around 300 men about 60 miles up the James River to build the new settlement at a location that was "a place of high ground, strong and defensible by nature, a good air, wholesome and clear, unlike the marshy seat at Jamestown, with fresh and plenty of water springs, much fair and open grounds freed from woods, and wood enough at hand." Being much further up the James than the original settlement, it was better defended against potential Spanish attacks. And because it was located on a peninsula in the James River (later an island known as Farrar's Island), it was seen as more secure from Indian advances. In fact, it was converted into an "island" by constructing Dale's Dutch Gap, a palisaded ditch across the neck of the peninsula.

Throughout the life of the settlement—indeed, during the expedition to reach the location and intermittently until its destruction in the massacre in March 1622—Henricus was plagued by Indian attacks, hardships, and harsh discipline. As George Percy wrote,

> [A]fter divers encounter and skirmishes with the savages, [the colonists] gained a convenient place for fortification, where presently they did begin to build a fort; and Sir Thomas Dale named the same "Henericus Fort," in honor of Prince Henry. The savages were not idle all this time but hind'red their designs as much as they could, shooting arrows into the fort, wherewith divers of our men were wounded and others endangered. And some having employment without the fort did come short home and were slain by the savages.

Attacks by the Indians were not the only threats to life and limb of the settlers. Due to desertions, theft, and general lack of discipline, Dale implemented the *Lawes Divine, Morall and Martiall* that he, Governor Gates, and Sir Thomas Smythe had developed for the Jamestown colony. These were harsh times for the colonists; the leadership felt that harsh measures were needed in order to achieve what they had been sent to do. In keeping with this line of reasoning, Dale did not hesitate to use these laws at his new settlement at Henricus. Percy wrote that the worst offenders were

> appointed to be hanged, some burned, some to be broken upon wheels, others to be staked, and some

Coxendale: Forgotten Town

"On the other side of the River, for the securitie of the towne, is intended to be impaled for the securitie of our Hogs, about two miles and a halfe, by the name of Hope in Faith, and Coxendale, secured by five of our manner of Forts, which are but Palisadoes, called Charitie Fort, Mount Malado, a guest house for sicke people, a high seat and wholsome aire Elisabeth Fort, and Fort Patience: And here hath Master Whitaker chosen his Parsonage, impaled a faire framed Parsonage, and one hundred acres called Rocke hall, but these are not halfe finished." *Travels of Captain John Smith,* 1630 (vol. 1)

The town of Coxendale on the James River was settled as part of Virginia military governor Thomas Dale's effort to bring security to the Jamestown colony. Situated directly across the river from Henricus (present-day Chesterfield County), it was an impaled enclosure protected by the four aforementioned forts; within the town's walls were areas for the growing of crops and the raising of hogs and cattle. Because it was midway between the parishes of Henrico and Bermuda Hundred, Reverend Alexander Whitaker made his home there. The settlement was abandoned after the 1622 Indian raids and later became known as the Coxendale plantation or the Osborne tract, after the family who later took over the property. Coxendale appears on a map drawn in 1611.

> to be shot to death. All these extreme and cruel tortures he used and inflicted upon them to terrify the rest for attempting the like; and some which robbed the store, he caused them to be bound fast unto trees and so starved them to death.

Nonetheless, Henricus did prosper and grow for a few years. Writing in 1614, the secretary to the Virginia colony, Ralph Hamor, noted that Henricus had

> three streets of well framed houses, a handsome Church, and the foundation of a better laid (to bee built of Bricke), besides Store-houses, Watch-houses, and such like. Upon the verge [edge] of the River there are five houses, wherein live the honester sort of people, as Farmers in England, and they keepe continuall centinell for the townes securitie.

Besides being the relatively brief center of attention as an improvement over Jamestown, Henricus was also the site of other notable events. When Pocahontas was taken captive in April 1613 by Captain Samuel Argall and held as ransom for the return of English prisoners, weapons, and tools in the hands of Powhatan's people, she evidently was taken to the area, said to be about fifteen miles south of the falls on the James River. It was at Henricus that she received tutoring in the English language and in Christianity by Parson Alexander Whitaker at his Rocke Hall parsonage. While there, Pocahontas was courted by her soon-to-be husband, John Rolfe, and may have been married at the church at Henricus in April 1614, although it is usually assumed that the marriage took place at Jamestown's church. Some have speculated that the first English hospital in the New World was built at Henricus; the first university charter was established there as well, although Williamsburg was later chosen as the institution's site. Also, Henricus supposedly was the site where Dale instituted the first instance of private land ownership in Virginia.

By 1616, Henricus had begun to decline as attention shifted to new settlements elsewhere. Only about thirty-eight men and boys remained there by then, and by 1619 only a few old houses and out buildings and a church remained. The massacre of colonists all along the James River on 22 March 1622 was the last gasp for what once had been considered the replacement for Jamestown.

Apparently, it was abandoned for other sites after that time.

In 1864, Union forces tried to deepen Dale's ditch in an effort to bypass Confederate gun emplacements, but rebel sharpshooters ended the attempt. It was not until 1871–1872 that the U.S. government sufficiently improved the passage, thereby shortening the water distance to Richmond by about seven miles. Today, a re-creation of the 1611 "Citie of Henricus" is being constructed at the thirty-two-acre Henricus Historical Park near the original site just below Richmond. Examples of both European and Indian buildings and gardens are represented.

Related entries: College at Henricus; Dale, Sir Thomas; Massacre of 1622; Rolfe, John

Suggestions for further reading

Edward Arber, ed. 1910. *Travels and Works of Captain John Smith* (part 2). Edinburgh, Scotland: J. Grant.

Philip L. Barbour, ed. 1986. *The Complete Works of Captain John Smith (1580–1631)* (vol. 2). Chapel Hill and London: University of North Carolina Press.

Edward Wright Haile, ed. 2001. *Jamestown Narratives: Eyewitness Accounts of the Virginia Colony: The First Decade: 1607–1617.* Champlain, VA: Round House.

Charles E. Hatch, Jr. 1995. *The First Seventeen Years: Virginia, 1607–1624.* Charlottesville: University Press of Virginia.

Ivor Noël Hume. 1994. *The Virginia Adventure: Roanoke to James Towne: An Archaeological and Historical Odyssey.* New York: Alfred A. Knopf.

David A. Price. 2003. *Love and Hate in Jamestown: John Smith, Pocahontas, and the Heart of a New Nation.* New York: Alfred A. Knopf.

Lyon Gardiner Tyler. 1906. *The Cradle of the Republic: Jamestown and James River.* Richmond, VA: Hermitage Press.

Alden T. Vaughn. 1975. *American Genesis: Captain John Smith and the Founding of Virginia.* Boston: Little, Brown.

Hog Island

It would seem that the marshy bend that dominates the James River directly across from Jamestown Island's easternmost shore, Hog Island, would have played an important part in the founding of the first English colony, if for no other reason than its proximity to the settlers. Surprisingly, however, the role of the peninsula was minor in the early years, with one near-fatal exception—the placing there of the livestock from which it draws its name. The colonists decided that raising hogs near or within the confines of the fort was unacceptable by 1609, when "the hogges were transported to Hog Ile, where also we built a blocke house, with a garrison, to give us notice of any shipping; and for their exercise, they [the company within the garrison] made clapbord, waisncot, and cut downe trees against the ships comming." Considering the effect that hogs have on both the land they inhabit and the air surrounding, it appeared to be a good idea to move them at the time, especially because "of 3 sowes, in one yeare increased 60 and od[d] pigges." It soon proved to be an unwise decision—at least to the handful of colonists who lived long enough to regret its making—for the nearly three-mile distance between Hog Island and Jamestown meant that there was little the settlers could do to protect the livestock from the depredations of Indians.

Thus, with so much of what the colonists depended upon for survival running wild and unprotected across the river, Hog Island became an easy target when relations between the settlers and Indians began to sour. During the winter of 1609–1610, known as the Starving Time, when the colonists desperately needed every scrap of food they could find, the Indians took advantage of Hog Island's isolation and slaughtered all the hogs, exacerbating the famine that nearly wiped out the whole settlement. When the survivors decided to abandon Jamestown in June 1610, it was to Hog Island that they "fell downe to" and anchored for the night, before "the morning tide brought us to another Iland, which we have called Mulberry Iland," about four more miles downriver where Lord De La Warr's men intercepted them that afternoon and turned them back to Jamestown.

One other major event is recorded about Hog Island during the English settlement years, when in 1609

> Master [Matthew] Scrivener willing to crosse the surprizing of Powhatan; 9 daies after the Presidents [John Smith] departure, would needs visit the Ile of Hogges, and took with him Captaine [Richard] Waldo . . . with Master Anthony Gosnoll [brother to Bartholomew Gosnold] and eight others but so violent was the wind (that extreame frozen time) that the boat sunke, but where or how, none doth knowe, for they were all drowned.

Following the settlers' attempt to abandon Jamestown in 1610, not much of significance can be found recorded about Hog Island until 28 March 1619, when Governor Samuel Argall included the area within the boundaries of allowed settlement by the Jamestown colonists. Even then the Hog Island area developed rather slowly; only thirty-one inhabitants were listed in 1624 and fifty-three the following year. Hog Island is today one of three tracts of land that make up the 3,908-acre Hog Island Wildlife Management Area and is adjacent to the Surry Nuclear Power Station.

Related entries: Gosnold, Bartholomew; Mulberry Island; West, Thomas, Lord De La Warr

Suggestions for further reading

Edward Arber, ed. 1910. *Travels and Works of Captain John Smith* (part 1). Edinburgh, Scotland: J. Grant.

Philip L. Barbour, ed. 1986. *The Complete Works of Captain John Smith (1580–1631)* (vol.1). Chapel Hill and London: University of North Carolina Press.

Charles E. Hatch, Jr. 1995. *The First Seventeen Years: Virginia, 1607–1624.* Charlottesville: University Press of Virginia.

Ivor Noël Hume. 1994. *The Virginia Adventure: Roanoke to James Towne: An Archaeological and Historical Odyssey.* New York: Alfred A. Knopf.

David Beers Quinn, ed. 1979. *New American World: A Documentary History of North America to 1612* (vols. 1, 4). New York: Arno Press and Hector Bye.

House of Burgesses

See General Assembly

Hunt, Robert (c.1568–1608)

Robert Hunt was the first Anglican clergyman to serve in the Jamestown colony. He had agreed to serve as vicar of the colony, representing the Reverend Richard Hakluyt, the influential promoter of English colonization who himself had been named rector of Virginia by the Virginia Company. As vicar, Hunt was charged not only with overseeing the spiritual welfare of the settlers going to the New World but with converting the native inhabitants to Christianity—considered a major component of Hakluyt's colonization scheme. In fact, Edward-Maria Wingfield, the first president of the colony, declared that his own "first worke" concerning the establishment of a settlement in Virginia was to "make a right choice of a spirituall pastor." Hunt previously had served as vicar of Reculver, in Kent, from 1594 to 1602, and as vicar of All Saints Church at Old Heathfield, East Sussex, begining in 1602, and apparently had gained a reputation as a cleric dedicated to the English church. "All the world," continued Wingfield, "knoweth whome I took wth me: truly, in my opinion, a man not any waie to be touched wth the rebellious humors of a popish spirit, nor blemished wth ye least suspition of a factius scismatick, whereof I had a spiall care." In addition to Wingfield and Hakluyt, another of the colony's prime movers, Captain Bartholomew Gosnold, had entreatied Hunt to attach himself to the first colonizers.

Hunt, who had left his wife Elizabeth (b. 1581) and their two children behind, fell sick before his ship even left England's waters. Captain John Smith, who was much taken with Hunt's fortitude and judgment, describes Hunt's misfortune in his *Historie:*

> On the 19 of December, 1606. we set sayle from Blackwall, but by unprosperous winds, were kept six weekes in the sight of England; all which time, Mr. Hunt our Preacher, was so weake and sicke, that few expected his recovery. Yet although he were but twentie myles from his habitation (the time we were in the Downes) and notwithstanding the stormy weather, nor the scandalous imputations (of some few, little better then Atheists, of the greatest ranke amongst us) suggested against him, all this could never force

Colonists meet for a religious service under a canopy at Jamestown. (North Wind Picture Archives)

> from him so much as a seeming desire to leave the busines, but preferred the service of God, in so good a voyage, before any affection to contest his godlesse foes, whose disasterous designes (could they have prevailed) had even then overthrowne the businesse, so many discontents did then arise, had he not with the water of patience, and his godly exhortations (but chiefly by his true devoted examples) quenched those flames of envie, and dissention.

Yet Hunt, who probably was ill with typhoid, survived the four-month voyage.

Hunt's actual mission in Virginia began on 29 April 1607, when he and the other passengers aboard the three English vessels disembarked and, according to George Percy in his *Observations,* "set up a cross at Chesupioc Bay, and named the place Cape Henry." From Cape Henry, the colonists traveled upriver to Jamestown, where Hunt's work was to begin in earnest. His first act at Jamestown was to dedicate a piece of ground to the glory of God, where the colonists could begin "in the name of God to raise a fortresse." Although the passenger lists named Hunt as a gentleman, he worked alongside the colonists, giving an example of his favorite saying, "We are all laborers in a common vineyard." He built the colony's first grist mill, for instance, in addition to tending to the ever-present needs of the sick and dying. In June 1607, when food was in short supply and tempers flared (especially at Captain John Smith, the most capable of the leaders), it was Hunt who was able to bring reason to bear:

> Many were the mischiefes that daily sprung from their [the colonizers'] ignorant (yet ambitious) spirits; but the good Doctrine and exhortation of our Preacher Mr. Hunt reconciled them, and caused Captaine Smith to be admitted of the Councell; the next day all received the Communion, the day following the Salvages voluntarily desired peace, and Captaine Newport returned for England with newes; leaving in Virginia 100 [of the settlers].

When disaster struck and the fort was accidently burned in the winter of that "extreame frost" (1607–1608), "Good Master Hunt our Preacher lost all his Library and all he had but the cloathes on his backe: yet none never heard him repine at his losse."

Captain Smith labeled Hunt an "honest, religious, courageous divine," and described the church in which Hunt preached:

> When I first went to Virginia, I well remember we did hang an awning (which is an old sail) to three or four trees to shadow us from the sun. Our walls were rails of wood, our seats unhewn trees till we cut planks, our pulpit a bar of wood nailed to two neighboring trees. In foul weather, we shifted into an old rotten tent, for we had few better. . . . This was our church, till we built a homely thing like a barn.

Under Hunt, attendance at prayers (morning and evening) and church services (two sermons each Sunday) was mandatory.

The exact date of Reverend Hunt's death is unknown, as is the name of his immediate successor. Apparently, the latter neither had Hunt's demeanor nor set the same example, for the colonists complained that he was "somewhat a puritane" and refused "to go to his service & to heare his sermons." The colony's third minister, Richard Buck, was more in line with what the colonists had learned to expect under Hunt, and he served the colony from 1610 to 1624. At Jamestown Island, Hunt is honored with a shrine dedicated to his memory. Erected by the Colonial Dames of America in the State of Virginia, it commemorates the earliest celebration of the Holy Communion in the first permanent English settlement in America. As for Hunt's heirs, it is said that his son, Thomas, may be the man of that name who came to Virginia and settled in Accomack County in 1636.

Related entries: Buck, Richard; Crashaw, Reverend William; Jamestown Church Tower; Newport, Sir Christopher; Smith, Captain John

Suggestions for further reading

E. Clowes Chorley. 1930. "The Planting of the Church in Virginia" (*William and Mary Quarterly,* 2d ser., vol. 10).

Captain John Smith. 1907. *The Generall Historie of Virginia, New England & The Summer Isles Together with The True Travels, Adventures and Observations, and A Sea Grammar* (vol. 1). Glasgow, Scotland: MacLehose and Sons.

Jack-of-the-Feather

See Nemattanew

James Fort

Located just over 30 miles up the James River on the 1,500-acre Jamestown Island is the site of the original James Fort, constructed by the English settlers in 1607. Long thought to have eroded into the river, the fort site had been given up as lost by most who had considered its fate. But in 1994, William Kelso, Director of Archaeology at Jamestown, uncovered what was soon to be identified as artifacts from the original settlement. Within two years of the start of excavations, the announcement was made that the original fort site had been discovered and that a substantial portion of its outline and many thousands of artifacts still remained to be uncovered. The success of Kelso's efforts launched a major archaeological endeavor to rediscover James Fort in preparation for the 2007 celebration of the 400th anniversary of Jamestown's founding.

When the first Jamestown settlers departed London for the New World in 1606, they left with instructions from the Virginia Company of London to

> do your best endeavor to find out a safe port in the entrance of some navigable river making choice of such a one as runneth furthest into the land, and if you happen to discover divers portable rivers, and amongst them any one that hath two main branches, if the difference be not great make choice of that which bendeth most toward the North-West, for that way you shall soonest find the other sea [the Pacific Ocean]. . . . if you choose your place so far up as a bark of fifty tuns will float, then you may lay all your provisions ashore with ease, and the better receive the trade of all the countries about you in the land, and such a place you may perchance find a hundred miles from the river's mouth, and the further up the better, for if you sit down near the entrance, except it be in some island that is strong by nature, an enemy that may approach you on even ground may easily pull you out, and if he be driven to seek you a hundred miles in the land in boats you shall from both sides of the river, where it is narrowest, so beate them with your muskets as they shall never be able to prevail against you.

It was with these orders in mind that the settlers traveled as far up the James River as perhaps one hundred miles before returning to the Jamestown Island area. On 12 May 1607, they landed at what became known as Archer's Hope, just slightly downriver from Jamestown Island. There, George Percy described the land as a virtual paradise,

Illustration of James Fort in Virginia, one of the earliest colonial settlements in North America. (MPI/Getty Images)

> which was sufficient with a little labour to defend ourselves against any Enemy. The soile was good and fruitfull, with excellent good Timber. There are also great store of Vines in bignesse of a man's thigh, running up to the tops of the Trees in great abundance.
>
> We also did see many squirels, conies, Black Birds with crimson wings, and divers other Fowles and Birds of divers and sundrie collours of crimson, watchet, Yellow, Greene, Murry, and of divers other hewes naturally without any art using. We found store of Turkie nests and many Egges. . . . If it had not beene disliked, because the ship could not ride neere the shoare, we had setled there to all the Collonies contentment.

Finally, the next day, they sailed to Jamestown Island and "came to our seating place in Paspihas countrey, some eight miles from the point of Land, which I made mention before; where our shippes doe lie so neere the shoare that they are moored to the Trees in six fathom water."

It would appear that the choice of location for the first settlement was made for convenience—the ability to anchor so near the shore—and defense. Jamestown Island, and the area where the fort first was built, is located at a point in the James River where waterborne traffic can be seen coming from quite some distance in both directions, thereby allowing greater time to prepare for possible attack. And at the time of first settlement, the only connection to the mainland was a narrow strip of land that might disappear at high tide, making the approach by land more defensible. Compared to other possible choices, particularly Archer's Hope, it was certainly not the most favorable location in terms of the land and resources. The surrounding marshes were breeding grounds for disease-carrying mosquitoes, and there were no freshwater springs, so brackish water and shallow wells were the main sources of water. As well, most of the island was below the 100-year flood level. But the island appeared to be uninhabited, and it met their requirements as seen at the time, so after the colonists began unloading their provisions, tools, and weapons on 14 May 1607, work on their first fort began.

Artist's rendering of a seventeenth-century sentry in the Virginia colony. (Library of Congress)

The first fort, because of the "Precidents overweening jealousie would admit no exercise at armes, or fortification," apparently was nothing more than the "boughs of trees cast together in the forme of a halfe moone by the extraordinary paines and diligence of Captaine Kendall." This casual approach to defense did not last long, however. Within days of beginning settlement, Captains Christopher Newport and John Smith and about 20 others returning from an expedition to discover the head of the James River, "found 17 men hurt, and a boy slaine by the Salvages, and had it not chanced a crosse barre shot from the ships strooke down a bough from a tree amongst them that caused them to retire, our men had all been slaine." This prompted the necessary action, and "the President was contented the Fort should be palisadoed, the ordinance mounted, his men armed and exercised, for many were the assaults." As Percy described it,

> The fifteenth day of June, we had built and finished our Fort which was triangle wise, having three Bulwarkes at every corner like a halfe Moone, and foure or five pieces of Artillerie mounted in them, we had made ourselves sufficiently strong for these Savages, we had also sowne most of our Corne on two Mountaines.

This fort lasted only until January 1608, when a fire destroyed it. But, as written in words attributed to John Smith,

> wee rebuilt it and three Forts more, besides the Church and Store-house, we had about fortie or fiftie severall houses to keepe us warme and dry, invironed with a palizado of foureteene or fifteene foot, and each as much as three or foure men could carrie. We digged a faire Well of fresh water in the Fort, where wee had three Bulwarks, foure and twentie peece of Ordnance, of Culvering, Demiculvering, Sacar and Falcon, and most well mounted upon convenient plat-formes, planted one hundred acres of Corne.

This third fort, the second with wooden walls, was the structure standing during the winter of 1609–1610, during the period that came to be known as the Starving Time. Although this was the most substantial fort yet, it could not withstand the neglect and abuse it suffered while its inhabitants were slowly starving to death, dying from disease, and being picked off one by one by Powhatan's warriors if they dared to venture outside of the fortification's walls to search for food or relief. William Strachey, secretary to the colony, described the condition of the fort upon his arrival there with Governor Thomas Gates in May 1610:

> Viewing the fort, we found the palisadoes torn down, the ports open, the gates from off the hinges, and empty houses, which [the] owners' death had taken from them, rent up and burnt, rather than the dwellers would step into the woods a stone's cast off from them to fetch other firewood. And it is true the Indian killed as fast without, if our men stirred but beyond the bounds of their blockhouse, as famine and pestilence did within, with many more particularities of their sufferances brought upon them by their own disorders the last year than I have heart to express.

After a few days of considering the situation and determining whether or not there were enough supplies to bring the fort back to life, Gates gave the orders "to abandon the country." The remaining supplies were loaded aboard ships,

> and burying our ordnances before the fort gate, which looked into the river, the seventh of June, having appointed to every pinnace likewise his complement and number, also delivered thereunto a proportionable rate of provision, he commanded every man at the beating of the drum to repair aboard. And because he would preserve the town (albeit now to be quitted) unburned, which some intemperate and malicious people threat'ned, his own company he caused to be last ashore, and was himself the last of them, when about noon giving a farewell, with a peal of small shot, we set sail.

The abandonment of Jamestown lasted little more than a day. Only a few miles downriver, they were greeted by members of the next governor's party and turned back to Jamestown. New leadership, settlers, and supplies brought new vitality to the colony and to the fort itself. As Strachey described it:

> A low level of ground about half an acre . . . on the north side of the river, is cast almost into the form of a triangle, and so palisadoed. The south side next the river, howbeit extended in a line, or curtain, sixscore foot more in length than the other two by reason the advantage of the ground doth so require, contains one hundred and forty yards, the west and east sides a hundred only. At every angle, or corner, where the lines meet, a bulwark or watchtower, is raised, and in each bulwark a piece of ordnance or two well mounted. To every side, a proportioned distance from the palisado, is a settled street of houses that runs along so as each line of the angle hath his street. In the middest is a marketplace, a storehouse, and a *corps du guard,* as likewise a pretty chapel, though at this time when we came in as ruined and unfrequented; but the lord governor and captain general hath given order for the repairing of it, and at this instant many hands are about it.
>
> And thus enclosed, as I said, round with a palisado of planks and strong posts, four foot deep in the ground, of young oaks, walnuts, etc., the fort is called, in honor of His Majesty's name, James Town. The principle gate from the town through the palisado opens to the river, as at each bulwark there is a gate likewise to go forth, and at every gate a demi-culverin, and so in the marketplace.

The chapel described by Strachey appears to have been one of the finer structures at the fort:

> It is in length threescore foot, in breadth twenty-four, and shall have a chancel in it of cedar and a communion table of the black walnut, and all the pews of cedar with fair broad windows to shut and open, as the weather shall occasion, of the same wood, a pulpit of the same with a font hewn hollow like a canoa, with two bells at the west end. It is so cast as it be very light within and the lord governor and captain general doth cause it to be kept passing sweet and trimmed up with divers flowers, with a sexton belonging to it.

The houses, while lacking "hangings, tapestry, and gilded Venetian cordovan, or more spruce household garniture, and wanton city ornaments," still afforded reasonable shelter due, in part, to techniques learned from the Native Americans.

> The houses first raised were all burnt by a casualty of fire the beginning of the second year of their seat, and in the second voyage of Captain Newport—which since have been better rebuilded, though as yet in no great uniformity, either for the fashion or beauty of the street.
>
> A delicate-wrought fine kind of mat the Indians make, with which, as they can be trucked for or snatched up, our people do dress their chambers and inward rooms, which make their houses so much the more handsome. The houses have wide and large country chimneys in the which is to be supposed, in such plenty of wood, what fires are maintained. And they have found the way to cover their houses now as the Indians, with barks of trees as durable and as good proof against storms and winter weather as the best tile, defending likewise the piercing sunbeams of summer, and keeping the inner lodgings cool enough, which before in sultry weather would be like stoves whilest they were, as at first, pargeted and plastered with bitumen or tough clay.

While Strachey wrote of the much-improved fort and living quarters, he still recognized the problems with the location first chosen. "True it is, I may not excuse this our fort or James Town, as yet seated in somewhat an unwholesome and sickly air, by reason it is in a marish ground, low, flat to the river, and hath no fresh water springs serving the town but what we drew from a well six or seven fathom deep, fed by the brackish river oozing into it from whence I verily believe the chief causes have proceeded of many diseases and sicknesses which have happened to our people, who are indeed strangely afflicted with fluxes and agues."

In contrast to Strachey's account of the environment surrounding James Fort, but in agreement with the better living conditions there, Ralph Hamor's 1615 report recounts that the settlement sits

> upon a goodly and fertile island which, although formerly scandaled with unhealthful air, we have since approved as healthful as any other place in the country. And this I can say by mine own experience that that corn and garden ground, which with much labor (being when we first seated upon it a thick wood) we have cleared and impaled, is as fertile as any other we have had experience and trial of. The town itself by the care and providence of Sir Thomas Gates, who for the most part had his chiefest residence there, is reduced into a handsome form and hath in it two fair rows of houses, all of framed timber, two stories, and an upper garret, or corn loft, high, besides three large and substantial storehouses joined together in length some hundred and twenty foot, and in breadth forty. And this town hath been lately newly and strongly impaled, and a fair platform for ordnance in the west bulwark raised. There are also without this town in the island some very pleasant and beautiful houses, two blockhouses to observe and watch lest the Indians at any time should swim over the back river and come into the island, and certain other farm houses.

James Fort continued to be used for the next few years, but, as the settlement began to grow and expand beyond the fort's walls, it eventually began to deteriorate from inattention. By late 1623, the Virginia Company's reports indicated that "the fortifications about James Citie . . . [have been allowed] by the Colonye of late to grow to such decay that they . . . are become of no strength or use so that . . . at this tyme there are no places fortified for defence & safetie for the Access of Shipping from the Sea and Boates uppon the Rivers." Eventually, as settlement focus shifted from the island to the mainland, especially after the capital was officially moved to Williamsburg at the end of the seventeenth century, the original fort site began to fade from memory. During the American Civil War, Confederate forces destroyed part of the archaeological remains while digging and building earthen fortifications. The island eventually became agricultural land, and plowing destroyed or displaced many more traces and artifacts. But as Kelso relates, the fort would hold on through the ravages of time, war, tillage, and flood and wait for its rediscovery.

Related entries: Archaeology; Jamestown Church Tower; Kelso, William M.; Newport, Sir Christopher; Smith's Fort

Suggestions for further reading

Alexander Brown. 1890. *The Genesis of the United States* (vol. 1). Boston: Houghton Mifflin.

Edward Wright Haile, ed. 2001. *Jamestown Narratives: Eyewitness Accounts of the Virginia Colony: The First Decade: 1607–1617.* Champlain, VA: Round House.

William M. Kelso with Beverly Straube. 2004. *Jamestown Rediscovery, 1994–2004.* Richmond, VA: Association for the Preservation of Virginia Antiquities.

William M. Kelso et al. 1995–2001. *Jamestown Rediscovery.* 7 vols. Richmond, VA: Association for the Preservation of Virginia Antiquities.

Susan Myra Kingsbury, ed. 1933. *The Records of The Virginia Company of London* (vol. 4). Washington, DC: Government Printing Office.

Ivor Noël Hume. 1994. *The Virginia Adventure: Roanoke to James Towne: An Archaeological and Historical Odyssey.* New York: Alfred A. Knopf.

James River

The James River has played a vital role in the history of Virginia. On its shores was established the first permanent English settlement in America, Jamestown, in 1607. Within weeks, Captains

Christopher Newport and John Smith led expeditions up the James to discover how far it could be navigated. At the falls, some sixty miles above Jamestown, the site of Virginia's present capital, Richmond, they discovered the seat of Powhatan, the powerful Algonquin chief who ruled the region encompassing Jamestown. In fact, the Indians called the river by the name of Powhatan. Newport claimed the river for England and named it after James I, and it was not long before the colonists had established an outpost at the falls in an effort to control the river. Thomas Stegge, Jr., a prominent Indian trader and the auditor general of the colony, was an early settler at the falls, living there until his death in 1671, when his estate passed to his nephew, William Byrd I. Byrd was named captain of the Henrico County militia and charged with defending the frontier, in effect making the falls area the buffer zone between the English settlement area and the natives that were steadily being pushed back. Above the falls, the French Huguenots made a settlement at Manakin Town, and shortly after the end of the seventeenth century Thomas Jefferson's ancestor, Thomas Randolph, acquired a tract of land even further upstream, which he named Tuckahoe.

During the colonial period, the James River was Virginia's main water route for commerce, connecting the seaports to the backcountry. In later centuries, the James, through the Kanawha River, with the help of the James River and Kanawha Canal, became the route by which produce could be transported all the way from the Ohio River Valley to the Atlantic Ocean. Above the falls, communities grew up and thrived on the James: Columbia, Scottsville, Lynchburg, Warminster, Buchanan. Below the falls but above Jamestown, great tobacco plantations were established, of which more than a dozen have survived, including Sherwood Forest, Westover, Shirley, Evelynton, and Berkeley. Closer to the sea, Hampton Roads became the world's largest shipyard. A bridge across the James at Newport News (connecting the counties of Warwick and Isle of Wight) opened in 1928 as the world's longest bridge across water, some five miles long. During the American Civil War, Union and Confederate naval forces both vied for control of the James.

At 340 miles, the James River is Virginia's longest waterway and a large tributary of the Chesapeake Bay. Formed by the confluence of the Cowpasture and Jackson Rivers near Iron Gate in the Appalachian Mountains, the James's watershed drains some 10,000 square miles. In recent years, with nearly 3 million people living in its watershed and using its waters, the James has faced significant challenges regarding pollution. Toxicity levels have been dangerous for decades, and contamination of fish has been an ongoing problem; the size of the river's freshwater spawning grounds for oysters, shad, and striped bass are a fraction of what they were in the past. In addition, significant flooding of the banks of the James at various points, especially at Richmond and Scottsville, has caused great property damage; Hurricane Camille in 1969 caused flooding along the river that took 151 lives. Nevertheless, the river remains vibrant and appealing, and recreational use of the James is a major industry, consisting of canoeing, rafting, speed boating, fishing, camping, sightseeing, and riverboats. An annual James River Batteau Festival is held each spring at Lynchburg. The Virginia General Assembly named the James River to its state scenic river system, and the James River Association formed to promote conversation and responsible stewardship of the river's natural resources and fish and habitat restoration.

Related entries: Byrd, William, I; Chickahominy River; Elizabeth River; Mattaponi River; Nansemond River; Newport, Sir Christopher; Newport News; Pamunkey River; Rappahannock River; York River

Suggestions for further reading

Philip L. Barbour. 1969. *The Jamestown Voyages Under the First Charter: 1606–1609* (vol. 1). Cambridge, England: Cambridge University Press.

A. J. Foster. 1965. *Early James River History in and Around Hopewell, Virginia.* Falls Church, VA: Falcon.

Lyon Gardiner Tyler. 1906. *The Cradle of the Republic: Jamestown and James River.* Richmond, VA: Hermitage Press.

Jamestown Church Tower

What could be considered the first church in Virginia "was a simple shrine in the forest covered with a tattered sailcloth." As Captain John Smith described it,

> we did hang an awning (which is an old saile) to three or foure trees to shadow us from the Sunne, our walls were rales of wood, our seats unhewed trees, till we cut plankes, our Pulpit a bar of wood nailed to two neighbouring trees, in foule weather we shifted into an old rotten tent, for we had few better . . . this was our Church.

As the Church of England was the official church of the Jamestown colony for the settlement's first century and a half, this structure was Anglican, as were all the priests and vicars sent there during that time. "It was intended that the settlement would be a full-fledged Parish of the Church of England, an overseas extension of the ancient Diocese of London." To perform the first services there, the Bishop of London sent the Reverend Robert Hunt who, at the age of around thirty-seven, came to be a great benefit and comfort to the colony until he was tragically lost the year following their arrival.

Perhaps by the early autumn of 1607, a timber church had been completed at the new settlement. According to John Smith, it was not yet a majestic edifice, as evidenced by his written description of it as

> a homely thing like a barne, set upon Cratchets, covered with rafts, sedge, and earth, so was also the walls . . . that could neither well defend [provide shelter from] wind nor raine, yet wee had

Present-day view of the seventeenth-century Jamestown church tower. The church behind the tower was constructed in 1906. (Photo by Frank E. Grizzard, Jr.)

> daily Common Prayer morning and evening, every Sunday two Sermons, and every three moneths the holy Communion.

This church was in service for only a few weeks, however, because along with most of the rest of the fort, it burned in January 1608. But as they did with the rest of the settlement, the colonists soon built a new church. It has been suggested by some that this newest church was the one in which Pocahontas married John Rolfe in April 1614, although some evidence indicates they were married at what was first intended to be a replacement for the original settlement site, Henricus, a few miles further up the James River.

Ten years after the colonists first arrived, Governor Samuel Argall had another wooden church built. It was in this building in 1619 that "the first representative legislative assembly in the New World" met. This church served the colony until about 1639, when Governor John Harvey began the process of having a slightly larger brick church built. As was the custom among builders at the time, the church tower was constructed after the church had been built. Sometime after 1647, the brick tower, originally about forty-six feet high and three feet thick at the base, was built as an addition to the 1639 church. The tower had two upper floors, with six small windows in the highest level. On 19 September 1676, that church was burned by the insurgents during Bacon's Rebellion. The tower, however, was undamaged. A new church was constructed on the site and served until the 1750s. By the 1790s, the tower was still standing strong, but the church had fallen into disrepair, and its bricks had been used to build the existing graveyard wall.

In 1906, the National Society of Colonial Dames of America provided for the construction of the Memorial Church that now stands adjacent to the original tower. It was dedicated on 13 May 1907, 300 years after the original colonists first moored their ships to a tree on Jamestown Island. Inside this building can be seen the foundations of the 1617 and 1639 churches as well as a number of graves, one apparently of a prominent early Jamestown resident, as indicated by the method of burial. Shortly after acquiring the property in the 1890s, the Association for the Preservation of Virginia Antiquities (APVA) began work to reinforce and preserve the tower. As a result, it still stands, the oldest above-ground structure on Jamestown Island and one of the oldest standing English-built structures in America today.

Related entries: Archaeology; Association for the Preservation of Virginia Antiquities; Buck, Richard; Henricus; Hunt, Robert; James Fort; Kelso, William M.

Suggestions for further reading

Philip L. Barbour, ed. 1986. *The Complete Works of Captain John Smith (1580–1631)* (vol. 3). Chapel Hill and London: University of North Carolina Press.

Paul J. Hudson. 1970. *Jamestown Church.* Jamestown, VA: Jamestown Foundation.

William M. Kelso. 1984. *Kingsmill Plantations: Archaeology of Country Life in Colonial Virginia.* San Diego, CA: Academic Press.

—— with Beverly Straube. 2004. *Jamestown Rediscovery, 1994–2004.* Richmond, VA: Association for the Preservation of Virginia Antiquities.

William M. Kelso et al. 1995–2001. *Jamestown Rediscovery.* 7 vols. Richmond, VA: Association for the Preservation of Virginia Antiquities.

Ivor Noël Hume, 1994. *The Virginia Adventure: Roanoke to James Towne: An Archaeological and Historical Odyssey.* New York: Alfred A. Knopf.

Jesuit Mission (Chesapeake)

Fifteen years before England attempted to establish a colony on Roanoke Island and thirty-seven years before the first permanent English settlement in North America was realized at Jamestown, representatives of Spain's King Philip II planted a Jesuit mission only a few miles northeast of the site where England finally gained its foothold in 1607. Located possibly on the Rappahannock or the Potomac River but more likely between the King and the Queen Creeks where they empty into the York River, this mission was the result of a second attempt by Spain to extend its domination of North America into the Chesapeake Bay, or as they called it, Bahía de Santa

María, or Bahía de Madre de Dios. The first attempt had been made in August 1566, when two Dominican friars and thirty-seven Spanish and Portuguese soldiers sailed to that area, called Ajacán by their guide and interpreter, Don Luis de Velasco, a converted, hispaniolized Algonquian Indian who had been taken from the area on an earlier voyage in 1561. While searching for a landing site, Don Luis claimed to not recognize the surroundings, and after a strong storm arrived, this first attempt was abandoned. On 10 September 1570, the members of the second colonizing expedition, after making their first landfall probably at either Cape Henry, Point Comfort, or the southeastern tip of present-day Newport News, decided to disembark at what may have been College Creek, just east of Jamestown, and travel by smaller boat and foot to their preferred site on the York River. The colonists consisted of two Jesuit priests, including Father Juan Baptista de Segura as leader, one other priest, three Jesuit brothers, three lay catechists, the young son of a Spanish colonist from Santa Elena (present-day Parris Island, South Carolina), and Don Luis de Velasco, once again as guide and interpreter. They arrived at an inopportune time in that the Indians whose territory they chose to settle were experiencing a drought, and food was in short supply. Having to rely on the local inhabitants for sustenance, many of whom had left the area to search for food elsewhere, the Jesuits soon became more of an irritant than an inspiration, especially to Don Luis. Back in his homeland once again, he was no longer interested in following the strict Jesuit dictates that were so contrary to the lifestyle he had known before his experiences with the Spanish. He left their company to live with relatives and, despite many pleas from the Jesuits to return, he resisted until the morning of 9 February 1571, when Don Luis and a number of his tribe appeared at the mission and killed the remaining five Jesuits, after having killed three others who had gone to seek his return a few days earlier. Only the young boy, Alonso de Olmos, was spared.

In the spring of 1571, a relief ship was sent from the Spanish settlement in Cuba, but the crew was attacked by a group of Indians before disembarking. At least one Indian was taken and held captive, and it was learned from him that the mission had been destroyed but the boy had survived. Two more relief efforts were made during that year, but were stopped at Santa Elena by Spanish officials. In the summer of 1572, a rescue and punitive expedition was sent to the area, during which the boy was recovered and a number of the native people were killed; some were captured, tried for the murders of the Jesuits, and executed. Although the Spanish made a few more voyages to the area, the destruction of the Jesuit mission in 1571 marked the end of Spain's land presence in the Chesapeake Bay.

Related entries: Cape Henry; College at Henricus; Sagadahoc (Popham) Colony

Suggestions for further reading

Clifford M. Lewis and Albert J. Loomie. 1953. *The Spanish Jesuit Mission in Virginia: 1570–1572.* Chapel Hill: University of North Carolina Press for the Virginia Historical Society.

David Beers Quinn, ed. 1979. *New American World: A Documentary History of North America to 1612* (vol. 2). New York: Arno Press and Hector Bye.

Helen C. Rountree. 1993. *Powhatan Foreign Relations: 1500–1722.* Charlottesville: University Press of Virginia.

Kecoughtan

The site of present day Hampton, Virginia, Kecoughtan bears the name of the Native Americans who once lived there. Never accepting Powhatan's authority over them, they were driven out of their ancestral town by him and later resettled in former Piankatank territory. Powhatan repopulated the former Kecoughtan town site with other natives loyal to him, with his son Pochins as their leader. It was apparently these people whom the colonists encountered shortly after arriving in the New World.

After first landing at Cape Henry on the southern side of the mouth of the Chesapeake Bay, George Percy records that later they "rowed over to a point of land where we found a channel and sounded six, eight, ten, or twelve fathom, which put us in good comfort; therefore we named that point of land 'Cape Comfort.'" After returning to Cape Henry and placing a cross there, they took their ships to Cape Comfort, where they "saw five savages running on the shore." The crew launched a small boat to meet them, and

> the captain called to them in sign of friendship, but they were at first very timorsome until they saw the captain lay his hand on his heart. Upon that they laid down their bows and arrows and came very boldly to us, making signs to come ashore to their town, which is called by the savages Kecoughtan.

After much drinking, dancing, and merriment, the colonists returned to their search for a permanent settlement site. John Smith noted a similarly pleasant encounter with the inhabitants while searching for provisions in the cold months of 1608. He wrote,

> [For] six or seaven dayes the extreame winde, rayne, frost and snow caused us to keep Christmas among the Salvages, where we were never more merry, nor fed on more plentie of good Oysters, Fish, Flesh, Wild-foule, and good bread; nor never had better fires in England, then in the dry smoaky houses of Kecoughtan.

But these good relations did not last. On 9 July 1610, after the inhabitants killed Humphrey Blunt at Blunt Point, Sir Thomas Gates attacked the settlement and drove away Pochins and his followers. Gates then built two forts there, Henry and Charles, named after the sons of King James I. During that year, the settlers established St. John's Episcopal Church, now the oldest Anglican church in America.

By 1616, the area was mainly a farming community with about twenty English colonists. Kecoughtan's first two representatives to the House of Burgesses, military commander Captain William Tucker, and landowner William Capps, petitioned the House of Burgesses in 1619 to change the name of their settlement; although the name Kecoughtan remained associated with the area throughout the seventeenth century, by 1620 it had become known as Elizabeth City, after the daughter of King James. This remained the name of the county until 1952. It was not until 1680 that the town of Hampton was established there.

Kecoughtan continued to grow and prosper, and in 1621 French vignerons were established in the place known as Buck Roe, on the bay side of the settlement, to teach the inhabitants the process of growing grapes and making wine. And on 27 February 1634, Leonard Calvert and a group of emigrants stopped there on their way to found the state of Maryland.

By 1716, there were around 100 houses at Kecoughtan (or Hampton), with a great deal of Virginia's trade being conducted from its ports, especially with New York and Pennsylvania. Just two years later, Captain Henry Maynard landed there after defeating the pirate Blackbeard at Pamlico Sound in North Carolina on 21 November. Among Maynard's cargo was Blackbeard's head, which hung from the ship's bowsprit. Maynard also was transporting the survivors of the pirate's crew, most of whom were destined for Williamsburg, where they later would be hung. Nearly a century later, during the War of 1812, Hampton was captured and ravaged by the British, and during the American Civil War the city once again was damaged badly when the citizens set fire to their buildings to keep them from falling into the hands of enemy troops.

Today, what was once known as Kecoughtan is now part of the city of Hampton with about 140,000 inhabitants. It is host to the National Aeronautics and Space Administration's (NASA) Langley Research Center, where America's first astronauts were trained; to Fort Monroe, established in 1819 and now home to the U.S. Army's Training and Doctrine Command; to Langley Air Force Base, where the First Fighter Wing is stationed; and to Hampton University.

Related entries: Kecoughtan Indians; Percy, George; Powhatan; Smith, Captain John

Suggestions for further reading

Alexander Brown. 1890. *The Genesis of the United States* (vol. 2). Boston: Houghton Mifflin.

Edward Wright Haile, ed. 2001. *Jamestown Narratives: Eyewitness Accounts of the Virginia Colony: The First Decade: 1607–1617.* Champlain, VA: Round House.

Helen C. Rountree. 1989. *The Powhatan Indians of Virginia: Their Traditional Culture.* Norman and London: University of Oklahoma Press.

Lyon Gardiner Tyler. 1906. *The Cradle of the Republic: Jamestown and James River.* Richmond, VA: Hermitage Press.

Kecoughtan Indians

> Thirtieth day [April 1607], we came with our ships to Cape Comfort; where we saw five Savages running on the shore. Presently the Captain [Christopher Newport] caused the shallop to be manned, so rowing to the shore, the Captain called to them in sign of friendship, but they were at first very timersome, until they saw the Captain lay his hand on his heart: upon that they laid down their Bows and Arrows, and came very boldly to us, making signs to come ashore to their Town, which is called by the Savages Kecoughtan.

By the time George Percy made this record of the first friendly contact between the English colonists who would settle Jamestown and the natives who had long inhabited Virginia, the Kecoughtan Indians had been reduced to a clan of only about twenty to thirty warriors, plus women and children. The natives, said Percy,

> goe altogether naked, but their privities are covered with Beasts skinnes beset commonly with little bones, or beasts teeth: some paint their bodies blacke, some red, with artificiall knots of sundry lively colours, very beautifull and pleasing to the eye, in a braver fashion than they in the West Indies.

The Kecoughtan entertained the English "very kindly," presenting them with gifts of dainties, bread, and tobacco, all the while performing a ceremonial welcome dance and song. In exchange, the English gave the Kecoughtans "Beades and other trifling Jewells."

William Strachey, appointed secretary and recorder of the Jamestown colony in 1610, learned

Native Americans and colonists meet. (Smith, John. The True Travels, Adventures, and Observations of Captaine John Smith, *1630)*

upon his arrival at Jamestown that the Kecoughtans had been a part of the Powhatan Confederacy for only about a decade, having been conquered by Powhatan in 1597 or 1598. Until then, said Strachey, the Kecoughtan had been a people 1,000 strong, living in some 300 houses. By the time John Smith observed them in 1608, they were confined to a village of 18 houses on 3 acres of land. The Kecoughtan had met Europeans as early as the late 1560s, when Spanish Jesuits had traveled to the area in pursuit of an ideal spot to establish a mission. Ralph Lane, the founder of the tiny settlement on Roanoke Island that came to be known as the Lost Colony, had learned of the Kecoughtan in the 1580s but was unable to find them. (In fact, some scholars have suggested that the lost English of Lane's colony went to live with the Kecoughtan, either by force or by their own volition.) The Kecoughtans, situated as they were near the Atlantic coast in the Chesapeake Bay, most likely had met other Europeans or at least had seen their vessels sailing in the Atlantic from time to time. Perhaps their knowledge of the existence of other peoples and societies made them more resolute in supporting their chief's resistance against Powhatan, who wanted to bring the tribe into his confederacy. In any event, when the Kecoughtan chief died (about 1597), Powhatan "subtilly stepped in, and conquered the People killing the Chief and most of them;" those left alive, except for a handful loyal to Powhatan, were taken into captivity and their lands occupied by Pochins (b. 1583), one of Powhatan's sons. The displaced Kecoughtans were later allowed by Powhatan to live on lands once occupied by the Piankatank, a tribe in Powhatan's dominion that he considered disloyal and thus expelled in 1608.

The next encounter between the Kecoughtan and the colonists took place in September 1607, when the colonists were in dire need of food; Captain John Smith led a party of six or seven men to barter with the Indians. Smith went down the river from Jamestown to Kecoughtan "where at first they scorned him, as a famished man, and would in derision offer him a handfull of Corne, a peece of bread, for their swords and muskets, and such like proportions also for their apparell." Smith put up with the Indians' mocking long enough to learn for sure that they were not going to trade away their corn, at which time he

> made bold to try such conclusions as necessitie inforced, though contrary to his Commission: Let fly his muskets, ran his boat on shore, whereat they all fled into the woods. So marching towards their houses, they might see great heapes of corne: much adoe he had to restraine his hungry souldiers from present taking of it, expecting as it hapned that the Salvages would assault them, as not long after they did with a most hydeous noyse.

Although the Indians outnumbered Smith's party ten to one, they were no match for the colonists' gunfire, and in the end the warriors sought peace. They then traded venison, turkey, fowl, and bread for English beads, copper, and hatchets. The following summer, 1608, Smith stayed several days at Kecoughtan, where their chief, thinking Smith was going to attack their enemy the Massawomecks, "feasted us with much mirth." That December, while enroute to the Pamunkey town in search of Chief Powhatan, Smith stayed six or seven days at Kecoughtan, where

> the extreame winde, rayne, frost and snow caused us to keepe Christmas among the Salvages, where we were never more merry, nor fed on more plentie of good Oysters, Fish, Flesh, Wild-foule, and good bread; nor never had better fires in England, then in the dry, smoaky houses of Kecoughtan.

This is the first recorded Christmas celebration of the English in the New World.

After Smith's December 1608 stay with the Kecoughtans, other colonists routinely visited the tribe's town, although not all of the enounters were pleasant ones. The Kecoughtans joined some of their native neighbors in resisting both the establishment of an English settlement in Nansemond territory in the summer of 1609 and the erection of Fort Algernon at Old Point Comfort, only a half mile from the Kecoughtan settlement, the following fall. In the summer of 1610, Lord De La Warr and Sir Thomas Gates retaliated against the Kecoughtan for their part in trying to fend off the English move into the region, by driving them away and occupying their town. The English occupation of the town and surrounding territory brought to an end Kecoughtan occupation of the small peninsula on the Chesapeake Bay. By 1611, two other English fortifications were erected in Kecoughtan territory, Fort Henry and Fort Charles. Although the Virginia General Assembly voted to "change the savage name of Kicowtan" to Elizabeth City when it incorporated the county at its first session (the county name was retained until mid-twentieth century), the name Kecoughtan persisted, especially in reference to the area bordering the waterfront and even after the founding of Hampton in the 1690s.

The eviction of the Kecoughtans from the land of their ancestors by the English, coming on the heels of Powhatan's complete subjugation of the tribe, resulted in the total disappearance of the Kecoughtan people in the very early years of English settlement. Strachey claimed that the Kecoughtans had been "better husbands then in any parte else that we have observed," having cultivated great fields of maize, the product of which they apparently exported to neighboring tribes, and mulberry groves. The Kecoughtans also gathered shells from the nearby bay to make beads for

Powhatan's people, but otherwise little else is known about the now lost Algonquin tribe. The Peninsula Council of the Boy Scouts of America in 1951 honored the Kecoughtan tribe by chartering the council's Order of the Arrow lodge in its name. In 1996, the Kecoughtan Lodge merged with nearby Chanco Lodge of the Old Dominion Area Council (when the two councils merged) to create Wahunsenakah Lodge, named in honor of Chief Powhatan.

Related entries: Accohannock Indians; Accomac Indians; Chesapeake Indians; Chickahominy Indians; Early European Exploration of North America; Lost Colony; Manahoac Indians; Mattaponi Indians; Monacan Indians; Nansemond Indians; Pamunkey Indians; Paspahegh Indians; Powhatan; Three Ships; Warraskoyak Indians; West, Thomas, Lord De La Warr

Suggestions for further reading

David Beers Quinn, ed. 1967. *Observations Gathered Out of "A discourse on the Plantation of the Southern Colony in Virginia by the English, 1606," Written by that Honorable Gentleman, Master George Percy.* Charlottesville: University Press of Virginia.

Helen C. Rountree. 1990. *Pocahontas's People: The Powhatan Indians of Virginia Through Four Centuries.* Norman: University of Oklahoma Press.

Captain John Smith. 1907. *The Generall Historie of Virginia, New England & The Summer Isles Together with The True Travels, Adventures and Observations, and A Sea Grammar* (vol. 1). Glasgow, Scotland: MacLehose and Sons.

Kelso, William M. (b. 1941)

The driving force behind the rediscovery of the original James Fort site in Jamestown, Virginia, and the recovery of hundreds of thousands of related early seventeenth-century artifacts, is William M. Kelso.

After having served as director of archaeology at Carter's Grove in Williamsburg, Virginia, and Thomas Jefferson's Monticello and Poplar Forest, as well as being commissioner of archaeology for the Virginia Historic Landmarks Commission, Kelso became the director of archaeology for the

William Kelso examines a seventeenth-century entrenching tool found in a dry moat at Jamestown. (Courtesy of APVA Preservation Virginia)

Association for the Preservation of Virginia Antiquities (APVA) Jamestown Rediscovery project. This was the result of a decades-long dream that began, as he writes, "one typical gray March day" in the library at his *alma mater,* Baldwin-Wallace College in Berea, Ohio, when, "Tired of memorizing names and dates for a history exam . . . I decided to cheer up by reading about Virginia where I heard the sun usually shines and American colonial history, second only to football as a passion in my life, was taken to be a serious subject." While perusing through back issues of *National Geographic,* he came across an aerial color photograph of Jamestown Island showing results of archaeological excavations conducted there in association with the 350th Jamestown founding celebration in 1957. As he related, he was "totally mesmerized" by what he saw. He later traveled to Jamestown Island and asked a park ranger there about the location of the original fort site, only to be told that it had been washed away by the James River. Fortunately, he did not take the ranger's response as the definitive answer.

Kelso's interests led him to graduate studies at the College of William and Mary in Williamsburg, Virginia, where he earned a Master's degree in history. While there, he studied under historian and editor W. W. Abbot, author of, among other works, *A Virginia Chronology 1585–1783,* written for the Virginia 350th Anniversary Celebration Corporation in Williamsburg as part of a 1957 series of publications in the Jamestown 350th Anniversary Historical Booklets project. (Abbot later became professor of history at the University of Virginia and, still later, editor of the *Papers of George Washington.*) Following his studies at William and Mary, Kelso earned a doctorate at Emory University in Atlanta, Georgia, but his fascination with Jamestown would eventually draw him back to Virginia, where he built a distinguished career rediscovering some of America's greatest history while uncovering some of its most important archaeological sites.

Following his studies, Kelso became a field archaeologist of colonial America, especially the much-neglected period of the seventeenth century. Much of his attention was given to farms and plantations along the James River that were slated for real estate development. As he and his colleagues worked at these sites, they became convinced that the "colonial level" on display under glass at Jamestown appeared to indicate that much of the original settlement could still be there. After reviewing the field notes from the 1955 National Park Service excavations at the Jamestown site, he noticed that some of the work done had uncovered what looked like signs of slot trenches of the type used when building seventeenth-century fort palisades. Also, pieces of pottery and iron found appeared to be of the correct date and design to be contemporaneous with the original fort period.

When the APVA decided to proceed with further excavations at the site, Kelso was ready to serve history once again. As he points out, at the time he did not have much competition when it came to searching for the original fort site. Most archaeologists had already given up on the original fort site as having been washed away many years before by the James River. Nonetheless, Kelso pressed on. "Consequently, 33 years to the day when I first set foot on the island, Governor George Allen of Virginia announced that the remains of the 1607 James Fort had been found. Fortunately for me, I did not have to miss out on digging at the James Fort after all."

Kelso writes that from the beginning of the digging at Jamestown on 4 April 1994, he had two major goals: to discover, reveal, and preserve whatever had survived at the site from the seventeenth century, and to make that "process of discovery" as visible to the public as possible. Both goals have been met with great success in that the original James Fort site has been found, mapped, and is in the process of being excavated and interpreted; and Kelso has written and lectured prolifically about his discoveries there. When not researching and writing the various publications about the excavations at Jamestown, including at least eight booklets on the findings, or giving lectures around the United States and Europe, he can be seen walking among the sites, working alongside fellow archaeologists, or discussing the latest finds with the increasing numbers of curious visitors. Additionally, in the summer he heads a field school for students and archaeologists from around the world to take part in the ongoing excavations.

The author of numerous other articles and books in addition to his publications about Jamestown, Kelso currently resides on Jamestown Island.

Related entries: Archaeology; James Fort; Martin's Hundred

Suggestions for further reading

William M. Kelso. 1984. *Kingsmill Plantations: Archaeology of Country Life in Colonial Virginia.* San Diego, CA: Academic Press.

——. 1997. *Archaeology at Monticello: Artifacts of Everyday Life in the Plantation Community.* Charlottesville: University Press of Virginia.

—— with Beverly Straube. 2004. *Jamestown Rediscovery, 1994–2004.* Richmond, VA: Association for the Preservation of Virginia Antiquities.

—— et al. 1995–2001. *Jamestown Rediscovery.* 7 vols. Richmond, VA: Association for the Preservation of Virginia Antiquities.

Kendall, George (d. 1608)

The distinction of being the first recorded Englishman to be executed in America falls to George Kendall, a member of the first council at Jamestown. George Kendall's activities at Jamestown are rather cryptic. Captain John Smith noted that Kendall through "extraordinary paines and diligence" formed the first crude defensive structure for the colonists, consisting of the "boughs of trees cast together in the forme of a halfe moone." Even that necessary work seems to have been only grudgingly allowed by the colony's president, Edward-Maria Wingfield, and before long Kendall was stirring up discontent among Wingfield and his fellow councilors. Kendall's continual harpings against Wingfield temporarily backfired, however, and he was voted off the council, arrested, and confined to the *Discovery*. The machinations of settler Gabriel Archer finally succeeded in having Wingfield himself ejected from his position of authority, arrested, and confined, however. John Ratcliffe was chosen to replace Wingfield, and Kendall was released on the condition that he would not carry a weapon. The situation continued hence for some weeks until the colony's blacksmith, James Read, was charged with treason for angrily attempting to strike President Ratcliffe. Read was condemned to death but saved himself by revealing that Kendall was plotting a mutiny. Kendall was tried, condemned, and executed.

Captain Smith, in his *Generall Historie of Virginia,* tells us as much as anyone about the how the disagreement between Wingfield and Kendall arose:

> Smith perceiving (notwithstanding their late miserie) not any regarded but from hand to mouth (the company being well recovered) caused the Pinnace to be provided with things fitting to get provision for the yeare following; but in the interim he made 3. or 4. journies and discovered the people of Chickahamania: yet what he carefully provided the rest carelessly spent. Wingfield and Kendall living in disgrace, seeing all things at randome in the absence of Smith, the companies dislike of their Presidents weaknes, and their small love to Martins never mending sicknes, strengthened themselves with the sailers, and other confederates to regaine their former credit and authority, or at least such meanes abord the Pinnace, (being fitted to saile as Smith had appointed for trade) to alter her course and to goe for England. Smith unexpectedly returning had the plot discovered to him, much trouble he had to prevent it, till with store of sakre and musket shot he forced them stay or sinke in the river, which action cost the life of captaine Kendall. These brawles are so disgustfull, as some will say they were better forgotten, yet all men of good judgement will conclude, at were better their basenes should be manifest to the world, then the busines beare the scorne and shame of their excused disorders. The President and captaine Archer not long after intended also to have abandoned the country, which project also was curbed, and suppressed by Smith. The Spaniard never more greedily desired gold then he victuall, nor his souldiers more to abandon the Country, then he to keepe it.

Smith elsewhere elaborated on Kendall's removal from the council for "divers reasens," in his *A True Relation of Such Occurrences and Accidents of Note as Hath Hapned in Virginia Since the First Planting of that Colony, 1608:*

> Having thus by Gods assistance gotten good store of corne, notwithstanding some bad spirits not content with Gods providence, still grew mutinous; in so much, that our president having occasion to chide the smith for his misdemeanour, he not only gave him bad language, but also offred to strike him with some of his tooles. For which rebellious act, the smith was by a Jury condemned to be hanged, but being uppon the ladder, continuing very obstinate as hoping upon a rescue, when he saw no other way but death with him, he became penitent, and declared a dangerous conspiracy: for which, Captaine Kendall, as principal, was by a Jury condemned, and shot to death.

Other contemporary accounts agreed but were vague. George Percy, in his *Observations,* wrote that "After Captaine Gosnols death, the Councell could hardly agree by the dissention of Captaine Kendall, which afterward was committed about hainous matters which was proved against him." Wingfield himself simply declared that Kendall "was put of from being of the Counsell, and comitted to prison; for that it did manyfestly appeare he did practize to sowe discord betweene the President and Councell." Here the matter rested for three and a half centuries, until historian and editor Philip L. Barbour delved into Kendall's identity in the 1960s.

Barbour discovered that a George Kendall of Westminster, "brought up as Her Majesty's Scholar" (in Kendall's own words), was spying for England's secretary of state, Sir Robert Cecil, as early as 1600. Moreover, by that time (1600), Kendall had been a spy for as long as seven years. What Cecil or the Virginia colonists did not know was that Kendall went to Virginia as a double-spy, in the service of Spain! A Roman Catholic and quite possibly Irish, a gentleman of standing with family connections to Cecil and to Sir Edwin Sandys, one of the colony's main promoters, Kendall had switched his allegiance to Philip III. Kendall was eager to pass on intelligence about England's attempts to get a foothold in the New World, and these were the "hainous matters" for which he was shot—matters of much greater consequence than sowing discord, of which all the councilors at one time or another were accused.

The latest concerning George Kendall the Mutineer, or the Intelligencer, may be the discovery of his skeleton by archaeologists digging at the walls of the original Jamestown fort, in 1996. The young white male had been shot, possibly several times, and was buried in a coffin—both the style of execution (rather than hanging) and the burial indicate a person of status, and there is no surviving record of other colonists being thus shot. Whether it is really Kendall or not, like so much more surrounding his life, may always remain a mystery.

Related entries: Archer, Gabriel; Sandys, Sir Edwin; Smith, Captain John; Wingfield, Edward-Maria

Suggestions for further reading

Philip L. Barbour. 1962. "Captain George Kendall, Mutineer or Intelligencer?" (*Virginia Magazine of History and Biography,* vol. 70).

Captain John Smith. 1907. *The Generall Historie of Virginia, New England & The Summer Isles Together with The True Travels, Adventures and Observations, and A Sea Grammar* (vol. 1). Glasgow, Scotland: MacLehose and Sons.

L

Lawes Divine, Morall, and Martiall (Dale's Laws)

See Dale, Sir Thomas

Lee, Richard (c.1613–1664)

The Jamestown colony was only a little over three decades old when Richard Lee first crossed the Atlantic to explore the bounties of the Virginia countryside. Although not much is known of his life in England—Lee's ancestors were seen as hailing from Shropshire, until recently, when researchers turned their attention toward Worcester—Lee apparently had already set himself up as a London merchant in the tobacco trade. Interested in seeing firsthand how the lucrative crop was grown and shipped, as well as what other opportunities the New World offered, he sailed for Virginia in late 1639 or early 1640. He liked what he saw, and in 1640, not long after his arrival, he acquired his first lands, at Tindall's Point in present-day Gloucester County, on the north side of the York River directly across from where Yorktown was later established. Two years later, in 1642, Lee patented a thousand-acre tract on Poropotank Creek, a tributary of the York about twenty miles above the river's mouth. The region on the north side of the York River was still controlled by natives inhospitable to the English, but Lee, exhibiting the adventurous spirit that came to characterize his descendants, discarded any fears he may have held of Indians, not only cultivating his fields in their midst but trading furs and skins with them directly. Lee's land contained virgin soil, its richness was perfect for the planting of tobacco, and he soon saw the wisdom in adding to it. After the Indian Massacre of 1644, Lee moved to the south side of the York, where he remained for nearly a decade; but in 1653 he resettled on Poropotank Creek, establishing a trading post and tobacco warehouse. He named this estate Paradise.

Richard Lee and his young wife, Anne Constable, who was born in London and may have come to America at the same time as Richard, were parents to an ever-increasing brood of children. Between 1645 and 1656, in quick succession, Anne delivered at least ten children, including two girls and six boys who survived infancy: John, Richard, Francis, William, Hancock, Elizabeth, Anne, and Charles. In a short time, Lee began to prosper; with prosperity came the ability to cultivate more tobacco fields; with increased cultivation came more prosperity and the ability to supplement his land holdings. His tobacco plantation eventually grew to 1,500 acres and became home to seventeen laborers—indentured servants who paid for their voyage from England to Virginia with seven years of service in

Lee's tobacco fields. More important, prosperity brought Lee prestige and, with it, political appointments: clerk of the Quarter Court in 1641; attorney general in 1643; sheriff and burgess of York County in 1646 and 1647; secretary of state in 1649; and the Governor's Council in 1651. As secretary of state, Lee was the most valuable assistant to the colony's royal governor, Sir William Berkeley (whose estate, Green Spring, was later inherited by one of Lee's descendants), and the most powerful man in the colony after Berkeley. As a member of the Governor's Council, Lee set a precedent for his offspring, who in succeeding generations occupied a seat on the Council until it was dissolved in 1776.

Richard Lee led an active life, one of much hustle and bustle, as he kept the official records at Jamestown, issued marriage and travel and hunting licenses, recorded wills and land titles, and made transatlantic trips in the governor's name—all the while managing his tobacco fields; he also entered the shipping business, becoming part owner of at least two ships, the *Susan* and the *Elizabeth and Mary.* Along with Governor Berkeley, Lee was a loyal supporter of the Crown; like Berkeley's, his career as a public official ended with Cromwell's seizure of power in England. Lee retired quietly to land on Virginia's Northern Neck, four days' distance from Jamestown, to wait out the Interregnum on land that was not his, that had been given to the Indians in treaty. He began to amass more tracts of land, in present-day Northumberland County, where he lived out the rest of his life (when he was not in England), and in present-day Fairfax County, including the plantation later inherited by George Washington and known as Mount Vernon. At the Restoration, Governor Berkeley returned to power in Virginia, and Lee returned to his seat on the Governor's Council, although for Lee the colony's politics no longer held any interest. At his death in 1664, which took place at his home on Dividing Creek (near present-day Kilmarnock, Virginia), Richard Lee owned 13,000 acres of land, more than anyone else in the colony, which made him probably the richest man in Virginia. Lee also owned a large estate outside London at Stratford-Langton. At the village, an important road (or street) crossed the River Lea by a ford—and hence originally was known as "Strat by the ford"—which in Virginia became the name that Lee's grandson Thomas Lee attached to the most famous of all Lee family homes when he built it in the 1700s—Stratford Hall.

The success of Richard Lee, the Virginia immigrant, destined his children for a life consistent with their father's fortune and status. John, the eldest, attended Oxford University, taking a medical degree; Richard, the second eldest and his father's namesake, also attended Oxford; Francis, the third child, became the family's factor in London. The fourth son, William, died in his mid-forties, apparently without marrying or issue. The fifth son of the family founder, Hancock, married (the second time) Sarah Allerton, a granddaughter of Isaac Allerton, who was a passenger on the *Mayflower.* Charles, the youngest of all the children, inherited the part of his father's Dividing Creek lands that came to be known as Cobbs Hall, Cobb being the name given to Charles's line of descendants. Hancock Lee built a mansion house called Ditchley, after which his descendants are known to history; this illustrious line includes descendants who were a surveyor for the Ohio Company, the founder of Leestown on the Kentucky River, and the mother of President Zachary Taylor. John Lee, the physician, although he died before marrying at age twenty-eight, managed to build a mansion on the Potomac River, Mount Pleasant, and to serve as high sheriff and burgess from Westmoreland County.

Richard, the second child, said family biographer Burton Hendrick, was "a man thoughtful, serious, quiet, devoted to the domestic virtues, deeply loyal in his political convictions, prepared, at times, to sacrifice personal fortune for things in which believed." If Hendrick can be believed, Richard, sometimes called "the Scholar," was given to melancholy and even despair. His grandson, William, claimed that Richard's management of his inheritance was one of lost opportunities, despite the fact that his quite abundant estate was diminished in no respect. Richard, the younger, nevertheless held public office, including sitting on the Governor's Council and serving as a burgess, a naval officer, receiver of duties on the Potomac River, and colonel of the Westmoreland militia (his father had been a militia colonel as well). During Bacon's Rebellion in 1676, it was the younger Richard's fate to be labeled by Nathaniel Bacon as one of the "wicked and pernitious" culprits responsible for having "sucked up the public Treasury;" Richard was captured by Bacon, hauled a hundred miles from his home, and held for seven weeks. Bacon's Rebellion, rightly or wrongly, has been interpreted by some to presage the popular uprising that took place a hundred years later in the American War for Independence. Ironically, given the Lee family's prominent role in that rebellion, Richard Lee was firmly on the side of the established order.

The eighteenth century brought changes to Virginia—including the end of the glory of Jamestown—and to its families of Lees. Virginia was entering its golden age, and perhaps no one in the colony represented more the changes and the splendor of the age than Richard the elder's grandson, Thomas Lee, the builder of Stratford Hall. Although Paradise on the York was still in family hands—occupied by another grandson, Francis, a physician—its day was giving way to the estates that the founder had settled in the Northern Neck, especially to the one upon which Thomas built his great brick Georgian mansion. Later in the century, several of Richard Lee's descendants became prominent players in the coming Revolution against Great Britain; in the following century, the family name burned brightest in the person who commanded the Confederacy's Army of Northern Virginia, General Robert E. Lee.

Related entries: Culpeper, Lord Thomas, Second Baron of Thoresway; Northern Neck; York River

Suggestions for further reading

Burton J. Hendrick. 1935. *The Lees of Virginia: Biography of a Family.* Boston: Little, Brown.

Paul C. Nagel. 1990. *The Lees of Virginia: Seven Generations of an American Family.* New York and Oxford, England: Oxford University Press.

London Company

Joint-stock ventures were nothing new for England when the Virginia Company received its charter from James I in April 1606. Indeed, the Virginia Company was patterned after the East India Company, a private trade company chartered by Queen Elizabeth in 1600 that exercised a trade monopoly and territorial powers within the boundaries allocated to the company's investors. As the private voyages and attempts to settle English colonies in the New World undertaken by such visionaries as Sir Humphrey Gilbert and Sir Walter Raleigh, along with the corporate venture of Bartholomew Gosnold, had all ended in failure, it is no wonder that those interested in colonization would turn to the Crown for the creation of a public–private venture charged with establishing a permanent presence in America.

James granted authority for two colonies in Virginia (meaning the New World): one in Northern Virginia, to be colonized by the Plymouth Company, and one in Southern Virginia, to be settled by the London Company. The territories granted to the two companies overlapped, the northern boundary of Southern Virginia being the Hudson River and the southern boundary of Northern Virginia being the Potomac River. With restrictions on proximity (colonies had to be situated at least 100 miles apart in every direction), the joint territory ultimately would be conceded to the company that settled the most lands. Granted to the respective companies were the territories north and south of the Hudson and Potomac Rivers to the 41st and 34th parallels (unless the borders would be limited by England's enemies). Both the London and the Plymouth Companies made early attempts at settlement, in 1607. The Plymouth group settled more than 100 colonists near the mouth of the Sagadahoc (later Kennebec) River at present-day Phippsburg, Maine, where they built Fort St. George (also named Fort Sagadahoc). The colony was abandoned in 1608 after the death of its leader, George Popham, and the Plymouth Company made no further efforts to establish a foothold in the New World. The London Company was

The seal of the Virginia Company. The Virginia Company of London was founded in 1606 as a private business, intent on gaining profit by exploiting the resources of the Chesapeake region in Virginia. (North Wind Picture Archives)

more fortunate in that the colony it established at Jamestown survived its initial years.

The London Company's charter was issued to Sir Thomas Gates, Sir George Somers, Richard Hakluyt, and Edward-Maria Wingfield. Under the terms of its charter, the Crown would exercise authority over the company through a royal council in London that would set up a subordinate council to travel to and govern the colony. The company was responsible for promoting the Virginia adventure, for recruiting investors and settlers, for outfitting vessels of transportation to and from Virginia, and for administering all of the colony's financial affairs. Although the company was to become England's foremost proponent of the Virginia settlement, neither the company nor its potential emigrant settlers would actually own any of the land it settled; rather, all English-claimed lands in the New World would remain in the possession of the king. The primary goal of the company was to turn a quick profit for its investors, who included not only merchants but noblemen, knights, clerics, physicians, and other gentlemen. These investors were not as interested in seeing the virgin land settled by the immigrants that they sent over as they were in finding raw materials and setting up small manufactories for goods to be shipped back to England.

The eight months between James's granting of the charter and the launching of the expedition were busy ones for London Company investors in England. Three sailing vessels, the *Susan Constant,* the *Godspeed,* and the *Discovery,* were outfitted to make the hazardous ocean voyage to what would become Virginia; in the golden age of seafaring it was easy to engage mariners for the ships' crews. Men looking for adventure or a new life were also abundant, and more than 100 men were recruited to settle the colony. Unfortunately

Virginia

Virginia, as you have heard before, was a name at first given to all the northern part of the continent of America; and when the original grant was made, both to the first and second colonies, that is, to those of Virginia and New England, they were both granted under the name of Virginia. And afterwards, when grants for other new colonies were made by particular names, these names for a long time served only to distinguish them as so many parts of Virginia; and until the plantations became more familiar to England, it was so continued. But in process of time, the name of Virginia was lost to all except to that tract of land lying along the bay of Chesapeake, and a little to the southward, in which are included Virginia and Maryland; both which, in common discourse, are still very often meant by the name of Virginia.

The least extent of bounds in any of the grants made to Virginia, since it was settled, and which we find upon record here, is two hundred miles north from Point Comfort, and two hundred miles south, winding upon the sea coast to the eastward, and including all the land west and northwest, from sea to sea, with the islands on both seas, within an hundred miles of the main. But these extents, both on the north and south, have been since abridged by the proprietary grants of Maryland on the north, and Carolina on the south.

—Robert Beverley, *The History and Present State of Virginia* (1705)

for the company and for the settlers themselves, not many of these recruits were adequately prepared to survive life in the uncharted and formidable wilderness, much less to establish profitable commercial enterprises for their London sponsors. The first two years following the initial landing at Jamestown in May 1607 were challenging ones for the immigrants, who faced illness, starvation, and Indian raids, and the company's grip on its settlers was tenuous at best. Nevertheless, with the recruitment of investors and willing immigrants, the sailing and safe arrival of the ships, the choosing of a settlement location and the construction of a fort, and the continuing survival of some of the settlers, the London Company was well on its way toward establishing what it hoped to be a permanent and lucrative settlement in the New World.

The company expanded its power somewhat during the first two years of the colony, and in 1609 the company petitioned James for a new charter extending its territorial boundaries and conferring even more authority, replacing the royal council with a treasurer and a company council, and the local (Jamestown) council with a company-appointed governor responsible for directly governing the colony. (Lord De La Warr was appointed first governor, with Sir Thomas Gates as his deputy.) Under the new charter, the company itself would own the land it settled, and stock could be sold to both individuals and merchant guilds for the purpose of infusing more money into the Virginia venture; by June 1609, nine ships were outfitted and more than 500 additional emigrants recruited for the Jamestown settlement. (News of the colony and of life in Virginia had created a stir in England, and the London Company benefited from it by attracting many more investors—more than 650 individuals and nearly 60 companies.) Changes in the company charter and the infusion of more money and people into the colony were not enough to get the Jamestown settlement onto a sound basis, however. Calamities, especially the Starving Time in the winter of 1609–1610, left the stockholders disillusioned with Jamestown's chances of survival; yet a third royal charter was granted in March 1612, authorizing the company to become a self-governing body (at the expense of the authority of the treasurer and council). The

VIRGI
POWHATAN
Held this state & fashion when Capt. Smith was deliuered to him prisoner 1607
MONACANS
MANNAHOACKS
POWHATAN
Iames towne
Cape Henry
Cape Charles
Point comfort
PEACK BAY
KUSKARAWAOKS
Scale of Leagues
THE VIRGINIAN SEA
Discouered and Discribed by Captayn John Smith 1606
Grauen by William Hole

Map of Virginia, as described by John Smith in 1606. Smith was one of the founders of the Jamestown colony and helped ensure its survival. The map depicts Native American leader Powhatan, Chesapeake Bay, and the Potomac River. (Library of Congress)

boundaries of settlement were expanded once again, this time to include the Bermuda Islands, and a lottery was started in an attempt to ensure a more secure financial foundation for the colony. For the next decade, factions within the London Company led to internal disputes and uneven governance—reflecting the ongoing struggle for power between the king and Parliament—although the colony's government was reorganized in 1618 to allow for representative oversight, leading to the establishment of the Virginia General Assembly in 1619.

In the wake of the Indian Massacre of 1622, the London Company came under close scrutiny and criticism. In April 1623, the king was petitioned to appoint a commission to investigate how well the London Company was running the colony. Before the commission could look into the colony's affairs, a tract critical of the company's policy in Virginia was published, *The Unmasked Face of Our Colony in Virginia, as it was in the Winter of the Year 1622,* written by Captain Nathaniel Butler, the former governor of the Somers Islands, who had traveled to Virginia shortly after the Indian attack. Butler found conditions in the colony abject: The settlers were malnourished and completely demoralized; their houses were mere shanties; the businesses and plantations were unprofitable; and the people had abandoned English law. The royal commissioners began to investigate the London Company in the spring of 1623, confiscating the company's financial records and other papers and hearing witnesses from company officials as well as their detractors. The commission found the company wanting, and its initial report was negative—the company was bankrupt with no chance for recovery in sight. When the commissioners finally reached Virginia in March 1624, they, like Captain Butler, did not like what they found. The governor and General Assembly defended the company's role in running the colony, but their avowals were not enough to save the company. King Charles revoked the company's charter in May 1624. Nevertheless, by the time of the London Company's demise, the Jamestown colony had experienced its formative years, surviving the trials of the initial landing and settlement, the misery of the Starving Time of 1609–1610, the dubious introductions of tobacco and slavery into the colony, and the devastating Indian Massacre of 1622, as well as the first attempt to establish a college and the beginnings of representative government in the New World. All told, it was quite an achievement, considering that the company failed to achieve its primary goal: to turn a profit.

Related entries: General Assembly; Gosnold, Bartholomew; Sagadahoc (Popham) Colony; Smythe, Sir Thomas; Somers, Sir George; Three Ships; West, Thomas, Lord De La Warr; Wingfield, Edward-Maria

Suggestions for further reading

James Taylor Ellyson. 1908. *The London Company of Virginia: A Brief Account of its Transactions in Colonizing Virginia with Photogravures of the More Prominent Leaders . . .* New York and London: De Vinne Press.

Herbert L. Osgood. 1904. *The American Colonies in the Seventeenth Century* (vol. 3). New York: Columbia University Press.

Lost Colony

In the last quarter of the sixteenth century, England seriously began to consider establishing a presence in the New World. In late 1578, Sir Humphrey Gilbert sailed west to act on those intentions, but he was unable to reach his destination. He made another attempt in mid-1583 and succeeded in settling some men on the shores of Newfoundland. This colony lasted only a few weeks, however, and Gilbert's attempts came to a final end when he was lost at sea on his return voyage to England. Gilbert's royal patent and goal were to be taken up a few years later by his half brother, Sir Walter Raleigh, whose efforts in 1585 and 1587 would lead to one of the greatest mysteries in American history.

In 1584, Sir Walter Raleigh began a quest to become the first Englishman to establish a permanent presence in the New World for his queen. Raleigh sent Philip Amadas and Arthur Barlowe on a reconnaissance mission to America to seek a planting site for his envisioned colony. After sailing to the West Indies, they proceeded northward in search of a suitable location, arriving in the Outer Banks region of present-day North Car-

John White finds Roanoke Colony abandoned without a trace except the word "Croatoan" carved on a tree, 1591. (North Wind Picture Archives)

olina in July 1584. After sailing along the coast, they found an opening in the banks near the site of Raleigh's future settlement sites, Roanoke Island. After laying claim to the region in the name of Queen Elizabeth, a smaller boat was taken to explore the area—the water between the mainland and the Outer Banks being too shallow for the larger ships—during which time they met with the native inhabitants and established friendly relations. Two of these people, Manteo and Wanchese, returned to England with them later that year on a voyage that may have sailed into the Chesapeake Bay before turning eastward.

After considering the report from Amadas and Barlowe upon their return to England, Raleigh decided that the Outer Banks would be the future site for his colony. In April 1585, the first group of settlers—500 or 600 men and seven ships under the command of Richard Grenville and Ralph Lane, with the *Tiger* as flagship—set sail from England for Virginia once again, along with Manteo and Wanchese. After sailing through the Caribbean on their way and establishing a brief base in Puerto Rico, the expedition reached the Outer Banks in June. In July, they landed at Roanoke Island and began preparations to establish their colony, with Grenville leaving in August to return to England for supplies. Lane was left in charge as governor of the colony of about 107 men, including John White to map and to record in watercolors and sketches their findings on the flora and fauna, Thomas Hariot as naturalist and scientist for the expedition, and Joachim Ganz to conduct metals and minerals tests.

Part of the settlement's mission was to serve as a military outpost and base for privateering against the Spanish, who had become established in the southern part of the region. As a result, most of the colonists were men of military background, including Ralph Lane. This was useful for dealing with the Spanish threat, but when considering the necessity of producing crops for survival and establishing good relations with the native inhabitants, these men were not well prepared.

Indeed, as relations worsened with the indigenous people because of attempts to extract food and concessions from them, tensions escalated until Lane, fearing an attack from the Roanokes, led an attack against them, killing and beheading their leader, Wingina (Pemisapan). Lane's short-sighted actions during this first attempt at settlement on Roanoke Island were to have serious repercussions for the English presence there.

During the eleven months that Raleigh's first colony remained on Roanoke Island, a fort and some structures were built, and explorations were carried out in the surrounding waters and land, including expeditions up the Chowan and Moratuc (Roanoke) Rivers and in the Albemarle Sound. A hoard of rich information was collected and recorded, especially by John White and Thomas Hariot. During this time, Sir Richard Grenville was in England gathering supplies and preparing for his return trip to the new colony. Grenville finally set sail for Roanoke Island in the spring of 1586 with the intention of resupplying Lane's group. Meanwhile, conditions had worsened for the struggling colony, and by the time Sir Francis Drake arrived in June (after spending time raiding Spanish outposts in the Caribbean and nearly destroying their settlement in St. Augustine, Florida), Lane and his men were ready to abandon the colony altogether and return home. After weathering a hurricane, in which Drake lost some of his smaller ships, in mid-June Drake left and returned to England with Lane, the other colonists, and the Indian Manteo. Not long after their departure, a supply ship arrived; finding none of the first colonists, it returned to England. Sometime in July or August, Grenville arrived with fresh supplies and men, only to find the settlement abandoned. With the intention of keeping an English presence in Virginia (as it became known, in honor of Queen Elizabeth I, the Virgin Queen), Grenville left about fifteen men with ample supplies and once again set sail for England. Local Indians soon attacked the men left behind on the island, no doubt wanting to settle scores for Lane's misguided attacks against them. Some of the Englishmen were killed, and the rest fled by boat to an as-yet-unknown ending.

Although the first attempt to settle Roanoke Island had ended without success, Raleigh was anxious to try again. This time, however, his plan was to make a more natural and sustainable settlement, one that included families and that was based on self-sufficiency rather than on reliance on the native inhabitants to supply food and labor. The goal was to plant this colony in the Chesapeake Bay area, stopping only briefly at the Roanoke Island settlement to resupply and check on the men left there by Grenville the preceding year. With John White as their governor and Manteo ready to return from his second visit to England, a group of about 115 men, women, and children left for the venture in May 1587. After several stops in the Caribbean and Puerto Rico, they made their way northward to establish their "Cittie of Ralegh," with each settler anticipating starting life anew on the promised 500 acres of land. But after their ships weighed anchor near Roanoke Island in July, the expedition's Portuguese pilot, a sometime privateer by the name of Fernandez, was anxious to continue his other, more profitable activities. He set the colonists ashore and left them at Roanoke Island instead of taking them to their intended destination on the Chesapeake Bay. The colonists made their way to the seat of the first attempt at Lane's fort and the few buildings on the northern end of the Island. The settlement was in much disrepair because of its abandonment and Indian reprisals, yet the colonists began the arduous task of rebuilding and expanding what remained.

Time and distance between the English and indigenous peoples had not led to much improvement in their relations. Hostility between the groups existed still, and the Indians killed one of the colonists not long after their return. With Manteo's help, Governor White attempted to make amends to those groups closest to the settlement so that the business of building the colony could proceed. A parley was arranged in which differences were to be discussed and an attempt made to ease tensions. The meeting never took place, however, and White soon ordered an attack against an (unbeknownst to him) innocent group of Indians in retaliation for the killing of the colonist. Although Manteo's intervention kept the incident from getting any further out of hand at the time, the English colonists were experiencing a somewhat inauspicious beginning to their venture.

John White's Account of the Lost Colony

The 15 of August [1590] towards Evening we came to an anker at Hatorask, in 36 degr. and one third, in five fadom water, three leagues from the shore. At our first comming to anker on this shore we saw a great smoke rise in the Ile Roanoak neere the place where I left our Colony in the yeere 1587, which smoake put us in good hope that some of the Colony were there expecting my returne out of England.

The 16 and next morning our 2 boates went a shore, and Captaine Cooke, and Cap. Spicer, and their company with me, with intent to passe to the place at Roanoak where our countreymen were left. At our putting from the ship we commanded our Master gunner to make readie 2 Minions and a Falkon well loden, and to shoot them off with reasonable space betweene every shot, to the ende that their reportes might bee heard to the place where wee hoped to finde some of our people. This was accordingly performed, and our twoe boats put off unto the shore, in the Admirals boat we sounded all the way and found from our shippe untill we came within a mile of the shore nine, eight, and seven fadome: but before we were halfe way betweene our ships and the shore we saw another great smoke to the Southwest of Kindrikers mountes: we therefore thought good to goe to that second smoke first: but it was much further from the harbour where we landed, then we supposed it to be, so that we were very sore tired before wee came to the smoke. But that which grieved us more was that when we came to the smoke, we found no man nor signe that any had bene there lately, nor yet any fresh water in all this waye to drinke. Being thus wearied with this journey we returned to the harbour where we left our boates, who in our absence had brought their caske a shore for fresh water, so we deferred our going to Roanoak untill the next morning, and caused some of those saylers to digge in those sandie hills for fresh water whereof we found very sufficient. That night wee returned aboord with our boates and our whole company in safety.

The next morning being the 17 of August, our boates and company were prepared againe to goe up to Roanoak, but Captaine Spicer had then sent his boat ashore for fresh water, by meanes whereof it was ten of the clocke afternoone before we put from our ships which were then come to an anker within two miles of the shore. The Admirals boat was halfe way toward the shore, when Captaine Spicer put off from his ship. The Admirals boat first passed the breach, but not without some danger of sinking, for we had a sea brake into our boat which filled us halfe full of water, but by the will of God and carefull styrage of Captaine Cooke we came safe ashore, saving onely that our furniture, victuals, match and powder were much wet and spoyled. For at this time the winde blue at Northeast and direct into the harbour so great a gale, that the Sea brake extremely on the barre, and the tide went very forcibly at the entrance. By that time our Admirals boat was halled ashore, and most of our things taken out to dry, Captaine Spicer came to the entrance of the breach with his mast standing up, and was halfe passed over, but by the rash and undiscreet styrage of Ralph Skinner his Masters mate, a very dangerous Sea brake into their boate and overset them quite, the men kept the boat some in it, and some hanging on it, but the next sea set the boat on ground, where it beat so, that some of them were forced to let goe their hold, hoping to wade ashore: but the Sea still beat them downe, so that they could neither stand nor swimme, and the boat twise or thrise was turned the keele upward, whereon Captaine Spicer and Skinner hung untill they sunke, and were seene no more. But foure that could swimme a litle kept themselves in deeper water and were saved by Captaine Cookes meanes, who so soone as he saw their oversetting, stripped himselfe, and foure other that could swimme very well, and with all haste possible rowed unto them, and saved foure. There were 11 in all and 7 of the chiefest were drowned, whose names were Edward Spicer, Ralph Skinner, Edward Kelly, Thomas Bevis, Hance the Surgion, Edward Kelborne, Robert Coleman. This mischance did so much discomfort the saylers, that they were all of one mind not to goe any further to seeke the planters. But in the end by the commandement and perswasion of me and Captaine Cooke, they prepared the boates: and seeing the Captaine and me so resolute, they seemed much more

(*continued on next page*)

John White's Account of the Lost Colony, continued

willing. Our boates and all things fitted againe, we put off from Hatorask, being the number of 19 persons in both boates: but before we could get to the place where our planters were left, it was so exceeding darke, that we overshot the place a quarter of a mile: there we espied towards the North ende of the Island the light of a great fire thorow the woods, to which we presently rowed: when wee came right over against it, we let fall our Grapnel neere the shore and sounded with a trumpet a Call, and afterwardes many familiar English tunes of Songs, and called to them friendly; but we had no answere, we therefore landed at day-breake, and comming to the fire, we found the grasse and sundry rotten trees burning about the place. From hence we went thorow the woods to that part of the Iland directly over against Dasamongwepeuk, and from thence we returned by the water side, round about the North point of the Iland, untill we came to the place where I left our Colony in the yeere 1586. In all this way we saw in the sand the print of the Salvages feet of 2 or 3 sorts troaden the night, and as we entred up the sandy banke upon a tree, in the very browe thereof were curiously carved these faire Romane letters CRO: which letters presently we knew to signifie the place, where I should find the planters seated, according to a secret token agreed upon betweene them & me at my last departure from them, which was, that in any wayes they should not faile to write or carve on the trees or posts of the dores the name of the place where they should be seated; for at my comming away they were prepared to remove from Roanoak 50 miles into the maine. Therefore at my departure from them in An. 1587 I willed them, that if they should happen to be distressed in any of those places, that then they should carve over the letters or name, a Crosse + in this forme, but we found no such signe of distresse. And having well considered of this, we passed toward the place where they were left in sundry houses, but we found the houses taken downe, and the place very strongly enclosed with a high palisado of great trees, with cortynes and flankers very Fort-like, and one of the chiefe trees or postes at the right side of the entrance had the barke taken off, and 5 foote from the ground in fayre Capitall letters was graven CROATOAN without any crosse or signe of distresse; this done, we entred into the palisado, where we found many barres of iron, two pigges of Lead, foure yron fowlers, Iron sacker-shotte, and such like heavie thinges, throwen here and there, almost overgrowen with grasse and weedes. From thence wee went along by the water side, towards the poynt of the Creeke to see if we could find any of their botes or Pinnisse, but we could perceive no signe of them, nor any of the last Falkons and small Ordinance which were left with them, at my departure from them. At our returne from the Creeke, some of our Saylers meeting us, told us that they had found where divers chests had bene hidden, and long sithence digged up againe and broken up, and much of the goods in them spoyled and scattered about, but nothing left, of such things as the Savages knew any use of, undefaced. Presently Captaine Cooke and I went to the place, which was in the ende of an olde trench, made two yeeres past by Captaine Amadas: wheere wee found five Chests, that had bene carefully hidden of the Planters, and of the same chests three were my owne, and about the place many of my things spoyled and broken, and my bookes torne from the covers, the frames of some of my pictures and Mappes rotten and spoyled with rayne, and my armour almost eaten through with rust; this could bee no other but the deede of the Savages our enemies at Dasamongwepeuk, who had watched the departure of our men to Croatoan; and assoone as they were departed digged up every place where they suspected any thing to be buried: but although it much grieved me to see such spoyle of my goods, yet on the other side I greatly joyed that I had safely found a certaine token of their safe being at Croatoan, which is the place where Manteo was borne, and the Savages of the Iland our friends.

—From White's account of his fifth voyage to the New World, 1590, written to Richard Hakluyt

Despite the hardship and disappointment, in the colonists' view there were some positive developments. Manteo, who had been their faithful guide, interpreter, and ambassador to the indigenous peoples, was baptized on 13 August 1587 and made "Lord of Roanoke." Shortly after these events, on 18 August, Virginia Dare, the first English child born in America, was delivered to White's daughter, Eleanor, and her husband, Ananias Dare. But because of inadequate supplies and the generally hostile environment in which they found themselves, the colonists soon became desperate to alleviate the pressures they were facing. It was decided that John White should return to England for supplies, and he did so, leaving on 27 August.

What happened to Raleigh's second colony after White's departure is as yet unknown, despite centuries of investigation. When White reached England, open hostilities with Spain appeared imminent and, despite great efforts by both White and Raleigh, no English supply or relief ships reached Roanoke Island again until August 1590, a full three years after White had left the settlement for England. It is interesting to speculate what might have been the outcome had White's April 1588 attempt to reach the colony been successful, but that can never be known. He set sail with two small vessels and supplies, but larger French ships attacked and looted his vessels, and he was forced to return to England without making his way to Virginia.

John White finally made a successful return to Roanoke Island in August 1590. He had hopes of finding the colony somehow surviving, along with his daughter and granddaughter, but to no avail. All were gone except the remnants of the settlement structures and gear, and a few personal items scattered about. As White later related about his search for the colonists,

> as we entred up the sandy banke upon a tree, in the very browe thereof were curiously carved these faire Romane letters CRO: which letters presently we knew to signifie the place, where I should find the planters seated, according to a secret token agreed upon betweene them & me at my last departure from them, which was, that in any wayes they should not faile to write or carve on the trees or posts of the dores the name of the place where they should be seated . . . [and] if they should happen to be distressed in any of those places, that then they should carve over the letters or name, a Crosse . . . but we found no such signe of distresse. And having well considered of this, we passed toward the place where they were left in sundry houses, but we found the houses taken downe, and the place very strongly enclosed with a high palisodo of great trees . . . very Fort-like, and one of the chiefe trees or postes at the right side of the entrance had the barke taken off, and 5 foote from the ground in fayre Capitall letters was graven CROATOAN without any crosse or signe of distresse.

Finding the colony abandoned, and mindful of the agreed-upon method of indicating where the colonists would have gone if abandonment became necessary, White had every intention of sailing to Croatoan, which was Manteo's homeland, at the time an island composed of part of present-day Hatteras and Ocracoke Islands, in search of the missing settlers. But weather and other priorities (mainly privateering) of the crew of the ship on which he had arrived prevented his reaching the island. Once again, he sailed back to England, and he never returned to Virginia.

What became of the "Lost Colonists" is a mystery to this day. There have been many theories, one of the most interesting being that at least some of the colonists may have moved northward to a friendly Native American tribe living on or near the Chesapeake Bay, only to be massacred along with those people by Powhatan's warriors shortly before, or coincident with, the arrival of the Jamestown colonists in 1607. Others speculate that the surviving settlers did indeed move to Croatoan with Manteo and finished their days there. Considering the hostile conditions in which they found themselves, perhaps their actual fate was what many have assumed: they all starved or were killed by local tribes who still held the English in contempt as a result of Ralph Lane's hostile actions against the indigenous people he encountered. The answer probably will never be known. What is certain, however, is that their bold and courageous attempts to establish a permanent presence for England in America produced a wealth of information still fascinating to this day, and the groundwork they laid became, some twenty years later at Jamestown, the base upon which the promise of the New World became reality.

Related entries: Early European Exploration of the North America; Gosnold, Bartholomew; Kecoughtan Indians; Newport, Sir Christopher; Raleigh, Sir Walter; White, John

Suggestions for further reading

Michael Golay and John S. Bowman. 2003. *North American Exploration.* Hoboken, NJ: John Wiley.

Karen Ordahl Kupperman. 1984. *Roanoke: The Abandoned Colony.* Totowa, NJ: Rowman & Littlefield.

Lee Miller. 2002. *Roanoke: Solving the Mystery of the Lost Colony.* New York: Penguin Books.

Samuel Eliot Morison. 1971. *The European Discovery of America: The Northern Voyages A.D. 500–1600.* New York: Oxford University Press.

David Beers Quinn. 1985. *Set Faire for Roanoke: Voyages and Colonies, 1584–1606.* Chapel Hill and London: University of North Carolina Press.

David Stick. 1983. *Roanoke Island: The Beginnings of English America.* Chapel Hill: University of North Carolina Press.

Ludwell, Lady Frances Culpeper Berkeley

See Berkeley, Lady Frances Culpeper

Ludwell, Philip

See Berkeley, Lady Frances Culpeper

M

Manahoac Indians

A confederation of about a dozen nomadic, Siouan-speaking Native American tribes in Piedmont, Virginia, are known by the name Manahoac, dubiously translated into English in the nineteenth century as "the very merry." Living in the region bordered by the falls of the rivers to the east, the mountains to the west, the Potomac River to the north, and the North Anna River to the south, the Manahoac tribal names that have come down through history coalesced mostly near the Rappahannock and Rapidan Rivers in the present-day counties of Culpeper, Fauquier, Orange, Spotsylvania, and Stafford. In addition to the Manahoac tribe proper, sometimes shortened to Mahoc, the peoples included the Stegaraki, the Ontponea, the Shackaconia, the Tanxnitania, the Whonkentia, the Tegninateo, and the Hassinunga. Estimates of the total Manahoac population range from about 500 up to 1,500. The Manahoac culture centered on the buffalo, plentiful in the Virginia Piedmont, and in fact their ancestors are thought to have come into the area by following great herds of migrating buffalo from the Ohio River Valley. The Manahoac tribe was closely allied with two other Siouan peoples, the Monacan and the Tuscarora, against the Algonquin nations of Powhatan's empire to the east and south and the Iroquois to the west.

Although the Manahoac followed the buffalo, few, if any, of the tribes subsisted solely on hunting, fishing, and the gathering of fruits and nuts; like other native peoples, they practiced agriculture as well. The Manahoac had few permanently settled towns or villages, and in fact the European colonists apparently never visited a Manahoac village. Captain John Smith set out for Manahoac territory in 1608 but got no farther than the outer edges of their region when warriors from a Manahoac fishing camp on the Rappahannock River attacked his party of explorers. The conflict resulted in casualties, including that of a Manahoac combatant who was taken prisoner and interrogated by the English. The colonists prevailed upon the wounded warrior to serve as an intermediary between the adversaries and establish a truce. A feast followed, during which Smith was able to learn something about the Manahoac tribes and their villages, but with that the expedition ended, and the English turned back without having visited a Manahoac settlement. After meeting Smith, the Manahoac had little other contact with the Europeans who would settle and conquer the New World.

By mid-century, the Manahoac had retreated farther from English-occupied territory because they were squeezed by the Iroquoian Susquehanna and the Algonquian Powhatan (who were themselves squeezed by the expanding English). Some Manahoac apparently joined with their

Manahoac Confederacy: Enemies of Powhatan

West of the fall line in the Virginia Piedmont, to the mountains and between the Potomac and North Anna Rivers, lived an Indian people who at the time of the settling of the English were enemies of the Powhatans—the Manahoacs. The Manahoacs were not only a tribe but also a confederacy that included the clans of the Hassinunga, Ontponea, Shackaconia, Stegaraki, Tanxnitania, Tegninateo, and Whonkentia. Allied with other tribes of the Siouan language group, including the Monacans and the Tuscaroras, against the Algonquians, of whom the Powhatan Confederacy was the most powerful, the tribes of the Manahoac Confederacy embraced the geographical areas of Manahoac proper (Stafford and Spottsylvania Counties) as well as the counties of Fauquier, Culpeper, and Orange. Like their enemy the Powhatans, the Manahoac people cultivated crops, gathered fruit, nuts, and vegetables, and hunted and fished. The Manahoacs apparently lived in the Ohio Valley before being forced east and south by the tribes of the Susquehanna, and most of the tribes of the confederacy were forced out of the Virginia Piedmont around 1650, when the Iroquois claimed their lands for hunting grounds. Warfare and disease took a terrible toll on the Manahoac; the people had largely disappeared altogether by 1667, although some apparently joined up with other tribes, including the Monacans to the south. The English settlers never visited a Manahoac village, and the explorer John Lederer, who crossed the Rappahannock River on his way to the Blue Ridge Mountains in 1669–1670, did not find the one identified by Captain John Smith. It has been said that the name Manahoac means "very merry," but no evidence has been found to substantiate it.

Monacan allies, and many may have migrated south and west to unite with the Saponi and the Occoneechee. In either case, they left behind few traces of their long occupation of the Piedmont other than artifacts that occasionally turn up at their former river camps. In fact, only one name of a Manahoac town has even come down to us: Mahaskahod, a village on the Rappahannock River near Fredericksburg. Others may have borne the names of the tribes of the confederacy.

Related entries: Accohannock Indians; Accomac Indians; Chesapeake Indians; Chickahominy Indians; Kecoughtan Indians; Monacan Indians; Mattaponi Indians; Nansemond Indians; Pamunkey Indians; Paspahegh Indians; Rappahannock River; Smith, Captain John; Warraskoyak Indians

Suggestion for further reading

David I. Bushnell. 1935. *The Manahoac Tribes in Virginia, 1608.* Washington, DC: Smithsonian Institution.

Martin's Hundred

Even after nearly 400 years, the origins of Martin's Hundred are clouded in obscurity. A private or "particular" plantation made possible by reforms instituted at the end of colonial Jamestown's first decade, Martin's Hundred consisted of 20,000 acres of land sold to investors at 100 acres per share. The largest of Jamestown's particular plantations, it was situated on the northern banks of the James River about 6 miles south of Jamestown and included within its perimeter a settlement of Kiskiack Indians. The investors' company, the Martin's Hundred Society (mostly London businessmen), apparently formed in 1617, was charged with the recruitment of settlers—both men and women—and the administration of the Hundred. The society and the Hundred bore the name of Martin apparently in honor of a principle promoter or shareholder in England, possibly Sir Richard Martin (1534–

1617), master of the mint under Elizabeth I and James I. Martin's Hundred was populated by 72 people (45 men, 14 women, and 13 children) at the time of the March 1619 census of Virginia, but evidence linking those settlers to the society has yet to be discovered.

The first colonists known to have been associated legitimately with Martin's Hundred were 220 men and women recruited in England who arrived in Virginia (minus 14 who died en route) aboard the *Guift of God,* a vessel owned by the society, in April 1619 after a 3-month voyage from London. Once at Jamestown, however, these settlers—for reasons unknown—failed to settle at Martin's Hundred but instead began clearing land and growing crops on ground that had been allotted to the colony's governor, Samuel Argall. More than a year passed before any of the 1619 immigrants were allowed to settle at Martin's Hundred. The Hundred's leader, John Boyse, who along with one John Jackson served as bailiffs or wardens for the Hundred and represented the Hundred to the General Assembly, oversaw the erection of a palisades fort at the settlement's town, which was named for Sir John Wolstenholme, one of the society's large shareholders. A maverick, Boyse also elected to live apart from the other colonists and built his own fort on the James a few miles from Wolstenholme Town.

Meanwhile, in August 1620, William Harwood, Martin's Hundred's future leader and the most "dominant figure" of its history, arrived at Jamestown on board the *Francis Bonaventure.* Inexplicably, Harwood, who was styled "governor" of the Hundred, was himself waylaid at Jamestown for a year before stepping into his leadership role at the Hundred. Perhaps he was waiting for instructions from the society that arrived at Jamestown in June 1621 and of which no record exists. In any event, Harwood's tireless efforts on behalf of Martin's Hundred throughout most of the 1620s were of the sort that prevented him from engaging in other business, including attending the meetings of the Governor's Council, to which he had been appointed before his arrival in Virginia. (Harwood apparently took care of his own interests, however, causing one resident to complain that "Mr Harwood wil have half of what little we do get.")

According to surviving records, about 280 colonists were sent from England to Martin's Hundred between 1618 and 1621. However, only about 140 people were living at the Hundred when the most important event of its history took place, the Indian Massacre of 1622. Between 58 and 118 settlers were killed—the highest number of casualties in the colony—the latter figure apparently including deaths that occurred at some smaller farms or settlements away from Martin's Hundred proper. In addition, the only settlers taken prisoner during the massacre, about 15 women and 5 men, were taken from Martin's Hundred and held as hostages. (The men were soon killed, but the women were held in servitude and used in peace and trade negotiations between 1624 and 1630.) The precariousness of life in early seventeenth-century Virginia, combined with some settlers working (either willingly or unwillingly) at other plantations, had kept down the population of Martin's Hundred; otherwise the number of settlers slain by the Indians probably would have been even higher. Governor Harwood survived the great Indian massacre, but he did not take part in the effort afterward to defend Martin's Hundred or to punish the Indians—despite the fact that Harwood was the only person in the Hundred who owned a piece of ordnance. That task fell to Captain Ralph Hamor, a sometime rival of Harwood, who evacuated the survivors before leading counterattacks against the Indians. (Harwood may have been in London on society business, for his name does not appear in any of the surviving records for the period.)

The Massacre of 1622 all but destroyed Martin's Hundred, and those settlers who attempted to carry on—without adequate provisions, shelter, clothing, or support from the other colonists—were paralyzed with fear. It was during the aftermath of the massacre that Harwood emerged as the leader at Martin's Hundred and served in that capacity until his death in 1629. Even so, rebuilding was painfully slow, and the Hundred failed to prosper. The society recruited and sent over more new settlers, but those who managed to survive and prosper were outnumbered by those who died during the passage or in the first few months after their arrival; the total number of settlers at Martin's Hundred did not surpass the number of pre-massacre settlers until long after the Hundred ceased to exist as a particular plantation. By the mid-1630s, Martin's Hundred had lost its distinction as a landed unit and was no longer sending representatives to the General Assembly. Its mother, the Martin's Hundred Society, had dissolved, and its acreage was broken into numerous tracts for small farmers; Wolstenholme Town was completely abandoned. Over time, even the name Martin's Hundred became distorted, to Merchant's Hundred. By the time it came into the possession of Robert King Carter, in 1722, most of the Hundred's history had been long forgotten—it is not even known from whom Carter acquired the property. Yet, Martin's Hundred's glory days as a plantation were still to come, for Carter's Grove (as it was renamed) became perhaps the most important of Virginia's tobacco estates and the home of one of the finest mansions in America (built by Carter's grandson, Carter Burwell, between 1750 and 1755).

In the 1970s, Martin's Hundred was the subject of some of the most extensive and remarkable archaeology excavations ever undertaken in the United States, led by archaeologists Ivor Noël Hume and his wife Audrey Noël Hume and funded in part by the National Geographic Society. The team not only identified and uncovered Wolstenholme Town (c.1620–1622) but made a stunning discovery: a hitherto-unknown company compound and military fort—a trapezoidal palisade fort about 93 feet by 130 feet. Other buildings at Wolstenholme Town included a church (not yet discovered), a barn or storehouse, and several small houses and sheds. Also identified during the excavations were the Boyse Homestead (c.1619–1622); the Jackson/Ward site (c.1623–1640), consisting of a dwelling and a large drying shed for pottery; the Harwood Plantation (c.1623–1645), described by the Noël Humes as Martin's Hundred's "most varied and extensive complex," which included three dwellings, a store (apparently for the Martin's Hundred Society), and a half-dozen other buildings. Relics uncovered at the various sites include body armor (helmets, gorget, and coat of mail), a gun barrel, musket firing mechanisms, and daggers; a shackle padlock, horseshoes and a stirrup, an iron key, a brass thimble, and a cleaver; coins, tobacco pipes, buttons, shoes, bale seals, table knives, spoons, scissors, fire tongs, nails, and tools; imported jars, window glass, and large amounts of locally made pottery. And finally, an unusually large number (40) of human graves were discovered and opened. Twenty-three buried in proximity had been interred "at different times and with differing degrees of deference"; some were victims of the Indian Massacre of 1622, the event that forever hung its shadow on Martin's Hundred.

Related entry: Massacre of 1622

Suggestions for further reading

Ivor Noël Hume. 1982. *Martin's Hundred.* New York: Alfred A. Knopf.

—— and Audrey Noël Hume. 2001. *The Archaeology of Martin's Hundred.* 2 vols. Philadelphia and Williamsburg, VA: University of Pennsylvania Museum of Archaeology and Anthropology.

Mary A. Stephenson. 1964. *Carter's Grove Plantation: A History.* Williamsburg, VA: Colonial Williamsburg Foundation.

Massacre of 1622

On the morning of 22 March 1622, colonists and Indians all along the James River were intermingling and carrying on their business together as they had been for quite some time. Some were having breakfast, others working in the fields or bartering for goods and services. Then, with a swiftness and fierceness so intense that many of the settlers never knew they were breathing their last breath, the Indians seized whatever weapons they could find, from swords and firearms to hoes and cooking utensils, and killed possibly as many as one quarter to one third of the European colonists. What had taken the settlers fifteen years to build was nearly wiped out within minutes.

One reason the attack was so effective and such a complete surprise to the Europeans was

Opechancanough's warriors attack settlers at Jamestown on 22 March 1622 in this engraving by Matthaeus Merian. (de Bry's, America, *Frankfurt, Germany, 1628)*

that their interpretation and pursuit of prosperity in the New World meant something entirely different to their indigenous neighbors. Where the settlers saw the opportunity for the growth of their wealth and community, the Native Americans saw continued encroachment on their lands and culture. They came to realize that speed and ferocity were of the essence if they were to have any chance of at least halting, if not recouping, losses of land and liberty they had enjoyed before the arrival of the English. Opechancanough, who, along with his half brother Opitchapam, had assumed control of Powhatan's empire after his death, had been planning for years to end the growing European presence in his territory. On one "fatal day"—another typical Friday morning to most of the colonists—he put his nearly perfect plan into action.

As related in the official account of the attack written by Edward Waterhouse, secretary to the Virginia Company in London at the time, when Sir Francis Wyatt arrived in Virginia as governor in November 1621,

> [H]e found the Country setled in a peace (as all men there thought) sure and unviolable, not onely because it was solemnly ratified and sworne, and at the request of the Native King [Opechancanough] stamped in Brasse, and fixed to one of his Oakes of note, but as being advantagious to both parts; to the Savages as the weaker, under which they were safely sheltred and defended; to us, as being the easiest way then thought to pursue and advance our projects of buildings, plantings, and effecting their [the Indians] conversion [to Christianity] by peaceable and fayre meanes.

Indeed, the colonists had become dangerously inattentive to their security. As Waterhouse writes,

> [S]uch was the conceit of firme peace and amitie, as that there was seldome or never a sword worne, and a Peece [firearm] seldomer, except for a Deere or Fowle. . . . The Plantations of particular Adventurers and Planters were placed scatteringly and straglingly as a choyce veyne of rich ground invited them, and the further from neighbors held the better. The houses generally set open to the Savages, who were alwaies friendly entertained at the tables of the English, and commonly lodged in their bed-chambers.

To gain greater assurance of the peace between the two groups, a messenger was sent to Opechancanough just days before the planned attack; he returned with the statement of the Indian leader "that he held the peace concluded so firme, as the Skie should sooner fall then it dissolve." But Opechancanough's message was intended only as a disguise for his real intentions. As Waterhouse relates,

> yea, such was the treacherous dissimulation of that people who then had contrived our destruction, that even two dayes before the Masssacre, some of our men were guided thorow the woods by them in safety: and one Browne, who then to learne the language lived among the Warrascoyacks (a Province of that King) was in friendly manner sent backe by them to Captaine Hamor his Master, and many the like passages, rather increasing our former confidence, then any wise in the world ministring the least suspition of the breach of the peace, or of what instantly ensued; yea, they borrowed our owne Boates to convey themselves crosse the River (on the bankes of both sides whereof all our Plantations were) to consult of the divellish murder that ensued, and of our utter extirpation, which God of his mercy (by the meanes of some of themselves converted to Christianitie) prevented.

Opechancanough's protestations of peace long had masked his true intention of removing what he saw as the virulent infestation of the English pestilence. The previous summer, he had planned an attack to exterminate the colonists through the use of a poison potion made from a plant that grows mainly on the Eastern Shore. He sent a messenger to one of the Indian leaders there asking for enough of the material to carry out his scheme. The plot was foiled, however, when the leader contacted reported the incident to the English, and Opechancanough was forced to deny his plans and wait a few more months for the colonists to once again let down their guard.

What may have prompted the next attempt the following March was the death of one of the main plotters against the English, Nemattanew, also known as Jack-of-the-Feathers because of his preference for wearing "feathers and Swans wings fastened unto his showlders as thowghte he meante to flye" when he appeared on the battlefield. According to the account of John Smith (who was not in Virginia at the time), around two weeks before the attack, Nemattanew had gone to the house of a colonist named Morgan because "he had many commodities that hee [Nemattanew] desired." With the apparent intention of luring Morgan to his death in order to possess those "commodities," Nemattanew

> perswaded Morgan to goe with him to Pamaunke to trucke [trade], but the Salvage murdered him by the way; and after two or three daies returned againe to Morgans house, where he found two youths his Servants, who asked for their Master: Jack replied directly he was dead; the Boyes suspecting as it was, by seeing him weare his [Morgan's] Cap would have had him to Master Thorp: But Jack so moved their patience, they shot him.

There is some dispute as to the immediate cause of the March 1622 attack and even as to the exact time of Nemattanew's death, but the details and results of the events soon became well known throughout Virginia and England.

As Waterhouse related it,

> on the Friday morning (the fatal day) the 22 of March, as also in the evening, as in other dayes before, they came unarmed into our houses, without Bowes or arrowes, or other weapons, with Deere, Turkies, Fish, Furres, and other provisions, to sell and trucke with us, for glasse, beades, and other trifles: yea in some places sate downe at Breakfast with our people at their tables.

But the morning soon became nothing like "other dayes before" because in an instant,

> with their owne [the colonists'] tooles and weapons, eyther laid downe, or standing in

> their houses, they basely and barbarously murthered, not sparing eyther age or sexe, man, woman or childe; so sodaine in their cruell execution, that few or none discerned the weapon or blow that brought them to destruction. In which manner they also slew many of our people then at their severall workes and husbandries in the fields, and without their houses, some in planting Corne and Tobacco, some in gardening, some in making Bricke, building, sawing, and other kindes of husbandry, they well knowing in what places and quarters each of our men were, in regard of their daily familiarity, and resort to us for trading and other negotiations, which the more willingly was by us continued and cherished for the desire we had of effecting that great master-peece of workes, their conversions.

The Indians' resentment of the colonists had built to such a degree that just killing them was not enough:

> Not being content with taking away life alone, they fell after againe upon the dead, making as well as they could, a fresh murder, defacing, dragging, and mangling the dead carkasses into many pieces, and carrying some parts away in derision, with base and bruitish triumph.

Although the true number is not known, by the reckoning of the survivors, as many as 347 colonists perished during the attacks.

Whether it was the increasing pressure of continued English encroachment, the death of Nemattanew, or, as John Smith testified when asked by a commission for the reformation of Virginia what he thought had been the cause of the so-called massacre—"the want of marshall discipline, and because they would have all the English had by destroying those they found so carelesly secure, that they were not provided to defend themselves against any enemy, being so dispersed as they were"—no doubt a combination of these and many other reasons, some saw the attack as an excuse to remove all semblance of civility towards the indigenous populations and commence a full-scale expropriation of the best land which, until that time, had been held mainly by the Indians. As Waterhouse states ominously in his report,

> Thus have you seene the particulars of this massacre, out of Letters from thence written, wherein treachery and cruelty have done their worst to us, or rather to themselves; for whose understanding is so shallow, as not to perceive that this must needs bee for the good of the Plantation after, and the losse of this blood to make the body more healthfull.

He then proceeds to explain what is meant by his thought:

> First, Because betraying of innocency never rests unpunished: And therefore Agesilaus, when his enemies (upon whose oath of being faithfull hee rested) had deceived him, he sent them thankes, for that by their periury, they had made God his friend, and their enemy.
>
> Secondly, Because our hands which before were tied with gentlenesse and faire usage, are now set at liberty by the treacherous violence of the Savages, not untying the Knot, but cutting it: So that we, who hitherto have had possession of no more ground then their waste . . . may now by right of Warre, and law of Nations, invade the Country, and destroy them who sought to destroy us: whereby wee shall enjoy their cultivated places . . . and possessing the fruits of others labours. Now their cleared grounds in all their villages (which are situate in the fruitfullest places of the land) shall be inhabited by us, whereas heretofore the grubbing of woods was the greatest labour.
>
> Thirdly, Because those commodities which the Indians enjoyed as much or rather more than

A Narrow Escape

I had almost forgott, That all our peoople in Virginia in all places should on March 22 at 8 in the morning, under pretence of freindship have bin murthered by the Natives; & had bin, had not an Indian boy the night before discovered it to his Master, who all night sent about to give notice.

—Unknown Correspondent
to the Reverend Joseph Meade,
London, 12 July 1622

we, shall now also be entirely possessed by us. The Deere and other beasts will be in safety, and infinitly increase, which heretofore not onely in the generall huntings of the King (whereat foure or five hundred Deere were usually slaine) but by each particular Indian were destroied at all times of the yeare, without any difference of Male, Damme, or Young. The like may be said of our owne Swine and Goats, whereof they have used to kill eight in tenne more than the English have done. There will be also a great increase of wild Turkies, and other waighty Fowle, for the Indians never put difference of destroying the Hen, but kill them whether in season or not, whether in breeding time, or sitting on their egges, or having new hatched, it is all one to them: whereby, as also by the orderly using of their fishing Weares, no knowne Country in the world will so plentifully abound in victuall.

Fourthly, Because the way of conquering them is much more easie then of civilizing them by faire meanes, for they are a rude, barbarous, and naked people, scattered in small companies, which are helps to Victorie, but hinderances to Civilitie: Besides that, a conquest may be of many, and at once; but civility is in particular, and slow, the effect of long time, and great industry. Moreover, victorie of them may bee gained many waies; by force, by surprize, by famine in burning their Corne, by destroying and burning their Boats, Canoes, and Houses, by breaking their fishing Weares, by assailing them in their huntings, whereby they get the greatest part of their sustenance in Winter, by pursuing and chasing them with our horses, and blood-Hounds to draw after them, and Mastives to teare them, which take this naked, tanned, deformed Savages, for no other then wild beasts, and are so fierce and fell upon them, that they feare them worse then their old Devill which they worship, supposing them to be a new and worse kinde of Devils then their owne. By these and sundry other wayes, as by driving them (when they flye) upon their enemies, who are round about them, and by animating and abetting their enemies against them, may their ruine or subjection be soone effected. . . . In VIRGINIA the many divers Princes and people there are at this day opposite in infinite factions one unto another, and many of them beare a mortall hatred to these our barbarous Savages, that have beene likely as false and perfidious heretofore to them, as unto us of late. So as the quarrels, and the causes of them, and the different humours of these people being well understood, it will be an easie matter to overthrow those that now are, or may bee our enemies hereafter, by ayding and setting on their enemies against them. . . .

Fifthly, Because the Indians, who before were used as friends, may now most justly be compelled to servitude and drudgery, and supply the roome of men that labour, whereby even the meanest of the Plantation may imploy themselves more entirely in their Arts and Occupations, which are more generous, whilest Savages performe their inferiour workes of digging in mynes, and the like, of whom also may be sent for the service of the Sommer Ilands.

Sixtly, This will for ever hereafter make us more cautelous and circumspect, as never to bee deceived more by any other treacheries, but will serve for a great instruction to all posteritie there, to teach them that Trust is the mother of Deceipt, and to learne them that of the Italian. . . . Hee that trusts not is not deceived: and make them know that kindnesses are misspent upon rude natures, so long as they continue rude; as also, that Savages and Pagans are above all other for matter of Justice ever to be suspected. . . . And so we may truly say according to the French Proverb . . . Ill lucke is good for something.

Lastly, We have this benefit more to our comfort, because all good men doe now take much more care of us then before, since the fault is on their sides, not on ours, who have used so fayre a cariage, even to our owne destruction. Especially his Majesties most gratious, tender and paternall care is manifest herein, who by his Royall bounty and goodnesse, hath continued his many favors unto us, with a new, large, & Princely supply of Munition and Armes, out of his Majesties owne store in the Tower, being gratiously for the safety and advancement of the Plantation. As also his Royall favor is amply extended in a large supply of men and other necessaries throughout the whole Kingdome, which are very shortly to bee sent to VIRGINIA.

To underscore the commitment to the Virginia enterprise and to bolster needed manpower and resources, Waterhouse concluded with the notice,

Neyther must wee omit the Honourable City of London, who to shew their zeale at this time (as

The Other Massacre

Everyone has heard of the famous Indian Massacre of 1622, but few know about the so-called Poison Massacre of 22 May 1623—an English reprisal against the Powhatan Indians in which some 200 natives were feasted with laced wine by officials of the Virginia Company, Captain William Tucker and Dr. John Pott. Knowledge of the supposed event reached England via a single report written by colonist Robert Bennett to a relative but was vehemently denied by the Governor, Francis Wyatt, and others in Virginia as a malicious attack by Wyatt's enemies. Whether true or not, the report outraged James I and contributed to the royal dissolution of the London Company the next year. The affair did not touch Tucker and Pott, however, for both men continued prominent in the colony; Pott eventually became governor of the colony.

> they have alwayes done upon all Honourable occasions to their endlesse praise) are now setting forth one hundred person, at their owne charges, for the advancement of the Plantations. . . . And whosoever transports himselfe or any other, at his charge into VIRGINIA, shall for himselfe and each person so transported, before Midsummer, 1625, have to him and his heyres forever, fifty Acres of land upon a first Division, and as much more upon a second: the first fifty being cultivated or manured, if such person continue there three yeares, eyther at once or severall times, or dye after hee bee shipped for that Voyage."

Although the initial attack was swift and devastating, it was not as thorough and effective as Opechancanough had desired. Partly due to warnings given to some of the settlers by sympathetic Indians, Chanco (or Chauco) being the best known, but just as important, because of the tenacious hold the English finally had established in the New World, Jamestown and surrounding settlements would survive and expand. Following a brief retraction of settlement just after the attack, the English settlers returned to most of the previously destroyed or abandoned outposts and homesteads. At the same time, a more organized and systematic destruction of the neighboring indigenous presence was initiated with a vengeance. Ships, supplies, and settlers were poured increasingly into the New World venture, but great challenges still lay ahead in Virginia for the British dream of empire.

Related entries: Chanco; London Company; Massacre of 1644; Nemattanew; Opechancanough

Suggestions for further reading

James Axtell. 1995. *The Rise and Fall of the Powhatan Empire: Indians in Seventeenth-Century Virginia.* Williamsburg, VA: Colonial Williamsburg Foundation.

Robert C. Johnson, ed. 1963. "The Indian Massacre of 1622: Some Correspondence of the Reverend Joseph Mead" (*Virginia Magazine of History and Biography,* vol. 71).

Susan Myra Kingsbury, ed. 1933. *The Records of The Virginia Company of London* (vol. 3). Washington, DC: Government Printing Office.

Karen Ordahl Kupperman. 2000. *Indians & English: Facing Off in Early America.* Ithaca, NY: Cornell University Press.

Helen C. Rountree. 1990. *Pocahontas's People: The Powhatan Indians of Virginia Through Four Centuries.* Norman: University of Oklahoma Press.

Captain John Smith. 1907. *The Generall Historie of Virginia, New England & The Summer Isles Together with The True Travels, Adventures and Observations, and A Sea Grammar* (vol. 1). Glasgow, Scotland: MacLehose and Sons.

Massacre of 1644

Twenty-two years after Opechancanough, brother and successor of Powhatan, launched his massive attack against the English colonists along the James River in Virginia, he tried once again to eradicate the settlers from his inherited empire. On 18 April 1644, a force composed of Nansemonds, Chickahominies, and Weyanocks, possibly with help from the Rappahannocks and other local chiefdoms, attacked the English settlements, killed around 400 colonists, and took many others prisoner. This time, there were no warnings delivered by sympathetic Indians, as in the March 1622 attack, but because the English population had increased so dramatically in the intervening years, the number of casualties amounted to about only about one-twelfth of the population—whereas it had been as much as one-quarter to one-third in the first attack.

Few records about the event survive from the period, but it is known that in the days and weeks following the attack the English once again consolidated their forces and set out on punitive, if not annihilative, expeditions against the groups known, or thought, to have taken part. During the summer of 1644, attacks were made against the Chickahominies, Weyanocks, Nansemonds, Appamattucks, and Powhatans. Although some English lost their lives during the retaliatory raids, many more Indian lives were taken, and many of the natives who were not killed were taken prisoner and sold as slaves or servants. In some cases, whole settlements were destroyed.

In addition to reprisals by the English, other measures were taken in an attempt to ensure that other such disasters could be avoided. Trade with the Indians by individual settlers was halted because it was generally believed that such was

> the cause of their [the Indians] enabling and furnishing themselves with such necessaries whereby they may be strengthened and fitted for their defense and subsistence, and that it is generally suspected under the color of license for commerce the natives have been furnished both with guns, powder, and shot, and with other offensive instruments, thereby tending to our utter ruin.

Chief Necotowance on the Treaty of 1646

Nickotawance came to *James* town to our Noble Governour Sir William Bearkley with five more petty Kings attending him, and brought twenty Beavers-skinnes to be sent to King Charles as he said for Tribute; *and after a long Oration, he concluded with this Protestation; That the Sunne and Moon should first lose their glorious lights and shining, before He, or his People should evermore hereafter wrong the English in any kind, but they would ever hold love and friendship together.*

—*A Perfect Description of Virginia,* 1649

To ensure that lands already settled by the colonists were not recovered by the natives, acts were passed stating

> that it shall not be lawfull for any person holding land by patent or who soe hath held land since the 20th of November last, voluntarily to leave the same upon penaltie of forfeiture thereof, so as it may be lawfull for any person whatsoever to take up the same by patent as land deserted.

Additionally, three new forts were ordered built: "one at Pomunkey to be called Fort Royal; another to the Falls of James River to be called Fort Charles, and the third on the Ridge of Chiquohomine, and to be called Fort James."

The renewed hostilities lasted for two years until the late summer of 1646, when Opechancanough, possibly 100 years old and so physically weakened by age "that he was not able to walk alone, but was carried about by his men wherever he had a mind to move," and whose "flesh was all macerated, his sinews slackened, and his eyelids became so heavy, that he could not see, but as they were lifted up by his servants," was taken captive by an expedition led by Governor Berkeley and held at Jamestown. The intention was to take the great Indian leader to England to be presented to King Charles as a "Royal Captive." And, indeed, Opechancanough considered himself royal and unbowed even during his captivity. While being held prisoner,

> [H]e heard one day a great noise of the treading of people about him; upon which he caused his eyelids to be lifted up, and finding that a crowd of people were let in to see him he called in high indignation for the governor, who being come, Oppechancanough scornfully told him, that had it been his fortune to take Sir William Berkeley prisoner, he should not meanly have exposed him as a show to the people.

Opechancanough never made the voyage to England. Within two weeks of his delivery to Jamestown, a soldier at the fort, apparently in retaliation for all the suffering that Opechancanough inflicted upon the settlers, "shot him through the back" and killed him.

Following the capture and death of Opechancanough, a peace treaty was established between the colonists and the man who was considered by the English to be the successor to Opechancanough's inherited chiefdom. Little is recorded about this leader, Necotowance, who disappears from English writings shortly after the treaty's enactment. But the treaty, in which Necotowance is referred to as the "King of the Indians," is clear in setting forth the new relationship between the settlers and the remnants of the once mighty empire of Powhatan. In the treaty, Necotowance acknowledges that he "holds his kingdome from [by the permission of] the King's Ma'tie of England, and that his successors [will] be appointed or confirmed by the King's Governours from time to time." In tribute to his new sovereign, "Necotowance and his successors are to pay unto the King's Govern'r the number of twenty beaver skins att the goeing away of Geese yearely." New borders between the settlers and Indians are delineated—Necotowance and his people were restricted to "inhabit and hunt on the north-side of Yorke River, without any interruption from the English . . . [unless] It shall be thought fitt by the Governer and Council to permitt any English to inhabitt from Poropotanke [on the north side of the York river near the Poropotank River] downewards." For their part, the English have

> that tract of land betweene Yorke river and James river, from the falls of both the rivers to Kequotan [present day Hampton] . . . and that neither he the said Necotowance nor any Indians do repaire to or make any abode upon the said tract of land, upon paine of death, and it shall be lawfull for any person to kill any such Indian.

If Necotowance needed to send a messenger into the English territory, or if any of his people had any reason to go there, a special striped badge would have to be worn to identify him as being on approved business. Under no circumstances could they enter without this identification. Punishment for violating this part of the treaty was harsh, even for the colonists. As written, "if any English do entertain any Indian or Indians or doe conceale any Indian or Indians that shall come within the said limits, such persons being lawfully convicted thereof shall suffer death." The English, however, were allowed to cross into Necotowance's lands if forced to by "stresse of weather," or "to fall timber trees or cut sedge" provided "theyre soe doeing under the hand of the Gov."

In the end, this second all-out attempt to remove the English from Virginia was even less successful than the first. The settlers had become too strong and too numerous for the Virginia Indians with their smaller numbers and weaker technologies. Still, like the date of the 1622 massacre, the day of this attack was set aside as a holiday to be "celebrated by thanksgivinge for our deliverance from the hands of the Salvages." But it was perhaps the last gasp of a once powerful and dominant empire. The warnings of Powhatan's prophets that enemies from the east would come and threaten to take away his empire had come to pass at last. But it was not his eastern enemies the Chesapeakes—whom Powhatan suspected and had slaughtered sometime near the arrival of the first Jamestown colonists—who were the subject of the prophecies. His greatest enemies did indeed come from the east, but they traveled thousands of miles across the Atlantic, eastward from England.

Related entries: Chanco; Massacre of 1622; Nemattanew; Opechancanough

Suggestions for further reading

James Axtell. 1995. *The Rise and Fall of the Powhatan Empire: Indians in Seventeenth-Century Virginia.* Williamsburg, VA: Colonial Williamsburg Foundation.

Robert Beverley. 1855. *The History of Virginia, in Four Parts.* Richmond, VA.

Frederic W. Gleach. 1997. *Powhatan's World and Colonial Virginia: A Conflict of Cultures.* Lincoln and London: University of Nebraska Press.

William Waller Hening. 1823. *The Statutes at Large, being a Collection of All the Laws of Virginia from the First Session of the Legislature, in the Year 1619* (vol. 1). New York: R. & W. & G. Bartow.

Helen C. Rountree. 1990. *Pocahontas's People: The Powhatan Indians of Virginia Through Four Centuries.* Norman: University of Oklahoma Press.

Mathew, Thomas (died c.1705)

Burgess, planter, and businessman Thomas Mathew of Cherry Point in Northumberland County, Virginia, wrote an early and judicious narrative of Bacon's Rebellion, in 1705. Although almost three decades had passed by the time he penned his account, Mathew had witnessed much of the affair from the vantage point of a landholder in the region where the Indian hostilities first broke out that gave rise to the insurrection, for he owned vast tracts of land in the Northern Neck counties of Northumberland and Stafford. A county justice at the time of the insurrection, Mathew was elected to the House of Burgesses as one of the members from Stafford County when Governor Sir William Berkeley in 1676 allowed the first new elections to the General Assembly since 1660. As a burgess, Mathew played an active role in the famous June session, even though he apparently was more interested in his business pursuits than in politics; he studiously avoided being drawn into the contest of wills that Bacon and the governor fought out in the following summer and fall. Following the sudden death of Bacon and the squelching of the rebellion, Mathew returned home, where he experimented with linen manufacture. He was living in Westminster, England, at the time he wrote his narrative, which he finished shortly before his death.

Mathew relied on firsthand accounts, including his own, when writing *The Beginning, Progress, and Conclusion of Bacon's Rebellion.* One editor of the work described it as "straightforward and concise, such as one would expect from a man of business, and it is manifestly fair and honest," and the author as a man who "certainly at first had much sympathy with the cause they represented, though not with its excesses." Mathew wrote his little history for Robert Harley, first Earl of Oxford (1661–1724), the British statesman and bibliophile who at the time served on the Privy Council and as principal secretary of state. The original manuscript was not included in the 1764 sale of Harley's library to the British Museum, and in 1801 it was acquired by Rufus King, the U.S. minister plenipotentiary to Great Britain. King gave it to President Thomas Jefferson in 1803, and it is now in the Jefferson Papers in the Library of Congress. Jefferson made two copies of the manuscript, one of which is in the Virginia Historical Society and the other in the American Antiquarian Society. The latter copy was used as the source for the first printing of the narrative, which took place in the 1, 5, and 8 September 1804 issues of the *Richmond Enquirer.* Subsequent printings in 1820, 1836, 1850, 1897, and 1914 relied variously on all three manuscripts.

Related entries: Bacon's Rebellion; Berkeley, Sir William; General Assembly

Suggestions for further reading

Charles M. Andrews, ed. 1915. *Narratives of the Insurrections, 1675–1690.* New York: Charles Scribner's Sons.

Thomas Jefferson Wertenbaker. 1914. *Virginia Under the Stuarts: 1607–1688.* Princeton, NJ: Princeton University Press.

Mattaponi Indians

Members of the Algonquian-speaking Native American tribe Mattaponi first encountered

English colonists in late 1607, when Captain John Smith visited their capital town, "Matapamient," one of eight named villages that Smith recorded having discovered while searching for food and the headwaters of the Chickahominy River. Living in present-day King William County, estimates of the tribe's number of inhabitants at the time range from 30 to 140, not counting women and children. In his *Map of Virginia* (1612), Smith indicates that he encountered Mattaponi warriors living in villages along the banks of both the Mattaponi and Pamunkey Rivers. Counted among the native peoples dominated by Chief Powhatan, the Mattaponi made their living off the rich natural resources available in the river basins of the Chesapeake watershed. Their name or its derivative might translate roughly as "Landing Place."

Initially, the Mattaponi found the European arrivals intriguing and befriended them, willingly trading away surplus corn and even hosting a mock Indian battle for English observation. But rather quickly the relations between the Mattaponi and the settlers began to resemble those of surrounding tribes and the English—they became strained, and hostilities broke out. The English easily subdued the Mattaponi and began to treat their lands as a sort of buffer between the settlement expanding from Jamestown and the territory more easily controlled by Powhatan. When William Claiborne waged war on the Indians after the Massacre of 1644, he drove the Mattaponi away from Pamunkey Neck to a site near the Rappahannock River. A peace settlement resulted in the Mattaponi paying tribute to the colony's governor in 1646, beginning an annual practice that has continued for over three and one-half centuries; each November, a tribal delegation (along with representatives of the Pamunkey tribe) meets with the Virginia governor to present a payment of game or fish.

In 1658, the General Assembly set aside some of the tribe's ancestral lands on the western banks of Mattaponi River as a permanent reservation. The Mattaponi lived there peacefully until 1676, when they were attacked by Nathaniel Bacon and his followers. The tribe fled the reservation, seeking safety in Gloucester County, but eventually Yau-na-hah, the tribe's chief, was apprehended and slain by being nailed to the ground with a wooden stake. Yau-na-hah's eldest son, Mahayough, became chief in his father's stead and in time led his people back to their reservation village. The present-day reservation consists of only about 150 acres, inhabited by about 60 of the tribe's 450 members. These descendants of the original natives carry on many of the cultural traditions of their ancestors, although they converted to Christianity and worship as Southern Baptists. The reservation community's facilities consist of residences, a church, a museum, a fish (shad) hatchery, and a former reservation school building that now serves as a community center.

At present, the Mattaponi reservation is not large enough to accommodate more inhabitants without expansion of its acreage, so the likelihood of additional descendants returning to their ancestral homelands is unlikely in the near future. The tribe has sought to reclaim some of its former reservation lands, where it plans to build more housing and establish a Living History Center for the education of future generations of Mattaponi, but thus far they have met with little success. A proposal by the city of Newport News to build a 1,500-acre reservoir adjacent to the reservation makes land reclamation even more difficult and threatens to disrupt shad spawning grounds and destroy the tribe's fish hatchery, which would adversely affect the economic and cultural life of the tribe. Although the Mattaponi tribe lives as a sovereign nation and is governed by a chief, assistant chief, and seven councilors, in 1995 the Mattaponi Heritage Foundation was established at West Point, Virginia, to assist in furthering the tribe's goals.

The Mattaponi tribe of Native Americans has a sister tribe known as the Upper Mattaponi, which lives further up the Mattaponi River in King William County near Aylett, Virginia. Its principle town, Passaunkack, was located on the south bank of the river in the northwest part of the county and was visited by John Smith in 1608. Throughout the seventeenth, eighteenth, and nineteenth centuries, the Upper Mattaponi people inhabited the same land, and over time they began to be called the Adamstown Indians because so many of them had the surname

Adams—apparently as a result of British interpreter James Adams's service in the region from 1702 to 1727. The origins of the Upper Mattaponi can be traced to the Mattaponi and Pamunkey reservations; the tribe officially adopted the name Upper Mattaponi in 1921. Like the Mattaponi, the Upper Mattaponi people are Baptists, and their community revolves around the Indian View Baptist Church, which is located next to the tribal community center in a former school building. Extensive archaeological excavations on Upper Mattaponi ancestral lands found evidence of Indian habitation for thousands of years into prehistory. The Upper Mattaponi tribe presently owns thirty-two acres of land and hosts an annual powwow or spring festival for the public to learn about their history and culture. Members of the tribe make and sell pottery in the region.

Both the Mattaponi and the Upper Mattaponi are among the eight tribes officially recognized by the State of Virginia, and the Upper Mattaponi is one of six tribes seeking recognition by the federal government.

Related entries: Accohannock Indians; Accomac Indians; Chesapeake Indians; Chickahominy Indians; Kecoughtan Indians; Manahoac Indians; Mattaponi River; Monacan Indians; Nansemond Indians; Newport News; Pamunkey Indians; Paspahegh Indians; Warraskoyak Indians

Suggestions for further reading

Helen C. Rountree. 1989. *The Powhatan Indians of Virginia: Their Traditional Culture.* Norman and London: University of Oklahoma Press.

Captain John Smith. 1612. *Map of Virginia.* London: S.I.

Mattaponi River

Often described as one of the most pristine of the waterways making up the Chesapeake Bay river system, the Mattaponi takes its name from the tribe of Native Americans that lived along its banks when the English settled the Jamestown colony in 1607. The people of the Mattaponi considered the river sacred, believing that the stream gave rise to life itself, and even today their tribal descendants depend on the river as the cultural and economic lifeblood of their community. Captain John Smith became the first Englishman to see the river when the Chickahominy Indians who had taken him prisoner used that water route to deliver him to Chief Powhatan in December 1607.

The Mattaponi is one of the two tributaries (the other being the Pamunkey) that meet to form the York River at the site of the old Indian town Cinquoteck (present-day West Point, Virginia), about halfway between Richmond and Tindall's Point, the important commercial center that developed at the mouth of the York. Robert Beverley, in his *History and Present State of Virginia* (London, 1705) included the Mattaponi in his list of about a dozen "lesser rivers" capable of receiving the largest merchant ships of the period. Beverley, in fact, resided near the head of the Mattaponi, cultivating on his plantation a variety of native and French grapes in a three-acre vineyard from which he produced as much as 400 gallons of wine annually.

The Mattaponi stretches about the Virginia landscape for about 85 miles before emptying into the York. The river and its freshwater tidal wetlands are home to many species of plants and a variety of birds and fish, including ducks, geese, herons, osprey, bald eagles, blueback herring, striped bass, shad, and shellfish. It is good for canoeing as well as recreational and commercial fishing. For two decades, the city of Newport News has been attempting to build a dam and a 1,500-acre reservoir near the Mattaponi Indian reservation at Cohoke Creek in King William County, where the Mattaponi and the Pamunkey flow together, to provide an additional source of water for the eastern Tidewater region. Opponents of the proposal say its implementation would submerge 21 miles of free-flowing streams, 1,100 acres of land (including 440 acres of wetlands), and at least 100 historical, archaeological, and cultural sites plus a sacred Mattaponi site the location of which is known only to tribal elders. The disruption of the river's shad spawning grounds and destruction of the Mattaponi Indian reservation's fish hatchery and some of the tribe's traditional Indian hunting grounds would adversely affect the economy and culture of the tribe.

In 1992, as a result of the dispute about the proposed reservoir, local citizens formed the Mattaponi and Pamunkey Rivers Association, a public interest group dedicated to preserving the "history, ecology, scenic landscape, recreation, and economy" of the two rivers. In 2003, American Rivers, the foremost river conservation organization in the United States, designated the Mattaponi as one of America's most endangered rivers, one of only three East Coast rivers placed on the list.

Related entries: Chickahominy River; Elizabeth River; James River; Mattaponi Indians; Nansemond River; Newport News; Pamunkey River; Rappahannock River; Smith, Captain John; York River

Suggestion for further reading

Captain John Smith. 1612. *Map of Virginia.* London: S.I.

Robert Beverley. 1855. *The History of Virginia, in Four Parts.* Richmond, VA.

Merchant's Hundred

See Martin's Hundred

Monacan Indians

It was Whitsunday—24 May 1607—just eleven days after the Englishmen had planted their banner on the marshy Jamestown peninsula, when Captain Christopher Newport and a party of twenty-three ocean-weary adventurers at the falls of the James, some sixty miles upstream from their newly established settlement, first heard the tale of a powerful tribe of Native Americans who were not under the sway of Chief Powhatan. With the help of a native guide named Nauiraus, Newport and his matchlock-wielding mariners laid out a banquet for the natives watching from the woods at the falls, and enticed their leaders out of the woods. They came wearing mantles of raccoon fur and copper, escorted by men with painted faces and strangely cut manes. At the appearance of a chief, "Pawatah, Nauiraus made signe to us we must make a shoute," wrote Gabriel Archer, "which we Dyd." Then a feast of roasted wildfowl and venison began.

> Now sitting upon the banck by the overfall . . . [Pawatah] began to tell us of the tedyous travell we should have if wee proceeded any further, that it was a Daye and a halfe Journey to Monanacah, and if we went to Quiranck, we should get no vittailes and be tyred, and sought by all means to Disswade our Captayne from going any further.

Continued Archer,

> Also he tolde us that the Monanacah was his Enmye, and that they came Downe at the fall of the leafe and invaded his Countrye. But our Captayne out of his Discreyton (though we would faine have seen further, yea and himselfe as desirous also) Checkt his intentyon and retorned to his boate.

Discouraged from further exploration at that time, the colonists unfettered their craft and fell back downstream—but not until Captain Newport had planted a cross on one of the many islets below the falls and christened the river the James in honor of James I, king of all England and Scotland.

Thus did the Jamestown settlers first learn of the Monanacah—or Monacan—nation, a confederacy of Native Americans that dominated the Virginia Piedmont, living under the protective shadows of the Quiranck, the beautiful Blue Ridge Mountains. Like other Native American tribes of the period, they left behind a rich archaeological record but no written records. In 1780, Thomas Jefferson named the Monacan, along with the Powhatan and the Manahoac, the most powerful of the more than forty different groups of "aboriginies" occupying Virginia. Thus penned the master of Monticello:

> Those between the sea-coast and falls of the rivers, were in amity with one another and attached to the Powhatans as their link of union. Those between the falls of the rivers and the mountains, were divided into two confederacies; the tribes inhabiting the head waters of the Potomac and Rappahannock being attached to the Mannahoacs; and those on the upper parts of James River to the Monacans.

These divisions marked by the limits of navigation, however, were rather loose and in constant dispute for, wrote Jefferson, "the Monacans and their friends were in amity with the Manahoacs

Native American town in pre-colonial Virginia, surrounded by a palisade. (Library of Congress)

. . . and waged joint and perpetual war against the Powhatans" to the east.

The region controlled by the Monacan, therefore, was vast and fertile. It included the valleys of the James and Rivanna Rivers and the fabulous country drained by their tributaries both north and south. The Indians and the early English colonists regarded it as a separate and distinct land. Sir Henry Payton, writing in 1610, referred to the area as "the Land called the Monscane." (Later, William Strachey was hopeful that the area would prove rich in minerals or, failing that, the long-imagined passage to the Pacific Ocean.) The armored Englishmen did discover that "Monscane" embraced at least five large villages, centers of the Indian population. Mowhemcho and Massinacack rested on the right bank of the James (in present-day Powhatan County), whereas Rassawek—often called the Monacan's "principal town"—had been set up at or near the confluence of the James and the Rivanna (present-day Fluvanna County). Further up the James, the ancient village of Monahassanugh was built on the broad bottomland of the left bank (present-day Nelson County), approximately ten miles upstream from the mouth of the Rockfish River. Monasukapanough occupied both sides of the Rivanna River at a beautiful site two miles above its principal fork, where a convenient ford made passage easy (present-day Albemarle County).

Most scholars agree that the Monacan people—including their "contributors," the Tutelo and Saponi tribes—spoke a Siouan language, unlike their Algonquian-speaking rivals to the east. Exactly when they first moved into the Virginia Piedmont most likely will forever remain a mystery, although their place of origin was the Ohio River valley. Possibly these early Sioux were driven over the Alleghenies by enemies farther to the north, or perhaps they came voluntarily in search of better game. In any event, the Monacan flourished in the Virginia Piedmont, a vast, forested land full of deer, bear, elk, and a variety of fowl and fish. Buffalo were not uncommon, and a buffalo trail wound over the mountains and into the Shenandoah Valley. But the Monacan lived an existence that left few traces, an existence described in but a small number of firsthand accounts. Of the original Monacan villages, white men visited only Massinacack and Mowhemcho. Captain Newport and his men passed through in a 1608 expedition beyond the falls of the James. And a colony of Huguenots who settled along the James in 1699 briefly detailed the Indians still in residence. Perhaps the best description of the Monacan came from the hand of Huguenot John Fontaine, who in 1716 toured a Saponi village established outside Fort Christianna in Brunswick County. It is believed that these people were the direct descendants of the inhabitants of Monasukapanough. (The inhabitants of Monasukapanough inexplicably abandoned the town in the 1670s.) What little else we know of the Monacan is based on the assumption that their way of life resembled that of the Powhatan.

The Monacan were hunters, gatherers, and subsistence farmers (with the women doing the gardening). They lived in villages that resembled the palisaded forts erected by the white colonists. According to John Fontaine, the Saponi village he visited was constructed right alongside a river:

> The houses join all the one to the other, and altogether make a circle . . . the walls are large pieces of timber which are squared, and being sharpened at the lower end, are put down two feet in the ground, and stand about seven feet [high]. These posts are laid as close together as possible . . . and when they are all fixed after this manner, they make a roof with rafters, and cover the house with oak or hickory bark, which they strip off in great flakes, and lay it so closely that no rain can come in.

Other Monacan shelters were described as circular, made up of a framework of flexible saplings with both ends in the ground, the whole covered with bark or grass mats. Across the entranceway would be hung a deerskin. These houses would certainly have been dark, smoky affairs: One portal provided the only light; one hole in the roof, the only escape for the smoke. Wrote Fontaine,

> They make their fires always in the middle of the house; the chief of their household goods is a pot and some wooden dishes and trays, which they make themselves; they seldom have any thing to sit upon, but squat upon the ground. They have small divisions in their houses to sleep in, which they make of mats made of bullrushes; they have bedsteads, raised about two feet from the ground, upon which they lay bear and deer skins, and all the covering they have is a blanket. These people have no sort of tame creatures, but live entirely upon their hunting and the corn which their wives cultivate. They live as lazily and miserably as any people in the world.

Fortunately, Fontaine also described the appearance of the Monacan at Fort Christianna. For their war dress, the young men of the tribe decorated themselves

> with feathers in their hair and run through their ears, their faces painted with blue and vermilion, their hair cut in many forms, some on one side of the head, and some on both, and others on the upper part of the head making it stand like a cock's-comb.

These proud warriors—wrapped in blue and red blankets—strutted back and forth in their "abominable dress," looking for all the world, wrote Fontaine, "like so many furies." The Monacan women at Fort Christianna had long, straight, black hair reaching down to their waists. They used nothing to cover their upper bodies, but each of them wore, wrote Fontaine, "a blanket tied round the waist, and hanging down about the legs like a petticoat." These women were wild looking and very shy around Europeans. But despite the fact that they were covered head to toe in horrible-smelling bear grease, Fontaine found them "straight and well limbed, good shape, and extraordinary good features." Fontaine claimed that these natives lived a monogamous life—that is, until the woman could no longer bear children. "Then the man may take another wife," he wrote, "but is obliged to keep them both and maintain them."

The Monacan had a great burial mound near Monasukapanough not far from Thomas Jefferson's Monticello. Endlessly fascinated by Native American culture, Jefferson took it upon himself to make a personal investigation of the mound. (His careful analysis of this barrow, in fact, won for him the title "Father of Modern Archeology.") According to Jefferson, the mound

> was situated on the low grounds of the Rivanna . . . and opposite to some hills, on which had been an Indian town. . . . It was of spheroidical form, of about 40 feet diameter at the base, and had been of about twelve feet altitude, though now reduced by the plough to seven and a half, having been under cultivation about a dozen years . . . round the base was an excavation of five feet depth and width, from whence the earth had been taken of which the hillock was formed. I first dug superficially in several parts of it, and came to collections of human bones at different depths, from six inches to three feet below the surface.

Jefferson's systematic dig revealed about 1,000 skeletons arranged in rough layers with no apparent plan. The bones did not seem to show wounds acquired in battle, and he did not believe that the barrow was simply Monasukapanough's "common sepulchre." Jefferson thought it obvious that

> the first collection had been deposited on the . . . surface of the earth, a few stones put over it, and then a covering of earth, that the second had been laid on this, had covered more or less of it in proportion to the number of bones, and was then also covered with earth; and so on.

Because the tall mass of dirt and stones contained so many bodies, had it been, for a time, the main burial mound of the northern part of the Monacan nation? There is evidence that it was revered and long remembered by the Indians. Writing in 1780, Jefferson recalled

> a party passing, about thirty years ago, through the part of the country where this barrow is, went through the woods directly to it, without any instructions or enquiry, and having stayed about it some time, with expressions which were construed to be those of sorrow, they returned to the high road . . . and pursued their journey.

Bushnell concluded that "only those who had retained a memory of the burial place could, or would, have made such a pilgramige." Why was Monasukapanough abandoned? No one knows for sure, but probably the tribe was forced out as the English crept in from the east and the Iroquois raided from the north. In western North Carolina along the Virginia border, say most of the sources, the Monacan tribe was assimilated by the Tuscarora. Ironically, these people later moved north and were received in 1712 as the Sixth Nation. During the American Revolution, unfortunately, several of these tribes sided with the British. For this reason, George Washington dispatched General John Sullivan with orders that the territory occupied by these Indians was "not to be merely overrun, but destroyed." Forty villages were put to the torch, including, probably, the remnants of the Monacan.

Today, there are approximately 1,400 members of the Monacan tribe, about two-thirds of whom live in Virginia in Amherst County. Centered at Bear Mountain, the tribe operates an ancestral museum and hosts an annual powwow in Elon, Virginia, each spring. A living history Monacan village complex near the Natural Bridge of Virginia interprets Monacan life at about the time of English settlement.

Related entries: Accohannock Indians; Accomac Indians; Chesapeake Indians; Chickahominy Indians; Kecoughtan Indians; Manahoac Indians; Mattaponi Indians; Nansemond Indians; Newport, Sir Christopher; Pamunkey Indians; Paspahegh Indians; Warraskoyak Indians

Suggestions for further reading

Rick Britton. 1999. "The Lost Culture of the Monacans: People of the River Banks" (*Albemarle,* vol. 11).

David I. Bushnell, Jr. 1930. *The Five Monacan Towns in Virginia, 1607.* Washington, DC: Smithsonian Institution.

———. 1935. *The Manahoac Tribes in Virginia, 1608.* Washington, DC: Smithsonian Institution.

Samuel R. Cook. 2000. *Monacans and Miners: Native American and Coal Mining Communities in Appalachia.* Lincoln: University of Nebraska Press.

Jeffrey L. Hantman. 1990. "Between Powhatan and Quirank: Reconstructing Monacan Culture and History in the Context of Jamestown" (*American Anthropologist,* vol. 92).

Karenne Wood and Diane Shields. 1999. *The Monacan Indians: Our Story.* Madison Heights, VA: Office of Historical Research, Monacan Indian Nation.

Helen C. Rountree. 1993. *Powhatan Foreign Relations: 1500–1722.* Charlottesville: University Press of Virginia.

Thomas Jefferson. 1787. *Notes on the State of Virginia.* London.

Sandra F. Waugaman and Danielle Moretti-Langholtz. 2000. *We're Still Here: Contemporary Virginia Indians Tell Their Stories.* Richmond, VA: Palari Publishing.

Mt. Malady

By 1612, the population of the Jamestown colony had grown to more than 700, and it was found necessary to construct a retreat for "harboring sick men and receiving strangers." This hospital, the first in English America, was constructed inland near Henricus, described at the time as a "place of higher ground, strong and defencible by nature, a good aire, wholesome and cleere (unlike the marish seate at James towne) with fresh and plentie of water springs, much faire and open grounds freed from woods, and wood enough at hand." The healthy settlers built a sturdy building that by the standards of the time was commodious enough to accommodate as many as 80 men, women, and children at once. As an eyewitness described it, "Here they were building also an

Hospitall with fourescore lodgings (and beds alreadie sent to furnish them) for the sicke and lame, with keepers to attend them for their comfort and recoverie." It was used both as a place to treat those suffering from illnesses typical in the colony (malaria, typhoid fever, dysentery, and infections) and as a holding area to allow recent arrivals time to recuperate from their long and exhausting ocean voyages. Little is known about the actual patients treated at Mt. Malady, which may have already fallen into disuse by the time of the Indian Massacre of 1622.

Mt. Malady hospital is represented in the partially recreated Henricus Historical Park, a thirty-two acre settlement south of Richmond in Chesterfield County.

Related entry: Henricus

Suggestion for further reading

R. I. 1612. *The New Life of Virginea: Declaring the Former Success and Present Estate of that Plantation. Being the Second Part of Nova Britannia.* London.

Mulberry Island

About ten miles downriver from Jamestown Island lay a point of land the colonists knew as Mulberry Island, Mulberry Point, or Cedar Island. Like Jamestown Island, it was not a true island when the colonists arrived, but unlike Jamestown, it still is not one today. It was just offshore there on Friday afternoon, 8 June 1610, that the departing colonists were met and turned back by Lord De La Warr's representative, Captain Edward Brewster, in command of the pinnace *Virginia,* after they had abandoned Jamestown the previous day as a result of the tragic Starving Time of 1609–1610. As related by William Strachey, then secretary to the colony, in his *True Reportory,* "the morning tide brought us to another Iland, which we have called Mulberry, Iland; where lying at an ancor, in the afternoone stemming the tide, wee discovered a long Boate making towards us, from Point Comfort." Lord De La Warr had landed at Fort

Mulberry Shade

"In different parts of Virginia there were beautiful groves of mulberry. So numerous were they in Arrahattock, a country situated on the north side of the Powhatan and to the east of the Falls, that the name of Mulberry Shade was given to one spot in that region." That is historian Philip Alexander Bruce's description of the location where, according to Jamestown settler Gabriel Archer, Captain Christopher Newport and a band of "discoverers" made up of "5 gentlemen, 4 marines and 14 sailors," met Pawatah, the chief of all the native kingdoms in the area. The explorers were more than forty-five miles up the James River from the Jamestown fort when contact took place on Monday, 25 May 1607. The writer Charles Dudley Warner described the encounter this way, in his *Captain John Smith* (1881):

> They dropped down the river to a place called Mulberry Shade, where the King killed a deer and prepared for them another feast, at which they had rolls and cakes made of wheat. "This the women make and are very cleanly about it. We had parched meal, excellent good, sodd [cooked] beans, which eat as sweet as filbert kernels, in a manner, strawberries; and mulberries were shaken off the tree, dropping on our heads as we sat. He made ready a land turtle, which we ate; and showed that he was heartily rejoiced in our company." Such was the amiable disposition of the natives before they discovered the purpose of the whites to dispossess them of their territory. That night they stayed at a place called "Kynd Woman's Care," where the people offered them abundant victual and craved nothing in return.

Algernon there on June 6. The encounter at Mulberry Island marked, in both distance and time, the limits of the colonists' attempts to abandon Jamestown.

Settlement of the island, which was possibly named for its growth of Virginia mulberry trees, was not a priority for the colonists. In fact, settlement did not begin until perhaps 1617 or later. But the island did contain enough inhabitants to be targeted by Indians during the March 1622 massacre; its victims included "Thomas Pierce . . . his wife and child, two men and a 'French boy'." The massacre temporarily delayed further settlement for a few years, but in the January 1625 census, thirty persons were listed as living there. Bounded by the James River to the south and west, the Warwick River to the east, and Skiffes Creek to the northwest, Mulberry Island is today within the city limits of Newport News, Virginia, and is the site of Fort Eustis, a U.S. military transportation installation.

Related entries: Hog Island; Newport News; West, Thomas, Lord De La Warr

Suggestions for further reading

Edward Arber, ed. 1910. *Travels and Works of Captain John Smith* (part 2). Edinburgh, Scotland: J. Grant.

Charles E. Hatch, Jr. 1995. *The First Seventeen Years: Virginia, 1607–1624.* Charlottesville, VA: University Press of Virginia.

David Beers Quinn, ed. 1979. *New American World: A Documentary History of North America to 1612.* 5 vols. New York: Arno Press and Hector Bye, Inc.

Conway Whittle Sams. 1929. *The Conquest of Virginia: The Second Attempt: An Account, Based on Original Documents, of the Attempt, Under the King's Form of Government, to Found Virginia at Jamestown, 1606–1610.* Norfolk, VA: Keyser-Doherty.

Lyon Gardiner Tyler. 1906. *The Cradle of the Republic: Jamestown and James River.* Richmond, VA: Hermitage Press.

N

Nansemond Indians

Separated from most of their Powhatan allies by the James River at one of its widest points, the Native Americans who made up the Nansemond tribe at first contact were perhaps more susceptible to English incursion than any in Virginia. Captain John Smith became the first Englishman to explore the neighborhood of the Nansemond when, on his return voyage from exploring the Eastern Shore in early September 1608, a storm blew his boat across the Chesapeake Bay into the Nansemond River. Characterizing the Nansemond as "a proud warlike Nation, as well we may testifie," Smith's band apparently made it as far as the Nansemond's principle seat, Dumpling Island, where the natives greeted them with friendly gestures and encouraged them to sail even farther up the river. This the English did until a Nansemond force made up of more than 200 warriors suddenly appeared and launched a concerted assault on the party. The natives could make no headway against the colonists' armor, however, and Smith's men retaliated against the Nansemond by setting fire to their cornfields and making off with their canoes, which they proceeded to destroy in the middle of the river. Seeing this destruction, the Nansemond backed off, and before Smith left their town, he concluded a "peace" that required the Nansemond to surrender their weapons and give the English a pearl necklace as a conciliatory gesture and as much corn as their vessel could carry. It was an uneasy accord, however, as both sides would learn in the coming months.

At the time the English collided with the Nansemond in 1608, the tribe had occupied the same lands for more than 1,000 years. Like the other Native American peoples living in Tidewater Virginia when the English arrived in the early seventeenth century, the Nansemond lived along a coastal stream that bore the tribe's name. About 1,200 men, women, and children (including 200 to 300 warriors) lived in several villages scattered along both sides of the river on land in the vicinity of Reids Ferry. The tribe's ceremonial area was on Dumpling Island and included the chief's principal seat and tribal treasure house (Dumpling Island is incorporated in the present-day city of Suffolk, Virginia). As was not uncommon, the Nansemond had its own Algonquian dialect, probably very similar to other Powhatan dialects. John Smith later wrote that the Nansemond territory was excellent and beautiful, and about 1,000 acres of it impressed him as some of the most fertile land in the colony. To the English, Dumpling Island especially seemed suitable for the defensive fort they wanted to erect downriver from Jamestown, so they set their sights on the seat of the Nansemond chief. Thus, only a few weeks passed before the uneasy alliance with the English, forced upon the Nansemond by Smith, threatened to fall apart. Fortunately for the Nansemond, the settlers hardly were in a position to survive, much less to construct a new fort, so the inhabitants won a respite for a few months until the summer of 1609.

When the English did get serious about the new settlement, George Percy, the colony's governor, naively sent two representatives to the Nansemond chief with an offer to buy Dumpling Island. The emissaries were not received kindly, however, and they failed to return to Jamestown. According to Percy, the colonists eventually learned the fate of their cohorts: "their Braynes weare cutt and skraped outt of thier heads wth mussell shelles." The English commandeered Dumpling Island anyway, but its nine-mile distance from the James made it untenable at that time, and it was abandoned before any real settlement could be established. Sir Thomas Dale arrived in the colony in the spring of 1611, repaired Jamestown, and renewed the effort to set up a new town. The Nansemond River was the first of several that he and a force of 100 men explored with this view in mind, but in the end Dale chose a site nearer the falls of the James. Dale next turned his attention to subjugating the unruly Nansemond, described by now former governor George Percy in his "Trewe Relacyon" (1612):

> All things in Tyme beinge well settled and ordered Sr Thomas DALE made preparatyon and wente ageinste the NANCEMONDIES wth a hundrethe men in Armour where he had dyvrs encownters and skirmishes wth the Salvages bothe by Lande and water dyvrs of his company beinge wownded.

During the conflict Dale himself narrowly escaped serious injury when an arrow bounced off the brim of his headpiece. Unfamiliar with opponents protected by full armor, the Nansemond resorted to war dances and appeals to the supernatural, described by Percy as devilish conjuring:

> they did fall into their exorcismes conjuracyons and charmes throweinge fyre upp into the skyes Runneinge up and downe wth Rattles and makeinge many dyabolicall gestures wth many irigramantcke Spelles and incantacionus Imageinge thereby to cawse Raine to fall from the Clowdes to extinguishe and putt owtt our mens matches and to wett and spoyle their powder butt nether the dievall whome they adore nor all their Sorcerres did anytheinge Avayle them for our men Cutt downe their Corne Burned their howses and besydes those wch they had slayne browghtt some of them prissoners to our foarte.

It did not take long for the better-armed English to subdue the Nansemond and drive them away from their habitations.

The colonists were beginning to understand just how unhealthy Jamestown could be, and under Captain Francis West, 100 settlers established a new settlement in Nansemond territory. The "Countrie of *Nansemunds*" proved to be a good choice for the colonists who went there, for "did not so much as one man miscarrie: when in *James* Towne, at the same time, and in the same moneths, 100. sickened, and halfe the number died." The colonists later established another settlement on the far side (from Jamestown) of the mouth of the Nansemond. Known as Nansemond Fort or Harbourview, the site has been thoroughly excavated in the last few years, yielding artifacts suggesting extensive English occupation for about two decades beginning about 1636, the period when the land was first patented. In just a few decades, the Nansemond lost most of their ancestral lands, and the treaty following the Indian Massacre of 1644 confined them to a reservation. Even the reservation lands were not secure, and the tribe moved farther up river several times by the end of the century. In his *History and Present State of Virginia* (1705), Robert Beverley observed that the "Indians of Virginia are almost wasted" and estimated the Nansemond tribe consisted of about 30 bowmen, "they have increased much of late." Living alongside the Nansemond was a group of Iroquoians of the same size who had been driven from their lands, the Meherrin ("People of the Muddy Water"). By the 1740s, many of the Nansemond had migrated eastward to the settlements in Southampton County of another Iroquoian tribe, the Nottoway (Nadowa, Algonquian for "adders," or "enemy"). After living with their newfound friends for about seven years, the Nansemond tribe exchanged its 300-acre reservation for a similarly sized tract of land nearer to their new home. That land apparently was sold by the end of the century.

Before the end of the seventeenth century Nansemond had gone through a number of reiterations of its name: Nansimum, Nancemond, Nantzemund, Nansemunde, Nansammand, Nansemunds, and Nantzemond. The Nansemond lent its name to one of the counties lying on the south side of the James River, the only one named after the natives, consisting of three parishes, Lower Parish, Upper Parish, and Chickaluck. Formed in 1637 out of Upper Norfolk, it became an independent city in July 1972, and in 1974 it lost its name when it merged with Suffolk to become Virginia's largest city in acreage. *An Act for Establishing Ports and Towns* in 1705 designated the English settlement at Nansemond a port and a town, appointing Mondays and Thursdays in each week as market days, and 15 October and the four following days, exclusive of Sundays, as the days of the annual fair. Quakers moved onto former tribal lands by the end of the seventeenth century and have maintained an active meeting ever since. Also on their former lands are substantial Civil War earthworks, including Battery Onondaga from the Siege of Suffolk in 1863, which was lucky enough to survive the ravages of development. Current Nansemond tribe members living in the area trace their lineage back to a daughter of Chief Powhatan, Elizabeth, who married Englishman John Basse in 1638. The tribe meets at the Indian United Methodist Church, originally founded as a mission church to the Nansemond in 1850. One of eight tribes officially recognized by the State of Virginia, the tribe operates the Nansemond Indian Museum in the Chuckatuck area of Suffolk and has plans to reconstruct Mattanock Town on lands once occupied by their ancestors.

Related entries: Accohannock Indians; Accomac Indians; Chesapeake Indians; Chickahominy Indians; Kecoughtan Indians; Monacan Indians; Manahoac Indians; Mattaponi Indians; Nansemond River; Pamunkey Indians; Paspahegh Indians; Percy, George; Smith, Captain John; Warraskoyak Indians

Suggestions for further reading

Ivor Noël Hume. 1994. *The Virginia Adventure: Roanoke to James Towne: An Archaeological and Historical Odyssey.* New York: Alfred A. Knopf.

George Percy. 1922. "'A Trewe Relacyon'—Virginia from 1609 to 1612" *(Tyler's Quarterly Historical and Genealogical Magazine,* vol. 4).

Captain John Smith. 1608. *A True Relation of Such Occurrences and Accidents of Noate as Hath Hapned in Virginia Since the First Planting of that Colony, which is now Resident in the South Part Thereof, till the Last Returne from Thence.* London: Edward Alde for John Tappe.

Virginia General Assembly, The Governor, Council, and Burgesses of the. 1705. "An Act for Establishing Ports and Towns" (William Waller Hening, ed., *The Statutes at Large, being a Collection of All the Laws of Virginia from the First Session of the Legislature, in the Year 1619* (vol. 3). Philadelphia.

Nansemond River

Named after the "proud and warlike" natives who lived alongside both its banks, the Nansemond is one of the Chesapeake Bay's major coastal streams south of the James River. From the river's headwaters to the James is about 20 miles as the crow flies but lengthened by about 25 percent as it leisurely winds its way to the northeast. It drops only 65 feet in elevation from the headwaters to the mouth, where it empties into the tidal waters of the James at Hampton Roads. The Nansemond runs through the present-day city of Suffolk, Virginia, and roughly parallels the northern part of the Great Dismal Swamp, two to three miles to the river's east. Thomas Jefferson, in his *Notes on the State of Virginia* (1781), recorded that the Nansemond was "navigable to Sleepy hole, for vessels of 250 tons; to Suffolk, for those of 100 tons; and to Milner's, for those of 25." Because the entrance to the Nansemond was some 20 miles downstream from Jamestown and across the James at its widest point, the river and its native inhabitants escaped the notice of the English colonists for more than a year after their settlement of Jamestown.

Led by Captain John Smith, the first Englishmen sailed up the Nansemond in September 1608, encountering along the way the people who by then had lived on the river's banks for about 1,200 years. Smith later described the river as a "musket shot broad, each side being should bayes, a narrow channell, but three fadom, his course for eighteen miles, almost directly South, and by west." Smith delineated some of the river's twists and turns and gave his impressions of the landscape, the luxuriance of which awed him. Smith also noticed the river's significant oyster beds, at 7 miles thought to be the world's longest, known as Nansemond Ridge. Nansemond Ridge gave rise in colonial times to a major oyster industry that declined only with the onslaught of disease in the present era. The abundant supply of oyster shells in the river was exported across the region for use in agricultural and construction settings in the eighteenth and nineteenth centuries.

Since John Smith first explored the Nansemond River in 1608, dramatic changes have taken place along its shores, beginning with its native inhabitants, who all but disappeared from its banks in the first few decades of colonization as the English claimed the area and established plantation settlements. During the American Civil War, Federal gunboats frequently patrolled the Nansemond as part of the effort to prohibit Confederate ships from running the blockade on the James. A hexagonal woodpile cottage-style lighthouse was erected in the entrance to the Nansemond in 1878 and operated until 1935. Today, the Nansemond contains a series of monitoring stations as part of the complex reservoir system that provides water for the Hampton Roads area cities of Suffolk, Norfolk, Chesapeake, Portsmouth, and Virginia Beach. In 1973, the U.S. Navy transferred 207 acres of salt marsh in Suffolk to the U.S. Fish and Wildlife Service, creating the Nansemond National Wildlife Refuge, a non-staffed satellite refuge managed by the Great Dismal Swamp National Wildlife Refuge. It was supplemented in 1999 by the transfer of 204 acres of upland grassland and forest stream corridors.

Related entries: Chickahominy River; Elizabeth River; James River; Mattaponi River; Nansemond Indians; Pamunkey River; Rappahannock River; York River

Suggestions for further reading

George Percy. 1922. "'A Trewe Relacyon'—Virginia from 1609 to 1612" *(Tyler's Quarterly Historical and Genealogical Magazine,* vol. 4).

Captain John Smith. 1608. *A True Relation of Such Occurrences and Accidents of Noate as Hath Hapned in Virginia Since the First Planting of that Colony, which is now Resident in the South Part Thereof, till the Last Returne from Thence.* London: Edward Alde for John Tappe.

Nemattanew (died c.1622)

Also known to the English colonists as "Jack-of-the-Feather" because "he used to come into the felde all covered over wth feathers and Swans wings fastened unto his showlders as thowghe he meante to flye," Nemattanew (also Nemattanow and Munetute) was one of Powhatan's (and later Opechancanough's) greatest warriors. He died sometime just before the widespread attack on the English settlements by Opechancanough's forces along the James River on 22 March 1622. Nemattanew was considered a great war leader by the warriors, who followed him into battle under the belief (apparently promulgated by Nemattanew as part of the plan to help revitalize the empire that Opitchipam and Opechancanough had inherited from their brother Powhatan upon the latter's death in 1618) that he was invincible to bullets and could lead his people eventually to vanquish and drive out their mortal enemies, the English.

For a period of about eleven years, Nemattanew was one of the most effective Indian battle leaders. George Percy, in his "A Trewe Relacyon," writes that when Sir Thomas Dale was sent further up the James River in 1611 to establish what became known as the Cittie of Henricus, some of the men traveling on foot were many times "assawlted and encouwntered by the salvages beinge sente from Powhatan haveinge for their Leader one Munetute." After Dale's men finally reached the location where the new settlement was to be established and began to build the fortifications,

> The Salvages weare nott Idle all this Tyme butt hindred their designes as muche as they colde shoteinge Arrowes into the foarte where wth dyvrs of our men weare wownded & others indangered And some haveinge inploymentt wthoutt The foarte did come shorte hoame and weare slayne by the Salvages.

Nemattanew apparently led a number of daring actions against the English in the years leading up to the Massacre of 1622, but shortly before the massive attack against the colonists took place, he was shot and killed by two friends of a settler named Morgan, to which event some have attributed the timing of the attack.

> The Prologue to this Tragedy, is supposed was occasioned by Nemattanow, otherwise called Jack of the Feather, because hee commonly was most strangely adorned with them; and for his courage and policy, was accounted amongst the Salvages their chiefe Captaine, and immortall from any hurt could bee done him by the English. This Captaine comming to one Morgans house, knowing he had many commodities that hee desired, perswaded Morgan to goe with him to Pamaunke to trucke, but the Salvage murdered him by the way; and after two or three daies returned againe to Morgans house, where he found two youths his Servants, who asked for their Master: Jack replied directly he was dead; the Boyes suspecting as it was, by seeing him weare his [Morgan's] Cap, would have had him to Master Thorp: But Jack so moved their patience, they shot him, so he fell to the ground, put him in a Boat to have him before the Governor, then seven or eight miles from them. But by the way Jack finding the pangs of death upon him, desired of the Boyes two things: the one was, that they would not make it knowne hee was slaine with a bullet; the other, to bury him amongst the English. At the losse of this Salvage Opechankanough much grieved and repined, with great threats of revenge; but the English returned him such terrible answers, that he cunningly dissembled his intent, with the greatest signes he could of love and peace.

Yet fourteen days later, Opechancanough launched the attack that came to be known as the Massacre of 1622.

Scholars disagree as to whether or not Nemattanew's death was the direct cause of the choice of time for the attack. There is even debate over whether Nemattanew was still an ally of Opechancanough at the time of his death, as evidenced in a letter from the Council in Virginia addressed to the London Company in England. In it, they wrote:

> Neither was it to be imagined yt uppon ye death of Nenemachanew, a man soe farr owt of the favor of Apochancono yt he [Opechancanough] sent worde to Sr. George Yardley beinge then Govrnor by his interpreter, yt for his p[ar]te he could be contented his [Nemattanew's] throte were Cutt, there w[ould] falle owte a generall breach, wee beinge intreatie wth him and offeringe to doe him Justice Accordinge to the Articles of the peace, yt uppon the takinge upp of the dead bodies yt might appere yt Nenemachanew had noe hande in theire deaths wch was all yt Apochancon[o] required and ther uppon sent oute as he fainde to search for ye bodies, and in the mean tyme sent woorde yt the death of Nenemachanew beinge but one man should be noe occasione of the breach of ye peace, and yt the Skye should sooner falle then [ye] Peace be broken, one his p[ar]te, and that he had given order to all his People to give us noe offence and desired the like from us.

Whether or not Nemattanew was out of favor—and the statement sent against him may have been made by Openchancanough to cover his true intent, to attack the English settlements soon—his abilities as a war leader and symbol of revitalization of the Indians' hopes was a great loss to Opechancanough and his people. This "Jack-of-the-Feather" had so long defied the English and their superior firepower while inflicting real damage on them that he had given hope to his people that perhaps there was still a chance to recover their lands and remove what they saw as foreign invaders threatening their world. But just as Powhatan had tried, and as Opechancanough continued to try for twenty-two years more following Nemattanew's death, the quest was futile. The English had established a strong foothold on the Chesapeake Bay, and even supposed invincibility against their weapons was no match for the reality of their determination to keep it.

Related entries: Massacre of 1622; Opechancanough; Powhatan

Suggestions for further reading

James Axtell. 1995. *The Rise and Fall of the Powhatan Empire: Indians in Seventeenth-Century Virginia.* Williamsburg, VA: Colonial Williamsburg Foundation.

Susan Myra Kingsbury, ed. 1935. *The Records of The Virginia Company of London* (vol. 4). Washington, DC: Government Printing Office.

George Percy. 1922. "'A Trewe Relacyon'—Virginia from 1609 to 1612" *(Tyler's Quarterly Historical and Genealogical Magazine,* vol. 4).

Captain John Smith. 1907. *The Generall Historie of Virginia, New England & The Summer Isles Together with The True Travels, Adventures and Observations, and A Sea Grammar* (vol. 1). Glasgow, Scotland: MacLehose and Sons.

New Fort

See Smith's Fort

Newport News

Listed in Captain John Smith's 1612 *Map of Virginia* as Point Hope, the land bordering the James River just to the west of Kecoughtan (modern-day Hampton) had been renamed "Newporte Newes" by November 1619, when it first appeared in the records of the Virginia Company of London. The origin of the name is not certain, but there are at least two and possibly three plausible explanations. The first is that it was named for Captain Christopher Newport after he intercepted the Jamestown colonists attempting to abandon Jamestown following the Starving Time, the disastrous winter of 1609–1610. Newport had just returned from England with enough supplies to sustain the colonists for many months, and as a result of this good news, the spot became known as Newport's News. Another possible source of the name is Newce's Town, or Port Newce, in County Cork, Ireland. From there in late 1621, Daniel Gookin, preceded by Captain Thomas Newce and Sir William Newce, traveled to what is now Newport News with forty head of cattle, fifty men, thirty other passengers, and the desire to build a new settlement. "According to their desire the Governor seated them at New Porte Newce, and he conceived great hope if this Irish plantation prospered that from Ireland great multitude of people wilbe like to come hither." A third possibility is that Newport News was named after a member of the Newce (Newse, Nuce) family.

For some years, the settlement at Newport News appeared to prosper. It was reported that

> at Nuports-newes: the Cotten trees in a yeere grew so thicke as ones arme, and so high as a man: here any thing that is planted doth prosper so well as in no place better. For the mortality of the people accuse not the place, for of the old Planters and the families scarce one of twenty miscarries, onely the want of necessaries are the occasions of those diseases.

Apparently, Newport News provided some sense of security to its inhabitants as well. Immediately following the 1622 Massacre, Gookin refused to abandon his settlement and "would not obey the Commanders command in that, though hee had scarce five and thirty [men] of all sorts with him, yet he thought himselfe sufficient against what could happen, and so did to his great credit and the content of his Adventurers." Although the settlement survived the immediate aftermath of the massacre, by 1623 conditions had deteriorated. When forty new colonists arrived at the settlement in the spring of that year, they reported that "Of all Mr. Gookins men which he sent out the last year we found but seven, the rest being all killed by the Indians, and his plantation ready to fall to decay." By the 1625 census, only twenty servants are listed with a total of four houses.

Although Newport News experienced a decline from its height at the time of Daniel Gookin's estate, by the 1630s it had become a well-known and much-frequented stop for ships traveling to and from the New World. A Dutch shipmaster by the name of David Pietersz de Vries writes in 1633 that, while sailing up the James River,

> When we came to the before-mentioned point of Newport-Snuw, we landed and took in water. A fine spring lies inside the shore of the river, convenient for taking water from. All the ships come here to take in water on their way home.

On his return trip downriver, he notes that again he "anchored at evening before the point of Newport-Snuw, where we took in water."

Newport News has been the site of some of America's most important early history. In the American Civil War, the famous Battle of the Ironclads, the *Monitor* and the *Merrimack,* took place just off its shores, and many earthen fortifications from the Peninsula Campaign are still to be found there in its fields and parks. With the entry of the United States into World War I, Newport News became a port of embarkation for the army, and it was the site of Camp Eustis, now known as Fort Eustis. And it was to play an important role in future wars as well. The Newport News Shipbuilding and Dry Dock Company, established in 1886, became a major source of naval power by building many of America's aircraft carriers, including the *Roosevelt,* the *Kennedy,* the *Enterprise,* the *Vinson,* and the *Washington.* Today, the city of Newport News is about twenty-two miles long by four miles wide, with a population of about 170,000 people, and it has become a center of international research, technology, and commerce.

Related entries: Cape Charles; Cape Henry; Kecoughtan; Kecoughtan Indians; Massacre of 1622; Mulberry Island; Newport, Sir Christopher; Smith, Captain John

Suggestions for further reading

Philip L. Barbour, ed. 1986. *The Complete Works of Captain John Smith (1580–1631)* (vol. 2). Chapel Hill and London: University of North Carolina Press.

Alexander Brown. 1890. *The Genesis of the United States* (vol. 2). Boston: Houghton Mifflin.

——. 1898. *The First Republic in America.* Boston: Houghton Mifflin.

Charles E. Hatch, Jr. 1957. *The First Seventeen Years: Virginia 1607–1624.* Charlottesville, VA: University Press of Virginia.

Lyon Gardiner Tyler. 1906. *The Cradle of the Republic: Jamestown and James River.* Richmond, VA: Hermitage Press.

Newport, Sir Christopher (1560–1617)

Perhaps not widely celebrated as such, but just as deserving as most others in the earliest years of the Jamestown colony, Captain Christopher Newport can be considered one of the most important members of the company of bold and adventurous individuals who founded the first permanent English settlement in the New World. It was he who led the first voyage to Jamestown and was the ultimate authority for the crew and colonists until they landed in Virginia and read the sealed orders designating who would comprise the king's representatives in the new colony. And as those orders were read, Christopher Newport's name was found among the list of first councilors, who were charged with guiding the colony in the king's name. Not only had he been the ultimate authority at sea, Newport would continue in authority on land, sharing governance of the other colonists with his fellow council members. Although he left the colony a few weeks after his first arrival (which had been the plan, as he was admiral of the expedition and not a "planter"), it was Newport who returned four more times over the next four years with crucial shipments of colonists and supplies to sustain and build the settlement. His role was vital and essential, and under less capable leadership the expeditions might never have reached their destinations.

Even before his voyages to Virginia, Captain Newport had begun to earn the respect of his fellow mariners and countrymen. After a somewhat interesting entry into the historical record, in which it is seen that, following a quarrel on a voyage to Brazil in 1581, he jumped ship before returning to England, he served as a privateer in the West Indies, during which time he lost an arm while attempting to take a Spanish galleon. It was also on one of these expeditions in 1592 that he was involved in the capture of the prize *Madre de Dios.* Newport's contribution was so valued that he was given command of the ship for its voyage to Dartmouth.

Shortly after arriving in Virginia in 1607, Newport led a small exploratory expedition up the James River as far as the falls at present-day Richmond. There he placed a cross with the inscription "Jacobus Rex, 1607" to make claim for England before returning to the new settlement to load those commodities most easily collected, mainly "sassafrax rootes," for the return voyage to England. Although accused by Captain John Smith of trading too liberally with the indigenous peoples and thus making future negotiations more difficult, Newport did contribute much to the survival of the colony during its first years. His five voyages between England and Virginia

> ### *First Christian Marriage*
>
> Anno 1609, John Laydon and Anna Burras were married together, the first Christian marriage in that part of the world; and the year following the plantation was increased to near five hundred men.
>
> —Robert Beverley, *History and Present State of Virginia* (London, 1705)

from 1606 through 1611 brought many needed supplies and workers; he sometimes arrived when the permanent settlers were on the verge of total collapse. His arrival with relief at the end of the Starving Time in 1610, after finally reaching Virginia following the wrecking of his *Sea Venture* at Bermuda the previous year, found the colony all but destroyed through disease, starvation, neglect, and Indian attack. And much to the delight of the men to whom he returned in late 1608, he brought the first women to the colony, a Mrs. Forrest and her maid, Anne Burras. The latter soon married a carpenter of the colony by the name of John Laydon, with whom she had a daughter, Virginia, who became the first child born of English parents at Jamestown.

Captain Christopher Newport served England well for many years, and he contributed greatly to the founding of Jamestown as well as the state and nation that grew from it. It is speculated that Newport News, just downriver from Jamestown Island, was named for him, as a result of his arrival and interception of the remaining colonists near there as they attempted to abandon Jamestown following the disastrous winter of 1609–1610. Newport had brought with him enough supplies to sustain the colonists for many months, and as a result of the news of this good fortune, the spot may have become known as Newport's News. Whether or not that is the origin of that city's name, or whether it was simply named in honor of Newport, the Jamestown colonists owed much gratitude to Newport for his many contributions, most important of which were the safe delivery of people and supplies.

Following his years of leading expeditions for the Virginia Company, Newport joined the service of the East India Company in 1612 and became one of the six masters of the Royal Navy. He made voyages to India and the Persian Gulf; while upon one of these voyages, he died at Bantam on Java in August 1617.

Related entries: Cape Henry; Early European Exploration of North America; Gosnold, Bartholomew; James Fort; James River; Lost Colony; Newport News; Powhatan; Smith, Captain John; Three Ships

Suggestions for further reading

Philip L. Barbour, ed. 1986. *The Complete Works of Captain John Smith (1580–1631)* (vol. 2). Chapel Hill and London: University of North Carolina Press.

Alexander Brown. 1890. *The Genesis of the United States* (vols. 1, 2). Boston: Houghton Mifflin.

Charles E. Hatch, Jr. 1995. *The First Seventeen Years: Virginia 1607–1624.* Charlottesville, VA: University Press of Virginia.

Samuel Eliot Morison. 1971. *The European Discovery of America: The Northern Voyages A.D. 500–1600.* New York: Oxford University Press.

Northern Neck

The Northern Neck of Tidewater Virginia is the largest of the several great peninsulas formed by the rivers that drain into the Chesapeake Bay. Bounded by water on the east and north, on the south by the bay and the Potomac and Rappahannock Rivers, its western boundary was originally defined as the line between the headwaters of the rivers, more than 120 miles from the ocean. The region was hardly considered for settlement during the initial period of English colonization because of its distance from Jamestown and the inability of the settlers to provide a defense against Indians. When people did begin to think about settling in the Neck, in 1642 the Virginia General Assembly officially declared it off limits,

Sir William Morton and "The Royal Feast"

(*Sung to the popular tune of "Chevy Chace"*)

Will Morton's of that Cardinal's race,
Who made that blessed maryage;
He is most loyall to his King,
In action, word, and carryage;
His sword and pen defends the cause,
If King Charles thinke not on him,
Will is amongst the rest undone,—
The Lord have mercy on him!
The King sent us, etc.
(chorus:)
The King sent us poor traytors here (But you may guesse the reason) Two brace of bucks to mend the cheere, Is't not to eat them treason?

—"A Loyall Song of the Royall Feast kept by the Prisoners in the Towre . . . with the Names, Titles, and Characters of every Prisoner," by Sir Francis Wortley, Knight and Baronet, Prisoner (1647)

making it illegal to settle in the Neck without the express permission of the governor and council. In 1647, the Assembly reconfirmed the prohibition of settlement in the Neck, although by then the county of Northumberland had been formed (in 1644 or 1645). Northumberland County, or Chickcoun as it was first called, covered the entire Northern Neck until Lancaster County was carved out of it in 1652.

In September 1649, from exile King Charles I granted the Northern Neck to seven English noblemen who were among his staunchest supporters: Sir Ralph, Lord Hopton of Stratton (1596–1652), Henry, Lord Jermyn, later Earl of St. Albans (c.1604–1684), John, Lord Culpeper, First Baron of Thoresway (1600–1660), Sir John, Baron of Berkeley of Stratton (1606–1678), Sir William Morton of Gloucestershire (d. 1672), Sir Dudley Wyatt (d. 1651), and Lieutenant Colonel Thomas Culpeper (c.1602–c.1652). (The latter two died in Virginia.) Charles II confirmed the grant after his restoration in the spring of 1660 and exchanged it for a new charter in May 1669. Although all the original patentees would be dead long before the final boundary lines would be drawn, the Northern Neck Proprietary, as it was known, encompassed some 5,282,000 acres. According to later versions of the patent, the king gave his seven loyal subjects and their heirs and assigns

> for ever, all that intire tract, territory, or parcel of land . . . together with the rivers themselves, and all the islands within the banks of those rivers, and all woods, under-woods, timber and trees, ways, waters and rivers, ponds, pools, water-courses, fishings, streams, havens, ports, harbours, creeks, wrecks of sea, fish-roial, deer, wild beasts and fowl, of what nature and kind soever, mines of gold and silver, lead, tin, iron, and copper, and quarries of stone, and coal . . . together with the roialty of hawking and hunting.

The King did reserve for himself and his heirs one-fifth of all gold and one-tenth of all silver that might be mined in the Neck.

The Northern Neck would prove to play an interesting and conspicuous role in the Virginia colony's history. Lord Culpeper's son Thomas, Second Baron of Thoresway, eventually acquired the interests of the other patentees and was appointed captain and governor of Virginia. He visited Virginia twice in efforts to solidify his ownership, the first time when the colony was still reeling from the aftermath of Bacon's Rebellion. Settlement of the Neck opened up but did not prove as lucrative as Culpeper had hoped, and after a second brief visit to the colony, he returned to England, relinquished the governor's office, and sought to capitalize on the Proprietary from afar. When Culpeper died, the grant went to his heirs, eventually passing to Thomas, Lord Fairfax, sixth Baron of Cameron, who became the first proprietor to actively exercise control over the lands. Fairfax's agent for the Proprietary, Robert "King" Carter of Corotoman (1663–1732) became the wealthiest man in the colonies. Lord Fairfax, an eccentric bachelor who lived in isolation on the western edge of the Proprietary, was the patron of George Washington, who got his start in life surveying the Neck's western lands. Both Washington's birthplace and his eventual home at Mount Vernon were located in the Northern Neck; his great-grandfather had been among the few colonists who dared venture so far away from Jamestown in the early years. Indeed, the great-grandfathers of three early U.S. presidents—Washington, Madison, and Monroe—established tobacco plantations in the Northern Neck in the 1650s, making their homes in what became Westmoreland County. After them came the Carters, the Lees, and others with names that resound across Virginia history. The Northern Neck became a prosperous plantation society with mansion houses like Cobbs Hall, Stratford Hall, Sabine Hall, and Nomini Hall—all undergirded by tobacco and slavery. In the second half of the eighteenth century, the Neck became a hotbed of revolutionary activity. With English settlement came the dislocation of most of the territory's Native Americans.

In the modern era, the Northern Neck usually is defined by the present-day counties of Northumberland, Lancaster, Richmond, and Westmoreland, and sometimes King George—about one-tenth of the original claim. The area is still largely rural with a population of about 50,000 people (70,000 when King George County is included). Historic sites open to the public in the Northern Neck include the George Washington Birthplace National Monument, Stratford Hall Plantation (birthplace of Robert E. Lee), Menokin (home of Francis Lightfoot Lee, a signer of the Declaration of Independence), Historic Christ Church (the best preserved Anglican parish church from colonial Virginia), and the Mary Ball Museum and Library, which includes Lancaster County's old clerk's office, jail, and courthouse. The original Northern Neck land grants are in the Library of Virginia.

Related entries: Culpeper, Lord Thomas, Second Baron of Thoresway; Rappahannock River; Slavery

Suggestions for further reading

Fairfax Harrison. 1926. *The Proprietors of the Northern Neck: Chapters of Culpeper Genealogy.* Richmond, VA: Old Dominion Press.

Mary R. Miller. 1983. *Place-Names of the Northern Neck of Virginia: From John Smith's 1606 Map to the Present.* Richmond: Virginia State Library.

John C. Wilson. 1984, 2003. *Virginia's Northern Neck: A Pictorial History.* Virginia Beach, VA: Donning.

O

Occohannock Indians

See Accohannock Indians

Opechancanough (d. 1646)

Like Powhatan (or Wahunsonacock), who preceded him as mamanatowick, or "great king" of the Powhatan Indians of Virginia, Opechancanough probably was born in the 1540s or 1550s. He apparently was a half brother to Powhatan and, along with another brother, Opitchapam, who immediately succeeded Powhatan as ruler of the Algonquin tribes of Virginia after Powhatan's death in April 1618, Opechancanough took a dramatically different approach to relations with the Jamestown colonists than had Powhatan in his reign.

During the early years of the Jamestown colony, interaction between the Native Americans and the Europeans had been a mixture of cautious cooperation and low-intensity warfare. At times, Powhatan would help the colonists when they were most in need; at other times, he would watch and help them starve because of their own lack of skills in providing for themselves in their new environment. And, apparently, on many occasions Powhatan would order his people to harass and attack the colonists if the opportunity presented itself. But during his reign, no large-scale, concerted effort ever was made to totally destroy and remove the colony, although it was seen as at least a nuisance if not a direct threat to the native people's very existence. It was not long after Powhatan's passing that all this changed.

Long before Powhatan handed over power to his rightful heir and brother Opitchapam in 1617, there were rumors that the actual power of the mamanatowick was beginning to be consolidated into the person of Opechancanough. As Ralph Hamor wrote while quoting a letter from Sir Thomas Dale written on 18 June 1614, "*This* Opocankano *is brother to* Powhatan, *and is his and their chiefe* Captaine: *and one that can as soone (if not sooner) as* Powhatan *commaund the men.*" Indeed, Opechancanough appears to have overshadowed Opitchapam from the start and, aside from what he saw and understood to be the European infringement and occupation of his hereditary lands, he had another major grievance with the colonists, particularly Captain John Smith. After having captured Smith during one of Smith's expeditions shortly after the colonists landed, following which Smith was taken to Powhatan and subsequently released, Opechancanough was captured and briefly held prisoner by Smith. While Smith was meeting with Opechancanough on one of the unending and increasingly difficult quests to obtain food for the colony, the Captain began to detect a trap set by

Opechancanough was a leader of the Powhatan Indians in Virginia and the younger half brother of Powhatan, the powerful sachem who ruled the vast Indian empire around the Chesapeake Bay. An important negotiator with the English settlers in Virginia during the early seventeenth century, Opechancanough later led raids against them, including the Massacres of 1622 and 1644. (North Wind Picture Archives)

his host. Not wasting any time to secure his and his men's safety, Smith "in such a rage snatched the King by his long locke in the middest of his men, with his Pistoll readie bent against his brest. Thus he led the trembling King, neare dead with feare amongst all his people." Addressing Opechancanough's warriors, Smith caused them "to cast downe their Armes, little dreaming any durst in that manner have used their King." Having little affection for the invading Europeans in the first place, this plain humiliation in front of his people allowed the brave and proud man to develop an even greater hatred for Smith and his fellow colonists. This sentiment would eventually lead to grave consequences for the colonists and, eventually, for Opechancanough himself.

Following the few relatively peaceful years after Pocahontas married John Rolfe on 5 April 1614, relations between the ever-expanding, demanding English and their native hosts became strained once again. As much as possible, however, Opechancanough attempted to appear as if he and his people (as noted, Opitchapam appears to have been titular ruler after Powhatan relinquished power, with Opechancanough being the *de facto* leader) finally were beginning to accept the presence of the colonists. The colonists, likewise, were becoming more comfortable with having the "savages" live, work, and play among them. The Indians were often within the confines of the colonists' fortifications, even in their houses, participating in everything from tilling the crops, using the colonists' sharp, metal tools, to providing wild game, using the European weapons. Other than a relatively few unpleasant incidents, everything appeared to be progressing rather nicely for the colonists—until the morning of 22 March 1622. At a predetermined time, the original inhabitants of the land took up any weapons and tools they could find and killed and wounded as many colonists as they could, all the while destroying as much of the colony as could be effected before the English had a chance to regroup and respond. Hundreds of the settlers were killed and many wounded. Opechancanough's plan to eradicate the foreign encroachment had struck a devastating, and apparently unsuspected, blow to England's most successful New World foothold.

Despite the tremendous effectiveness of this attack on Opechancanough's most dangerous and hated enemies, it was not enough to bring the results he and his brothers wanted most—the removal of these invaders and interlopers from the lands of his people. In fact, the attack led to severe and effective reprisals against the native inhabitants, with Opechancanough suffering a near fatal encounter with his tormentors. About a year after the attack, and following much more bloodshed, a meeting was held between the English and Indians under the pretense of establishing some semblance of peace, and obtaining the release of English prisoners held by Opechancanough's forces. At some time during the occasion, the English offered wine to the assembled native leaders. Unbeknownst to Opechancanough and his people, the wine had been laced with poison. Apparently, the poison had enough effect to allow the English to attack and shoot many of their already poisoned hosts. The English thought the attack quite successful in that they

> not only regained their people but cutt of divers of the Indian Kinges and great Comaunders: Amongst whome they are confident that Opachankano was one it beinge impossible for him to escape, beinge the designe was chiefely on his person and that exposed to the principall danger.

For quite some time after this event, the English believed they had achieved their goal of eliminating Opechancanough, thus removing one of the main obstacles to their continuing expansion in the New World. It was not until Opitchapam's death in 1629 that they learned that Opechancanough in fact had survived and was finally the *de jure* leader, or mamanatowick, of the remaining yet much diminished Powhatan empire.

Not many accounts remain of the next few years after the 1622 attack, and Opechancanough is mentioned in very few of those. But he was not idle during that time, and he was not ready to be written entirely out of the history of his people and their land. Following more or less the same tactics he had used before the 1622 actions—having his warriors become familiar to and friendly with the colonists—on 18 April 1644 his forces struck again. They killed even more colonists than the first time, but because of the increased numbers of the settlers, this time the effect was not as devastating to the colony. As before, English reprisals followed the attack, with the result that, after two more years of evading English capture and judgment, during which time he continued to cause much damage to be inflicted on the English as well, Opechancanough was finally apprehended in the summer of 1646. According to some accounts, he had reached nearly 100 years of age. By that time, according to an account written by Robert Beverley many years later in his *History of Virginia,* the man who had been "a man of large stature, noble presence, and extraordinary parts" who "Though he had no advantage of literature . . . was perfectly skilled in the art of governing his rude countrymen" and who "caused all the Indians far and near to dread his name,"

> [had]grown so decrepit, that he was not able to walk alone, but was carried about by his men wherever he had a mind to move. His flesh was all macerated, his sinews slackened, and his eyelids became so heavy, that he could not see, but as they were lifted up by his servants.

On the day of his capture, this formerly great warrior had been discovered nearby and was pursued and captured by a party led by Sir William Berkeley, who took him to Jamestown, where "he was treated with all the respect and tenderness imaginable." Berkeley intended to send Opechancanough to England, "hoping to get reputation by presenting his majesty with a royal captive, who at his pleasure, could call into the field ten times more Indians, than Sir William Berkeley had English in his whole government." But that trip and presentation would not take place. Not long after Opechancanough's capture, "one of the soldiers, resenting the calamities the colony had suffered by this prince's means, basely shot him through the back, after he was made prisoner; of which wound he died." Befitting a man as courageous and dedicated to the cause of protecting his people, land, and way of life, Opechancanough had, as Beverley wrote, "continued brave to the last moment of his life."

Related entries: James Fort; Kecoughtan Indians; Massacre of 1622; Massacre of 1644; Opitchapam; Pamunkey Indians; Pocahontas; Powhatan; Smith, Captain John

Suggestions for further reading

Edward Arber, ed. 1910. *Travels and Works of Captain John Smith* (parts 1, 2). Edinburgh, Scotland: J. Grant.

Philip L. Barbour. 1964. *The Three Worlds of Captain John Smith.* Boston: Houghton Mifflin.

——, ed. 1986. *The Complete Works of Captain John Smith (1580–1631)* (vol. 1). Chapel Hill and London: University of North Carolina Press.

Robert Beverley. 1855. *The History of Virginia, in Four Parts.* Richmond, VA.

Edward Wright Haile, ed. 2001. *Jamestown Narratives: Eyewitness Accounts of the Virginia Colony: The First Decade: 1607–1617.* Champlain, VA: Round House.

James Horn. 2005. *A Land as God Made It: Jamestown and the Birth of America.* New York: Basic Books.

Helen C. Rountree. 2005. *Pocahontas, Powhatan, Opechancanough: Three Indian Lives Changed by Jamestown.* Charlottesville: University Press of Virginia.

William Strachey. 1953. *The Historie of Travell into Virginia Britania (1612)* (Louis B. Wright, and Virginia Freund, eds.) London: Hakluyt Society.

Opitchapam (d. 1630)

Oldest brother or half brother to Powhatan, Opitchapam co-ruled possibly the most important of the Powhatan chiefdoms from an undetermined date until 1618, when he became paramount chief of all of Powhatan's domain following Powhatan's death in April of that year. His chiefdom prior to 1618, the Pamunkey located at Cinquoateck, just above present-day West Point, Virginia, held the holiest temple of the Powhatans and was ruled by Opitchapam and his two younger brothers, Opechancanough and Kekataugh. According to Powhatan succession customs, the brothers would succeed the deceased ruler beginning with the oldest, then the sisters, followed by the sisters' (but not the brothers') children from oldest to youngest. Thus, Opitchapam was essentially the titular paramount chief following Powhatan's death; titular because his younger brother, Opechancanough, was the true power during and after Opitchapam's reign, except for a relatively brief period during which his younger brother may have been recovering from wounds that he received in an ambush by the English in 1623. During that period, in July 1624, as part of the ongoing animosity between the Indians and the English, Opitchapam led a major battle in which as many as 800 Indian bowmen faced about 60 colonists, who were trying to destroy Opitchapam's corn fields. The battle lasted for two days and ended when the Powhatans became disheartened after seeing that the English had succeeded in cutting down much of their corn.

Following his generally overshadowed tenure, Opitchapam died around 1630, and Opechancanough became in name what he had been in fact since 1618, paramount chief of Powhatan's domain. Opitchapam's unusual name appears in the sources in a variety of spellings, including: Itoyatin, Otiotan, Sasaupen, Taughaiten, Istan, Sassapen, Toyatan, Opochoppam, Itoyatene, and Opicham.

Related entries: Opechancanough; Powhatan

Suggestions for further reading

Edward Arber, ed. 1910. *Travels and Works of Captain John Smith* (parts 1, 2). Edinburgh, Scotland: J. Grant.

Philip L. Barbour, ed. 1986. *The Complete Works of Captain John Smith (1580–1631)* (vol. 2). Chapel Hill and London: University of North Carolina Press.

Edward Wright Haile, ed. 2001. *Jamestown Narratives: Eyewitness Accounts of the Virginia Colony: The First Decade: 1607–1617.* Champlain, VA: Round House.

Ivor Noël Hume. 1994. *The Virginia Adventure: Roanoke to James Towne: An Archaeological and Historical Odyssey.* New York: Alfred A. Knopf.

Helen C. Rountree. 1990. *Pocahontas's People: The Powhatan Indians of Virginia Through Four Centuries.* Norman: University of Oklahoma Press.

——. 1993. *Powhatan Foreign Relations: 1500–1722.* Charlottesville: University Press of Virginia.

Lyon Gardiner Tyler. 1906. *The Cradle of the Republic: Jamestown and James River.* Richmond, VA: Hermitage Press.

——, ed. 1907. *Narratives of Early Virginia: 1606–1625.* New York: Charles Scribner's Sons.

P

Pamunkey Indians

The most prominent and powerful of the Algonquin tribes that made up the Powhatan Confederacy at the time of the English settling of Jamestown was the Pamunkey, who lived along the river that takes its name from the tribe, in the present-day counties of King William and New Kent, Virginia. Consisting of about 300 braves at the time of first contact, the tribe was by far the largest in the region, seconded by the Chickahominy. Even today, nearly 400 years later, the tribe remains the most prominent of those that have survived in the state.

Captain John Smith was the first Englishman of note to encounter the Pamunkey people and visit their town. Smith was exploring the rivers of the Chesapeake in December 1607 when a hunting party, including several Pamunkey, managed to take him captive after killing two of his comrades. What followed were "sixe or seven weekes" during which Smith was alternately feasted and threatened with death. He finally was taken to the tribe's chief, Powhatan, who in fact was the most powerful native chief in the region where the colonists would settle. After consulting with his braves, Powhatan seemed ready to allow them, "ready with their clubs, to beate out his braines"; his salvation, Smith later claimed, was due in part to the intervention of Powhatan's princess daughter, Pocahontas. Smith described in detail the ceremonies "where they entertained him with most strange and fearefulle Conjurations;

> As if neare led to hell,
> Amongst the Devils to dwell."

Smith's captivity among the Pamunkey proved to be a lucky event for the Jamestown colonists, for until his capture the colonists were unaware of the "state and bountie" of Powhatan or even where the great chief lived. Over the next year, 1608, Powhatan and Smith met several times, each vying for the upper hand in an uneven alliance.

In January 1609, Smith led a trading expedition up the Pamunkey River, where he encountered Chief Opechancanough, Powhatan's younger half brother, whom Smith had met during his captivity the year before. After negotiations for foodstuffs did not go as smoothly as either side wished, Opechancanough ambushed the Englishmen. He was, however, repulsed by Smith, who jabbed his pistol onto the Indian's chest and led him trembling "near dead with feare" among his people, who then were forced to trade away their winter supply of corn (which the English used up before the end of the ensuing spring). The affront humiliated Opechancanough and fueled his hatred of the English, bringing on years of mutual distrust that culminated finally in the devastating Indian attack of 1622, followed

John Smith is saved from execution by Pocahontas. (Smith, John. The True Travels, Adventures, and Observations of Captaine John Smith, *1630)*

by ten years of warfare. Both sides were leery of one another during the whole time between Smith's initial contact and the great massacre; the capture and year-long captivity of Pocahontas and the uneasy peace that followed her release after John Rolfe and Robert Sparkes traveled up the Pamunkey River in 1612 to look for Powhatan, represent the precariousness of the Pamunkey–English relationship during the early years of the English settlement at Jamestown.

Following the Massacre of 1622 (of which the only warning the settlers received was given by a Pamunkey youth, Chanco), the Pamunkeys hid their corn supplies, burned their houses, and went into hiding, carrying with them English hostages captured during their attacks. Two years later, while keeping their distance from the settlers, they increased their corn cultivation in order to assist neighboring tribes who also were being harassed by the English. A treaty between the English colonists and the Pamunkey and Chickahominy Indian tribes was finally ratified in September 1632. Animosity continued to characterize the relationship between the colonists and the Pamunkey, however, and when Opechancanough led his second major (and final) assault on the English colony in April 1644, killing more than 400 men, women, and children, the Pamunkey were among the Indian coalition leading the attack. The English retaliation that followed was swift and severe; Opechancanough was imprisoned (and later murdered) and the Pamunkey people completely subjugated.

A treaty in October 1646 between the settlers and the Pamunkey tribe officially ended hostilities and explicitly recognized the king of England as supreme over both groups. The treaty required the Pamunkey to pay tribute to the colony's governor, but at the same time it recognized the Indians' rights to territory and established clear land boundaries for both sides. Although the settlers honored the land agreements for only three years, the treaty did ease tensions and usher in a period of peaceful coexistence that lasted until 1676, when Nathaniel Bacon occupied the main Pamunkey town on two separate occasions. An investigation into the rebellion after Bacon's

Canoeing on the Thames

An unusual spectacle took place on the Thames River on 2 September 1603 when three young Native Americans from Virginia demonstrated for Sir Robert Cecil, Earl of Salisbury, how to paddle a canoe. Dressed in fashionable English apparel, the canoeists were a great hit with Cecil and the London social elite who turned out for the event, many of whom presented the Indians with gifts. How the canoeists came to be in England is not known for sure, nor is the origin of their dugout. Speculation has it that they were Pamunkey Indians taken prisoner by Captain Samuel Mace while he was on a reconnaissance voyage to the Chesapeake Bay in preparation for English colonization of Virginia. After two separate demonstrations, Sir Cecil paid the canoeists a total of nine pence for their efforts.

Captain John Smith's Capture by the Pamunkey Indians

The Salvages having drawne from George Cassen whether Captaine Smith was gone, prosecuting that opportunity they followed him with 300. bowmen, conducted by the King of Pamaunkee, who in divisions searching the turnings of the river, found [Jehu] Robinson and [Thomas] Emry by the fire side, those they shot full of arrowes and slew. Then finding the Captaine, as is said, that used the Salvage that was his guide as his shield (three of them being slaine and divers other so gauld) all the rest would not come neere him. Thinking thus to have returned to his boat, regarding them, as he marched, more then his way, slipped up to the middle in an oasie creeke & his Salvage with him, yet durst they not come to him till being neere dead with cold, he threw away his armes. Then according to their composition they drew him forth and led him to the fire, where his men were slaine. Diligently they chafed his benummed limbs. He demanding for their Captaine, they shewed him Opechankanough, King of Pamaunkee, to whom he gave a round Ivory double compass Dyall. Much they marvailed at the playing of the Fly and Needle, which they could see so plainely, and yet not touch it, because of the glasse that covered them. But when he demonstrated by that Globe-like Jewell, the roundnesse of the earth, and skies, the spheare of the Sunne, Moone, and Starres, and how the Sunne did chase the night round about the world continually; the greatnesse of the Land and Sea, the diversitie of Nations, varietie of complexions, and how we were to them Antipodes, and many other such like matters, they all stood as amazed with admiration. Notwithstanding, within an houre after they tyed him to a tree, and as many as could stand about him prepared to shoot him, but the King holding up the Compass in his hand, they all laid downe their Bowes and Arrowes, and in a triumphant manner led him to Orapaks, where he was after their manner kindly feasted, and well used.

Engraving of Captain John Smith's capture by the Pamunkey Indians. (Smith, John. The True Travels, Adventures, and Observations of Captaine John Smith, *1630)*

—*Travels of Captain John Smith,* 1630 (vol. 1)

death revealed that the Pamunkey (and other tributary tribes) had been attacked without provocation by frontier landholders hoping to increase their plantations at the Indians' expense. In May 1677, a new agreement, the Treaty of Middle Plantation, was ratified that reaffirmed Pamunkey rights to land ownership, prohibiting English settlement within three miles of any Indian town. The treaty also established guidelines for Indian hunting, fishing, and gathering expeditions, and for trading with the English. (The 1,200 acres that make up the present

Pamunkey Indian reservation dates from that treaty, as does the annual custom of paying a tribute of venison or turkey to the governor of Virginia every Thanksgiving Day.) The Pamunkey signatories of the Treaty of Middle Plantation were Queen Cockacoeske, a descendant of Opechancanough who had fled in terror from Bacon's invaders and lived alone in the Virginia forests for two weeks, and her son, known as Captain John West (apparently the son of an English colonel named John West who owned a plantation on the Pamunkey River), Cockacoeske's presumed successor. As it turned out, the reign until 1718 of Cockacoeske's successor, a niece known to history only as Queen Ann, foreshadowed the history of the Pamunkey people as it would play out for the next century and a half: increased isolation, dwindling population, declining fortunes, and continued loss of land. The low point appears to have occurred in the eighteenth century, when the tribe consisted of fewer than ten families with about seven to a dozen adult men; in the second half of the eighteenth century (after the tribe's conversion to Christianity, which in part resulted from the missionary outreach efforts of William and Mary College), a few white men took Pamunkey wives and lived among the Indians.

Today, about three dozen families reside on the Pamunkey reservation, although many tribal members live in other parts of Virginia and the United States. The Pamunkey tribe has an elected governing body, including a chief and seven council members elected every four years. The surviving Pamunkey culture revolves around interests that the tribe has maintained since precolonial times: hunting, trapping, fishing, and pottery making. Since 1918, the tribe has operated a shad hatchery on the Pamunkey River, and in April 1998 the tribe, in cooperation with federal and state governmental agencies (including the Virginia Department of Game and Inland Fisheries) opened a renovated shad hatchery aimed at greatly increasing the number of American shad. A pottery school established in the 1930s helps to preserve the art as carried on by the Pamunkey women, making pottery of local clay in the style of their ancestors. In 1979, the tribe opened the Pamunkey Indian Museum, an extensive museum that exhibits 12,000 years of Indian artifacts chronologically, from prehistory to the present. Also on the reservation are burial mounds that, according to legend, contain the resting place of Powhatan. The Pamunkey tribe is one of eight officially recognized by the State of Virginia.

Related entries: Accohannock Indians; Accomac Indians; Chanco; Chesapeake Indians; Chickahominy Indians; Kecoughtan Indians; Manahoac Indians; Massacre of 1622; Mattaponi Indians; Monacan Indians; Nansemond Indians; Pamunkey River; Paspahegh Indians; Pocahontas; Powhatan; Smith, Captain John; Warraskoyak Indians

Suggestions for further reading

Helen C. Rountree. 1990. *Pocahontas's People: The Powhatan Indians of Virginia Through Four Centuries.* Norman: University of Oklahoma Press.

Captain John Smith. 1907. *The Generall Historie of Virginia, New England & The Summer Isles Together with The True Travels, Adventures and Observations, and A Sea Grammar* (vol. 1). Glasgow, Scotland: MacLehose and Sons.

Pamunkey River

One of what Robert Beverley in 1705 called the "abundance of lesser rivers, many of which are capable of receiving the biggest merchant ships," the Pamunkey River takes its name from the Native American tribe to which Chief Powhatan belonged. The Pamunkey is formed about twenty miles north of Richmond when its two tributary rivers, the North and South Anna, converge. From there the Pamunkey flows (roughly parallel with the James) for about ninety miles, the lower fifty of which are navigable, before joining the Mattaponi to form the York River. The river's basin drains from the Virginia counties of Caroline, Hanover, King William, and New Kent.

The Pamunkey River basin was still uncharted territory as far as Europeans were concerned when German explorer John Lederer in March 1669 made the first of his three trips up the river. He wrote,

> I reached the first Spring of *Pemaeoncock,* having crossed the River four times that day by reason of its many windings; but the water was so shallow,

> that it hardly wet my horses patterns. Here a little under the surface of the earth, I found flat pieces of petrified matter, of one side solid Stone, but on the other side Isinglas, which I easily peeled off in flakes about four inches square: several of these pieces, with a transparent Stone like Crystal that cut Glass, and a white Marchasite that I purchased of the Indians, I presented to Sir *William Berkley* Governour of *Virginia*.

Lederer also noted in detail the wildlife that he encountered—squirrels, wolves, grey foxes, wild cats and "Small Leopards," rattle snakes, bears, beavers, otters, and "Great herds of Red and Farrow Deer." Lederer described the view that opened to him from the Pamunkey's headwaters: "from the top of an eminent hill, I first descried the Apalatean Mountains, bearing due West to the place I stood upon: their distance from me was so great, that I could hardly discern whether they were Mountains or Clouds."

Modern travelers find that much of the Pamunkey remains as Lederer experienced it, for development has been almost nonexistent, tidal marshes and forestation remain intact, and the river is clean. Indeed, many formerly improved lands that included Native American villages and colonial plantations have reverted back to natural habitat. In addition to the wildlife that Lederer described, bird life includes osprey, bald eagles, great blue herons, and a wide variety of waterfowl and songbirds. The river is filled with abundant fish, bluegill, redbreast sunfish, stripers, white and yellow perch, blue and white and channel catfish, small- and largemouth and spotted bass, crappie, carp, long-nose gar, and shad (a shad hatchery is operated by the Pamunkey Indians at the tribe's reservation in King William County). The Pamunkey River's recreational uses include hunting, fishing, camping, canoeing, kayaking, boating, and bird watching.

Perhaps the most famous Pamunkey River settlement was the White House Plantation, the Custis family estate where George Washington and Martha Custis were married in 1760 and which was later owned by Martha's great-granddaughter, Mary Anna Randolph Custis, the wife of Robert E. Lee. During the American Civil War, operations along the Pamunkey were especially important during the Peninsula Campaign of 1862 and the Overland Campaign of 1864.

Related entries: Chickahominy River; Elizabeth River; James River; Mattaponi River; Nansemond River; Pamunkey Indians; Rappahannock River; York River

Suggestion for further reading

William Talbot, trans. 1672. *The Discoveries of John Lederer, In Three Several Marches from Virginia, to the West of Carolina, And Other Parts of the Continent: Begun in March 1669, and Ended in September 1670. Together with A General Map of the Whole Territory which He Traversed.* London: J.C. for Samuel Heyrick.

Paspahegh Indians

It was an unhappy fate that frowned upon the people occupying the James River countryside where the English chose to establish their fort and settlement in 1607. Those inhabitants, Native Americans called the Paspahegh, were an Algonquian-speaking nation closely allied with Chief Powhatan, to whom they paid tribute. From their principal town at what was later Middle Plantation (still later, Williamsburg), these natives of the north side of the James, which lies in present-day Charles City and James City Counties, already knew of Europeans and the potential threat to their sovereignty presented by those foreigners. In fact, by the time the three English ships sailed into the Chesapeake Bay and up the James, the Paspahegh already had moved further up the James to Sandy Point in anticipation of the white man's arrival. That act of prudence—or fear—would not be enough to prevent the inevitable confrontations that soon would arise between them and the intruders who would lay claim to the territory where they and their ancestors had lived for generations beyond remembrance.

The settlers hardly had begun to construct a fort when the Paspahegh violently assaulted them on 26 May (less than a fortnight after their arrival)—from the English perspective, an unprovoked, violent attack aimed at wiping them out. The colonists suffered a dozen casualties, including one or two killed, and the Paspahegh lost its chief, Wowinchopunk. The colonists were in no position to retaliate at that time, but this turbulent prelude set the tone for what would follow: a

Native Americans dance in this sixteenth-century illustration by John White, engraved by Theodor de Bry. (Library of Congress)

decades-long struggle for supremacy between the native peoples and the white settlers that would end with the total subjugation of the Powhatan peoples. As Chief Okaning later told Captain John Smith, "We perceive and well know you intend to destroy us." Smith met with the Paspahegh on several occasions, including one rendezvous in which Smith characterized the Paspahegh as a "churlish and trecherous nation" looking to deal with him "by stelth, but seeming to dislike it, they were ready to assault us." Standing their guard, neither side trusting the other, the Paspahegh and the settlers traded with one another, the natives giving up ten or twelve bushels of corn for whatever trinkets or goods the English had with them. (The Paspahegh also traded corn to Captain John Martin, one of the original Jamestown councilors, on at least two occasions.)

When Smith was captured by a group of native hunters in December 1607, one of the chiefs he was paraded before was the king of the Paspahegh. The two men exchanged knowledge and beliefs; according to Smith,

> the King tooke great delight in understanding the manner of our ships, sayling the seas, the earth and skies, and of our God: what he knew of the dominions he spared not to acquaint me with, as of certaine men cloathed at a place called Ocanahonan, cloathed like me: the course of our river, and that within 4 or 5 daies journey of the falles, was a great turning of salt water.

When Smith's captors carried him back to the English settlement, they did so by way of the Jamestown isthmus, long a Paspahegh possession. "The Indians trifled away that day," wrote Smith, "and would not goe to our Forte by any persuasions: but in certaine olde hunting houses of Paspahegh we lodged all night." Almost a year after Smith had left the colony, the day of reckoning finally came for the Paspahegh, on 9 August 1610, for on that date the governor of the colony sent a strong force of more than seventy English soldiers to lay waste to the Paspahegh town. Fifteen or sixteen Paspahegh were killed, their heads cut off, the tribe's corn crop destroyed, and the tribal queen and her children taken into custody. According to George Percy, who led the expedition, events then took an even uglier, more gruesome turn, as the soldiers

> did begin to murmur becawse the quene and her Children weare spared. So upon the same A Cowncell beinge called itt was Agreed upon to putt the Children to deathe the wch was effected by Throweinge them overboard and shoteinge owtt their Braynes in the water yett for all this Crewellty the Sowldiers weare nott well pleased And I had mutche to doe To save the quenes lyfe for thatt Tyme.

Alas for the queen; she also was put to the sword shortly after being taken to the Jamestown fort.

After the English attack on Paspahegh Town, the Paspahegh ceased to be a threat to the colonists. The tribe's occupation of Sandy Point ended by 1617, when Smythe's Hundred (Southampton Hundred after 1619) was established there, and in 1618 some 3,000 acres in the center of the Paspahegh region were set aside by the Virginia Company as the "Governor's Land" tract for the new incoming governor of the colony, George Yeardley. During Bacon's Rebellion in 1676, the insurgents directed their siege of Jamestown from a 44-acre clearing where the colony's original glass factory had once stood, by then a small plantation owned by Colonel Francis Moryson (elected governor and captain general of Virginia in 1661) but known as Paspahegh Old Fields.

The principle seat of the Paspahegh was excavated in the early 1990s by a team representing the Williamsburg-based James River Institute for Archaeology. Added to the National Register of Historic Places in 1993, the Paspahegh settlement site revealed occupation as far back as 500 B.C. The dig uncovered three large buildings and several small houses from the Jamestown settlement period, and the layout of the site has been incorporated into the Powhatan Indian village living history area at Jamestown Settlement.

Related entries: Accohannock Indians; Accomac Indians; Chesapeake Indians; Chickahominy Indians; Kecoughtan Indians; Manahoac Indians; Mattaponi Indians; Monacan Indians; Nansemond Indians; Pamunkey Indians; Smith, Captain John; Warraskoyak Indians

Suggestions for further reading

Nicholas M. Lucketti, Mary Ellen N. Hodges, and Charles T. Hodges, eds. 1994. *Paspahegh Archaeology: Data Recovery Investigations of Site 44JC308 at the Governor's Land at Two Rivers, James City County, Virginia.* Williamsburg, VA: Colonial Williamsburg Foundation.

George Percy. 1922. "'A Trewe Relacyon'—Virginia from 1609 to 1612" *(Tyler's Quarterly Historical and Genealogical Magazine,* vol. 4).

Captain John Smith. 1608. *A True Relation of Such Occurrences and Accidents of Noate as Hath Hapned in Virginia Since the First Planting of that Colony, which is now Resident in the South Part Thereof, till the Last Returne from Thence.* London: Edward Alde for John Tappe.

Percy, George (1580–1632)

George Percy was born on 4 September 1580 into a distinguished and ancient English family. He was the son of the eighth earl of Northumberland, Henry, and brother to the ninth, also Henry. His mother was the eldest daughter of Lord Latimer, John Neville. He was educated in Oxford and Middle Temple, and saw service as a soldier in the Netherlands before taking part in the original Jamestown settlement, arriving in May 1607.

Given his heritage, it was somewhat of a surprise that Percy's name was not on the list of the Council for Virginia when the King's instructions were opened and read on the colonists' first landing at Cape Henry on 26 April 1607. Others from less distinguished families, John Smith for one, had been included. This may have been due to the fact that his brother, Henry, had been arrested and held in the Tower of London under suspicion of involvement in the 1605 Gunpowder Plot to assassinate King James I with the Lords and the Commons. Nonetheless, he would become governor of the colony and serve as such from September 1609 until May 1610, during the tragic period known as the Starving Time, and again from March 1611 until April 1612.

During his first term as governor, Percy sent Captain John Ratcliffe to build a fort at the mouth of the James River as a defense against the Spanish. A fort was built in 1609 at Point Comfort and named Fort Algernon after one of Percy's ancestors, William Algernourne de Percy.

George Percy left Virginia, never to return, on 22 April 1612. In 1625, he again saw military action in the Netherlands, during the war with Spain, losing a finger in battle while commanding a company. His *Observations Gathered Out of a Discourse of the Plantation of the Southerne Colonie in Virginia by the English, 1606,* along with the writings of John Smith, contains some of the most important and detailed accounts of the first few years of the Jamestown settlement. (The original *Observations* was lost, but an abridged version was published in volume 4 of *Purchas his Pilgrimes* [London, 1685–1690].) Percy also left another important account of the early years of Jamestown, "A Trewe Relacyon of the Proceedings and Ocurrentes of Momente wch have hapned in Virginia from 1609 to 1612," written to his brother, Lord Percy, which details the Starving Time of the winter of 1609–1610. George Percy died in 1632.

Related entry: Algernon, Fort

Suggestions for further reading

Philip L. Barbour, ed. 1986. *The Complete Works of Captain John Smith (1580–1631)* (vol. 1). Chapel Hill and London: University of North Carolina Press.

Edward Wright Haile, ed. 2001. *Jamestown Narratives: Eyewitness Accounts of the Virginia Colony: The First Decade: 1607–1617.* Champlain, VA: Round House.

George Percy. 1612. *Observations Gathered Out of a Discourse of the Plantation of the Southerne Colonie in Virginia by the English, 1606* (In *Purchas his Pilgrimes,* London, 1685–1690).

——. 1922. "'A Trewe Relacyon'—Virginia from 1609 to 1612" *(Tyler's Quarterly Historical and Genealogical Magazine,* vol. 4).

Lyon Gardiner Tyler. 1906. *The Cradle of the Republic: Jamestown and James River.* Richmond, VA: Hermitage Press.

——, ed. 1907. *Narratives of Early Virginia: 1606–1625.* New York: Charles Scribner's Sons.

Plymouth Company

See London Company

Pocahontas (c.1595–d. 1617)

Perhaps no other name except that of Captain John Smith is more associated with the Jamestown colony than that of Pocahontas. While her place in the history of the first permanent English settlement in the New World is not well documented in the earliest records of the colony, her legend has overshadowed the history of almost all others who participated in that venture. She took a central role in some of the most

St. George at Gravesend

The parish death registry of the church at St. George, Gravesend, contains an interesting entry: "Rebecca Wrolfe, wyffe of Thos. Wrolfe, gent, a Virginia lady born, was buried in ye chauncel." Pocahontas, alias Matoaka, the daughter of the paramount chief of the Powhatan Indians, was baptized as Rebecca after her conversion to Christianity at Jamestown before her marriage to tobacco planter John Rolfe in 1614. In the early twentieth century, the rector of St. George placed a marble monument dedicated to the "Virginia lady born" and chronicling her services in assisting the colony at Jamestown.

Kewasa (The Deity)

They believe that there are many Gods which they call "Mantóac," but of different sortes and degrees; one onely chiefe and great God, which hath bene from all eternitie. Who as they affirme when hee purposed to make the worlde, made first other goddes of a principall order to bee as meanes and instruments to bee used in the creation and government to follow; and after the Sunne, Moone, and Starres, as pettie goddes and the instruments of the other order more principall. First they say were made waters, out of which by the gods was made all diversitie of creatures that are visible or invisible. . . .

They thinke that all the gods are of humane shape, & therfore they represent them by images in the formes of men, which they call "Kewasowok" one alone is called "Kewás"; Them they place in houses appropriate or temples which they call "Mathicómuck"; Where they woorship, praie, sing, and make manie times offerings unto them. In some "Machicómuck" we have seene but one "Kewas," in some two, and in other some three; The common sort thinke them to be also gods.

—Thomas Hariot, *A Briefe and True Report of the New Found Land of Virginia,* 1588

important aspects of the early years of the settlement, as documented in some of Smith's later writings, but received little, if any, mention in the reports of others. Indeed, her importance to the survival of the colony, and of Smith, increased as Smith rewrote his accounts of his two and one-half years in Virginia. She was one of the rare few whom appeared to have contributed in a positive way to both cultures struggling to survive during the early years of the Jamestown colony.

Probably born in the mid-1590s, Pocahontas was one of several children of the then great chief of the region, Powhatan (or Wahunsonacock). She was not, as the current interpretations of her life would have it, actually a princess. Because of the traditions of succession in her society, Pocahontas was not considered "royalty" among her people, at least not in the European sense of the word. However, she was described as having been a favorite of her father, one whom he "most esteemed," as well as being admired by many of the English with whom she came in contact. As Smith related, Pocahontas was exceptional even as "a child of tenne yeares old: which, not only for feature, countenance, and proportion, much exceedeth any of the rest of his [Powhatan's] people: but for wit and spirit, [is] the only *Nonpariel* of his Country."

Pocahontas, whose actual public name was Amonute (she also had a secret name, Matoaka, revealed only to a few), was best known at James Fort as a young girl who came to play with the other children and who would "gett the boyes forth with her into the markett place and make them wheele, falling on their handes turning their heeles upwardes, whome she would follow, and wheele so her self naked as she was all the Fort over." It was perhaps this sort of activity which earned her the nickname she is best known by, Pocahontas, sometimes interpreted to mean "little wanton," which her father had given to her as a result of her playful antics designed to get his attention, for which she had to compete against all of her sisters and brothers. Whatever the meaning and origin of the word, Pocahontas's charm and vibrancy appeared to have gained the affection of many she encountered.

Along with their fondness for her, the colonists also owed Pocahontas a great deal of gratitude, according to the writings of some of the English observers. Not only is she credited with saving John Smith's life during what may

The daughter of Powhatan, Pocahontas played a crucial role in negotiating a stable relationship between the Jamestown colonists and the Powhatan nation during the early seventeenth century. (Ellyson, J. Taylor. The London Company of Virginia, *1908)*

have been an initiation right staged by her father, Pocahontas apparently was instrumental in saving the colony on more than one occasion. In a letter Smith addressed to Queen Anne on behalf of Pocahontas during the latter's visit to England, he stated that she had been of great importance in helping to sustain the colony. He wrote that

> such was the weaknesse of this poore Commonwealth, as had the Salvages not fed us, we directly had starved.
>
> And this reliefe, most gracious Queene, was commonly brought us by this Lady Pocahontas, notwithstanding all these passages when inconstant Fortune turned our peace to warre, this tender Virgin would still not spare to dare to visit us, and by her our jarres have beene oft appeased, and our wants still supplyed; were it the policie of her father thus to imploy her, or the ordinance of God thus to make her his instrument, or her extraordinarie affection to our Nation, I know not: but of this I am sure; when her father with the utmost of his policie and power, sought to surprize mee. . . . the darke night could not affright her from comming through the irkesome woods, and with watered eies gave me intelligence, with her best advice to escape his furie; which had hee knowne, hee had surely slaine her. James towne . . . she as freely frequented, as her fathers habitation; and during the time of two or three yeeres, she next under God, was still the instrument to preserve this Colonie from death, famine and utter confusion.

Some have questioned Smith's objectives for writing about Pocahontas as he did in this letter, but it was clear that one of the most important participants in the earliest years of the colony presented her as integral to its survival. It was another occurrence, however, that solidified the importance of Pocahontas's role in the thinking and plans of others involved in the colonization of the New World.

In 1613, Pocahontas was visiting the Patawomekes when she learned that an English ship was in the area. Having been friendly with the

Pocahontas's Brothers

Pocahontas is one of the most famous names in American history, but hardly anyone knows that she had two brothers just slightly older than she, Matachanna (b. 1593) and Nantaquaus (b. 1594). Of the younger brother, Nantaquaus, Captain John Smith wrote, in his petition to Queen Anne on behalf of Pocahontas, that when he was "taken prisoner by the power of Powhatan, their chief king, I received from this great savage exceeding great courtesy, especially from his son, Nantaquaus; the manliest, comeliest, boldest spirit I ever saw in a savage." Unfortunately, little else is known of the brothers, other than that they attended the wedding of Pocahontas and John Rolfe in 1616.

Kocoum: Pocahontas's First Husband?

Because of the popularity of the Disney film, *Pocahontas,* many know that the legendary Indian princess already may have been married when she wed John Rolfe in 1614. But of her reputed first husband, an Indian warrior named Kocoum, not much is known other than that he apparently was a "pryvate Captayne" of Chief Powhatan and may have been a Patawomeke warrior. The marriage is said to have taken place in 1610, a few months after Pocahontas went to live at the Patawomeke village in the fall of 1609, long before the English settlers captured her and held her for ransom in 1613. When in England, Pocahontas became the subject of accusations that she was living in sin because she was married to both Kocoum and John Rolfe at the same time. Although rumors apparently swirled, no one took the trouble to record them for posterity. Some have theorized that Kocoum had been killed fighting the English, or that he was unable or unwilling to rescue her after her kidnapping, and thus she became free to remarry according to an Indian tradition of "divorce by capture." Some have suggested the marriage was honorary only, possibly the product of a tribal alliance ritual, and never consummated because of her youth. Still others have wondered whether jealous enemies concocted the story altogether. Whatever the truth, Kocoum remains buried in obscurity forever.

colonists since their earliest years at Jamestown, she decided to visit the ship. Prior to this time, her father's people had captured and still held a number of the colonists, as well as arms and tools from the colony. The ship's captain, Samuel Argall, realized how valuable Pocahontas could be in negotiating for the return of the captives and goods. He devised and executed a plan to lure her aboard the ship and proceeded to detain her with the intention of holding her for ransom to force negotiations with Powhatan. Pocahontas, distressed and unwilling, was taken to Jamestown to be held until the colonists' demands were met. The exchange between Powhatan and the English dragged on for months, during which time Pocahontas was indoctrinated into the behaviors and religion of her captors. It was during this time that she met John Rolfe who, apparently becoming infatuated with her, asked that they be married, which they were on 5 April 1614. Both the English and Rolfe, who implied as much in his petition to the governor to allow him to marry her, saw great potential in Pocahontas as a model and example of what could be accomplished with the native inhabitants of Virginia if the proper techniques were employed to convert them to English customs and religion. Along with the search for viable commodities, bringing the English understanding of salvation to the Indians was one of the stated goals of the quest to colonize the New World. Pocahontas's conversion to Christianity and marriage to Rolfe were seen as substantial steps toward "civilizing" her people. It did not appear to be important, or obvious, to the English that the Powhatans already had their own civilization and religious beliefs, or that Pocahontas already had a husband, a Powhatan warrior named Kocoum. The conversion and ceremony were concluded, and the English had their most important convert to date, now known as Rebecca.

Following their marriage, Pocahontas and John Rolfe had one child, a son they named Thomas, and for the remainder of Pocahontas's life there was relative peace between the Powhatans and the English. In 1616, the Rolfe family traveled to England, where Pocahontas was received as a princess from the New World and enjoyed a number of festivities given on her behalf. It was during this time that the only visual

Queen Anne (1574–1619)

Anne of Denmark, the queen consort of James I, was the daughter of Frederick II, King of Denmark, and Sophia of Mecklenburg-Güstrow. She married James in 1589 before he ascended to the throne.

Anne and James had eight children but only three survived childhood, including Charles I, the British monarch from 1625 to 1649. Anne was raised a Lutheran but in the 1590s converted to Roman Catholicism, and when she and James were crowned she refused to take the Anglican sacrament. Her religious sympathies remained an embarrassment to her husband throughout his reign. After the death of her last infant, Anne and James consented to live apart.

Queen Anne was greatly interested in the Jamestown colony, and her royal reception of Pocahontas in London had the effect of promoting English interest in Virginia at a critical time in the colony's history. The Rappahannock River in Virginia was at one time called the Anne River in her honor; Cape Ann in Massachusetts was also named for her.

Anne of Denmark, wife of James I and Queen of England, who entertained Pocahontas on her visit to London in 1616. (Ellyson, J. Taylor. The London Company of Virginia, *1908)*

representation known of her was made, an engraving by Simon van de Passe. In it, she is dressed in the customary fashion of an English lady of her day and, fortunately, her features do not appear to have been "anglicised" to a great degree, so perhaps the engraving may be a glimpse of her actual appearance. It was also during this time that she once again met John Smith, whom she had previously believed dead following his sudden departure from Jamestown after receiving a serious injury in late 1609. The meeting was brief and possibly not as amiable as either would have preferred because of Pocahontas's disappointment with Smith for not having contacted her during the years since their last meeting in Virginia. As is often the case, too few records remain of what may have transpired in what probably was an interesting reunion between two of the best-known personalities from the founding of Jamestown.

After being displayed and entertained for some time in England, Pocahontas and her family prepared to return to Virginia. She never saw her homeland again, however. On the voyage back, she became so ill that she had to be taken ashore at Gravesend, where, around the age of twenty, she died and was buried at St. George's Church on 21 March 1617. Her husband John Rolfe continued his journey back to the New World, where he would help establish a thriving tobacco industry. Thomas, their son, due to a temporary illness of his own, would remain in

England under the care of an uncle, returning to Virginia only after reaching adulthood.

Pocahontas was many things to many people during her short life. To her father and their people, she was a playful and mischievous youngster who grew into an important link between themselves and those whom they saw as the "other." To the English, she was seen as the same while she was a child but, according to John Smith, one of the few who left a written record of the time, the link Pocahontas provided was vastly more important to the English in that it helped them survive during their first years in the New World. Whatever the full facts of her life and contributions, there is little doubt that Pocahontas was one of the most important and legendary figures in the history of Jamestown and America.

Related entries: Dale, Sir Thomas; Henricus; James Fort; Powhatan; Rolfe, John; Smith, Captain John

Suggestions for further reading

Edward Arber, ed. 1910. *Travels and Works of Captain John Smith* (part 1). Edinburgh: J. Grant.

Philip L. Barbour. 1964. *The Three Worlds of Captain John Smith.* Boston: Houghton Mifflin.

——. 1969. *Pocahontas and her World.* Boston: Houghton Mifflin.

James Horn. 2005. *A Land as God Made It: Jamestown and the Birth of America.* New York: Basic Books.

Karen Ordahl Kupperman. 1988. *Captain John Smith: A Select Edition of His Writings.* Chapel Hill and London: University of North Carolina Press.

Helen C. Rountree. 2005. *Pocahontas, Powhatan, Opechancanough: Three Indian Lives Change by Jamestown.* Charlottesville: University Press of Virginia.

Lyon Gardiner Tyler, ed. 1907. *Narratives of Early Virginia: 1606–1625.* New York: Charles Scribner's Sons.

Grace Steele Woodward. 1969. *Pocahontas.* Norman: University of Oklahoma Press.

Point Hope

See Newport News

Polish Workers

"There are no better workers than Poles." At least, that is what Captain John Smith thought about the workforce of the flourishing pitch, tar, and glass industries that he observed when traveling through Poland after escaping his Turkish captors in 1602. Thus, it was to Poland that he turned for skilled artisans for Jamestown, and "eight Dutchmen [Germans] and Poles" were among the second supply of colonists who landed aboard the *Mary and Margaret* in October 1608. Two of the Polish workers later saved Smith's life when Indians attacked him.

The Polish craftsmen immediately constructed a glass house and pitch and potash burners, and products of those manufactories became the first exports from the colony to England. As the luxuriant Virginia landscape was abundant with pine trees, the settlers soon realized the potential for a thriving timber industry, and more Poles were brought to the colony, in 1619, to manufacture pitch, tar, resin, and turpentine for shipbuilding.

The early Polish workers were denied the right to vote by the governor when the first elections were held in 1619, on the grounds that they were not of English origin, but after they refused to work, the Virginia General Assembly reversed the decision and extended the privilege:

> Upon some dispute of the Polonians resident in Virginia, it was now agreed . . . they shallbe enfranchized, and made as free as any inhabitant there whatsoever: and because their skill in making pitch and tarr and sope-ashees shall not dye with them, it is agreed that some young men, shallbe put unto them to learne their skill and knowledge therein for the benefitt of the Country hereafter.

The Poles' refusal to work has been called the first labor strike in American history.

Related entries: Falling Creek Ironworks; French Huguenots; Glassmaking

Suggestions for further reading

Philip L. Barbour. 1964. "The Identity of the First Poles in America" (*William and Mary Quarterly*, vol. 21).

Philip Alexander Bruce. 1896. *Economic History of Virginia in the Seventeenth Century: An*

Inquiry into the Material Condition of the People, Based on Original and Contemporaneous Records. New York: Macmillan.

Captain John Smith. 1907. *The Generall Historie of Virginia, New England & The Summer Isles Together with The True Travels, Adventures and Observations, and A Sea Grammar* (vol. 1). Glasgow, Scotland: MacLehose and Sons.

Popham Colony

See Sagadahoc (Popham) Colony

Pory, John (1572–1636)

When the first representative assembly in the New World was convened at Jamestown on 30 July 1619, John Pory was its speaker and secretary. One of the grantees of the Second Virginia Charter of 1609, Pory already had experience serving in deliberative bodies, having served in the English Parliament from 1605 to 1611. He sailed for Virginia in January 1619, only one month after his election to the office of secretary, landing at Jamestown in mid-April. He served as secretary and as speaker until 1621. In those roles, at the assembly's initial session, Pory thus presided over the assembly's ratification of the Great Charter of 1618 and the passage of acts regulating and taxing the settlers and establishing guidelines for dealing with their Indian neighbors. Heat, humidity, and illness brought the first session to a halt after only a few days, however, and Pory as speaker drafted a petition on behalf of the delegates to the London Company seeking more power for the assembly when reconvened. Although the 1619 session was brief, it was nevertheless historic and precedent setting, and Pory was commended by his fellow legislators for his leadership role as speaker and secretary. It proved to be Pory's only service in the General Assembly, however, for his term expired before another session was called. As it turned out, Pory's minutes were the only record of what took place during that first meeting of the General Assembly, and even they were lost to history until after 1850.

Before going to America, Pory had traveled to Ireland, France, Padua, Turin, Constantinople, and The Hague, finding employment as a scribe, a translator, and a writer of newsletters for a variety of political and other wealthy patrons. His works included English translations of Johannes Leo's *Geographical Historie of Africa, Written in Arabicke and Italian* and of Leo Africanus's *A Geographical History of Africa* (3 vols.), which had been a minor source for Shakespeare's *Othello,* both published in 1600. His interest in Africa was a result of his association with Richard Hakluyt, the architect of English colonization, whom he had met while teaching Greek at Gonville and Caius College, Cambridge University (which Pory attended from 1588 to 1595).

In Virginia, Pory did not limit himself to colonial governance. Of particular importance was his willingness to travel and describe what he found in the colony. He made observations about the timber, pitch, tar, silk, and wine industries, and he attempted to discover iron and salt deposits that could be mined. He explored the Eastern Shore, noting the "incomodity of Musquitos" but also the beauty of the place, and decided to settle a 500-acre plantation, where he built a house. (The London Company had awarded Pory a land grant in lieu of pay for his service as secretary.) He also explored the Chesapeake Bay, making a trip up the Potomac River; to the south he made a land trip to the Chowan River in what later became North Carolina, becoming the first to write a description of the region. In addition, Pory sailed with the *Discovery* to New England and Newfoundland, visiting the Plymouth colony in 1622 and writing one of the earliest descriptions of that colony.

Unfortunately for Pory, the *Discovery* was shipwrecked in the Azores, and Pory was held prisoner for more than a year. Upon his release, he returned to London, where he was appointed to a commission that had been set up to investigate the Virginia colony; he returned to Virginia in 1624 but went back to London the following year, where he lived for the rest of his life. In England, he returned to writing newsletters and engaged to attend Court on behalf of the Earl of Warwick; in 1630, he published a final work, *The Summe and Substance of a Disputation.* Pory is buried at Sutton Saint Edmunds in Lincolnshire.

Related entries: General Assembly; Three Ships

Suggestions for further reading

Johannes Leo. 1600. Reprint, 1969. *A Geographical Historie of Africa, Written in Arabicke and Italian.* Amsterdam and New York: Theatrum Orbis Terrarum and Da Capo Press.

John Pory. 1915. *A Report of the Manner of Proceeding in the General Assembly Convented at James Citty in Virginia, July 30, 1619. . . .* (H. R. McIlwaine, ed. *Journals of the House of Burgesses of Virginia, 1619–1658/59.* vol. 6.) Richmond: Virginia State Library.

William S. Powell. 1977. *John Pory, 1572–1636: The Life and Letters of a Man of Many Parts.* Chapel Hill: University of North Carolina Press.

Powell, Captain Nathaniel (d. 1622)

Listed as a gentleman on the roster of the first colonists to come to Jamestown, Nathanial Powell was present at the colony during some of its most trying and dangerous times. Not only did he survive the Starving Time in the winter of 1609–1610, he also was involved in a number of hostile encounters with some of Powhatan's subjects while a member of various expeditions exploring the areas surrounding Jamestown. In the winter of 1608, he accompanied Captain Christopher Newport on a journey up the York River after having been a member of Captain John Smith's second exploration of the Chesapeake Bay from 24 July through 7 September of the same year. As a result of his records of the trip with Smith, he is credited with probable authorship of the "Diarie of the second voyage in discovering the Bay," sent to England in December 1608 by Newport, and it was from this account that content was probably drawn for chapter six of Smith's *Generall Historie.* In late 1608 and early 1609, he accompanied Smith in an effort to trade for food with the Pamunkeys. It was during that trip that Smith, infuriated by the unfolding events, ordered Powell to stand guard while Smith seized Opechancanough, Powhatan's half brother, by the hair in order to escape what appeared to be an imminent attack from hundreds of warriors surrounding Smith's group.

Later, in February 1610, Powell had an even more treacherous encounter. After learning of an Indian plot to attack the colonists, George Percy sent Powell to Wowinchopunk to capture alive, if possible, the king of the Paspaheghs, "he being one of the mightiest and strongest savages that Powhatan had under him, and was therefore one of his champions, and one who had killed treacherously many of our men as he could beguile them." But the king had no desire to be taken alive. As the colonists approached and "caught hold of him," a number of previously unseen warriors appeared and shot "their arrows freely amongst our men. The which Captain Powell seeing did apprehend that there was small hope to bring in Paspahe alive, for he struggled mainly, whereupon he thrust him twice through the body with his sword." These and other events, including an expedition guided by the Quiyoughquohanocks to the Mangoag territory to search for survivors of the lost Roanoke Colony, seasoned and toughened Powell, preparing him for greater service to the colony.

Powell eventually acquired his own holdings in the New World, and with his wife, daughter of Master William Tracy, had a 600-acre tract on the west side of Powell's Creek. As well as being a brave and dependable soldier for the colony, among his other duties were included those of deputy governor following Captain Samuel Argall's departure from Jamestown on 10 April 1619. Upon the arrival, nine days later, of Sir George Yeardley as governor and captain-general of Virginia, Powell was made a member of the Council, on which he served until 1622. It was in that fateful year that Powell's service in Virginia came to an end.

After having served so well for so long, and through some of the harshest and most desperate and deadly years of the colony, Nathaniel Powell, "one of the first Planters, a valiant Soulder, and not any in the Countrey better knowne amongst them," was finally taken, along with hundreds others, in the 22 March 1622 attack launched by members of Powhatan's confederacy all along the James River. When the attack came to Powell's home, Powhatan's warriors did their best to express their hatred of what they saw as the English invaders. Not only did they kill Powell and his wife, who was "great with childe," but they "butcher-like hagled their bodies, and cut off his head."

Among his other achievements, Powell has been cited as contributing to other accounts of the early years of Jamestown, including the 1612 *Proceedings of the English Colonie in Virginia* and Smith's *Map of Virginia* of the same year.

Related entries: Lost Colony; Massacre of 1622; Newport, Sir Christopher; Opechancanough; Pamunkey Indians; Smith, Captain John; York River

Suggestions for further reading

Philip L. Barbour. 1969. *The Jamestown Voyages Under the First Charter: 1606–1609* (vol. 2). Cambridge, England: Cambridge University Press.

——, ed. 1986. *The Complete Works of Captain John Smith (1580–1631)* (vol. 2). Chapel Hill and London: University of North Carolina Press.

Alexander Brown. 1890. *The Genesis of the United States* (vol. 2). Boston: Houghton Mifflin.

Edward Wright Haile, ed. 2001. *Jamestown Narratives: Eyewitness Accounts of the Virginia Colony: The First Decade: 1607–1617*. Champlain, VA: Round House.

Edward D. Neill. 1869. *History of the Virginia Company of London, with Letters to and from the First Colony Never Before Printed.* Albany, NY: Joel Munsell.

Lyon Gardiner Tyler. 1906. *The Cradle of the Republic: Jamestown and James River.* Richmond, VA: Hermitage Press.

Powhatan (d. 1618)

Born in the 1540s or 1550s, Powhatan—or, more exactly, Wahunsonacock—was the ruler of as many as twenty to thirty Indian tribes when the first Jamestown colonists arrived in the New World. According to John Smith's writings, Powhatan had inherited six tribes in the surrounding area—"Powhatan, Arrohateck, Appamatuke, Pamaunke, Youghtanu[n]d, and Mattapanient"—with the remainder of the tribes joining him as a result of his "severall conquests" of them. The English saw him as an "Emperour" and, as William Strachey wrote, "we Commonly call [him] Powhatan for by that name true it is, he was made known unto us, when we arrived in the

Powhatan was the principal chief of the so-called Powhatan Confederacy in Virginia during the late-sixteenth and early seventeenth centuries. (Library of Congress)

Country first . . . but his proper right name which they salute him with (himself in presence) is *Wahunsenacawh.*" Smith concurred on this and noted that they referred to him as Powhatan, who "taketh his name of the principall place of dwelling called *Powhatan.* But his proper name is *Wahunsonacock.*"

Both Smith and Strachey gave brief but useful descriptions of Chief Powhatan, Smith in his *Map of Virginia* and Strachey in his *Historie of Travell into Virginia Britania,* both written in 1612. Smith wrote,

> He is of parsonage a tall well proportioned man, with a sower looke; his head somwhat gray, his beard so thinne that it seemeth none at al. His age neare 60; of a very able and hardy body to endure any labour.

Strachey's description contained a bit more detail:

Of the Natives

Their Habit, Costumes & Manner of Living

Sixteenth-century illustration of a Chesapeake man by explorer and artist John White, engraved by Theodor de Bry. (Library of Congress)

I cannot learn that there are (either to the Northward or Southward of us) any people remarkable for their gigantick or dwarfish stature. The Susque Hanoughs & Wickacommacos are said to be so but are not: their bodies are generally straight, clean limbed, & well proportioned, not black like Negroes, but of a complexion like a chestnut colour, & would (I suppose) be less swarthy, were it not for their anointings, paintings, & fuligenous smoke of light-wood, i.e., Pine whose sap is rotted away: this thô it blacks the face, offends not the eyes, & is used by the Indians far & near. Peter Martyr tell us that the Mexicans at the first coming of the Spaniards had no other candles, though they neither wanted hony or wax. Their hair is black & straight, which the men cut after divers manners, but the women wear long, hanging at their backs & bound up in one lock with a fillet of white beads. That of their beards & other parts they pull up with Muscleshells; so do the inhabi[tants] of Chili & Brasil: the ancient Britains left none but on their upper lip. The like custom is also among the Turks, where the men take it off with a razour, but the softer sex use a Psilothrim of Rusma & unslak'd lime. The Caribbies call all bearded men wild beasts.

The women go bareheaded, & so do the men too unless it be those of the better sort, who sometimes put on a border or Coronet of black & white Peak prettily wrought, but more for ornament than use, being

(*continued on next page*)

Of the Natives, continued

open at top like the Peruvian ffeather-crown. The beads of which this crown is wove are small Cylindres. . . . They are made out of a large kind of Cockle. . . . About their neck they wear a broad belt, or rather collar of the same, as also a round tablet of about 3 or 4 inches wrought out of large Cunk shell, & some too wear a bracelet of great bulging beads made of the same shell, which the Southern Indians call Rantees: in their ears they hang a pipe about the bigness of the stem of a tobacco pipe smoothly worked out of the string or middle part of a Cunk drilled from end to end, or else a fingers length of smooth Roanoak, which is a kind of bead mony also, about the bigness of a large spangle: it is gotten on the eastern shore out of I know not what thin shell: the new is rough or cragged on the edges, & tis not so much esteemed as that which is new & worn. . . . Their clothing was with skins which they sewed together with Deer sinews, like the ancient Britains, & other barbarous nations; but since the Europeans have traded among them, they cover their nakedness with a flap of red or blew cotton, & wrap themselves up in a mantle or matchcoat of Daffields. Those that wear coats after the English fashion, are very desirous of having them of divers colours, like that Jacob made for his son Joseph, & therefore the traders have them cut partly from pale, gules, & azure. They wear no breeches; their buskins are of cotton or leather, without feet sown down with a wing on the outside of the leg about an inch wide, & their shooes of Buckskin all of a piece & drawn together in a purse with a running string on the top of the foot. The Indians call them Mockasins & therefore that sort of Helleborine which is called ladeis-sliper we call Mockasinflower: those that wear leather coats & stockins, sew them with Deers sinews as the Samoides & those of Rene.

—Excerpt from John Banister's description of the native peoples of Virginia, as rendered in Robert Beverley's *History and Present State of Virginia* (London, 1705)

> He is a goodly old-man, not yet shrincking, though well beaten with many cold and stormy winters, in which he hath bene patient of many necessities and attempts of his fortune, to make his name and famely great, he is supposed to be little lesse than 80. yeares old, (I dare not say how much more, others say he is). Of a tall stature, and cleane lymbes, of a sad aspect, rownd fat visag'd with gray haires, but plaine and thin hanging upon his broad showlders, some few haires upon his Chinne, and so on his upper lippe. He hath bene a strong and able salvadge, sinowie, active, and of daring spiritt, vigilant, ambitious, subtile to enlarge his dominions.

As mentioned, Powhatan had inherited a number of territories, and in these he had many "houses built after their manner like arbours; some 30, so 40 yardes according to the time. At *Werow*[o]*comoco,* he was seated upon the North side of the river *Pamaunke* [Pamunkey, or today's York River], some 14 miles from *James* Towne." It was not long, however, before the meddling of the Europeans caused Powhatan to move his base farther away from Jamestown.

> He tooke so little pleasure in our neare neighbourhood, that were able to visit him against his will in 6 or 7 houres, that he retired himself to a place in the deserts at the top of the river *Chickahamania* betweene *Youghtanund* and *Powhatan.* His habitation there is called *Orapacks,* where he ordinarily now resideth.

About a mile from this location, "in a thicket of wood," Wahunsonacock had constructed

> a house, in which he keepeth his kind of Treasure, as skinnes, copper, pearle, and beades; which he storeth up against the time of his death and buriall. Here also is his store of red paint for ointment, and bowes and arrowes. This house is 50 or 60 yards in length, frequented only by Priestes. At the 4 corners of this house stand 4 Images as Sentinels; one of a Dragon, another a Beare, the 3 like a Leopard, and the fourth like a

> giantlike man: all made evill favordly, according to their best workmanship.

According to Smith, Powhatan was well attended by warriors for protection and by women as wives and servants:

> About his person ordinarily attendeth a guard of 40 or 50 of the tallest men his Country doth afford. Every night upon the 4 quarters of his house are 4 Sentinels, each standing from other a flight shoot: and at every halfe houre, one from the Corps du guard doth hollowe; unto whom every Sentinell doth answer round from his stand. If any faile, they presently send forth an officer that beateth him extreamely.

His chosen women were omnipresent as well:

> He hath as many woman as he will: whereof when hee lieth on his bed, one sitteth at his head, and another at his feet; but when he sitteth, one sitteth on his right hand, and another on his left. . . . When he dineth or suppeth, one of his women, before and after meat, bringeth him water in a wo[o]den platter to wash his hands. Another waiteth with a bunch of feathers to wipe them insteed of a Towell, and the feathers when he hath wiped are dryed againe.

Being a chosen woman or wife had no guarantees, however. "As he is wearie of his women, hee bestoweth them on those that best deserve them at his hands." As to his women, Strachey added that

> there are said to be about some dozen at this present, in whose Company he takes more delight then in the rest, being for the most parte very young women, and these Commonly remove with him from howse to howse, either in his tyme of hunting, or visitation of his severall howses.

Although there were no written laws, there were customary practices and rules to be obeyed. Powhatan was, essentially, the law. Although he, too, knew and followed custom, "his will is a law and must bee obeyed: not only as a king, but as halfe a God they esteeme him." The punishments for not obeying the law, either customary or those decreed by Powhatan, were severe "for he is very terrible and tyrannous in punishing such as offend him." Smith gave examples of the forms of punishments meted out for the worst offenses. Burning coals would be raked into the shape of a "cockpit," and binding the victims hand and foot, "in the midst [of the coals] they cast the offenders to broyle to death." Some met their fate by having their heads forced onto an "altar or sacrificing stone, and one with clubbes beates out their braines." For the "notorious enimie or malefactor" a far more terrible end awaited:

> [He would] be tied to a tree, and, with muscle shels or reeds, the executioner cutteth of[f] his joints one after another, ever casting what they cut of[f] into the fire; then doth he proceed with shels and reeds to case the skinne from his head and face; then doe they rip his belly, and so burne him with the tree and all.

Powhatan's harsh justice was not reserved for individuals alone. Entire neighboring tribes were wiped out for refusing to join him or show him what he saw as due fealty, and, as William Strachey related, for other reasons as well. The chief's priests earlier had warned him of a prophecy that "from the Chesapeack Bay a Nation should arise, which should dissolve and give end to his Empier." Concerned that this prophesy might be realized (which it essentially was, but not from indigenous peoples), Powhatan

> put to the sword, all such who might lye under any doubtfull construccion of the said prophesie, as all the Inhabitants, the weroance and his Subjects of that province and so remayne all the *Chessiopeians* at this daie, and for this cause extinct.

Another theory suggests that the removal of the Chesapeakes was the result of an earlier attempt by members of the Lost Colony from England to settle the area, migrating northward and joining the Chesapeakes for succor when they could no longer sustain their existence on Roanoke Island. Whatever the cause of Powhatan's action against them, the Chesapeakes were apparently exterminated just before, or coincident with, the arrival of the Jamestown colonists.

Captain Smith relates another exhibition of Powhatan's wrath. He wrote,

> In the yeare 1608, hee surprised the people of *Paiankatank,* his neare neighbours and subjects. The occasion was to us unknowne, but the manner was thus. First he sent diverse of his men as

Patawomeke Indians: Allied with Powhatan

On the Virginia side of the Potomac River, in present-day Stafford County, lived the Patawomeke, an Algonquian tribe of the Powhatan Confederacy from which the Potomac River derives its name. Captain John Smith said the tribe consisted of "160 able men" in 1612. Smith first visited the fortified village of Patawomeke in 1608, and English settlers routinely visited the area to trade with the natives until 1623, when the Patawomeke's enemies, the Nacotchtank (Anacostan) Indians, raided the town, killing and capturing both English settlers and Patawomekes. Pocahontas lived with the Patawomeke people in the fall of 1609, and it has been suggested that her reputed first husband, Kocoum, was a Patawomeke warrior. The town, located at Indian Point, the juncture of Accokeek and Potomac Creeks, was abandoned by 1635, when English settlers began to move into the area. The word Patawomeke means "gathering space" or "marketplace," or more precisely, "where the goods are brought in." Archaeological excavations at the site of the Patawomeke village in 1935–1937 and 1939–1940 by William J. Graham and T. Dale Stewart, respectively, revealed a late-Woodland (1300–1600) palisaded village of slightly less than an acre and a half, enclosing circular and elongated houses, storage pits, and mass graves. Patawomeke Village was added to the National Register of Historic Places in 1969.

> to lodge amongst them that night, then the *Ambuscadoes* invironed [occupied] al[l] their houses, and at the houre appointed, they all fell to the spoile: 24 men they slewe, the long haire of the one side of their heades with the skinne cased off with shels or reeds, they brought away. They surprised also the women and the children and the *Werowance.* All these they present[ed] to *Powhatan.* The *Werowance,* women and children became his prisoners, and doe him service.

The scalps of the slain men were then

> hanged on a line unto two trees. And thus he made ostentation as of a great triumph at *Werowocomoco;* shewing them to the English men that then came unto him. . . . supposed to halfe conquer them, by this spectacle of his terrible crueltie.

Indeed, the Jamestown colonists became fully aware of Chief Powhatan's power and wrath during their first eleven years in the New World. The Europeans were at times killed on sight by Powhatan's warriors or starved, either through the refusal of goods for food or by attack and capture or killing of any colonists who left the fort to hunt, fish, or forage for food.

Although Powhatan could be lethal and harsh, he could also be sociable and congenial. He entertained a number of European visitors without harm coming to them, and his people both admired and respected him, according to accounts given by colonists who saw their interactions. As with any successful leader, however, his primary responsibility was to protect his people and his domains, and when others threatened with deadly force or menacing encroachment, he had to respond with the most effective means at his disposal.

Powhatan distanced himself from the Jamestown colonists and settlement as much as he could. Not once did he visit the site after the Europeans arrived—perhaps fearing capture or desirous of showing his authority by making the colonists come to him, or both—and he moved his domicile farther away from them when he realized the English had no intentions of leaving. His was a life of great power and accomplishment as he built his empire. But the forces of change were too strong for him to resist the numbers of people and the technology that the Europeans brought with them to the New World. Powhatan turned over power to his brother Opitchapam in 1617, not long after hearing of the death of his daughter Pocahontas while she was visiting England with her husband John Rolfe and their infant son, Thomas. He once again moved further away from the colonists, possibly to live with the Patawomekes, and died there the following year in April 1618.

Interestingly, one artifact probably associated with the great chief has survived, the so-called Powhatan's Mantle, an apparent garment made of four white-tailed deer hides held together with sinew and embroidered with thousands of shell beads. Overall, the mantle measures 7 1/2 by 5 1/2 feet and contains the figures of a human and two animals, possibly a deer and a cougar or mountain lion. Described variously as the "robe of the king of Virginia" and the "King of Virginia's habit," it was carried to England within twenty years of Powhatan's death by John Tradescant, Sr. (c.1570–1638), or his son, John, Jr. (1608–1662), both royal gardeners who made numerous voyages to the New World in search of curiosities. Powhatan's Mantle and the rest of the Tradescant collection went to Oxford University in 1683, forming the basis of what is today Oxford's Ashmolean Museum of Art and Archaeology.

Related entries: James Fort; Kecoughtan Indians; Opechancanough; Opitchapam; Pamunkey Indians; Pocahontas; Rolfe, John; Smith, Captain John

Suggestions for further reading

Edward Arber, ed. 1910. *Travels and Works of Captain John Smith* (parts 1, 2). Edinburgh, Scotland: J. Grant.

Philip L. Barbour. 1964. *The Three Worlds of Captain John Smith.* Boston: Houghton Mifflin.

——, ed. 1986. *The Complete Works of Captain John Smith (1580–1631)* (vol. 1). Chapel Hill and London: University of North Carolina Press.

Edward Wright Haile, ed. 2001. *Jamestown Narratives: Eyewitness Accounts of the Virginia Colony: The First Decade: 1607–1617.* Champlain, VA: Round House.

James Horn. 2005. *A Land as God Made It: Jamestown and the Birth of America.* New York: Basic Books.

Susan Myra Kingsbury, ed. 1933. *The Records of the Virginia Company of London.* (vol. 3) Washington, DC: Government Printing Office.

Karen Ordahl Kupperman, ed. 1988. *Captain John Smith: A Select Edition of His Writings.* Chapel Hill and London: University of North Carolina Press.

Helen C. Rountree. 2005. *Pocahontas, Powhatan, Opechancanough: Three Indian Lives Changed by Jamestown.* Charlottesville: University Press of Virginia.

William Strachey. 1953. *The Historie of Travell into Virginia Britania (1612)* (Louis B. Wright, and Virginia Freund, eds.) London: Hakluyt Society.

Lyon Gardiner Tyler, ed. 1907. *Narratives of Early Virginia: 1606–1625.* New York: Charles Scribner's Sons.

Grace Steele Woodward. 1969. *Pocahontas.* Norman: University of Oklahoma Press.

R

Raleigh, Sir Walter (c.1552–1618)

Tall, handsome, dashing, bold, adventurous—all these terms appear to be applicable to the man who, arguably, was the most successful advocate of the establishment of a permanent English presence in the New World. Although both of his attempts to settle a colony in what was at the time considered Virginia ended in abandonment, his ventures laid the foundation for all the English efforts that followed.

Sir Walter Raleigh (his last name was spelled in a dozen ways but typically signed as "Ralegh" during his later years) was not the first of his countrymen to attempt to establish a colony in the New World. His half brother Sir Humphrey Gilbert had set sail on at least two attempts before Raleigh's, the first of which never reached the shores of North America, and the second lasted only a few weeks on Newfoundland. But the two colonies that were settled, however briefly, on Roanoke Island in the Outer Banks of present-day North Carolina lasted long enough to provide useful and badly needed information about the people, flora, fauna, and environment of that region. The documentation of these attempts and experiences, particularly that by John White and Thomas Hariot, would be extremely helpful to those who followed, specifically the Jamestown colonists twenty years later. Indeed, Raleigh's second attempt to settle in 1587 was planned for somewhere on the Chesapeake Bay, probably not far from where Jamestown was later seated. Apparently, it was the reluctance of the expedition's chief pilot to take the colonists northward that prevented the second set of settlers, led by Governor John White and later known as the Lost Colony, from reaching its intended destination. Still, the data collecting, exploring, and mapmaking done during those Roanoke voyages later led to the realization of Raleigh's quest for an English presence in the New World.

Raleigh was born in the early 1550s in Hayes Barton, Devon, to father Walter and mother Katherine. Around 1568, he went to study at Oriel College at Oxford, after which he served for a time with the Huguenots in France, fighting the Catholics. He also may have studied law at the Inner Temple in London before going to Ireland in 1580 to help suppress an insurrection, during which time he distinguished himself and gained favor with England's Queen Elizabeth I. The results of such favor were, among other things, receipt of the patent previously held by his half brother Gilbert to explore, exploit, and colonize much of North America; grants of land in Ireland totaling thousands of acres; licenses to profit from the sale of wine and cloth; titles such

Thomas Hariot: New World Enthusiast

Perhaps the leading English authority on the New World before the Virginia settlement in 1607 was Thomas Hariot (c. 1560–1621), an Oxford-educated mathematician and astronomer. Described as the quintessential Renaissance man, Hariot was also expert in navigation, cartography, optics, physics, chemistry, hydraulics, and the science of gunnery. He single-handedly founded the English school of algebra. While at Oxford, Hariot became friends with Richard Hakluyt, a university lecturer who was also the principal promoter of New World colonization and who later described Hariot as "a man pre-eminent" in the arts and sciences. Hariot entered the patronage of Sir Walter Raleigh about 1583 as a tutor in the art of navigation; he quickly became involved in all facets of Raleigh's voyages to America, from the design and construction of his sea vessels to fund-raising and accounting for the expeditions. He made at least one trip to the New World in the 1580s, on which he based his *A Briefe and True Report of the New Found Land of Virginia* (1588), which described his experience at Roanoke Island on the Carolina coast. Published with engravings of John White's paintings, *A True Report* extolled the potential of the region and helped prepare Englishmen for what to expect in the New World. In the 1590s, while remaining in Raleigh's employ, Hariot also entered the service of Henry Percy, Duke of Northumberland. Hariot was detained briefly during the so-called Gunpowder Plot of November 1604, but no evidence has ever surfaced that connects him to the affair.

as warden of the Stannaries, gained in July 1585, member of the council of war and captain of the Queen's Guard; and the highest honor, his knighthood, granted by Queen Elizabeth on 6 January 1585. In addition, Raleigh also served as a member of Parliament and participated in a number of voyages of exploration, including trips to South America, during his long career. Although he was responsible for the 1584 voyage of Philip Amadas and Arthur Barlowe to scout the eastern North American coast for suitable settlement sites, and the two attempts to establish the colonies there in 1585 and 1587, as well as the relief and rescue missions sent to them, he never visited his North American holdings.

While Raleigh had the favor of Queen Elizabeth for some years, in 1592 he secretly married Elizabeth Throckmorton and had a son, Carew. This apparently was not acceptable to the queen, however, and Raleigh soon found himself under arrest and imprisoned in the Tower of London. After his release, Raleigh once again set out on voyages of discovery and exploration, among other endeavors, and published an account of his 1595 expedition to Guiana. Queen Elizabeth I died in 1603; her successor, James I, was not as charmed by the bold adventurer as Elizabeth had been. Raleigh was accused of plotting against the king, and he was once again returned to the Tower, this time spending thirteen years there until his release in January 1616. His time in prison was not entirely wasted, however. During his confinement in the Tower, he wrote his *Historie of the World,* which was published in 1614, and throughout his time there he worked to gain his release, finally succeeding in March 1616 by convincing the king that he could be of much better use to the crown by generating revenue for it. His plan was to return to South America and search for gold along the Orinoco River. He did make the voyage, but it met with little success. Upon his return to England in June of 1618, he was once again arrested on the orders of the still distrustful and disappointed king. This time, his imprisonment ended less satisfactorily: Raleigh was beheaded on 29 October of that year.

Sir Walter Raleigh lived a relatively long, eventful, and fruitful life for a man of his time.

As an English naval commander and favorite courtier of Queen Elizabeth I, Sir Walter Raleigh played an important role in initiating and sponsoring the establishment of English settlements in North America. (Library of Congress)

He attempted much and achieved a great deal of what he set out to do. Although his two colonies on Roanoke Island did not survive, his goal—to give England a permanent foothold in the New World—did. Other attempts would follow, succeeding where his had not, but that should not reflect badly on the man who dared to do so much when knowledge of how to do it was nearly nonexistent. It would take many more decades and thousands of lives before the permanent, thriving English presence would be established that eventually grew into the United States of America. Many challenges and much learning awaited those who would follow Raleigh's lead, but follow they did. Raleigh and his colonists risked everything as they ventured into the virtually unknown; those who followed were the beneficiaries of lives boldly and bravely led.

Related entries: Early European Exploration of North America; Gosnold, Bartholomew; London Company; Lost Colony; White, John

Suggestions for further reading

Alexander Brown. 1890. *The Genesis of the United States* (vol. 2). Boston: Houghton Mifflin.

Michael Golay and John S. Bowman. 2003. *North American Exploration.* Hoboken, NJ: John Wiley.

Karen Ordahl Kupperman. 1984. *Roanoke: The Abandoned Colony.* Totowa, NJ: Rowman & Littlefield.

Lee Miller. 2002. *Roanoke: Solving the Mystery of the Lost Colony.* New York: Penguin Books.

Samuel Eliot Morison. 1971. *The European Discovery of America: The Northern Voyages A.D. 500–1600.* New York: Oxford University Press.

David Stick. 1983. *Roanoke Island: The Beginnings of English America.* Chapel Hill: University of North Carolina Press.

Rappahannock Indians

At the time of the English colonization of Virginia, Powhatan's empire stretched northward from its center near the James River to territory occupied by natives of possible Iroquoian Owasco origin, who are known to history as the Potomac Indians and who lived along the Potomac River border of present-day Virginia and Maryland. Below the Potomac lived the Rappahannock, a numerous group who were perhaps the most ancient of Virginia's native peoples. Settled in thirteen villages or towns along both sides of the river that bore its name—one of Virginia's largest river systems—the Rappahannock tribe first encountered Europeans about 1606, when Englishmen exploring the mouth of their river killed one of their chiefs and kidnapped several of their people. That hostile event resulted in another Rappahannock chief going to the Powhatan town of Quiyocohannock to interrogate Captain John Smith after his capture in December 1607. The chief concluded that Smith had not been part of the 1606 party and carried

Native Americans smoke fish in this sixteenth-century illustration by John White, engraved by Theodor de Bry. (Library of Congress)

him to the Rappahannock capital Toppahanoke (or Dancing Point and Cat Point Creek overlooking the Menokin Bay, near present-day Warsaw, Virginia) for public exhibition and a meeting with the tribe's king. Smith apparently made a positive impression on the paramount chief, for the following summer, when Smith was exploring the Chesapeake Bay, he called upon Smith to intervene with unfriendly (but Powhatan-allied) Moraughtacund Indians who had kidnapped three Rappahannock women during a violent confrontation. Smith brought the warring parties together and, like King Solomon of old, made peace by separating the persons in question and giving one woman each to the Rappahannock and Moraughtacund kings and the third to Mosco, a Wighcocomoco guide.

Smith's was not the only early dealing between the Rappahannock and the colonists. In his *Observations* (1612), Jamestown president George Percy vividly described one of the earliest meetings, which took place on 5 May 1607:

> The Werowance of Rapahanna sent a Messenger to have us come to him. We entertained the said Messenger, and gave him trifles which pleased him. Wee manned our shallop with Muskets and Targatiers sufficiently: this said Messenger guided us where our determination was to goe. When wee landed, the Werowance of Rapahanna came downe to the water side with all his traine, as goodly men as any I have seene of Savages or Christians: the Werowance coming before them playing on a Flute made of a Reed, with a Crown of Deares haire colored red, in fashion of a Rose fastened about his knot of haire, and a great Plate of Copper on the other side of his head, with two long Feathers in fashion of a paire of Hornes placed in the midst of his Crowne. His body was painted all with Crimson, with a Chaine of Beads about his necke, his face painted blew, besprinkled with silver Ore as wee thought, his eares all behung with Braslets of Pearle, and in either eare a Birds Claw through it beset with fine Copper or Gold, he entertained us in so modest a proud fashion, as

Rappahannock Indians: Reverence for the Sun

The seven and twentieth of July [1607] the King of Rapahanna, demanded a Canoa which was restored, lifted up his hand to the Sunne, which they worship as their God, besides he laid his hand on his heart, that he would be our speciall friend. It is a generall rule of these people when they swere by their God which is the Sunne, no Christian will keepe their Oath better upon this promise. These people have a great reverence to the Sunne above all other things at the rising and setting of the same, they sit downe lifting up their hands and eyes to the Sunne making a round Circle on the ground with dried tobacco, then they began to pray making many Devillish gestures with a Hellish noise foming at the mouth, staring with their eyes, wagging their heads and hands in such a fashion and deformitie as it was monstrous to behold.

—George Percy, *Observations,* 1607

> though he had beene a Prince of civill government, holding his countenance without laughter or any such ill behaviour; he caused his Mat to be spred on the ground, where hee sate downe with a great Majestie, taking a pipe of Tobacco: the rest of his company standing about him. After he had rested a while he rose, and made signes to us to come to his Towne: Hee went formost, and all the rest of his people and our selves followed him up a steepe Hill where his Palace was settled. Wee passed through the Woods in fine paths, having most pleasant Springs which issued from the Mountaines: Wee also went through the goodliest Corne fieldes that ever was seene in any Countrey. When wee came to Rapahannos Towne, hee entertained us in good humanitie.

English displacement of the Rappahannock took place somewhat less rapidly than among the southern Powhatan, perhaps because of the initial friendly footing on both parts, partly because of the tribe's distance from Jamestown, and partly because the Rappahannock did not take part in the Indian uprisings of 1622 and 1644. In the aftermath of the Massacre of 1644, Captain William Claiborne, as commander of the avenging colonial forces, attempted to conclude a treaty with the Rappahannock, who were viewed as unfriendly to Powhatan chief Opechancanough. Negotiations proved unsuccessful, and by the end of the decade the colonists had begun to settle on Rappahannock lands, forcing the natives to leave their towns and retreat inland. Rappahannock chief Accopatough ceded land to Colonel Morre Fauntleroy in April 1651, setting the stage for the transfer of other Rappahannock-occupied territory into the hands of the colonists. In September 1653, representatives of Lancaster County concluded a treaty with the Rappahannock that recognized tribal claims to land and gave individual members of the tribe the same rights (and responsibilities) under English law as white citizens. Exactly three years later, the Rappahannock signed a similar treaty with the Virginia counties of Essex and Richmond. By 1669, when the colonywide Indian census of Virginia was taken, the Rappahannock had abandoned most of their villages near the Rappahannock River, and about thirty warriors and their families had relocated to a hunting village on the Mattaponi River. The tribe built a defensive fortification between the two rivers in 1672 as a refuge from marauding Susquehannocks (about three miles northwest of present-day Tappahannock, Virginia). Five years later, Opechancanough's descendent, Queen Cockacoeske, represented the Rappahannock in negotiating the Treaty of Middle Plantation (May 1677), signing the treaty on their behalf, but before the agreement was even ratified, the

Pamunkey queen reported to colonial authorities that the Rappahannock had joined the Chickahominy in opposing her authority.

In November 1682, the Virginia Council set aside 3,474 acres (including the hunting village on the Mattaponi River) for a reservation for the Rappahannock, now estimated to consist of about 350 persons, including 70 warriors. Less than a year later, however, the Virginia authorities forced the Rappahannock to abandon the reservation and settle about 30 miles away on the northern side of the Rappahannock River at the Nanzatico Indian town in an effort to curb hostile Iroquoian assaults on frontier Indian and English settlements. A colonial treaty with the Iroquois resulted in yet another relocation of the Rappahannock, this time to Portobacco (Portobago) in present-day Essex County. The Rappahannock finally returned to its hunting village and reservation lands in the early eighteenth century, where the tribe has remained ever since. Of about 15 or 20 surnames of present-day tribal families, three of the most prominent—Saunders, Johnson, and Nelson—date back to the 1760s, when 3 Rappahannock girls raised on a plantation in King William County married white men of those names. By 1820, the Rappahannock were beginning to convert to Christianity, and within a half-century almost the entire tribe were members of the Baptist church. The Rappahannock Indian Baptist Church, established in 1964, serves the Rappahannock community today.

The history of the Rappahannock in the twentieth century was largely defined by their efforts to win state and federal recognition of the tribe's sovereignty. (The State of Virginia awarded the Rappahannock official status in 1983; efforts at the federal level are ongoing.) Currently led by the first female chief since the 1700s, the tribe operates the Rappahannock Cultural Center at Indian Neck in King and Queen County, Virginia; its mission is to assist the preservation of tribal culture and to educate the public about the tribe's history. The Rappahannock's annual Harvest Festival and Powwow, held the second Saturday of each October, is open to the public.

Related entries: Mattaponi Indians; Rappahannock River; Smith, Captain John

Suggestions for further reading

George Percy. 1612. *Observations Gathered Out of a Discourse of the Plantation of the Southerne Colonie in Virginia by the English, 1606* (In *Purchas his Pilgrimes,* London, 1685–1690).

Frank G. Speck. 1926. *The Rappahannock Indians of Virginia.* New York: Charles Scribner's Sons.

U.S. Senate, 109th Congress. 2005. *Thomasina E. Jordan Indian Tribes of Virginia Federal Recognition Act of 2005.* Washington, DC: Government Printing Office.

Rappahannock River

Roughly translated as "Quick-Rising Water," the Rappahannock is one of Virginia's four great river systems of the Chesapeake Bay watershed. Some early English writers thought the river issued out of low marshes rather than from the mountains like the other rivers of Virginia, but Governor Alexander Spotswood and the Knights of the Golden Horseshoe proved otherwise in 1716, when he and his band of inebriates made its historic exploratory trek to the summit of the Blue Ridge Mountains. As described by Captain John Smith, the "Toppahanock" was navigable for some 130 of its 184 miles, and its headwaters were inhabited by a people called the Manahoackes, allied with the Monacan. Downstream, the breadth of the Rappahannock reminded Smith of the James; at its mouth was "a Countrey called Cuttata women: upwards is Marraugh tacum, Tapohanock, Appamatuck, and Nantaugs tacum: at Topmanahocks." Altogether, the native peoples inhabiting the banks of the Rappahannock who were of interest to the colonists were a diverse lot and represented several hundred warriors. Smith himself explored the Rappahannock in 1608, taking with him twelve fellow colonists and an Indian guide, Mosco, "a lusty Salvage of Wighcocomoco."

The Native Americans who gave their name to the Rappahannock were a numerous and ancient people, and for much of the seventeenth century they were able to remain on their ancestral lands, albeit in much tension with the English settlers and bordering tribes. By 1670, the Rappahannock River was home to one of the Virginia colony's five forts (along with two on the James and one each on the York and Potomac Rivers), but, as the governor, Sir William Berkeley, noted,

> God knows we have neither skill or ability to make or maintain them; for there is not, nor, as far as my enquiry can reach, ever was one ingenier in the country, so that we are at continual charge to repair unskilfull and inartificial buildings of that nature.

In 1680, the Virginia General Assembly's *Act for Cohabitation and Encouragement of Trade and Manufacture* established a town on the Rappahannock at Hobbs Hole (later Tappahannock), and the Assembly's 1691 *Act for Establishing Ports and Towns* designated the town as the river's official port for shipping tobacco and other products, "the said land laid out by a formere law and paid for where the Court house, severall dwelling houses, and ware houses already built." The designation was reaffirmed by a similar act in 1705, and about ten years later Governor Spotswood began to encourage European settlement of the river basin. Throughout the eighteenth century, the Rappahannock's banks became home to an increasing number of tobacco plantations, including one near Fredericksburg where George Washington lived as a boy and which remained in his family until after the Revolutionary War. During the American Civil War, both sides sought to control the Rappahannock; intense battles at Fredericksburg and Rappahannock Station were fought in 1862. Confederate defenses on the river spoiled Federal advances into southern Virginia on several occasions, and it was not until the famous Overland Campaign of 1865 that the Union army under General Ulysses S. Grant finally was able to overcome the Confederates' use of the river as a defensive barrier.

The Rappahannock River watershed covers over 2,700 square miles (or about 13 percent of the Chesapeake Bay basin) and includes the counties of Culpeper, Madison, Rappahannock, Lancaster, Essex, Richmond, Orange, Fauquier, Middlesex, Greene, King George, Stafford, Westmoreland, Spotsylvania, Northumberland, and Albemarle, and the city of Fredericksburg. Below Fredericksburg, the last 50 miles of the river are a tidal estuary that was especially suited for oyster and crab fishing until the onslaught of aqua-related diseases in recent decades. Below the falls are also numerous fish, including crappie, blue and channel catfish, striped and largemouth bass, white and yellow perch, American and hickory shad, blueback herring, and alewife; above the falls the river is noted for redbreast sunfish, smallmouth bass, and tiger musky. Much of the Rappahannock remains in pristine condition, and in fact the 86-mile length from the headwaters at Chester Gap in Fauquier County to the Mayfield Bridge near George Washington's Ferry Farm outside of Fredericksburg has been officially designated a scenic river by the Virginia General Assembly. Recently, in early 2005, the 22-foot-high Ebrey Dam at Fredericksburg (constructed in 1910 to replace a dam built in the1850s) was removed to reopen some 71 miles of the Rappahannock's historic spawning habitat and to make the river more attractive for recreational canoeing, boating, and camping.

It is fortunate that many supporters have come to the assistance of the Rappahannock River in the last half century. In 1985, the Friends of the Rappahannock was formed as a grassroots conservation effort, and in 1996 the Rappahannock River Valley National Wildlife Refuge was established to protect 20,000 acres of wetlands and to support a variety of wildlife, including wood duck, geese, swans, songbirds, and several endangered species (among them the American bald eagle and the peregrine falcon). Two years later, the legal code of the State of Virginia established the Rappahannock River Basin Commission and charged it with providing "guidance for the stewardship and enhancement of the water quality and natural resources" of the river basin.

Related entries: Chickahominy River; Elizabeth River; James River; Mattaponi River; Nansemond River; Pamunkey River; Rappahannock Indians; Smith, Captain John; York River

Suggestions for further reading

Robert Beverley. 1855. *The History of Virginia, in Four Parts.* Richmond, VA.

Captain John Smith. 1608. *A True Relation of Such Occurrences and Accidents of Noate as Hath Hapned in Virginia Since the First Planting of that Colony, which is now Resident in the South Part Thereof, till the Last Returne from Thence.* London: Edward Alde for John Tappe.

Pocahontas, known to the English as Rebecca, married tobacco planter and colonist John Rolfe in 1614. (Library of Congress)

Rolfe, John (1585–1622)

Although Bartholomew Gosnold may have been a prime mover of the drive to establish the Jamestown colony, and Captain John Smith was arguably the most important of the colonists in keeping the colony alive during its first two and one-half years, John Rolfe must be recognized as preeminently important in helping to ensure the colony's viability during the remainder of its first decade. His marriage to Pocahontas in 1614 helped establish a peace between the Native Americans and the English that lasted long enough for the colony to gain a solid foothold in the New World, and his introduction of tobacco as a commercial crop in 1612 provided much of the economic basis and justification necessary to attract and keep new settlers and to stimulate interest in the colonizing endeavor.

Rolfe was born, with his short-lived twin brother Eustacius, to John and Dorothea Mason Rolfe of Heacham in Norfolk, England. He was baptized in the parish church there on 6 May 1585. After receiving his university education and marrying in England, Rolfe sailed for Jamestown in 1609 with Sir Thomas Gates aboard the *Sea Venture.* Rather than arriving at their planned destination, however, the ship encountered a storm that blew it off course and wrecked it on the shores of Bermuda. During their ten-month stay there, his wife gave birth to a daughter on 11 February 1610, whom they christened Bermuda and who later died before the construction of new transportation could be finished for the completion of the voyage to Jamestown. Shortly after their arrival at Jamestown, in May 1610, Rolfe's wife died, and he set about making his new home alone, during which time he was known as an industrious and hard worker.

Although Rolfe was an important member of the colony for many reasons, serving as, among other things, a member of the Council and the

House of Burgesses, he became best known for his work in establishing tobacco as a major commodity for the colony and for his marriage to Pocahontas. Tobacco was the most important product for the colony for some time, prompting some to comment that it was grown in nearly every patch of land the colonists had available. At least as important, if not more so, to his legacy and to the survival of the colony, however, was the peace brought by his marriage to the daughter of the chief of the Powhatan Indians during a time when the population and strength of the colony were too weak to resist an all-out attempt at extermination by the native forces had they chosen to attack. The lack of supplies, food, and fresh water, as well as disease and intermittent warfare with Powhatan's warriors, had kept the fledgling colony from becoming firmly established. With the drastic reduction in hostilities between the English and Native Americans brought about by the union of a prominent colonist with a daughter of the preeminent native leader of the region, it was safer to grow, hunt, and collect food beyond the heretofore somewhat limited confines. At the same time, the colonists were able to expand their settlement far beyond the immediate fort vicinity, where native hostilities had been instrumental in keeping expansion to a minimum. By the time the first great massacre of the Europeans by the Native Americans occurred in 1622, the colony's population and settlement base had grown so much that even that successful attack could not eradicate what the native peoples saw as a fatal threat to their homeland and way of life. As had Captain John Smith before him, John Rolfe helped the colony survive during a critical period in its first struggling years.

Following their marriage in early April 1614 and the birth of their son, Thomas, Rolfe and Pocahontas sailed to England and spent some months there in 1616–1617. Pocahontas (now called Rebecca after her baptism in Virginia prior to her marriage to John) was introduced to English society, while John spent time writing his *A True Relation of the State of Virginia,* a copy of which was delivered to King James I. Upon their planned return to Virginia, Pocahontas became too ill to continue and had to return to shore, where she died at Gravesend on 21 March 1617. Their son was ill as well; John Rolfe left him with family in England and returned to Virginia, once again alone, and busied himself with building his home. He eventually married again, this time to the daughter of Captain William Pierce, Jane, with whom he had a daughter they named Elizabeth, and continued to improve his tobacco endeavors until his death in 1622. His will was dated 10 March 1621, and although he apparently died near the time of the great massacre of that year, it is not known whether he was a victim of that attack.

Although he may be known to most as the husband of Pocahontas, John Rolfe was without doubt one of the most important figures in the early history of the Jamestown colony and a major reason for the success of the first permanent English settlement in the New World.

Related entries: Buck, Richard; Henricus; James Fort; Pocahontas; Powhatan; Smith, Captain John; Tobacco

Suggestions for further reading

Edward Arber, ed. 1910. *Travels and Works of Captain John Smith.* (parts 1, 2). Edinburgh, Scotland: J. Grant.

Philip L. Barbour. 1969. *Pocahontas and her World.* Boston: Houghton Mifflin.

Edward Wright Haile, ed. 2001. *Jamestown Narratives: Eyewitness Accounts of the Virginia Colony: The First Decade: 1607–1617.* Champlain, VA: Round House.

James Horn. 2005. *A Land as God Made It: Jamestown and the Birth of America.* New York: Basic Books.

Grace Steele Woodward. 1969. *Pocahontas.* Norman: University of Oklahoma Press.

Rolfe, Thomas (1615–c.1675)

See Pocahontas

S

Sagadahoc (Popham) Colony

On 19 August 1607, about four months after English settlers first landed at Jamestown, sea captains Raleigh Gilbert and George Popham (c.1550–1608) led one hundred and twenty men ashore at Sabino Point (present-day Phippsburg, Maine) at the mouth of the Sagadahoc (now Kennebec) River, on the New England coast. The small group of colonists and sailors had ventured across the Atlantic aboard the *Mary and John* and the *Gift of God,* two vessels financed by the Plymouth Company, of England. The chief patron of the Maine colonization effort was Sir John Popham (c.1531–1607), the lord chief justice of all pleas and an uncle of George Popham; the colonists named their settlement in honor of him.

The colonists' plan was an ambitious one: to build a stockade, a stone fort, a storehouse, a church, and fifty houses. (A diagram of the fort, drawn by John Hunt and christened Fort St. George, made only seven weeks after the colonists landed, has survived.) The settlers set to work immediately constructing not only buildings but also the first ship in Maine's history, a fifty-foot pinnace, the *Virginia of Sagadahoc,* which was used to explore the Kennebec and outlying areas. In December, the two original vessels returned to England, leaving behind only forty-five settlers. Gilbert and Popham proved to be incompentent leaders, the former given to anger and mismangement, the latter completely inept.

The settlers became unruly and apathetic and unwisely began to loaf in the face of a New England winter. Popham, the president, survived only until February, leaving the ineffectual Gilbert, "desirous of supremacy and rule," in control. Despite Gilbert's blunders—which apparently included provoking an attack by the local Wabanaki chiefs, Canibas and Arosaguntacooks, that resulted in the death of 13 settlers and the burning of storehouses and other buildings—the colonists did manage to survive the winter by trading with local natives. (The Wabanaki, or the People of the Dawn, were Algonquian-speaking hunters and farmers, about 20,000 in number.) A resupply mission from England, sponsored by Sir Francis Popham (son and heir of Sir John), arrived in the spring of 1608 and took some of the colonists back to England. (The younger Popham sent vessels to trade with the natives long after the settlement's demise, in 1610, 1611, 1612, and 1614.)

The colony might have survived but for the news brought by a supply vessel in September 1608—that Sir John Popham and Raleigh Gilbert's brother, Sir Walter Raleigh, were dead. As the heir to Sir Walter's substantial inheritance, Gilbert determined to return to England, and the colonists decided to quit the colony as well. Three ships and the pinnace *Virginia,* loaded with—so say recent historians—all the remaining settlers, sailed for England with as much as they could carry of the colony's goods. In the end, wrote Sir Ferdinando Gorges, a colonizer who also served as the military governor of Plymouth, England, the Sagadahoc colony was a "wonderful discouragement" that was killed off more by a failure of leadership than by any hardship it encountered. It would be 1620, with the arrival of the Pilgrims at Plymouth Rock, before the Plymouth Company was able to colonize New England,

Archaeological excavations begun at the site of Fort St. George in 1994 (based on John Hunt's drawing) have uncovered many artifiacts, including a caulking iron from the pinnace *Virginia,* and have confirmed the existence of the public storehouse and the house of Raleigh Gilbert. Efforts to reconstruct the *Virginia* for the 400th anniversary celebration of the construction of Maine's first ship in 2007 have been under way since 2000.

Related entries: Gosnold, Bartholomew; London Company; Three Ships

Suggestions for further reading

Jeffrey P. Brain. 1998. "Fort St. George on the Kennebec" (*Bermuda Journal of Archaeology and Maritime History,* vol. 10).

——. 2003. "The Popham Colony: An Historical and Archaeological Brief" (*Maine Archaeological Society Bulletin,* vol. 43).

Warner F. Gookin and Philip L. Barbour. 1963. *Bartholomew Gosnold: Discoverer and Planter, New England—1602, Virginia—1607.* Hamden, CT, and London: Archon Books.

R. H. Major, ed. 1849. *The Historie of Travaile into Virginia Britannia; Expressing the Cosmographie and Comodities of the Country, Together with the Manners and Customes of the People. Gathered and Observed as Well by Those Who Went First Thither as Collected by William Strachey, Gent., the first Secretary of the Colony.* London: Hakluyt Society.

Sandys, Sir Edwin (1561–1629)

Although he never visited the New World, few men were as important to the survival of the Jamestown colony as Sir Edwin Sandys, the second son and namesake of the eminent archbishop of York. Born in Worcestershire, Sandys received a classical education befitting a child of so powerful a father. Sandys's education began at age ten, when he entered Merchant Taylors' School, headed by Richard Mulcaster, England's leading humanist and pedagogical theorist. Sandys attended Merchant Taylors' until September 1577, when he entered Oxford University's Corpus Christi College. At Oxford, Sandys's tutor was the young but brilliant theologian Richard Hooker. (The archbishop was Hooker's patron; Hooker in gratitude named three children after members of the Sandys family.) At Oxford, Sandys also became close friends with fellow student George Cranmer, the great-nephew of the martyred archbishop Thomas Cranmer, and together they assisted Hooker in preparing his significant eight-volume work, *Of the Lawes of the Ecclesiasticall Politie* (London, 1593–1604). Before Sandys left Oxford some thirteen years after matriculating, he had taken B.A. and M.A. degrees, prepared for a law degree that he failed to take, and had been elected a fellow of Corpus Christi. Also while at Oxford, Sandys married the first of four wives, Margaret Eveleigh, with whom he had a daughter, Elizabeth, before Margaret died in childbirth along with their second child. (A subsequent marriage to Margaret's cousin Anne Southcote, who died in 1593, produced no children. Sandys's third wife, Elizabeth Nevinson, whom he married in 1601, and their daughter Anne were both dead by 1605, when he married Katherine Bulkeley, with whom he had twelve children. Katherine outlived her husband, dying in 1640.)

All told, Sandys's study of the classics, theology, and law during his Oxford years prepared him for the distinguished parliamentary career that lay ahead as well as for the important role that he would play in the history of England's commerce and colonization. But first he would be elected to Parliament (possibly in 1586 but certainly in 1589), leaving no mark of his attendance; enter the Middle Temple (with his old friend George Cranmer) in 1590; and bring the first four volumes of Hooker's *Ecclesiastical Polity* into print in 1593. In 1593, Sandys finally made his first speech in Parliament, during the debates over the religious nonconformity bill that was passed that spring, and he served on a couple of committees, but otherwise he again left little mark of his attendance. In 1596, Sandys and Cranmer began a three-year tour of the continent, spending time in the Netherlands, Germany, Switzerland, France, and Italy. (Cranmer was killed in Ireland while serving with Lord Mountjoy in 1601.) During his travels, Sandys wrote a ponderous but comprehensive and learned survey of European religious practices, *A Relation of the State of Religion, and With What Hopes and Pollicies it Hath Beene Framed, and is Maintained in the Severall States of These Westerne Partes of the World* (London, 1605). Sandys's analysis of the various Christian faiths (especially Roman Catholcism) as he had found them led him to conclude that their reunification was impossible, and hence some sort of toleration and coexistence was called for—an English version of *Cuius regio, eius religio* ("Whose region, his religion"). Wildly popular, by the 1660s the *Relation* had gone through sixteen editions or printings, including three different foreign-language translations. Sandys also published another work with religious themes, *Sacred Hymns, Consisting of Fifti Select Psalms of David and Others, Paraphrastically Turned into English Verse* (London, 1615).

As previously alluded to, Sandys's early parliamentary career was hardly worthy of notice. That changed in April 1604, when Parliament was debating James I's proposal for union between England and Scotland. By then, Sandys had been in the House of Commons for nearly two decades and was esteemed a learned, judicious, and flexible member from a distinguished family; he was also aligned with Sir Robert Cecil, Queen Elizabeth's chief minister, who had taken charge of James's government (in fact, Sandys's association with Cecil may have contributed to his knighthood by James in May 1603). In an atmosphere urging union, Sandys stood up and cautioned restraint, questioning both the propriety of union and the extent of the king's authority. His arguments, surprisingly, fell on fertile ground; other members stepped forward to present their own misgivings about union. After that, even direct appeals from James could not slow the momentum against union; the audacious

Portrait of Edwin Sandys, seventeenth-century Jamestown statesman. (Ellyson, J. Taylor. The London Company of Virginia, *1908)*

members of the Commons rejected the issue, and union was not realized until 1707. Meanwhile, the issue had thrust Sandys into a leadership role in the House of Commons that would last for twenty years. No matter the issues—union, ending monopolies and opening free trade, reform of the system of wardships, subsidies for the Crown, free speech, the abuses and limits of royal power—Sandys was, in the words of his biographer, the Lower House's "principal tactician and negotiator" with the government. Sandys proved to be a tireless and effective leader who with rare exception represented the ideals of the gentry and the rights of individuals.

In 1607, the year of Jamestown's founding, Edwin Sandys was named to the Council of Virginia, but it would be another decade before he would turn his attention in earnest to the New World (this despite his apparent active part in drafting the Second Charter, issued in the spring of 1609, and his fund-raising efforts on behalf of the Virginia venture). Amid his busy schedule as a leader in the Commons, he did manage somehow to find time to keep abreast of English colonization strategy and efforts and to contribute occasionally to the work of the London Company in his official capacity. In 1614, when James prorogued the so-called Addled Parliament, Sandys, along with some other ringleaders in the House of Commons, was confined to the city of London for what turned out to be only a month. With Parliament out of session and unlikely to be called back any time soon (indeed, it was 1621 before James called a new session), Sandys turned his attention elsewhere: He constructed a new mansion, Northbourne Court (finished in 1616; burned 1750), in Kent, and he began to take a renewed interest in the affairs of the East India Company and the Virginia Company. The following year, he published his *Sacred Hymns,* was appointed sheriff of Kent, and invested in the Bermuda Company (he unsuccessfully campaigned for the governor's office of the Bermuda Company in 1619). In 1617, he became a joint manager of the Virginia Company, and that marks the beginning of what soon became his almost total immersion in the affairs of the colonization of Virginia. In fact, from 1617 until the king dissolved the company in 1624, no one in London was more involved in the settling of Virginia than Sandys. Indeed, his House leadership in regulating monopolies and opening trade amply prepared him for the daunting task of stabilizing the ongoing effort to colonize the New World.

For Sandys, the central weaknesses of the Jamestown settlement could be overcome by infusions of money and people. The population seemed to advance and recede without any purpose, the colony was nowhere near self-sufficient and always seemed on the verge of toppling over, and the company was broke. To Sandys, these were not insurmountable problems, provided legitimate reforms could be introduced. He aimed his first efforts at increasing the number of settlers, and in mid-1618 he sent over about 600 people—many at his own expense—which more than doubled the colony's population. At the same time, he attempted to shift the colony away from its reliance on tobacco by encouraging the diversification of agriculture, especially foodstuffs. Next, he agitated to have the Company's financial accounts audited, an expediency aimed not so much at casting blame over past managerial practices but at discovering how to develop sound polices for the future. Finally, he formulated a blueprint for the future governance of Jamestown that, when enacted, would have far-reaching consequences for life in Virginia: the so-called Great Charter of 1618. The Great Charter contained a series of reform measures that touched on land, labor, agriculture, industry, government, and taxation; in effect, it completely reorganized nearly every aspect of the colony. The reforms would be carried out in Virginia by a new governor, one aligned closely with Sandys, Sir George Yeardley (who had already served in that capacity); Governor Thomas Smythe would return home to England. Sandys himself, already presiding over the company in London, would be elected treasurer, the company's most powerful officer, in April 1619; a very capable deputy treasurer, John Ferrar, would manage most day-to-day activities in England. Sandys lent vision to the undertaking; his personal motivation, he claimed, was simple: He was "grieved to see this great action fall to nothing."

Sandys's reforms at first seemed to place the Jamestown settlement on the threshold of finally fulfilling the mission originally intended for it by the investors of the Virginia Company. The host of new settlers going to the colony and the institution of the new charter and all that it represented (including the introduction into the New World of a measure of self-governance through the newly created General Assembly) brought dramatic changes in Virginia; hope was renewed not only within the colony but in England as well. Sandys's failure to win reelection to the treasurer's office in 1620 and his brief imprisonment (five weeks) in the London Tower by James the following year were minor setbacks, considering all the forward strides being made at Jamestown. (Sandys's younger brother George was elected treasurer in 1621.) The rapid expansion had come with tremendous costs that only showed up later, however: Death rates still remained high; company debts, although reduced, could not be eliminated; crop diversification and the introduction of new industries proved less lucrative than expected; and, most worrisome, the steady increase in population and the subsequent demand for more land exacerbated tensions with the Indians. The last was worse than any of the English had imagined; just how dangerous the situation had become was not made apparent until the morning of 22 March 1622, when the natives suddenly rose up and killed some 350 English settlers. The attack proved to be both Sandys's and the company's undoing, although it took two years for it all to unravel. Blame for the attack had to be laid somewhere, and the powerful Sandys, always with detractors and enemies, was the most visible target. Accusations and inquiries, along with what proved to be a false sense of despair at Jamestown, eventually took their toll; in June 1624 the Crown dissolved the Virginia Company and took control of the colony.

Sir Edwin Sandys lived another five years after the dissolution of the Virginia Company. He watched developments in Virginia from a respectable distance, not uninvolved or without interest or some influence. He thus was able to see Jamestown begin to recover from the Massacre of 1622. That Jamestown survived and ultimately flourished owed much, in fact, to Sandys's leadership during its crucial years. Sandys died at Northbourne Court and was buried nearby at the Church of St. Augustine. In 1957, the American and British Commonwealth Association honored his contributions to the founding of Virginia by placing a plaque near his tomb outlining his major successes.

Related entries: Massacre of 1622; Sandys, George

Suggestions for further reading

Wesley Frank Craven. 1957. *The Virginia Company of London, 1606–1624.* Charlottesville: University Press of Virginia.

Richard Hooker. 1593–1604. *Of the Lawes of the Ecclesiasticall Politie.* London: John Windet.

Theodore K. Rabb. 1998. *Jacobean Gentleman: Sir Edwin Sandys, 1561–1629.* Princeton, NJ: Princeton University Press.

Sir Edwin Sandys. 1605. *A Relation of the State of Religion, and With What Hopes and Pollicies it Hath Beene Framed, and is Maintained in the Severall States of These Westerne Partes of the World.* London: Val. Sims for Simon Waterson.

——. 1615. *Sacred Hymns, Consisting of Fifti Select Psalms of David and Others, Paraphrastically Turned into English Verse.* London: Thomas Snodham, by the assignment of the Company of Stationers.

Willard Mosher Wallace. 1940. "Sir Edwin Sandys and the First Parliament of James I" (Ph.D. Thesis). Philadelphia: University of Pennsylvania.

Sandys, George (1578–1644)

Described as having "a zealous inclination to all human learning" by an early nineteenth-century writer and as "a striking example of the well-rounded Renaissance man in his role of colonizer and empire-builder" by a twentieth-century biographer, George Sandys was one of the most important men in the history of colonial Jamestown. The youngest of the nine children (including seven boys) of Edwin Sandys (c.1516), the Archbishop of York, and his second wife, Cicely Wilford, George apparently was named for one of his godfathers, George, third Earl of Cumberland, a chivalrous champion of Elizabeth's against the Spanish. Sandys's classical study at Oxford's Corpus Christi College, which he began at age eleven, nourished his love of learning and enabled him to master several languages but was cut short by an arranged marriage to Elizabeth Norton (b. 1580), the daughter of a wealthy landowner of Ripon. The marriage produced no children and ended after a few years in permanent separation. Elizabeth survived at least until 1662.

Like many of the "adventurers" who made their way to Virginia during the first decade of the Jamestown colony, George Sandys already had spent time on mainland Europe, exploring the environs of Paris and northern Italy and traveling to Constantinople, Egypt, and Palestine before charting a course for the New World. The ancient lands with their rich history, famous landmarks, and foreign religions held an exotic sway on Sandys. He marveled at the wonders of the Turkish capital and Cairo, of Alexandria and Memphis, and of Bethlehem, Nazareth, Jerusalem, and Phoenicia; the Nile, the Pyramids, the Sphinx, and

George Sandys was an ardent proponent of the colony of Virginia and served as a colonial official in the 1620s, a pivotal period in Virginia's development, as it struggled financially to survive and suffered devastating losses in the Indian massacre of 1622. (Ellyson, J. Taylor. The London Company of Virginia, *1908)*

the camels of Arabia all made their lasting impressions. Sandys recorded his travel experiences in a journal that he used as the basis of an expanded travel narrative, *A Relation of a Journey Begun An: Dom: 1610 . . . Containing a Description of the Turkish Empire, of Ægypt, of the Holy Land, of the Remote parts of Italy, and Ilands Adjoyning* (London, 1615), which he dedicated to Prince Charles. The work was well received by the English literati and went through nine editions, including seven during Sandys's lifetime. Sandys also incorporated parts of the *Relation* into some of his other writings, and it was translated into Dutch and German as well; John Milton, Ben Jonson, and Francis Bacon are among the numerous seventeenth-century writers who used Sandys's *Relation* as a source for their own works. By 1619, when Sandys's name begins to appear significantly in relation to Jamestown, his natural talents and education had been supplemented by travel and experience in the world, and he was becoming known and respected throughout England.

The second and third charters of the London Company (in 1609 and 1612) list Sandys as a subscriber, or stockholder. He and three of his brothers (and other family members) likely were recruited to the company by older brother Edwin, a leading force in the early colonization of Jamestown and a member of the Royal Council beginning in 1606. A strong advocate of the Virginia experiment in both the London Company and in Parliament, Sir Edwin Sandys was not afraid to become embroiled in the politics of colonization and led a multi-year effort to reform the colony that culminated in 1619 with his election as treasurer—in effect, the governor of Jamestown under the company charter. Among the reforms that he championed were faster settlement, crop diversification, and increased industries—all badly needed—but the changes came with political costs, and he was not reappointed when his term ended, although he continued to play a prominent role in the company until the king revoked its charter in 1624. For the most part, George watched his brother's entanglements from the sidelines, or at least from behind the scenes, until February 1621, when he was named to serve on company committees with the resident governor-elect of Virginia, Sir Francis Wyatt, who was Sandys's own nephew.

Although one of the committees to which Sandys was appointed dealt with the important and delicate issues surrounding the tobacco monopoly in Virginia, Sandys's service on that committee was only the prelude to a far greater appointment—that of treasurer of the London Company. It was a new position, designed to collect the rents and other revenue owed the company; with it came a land grant of 1,500 acres and 50 indentured servants to settle it. The Earl of Southampton proposed Sandys's nomination, remarking that he was known to them all as "a man very fitt to take that charge . . . who indeed was generally so well reputed of, for his approved fidelity sufficiency and integrity: as they conceaved a fitter man could not be chosen for that place." His election took place in May 1621, at which time he also was put on both the royal council for Virginia and the council in Virginia, and in late July, after three months of preparation, he sailed for the New World on board the *George* with Governor Wyatt, William Claiborne, and others who would play important roles in the colony. The *George* arrived at Jamestown the following October.

Received warmly by the Englishmen already living at Jamestown, Sandys seems to have relished his responsibilities as treasurer, entering into them with great purpose. Along with the new governor and Council, he quickly instituted some badly needed improvements, but the promise of continuing reform was cut short the following March by the sudden Indian attack on the settlers, known as the Indian Massacre of 1622. Sandys survived the devastating assault; he was fortunate—six fellow counselors did not. He promptly commanded one of the retaliatory operations against the natives and then played an instrumental role in restoring order to the colony. Nevertheless, the London Company blamed the Jamestown colony's leaders for the attack, a group that of course included Sandys. In the aftermath of the massacre, Sandys wrote a series of letters to supporters back in England outlining what he thought had led to the massacre, at root the same problem that had plagued colonization efforts in the New World since the Lost Colony: sending over settlers without adequately supporting their needs. It was a lesson that cost many people their lives and led to the dissolution of the company two years later.

After the Indian attack on Jamestown, Sandys redoubled his efforts to improve the agriculture and industries of the colony, mostly to little avail, and took on increased responsibilities in the Council, which included hearing court cases and substituting for the colony's secretary when he was out of the colony; he also negotiated a treaty with the friendly Potomac Indians. In addition, Sandys managed a personal estate of almost 3,000 acres of his own land, consisting of several separate plantations on both sides of the James River. Altogether, his life was busy and prosperous, and he wielded great influence in the colony; on the other hand, little time was left for the intellectual pursuits that attracted his attention, such as translating from Latin Ovid's *Metamorphoses,* which he managed to do in his spare time. By 1625, Sandys was ready to end the Virginia phase of his life and go back to England, and that June he left the New World, never to return.

Sandys lived almost two decades after his return to England. He led a somewhat charmed life, thanks in great part to the patronage of Charles I, who was crowned king soon after Sandys's arrival in London. Sandys's publication of his English translation of Ovid's *Metamorphoses* (London, 1626, 1632), with his extensive and learned commentaries, earned him critical acclaim in England's highest literary circles. Scholarly pursuits engaged much of his time and led to the publication of other translations and commentaries, all published in London: *A Paraphrase upon the Psalmes of David* (1636), *A Paraphrase upon the Divine Poems* (1638), *A Paraphrase upon the Song of Solomon* (1640), and Hugo Grotius's play, *Christs Passion* (1640). He nevertheless kept abreast of changes in Virginia (where he stilled owned considerable property), and in the 1630s he served on various commissions, committees, and boards connected with oversight of the colony. In 1639, Sir Francis Wyatt returned to Jamestown as governor for a second term, and Sandys represented his nephew's interests in England until 1642, when Wyatt's term ended. After that, Sandys took no more part in the affairs of Virginia.

George Sandys is buried at the parish church at Boxley, in Kent, where he spent his last years. He is remembered today as much or more for his contributions to English literature as for his brief but important contribution to the Jamestown settlement at a crucial time in its history. A site near Jamestown on the James River at Kingsmill Neck, identified as being first owned by Sandys, yielded more than 25,000 artifacts during excavation by archaeologists working under the auspices of the Association for the Preservation of Virginia Antiquities (APVA) during the 1990s.

Related entries: London Company; Sandys, Sir Edwin

Suggestions for further reading

Richard Beale Davis. 1955. *George Sandys: Poet-Adventurer A Study in Anglo-American Culture in the Seventeenth Century.* New York and London: Columbia University Press.

James Ellison. 2002. *George Sandys: Travel, Colonialism and Tolerance in the Seventeenth Century.* Woodbridge, Suffolk, England, and Rochester, NY: Boydell and Brewer.

Jonathan Haynes. 1986. *The Humanist as Traveler: George Sandys's Relation of a Journey begun An. Dom. 1610.* Cranbury, NJ, and London: Associated University Presses for Fairleigh Dickinson University Press.

Seth W. Mallios. 2000. *At the Edge of the Precipice: Frontier Ventures, Jamestown's Hinterland, and the Archaeology of 44JC802.* Richmond, VA: Association for Preservation of Virginia Antiquities.

Shirley Hundred

Shirley Hundred is the oldest continuously inhabited plantation in English America. Its rich history began in 1613, when Thomas West, Lord Governor De La Warr, received a patent from King James I for a tract of 8,000 acres on the north side of the James River, about equidistant (25 miles) from Jamestown and Richmond, in the so-called New Bermudas near the mouth of the Appomattox River. Lord De La Warr named the tract West and Shirley Hundred (after himself and his wife, Lady Cessalye Sherley), and began extensive tobacco cultivation on the lands. After West's death in 1619, the original Hundred was divided into smaller tracts that were occupied by several owners; the Virginia censuses taken between 1623 and 1625 distinguished between West and Shirley Hundred and Shirley Hundred (listing together a total of 64 inhabitants). The Indian Massacre of 1622 apparently claimed the lives of less than a dozen Shirley Hundred settlers, leaving ample survivors in the Hundred for it to form its own militia company to retaliate against their attackers (3 men of the Hundred were "slaine by the indians" in 1624). About 15 additional men, women, and children moved into Shirley Hundred within the first 24 months after the Powhatan uprising.

About half of the original Shirley acreage was acquired by Edward Hill I beginning in 1638, and within twenty years he had built a home on the banks of the James in the area of the present-day Shirley mansion. A Hill descendant, John Carter (d. 1742), replaced that house with another, a stately three-story mansion measuring sixty by twenty-four feet, sometime after his marriage to Elizabeth Hill in 1723. Known as the Hill House, it was described on the eve of the American Revolutionary War, in 1773, with the other buildings at the plantation as

> large, convenient, and expensive, but now falling to decay. . . . The present proprietor has a most opulent fortune, and possesses such a variety of seats, in situations so exceedingly delightful, that he overlooks this sweet one of Shirley, and suffers it to fall to ruin, although the buildings must have cost an immense sum in constructing; and would certainly be expensive to keep in repair.

Despite its decline, Hill House lasted nearly another century until 1868, when it was torn down and its bricks used for another house, Upper Shirley, a half mile to the north. (Archaeological excavations at Shirley's Hill House site in the 1960s turned up 16,590 artifacts plus large amounts of prehistoric and construction residue.)

Adjacent to the Hill House was another John Carter mansion, the one that still stands at Shirley today. Built in the same period as the Hill House, the existing mansion and its main dependencies (four brick structures—kitchen, laundry, and two large barns) form a Queen Anne forecourt, possibly the only surviving example of this style in America. Archaeological digs around the mansion and in the plantation's slave quarters in 1979 and 1980 revealed much about the occupation of Shirley by its owners, its tenant farmers, and its slaves. In addition to the aforementioned archaeological inquiries, an archaeological field school at the College of William and Mary has surveyed three prehistoric sites at Shirley Hundred, formerly the domain of the Weanock (Weyanoke) Indians, an Algonquin tribe under Powhatan's control. Evidence of intermittent occupation as far back as 6,000 was uncovered, with a concentration in the region beginning about 3,000 years ago. In particular, the Weanock heavily occupied the Shirley settlement area at the time Lord De La Warr was granted his patent, and the mansion site may have even been the tribe's chief town.

Shirley Plantation witnessed both the American Revolutionary and Civil Wars, serving as a supply rendezvous for the Continental army in the former and as a hospital for Union troops wounded during the Battle of Malvern Hill in the latter. Ann Hill Carter, wife of the Revolutionary War cavalry hero Light-Horse Harry Lee and mother of the great Confederate general Robert E. Lee, was born and married at Shirley. Today, Shirley Plantation is a thriving if somewhat secluded historic attraction, run by Hill family descendants, now in their eleventh generation, who have lived at Shirley Hundred ever since Edward Hill took possession of the Charles City County property in the seventeenth century. Shirley was added to the National Register of Historic Places in 1969, and in 2002 the Historic Richmond Foundation partnered with Shirley to establish an annual Shirley Polo Cup as a fund-raiser for historic preservation.

Related entries: Martin's Hundred; Massacre of 1622; West, Thomas, Lord De La Warr

Suggestion for further reading

Theodore R. Reinhart, ed. 1984. *The Archaeology of Shirley Plantation.* Charlottesville: University Press of Virginia.

Depiction of the Dutch man-of-war thought to have brought the first African slaves to the Virginia Colony in 1619. The slaves were exchanged for a supply of corn. (Library of Congress)

Slavery

Slavery as a system of forced labor came slowly to colonial Jamestown. Early on, many of the settlers made their way to the New World by bartering several years' worth of their future labor to a benefactor (initially the Virginia Company) who in return paid their ocean passage and set them to work in a trade upon their arrival in the colony. These obligations were contractual and legally binding, and they were incurred within a fixed system of servitude that was governed by English law; they could be traded or sold (or renegotiated) at their owner's discretion. When settlers failed to comply with the terms of their agreements (a common occurrence, given the unforeseen harshness of life in early Virginia), often their only recourse to paying off their debts was to have the length of their servitude extended. But as a rule, the duration was for a set period of time and not permanent, and hence few servants actually entered into slavery. In fact, throughout the seventeenth century, said one prominent historian of slavery, "Virginia hardly qualified as a slave society" at all.

Europeans had enslaved natives very early and brought African slaves to the New World as early as 1517, but very little is known about slaves in colonial Virginia before 1630. The frustratingly sparse references to slaves in the colony indicate that the first people held as slaves by the English were not blacks but Indians who had been captured in warfare. When tobacco cultivation was introduced in the colony, the English impressed some of these captive natives to work in the fields. Land was inexpensive but settling it a labor-intensive and therefore expensive process. "Labor was," as Lorena Walsh observed about the cultivation of land in the Jamestown colony, "the critical ingredient." Tobacco planters eagerly vied for laborers, whether free or slave, black or white. Unfortunately, little is known about either group of laborers in the first half century of the colony.

As with slavery in general, very little is known about blacks at Jamestown before 1630. From the earliest, the role of blacks in the colony was ambiguous. In recent years, social and quantitative historians have concluded that the vast majority of Africans entered the colony as slaves, not as indentured servants as previously thought, although some did serve out periods of servitude and eventually earn their freedom. What has become clear is that white colonists considered and treated blacks not as their equals but as their inferiors. Skin color, language, religion, and place of origin all combined to make Africans even more alien to the European settlers than the Indians they routinely encountered in the Virginia countryside. African arrivals were assigned the coarsest, most menial tasks and subjected to the most squalid living conditions in the colony, and whether conscious or not on the part of the whites, blacks were effectively relegated to the very bottom of society. From the lowest station, it was difficult to rise, especially as the traffic in slaves began to increase.

The history of the importation of Africans into Virginia began in late August 1619, when "20. and odd Negroes" were brought into Point Comfort near Jamestown. John Rolfe gave the most accurate description of their arrival in a letter to colony promoter Sir Edwin Sandys, saying that they came in the *White Lion* (formerly known as the *Lea Branca* and the *Witte Leeuw*), a 160-ton Dutch man-of-war commanded by Captain John Colyn Jope of Cornwall. The Africans originally had been on board a Portuguese slaver in the West Indies that was taken by two privateers (apparently the *White Lion* and the *Treasurer*, an English man-of-war commanded by Marmaduke Rayner). Jope traded the Africans to Virginia Governor George Yeardley and cape merchant Abraham Piersey for a supply of corn. The next reference to Africans in Virginia is in November 1624, when John Phillip, a black man christened in England twelve years earlier, shows up in the court records. As Phillip was in court to testify against a white man, he apparently was not a slave. The court records provide other tantalizing bits of information from the early period, including the fact that Governor Sir Francis Wyatt owned a black servant man named Brase, although he apparently was not a slave either. In the same year, the Virginia census taken for the London Company provided information on twenty-three blacks in the colony, twenty-two living and one dead. Most had been in Virginia for five years, and nearly half were listed without a name, and those so accorded, without surnames—a deviation from the form for the other people listed in the census.

The Virginia census for 1625 listed twenty-three blacks, including two children. For only four of the adults was their time of arrival at the colony given, between 1621 and 1623. The others apparently were the survivors from the original group of twenty that arrived in 1619. The names given included some Spanish names, indicating that the first arrivals may have come from unnamed, Spanish-occupied Caribbean islands rather than directly from Africa. John Rolfe certainly thought they did. If so, then the first Africans in Virginia were most likely American born and raised as Catholics. These twenty-three men, women, and children lived at six different places, including nine at Jamestown and seven at Percy's Hundred. None are listed as free, despite the fact that most had been in the colony for six years. At least one other importation occurred in the 1620s, in 1627 or 1628, when a shipmaster (possibly Arthur Guy) brought in blacks seized from an Angolan man-of-war. These are the first recorded blacks to come directly from Africa into Virginia. Common names given to the Africans included Francisco, Pedro, Antonio, Isabella, Angelo, Domingo, and Mingo (Spanish and Portuguese); Caesar, Hannibal, Nero, Jupiter, Pluto, Minerva, Primus, Secundus (from ancient history and mythology); and, unflatteringly, Ape and Monkey. Males were more numerous than females, but the latter often worked in the fields, too, especially in the early years before substantial family units came into being.

The slave trafficking did not increase dramatically until the end of the century. From 1635 until about 1669, probably fewer than 1,200 slaves were brought into Virginia. The incoming number more than doubled between then and 1694. Beginning in 1699, the numbers increased dramatically (more than 6,600 between 1699 and 1708, and 43,000 by 1740). Until the 1670s, most ships brought slaves into the West Indies, from which some later would be sold to Virginia. In the 1690s, the labor source for white indentures fell off drastically, and planters turned to African slaves to replace them. In the 1670s, slaves made up about one-fifth of the colony's labor force. By the early 1690s, they made up four-fifths of the labor supply, although there was a temporary resurgence in the numbers of indentured servants at the end of the decade. The Royal African Company exercised an official monopoly of the slave trade until 1698, after which the trade was thrown open and numbers increased. Until then, it was both natural and not unusual for blacks and whites to work (and play) together in the Virginia colony.

The legal status of slaves and blacks in the Virginia colony changed over the course of the seventeenth century. Slavery at first was not codified in law, and it would have been exceedingly difficult intentionally to do so, especially for the purpose of enslaving free men. At the same time, the law's silence permitted colonists to acquire persons already held in bondage, whether indentured servants or outright slaves, in the same way that they purchased other property. Although a distinction between white and black servants arose very quickly, many of the early African indentures were able to work out their time and thereby earn their freedom, and some actually prospered in the years to come. Thus, the transformation from indentured servitude to slavery, indeed racial slavery, took place gradually over a matter of decades as the number of existing blacks and newly imported Africans increased, and by the end of the seventeenth century the colony's laws clearly had codified to the point where blacks were treated as slave chattel. As historian Warren M. Billings observed, "Slavery existed in fact long before it received statutory definition, a process that accelerated after 1662 and culminated in 1705, when the General Assembly wrote a slave code into the revised statutes."

On 3 August 1619, only three weeks before the Dutch vessel sailed into the James River bringing the first Africans into Virginia, during the first meeting of the General Assembly the earliest case of a dispute between a master and a servant was recorded. Captain William Powell petitioned the assembly to prosecute his servant, Thomas Garnett, for a number of serious charges, "extreame neglect of his business to the great loss and prejudice" of his owner, and "for openly and impudently abusing his house, in sight both of Master and Mistress, through wantonness with a woman servant of theirs, a widdowe." The Assembly, led by the governor, sentenced Garnett to "stand fower dayes with his eares nailed to the Pillory . . . and every of those dayes should be publiquely whipped."

"Antonio the Negro"

The 1625 Virginia census listed "Antonio the negro" as a servant who had come to the colony in 1621. Antonio eventually earned his freedom, changed his name to Anthony Johnson, and with his wife Mary, another African servant, raised four children. The Johnsons purchased land, cattle, and (eventually) indentured servants of their own. Johnson moved his family to Maryland in 1665, where he leased a 300-acre plantation, but at the same time, he forfeited the property he owned in Virginia to the government when a jury determined that he was a "negroe and by consequence an alien." Johnson died in 1670.

The General Assembly apparently thought miscegenation a greater crime than simple fornication, for in September 1630 it ordered Hugh Davis to be "soundly whipped, before an assembly of Negroes and others for abusing himself to the dishonor of God and shame of Christians, by defiling his body in lying with a negro." In 1639, a legal distinction was made between white and black men when the Assembly decreed to provide "ALL persons except negroes" with arms and ammunition. In 1640, one African, known as John Punch, was ordered to be held "for the time of his natural Life here or elsewhere" as partial punishment for having run away from the colony to Maryland. Two white accomplices were beaten, as was Punch, but sentenced to four extra years of indenture, one for their master and three for the colony. Two years later, the General Assembly imposed severe penalties for secret marriages and attempted escapes, and other decrees of the 1640s made distinctions between white women and black women and descendants of the latter. Commercial transactions between servants and freemen began to be regulated by changes in the laws in 1657, and in 1659, as Parliament attempted to strengthen English commerce at the expense of their Dutch rivals, the legislature reconfirmed the rights of Dutch slave traders to bring Africans into the colony. In 1660, the Virginia legal code for the first time reflected indications that blacks were being held in bondage in the colony, when the General Assembly set penalties for white servants attempting to run away in company with "negroes who are incapable of making satisfaction by addition of time." At the same time, the Assembly attempted to address the "barbarous usage" of servants by "cruell masters," who were bringing "much scandall and infamy to the country in generall" and thereby discouraging new immigrants from entering the colony.

A decade later, the laws made clear the difference in status between servants and slaves and between whites and nonwhites:

> Whereas it hat been questioned whither Indians or negroes manumitted or otherwise free, could be capable of purchasing christian servants, It is enacted that noe negroe or Indian though baptized and enjoyned of their owne freedome shall be capable of any such purchase of Christians, but yet not debarred from buying any of their owne nation.

In 1661, the General Assembly readdressed the status of Native Americans, prohibiting the selling of Indian servants into slavery and limiting the time of their indentured servitude to a period no longer than the "English of the like ages." In the same session, the Assembly ruled that the king of the Wainoake Indians had no right to sell "for life time" Metappin, a member of the Powhatan nation, to the colonist Elizabeth Short and ordered Metappin's release from servitude, "he speaking perfectly the English tongue and desiring baptism." In 1662, the Assembly, attempting to clear up "some doubts" about the status of children born to English fathers and black mothers, ruled that "all children borne in this country shal be held bond or free only according to the condition of the mother." The Assembly passed restrictions on unlawful meetings and unlicensed travel among servants in 1663, and in 1667 it ruled that the conferring of baptism did not exempt slaves from bondage.

From 1669 until the end of the century, a host of laws were passed limiting the rights and privileges of slaves, especially blacks—including the automatic acquittal of masters of charges of felony for the killing of their slaves ("since it cannot be presumed that prepensed malice . . . should induce any man to destroy his owne estate"); the prohibition against the purchasing of "christian" servants by blacks and Indians; the creation of distinctions between Indians captured in warfare and sold to Englishmen and blacks imported into the colony; the apprehension and suppression of "runaways, negroes and slaves"; the intermarrying of whites with nonwhites; the deportation within six months of all newly freed blacks and mulattoes; the limiting of black ownership of livestock; and several acts aimed at preventing insurrections by blacks and bringing about an easy and speedy prosecution of slaves who committed capital crimes. The so-called Slave Codes of 1705, for the purported purpose of "better settling and preservation of estates within this dominion," declared all servants brought into the colony who "were not Christians in their native Country" to be accounted as slaves, and for all "Negro, mulatto and Indian slaves" to be held as property. Punishments decreed for slaves included lashing, hanging, branding, maiming, mutilation, and placing in stocks. Moreover, after 1705 a slave could not bring suit against a master.

Virginia became more and more of a plantation society across the decades of the seventeenth century; its economy, based largely on tobacco cultivation, was completely dependent upon manual labor. Upon their arrival in Virginia, slaves immediately went to work, mostly in labor-intensive tobacco production. The seasoning time

Baptism of Slaves

ACT III. *An act declaring that baptisme of slaves doth not exempt them from bondage.*

WHEREAS some doubts have risen whether children that are slaves by birth, and by the charity and piety of their owners made pertakers of the blessed sacrament of baptisme, should by vertue of their baptisme be made ffree; *It is enacted and declared by this grand assembly, and the authority thereof,* that the conferring of baptisme doth not alter the condition of the person as to his bondage or ffreedome; that diverse masters, ffreed from this doubt, may more carefully endeavour the propagation of christianity by permitting children, though slaves, or those of greater growth if capable to be admitted to that sacrament.

—Virginia General Assembly, September 1667

in Virginia was especially harsh, and slaves seemed to suffer more than whites—about one quarter of new blacks died within one year of arriving—despite having some stronger immunities against malaria; wintertime respiratory problems caused many of the deaths. High rates of natural reproduction and fertility worked in their favor, however, giving rise to strong family units.

Work for everyone in the Jamestown colony was hard, especially for slaves. Skilled artisans and domestics more than likely fared better than hands toiling in the tobacco fields, but even they could not have had it easy. Unlike their fellow laborers—indentured servants—slaves could not look forward to the day that they would be free and hence had to look for personal motivation elsewhere. More likely than not, the absolute worst of the jobs fell to the slaves, who numbered far fewer than one-sixth of the manual labor workforce throughout most of the seventeenth century. To some extent, all seventeenth-century manual labor followed the cycles of the seasons. The planting, harvesting, curing, and shipping of tobacco—the colony's main crop—were all labor-intensive chores that required small groups of laborers to work together, slaves alongside indentures and, often, their masters. Even though the tobacco cycle lasted far less than a year, its heavy depletion of the soil meant that new land had to be cleared every year. After the demands of the main crop were satisfied, there might be other crops to tend to for the master (especially corn, a colonial Virginia staple food) in addition to taking care of his farm animals and property; and there was the daily grind of preparing food (and finding it) and maintaining one's own household.

The material life of the slaves, although not uniform, was for the most part beneath all but the poorest of whites. Slaves who worked as skilled artisans or in the master's household and those who lived on large plantations tended to have it somewhat better than slaves who worked in the fields and on smaller farms. Housing was at first rather crude but gradually improved over the decades. Skilled slaves might live where they worked, but for field slaves, a dormitory-style structure, called the quarter, developed early on, wherein a large number of slaves (or even several families) would live together in one or two rooms. Over time, separate post-supported huts became the norm, and, later, more substantial log cabins with fireplaces; a few lucky slaves were able to occupy houses abandoned by their masters or other whites. Also, as the slave population grew, clusters of houses and even small villages sprung up. And as the housing of whites improved, so did that of the slaves. Nevertheless, living quarters for slaves were cramped throughout the seventeenth century.

Food allowances for slaves fell far below those of white colonists. Corn was the staple of the slaves' diet, supplemented by small allowances of pork, beef, salted fish, milk, rum, and occasionally cider. Enterprising slaves often hunted wild game or planted a few vegetables to make up for deficiencies in quantity and quality. Despite the poor nourishment, however, slaves were expected to work hard, and work hard they did. Clothing tended to be shabby, more lightweight than that of whites and rationed out only once or twice a year. Typically, each person was given annually a suit of outerwear for the winter and the summer and a pair of shoes and stockings, plus a couple of shirts or shifts. More often than not, clothing came in the form of cloth that had to be cut and made up into garments. Blankets were parceled out parsimoniously and inadequate for the low temperatures of the Virginia winters. Patches, skins, and furs were commonplace; patterns and colors varied widely, although the latter tended to be drab. Likewise, caps or hats might be made out of anything and take on any of numerous shapes. The result was that slave dress rarely consisted of finery; rather, it was disparate, mismatched, and irregular, and it little resembled the more uniform look that evolved in subsequent centuries. Also, it was not uncommon for slaves, especially children, to be without shoes, nor was it unheard of for them even to be naked or half-naked.

Natural affinity to Virginia's other oppressed group, the Indians, did not work out in practice as one might think. Reputedly, Indians "hated and despised" the "very sight of a Negroe"—feelings that "seemed to be reciprocated." Indians no doubt looked down on slaves and no doubt must have been jealous of the influx of black people into the colony at the very time when their dominance in the area had ended and their numbers were quickly dwindling. Yet the two groups did occasionally commingle, intermarry, and have children together, partner in crime, and resist white rule together when they could. Likewise, blacks who were slaves had a complex relationship with free blacks, small in number in the seventeenth century. Free blacks, in addition to their better legal status, were in more constant contact with whites, were able to earn money and own property, and generally could forge a better life. Mulattos, whether of mixed black and white or black and Indian blood, made up perhaps the most ambiguous category.

Resistance to authority by slaves was likely to take the form of running away in small groups, although slaves sometimes joined resistance efforts organized by white servants. This increasingly was the case in the period leading up to and including Bacon's Rebellion. The rendezvous of rebels at planter John West's home (at West Point) numbered about 400, including at least 80 blacks. After uprisings and violence petered out in the early 1680s, poorer whites never again aligned with black slaves against either their masters or the government. Acceleration of Indian removal around the same time left blacks, already on the lowest rung of society's ladder, even more isolated from the rest of the colony's setters. Rising standards of living among laboring whites made the slaves' alienation from white society even starker. With increased numbers of blacks imported directly from Africa and arriving in Virginia completely unacculturated, the total degradation of slaves was ensured.

Related entries: Rolfe, John; Smith, Captain John; Tobacco; Trades and Artisans

Suggestions for further reading

Warren M. Billings. 1991. "The Law of Servants and Slaves in Seventeenth-Century Virginia" (*Virginia Magazine of History and Biography,* vol. 99).

Wesley Frank Craven. 1971. *White, Red, and Black: The Seventeenth-Century Virginian.* Charlottesville: University Press of Virginia.

Edmund S. Morgan. 1975. *American Slavery, American Freedom: The Ordeal of Colonial Virginia.* New York: W. W. Norton.

Philip D. Morgan. 1998. *Slave Counterpoint: Black Culture in the Eighteenth-Century Chesapeake and Lowcountry.* Chapel Hill: University of North Carolina Press for the Omohundro Institute of Early American History and Culture.

Alden T. Vaughn. 1972. "Blacks in Virginia: A Note on the First Decade" (*William and Mary Quarterly,* 3d series, vol. 29).

Susan Westbury. 1985. "Slaves of Colonial Virginia: Where They Came From" (*William and Mary Quarterly,* 3d series, vol. 42).

Smith, Captain John (1580–1631)

Vincere est Vivere. These words, translated from Latin as "To conquer is to live," are most appropriate as part of the inscription on John Smith's statue, which now stands inside the walls of the original James Fort site at colonial Jamestown. John Smith's life was one of constant effort to conquer every obstacle that he encountered in his life, from his humble beginnings (at least in comparison to the other great names associated with Jamestown's founding) to the three Turkish officers he defeated and beheaded in hand-to-hand combat in Transylvania, to the challenges of surviving the earliest period in Jamestown's founding. Indeed, had Smith not personified these words, Jamestown most likely would have floundered and faded away, as had the earlier English attempts on Roanoke Island that resulted in what has become known as the Lost Colony.

The son of George—a yeoman and landholder—and Alice (Rickard) Smith, and brother to four younger brothers and a sister, John Smith was baptized in Willoughby by Alford, Lincolnshire, on 9 January 1580. He received schooling in Alford and at the Free Grammar School of King Edward VI in Louth. He was not entirely contented with his life of studies and was moved to an apprenticeship with a merchant by the name of Thomas Sendall in King's Lynn. Shortly after his father died in 1596 and his mother remarried, Smith, still unhappy, left that life behind and joined English volunteers fighting in the Dutch wars of independence from Spain. After returning to England, Smith set off again to accompany the son of his patron, Lord Willoughby of Eresby, on the younger Willoughby's trip to Orléans for further education. Smith's time there was short, and soon he was on his way back to England. On the way, his ship was wrecked, and he was obliged to stay on Holy Island to recover from an incapacity that resulted, apparently, from the wreck. On his way again at last, Smith passed through Scotland and finally reached England in 1599, where he spent some period of time camping and reading Marcus Aurelius and Machiavelli. But Smith could not sit still for long, and he soon set off again, this time for the Mediterranean, with a captain not opposed to enriching himself and his crew through piracy, some of the booty of which Smith apparently shared in and took with him to Italy. It was not long, however, before Smith's thirst for adventure and fortune once again sent him to the battlefield, where in late 1600 he enlisted with the Austrian army to fight in Hungary against the Turks.

The English soldier and adventurer Captain John Smith not only helped to found the Virginia colony in 1607 but also, through his bold and vigorous leadership, played a crucial role in its survival. (Ellyson, J. Taylor. The London Company of Virginia, *1908)*

According to Smith's writings, it was during his service in Hungary that, through his bravery and fighting skills, he was promoted to captain and received his coat of arms, on which were depicted the heads of three Turkish officers he defeated in single combat. In a later battle, he was wounded and captured, as a result of which he was sold into slavery and became the property of a noblewoman whose name he recorded as

Captain John Smith

John Smith is one of those persons about whom historians are apt to lose their tempers.

—Historian John Fiske

Charatza Tragabigzanda. Smith and his owner eventually became very close friends, and she sent him to her brother near the Black Sea to "sojourne to learne the language, and what it was to be a Turke." The harsh treatment Smith received at the hands of the brother was more than he chose to bear, and after killing the brother Smith fled back through Russia and Poland to Transylvania before traveling on through North Africa and back to England, where he arrived in the winter of 1604–1605. It was here that Smith began his greatest journey into history.

In England, Smith became a shareholder of a new company founded for the exploration of North America. The Virginia Company of London received its first charter in April 1606, and John Smith was among the passengers and crew who first set sail for the company to the New World in December of the same year. Because of his naturally decisive, bold, and opinionated approach to whatever he undertook, Smith arrived in Virginia under arrest. Upon opening the sealed instructions the London Company had provided the colonists—orders that were to be opened only after the ships had arrived safely at their destination, which they did in late April 1607—it was with great chagrin that Smith's captors discovered his name listed in the documents as a member of the Council for Virginia as appointed by the company. Because of his current status as a prisoner, however, he was not immediately recognized as a legitimate council member by a majority of the others. Smith remained under restraint and did not take part in the first expeditions to scout the land that would be their new home.

After the colonists had spent about two weeks exploring and searching for a place to land and begin their settlement, Jamestown Island was finally chosen, and on 13 May 1607 the three ships were moored to the trees near the shore. The next day the unloading of cargo and supplies began. Smith still was not entirely free nor admitted to his appointed position, but by 21 May, when an expedition under Captain Christopher Newport was set to explore farther upriver, Smith was included as one of the members. At last, Smith was free to make his own place and legacy in the New World and its history, becoming one of the most important actors and, at times, the main force keeping the colony from total destruction.

Over the next two and one-half years, until Smith's forced return to England because of a serious injury resulting from burns sustained when his powder bag "accidentally" exploded into flames while he was resting, he served the colony as apparently only he could. He met with various Indian leaders, including Powhatan, the paramount leader of the Native Americans most often encountered during the earliest period of the colony. It was in one of these meetings that Smith later wrote how Pocahontas, a favorite daughter of the great leader, saved Smith's life by covering his body with hers when Smith was about to be executed by clubbing. Whether or not this story took place exactly as related by Smith may never be known, but the idea that it may have happened has some credence, as it is known that various tribes have an initiation rite that involves ceremonial sentencing to death, with an accompanying pardon, as part of the initiate's acceptance into the society. Because Smith did not mention this incident until his later writing, after he had returned to England, many believe that he later fabricated the story for dramatic effect in an attempt to bolster his own image or to gain a wider readership and respect for his writings and adventures. However, it must be remembered that, in the early years of the colony, the Virginia Company was keen to enlist the support and backing of investors and potential colonists. With that in mind, much of what was written by the colonists themselves, or by those who claimed some knowledge of the venture, may have been censored or at least sanitized so as not to scare away much-needed funding and recruits. Whatever the truth, it is entirely plausible that some sort of incident probably occurred that resembled Smith's description. In fact, more recent scholars who have conducted serious inquiry into the veracity of Smith's writings have helped substantiate some of Smith's previously doubted claims, particularly some of his exploits as a soldier in Europe before traveling to the New World. After consulting documents from the times and places to which Smith claims to have traveled and engaged in battle, and allowing for the practice, prevalent at the time, of variable spellings of many words (especially names of people and places only heard and not seen written) scholars have confirmed that many of Smith's statements are based in fact. Thus, although the incident described by Smith as his rescue by Pocahontas may not have been as dramatic as he and later writers claimed, something resembling it apparently happened.

Much of John Smith's time at Jamestown was spent exploring and documenting what he encountered. Of all of Jamestown's inhabitants, he was by far the most prolific recorder of facts and impressions of the colony's first two and one-half years. But in addition to what he produced, which included excellent and detailed maps of the Chesapeake Bay and its environs (and later the New England coast) as well as invaluable descriptions of the indigenous people and their cultures and languages, Smith was called upon to provide defense for the colony as well as to obtain enough food to keep the colonists alive through some very difficult and dangerous times. As a result of some of the necessarily harsh measures he put into effect, Smith made enemies among both the Europeans and the Native Americans. At times, his trading encounters with the Powhatan Indians and their affiliated tribes were peaceful and productive for both sides. At other times, hostility was initiated, and lives were lost on both sides. Smith was more than once taken captive by one native group or another and held for some time until he could escape or was released through his own wits, courage, and familiarity with confrontation. On one occasion, Smith was captured and held for some time by Opechancanough, a brother and successor of Powhatan. Later, during one of Smith's many efforts to obtain food for the colony through trade, he would take Opechancanough captive while escaping from an ambush orchestrated by his would-be captor.

Captain John Smith and New England

Captain John Smith is remembered for the vital role he played in the founding of Jamestown, but his influence stretched far to the north as well. In 1614, Smith led an expedition to New England, charting the coastline from Maine to Cape Cod, cataloging the region's natural resources, and doing what he is most noted for at Jamestown—encountering the native population. He later published a report of the expedition, *A Description of New England* (London, 1616), and a map based on discoveries became important when the Plymouth Company settled a colony in Massachusetts in 1620.

Smith's encounters with the native peoples were frequent and ran the gamut from happy and peaceful—such as the Christmas he spent among the Kecoughtans, "where wee were never more merrie, nor fedde on more plentie of good oysters, fish, flesh, wild foule, and good bread, nor never had better fires in England then in the drie warme smokie houses of Kecoughtan"—to his dealings with Opechancanough as described above. However his actions and observations are considered, they were, for the most part, very effective in helping to keep the colony viable during his time at Jamestown.

John Smith's dealings with his fellow colonists also included a complex mixture of action and reaction. As already noted, Smith arrived in the New World a prisoner of his fellow travelers. After his release from restrictions, he was a very productive, useful, and, without doubt, vital member of the settlement. In addition to his exploration and provisioning expeditions, he did serve

Captain John Smith, Panegyrick Verses

I honour thy faire worth and high desert;
And thus much I must say, they merits claime
Much praise & honor, both from Truth & Fame.
What Judge so e're thy Actions over-looke,
Thou need'st not feare a triall by thy Booke.

—George Bucke, in the preface to Smith's *A Sea Grammar* (1627)

out his appointments as a member of the Council and later as the president of the colony (but never as governor). And on more than one occasion, he had to save the colony from its members by initiating and enforcing harsh standards in order to establish basic survival conditions in terms of defense and the production of necessary materials and nourishment. These measures, along with the resentment felt by some born to higher station than Smith, who considered themselves above being ordered about and having restrictions imposed on their designs by someone they considered a commoner, led to what were apparently plots to rid the colony of Smith. One of the most notable examples, and effective if it was indeed the result of a plot by Smith's enemies, was the final blow that sent Smith back to England.

Around September 1609, John Smith, then president of the colony and much disliked by many there because of his strict rule, set out on an expedition to the falls of the James River, at present-day Richmond, to check on the progress of a settlement being established there. After some contentious exchange with those colonists over the location chosen, Smith left and headed back to Jamestown. After having traveled a short way back downriver, he heard a commotion at the settlement he had just left and so turned back to determine the cause of the noise. The colonists had been attacked by a group of Indians, who had killed a number of them and caused much damage to the settlement. After more confrontation with the unwilling settlers, the settlement was relocated (but later reversed), and Smith once more set off for Jamestown. Some time during this voyage, Smith was resting, when suddenly the power bag he wore about his waist exploded, causing severe burns on his thighs. He jumped overboard to put out the flames and shortly was pulled back into the boat, almost drowned, by his men. This, along with the battles he had been waging over the conduct of the other colonists and the running of the enterprise, proved to be too much, even for a man as strong, bold, and determined as John Smith. After what appeared to be a close encounter with an assassination attempt while he lay nursing his wounds, Smith finally set off for England sometime during the first week of October. He never again set foot in Virginia.

Back in England, Smith made a number of offers and attempts to return to the sea and to Virginia, his greatest accomplishment in that realm being his April 1614 voyage to present-day Maine and the Massachusetts Bay. He did quite a bit of valuable mapping there and was the prime force behind the naming of the area New England. His most important contribution—after, of course, helping to first establish and then save the Jamestown colony from extinction—was the record he left behind detailing his travels and adventures in words and maps. Following his last sea voyage, he spent the remainder of his years in England writing about his experiences and offering advice and encouragement to those who, following in his footsteps, endeavored to establish an English presence wherever the opportunity presented itself. In addition to his *A True Relation of Such Occurrences and Accidents of Noate as Hath Hapned in Virginia,* published in edited form without his consent or knowledge in London in 1608 from a letter he sent back while still in the colony, he also produced *A Map of Virginia. With a Description of the Countrey, the Commodities, Peo-*

ple, Government and Religion, and *The Proceedings of the English Colonie in Virginia since Their First Beginning from England in the Yeare of Our Lord 1606,* both in 1612; *A Description of New England,* in 1616; *New England Trials,* published in 1620 and again in 1622; *The Generall Historie of Virginia, New-England, and the Summer Isles: with the Names of the Adventurers, Planters, and Governours from Their First Beginning An: 1584. to This Present 1624,* in 1624; *An Accidence or the Path-way to Experience. Necessary for All Young Sea-men, or Those That are Desirous to Goe to Sea,* in 1626; *A Sea Grammar, with the Plaine Exposition of Smiths Accidence for Young Sea-men, Enlarged,* in 1627; *The True Travels, Adventures, and Observations of Captaine John Smith, in Europe, Asia, Affrica, and America, from Anno Domini 1593 to 1629,* in 1630; and finally *Advertisements for the Unexperienced Planters of New England, or Any Where. Or, the Path-way to Experience to Erect a Plantation,* in 1631.

Captain John Smith left behind a legacy like few others before or since. True to the words inscribed on his statue, he conquered, and in every sense of the word, he lived.

Related entries: Gosnold, Bartholomew; James Fort; Kecoughtan Indians; Opechancanough; Pamunkey Indians; Pocahontas; Powhatan; Rolfe, John; Smith's Fort; Warraskoyak Indians

Suggestions for further reading

Edward Arber, ed. 1910. *Travels and Works of Captain John Smith* (parts 1, 2). Edinburgh, Scotland: J. Grant.

Philip L. Barbour. 1964. *The Three Worlds of Captain John Smith.* Boston: Houghton Mifflin.

——, ed. 1986. *The Complete Works of Captain John Smith (1580–1631)* (vols. 1–4). Chapel Hill and London: University of North Carolina Press.

Edward Wright Haile, ed. 2001. *Jamestown Narratives: Eyewitness Accounts of the Virginia Colony: The First Decade: 1607–1617.* Champlain, VA: Round House.

Karen Ordahl Kupperman, ed. 1988. *Captain John Smith: A Select Edition of His Writings.* Chapel Hill and London: University of North Carolina Press.

Lyon Gardiner Tyler, ed. 1907. *Narratives of Early Virginia: 1606–1625.* New York: Charles Scribner's Sons.

Smith's Fort

Sometime in 1608 or early 1609, Captain John Smith decided that another fort should be erected not far from the original English fort on Jamestown Island. Apparently, this was to serve as a place of refuge in case of Indian or Spanish attack on the island. Smith later wrote, "We built . . . a fort for a retreat, neare a convenient river upon a high commanding hill, very hard to be assaulted, and easie to be defended." The fort was started directly across the James River from Jamestown, on a high hill about two miles up Grays Creek in present-day Surry County. (Grays Creek was known as Smith's Creek until the 1640s, when Thomas Gray patented the land at the mouth of the creek.) It was an excellent choice for a fort site in that three sides were high and steep and the fourth was relatively narrow such that a defensive wall could be constructed easily across its width with minimal labor and materials. "The New Fort," as it was referred to on Smith's map of Virginia, was never completed, however, because

> ere it was halfe finished this defect caused a stay; in searching our casked corne, wee found it halfe rotten, the rest so consumed with the many thousand rats (increased first from the ships) that we knewe not how to keepe that little wee had. This did drive us all to our wits ende, for there was nothing in the countrie but what nature afforded . . . this want of corne occasioned the end of all our workes, it being worke sufficient to provide victuall.

Tradition has it that the land chosen for Smith's New Fort had been part of a 1,200-acre wedding gift to Pocahontas from her father, Powhatan, although a mid-seventeenth-century deed casts some doubt on whether the land had in fact been given to Pocahontas's son, Thomas Rolfe, by her father's half brother, Opechancanough. In any event, Thomas Rolfe was born on the property, later inherited it, and built a house there in the early 1650s. That house subsequently was abandoned or destroyed (its foundations have been discovered), and in about 1763 another small manor house was constructed for Jacob Faulcon, later clerk of Surry County.

The manor house at Smith's Fort Plantation, built between 1751 and 1765, and restored by the Association for the Preservation of Virginia Antiquities in 1933. The house was built on the site of Smith's Fort, an unfinished fort erected by John Smith, c.1609. (Photo by Frank E. Grizzard, Jr.)

The one-and-a-half-story, Flemish-bond brick house, known today as the Rolfe-Warren House, has a gabled roof with three dormer windows and a massive chimney built into each of the end walls, and the interior contains much of the original heart-pine woodwork. It was restored after many years of neglect when the Association for the Preservation of Virginia Antiquities (APVA) took possession of Smith's Fort Plantation in 1933.

Today, all that remains of Smith's Fort are a ditch and mound running the width of the fourth side of the fort site. Yet, as the Commonwealth of Virginia historical marker for Smith's Fort Plantation states, the two-foot-high earthwork remnants "constitute the oldest extant structure of English origin in Virginia." Archaeological excavations in 1968 and 1981 confirmed the site's identity but found little evidence of early English occupation. Smith's Fort is open to the public seasonally and is noted for the English boxwood and herb garden that was established by the Garden Club of Virginia.

Related entries: Pocahontas; Powhatan; Rolfe, John; Smith, Captain John; Warraskoyak Indians

Suggestions for further reading

Edward Arber, ed. 1910. *Travels and Works of Captain John Smith* (part 1). Edinburgh, Scotland: J. Grant.

Philip L. Barbour, ed. 1986. *The Complete Works of Captain John Smith (1580–1631)* (vol. 3). Chapel Hill and London: University of North Carolina Press.

Ivor Noël Hume. *The Virginia Adventure: Roanoke to James Towne: An Archaeological and Historical Odyssey.* New York: Alfred A. Knopf.

Conway Whittle Sams. 1929. *The Conquest of Virginia: The Second Attempt: An Account, Based on Original Documents, of the Attempt, Under the King's Form of Government, to Found Virginia at Jamestown, 1606–1610.* Norfolk, VA: Keyser-Doherty.

Lyon Gardiner Tyler. 1904. *England in America, 1580–1652.* New York: Harper and Brothers.

Smythe, Sir Thomas (c.1558–1625)

Born in Oxford, England, around 1588 to Sir Thomas Smythe, who had amassed a great fortune as "Mr. Customer Smythe," Queen Elizabeth's collector of customs duties, Thomas Smythe was for thirty years "the most active single figure in English overseas commercial enterprise." Cousin by marriage to two early Jamestown settlers, Samuel Argall and Bartholomew Gosnold, Smythe was involved in a wide array of English trade, settlement, and foreign relations activities until the end of his life in 1625. In addition to serving in his father's position in London, he also served as sheriff of London, ambassador to Russia, and as a member of Parliament, and he was founder, governor, or among the leading backers of the Turkey, Muscovy (Russia), Levant, East India, North West Passage, and Sommer Isles (Bermuda) Companies. Despite having held so many important and influential positions, he was arrested in 1602 and held in the Tower of London under suspicion of plotting with Robert Devereaux, Earl of Essex, and Henry Wriothesley, Earl of Southampton, to overthrow the government of Queen Elizabeth I. Nonetheless, he was released and the following year knighted by King James I in that same tower. Most important for Jamestown, however, he became one of the prime movers of the Virginia Company of London and its efforts to establish the English settlement in Virginia and, as a result, one of the officials most loathed by many of the colonists there.

By the time England was ready to make another serious attempt at establishing a colony

Portrait of Sir Thomas Smythe, English politician and proponent of the settlement of Virginia. (Ellyson, J. Taylor. The London Company of Virginia, *1908)*

in the New World, Smythe had become an extremely wealthy and influential businessman in London. Any attempt that he approved and supported would ensure the backing of most of the leading merchants in London as well. As early as 1588, he "lent £31,000 to Queen Elizabeth and raised the necessary funds for her to finance the English fleet which would destroy the Spanish Armada." Because of his accomplishments, wealth, and influence, King James I named him to his Council for Virginia on 20 November 1606. By 1609, Smythe had become Treasurer—essentially acting as chief operating officer—a position he held until 1619, when he resigned under pressure.

Smythe was considered by the colonists the person mostly responsible for the distresses of his administration. He had developed, along with Governor Gates and Thomas Dale, the *Lawes Divine, Morall and Martiall,* which prescribed torture and execution for offenses that at other times and places might have drawn only imprisonment or fines. The settlers also held him at least partially responsible for the lack of adequate provisions that had led to so much disease and starvation. Even though the colony did experience some success and growth under his management, the enmity felt for him was very great among some, as evidenced by the statement in a 1624 letter from the Virginia General Assembly referring to the Starving Time of 1609–1610. The conditions were so desperate and the blame so firmly placed on Smythe, "that the happyest day that ever some of them hoped to see, was when the Indyans had killed a mare, they [the colonists] wishinge whilst she was a boylinge that Sr Tho: Smith were uppon her backe in the kettle."

Having been so closely identified with the Virginia Company from its inception, Smythe refused to hand it over quietly to his successor, Sir Edwin Sandys. Over the next few years following his resignation, bickering and recriminations were exchanged between the Smythe and Sandys factions; through the machinations and missteps on both sides, the government in London recalled its charter, and the Virginia Company was dissolved on 24 May 1624.

Because of, or perhaps in spite of, Sir Thomas Smythe's enthusiasm for the furtherance of English commercial interests around the world, both Jamestown and the Virginia Company of London were realized. Both probably would have existed without him, but based on accounts of his supporters and detractors, the path followed might have been a very different one indeed.

Related entries: Gosnold, Bartholomew; London Company; Sandys, Sir Edwin

Suggestions for further reading

Warner F. Gookin and Philip L. Barbour. 1963. *Bartholomew Gosnold: Discover and Planter, New England—1602, Virginia—1607.* Hamden, CT, and London: Archon Books.

Edward Wright Haile, ed. 2001. *Jamestown Narratives: Eyewitness Accounts of the Virginia Colony: The First Decade: 1607–1617.* Champlain, VA: Round House.

Edward D. Neill. 1869. *History of the Virginia Company of London, with Letters to and from the First Colony Never Before Printed.* Albany, NY: Joel Munsell.

Ivor Noël Hume. 1994. *The Virginia Adventure: Roanoke to James Towne: An Archaeological and Historical Odyssey.* New York: Alfred A. Knopf.

David Beers Quinn. 1977. *North America from Earliest Discovery to First Settlements: The Norse Voyages to 1612.* New York: Harper & Row.

———. 1985. *Set Faire for Roanoke: Voyages and Colonies, 1584–1606.* Chapel Hill and London: University of North Carolina Press.

Conway Whittle Sams. 1929. *The Conquest of Virginia: The Second Attempt: An Account, Based on Original Documents, of the Attempt, Under the King's Form of Government, to Found Virginia at Jamestown, 1606–1610.* Norfolk, VA: Keyser-Doherty.

Somers, Sir George (1554–1610)

Born in 1554 in Lyme Regis, Dorset, England, Sir George Somers played a relatively brief but invaluable part in the establishment of the enduring English presence in the New World.

Described as a "lamb on land . . . a lion at sea" by his contemporaries for his daring adventures at sea, Somers was knighted on 23 July 1603 and was elected to Parliament for Lyme Regis the following year. He served as mayor of the town in 1605. In 1606, he became one of the "chief movers" in the formation of the Virginia Company, becoming one of its four patentees. When James I granted a new charter to the company on 23 May 1609, Somers was named admiral of the association to command a fleet of nine vessels for the purpose of taking more settlers and supplies to Jamestown—the expedition known as the Third Supply. Leaving his Parliament seat vacant, he set sail for Virginia on 2 June 1609 on the *Sea Venture,* along with Lieutenant Governor Sir Thomas Gates, the minister Richard Buck, colony Secretary William Strachey, Captain Christopher Newport as commander of the vessel, and approximately 150 settlers, including John Rolfe. After many weeks at sea, a hurricane struck the fleet and scattered the vessels, and in late July the *Sea Venture* was wrecked in Discovery Bay off an island in the Bermudas. Fortunately,

Portrait of Sir George Somers, English explorer and proponent of the Virginia Company. (Ellyson, J. Taylor. The London Company of Virginia, *1908)*

no one was killed, and many of the supplies were gotten safely to shore, but it would take nearly a year for Somers and his men to build two small pinnaces, the *Patience* (30 tons) and the *Deliverance* (80 tons), from Bermuda cedar and wreckage salvaged from the *Sea Venture* and prepare to continue their voyage. (Seven of the nine ships managed to make it safely to Virginia, arriving in August 1609; the final vessel, the *Catch,* was lost at sea with all its passengers.) Meanwhile, Somers explored and mapped Bermuda and claimed it for the Crown, and when the colonists finally resumed their voyage the following spring, three men volunteered to remain behind on the island.

On 10 May 1610, Admiral Somers and the colonists once again set sail for Virginia and on 23 May, after a two-week voyage, made landfall at Jamestown. Much to their dismay, however, they found the Jamestown inhabitants weak and starving, many already dead from the effects of what came to be known as the Starving Time of the previous winter. Finding the survivors in such dire straits, the decision was made to abandon the colony, and on 7 June all were loaded onto his two ships and two others, with the intention of returning to England. They were met and turned back by representatives of Lord De La Warr, who had arrived at Point Comfort on 6 June. That same month, Somers and Captain Samuel Argall sailed from Jamestown to Bermuda seeking a badly needed supply of meat and other provisions for the colony. This expedition, too, was delayed by another severe storm; Argall, in fact, found it impossible to continue to Bermuda and ended up attempting to "fetch Cape Cod," but Somers somehow rode out the storm and made his way to Bermuda, finally arriving in early November. This proved to be Somers's final adventure, however; he died there on 9 November apparently after "a surfeit of eating of a pig."

Although Sir George Somers' connection to the founding of Jamestown was relatively brief, his was a key role in the establishment of the first permanent English settlement in North America. The Virginia Company acknowledged his importance to them by renaming "Virginiola" (previously and currently called Bermuda after Spanish seaman Juan Bermudes, who was first to sight the islands, in 1515) the Summer Isles in honor of Somers and because of the islands' pleasant climate. And it was in no small part due to Somers that other important figures in Jamestown's history survived to eventually arrive at Jamestown following the shipwreck of the *Sea Venture* on the coast of Bermuda in July 1609. Somers's heart was buried in Bermuda, but his body was pickled and sent to the village of Whitchurch Canonicorum in Dorset for interment. In Bermuda, a parish and a town as well as a garden and a wharf bear his name, and in 1911 a memorial monument with his statue was erected in St. George's (which Somers named after the patron saint of England). Interestingly, even William Shakespeare may owe a debt of gratitude to Sir George Somers, for Shakespeare based his *The Tempest* on William Strachey's account of his time spent with Somers on Bermuda following that 1609 shipwreck.

Related entries: London Company; Newport, Sir Christopher; West, Thomas, Lord De La Warr (1577–1618)

Suggestions for further reading

Philip L. Barbour. 1964. *The Three Worlds of Captain John Smith.* Boston: Houghton Mifflin.

Edward Wright Haile, ed. 2001. *Jamestown Narratives: Eyewitness Accounts of the Virginia Colony: The First Decade: 1607–1617.* Champlain, VA: Round House.

David Beers Quinn, ed. 1979. *New American World: A Documentary History of North America to 1612.* New York: Arno Press and Hector Bye.

Conway Whittle Sams. 1929. *The Conquest of Virginia: The Second Attempt: An Account, Based on Original Documents, of the Attempt, Under the King's Form of Government, to Found Virginia at Jamestown, 1606–1610.* Norfolk, VA: Keyser-Doherty.

Strachey, William (1572–1621)

It is ironic that until very recently not much was known about the man who told us more about the early days of colonial Jamestown than anyone, excepting, perhaps, Captain John Smith. Born in Saffron Walden, Essex, England, little is known of his childhood even now, other than that he lived with his parents, Mary (d. 1587) and William Strachey (d. 1598), on an estate purchased by his grandfather in the 1560s, and that he attended school taught by a graduate of Cambridge University's Trinity College. Strachey himself entered Cambridge's Emmanuel College in 1588 but left before graduating for Gray's Inn, where he wrote poetry and mingled with London's wealthier young men of the day. In 1595, he married Frances Forster and settled near her home in Crowhurst in Surrey, although he also continued to keep a residence in London. By the turn of the seventeenth century, Strachey had embraced the London stage scene, becoming a shareholder in the Blackfriars Theatre Company and making friends with Ben Jonson, John Donne, and others, who may have included William Shakespeare. Financial considerations, including setbacks coupled with the support of a growing family, forced him to seek the positions of secretary to the English Levant Company and to Thomas Glover, the English ambassador to Turkey; with the assistance of his wife's family, he won both appointments in 1606. Strachey's travels on behalf of the company took him to Constantinople, where he was dismissed after a quarrel with Glover in 1607. After his return to England, Strachey decided to seek his fortune in the New World as a "gentleman-adventurer," and it was there, in the Bermudas and Virginia, that his lasting contribution to history was made.

In May 1609, Strachey sailed for Virginia on board the *Sea Venture,* the lead ship among a flotilla of nine vessels loaded with as many as 800 new settlers. Thrown off course, the *Sea Venture* was wrecked in the Bermudas after six weeks at sea; Strachey's *True Reportory of the Wracke, and Redemption of Sir Thomas Gates Knight* (London, 1625) is the only detailed narrative of the disaster and the would-be colonists' ten-month effort to launch two replacement vessels and set sail again for Virginia. Addressed as a letter to an "Excellent Lady," Strachey's hair-raising tale of the seafarers' shipwreck begins:

> S. James his day, July 24, being Monday (preparing for no less all the black night before), the clouds gathering thick upon us, and the winds singing, and whistling most unusually, which made us to cast off our Pinnace. . . . a dreadful storm and hideous began to blow from out the North-east, which swelling, and roaring as it were by fits, some hours with more violence then others, at length did beat all light from heaven; which like an hell of darkness turned black upon us, so much the more fuller or horror, as in such cases horror and fear use to overrun the troubled, and overmastered senses of all, which (taken up with amazement), the ears lay so sensible to the terrible cries, and murmurs of the winds, and distraction of our company, as who was most armed, and best prepared, was not a little shaken.

Miraculously, no lives were lost during the storm or the beaching of the passengers, but the *Sea Venture* was damaged beyond repair. In the end, the castaways were successful in constructing makeshift crafts; the aptly named *Deliverance* and the *Patience* set sail in May 1610, a full year after the colonists had left England on their original voyage. Shakespeare relied heavily on a manuscript copy of Strachey's story when writing *The Tempest,* which was inspired by the calamity.

Almost immediately after Strachey's arrival in Virginia in June 1610, Lord De La Warr made

Strachey the secretary and recorder of the colony, owing to the accidental drowning of Matthew Scrivener, the Virginia Company's appointee to the post. Strachey first set down an account of what he had learned about the terrible Starving Time that took place at Jamestown over the winter of 1609–1610 (which Strachey had missed by being in the Bermudas) and the fortuitous arrival of Thomas West, Lord De La Warr, in June 1610, when the colony was literally on the verge of collapse. Before he sailed back to England, Sir Thomas Gates, who had taken command of the colony after his arrival from Bermuda, introduced martial law at Jamestown, and Strachey's *For the Colony in Virginea Britannia. Lawes Divine, Morall and Martiall, &c.* (London, 1612) codified the list of articles and instructions that were instituted by Gates and subsequently added to by Lord De La Warr and Sir Thomas Dale. Strachey declared that he had considered it his duty to attempt to be the "Remembrancer of all accidents, occurrences, and undertakings" of the colonists' plight in the Bermudas and in Virginia, especially since he himself had "*beene a sufferer and an eie witness*" to it all, and hence had collected the laws with the hopes that they would be "*right welcom to such young souldiers in the Colony who are desirous to learne and performe their duties.*" Strachey expanded the *Lawes* into a general description of English colonization and settlement schemes in the New World; the manuscript was finished in 1612, but it remained unpublished until the nineteenth century, when it appeared as *The Historie of Travaile into Virginia Britannia: Expressing the Cosmographie and Commodities of the Country, togither with the Manners and Customes of the People* (London, 1849). A detailed, judicious account of the early years of Jamestown, Strachey's *Historie* is especially valuable for its author's observations on Algonquin life and the inclusion of an Indian vocabulary (the most comprehensive ever compiled). Some of the passages in the writings of Strachey and Captain John Smith are identical, although it is not clear who copied whom.

Strachey's accurate description of Jamestown has proven invaluable to archaeologists digging in the ruins of the fort. In fact, a ring belonging to Strachey, with his family crest, was discovered in the 1990s in the pit where the colonists buried the canon and armor in preparation of abandoning the colony in 1610; it was the first artifact ever found at Jamestown connected with a specific person.

Related entries: Gates, Sir Thomas; London Company; Smith, Captain John; West, Thomas, Lord de la Warr (1577–1618)

Suggestions for further reading

S. G. Culliford. 1965. *William Strachey, 1572–1621.* Charlottesville: University Press of Virginia.

William Strachey. 1953. *The Historie of Travell into Virginia Britania (1612)* (Louis B. Wright and Virginia Freund, eds.) London: Hakluyt Society.

Susan Constant

See Three Ships

T

Thorpe, George (d. 1622)

Captain, gentleman pensioner, member of the King's Privy Council, Parliament, the London Company, and eventually Governor's Council in Virginia, and even recommended for governorship of the colony, George Thorpe sold his lands in England and in 1618 formed a partnership to establish a plantation in Virginia. The land chosen for the venture, which came to be known as Berkeley Hundred, was granted by the Virginia Company of London on 3 February 1619 to Thorpe, Sir George Yeardley, Sir William Throckmorton, Richard Berkeley, and John Smith of Nibley. Thorpe, who also was appointed deputy to manage the planned college near the Cittie of Henricus, arrived in Virginia in March 1620, about three months after the landing of the first settlers sent by the Berkeley Company to Virginia from Bristol, England. Before leaving for America, Thorpe had adopted an Indian boy, a member of Pocahontas's retinue when she made her famed trip to England, who apparently had decided that he did not want to return to his native soil. Thorpe already had three children of his own, two boys and a girl, by his second wife, Margaret Harris (d. 1629), in addition to at least one more who died in infancy; his first wife Margaret, née Porter (d. 1610) and their two children were also dead. The conversion of this young man, whom Thorpe had baptized as Georgious Thorpe, *Homo Virginiae,* shortly before the boy's death in September 1619, helped convince Thorpe that Virginia was ripe for his missionary intentions. As a result of this conversion and discussions with other Native Americans once he reached the New World, one of his greatest passions there (while dabbling in the production of wine and silk) was "civilizing" and converting the indigenous populations to Christianity. During his short time there, he devoted much of his time and resources to that purpose.

Without fully understanding the conditions in Virginia or the inclinations of the people he planned to convert, Thorpe believed that the bad impressions so many of the colonists had of their Indian neighbors was caused by misunderstandings. In a letter written in May 1621 to Sir Edwin Sandys, he writes that there was hardly a colonist

> amongest us that doth soe much as affoorde them a good thought in his hart and most men wth theire mouthes give them nothinge but maledictions and bitter execrations beinge thereunto falslye caried wth a violent misp[er]swation . . . that these poore people have done unto us all the wronge and injurie that the malice of the Devill or man cann affoord whereas in my poore understandinge if there bee wronge on any side it is on o[u]rs who are not soe charitable to them as Christians ought to bee, they beinge (espetiallye the better sort of them) of a peaceable and vertuous disposition.

George Thorpe

The valliant and noble gentleman George Thorpe, one of the most influential among the English in Virginia, took a great interest in these savages, and embraced every opportunity that presented itself to speak to them about the Christian religion, and was either held in such high esteem or so feared by the Indians that they would apparently not harm him in any way whatever. In fact, they submitted to punishment for misbehavior if Mr. Thorpe deemed such a course necessary. Mr. Thorpe in order to befriend King Powhatan as much as possible caused a good substantial house to be built for him, of which the King was very proud, in place of his hut built of mats and straw; he was particularly pleased with the locks and keys, amusing himself frequently for an hour or more at a time locking and unlocking the doors; by these means Mr. Thorpe tried to win the friendship and confidence of the King and his subjects, embracing every opportunity to speak on religious topics, until finally the King confessed that he had come to the conclusion that the God whom the English worshipped was mightier and far superior to the gods they served; for, he said, the God of the English had done him more good than all his gods combined, upon which Mr. Thorpe answered that if he and his subjects would be converted to the Christian religion, they would receive many more and much greater blessings.

The result of Mr. Thorpe's efforts was that the King and his subjects began to show much inclination to embrace the Christian religion, from which the English expected much good, but it was not long before they found out that the savages were false and great hypocrites, for in the general massacre mentioned heretofore even Mr. Thorpe was not spared though he could have saved his life by flight. An hour before his death he was warned of the danger by one of his Indian servants who had embraced the Christian religion, but he had such faith in these savages that he remained at his post; his servant though was more prudent and fled to Jamestown, a place fortified by the English to protect themselves against the attacks of the Indians.

—*Voyage of Anthony Chester to Virginia, Made in the Year 1620* (1707)

Thorpe was always trying his best to be kind and thoughtful when dealing with his potential converts, even going so far as to anger and endanger the other colonists. He "did so truly and earnestly affect their conversion, and was so tender over them, that whosoever under his authority had given them but the least displeasure or discontent, he punished them severely." Moreover, Thorpe considered nothing "too deare" for his native audience, and as

> being desirous to binde them unto him by his many courtesies, hee never denyed them any thing that they asked him, insomuch that when these *Savages* complained unto him of the fiercenese of our Mastives, most implacable and terrible unto them, (knowing them by instinct it seemes, to be but treacherous and false-hearted friends to us, better than our selves) he to gratifie them in all things, for the winning of them by degrees, caused some of them to be killed in their presence, to the great displeasure of the owners, and would have had all the rest guelt (had he not beene hindered) to make them the gentler and the milder to them.

Thorpe's attempts to win the trust and affections of the Native Americans were not limited to those with whom he had daily contact:

> Hee was not onely too kinde and beneficiall to the common sort, but also to their King, to whom hee oft resorted, and gave many presents which hee knew to be highly pleasing to him. And whereas this king before dwelt onely in a cottage, or rather a denne or hog-stye, [a term Captain John Smith, who wrote of the relative opulence of an Indian king's home, omitted when he borrowed the story from the official Virginia Company account written by Edward Waterhouse] made with a few poles and sticks,

> and covered with mats after their wyld manner, to civilize him, he first, built him a fayre house according to the English fashion, in which hee tooke such joy, especially in his locke and key, which hee so admired, as locking and unlocking his doore an hundred times aday.

In his own mind, Thorpe's conversion and assimilation efforts were coming to fruition, as evidenced by what he was told, apparently, by the primary Powhatan leader at the time, Opechancanough:

> Capt Thorpe found by discoursinge wth him, that he had more motiones of religione in him, then Coulde be ymmagined in soe greate blindnes, for hee willinglye Acknowledged that theirs was nott the right waye, desiringe to bee instructed in ours and confessed that god loved us better then them.

But all of this was a ruse on the part of Opechancanough. Two months after the council in Virginia reported that good news to the Virginia Company in London, George Thorpe would finally understand, briefly, the challenge he actually had been facing.

On the morning of 22 March 1622, Thorpe's "man" came running to him with a dire warning of an impending attack by the Indians. After delivering the message and trying to persuade Thorpe to seek shelter with him, he

> ranne away for feare of the mischiefe he strongly apprehended, and so saved his owne life; yet his Master, out of the conscience of his owne good meaning, and faire deserts ever towards them, was so void of all suspition, and so full of confidence, that they had sooner killed him, then hee could or would beleeve they meant any ill against him.

Without regard for his previous efforts at what he understood to be his mission to show them the err of their ways, "they not only wilfully murdered him, but cruelly and felly, out of devillish malice, did so many barbarous despights and foule scornes after to his dead corpes, as are unbefitting to be heard by any civill eare." He had become yet another victim of the attack that led to the death of hundreds of colonists all along the James River on that tragic day.

Although his intentions were good, George Thorpe, like almost all other Europeans who ventured into the New World during the earliest years of colonization, saw little fault in taking the land and resources found there and considering the indigenous peoples at best primitive heathens who only needed the guidance of his more civilized culture and teachings. He, at least, appears to have been guided by truly good intentions. What he failed to understand, however, was that what he saw as bringing salvation to innocents and infidels his "pupils" saw as an attempt to destroy their own history, culture, and way of life. For his misunderstanding, he paid the ultimate price.

Related entries: London Company; Massacre of 1622; Opechancanough

Suggestions for further reading

Eric Gethyn-Jones. 1982. *George Thorpe and the Berkeley Company: A Gloucestershire Enterprise in Virginia.* Gloucester, England: Alan Sutton.

Susan Myra Kingsbury, ed. 1933. *The Records of The Virginia Company of London* (vol. 3). Washington, DC: Government Printing Office.

David A. Price. 2003. *Love and Hate in Jamestown: John Smith, Pocahontas, and the Heart of a New Nation.* New York: Alfred A. Knopf.

Lyon Gardiner Tyler. 1906. *The Cradle of the Republic: Jamestown and James River.* Richmond, VA: Hermitage Press.

Three Ships

On 20 December 1606, a trio of square-rigged sailing vessels, the *Susan Constant,* the *Godspeed,* and the *Discovery,* set sail from London destined for the New World. Together, the three ships had on board approximately 144 passengers and crew members—all men and boys—and each ship was laden with cargo supplies and livestock thought necessary for life in Virginia. The *Susan Constant,* sometimes referred to as the *Sarah Constant* and by far the largest of the three at 120 tons burden, had Captain Christopher Newport, supreme commander of the expedition while at sea, and approximately 71 passengers on board. The next

Full of English colonists, Susan Constant, Godspeed, *and* Discovery, *arrive at Jamestown in 1607. (Corbis)*

largest was the *Godspeed,* or *Goodspeed* at 40 tons, commanded by Captain Bartholomew Gosnold, a Suffolk adventurer trained as a lawyer, who had made his first voyage to America in 1602 when he sailed to the coast of New England. (Gosnold died in Virginia and is buried on Jamestown Island.) The *Godspeed* sailed with 52 men—13 crew and 39 passengers (many of whom were from England's East Anglian region, which includes Suffolk). The smallest by far—only 49 feet 6 inches long and 11 feet 4 inches wide—but the one that saw the most duty for the colonists, was the *Discovery* at 20 tons, commanded by Captain John Ratcliffe and carrying about 20 other members of the expedition. (Exact numbers of passengers and crew are not known.) The ships belonged to a London-based company, the Merchant Adventurers for the Discovery of Regions Unknown, later known as the Muscovy Company or the Russia Company. The *Discovery* remained in Jamestown after the return to England of the two larger ships and probably was purchased at some point from the Merchant Adventurers by the Virginia Company; the *Susan Constant* may have been purchased by the merchant firm Colthurst, Dapper, Wheatley & Company.

The vessels' voyages to Virginia were by no means smooth or direct. The exit from the English Channel was attended by "unprosperous winds" and "great stormes," which kept the ships from leaving the coast of Kent until early February 1607, when they made their way across the Bay of Biscay into the Atlantic, sailing along the coast of Europe to the Canary Islands, where they took aboard new supplies before catching the trade winds across the ocean to the Caribbean. After taking on more fresh supplies at Martinique, the vessels sailed up the Atlantic

Atlantic Coast

The coast is a bold and even coast, with regular soundings, and is open all the year round; so that, having the latitude, which also can hardly be wanted upon a coast where so much clear weather is, any ship may go in by soundings alone, by day or night, in summer or in winter, and need not fear any disaster, if the mariners understand anything; for let the wind blow how it will, and chop about as suddenly as it pleases, any master, though his ship be never so dull, has opportunity, (by the evenness of the coast,) either of standing off and clearing the shore, or else of running into safe harbor within the capes. A bolder and safer coast is not known in the universe; to which conveniences, there is the addition of good anchorage all along upon it, without the capes.

—Robert Beverley, *The History and Present State of Virginia* (1705)

seaboard, occasionally stopping at other islands along the way. The ships encountered severe storms off the coast of Virginia before anchoring off Cape Henry on 26 April, four months after setting sail. After crossing the Chesapeake Bay, they stopped at Point Comfort, near the friendly Indian village of Kecoughtan, before choosing the settlement spot of Jamestown on 13 May. By the time the ships landed in Virginia, they had sailed more than 8,000 miles—3,300 to the Canary Islands, 3,500 across the Atlantic to the Caribbean, and the remainder up the Atlantic coastline.

After establishing the settlement at Jamestown, Captain Newport took the *Susan Constant* on a voyage of exploration up the James River, a trip that was supposed to last about two months, according to the Virginia Company's instructions. Because the falls near present-day Richmond, Virginia, prevented further passage by the ship, the expedition lasted only seven days, however, and the *Susan Constant,* after its crew had made some contact with local Indians, returned to Jamestown on 25 May 1607. The day before Newport returned, about 200 Indians attacked the newly arrived colonists at Jamestown, and the *Godspeed* fired on them to help end the assault.

After using the two larger ships for various duties, the *Susan Constant* and the *Godspeed* were loaded with sassafras, clapboard, samples of ore, and other specimens, and on 22 June 1607, Captain Newport left for England, arriving in Plymouth harbor on 29 July to make the first report of findings and to arrange for return supply missions. The *Discovery* remained behind and, notwithstanding the return supply trips of the other two ships, became the workhorse of the colony for years to come. The ship was sent on exploratory, fishing, and military missions throughout the area waters and served as the colony's jail and as the preferred sleeping quarters of a few for some time. The vessel sailed as far north as Cape Cod on a fishing expedition; twice guns were trained on it by John Smith when first George Kendall, and later another group of unnamed colonists, attempted to take the *Discovery* and return to England. It was onto the *Discovery* and three other ships—the *Deliverance,* the *Patience,* and the *Virginia*—that the colonists were loaded in June 1610 after the decision to abandon Jamestown was made following the Starving Time of the previous winter. Apparently, the *Discovery,* described as "a smale Barck . . . belonging to the company," finally left Jamestown for England in 1609 or 1610 after having been sent on what was supposed to be only a fishing expedition.

Before they brought the colonists to Jamestown, not much is certain of the three ships. The *Susan Constant* is known to have been commissioned for only about one year before its voyage to Jamestown; it had made one voyage to Spain and had been involved in a collision with another ship in the Thames on 23 November 1606, as a result of which charges were filed by both ships' owners against each other. The outcome of the litigation is not known. The *Discovery* and *Godspeed* may have been the two vessels that Captain George Waymouth took on his expedition to discover the Northwest Passage to China that began in May 1602. That mission was aborted and the ships returned to England in late August after the crew mutinied.

No record remains of the final disposition of the three ships, but replicas have been built and reside at Jamestown Festival Park near the original site of the fort. Construction of the replica of the *Godspeed* was begun in 1982 using long-leaf yellow pine harvested in southern Georgia. As many as a dozen men at a time worked on the vessel, which took more than two and one-half years to build. The size of the *Godspeed*, based on the replica, is 68 feet long and 14 feet 8 inches wide; it contains a 55-foot main mast, and 1,128 square feet of sail area. It was the mid-sized vessel of the three. The new *Godspeed* was christened on 14 May 1984 and retraced the historic 1607 voyage across the Atlantic in 1985. The *Godspeed* has since made numerous short voyages in eastern Virginia for educational and sail training programs. A replica of the *Susan Constant* was built beginning in December 1989, using tropical hardwoods from Guyana, South America, and long-leaf yellow pine from southern Georgia, in addition to white oak, hackmatack (or balsam poplar), juniper, and Douglas fir harvested from other places. The *Susan Constant* was christened and docked in the James River alongside the *Godspeed* and the *Discovery* on 14 December 1990, and commissioned on 26 April 1991. In its 2001 session, the Virginia General Assembly designated the replicas of the three ships the official fleet of the Commonwealth.

Related entries: Cape Henry; Gosnold, Bartholomew; London Company; Newport, Sir Christopher

Suggestions for further reading

Edward Wright Haile, ed. 2001. *Jamestown Narratives: Eyewitness Accounts of the Virginia Colony: The First Decade: 1607–1617.* Champlain, VA: Round House.

Jamestown-Yorktown Foundation. c.1985. *Sailing into History: The Story of the Godspeed.* Williamsburg, VA.

Edward D. Neill. 1869. *History of the Virginia Company of London, with Letters to and from the First Colony Never Before Printed.* Albany, NY: Joel Munsell.

Ivor Noël Hume. 1994. *The Virginia Adventure: Roanoke to James Towne: An Archaeological and Historical Odyssey.* New York: Alfred A. Knopf.

David Beers Quinn. 1977. *North America from Earliest Discovery to First Settlements: The Norse Voyages to 1612.* New York: Harper & Row.

Conway Whittle Sams. 1929. *The Conquest of Virginia: The Second Attempt: An Account, Based on Original Documents, of the Attempt, Under the King's Form of Government, to Found Virginia at Jamestown, 1606–1610.* Norfolk, VA: Keyser-Doherty.

Alden T. Vaughn. 1975. *American Genesis: Captain John Smith and the Founding of Virginia.* Boston: Little, Brown.

Tindall's Point

Tindall's Point in present-day Gloucester County, Virginia, is on the north side of the York River directly across from Yorktown. It originally was settled by Robert Tindall (Tyndall), a mariner who sailed to Virginia with Captain Christopher Newport in the First Supply in 1608. Tindall was among the crew with Newport that charted the James and York Rivers, and he lent his name to the point, which Captain John Smith popularized by including in his *Map of Virginia* (1612). Richard Lee, the prominent secretary to Governor William Berkeley, bought his first tract of Virginia land in the vicinity of the point in 1640.

The location of Tindall's Point at the confluence of the York River and the Chesapeake Bay destined the point to become an important commercial center, and its development can be traced in the acts of the Virginia General Assembly. The assembly established tobacco warehouses at Tindall's Point in acts passed in February 1633 and June 1680; the latter, *An Act for Cohabitation and Encouragement of Trade and Manufacture*, allocated fifty acres for the warehouse and led to the settlement of the town of Gloucester. Hostilities between England and Holland led to the Assembly's act of September 1667 establishing forts along the York and three other Virginia rivers that emptied into the Chesapeake Bay; it designated Tindall's Point as the location of the York River fort. (Fort James, as it was named in 1671, was erected by the counties of York, Gloucester, and New Kent.) In August 1702, the Assembly established a ferry between Tindall's Point and Yorktown, the price of crossing in either direction "for a man one royall, for a man and horse two royalls," and in October 1705 the Assembly established Tindall's Point as a port, along with Yorktown and West Point. Colonial, British, Confederate, and Union forces occupied military batteries on Tindall's Point at one time or another until 1862.

Tindall's Point, known since the American Revolutionary War period as Gloucester Point, is today an unincorporated town of about 8,500 people. The National Register of Historic Places recognized the historical importance of Tindall's Point by establishing the Gloucester Point Archaeological District in 1985. Archaeological discoveries at Tindall's Point in 1983 and 1984 are exhibited in Waterman's Hall at the Virginia Institute of Marine Sciences, located in the town of Gloucester Point.

Related entries: Lee, Richard; Newport, Sir Christopher; James River; York River

Suggestion for further reading

Captain John Smith. 1612. *Map of Virginia.* London: S.I.

Tobacco

The origins of tobacco cultivation are lost in the prehistory of the New World, having been introduced in the Andes 5,000 to 7,000 years ago. The indigenous peoples of Central and South America grew crops for medicinal and religious purposes more than 2,000 years back, so by the time Columbus discovered America in 1492, tobacco was widely used for simple physical gratification across both American continents. When the natives at San Salvador presented "some dry leaves" to Columbus, he calculated that they "must be something much valued among them," as they were offered as a gift. At Cuba, Columbus observed both "women and men, with a firebrand in the hand, [and] herbs to drink the smoke thereof, as they are accustomed." One of his crew, Rodrigo de Jerez, became an instant advocate and developed the habit of smoking daily, earning for himself the dubious distinction of becoming the first of an endless number of people who would not be able to stop using the herb after the first taste—as if that was not enough, when he returned home he was given a three-year prison term by wary Europeans who had long associated the human breath with the Holy Spirit of God and hence interpreted the blowing of smoke out of the mouth and nostrils as a demonic act. Spanish and Portuguese sailors, along with Catholic missionaries, quickly learned from the Native Americans how to smoke, chew, snort, and eat tobacco. Some immediately recognized tobacco use as a vice and a harbinger of death; others hailed it as a magical

Pleasing Aroma?

Whereas vast Improvements might be made thereof; for the generality of *Virginia* is a sandy Land with a shallow soil: so that after they have clear'd a fresh piece of Ground out of the Woods, it will not bear Tobacco past two or three Years, unless Cow-pened; for they manure their Ground by keeping their Cattle, as in the South you do your Sheep, every Night confining them within Hurdles, which they remove when they have sufficiently dung'd one spot of Ground; but alas! they cannot improve much thus, besides it produces a strong sort of Tobacco, in which the Smoakers say they can plainly taste the fulsomness of the Dung.

—The Reverend John Clayton to the Royal Society, 17 August 1688

Workers harvest tobacco in colonial Virginia, c.1650. (Library of Congress)

cure-all for almost any illness or injury. Frenchman Jean Nicot, the royal ambassador to Portugal and an early defender of tobacco as a medicine, lent his name to the plant's active ingredient, nicotine. Tobacco made its way to England by way of Spain and Portugal, which, as leaders of colonization of the New World, monopolized the trade, and Sir Walter Raleigh is said to have sought its introduction into England and encouraged its use.

One of England's guiding lights of colonization, mathematician and astronomer Thomas Hariot, described tobacco positively in his *A Briefe and True Report of the New Found Land of Virginia* (1588):

> There is an herb called uppowoc, which sows itself. In the West Indies it has several names, according to the different places where it grows and is used, but the Spaniards generally call it tobacco. Its leaves are dried, made into powder, and then smoked by being sucked through clay pipes into the stomach and head. The fumes purge superfluous phlegm and gross humors from the body by opening all the pores and passages. Thus its use not only preserves the body, but if there are any obstructions it breaks them up. By this means the natives keep in excellent health, without many of the grievous diseases which often afflict us in England.

Against this backdrop, the Jamestown colonists discovered tobacco. Their earliest attempts to grow tobacco were not productive, but John Rolfe, the English settler who in 1614 married Powhatan's daughter Pocahontas, introduced a hybrid tobacco as a successful cash crop in the colony in 1612. Soon other settlers were growing tobacco in the streets of Jamestown Fort, encouraged by the governor, George Yeardley, who "neglecting the corn, and applying all hands to plant tobacco, which promised the most immediate gain," "let the buildings and forts go to ruin." Less than twenty years later, the colony's exports to England surpassed 750 tons annually; the demand for Virginia tobacco in England greatly increased the demand in the colony for indentured servants and, later, for slaves. Because tobacco ravaged the soil very quickly, large tracts of arable land likewise were needed and grabbed up.

The sudden success of English tobacco grown in Virginia brought prosperity to the Jamestown colony, but not everyone was happy with this unexpected turn of affairs. In particular,

Tobacco: The Native American Way of Receiving Visitors

They have a peculiar way of receiving strangers, and distinguishing whether they come as friends or enemies, though they do not understand each other's language: and that is by a singular method of smoking tobacco, in which these things are always observed:

1. They take a pipe much larger and bigger than the common tobacco pipe, expressly made for that purpose, with which all towns are plentifully provided; they call them the pipes of peace.
2. This pipe they always fill with tobacco, before the face of the strangers, and light it.
3. The chief man of the Indians, to whom the strangers come, takes two or three whiffs, and then hands it to the chief of the strangers.
4. If the stranger refuses to smoke in it, 'tis a sign of war.
5. If it be peace, the chief of the strangers takes a whiff or two in the pipe, and presents it to the next great man of the town they come to visit; he, after taking two or three whiffs, gives it back to the next of the strangers, and so on alternately, until they have past all the persons of note on each side, and then the ceremony is ended.

After a little discourse, they march together in a friendly manner into the town, and then proceed to explain the business upon which they came. This method is as general a rule among all the Indians of those parts of America as the flag of truce is among Europeans. And though the fashion of the pipe differ, as well as the ornaments of it, according to the humor of the several nations, yet 'tis a general rule to make these pipes remarkable bigger than those for common use, and to adorn them with beautiful wings and feathers of birds, as likewise with peak, beads, or other such foppery.

—Robert Beverley, *The History and Present State of Virginia* (1705)

King James I—like many other European and Asian rulers—did not like smoking and sought to regulate it closely. James had written an anti-tobacco pamphlet even before the settlement of Jamestown, *A Counter-Blaste to Tobacco* (1604), and now sought to curb his subjects' appetite for the habit. He was especially appalled that the colonists abandoned the raising of badly needed foodstuffs and raised tobacco almost exclusively. But even a tax increase of 4,000 percent did not slow English demand for the product, and tobacco became the common currency of Virginia. Nor did the widening recognition that tobacco use brought with it diseases of the lungs, lips, and gums, or the assertions that it caused syphilis, have any effect on the demand. James's anti-tobacco crusade fared so poorly that in the end all he could do was declare an English ban against non-Virginia tobacco, place a production limit of 100 pounds per man, and institute a regulatory process of rigid inspection. Despite royal disfavor, high taxation and regulation, and knowledge of its negative effects, tobacco use in England mirrored that of the rest of Europe—tobacco was widely accepted for medicinal and recreational use throughout all levels of society. Production rose to such levels "as to overstock the market," the bottom fell out, and prices dropped drastically, yet even then the crop remained the colony's staple. Over the rest of the seventeenth and into the eighteenth century, tobacco would become king as all public offices and revenues became entangled with its production. As Governor William Berkeley described tobacco's importance to the Jamestown colony in 1663,

> Amongst many other weighty Reasons, why Virginia has not all this while made any progression into staple Commodities, this is the chief. That

Tobacco So Sweet

Tobacco, Tobacco sing sweetly for Tobacco, Tobacco is like love, O love it for you see I wil prove it Love maketh leane the fatte mens tumor, so doth Tobacco, Love still dries uppe the wanton humor, so doth Tobacco, love makes men sayle from shore to shore, so doth Tobacco Tis fond love often makes men poor so doth Tobacco Love makes men scorneal Coward feares, so doth Tobacco Love often sets men by the eares so doth Tobacco.

Tobaccoe, Tobaccoe Sing sweetely for Tobaccoe, Tobaccoe is like Love, O love it, For you see I have prowde it.

—Tobias Hume, *The first part of Ayres* (London 1605)

our Governours by reason of the corruption of those times they lived in, laid the Foundation of our wealth and industry on the vices of men; it, for about the time of our first seating of the Country, did this vicious habit of taking *Tobacco* possesse the English Nation, and from them has diffused it self into most parts of the World. . . . This was the first and fundamental hinderance that made the Planters neglect all other accessions to wealth and happiness, and fix their hopes only on this vicious weed of Tobacco, which at length has brought them to that extremity that they can neither handsomely subsist with it, nor without it.

Related entries: Bacon's Rebellion; Banister, John; Berkeley, Sir William; *A Counter-Blaste to Tobacco;* Lee, Richard; Raleigh, Sir Walter; Rolfe, John; Slavery

Suggestions for further reading

James I. 1604. *A Counter-Blaste to Tobacco.* London.

William Berkeley. 1663. *A Discourse and View of Virginia.* London.

Robert Beverley. 1855. *The History of Virginia, In Four Parts.* Richmond, VA.

Todkill, Anas

Like many of the early settlers at Jamestown, not much is known about Anas Todkill. Early census records in the colony listed him simply as "Soldier, Captain [John] Martin's servant" and as a carpenter. His family hailed from Lincolnshire, the home of Captain John Smith, with whom he voyaged to the New World, arriving in 1607. Although he took part in the crucial explorations of the Chesapeake Bay, his importance in Jamestown's history lies not so much in the role he played in those expeditions as in the written accounts of them that he left to posterity by way of his contributions to Captain Smith's writings.

The two voyages to "discover the Bay" and its bordering Virginia countryside took place in the spring and summer of 1608 and are described in great detail in chapters 5 and 6 of the first volume of Smith's *Generall Historie of Virginia.* Smith acknowledged Todkill's authorship (with fellow settlers) at the end of each chapter; chapter 5 was written with Walter Russell and Thomas Momford, and chapter 6 was written with Anthony Bagnall and Nathaniel Powell. Todkill also collaborated on some later chapters; moreover, Smith's modern-day editor, Philip L. Barbour, observing that the compelling early chapters of Smith's work were "carelessly" divided, speculates that Todkill may have written chapters 3 and 4. In addition, Todkill was named by Smith as one of the contributors to Smith's *A Map of Virginia* (London, 1612).

That material, recording as it does, in vivid manner, the places visited and the first contact between the colonists and the native peoples of Virginia, is some of the most exciting reading from the English settlement period. Take, for example, the hair-raising brush with unfriendly Rappahannock Indians that nearly cost Todkill his life:

> Notwithstanding, Anas Todkill, being sent on shore to see if he could discover any Ambuscadoes, or what they had, desired to goe over the playne to fetch some wood, but they were unwilling, except we would come into the Creeke, where the boat might come close ashore. Todkill by degrees having got some two stones throwes up the playne, perceived two or three hundred men (as he thought) behind the trees, so that

offering to returne to the Boat, the Salvages assayed to carry him away perforce, that he called to us we were betrayed, and by that he had spoke the word, our hostage was over-board, but Watkins his keeper slew him in the water. Immediately we let fly amongst them, so that they fled, and Todkill escaped, yet they shot so fast that he fell flat on the ground ere he could recover the boat. Here Massawomek targets stood us in good stead, for upon Mosco's words, we had set them about the forepart of our Boat like a forecastle, from whence we securely beat the Salvages from off the plaine without any hurt: yet they shot more then a thousand Arrowes, and then fled into the woods. Arming our selves with these light Targets (which are made of little small sticks woven betwixt strings of their hempe and silke grasse, as is our Cloth, but so firmely that no arrow can possibly pierce them:) we rescued Todkill, who was all bloudy by some of them who were shot by us that held him, but as God pleased he had no hurt; and following them up to the woods, we found some slaine, and in divers places much bloud. It seems all their arrowes were spent, for we heard no more of them.

Another tantalizing episode alludes to the settlers of the Lost Colony. It is spare but nevertheless evocative:

> Master [Michael] Sicklemore well returned from Chawwonoke; but found little hope and lesse certaintie of them were left by Sir Walter Raleigh. The river, he saw was not great, the people few, the countrey most over growne with pynes, where there did grow here and there straglingly Pemminaw, we call silke grasse. But by the river the ground was good, and exceeding furtill; Master Nathanael Powell and Anas Todkill were also by the Quiyoughquohanocks conducted to the Mangoags to search them there: but nothing could they learne but they were all dead.

As for Todkill, little else is known other than that his stay in Virginia was rather short and that he opted to return to England rather than settle in the New World permanently.

Related entry: Smith, Captain John

Suggestion for further reading

Philip L. Barbour, ed. 1986. *The Complete Works of Captain John Smith (1580–1631)* (vol. 1). Chapel Hill and London: University of North Carolina Press.

Trades and Artisans

The planners of the Jamestown settlement envisioned that a thriving community would be set up in Virginia in short order and therefore made plans to quickly establish a series of trades in their new colony. A variety of traditional artisans were thus included in the first wave of colonists sent to Jamestown during the colony's first years. Although not all these craftsmen ended up practicing their respective crafts, many contributed to the colonization effort in some significant ways.

Among the most important members of the new colony were the blacksmiths. Not only were they useful at their trade, which included forging and repairing building materials, eating and cooking utensils, tools, weapons, and armor, but they also were expected to participate in other activities from building to exploration and defense. In fact, Captain John Smith made it clear that blacksmiths and others of what he considered the more useful trades should be sent over instead of more of the sort of colonists who had arrived in the beginning. In a letter Smith wrote to the treasurer and Council of Virginia in London while he was president of the colony in 1608, he asks,

> When you send againe I intreat you rather send but thirty Carpenters, husbandmen, gardiners, fisher men, blacksmiths, masons, and diggers up of trees, roots, well provided; then [rather than] a thousand of such as we have: for except wee be able both to lodge them, and feed them, the most will consume with want of necessaries before they can be made good for any thing.

Obviously, Smith felt that individuals with trades specifically suited for establishing and maintaining a colony months from what was considered civilization were more necessary to the enterprise than were "Gentlemen," who had made up the bulk of the passengers so far.

The first blacksmith arrived at Jamestown with the original settlers in May 1607. He was James Read, and John Smith writes of him as having more than just blacksmithing to occupy his time. In addition to accompanying Smith on expeditions in June and December 1608, during which time Read had a point of land named after him, he

Tobacco pipe with distinctive markings, thought to be the product of Robert Cotten, "tobacco-pipe-maker," who arrived at Jamestown in January 1608. (Courtesy of APVA Preservation Virginia)

also received mention for nearly being hung in September 1607 because "he not only gave him [John Ratcliffe, the president of the colony at the time] bad language, but also offred to strike him with some of his tooles, for which rebellious act the smith was by a Jury condemned to be hanged." Read's fame within the colony does not end with his notoriety for bad language and violence, however. As he was threatened with execution,

> But being uppon the ladder continuing verry obstinate, as hoping upon a rescue, when he saw no other way but death with him, he became penitent, and declared a dangerous conspiracy, for which Captaine Kendall as principal, was by a Jury condemned and shot to death.

Not only did Read, a mere blacksmith, threaten the president of the colony with violence, his actions resulted in the execution of one of the original council members.

Another blacksmith, Richard Dole, and a gunsmith, Peter Keffer, arrived with the First Supply in January 1608. Their stories were not as colorful as Read's, however, and not much mention is made of their time at Jamestown. Various writings from the colonists lament having too few "useful" settlers, such as blacksmiths, and requests were made for more people with helpful trades. With successive arrivals of new colonists, those sentiments received appropriate attention, and blacksmith's tools found during archaeological investigations at Jamestown attest to the fact.

Bricklayers were among the first colonists at Jamestown. In his list of "first planters," Captain John Smith records the names of two—John Herd and William Garret. Edward-Maria Wingfield identified another man as "ould short, the Bricklayer." Not much was recorded about the bricklayers, and their skills were not put to extensive use as quickly as some of the other tradesmen's, perhaps because of the labor intensiveness of the brick-making process. Brick structures were not built on the island until some years after the colonists first arrived. Hearths, wells, and chimneys would be the main use of bricks for the first few decades of the colony, and no doubt the bricklayers often were involved in chores other than those associated with their profession. One mason was also listed among the first colonists: Edward Brinton, or Brinto, was included on the May 1607 roster. He would be put to more notable use later as a member of various expeditions and as the hunter left with Powhatan "to kill him foule," or to shoot fowl for the Indian leader as a goodwill gesture.

Also found in archaeological excavations are carpenters' tools. Carpenters were other members of the necessary trades residing at Jamestown, and four arrived with the first settlers. They, like the blacksmiths, were also assigned duties other than their listed trade, and Captain Smith made soldiers of them all. Robert Small and Edward Pising both accompanied Smith on his expeditions in July and December 1607, and both of them, like Read, had points of land named after them. William Laxon came to be known as an "Ensign" for his duties, and the fourth man of the original settlers listed as carpenter, Thomas Emery, was killed in an engagement with Indians while on Smith's December 1607 expedition. Although their skills would have been put to good use had they been allowed to practice them, conditions for the first few years of the settlement required each individual to contribute in whatever way was most needed. Carpentry, it would appear, was not the most pressing need in the beginning.

Coopers also were important tradesmen who accompanied the early colonists to Jamestown. John Lewes is listed as having arrived with the First Supply in January 1608. Lewes's skills would have been needed not only to make barrels to store the colonists' own food and supplies but also to prepare containers in which to ship commodities back to England—which, of course, was one of the main reasons the colony was established. Unfortunately, little is known of Lewes's cooper work.

Some of the more colorful figures listed as tradesmen on the rosters were the glassmakers. Variably referred to as Dutch, Germans, and Poles, glassmakers arrived at Jamestown on 29 September 1608 and were referred to by John Smith as "eight Dutch men and Poles." They made a somewhat successful attempt to produce glass and returned samples to England by the end of 1608. But what made the glassmakers even more interesting was the conduct of a number of them who were sent to build a house for Powhatan. Smith sent them to the chief in an attempt to make Powhatan more pliable in terms of supplying food, so as to alleviate some of the strain on the colony's food stores. Apparently, while the "Germans" were there, they decided they preferred to be allied with Powhatan's people and contrived to steal weapons from the colony's store to give to their Indian hosts. Smith even wrote of a plot against his own life in which the artisans were involved. In the end, the conspirators were discovered but not dealt with by the English; as fate would have it, their Indian hosts eventually dispatched them.

Among other professions represented at Jamestown but not often mentioned in the sources were jewelers and perfumers. Daniel Stallings (or Daniell Stalling) was listed as a "Jueller" and member of the First Supply, which arrived in January 1608. Rather than cutting and polishing jewels, his task, more likely, was to identify and send back to England any stones of value to be found within reach of the colony. Robert Alberton was included on the voyage as a perfumer. He probably was charged with the duty of searching for the raw materials to make masking scents. Bathing was not a common practice among Europeans at the time, and perfumes were used to cover some of the resulting unpleasant side effects. One more craftsman who arrived early but who was not much mentioned was "Tobacco-pipe-maker" Robert Cotten. He arrived in January 1608, and remnants of what may be his handiwork have turned up in archaeological digs. Tobacco had not yet become the huge commodity for the New World venture that it would within a few years, and Cotten's trade was one of the less-needed ones at the time of his arrival.

Other members of the colony who may have plied their listed trade often were the fishermen and fishmongers. Smith reports copious numbers of a variety of fish species, and the catch of fish was often so great that it was more than "could be devoured by Dog and Man, of which the industrious by drying and pounding, mingled with

Caviare, Sorell and other wholesome hearbes would make bread and good meate." But the fishermen were not exempt from the other duties of the colony. Two, fishmonger Richard Keale and "fisher" Jonas Profit, are reported by Smith to have been recruited to accompany him on expeditions in the Chesapeake Bay.

Compared to most other trades in the first two years, tailors were well represented. William Love, "Taylor," was listed as having arrived with the first colonists. The First Supply brought six more: John Powell, Thomas Hope, William Beckwith, William Yonge, Laurence Towtales, and William Ward. Some of these men also accompanied Smith on exploring expeditions; one, William Ward, was honored by having "Ward Poynt" named for him. Archaeologists have discovered a number of artifacts associated with their trade at Jamestown. Among the finds are pressing irons, straight pins, needles, bodkins, and thimbles.

Goldsmiths and refiners, in whom the London investors had placed great hopes but whom Smith came to consider superfluous, even detrimental, to the early colonial efforts, were also named among the early colonists. Goldsmiths Richard Belfield and William Johnson and refiners Abram Ransack and William Dawson were among the first colonists of their trade to arrive; another refiner by the name of William Callicut arrived not much later. Efforts to find gold and other precious metals were unproductive, however, and Smith let his sentiments be known about their use of resources and other colonists' time and labor in futile searches when he wrote,

> the worst was our guilded refiners with their golden promises made all men their slaves in hope of recompences; there was no talke, no hope, no worke, but dig gold, wash gold, refine gold, loade gold, such a bruit of gold, that one mad fellow desired to be buried in the sands least they should by there art make gold of his bones.

Many other individuals made those early voyages to Jamestown, the majority of whom were listed merely as "Gentlemen." But preachers, apothecaries, a barber, drummer, laborers, and some listed merely as "boy" came to the colony at its beginning. One profession that would be considered vital, but whose members received mere mention on the list of passengers, was the chirurgion, or surgeon. Thomas Wotton and William Wilkinson were listed as the first surgeons to arrive, and they did so with the first ships. Chirurgion Post Ginnat arrived in 1608, as did Walter Russell, "Doctor of Physicke," whose distinction lay in administering "soothing oil" to John Smith's arm after he was wounded by a stingray while fishing with his sword.

It can be seen that it took many different kinds of people and skills to found the colony in the New World. Some, as evidenced by the contemporaneous accounts, were considered more important than others. In the end, however, everyone contributed in his or her own way, and England's first permanent North American presence finally was established.

Related entries: Archaeology; Glassmaking; James Fort; Jamestown Church Tower; Polish Workers; Smith's Fort

Suggestions for further reading

"APVA Preservation Virginia Fact Sheet." 2003. Richmond, VA: Association for the Preservation of Virginia Antiquities.

Philip L. Barbour, ed. 1986. *The Complete Works of Captain John Smith (1580–1631)* (vols 1–3). Chapel Hill and London: University of North Carolina Press.

William M.Kelso, et al. 1995–2001. *Jamestown Rediscovery.* 7 vols. Richmond, VA: Association for the Preservation of Virginia Antiquities.

—— with Beverly Straube. 2004. *Jamestown Rediscovery, 1994–2004.* Richmond, VA: Association for the Preservation of Virginia Antiquities.

Ivor Noël Hume. 1994. *The Virginia Adventure: Roanoke to James Towne: An Archaeological and Historical Odyssey.* New York: Alfred A. Knopf.

Yonge, Samuel H. 1904. *The Site of Old "James Towne" 1607–1698.* Richmond, VA: Hermitage Press.

U–Y

Upper Mattaponi Indians

See Mattaponi Indians

Virginia Company

See London Company

Wahunsonacock

See Powhatan

Warraskoyak Indians

About twenty miles southeast of Jamestown, where the Pagan River flows into the south bank of the James River, in present-day Isle of Wight County, Virginia, lived a small tribe of native Algonquin Indians called the Warraskoyak. Their lands were situated along a river bend near Hog Island and in plain sight of the English ships sailing to and from Jamestown. Captain John Smith himself was the first to discover the village, while returning from a trading mission to the Kecoughtan in September 1607. The friendly Kecoughtan had provided Smith with a supply of badly needed foodstuffs—fish, oysters, venison, bread, and sixteen bushels of corn. Two canoes of Warraskoyak tribesmen Smith encountered provided another fourteen bushels of corn. After that, English foraging parties routinely called on the Warraskoyak when they needed food, for the natives were eager to barter for bells, beads, pins, cloth, and other English goods. At the end of December 1608, with the settlers desperate for sustenance again, Smith and thirty-eight colonists set out for Powhatan's capital in search of provisions, stopping overnight with the Warraskoyak. On that occasion, their leader, Tackonekintaco, desirous of cooperating with the English, warned Smith not to trust Powhatan, even if the chief treated the colonists kindly, "and be sure he have no opportunity to seize on your arms, for he hath sent for you only to cut your throats." Tackonekintaco's demeanor induced Smith to leave Samuel Collier, his attendant, to learn the Algonquian language, which until that time had not been mastered by any of the colonists. Indeed, the Warraskoyak continued to teach the language to other settlers until the 1622 massacre, and even then the friendly Warraskoyak saved the life of at least one Englishman by returning him to Jamestown before the attack. The Warraskoyak Indians were driven away in the wake of the massacre, and the colonists constructed a river fort (Smith's Fort) on their former lands in 1623. English plantations that encompassed the territory continued to use the

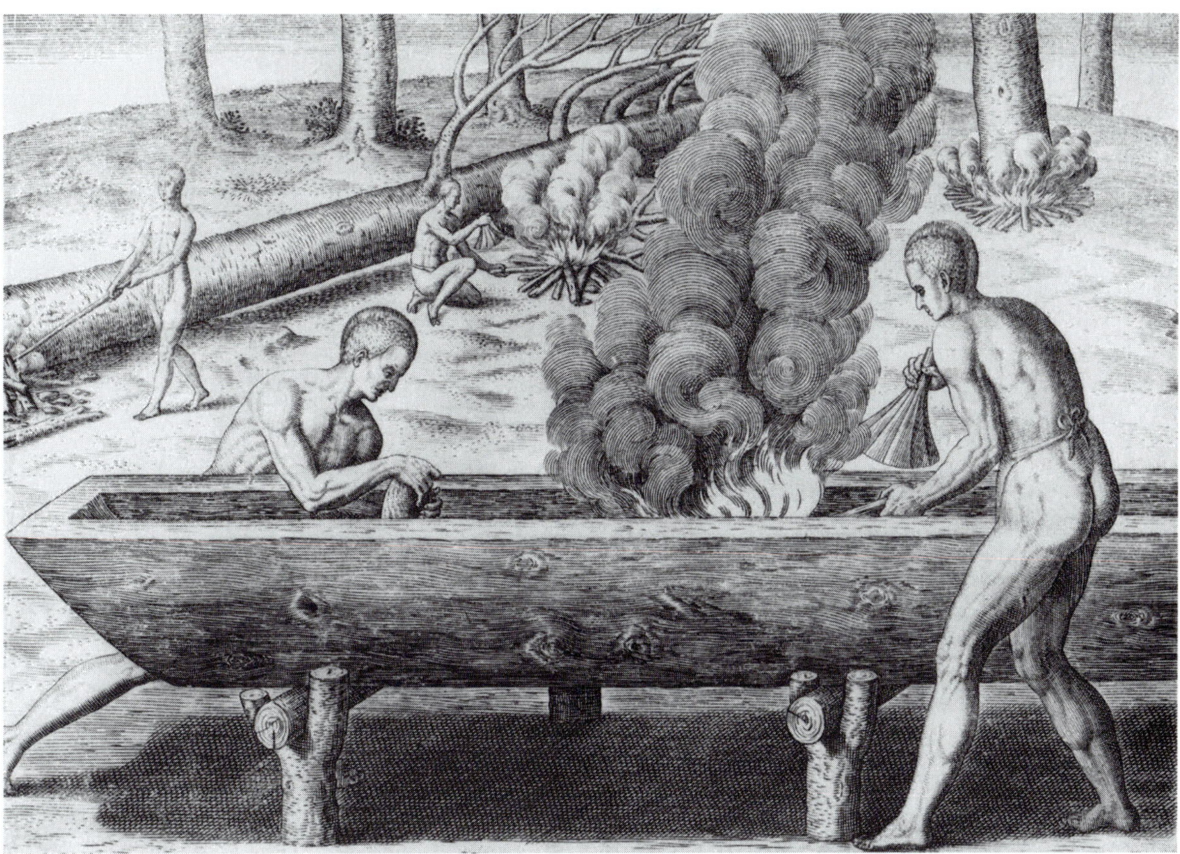

Native Americans build a canoe in this sixteenth-century illustration by explorer, John White, engraved by Theodor de Bry. (Library of Congress)

designation Warraskoyak for at least another decade.

Related entries: Accohannock Indians; Accomac Indians; Chesapeake Indians; Chickahominy Indians; Hog Island; Kecoughtan Indians; Manahoac Indians; Massacre of 1622; Mattaponi Indians; Monacan Indians; Nansemond Indians; Pamunkey Indians; Paspahegh Indians; Smith, Captain John; Smith's Fort

Suggestion for further reading

Ivor Noël Hume. 1994. *The Virginia Adventure: Roanoke to James Towne: An Archaeological and Historical Odyssey.* New York: Alfred A. Knopf.

Werowocomoco

See Powhatan

West, Thomas, Lord De La Warr (1577–1618)

Appointed first governor and captain-general of Virginia for life in 1610, Thomas West, who became the third Lord De La Warr (Delaware) following the death of his father in 1602, led an eventful and productive life, even though his time in the Virginia colony was very short considering the importance to the endeavor his title implies. Born to Sir Thomas West and his wife Ann, daughter of Sir Francis Knollys and Katherine Cary West, he was grandson of the first cousin of Queen Elizabeth and a second cousin of Henry, Earl of Dover. He received his master of arts from Oxford and married Cecily, the daughter of Sir Thomas Sherley, in 1596. After serving with distinction in the wars in the Netherlands, West was knighted at Dublin by the Earl of Essex on

Portrait of Thomas West, Lord De La Warr and first governor and captain general of Virginia. (North Wind Picture Archives)

12 July 1599. He was implicated in the Essex rebellion in 1601 and sent to prison but was released after a short confinement. West later became a member of the Privy Council of Queen Elizabeth and continued in the capacity under her successor, James I.

Although Lord De La Warr had already led an exciting and eventful life prior to the effort to establish the Jamestown colony, he became more thoroughly involved in England's designs on the New World when he became a member of the Virginia Company in 1609. The following year, on 29 February, he was named first governor and captain-general of Virginia and the next month sailed to Jamestown for the first time, along with about 150 others, mostly workmen, to help build the outpost into a viable settlement. He arrived in Virginia in June 1610 just as the Jamestown colonists were attempting to abandon the settlement following the desperate winter of 1609–1610, which came to be known as the Starving Time. After he turned the colonists back to the fort and, soon arriving there himself, saw the nearly total disarray and destruction of the fort, De La Warr ordered the reconstruction of the fort and its buildings and in general caused the settlement to be reestablished and put back in working order. He also had forts built near the mouth of the Chesapeake Bay and sent out expeditions in search of viable mines to supply the gold that the Virginia Company and its investors had been expecting since the first colonists' arrival at Jamestown three years earlier. Although West had great interest in and intentions for England's first permanent settlement in the New World, in June 1611 serious health issues forced his return to London. He remained in England until an attempted return voyage to Virginia in 1618, during which he died on 7 June. Two of his brothers, Francis and John, later served as governors of Virginia. His son Henry succeeded him to become the fourth Lord De La Warr.

Related entries: Algernon, Fort; James Fort; Shirley Hundred; Virginia Company

Suggestions for further reading

Alexander Brown. 1898. *The First Republic in America.* Boston: Houghton Mifflin.

Michael Golay and John S. Bowman. 2003. *North American Exploration.* Hoboken, NJ: John Wiley.

Charles E. Hatch, Jr. 1995. *The First Seventeen Years: Virginia, 1607–1624.* Charlottesville: University Press of Virginia.

Ivor Noël Hume. 1994. *The Virginia Adventure: Roanoke to James Towne: An Archaeological and Historical Odyssey.* New York: Alfred A. Knopf.

Lyon Gardiner Tyler. 1906. *The Cradle of the Republic: Jamestown and James River.* Richmond, VA: Hermitage Press.

White, John (c.1540–c.1618)

One of the more famous yet mysterious of all the Englishmen involved in the colonization of the New World was the talented John White. White's life before and after his involvement in the English voyages to Roanoke Island is not known well, and there is even room for dispute about the facts of his life during the years of those voyages (1584 to 1590). When and where he was

Sixteenth-century illustration of the English landing at Virginia, by John White, engraved by Theodor de Bry. (Library of Congress)

born is not certain, and who his parents were is unknown. The facts about his wife have never been discovered, but it is known that he had at least one child, Eleanor, whose place in history was assured when she arrived, pregnant, with her husband and the other members of the second group of colonists who reached Roanoke Island in 1587. Along with her husband, Ananias Dare, Eleanor became the parent of the first English child known to have been born in America, Virginia Dare, in August of that year.

White, an artist and member of the Painters-Stainers Company in London, may have accompanied Philip Amadas and Arthur Barlowe on their 1584 reconnoiter of the east coast of America for Sir Walter Raleigh when he was formulating plans to establish a colony there. White's presence on that voyage is not certain, but in his own writings he claimed to have made the Atlantic crossing five times which, considering the known voyages during the time in which he was active in the projects, would suggest that White was a member of the 1584 expedition. He was, however, a member of the 1585 voyage that placed a few more than 100 settlers on America's shores for about eleven months before being transported back to England by Sir Francis Drake in June 1586. Because of the list of colonists left on the island, there has been some speculation that John White was not actually there the entire eleven months and that he returned to England with Richard Grenville about a month after their arrival. Nonetheless, it was during this 1585 expedition that he produced many invaluable watercolors of the flora, fauna, maps, and indigenous peoples of the region. Considering the wealth and breadth of information that White conveyed through his watercolors, it would appear that he spent more than just a few short weeks exploring the island and its environs.

After this first colony was abandoned in 1586, Raleigh was anxious to make another attempt at colonization in the New World. This time, he planned to seat the colony on the Chesapeake Bay, north of his first attempt on Roanoke Island. To lead this endeavor, White was chosen as governor of the colony, and in July 1587 the expedition anchored off the Outer Banks of North Carolina near Roanoke Island. The intention of this stop was to check on the approximately fifteen men placed there in 1586 by Richard Grenville, who had left them there the previous year after finally returning in July or August with supplies for the first colonists. Finding the colonists gone, Drake having taken them back to England, Grenville left another small contingent to keep an English presence in the region. When the next group of settlers arrived with White as governor, no trace of Grenville's men was to be found.

White's tenure as governor of the Roanoke colony began against his own wishes as well as Raleigh's. As mentioned, their aim was to settle this second colony on the Chesapeake Bay. When White and the new colonists arrived at Roanoke Island, they disembarked to search for Grenville's men; but when they attempted to return to their ships, their pilot, a Portuguese privateer by the name of Fernandez, would not allow them back on board. With little room for maneuver, White returned to the site of the previous colony at the northern end of Roanoke Island and began to build anew. The previous colony, led by Ralph Lane, had been made up mostly of military men who had little desire for or skill in dealing with the indigenous peoples. That attitude resulted in hostilities between the Native Americans and the English, and White's colonists soon began to suffer the hardships of living in an alien and hostile environment with too few supplies or skills. The colonists, among them White's daughter and granddaughter, agreed that White should return to England for supplies and relief. He did so in August of 1587 with hopes of a rapid return. Other forces were at work, however, and his anticipated quick return became an agonizing wait.

Over the next three years, White made several attempts to gather the support, supplies, and ships needed to return to Roanoke Island and bring relief to the colony. Open hostilities between England and Spain, however, repeatedly thwarted White's efforts. He did manage to set sail with two small ships in April 1588, but larger French ships attacked and looted the vessels, and White had to return to England before reaching Virgini (as the territory was called by then). Finally, in August 1590, White did return to Roanoke Island, but the settlement had been destroyed, and none of the colonists were found. Carved on a tree or post at the fort the settlers had built was the word *Croatoan,* but White's attempts to sail to another island just south of the colony's last known location were stymied by weather and the reluctance of his ships' crews. White returned to England, and despite his desire to return, never again sailed in search of his lost family and friends.

As far as can be determined, John White, who contributed so much to the rare knowledge and understanding of the late sixteenth-century people, flora, and fauna of North America, ended his days at Newton in Kilmore, County Cork, Ireland; like all others who have yearned to do so ever since, he never learned the fate of his family or what came to be known to history as the Lost Colony.

Related entries: Gosnold, Bartholomew; Early European Exploration of North America; Kecoughtan Indians; Lost Colony; Powhatan; Raleigh, Sir Walter

Suggestions for further reading

Michael Golay and John S. Bowman. 2003. *North American Exploration.* Hoboken, NJ: John Wiley.

Karen Ordahl Kupperman. 1984. *Roanoke: The Abandoned Colony.* Totowa, NJ: Rowman & Littlefield.

Lee Miller. 2002. *Roanoke: Solving the Mystery of the Lost Colony.* New York: Penguin Books.

Samuel Eliot Morison. 1971. *The European Discovery of America: The Northern Voyages A.D. 500–1600.* New York: Oxford University Press.

David Beers Quinn. 1971. *North American Discovery: Circa 1000–1612.* Columbia: University of South Carolina Press.

——. 1974. *England and the Discovery of America, 1481–1620.* New York: Alfred A. Knopf.

——. 1985. *Set Faire for Roanoke: Voyages and Colonies, 1584–1606.* Chapel Hill and London: University of North Carolina Press.

Arthur M. Schlesinger, Jr., ed. 1993. *The Almanac of American History.* New York: Charles Scriber's Sons.

E. Thomson Shields, Jr., and Charles R. Ewen, eds. 2003. *Searching for the Roanoke Colonies: An Interdisciplinary Collection.* Raleigh, North Carolina.

David Stick. 1983. *Roanoke Island: The Beginnings of English America.* Chapel Hill: University of North Carolina Press.

Wingfield, Edward-Maria (1550–c.1614)

Perhaps no other person was more committed to the founding of an English colony in the New World than Edward-Maria Wingfield, Jamestown's first president. Intimately connected with all the organizers of the Virginia Company, heavily invested in the company as a stockholder, greatly experienced in military affairs, trusted by the Crown itself, and, importantly, willing to take the risk of personally going to the wilds of Virginia, it is no wonder that he was chosen to command the expedition charged with establishing a permanent presence in America. Wingfield's family was old, respectable, and somewhat prominent. He was one of ten children born to Thomas-Maria and his second wife, Margaret Kerry Wingfield, at Stonely Piory, Huntingdonshire. Wingfield began studying law at Furnivall's Inn in April 1576, and, although he did not take a degree, he was one of the five original Jamestown colonists who had attended law school. Toward the end of the decade, about 1579, Edward-Maria and his brother, Thomas-Maria Wingfield, volunteered to serve as captains of companies serving in the Low Countries under Colonel-General John Norris. Norris was an enemy of Robert Dudley, Earl of Leicester, with whom the Captains Wingfield were closely allied; the brothers passed information to Leicester until the early 1580s, when they went to Ireland to join some of their Wingfield relatives in the military service. After Ireland, Edward-Maria's military service carried him to Portugal, Brittany, and Normandy. He was captured by the Spanish near Bergen in 1587 and held for ransom for two years before being exchanged, despite his brother's heroic efforts to secure his release. In the 1590s he served again under John Norris and also with Ralph Lane, the unsuccessful colonizer of Roanoke Island.

Jamestown's First President

You were no lucky, Edward-Maria
  Wingfield,
Though I have no doubt you did as well as
  you knew.
You took your chance—had an arrow shot
  through your beard—
Starved and suffered—but *could not make
  ropes of sand . . .*
But now, for a while, you'll be President
  of Virginia,
And Smith, who will write you down,
  is under guard,
And the bitter days are not yet.

—Stephen Vincent Benét,
Western Star, Book One (1943)

When King James I issued the charter incorporating the two Virginia companies in April 1606, Wingfield was one of four persons named as "adventurers" for the London Company, the others being Sir Thomas Gates, Sir George Somers, and Richard Hakluyt, considered by many to be the grand architect of English colonization. Wingfield was related to many of the stockholders of the London Company, including another prime mover of colonization, Bartholomew Gosnold, who was his distant cousin. Together, Wingfield and Gosnold were responsible for recruiting nearly half of the 105 souls who sailed on that first voyage from England to the Chesapeake, to many of whom they were also related. Wingfield was fifty-seven years old by the time he arrived at Jamestown on board the *Susan Constant* with Captains Christopher Newport and John Smith in May 1607. Not only was he the eldest on the voyage, he was also the most experienced in military service—his service exceeded even Captain Smith's—and the only London Company "adventurer" among the colonists. Despite the fact that 10 captains (including Newport) had sailed to the Chesapeake, it came as no surprise to most of the settlers to learn that the Company had named Wingfield president of the colony in its secret instructions.

Wingfield accepted the appointment with all the soberness and decorum befitting the office. He declared that his own "first worke" concerning the establishment of a settlement in Virginia was to "make a right choice of a spirituall pastor," an appointment that he gave to the Reverend Robert Hunt, former vicar of Reculver, Kent, and vicar of All Saints Church at Old Heathfield, East Sussex. His second work was done in Virginia, when he chose the site of the settlement fort on the James River, picking the location because of its defensive position. The colonists had no way of knowing that it would prove to be an unhealthful site, and Captains Newport and Smith seconded Wingfield's choice, as did most of the sailors, although a vocal minority (including Gosnold) wanted to settle at Archer's Hope, a site a few miles downstream chosen by Captain Gabriel Archer. Wingfield wasted no time in beginning a palisade, using the labor of anyone and everyone—a measure not popular with the many gentlemen who had come to the colony. Wingfield summed up his attitude to service in the colony in his "Discourse of Virginia," written in 1608:

> I did so faithfully betroth my best endeavours to this noble enterprize, as my carriage might endure no suspition. I never turned my face from daunger, or hidd my handes from labour; so watchfull a sentinel stood myself to myself. I know wel, a troope of errors continually beseege men's actions; some of them ceased on by malice, some by ignorance. I doo not hoodwinck my carriage in my self love, but freely and humblie submit it to your grave censures.

Wingfield's brief term as president is illustrative of the internal squabbles that characterized the early council in Virginia as well as the settlers' relationship with the natives that the colonists encountered around Jamestown, both of which ultimately threatened the very existence of the settlement. There apparently were some rumblings very early on of what was to come; three or four days before taking leave of the colony, Captain Newport took Wingfield aside to ask him whether he "thought himself settled in the government," to which Wingfield replied in the affirmative, unless councilors Gosnold or Archer sought to interfere with his leadership. (Gosnold and Archer both had studied law in the early 1590s at Middle Temple and Gray's Inn, respectively.) Newport met with the other two parties and strongly urged them to be "myndefull of their dutyes" to the king and to the colony, and then he returned to England.

Three days after Newport's departure, representatives from Chief Powhatan showed up, bringing "the word of peace" with great expressions of friendship. This followed an attack that had occurred some weeks earlier while Captain Newport was exploring up river, when a native force of about 200 warriors led by Chief Wowinchopunk made the mistake of calling down upon itself artillery fire from the other English ships anchored near the fort. The Battle of Jamestown "endured hot about an hour," during which President Wingfield "showed himself a valiant gentlemen." He had "one shot clean through his beard" but was unharmed, and he personally directed the ship's ordnance against the attackers. After that it was over; twenty Indians and one English boy were dead, with many more wounded on each side. Now, with Newport gone, the natives had returned, seemingly in peace. Wingfield rewarded the messenger of peace with "many tryfles wch were great wonders to him." Wingfield knew that Powhatan's seat was about ten miles away on the Pamunkey River, but at that time no Englishman had yet laid eyes on the great chief. As for the overtures of peace, Wingfield said that Powhatan's "message fell out true" and that his people had "ever since remayned in peace and trade" with the English. More visits from warriors representing Powhatan and his younger half brother Opechancanough gave Wingfield a sense that the natives were much afraid of the English ships and were "well contented" with the "trifles" that the English presented in exchange for presents of game from the chiefs. About the same time, many of the settlers fell ill, and more than forty-five eventually died, including Captain Gosnold, who apparently had taken Newport's admonishments to heart. While Gosnold was sick, Wingfield began to realize how isolated he was among the councilors and how precarious was his grasp on power. Relations with the Indians were as good as they would ever be, but relations among the councilors had deteriorated so quickly that one councilor, Captain George Kendall, was charged with attempting to sow discord and imprisoned in a makeshift jail on a pinnace anchored in the river.

According to Wingfield, things really came to a head when he rejected pleas from the Council to provide better provisions for themselves and some of their sick friends. Attempting to make the colony's stores last as long as possible, the president prudently relied on the beneficence of the Indians, who "did daily relieve us wth corne and fleshe," and after several weeks he was able to muster back to work about twenty men who quickly replenished the colony's supply of rations. This success was not highly regarded by the Council, however, which by then had "fully plotted" to depose Wingfield. The councilors had gone so far as to draft "certeyne artycles in wrighting" and to swear oaths to follow through on their plans to rid themselves of the president. The councilors had decided to replace Wingfield with Captain John Ratcliffe and agreed to not allow Wingfield onto the Council ever again or to depose one another. Furthermore, they agreed not to take Archer back onto the Council either, unless the councilors accepted him unanimously. As John Smith, who years later seemed to regret his role in forcing Wingfield out of office, described their actions at the time, "About the tenth of September there was about 46. of our men dead, at which time Captaine Wingefield having ordred the affaires in such sort that he was generally hated of all, in which respect with one consent he was deposed from his presidencie, and Captaine Ratcliffe according to his course was elected." When Ratcliff, Smith, and John Martin delivered the warrant discharging him of his duties as president, Wingfield, who was confined to his tent because of illness, answered that they relieved him of a "great deale of care and trouble." A trial was conducted, the recounting of which Wingfield says amounted to being "forced to stuff my paper with frivolous trifles." Ratcliffe complained that the former president had "denyed him a penny whitle [a small pocket knife], a chickyn, a spoonfull of beere, and served him wth foule corne." Smith whined that Wingfield had told him "playnly how he lied," that Wingfield had said that, although they were equals at Jamestown, in England he would "scorne" to be Smith's companion because Smith had "begged in Ireland, like a rogue, wthout a lycence." Martin's accusations were similar in tone to those of Smith and Ratcliffe; he alleged that Wingfield had reported of him that, "I doe slack the service in the Collonye, and doe nothing but tend my pott, spitt, and oven; but he hath starved my sonne, and denyed him a spoonefull of beere." A host of other written charges were then read, against which the president was not allowed an adequate defense other than to appeal to the king's mercy. Wingfield said he had forgotten most of the complaints, "they were so slight." Wingfield was then confined to the pinnace, Kendall was given his liberty, and "all this while, the salvages brought to the towne such corn and fflesh as they could spare."

Wingfield's "Discourse of Virginia" is largely an account of his misfortune and a defense against the charges against him. In the "Discourse," he claimed that as president he did not abuse his station, did not "heate a flesh pott" unless the "comon pot was so used likewise," and went out of his way to share his own food with the sick. He contrasted his partaking of a gift of one roasted squirrel to that of his successor and fellow councilors, who routinely indulged in swans, ducks, and geese, asking "how many times their flesh potts have swelled, many hungry eies did behold, to their great longing; and what great theeves and theeving thear hath been in the comon stoare since my tyme?" He described the councilors' law as "speedie and cheape" and stated that, instead of making good men do better and staying the hand of the bad from doing worse, their law "did but rob us of tyme that might be better ymployed in service in the Collonye." Worse yet, beating and maiming had became commonplace at James Fort, and Wingfield feared that if "this whipping, lawing, beating, and hanging, in Virginia" became known in England it would "drive many well affected myndes from this honoble action of Virginia." Ultimately, Wingfield blamed his own misfortunes not on his accusers but on Archer, who he said was getting even with him because he had rejected Archer's choice for the site and laying out James Fort and had not allowed Archer onto the Council, "wch neyther I could doe or he deserve." After his trial, Wingfield's papers and accounts were seized and never returned; his trunk of books was broken up and lost. "Thus was I made good prize on all sides."

Wingfield languished on the pinnace from September 1607 to January 1608, when Captain Newport returned with the First Supply and set him free. It was another fourteen weeks before Wingfield sailed back to England with Newport on board the *John and Francis,* arriving at Blackwell in May 1608. Once in England, he immediately composed his "Discourse of Virginia" for Archbishop Richard Bancroft, who prudently kept it out of public view in order to protect the venture. Word of the adversities and factionalism in the colony got around to the stockholders anyway, and to the Crown, no doubt with the quiet assistance of Wingfield. The depravations, humiliations, and threats on his life had not soured Wingfield on the Jamestown settlement, however, and when James issued a new charter in 1609, Wingfield once again was on the short list of grantees. In fact, he was one of the Company's largest shareholders, and he kept a keen interest in its affairs up to the time of his death.

Related entries: Archer, Gabriel; Gosnold, Bartholomew; Kendall, George; London Company; Newport, Sir Christopher; Smith, Captain John

Suggestions for further reading

Charles Deane, ed. 1860. *"A Discourse of Virginia" by Edward-Maria Wingfield . . . now First Printed from the Original Manuscripts in the Lambeth Library.* Boston: J. Wilson and Son.

Jocelyn R. Wingfield. 1993. *Virginia's True Founder: Edward-Maria Wingfield and His Times, 1550–c.1614.* Athens, GA: Wingfield Family Society.

Winne, Peter (c.1560–1609)

Peter Winne (Wynn) was born in Wales, apparently near Mold in Flintshire, to an old but not very prominent or prosperous family. Whether he received an education or not is unknown, but as a younger son of the lesser gentry of that time, his options in life were limited, and like many of his sort, he chose to enter the military. It probably was with great pride and satisfaction that in 1586 he accepted a commission as captain of an Irish company in the regiment of Sir William Stanley, a colonel in the service of Robert Dudley, Earl of Leicester, who in the mid-1580s became embroiled in the ongoing war between Spain and the Netherlands. When Stanley deserted Leicester and sided with the Spanish in 1587, Winne, who had risen from lieutenant to captain while serving under Stanley, continued with his regiment for almost three years. After he and others in his regiment were pardoned by Queen Elizabeth for what amounted to treason, Winne aligned himself with Leicester's stepson, Robert Devereux, Earl of Essex, and over the next decade was involved in intelligence-gathering efforts in England and on the continent. An appointment in the service of the States General in the Netherlands by Essex's son brought Winne in contact with Sir Thomas Gates, who recommended him for service in the New World at the conclusion of the war in the Netherlands.

Winne was thus a seasoned soldier and officer by the time he joined the seventy men and women who made up the Second Supply of new colonists that sailed to Jamestown with Captain Christopher Newport on board the *Mary and Margaret,* arriving in September 1608. Shortly after his arrival at Jamestown, Winne accompanied Newport on a fruitless mission to the Monacan Indians; Winne was chosen because Newport erroneously thought Winne could serve as an interpreter, the languages of the natives and the Welsh sounding similar. Before returning to England later that fall, Newport swore Winne to the Council. Winne and Richard Waldo, the other captain who came in the Second Supply and who with Winne was appointed to the Council, were described by Captain John Smith as an "old soldiers and valiant gentlemen." Winne, in fact, had been named sergeant major of Jamestown Fort, a station of rank and consequence that indicates the esteem in which he was held by members of the London Company. Winne and Smith, however, apparently did not hit it off too well to begin with, and their relationship soured further when Winne joined fellow councilor and Smith's friend Matthew Scrivener in opposing Smith's plan to surprise Chief Powhatan and steal his supplies of corn. Smith considered the opposition of Winne and Scrivener a political ploy aimed at reducing his power, and thereafter he held Winne in little more than contempt. After Scrivener and Waldo drowned on a boating trip, Smith and Winne, as the two remaining councilors, were forced to work more closely together. Their relationship was not destined to last very long, however.

Unbeknownst to Winne or anyone else at Jamestown, Sir Thomas Gates had appointed Winne lieutenant governor to act in his stead when he was delayed in coming to the colony, but by the time news of the appointment arrived at Jamestown, Winne was dead. His death from fever (most likely malaria), occurred even before the Starving Time of 1609–1610 began to devastate the colony. It was an unfortunate end for a man whose experience and skills had so prepared him for life in the New World. Shortly after his arrival, he had written back to Sir John Egerton in England, "I was not so desirous to come into this country, as I am now willing here to end my dayes: for I finde it a farr more plesant, and plentifull country than any report made mention of." Winne's only biographer, Paul E. J. Hammer, noted that Winne, dying as he did before he could make his mark on the early history of Jamestown, personifies the age that produced him. For Winne, as for many, the early Jamestown colony "was a graveyard of hopes and dreams as much as of bodies."

Related entries: Newport, Sir Christopher; Smith, Captain John

Suggestions for further reading

Alexander Brown. 1890. *The Genesis of the United States* (vol. 2). Boston: Houghton Mifflin.

Paul E. J. Hammer. 1998. "A Welshman Abroad: Captain Peter Wynn of Jamestown." (*Parergon: Journal of the Australian and New Zealand Association for Medieval and Early Modern Studies,* vol. 16, July).

York River

Along with about a dozen rivers that include the Elizabeth, the Nansemond, the Rappahannock, the James, and the Potomac, the York River is one of the principal rivers feeding into the Chesapeake Bay from the bay's west side. It was named in honor of Charles, Duke of York (as were York Bay, York County, and Yorktown). At the time of first contact, according to Captain John Smith, Chief Powhatan's principal seat, Werowocomoco, was "upon the north side of York River" about fifteen miles from Jamestown (at present-day Wicomico in Gloucester County), and in February 1608 Smith led Captain Christopher Newport up the river to meet the powerful king. Smith recorded that Powhatan's half brother "Opechancanough, King of Pamaunkey, was also seated on the river of that name; the main part of which is now called York River." The York, like the James, the Rappahannock, and the Potomac, was explored early on by the colonists because it was "full of convenient and safe harbors." Although Smith and his companions eventually took control of the lands on either side of the York River, they were not the first Europeans to visit the region, for Jesuit priests had sailed up the river in 1570. A Powhatan-dominated tribe of forty or fifty warriors, the Kiskiack, lived in a wigwam village on the south side of the York that soon became a major trading site between the colonists and the natives.

The York's upper branches, the Pamunkey and the Mattaponi, meet to form the York at West Point, originally an Indian village named Cinquoteck, about halfway between the mouth of the river and Richmond. By the 1660s, the English had built three forts along the York River (in addition to two on the James), including Fort James at Gloucester (or Tindall's) Point across from Yorktown, the site of British and Confederate army batteries during the American Revolutionary and Civil Wars. The York, with the James to the south and the Rappahannock to the north, is bounded on either side by a great neck—large enough for the settlers to carve six counties on its northern side and seven and a half on its southern side. The first land patentee at what became Yorktown was a French Huguenot, Nicholas Marlier (Martian), said to be an ancestor of George Washington. Situated on the south bank of the York River a few miles southeast of Williamsburg, the Yorktown area was farmland for much of the seventeenth century, but it became an important port in the 1690s. Following Bacon's Rebellion in 1676, Governor William Berkeley presided over a court-martial held on board Captain John Martin's ship in the York River, on 11 January 1667, that convicted some of the ringleaders of the insurgency. (Indeed, the Indian attackers who helped spur Bacon to action had operated from the headwaters of the James, Rappahannock, and York Rivers.)

The act in the House of Burgesses that moved the capital from Jamestown to Williamsburg at the end of the seventeenth century cited "the conveniency of two navigable and pleasant creeks, that run out of *James* and *York* rivers, necessary for the supplying the place with provisions and other things of necessity." Land situated on a tributary of the York, Queen's Creek, was designated in the act for the port (Queen Mary's Port) of the new capital. After the move of the capital, the York River began to play an even more prominent role in the colony's commerce and history. Most of the colony's land was under tobacco cultivation, and the plantations along the river's edge were highly sought after because of their easy access to the ships that carried the tobacco back to England; large estates on the north side of the river included Rosewell (begun by Mann Page in 1725), perhaps the grandest colonial English brick mansion ever built in the New World, the magnificent ruins of which still stand; Clay Bank, a plantation established on land that colonist John Hansford bequeathed to two sons; Mulberry Hall (later Concord, the home of Colonels William and Catesby Jones of the War of 1812); and Valley Front (currently a horse farm). Five lighthouses were erected on the York in the nineteenth century, but none has survived into the twenty-first century.

Robert Beverley, in his *History and Present State of Virginia* (London, 1705), laid to rest the notion, taken from early maps, that the York and Rappahannock Rivers issued "out of low marshes, and not from the mountains as the other rivers." Beverley's own travels with Governor Alexander Spotswood had taken him to the "head spring of both those rivers, and their fountains are in the highest ridge of mountains"; the York River Watershed in fact encompasses much of present-day Louisa County and the lower half of Orange County, far above the fall line. The York proper flows 36 miles, but altogether from its headwaters to the bay, it extends 140 miles, and its watershed covers about 2,670 square miles, about 6 percent of Virginia's land base and 12 percent of Virginia's bay basin. One of the deepest rivers in the world, the York is as much as 80 feet deep at points, a mile wide at its head, and two and a half miles wide near its mouth.

Efforts to protect and restore the delicate ecosystem of the York River are ongoing, and much of the York's rich history still needs to be explored. Major archaeological excavations at the Kiskiack village site, now part of the Yorktown Naval Weapons Station, are ongoing. British ships sunk during the Revolutionary War have been explored and brought up since the 1930s. York River State Park, eleven miles west of Williamsburg in Gloucester County, preserves some of the unusual river marshes created by the meeting of salt and fresh waters. Croaker Landing, an early rendezvous spot for tobacco shipments at what was Taskinas Plantation, is an important archaeological site listed on the National Register of Historic Places and is on the park grounds. The park is a popular attraction for picnicking, hiking, bike riding, boating, canoeing, fishing, and hunting.

Related entries: Chickahominy River; Elizabeth River; James River; Jesuit Mission (Chesapeake); Lee, Richard; Mattaponi River; Nansemond River; Newport, Sir Christopher; Pamunkey

River; Powell, Captain Nathaniel; Rappahannock River; Tindall's Point

Suggestions for further reading

Sally Mills. 1997. *The York River Watershed Fact Sheet.* Waterton, VA: Friends of the York River.

U.S. Environmental Protection Agency, Chesapeake Bay Program. 2001. *Virginia's Tributary Strategies: A Customized Approach to Reduce Nutrient Pollution in the Rivers Flowing into the Chesapeake Bay, The York River.* Richmond: Virginia Department of Environmental Quality.

Selected Writings

Discovery of Virginia, 1170–1584

The following history of the discovery of Virginia is taken from the "First Booke" of Captain John Smith's Generall Historie of Virginia, New England & The Summer Isles, *first published in London in 1624. In this passage, Smith neatly summarizes the origins of European knowledge of the New World, up to the famous discovery by Columbus, along with Martin Frobisher's attempt to find the Northwest Passage and Sir Humphrey Gilbert and Sir Walter Raleigh's search for an adequate place to settle a colony on the Virginia coastline in present-day North Carolina.*

How Ancient Authors Report, the New-World, Now called America, was discovered: and part thereof, first Planted by the English, called Virginia, with the Accidents and Proceedings of the same.

For the Stories of Arthur, Malgo, and Brandon, that say a thousand yeares agoe they were in the North of America; or the Fryer of Linn that by his blacke Art went to the North pole in the yeare 1360. in that I know them not, let this suffice.

The Chronicles of Wales report, that Madock, sonne to Owen Quineth, Prince of Wales seeing his two brethren at debate who should inherit, prepared certaine Ships, with men and munition, and left his Country to seeke adventures by Sea: leaving Ireland North he sayled west till he came to a Land unknowne. Returning home and relating what pleasant and fruitfull Countries he had seene without Inhabitants, and for what barren ground his brethren and kindred did murther one another, he provided a number of Ships, and got with him such men and women as were desirous to live in quietnesse, that arrived with him in this new Land in the yeare 1170: Left many of his people there and returned for more. But where this place was no History can show.

The Spanyards say Hanno a Prince of Carthage was the first: and the next Christopher Cullumbus, a Genoesiar, whom they sent to discover those unknowne parts, 1492.

But we finde by Records, Cullumbus offered his service in the yeare 1488. to King Henry the seaventh; and by accident undertooke it for the Spanyards. In the Interim King Henry gave a Commission to John Cabot, and his three sonnes, Sebastian, Lewis, and Sautius. John and Sebastian well provided, setting sayle, ranged a great part of this unknowne world, in the yeare 1497. For though Cullumbus had found certaine Iles, it was 1498. ere he saw the Continent, which was a yeare after Cabot. Now Americus came a long time after, though the whole Continent to this day is called America after his name, yet Sebastian Cabot discovered much more then them all, for he sayled to about forty degrees Southward of the lyne, and to sixty-seaven towards the North: for which King Henry the eight Knighted him and made him grand Pilate of England. Being very aged King Edward the sixt gave him a Pention of 166l. 13S. 4d. yearely. By his directions Sir Hugh Willowby was sent to finde out the Country of Russia, but the next yeare he was found frozen to death in his Ship, and all his Company.

Mr. Martin Frobisher was sent in the yeare 1576. by our most gracious Queene Elizabeth, to search for the Northwest passage, and Meta incognita [the Artic]: for which he was Knighted, honored, and well rewarded.

Sir Humphrey Gilbert a worthy Knight attempted a Plantation in some of those parts: and obtained Letters Pattents to his desire: but with this Proviso, He should maintaine possession in some of those vast Countries within the tearme of sixe yeares. Yet when he was provided with a Navy able to incounter a Kings power, even here at home they fell in divisions, and so into confusion, that they gave over the Designe ere it was begun, notwithstanding all this losse, his undanted spirit began againe, but his Fleet fell with New-foundland, and he perished in his returne, as at large you may read in the third Volume of the English Voyages, written by Mr. Hackluit.

Upon all those Relations and inducements, Sir Walter Raleigh, a noble Gentleman, and then in great esteeme, undertooke to send to discover to the Southward. And though his occasions and other imployments were such he could not goe himselfe, yet he procured her Majesties Letters Pattents, and perswaded many worthy Knights and Gentlemen to adventure with him to finde a place fit for a Plantation. Their Proceedings followeth.

The most famous, renowned, and ever worthy of all memory, for her courage, learning, judgement, and vertue, Queene Elizabeth, granted her Letters Patents to Sir Walter Raleigh for the discovering and planting new Lands & Countries, not actually possessed by any Christians. This Patenty got to be his assistants Sir Richard Grenvell the valiant, Mr. William Sanderson a great friend to all such noble and worthy actions, and divers other Gentlemen and Marchants, who with all speede provided two small Barkes well furnished with all necessaries, under the command of Captaine Philip Amidas and Captaine Barlow. The 27. of Aprill they set sayle from the Thames, the tenth of May passed the Canaries, and the tenth of June the West Indies: which unneedfull Southerly course, (but then no better was knowne) occasioned them in that season much sicknesse.

The second of July they fell with the coast of Florida in shoule water, where they felt a most dilicate sweete smell, though they saw no land, which ere long they espied, thinking it the Continent: an hundred and twenty myles they sayled not finding any harbor. The first that appeared, with much difficulty they entred, and anchored, and after thankes to God they went to view the next Land adjoyning to take possession of it for the Queenes most excellent Majestie: which done, they found their first landing place very sandy and low, but so full of grapes that the very surge of the Sea sometimes over-flowed them: of which they found such plenty in all places, both on the sand, the greene soyle and hils, as in the plaines as well on every little shrub, as also climbing towardes the tops of high Cedars, that they did thinke in the world were not the like abundance.

We passed by the Sea-side towards the tops of the next hills being not high: from whence we might see of the Sea on both sides, and found it an Ile of twentie myles in length, and six in breadth, the vallyes replenished with goodly tall Cedars, Discharging our Muskets, such a flocke of Cranes, the most white, arose by us, with such a cry as if an Army of men had shouted altogether. This Ile hath many goodly Woods, and Deere, Conies, and Foule in incredible abundance, and using the Authors owne phrase, the Woods are not such as you finde in Bohemia, Moscovia, or Hercinia, barren and fruitlesse, but the highest and reddest Cedars of the world, bettering them of the Assores, Indies, or Libanus: Pynes, Cypres, Saxefras, the Lentisk that beareth Mastick, and many other of excellent smell and qualitie. Till the third day we saw not any of the people, then in a little Boat three of them appeared, one of them went on shore, to whom wee rowed, and he attended us without any signe of feare; after he had spoke much though we understood not a word, of his owne accord he came boldly aboord us, we gave him a shirt, a hat, wine and meate, which he liked well, and after he had well viewed the barkes and us, he went away in his owne Boat, and within a quarter of a myle of us in halfe an houre, had loaden his Boat with fish, with which he came againe to the poynt of land, and there derided it in two parts, poynting one part to the Ship, the other to the Pinnace, and so departed.

The next day came divers Boats, and in one of them the Kings Brother, with forty or fifty men, proper people, and in their behaviour very civill; his name was Granganamen, the King is called Wingina, the Country Wingandacoa. Leaving his Boats a little from our Ships, he came with his trayne to the poynt: where spreading a Matte he sat downe. Though we came to him well armed, he made signes to us to sit downe without any shew of feare, stroking his head and brest, and also ours, to expresse his love. After he had made a long speech unto us, we presented him with divers toyes, which he kindly accepted. He was greatly regarded by his people, for none of them did sit, nor speake a word, but foure, on whom we bestowed presents also, but he tooke all from them, making signes all things did belong to him.

The King himselfe in a conflict with a King his next neighbour and mortall enemy, was shot in two places through the body, and the thigh, yet recovered: whereby he lay at his chiefe towne six dayes journey from thence.

A day or two after shewing them what we had, Granganameo taking most liking to a Pewter dish, made a hole in it, hung it about his necke for a brestplate: for which he gave us twenty Deere skins, worth twenty Crownes; and for a Copper Kettell, fiftie skins, worth fiftie Crownes. Much other trucke we had, and after two dayes he came aboord, and did eate and drinke with us very merrily. Not long after he brought his wife and children, they were but of meane stature, but well favoured and very bashfull; she had a long coat of Leather, and about her privities a peece of the same, about her forehead a band of white Corrall, and so had her husband, in her eares were bracelets of pearle, hanging downe to her middle, of the bignesse of great Pease; the rest of the women had Pendants of Copper, and the Noblemen five or sixe in an eare; his apparrell as his wives, onely the women weare their haire long on both sides, and the men but on one; they are of colour yellow, but their hayre is blacke, yet we saw children that had very fayre Chesnut coloured hayre.

After that these women had beene here with us, there came downe from all parts great store of people, with Leather, Corrall, and divers kinde of dyes, but when Granganameo was present, none durst trade but himselfe, and them that wore red Copper on their heads, as he did. When ever he came, he would signifie by so many fires he came with so many boats, that we might know his strength. Their Boats are but one great tree, which is but burnt in the forme of a trough with gins and fire, till it be as they would have it. For an armour he would have ingaged us a bagge of pearle, but we refused, as not regarding it, that wee might the better learn where it grew. He was very just of his promise, for oft we trusted him, and he would come within his day to keepe his word. He sent us commonly every day a brace of Bucks, Conies, Hares, and fish, sometimes Mellons, Walnuts, Cucumbers, Pease, and divers rootes. This Author sayth, their corne groweth three times in five moneths; in May they sow, in July reape; in June they sow, in August reape; in July sow, in August reape. We put some of our Pease in the ground, which in ten dayes were 14. ynches high.

The soyle is most plentifull, sweete, wholesome, and fruitfull of all other, there are about 14. severall sorts of sweete swelling tymber trees: the most parts of the underwood, Bayes and such like: such Okes as we, but far greater and better. After this acquaintance, my selfe with seaven more went twenty myle into the River Occam, that runneth toward the Cittie Skicoack, and the evening following we came to an Ile called Roanoak, from the harbour where we entred 7. leagues; at the North end was 9 houses, builded with Cedar, fortified round with sharpe trees, and the entrance like a Turnpik. When we came towards it, the wife of Granganameo came running out to meete us, (her husband was absent) commanding her people to draw our Boat ashore for The Ile Roanoak. The great courtesie of a Woman beating on the billowes, other she appoynted to carry us on their backes aland, others to bring our Ores into the house for stealing. When we came into the other roome, (for there was five in the house) she caused us to sit downe by a great fire; after tooke off our clothes and washed them, of some our stockings, and some our feete in warme water, and she her selfe tooke much paines to see all things well ordered, and to provide us victuall.

After we had thus dryed our selves, she brought us into an Inner roome, where she set on the bord standing a long the house somewhat like frumentie, sodden venison, and rosted fish; in like manner mellons raw, boyled rootes and fruites of divers kindes. There drinke is commonly water boyled with Ginger, sometimes with Saxefras, and wholsome herbes, but whilest the Grape lasteth they drinke wine. More love she could not expresse to entertaine us; they care but onely to defend themselves from the short winter, and feede on what they finde naturall in sommer. In this feasting house was their Idoll of whom they tould us uncredible things. When we were at meate two or three of her men came amongst us with their Bowes and Arrowes, which caused us to take our armes in hand. She perceiving our distrust, caused their Bowes and Arrowes to be broken, and they beaten out of the gate: but the evening approaching we returned to our boate, where at she much grieving brought our supper halfe boyled, pots and all, but when she saw us, but put our boat a little off from the shoar and lye at Anchor, perceiving our Jelousie, she sent divers men & 30. women to sit al night on the shoare side against us, and sent us five Mats to cover us from the raine, doing all she could to perswade us to her house. Though there was no cause of doubt, we would not adventure: for on our safety depended the voyage: but a more kinde loving people cannot be. Beyond this Ile is the maine land and the great river Occam, on which standeth a Towne called Pomeiock, and six dayes higher, their City Skicoak: those people never saw it, but say there fathers affirme it to be above two houres journey about. Into this river falleth an other called Cipo, where is found many Mustells wherein are Pearles: likewise another River called Nomapona, on the one side whereof standeth a great towne called Chawanock, the Lord of the Country is not subject to Wingandacoa. Beyond him an other king they cal Menatonon. These 3. are in league each with other. Towards the south. 4. dayes journey is Sequotan, the southermost part of Wingandacoa.

Adjoyning to Secotan beginneth the country Pomovik, belonging to the King called Piamacum, in the Country Nusiok upon the great river Neus. These have mortall warres with Wingina, King of Wingandacoa. Betwixt Piemacum and the Lord of Secotan, a peace was concluded: notwithstanding there is a mortall malice in the Secotans, because this Piemacum invited divers men, and 30. women to a feast, and when they were altogether merry before their Idoll, which is but a meere illusion of the Devill, they sudainly slew all the men of Secotan, and kept the women for their use. Beyond Roanoak are many Isles full of fruits and other Naturall increases, with many Townes a long the side of the Continent. Those Iles lye 200. myles in length, and betweene them and the mayne, a great long sea, in some places, 20. 40. or 50. myles broad, in other more, somewhere lesse. And in this sea are 100. Iles of divers bignesses, but to get into it, you have but 3. passages and they very dangerous. Though this you see for most part be but the relations of Salvages, because it is the first, I thought it not a misse to remember them as they are written by them that returned & arived in England about the middest of September the same yeare. This discovery was so welcome into England that it pleased her Majestie to call this Country of Wingandacoa, Virginia, by which name now you are to understand how it was planted, disolved, reuned, and enlarged,

The Performers of this voyage were these following.

Captaines

Philip Amadas. Arthur Barlow.

Of the Companie.

William Grenvill. Benjamen Wood.
John Wood. Simon Ferdinando.
James Browewich. Nicholas Peryman.
Henry Greene. John Hewes.

Fifth Voyage of John White to Virginia, 1589

The following account of John White's final attempt to discover the fate of the colonists left behind on Roanoke Island (the Lost Colony) appeared in the "First Booke" of Captain John Smith's Generall Historie of Virginia, New England & The Summer Isles, *first published in London in 1624. Smith was an eclectic borrower of other people's writings, a number of which have survived only in his works.*

The fift Voyage to Virginia; undertaken by Mr. John White. 1589.

The 20. of March three ships went from Plimouth, passed betwixt Barbary and Mogadoro to his returne to Dominico in the West Indies. After we had done some Virginia. exployts in those parts, the third of August wee fell with the low sandy Iles westward of Wokokon. But by reason of ill weather it was the II. ere we could Anchor there; and on the 12. we came to Croatan, where is a great breach in 35 degrees and a halfe, in the Northeast poynt of the Ile. The 15. we came to Hatorask in 36. degrees & a terse, at 4. fadom, 3 leagues from shore: where we might perceive a smoake at the place where I left the Colony, 1587. The next morning Captaine Cooke, Captaine Spicer, & their companies, with two boats left our ships, and discharged some Ordnance to give them notice of our comming, but when we came there, we found no man, nor signe of any that had beene there lately: and so returned to our Boats. The next morning we prepared againe for Roanoack. Captaine Spicer had then sent his Boat ashore for water, so it was ten of the Clocke ere we put from the ships, which rode two myles from the shore. The Admirals boat, being a myle before the other, as she passed the bar, a sea broke into the boat and filled her halfe full of water: but by Gods good will, and the carefull stearage of Captaine Cook, though our provisions were much wet we safe escaped, the wind blew hard at Northeast, which caused so great a current and a breach upon the barre; Captaine Spicer passed halfe over, but by the indiscreet steering of Ralph Skinner, their boat was overset, the men that could catch hold hung about her, the next sea cast her on ground, where some let goe their hold to wade to shore, but the sea beat [the] Captaine [and] them downe. The boat thus tossed up and downe Spicer and Skinner hung there till they were but 4. that could swim a little, kept themselves drowned. in deeper water, were saved by the meanes of Captaine Cook, that presently upon the oversetting of their boat, shipped himselfe to save what he could. Thus of eleven, seven of the chiefest were drowned. This so discomfited all the Saylers, we had much to do to get them any more to seeke further for the Planters, but by their Captaines forwardnes at last they fitted themselves againe for Hatorask in 2 boats, with 19 persons. It was late ere we arrived, but seeing a fire through the woods, we sounded a Trumpet, but no answer could we heare. The next morning we went to it, but could see nothing but the grasse, and some rotten trees burning. We went up and downe the Ile, and at last found three faire Romane Letters carved. C.R.O. which presently we knew to signifie the place where I should find them, according to a secret note betweene them & me: which was to write the name of the place they would be in, upon some tree, dore, or post: and if they had beene in any distresse, to signifie it by making a crosse over it. For at my departure they intended to goe fiftie myles into the mayne. But we found no signe of distresse; then we went to a place where they were left in sundry houses, but we found them all taken downe, and the place strongly inclosed with a high Palizado, very Fortlike; and in one of the chiefe Posts carved in fayre capitall Letters CROATAN, without any signe of distresse, and many barres of Iron, two pigs of Lead, foure Fowlers, Iron shot, and such their like heavie things throwne here and there, overgrowne with grasse and weeds. We went by the shore to seeke for their boats but could find none, nor any of the Ordnance I left them. At last some of the Sailers found divers Chists had beene hidden and digged up againe, and much of the goods spoyled, and scattered up and downe, which when I saw, I knew three of them to be my owne; but bookes, pictures, and all things els were spoyled. Though it much grieved me, yet it did much comfort me that I did know they were at Croatan; so we returned to our Ships, but had like to have bin cast away by a great storme that continued all that night.

The next morning we weighed Anchor for Croatan: having the Anchor apike, the Cable broke, by the meanes whereof we lost another: letting fall the third, the ship yet went so fast a drift, we fayled not much there to have split. But God bringing us into deeper water; considering we had but one Anchor, and our provision neare spent, we resolved to goe forthwith to S. Johns Ile, Hispaniola, or Trinidado, to refresh our selves and seeke for purchase that Winter, and the next Spring come againe to seeke our Country-men. But our Vice Admirall would not, but went directly for England, and we our course for Trinidado. But within two dayes after, the wind changing, we were constrained for the Westerne Iles to refresh our selves, where we met with many of the Queenes ships our owne consort, and divers others, the 23. of September 1590. And thus we left seeking our Colony, that was never any of them found, nor seene to this day 1622. And this was the conclusion of this Plantation, after so much time, labour, and charge consumed. Whereby we see;

Not all at once, nor all alike, nor ever hath it beene,
That God doth offer and confer his blessings upon men.

—Written by Master John White

John Brereton's Account of the Aborted New England Colony, 1602

The following account of Captain Bartholomew Gosnold's ground-breaking expedition to explore the coast and plant a colony in New England in 1602, written by crew member John Brereton and published in London shortly after his arrival back in England the same year, is taken from the "First Booke" of Captain John Smith's Generall Historie of Virginia, New England & The Summer Isles, *first published in London in 1624. Gosnold's voyage was the first transatlantic crossing to New England, and although his colony lasted only a short time, it proved an invaluable precedent for the settlement at Jamestown only five years later.*

A briefe Relation of the Description of Elizabeths Ile, and some others towards the North part of Virginia; and what els they discovered in the yeare

1602. by Captaine Bartholomew Gosnoll, and Captaine Bartholomew Gilbert; and divers other Gentlemen their Associates.

All hopes of Virginia thus abandoned, it lay dead and obscured from 1590. till this yeare 1602. that Captaine Gosnoll, with 32. and himselfe in a small Barke, set sayle from Dartmouth upon the 26. of March. Though the wind favoured us not at the first, but force us as far Southward as the Asores, which was not much out of our way; we ran directly west from thence, whereby we made our journey shorter then heretofore by 500. leagues: the weaknesse of our ship, the badnes of our saylers, and our ignorance of the coast, caused us carry but a low sayle, that made our passage longer then we expected.

On fryday the 11. of May we made land, it was somewhat low, where appeared certaine hummocks or hills in it: the shore white sand, but very rockie, yet overgrowne with fayre trees. Comming to an Anchor, 8 Indians in a Baske shallop, with mast and sayle came boldly aboord us. It seemed by their signes & such things as they had, some Biskiners had fished there: being about the latitude of 43. But the harbour being naught, & doubting the weather, we went not ashore, but waighed, and stood to the Southward into the Sea. The next morning we found our selves imbayed with a mightie headland: within a league of the shore we anchored, and Captaine Gosnoll, my selfe, & three others went to it in our boat, being a white sand & a bold coast. Though the weather was hot, we marched to the highest hils we could see, where we perceived this headland part of the mayn, neare invironed with Ilands. As we were returning to our ship, a good proper, lusty young man came to us, with whom we had but small conference, and so we left him. Here in 5. or 6. houres we tooke more Cod then we knew what to doe with, which made us perswade our selves, there might be found a good fishing in March, Aprill, and May.

At length we came among these fayre Iles, some a league, 2. 3. 5. or 6. from the Mayne, by one of them Vineyard. we anchored. We found it foure myles in compasse, without house or inhabitant. In it is a lake neare a myle in circuit; the rest overgrowne with trees, which so well as the bushes, were so overgrowne with Vines, we could scarce passe them. And by the blossomes we might perceive there would be plenty of Strawberries, Respises, Gousberries, and divers other fruits: besides, Deere and other Beasts we saw, and Cranes, Hernes, with divers other sorts of fowle; which made us call it Martha's Vineyard.

The rest of the Iles are replenished with such like; very rocky, and much tinctured stone like Minerall. Though we met many Indians, yet we could not see their habitations: they gave us fish, Tobacco, and such things as they had. But the next Isle we arrived at was but two leagues from the Maine, & 16. myle about, invironed so with creekes and coves, it seemed like many Isles linked together by small passages like bridges. In it is many places of plaine grasse, and such other fruits, and berries as before were mentioned. In mid-May we did sow Wheat, Barley, Oates, & Pease, which in 14. dayes sprung up 9. inches. The soyle is fat and lusty: the crust thereof gray, a foot or lesse in depth. It is full of high timbred Okes, their leaves thrise so broad as ours: Cedar straight and tall, Beech, Holly, Walnut, Hazell, Cherry trees like ours, but the stalke beareth the blossom or fruit thereof like a cluster of Grapes, forty or fiftie in a bunch. There is a tree of Orange colour, whose barke in the filing is as smooth as Velvet. There is a lake of fresh water three myles in compasse, in the midst an Isle containing an acre or thereabout, overgrowne with wood: here are many Tortoises, and abundance of all sorts of foules, whose young ones we tooke and eate at our pleasure. Grounds nuts as big as egges, as good as Potatoes, and 40. on a string, not two ynches under ground. All sorts of shell-fish, as Schalops, Mussels, Cockles, Crabs, Lobsters, Welks, Oysters, exceeding good and very great; but not to cloy you with particulars, what God and nature hath bestowed on those places, I refer you to the Authors owne writing at large. We called this Isle Elizabeths Isle, from whence we went right over to the mayne, where we stood a while as ravished at the beautie and dilicacy of the sweetnesse, besides divers cleare lakes, whereof we saw no end, & meadows very large and full of greene grasse, &c.

Here we espyed 7. Salvages, at first they expressed some feare, but by our courteous usage of them, they followed us to the necke of Land, which we thought had beene severed from the Mayne, but we found it otherwise. Here we imagined was a river, but because the day was farre spent, we left to discover it till better leasure. But of good Harbours, there is no doubt, considering the Land is all rocky and broken lands. The next day we determined to fortifie our selves in the Isle in the lake. Three weekes we spent in building us there a house. But the second day after our comming from the Mayne, 11. Canows with neare 50. Salvages came towards us. Being unwilling they should see our building, we went to, & exchanged with them Knives, Hatchets, Beades, Bels, and such trifles, for some Bevers, Lyzards, Martins, Foxes, wilde Catte skinnes, and such like. We saw them have much red Copper, whereof they make chaines, collars, and drinking cups, which they so little esteemed they would give us for small toyes, & signified unto us they had it out of the earth in the Mayne: three dayes they stayed with us, but every night retyred two or three myle from us: after with many signes of love and friendship they departed, seaven of them staying behind, that did helpe us to dig and carry Saxafras, and doe any thing they could, being of a comely proportion and the best condition of any Salvages we had yet incountred. They have no Beards but counterfeits, as they did thinke ours also was: for which they would have changed with some of our men that had great beards. Some of the baser sort would steale; but the better sort, we found very civill and just. We saw but three of their women, and they were but of meane stature, attyred in skins like the men, but fat and well favoured. The wholesomenesse and temperature of this climate, doth not onely argue the people to be answerable to this Description, but also of a perfect constitution of body, active, strong, healthfull, and very witty, as the sundry toyes by them so cunningly wrought may well testifie. For our selves, we found our selves rather increase in health and strength then otherwise; for all our toyle, bad dyet and lodging; yet not one of us was touched with any sicknesse. Twelve intended here a while to have stayed, but upon better consideration, how meanely we were provided, we left this Island (with as many true sorrowfull eyes as were before desirous to see it) the 18. of June, and arrived at Exmouth, the 23 of July.

But yet mans minde doth such it selfe explay,
As Gods great Will doth frame it every way.
And, Such thoughts men have, on earth that doe but live,
As men may crave, but God doth onely give.

—Written by John Brierton one of the Voyage

First Virginia Charter, 10 April 1606

James, by the grace of God [King of England, Scotland, France, and Ireland, Defender of the Faith], etc. Whereas our loving and weldisposed subjects, Sir Thomas Gates and Sir George Somers, Knightes; Richarde Hackluit, Clarke, Prebendarie of Westminster; and Edwarde Maria Winghfeilde, Thomas Hannam and Raleighe Gilberde, Esquiers; William Parker and George Popham, Gentlemen; and divers others of our loving subjects, have been humble sutors unto us that wee woulde vouchsafe unto them our licence to make habitacion, plantacion and to deduce a colonie of sondrie of our people into that parte of America commonly called Virginia, and other parts and territories in America either appartaining unto us or which are not nowe actuallie possessed by anie Christian prince or people, scituate, lying and being all along the sea coastes between fower and thirtie degrees of northerly latitude from the equinoctiall line and five and fortie degrees of the same latitude and in the maine lande betweene the same fower and thirtie and five and fourtie degrees, and the ilandes thereunto adjacente or within one hundred miles of the coaste thereof;

And to that ende, and for the more speedy accomplishemente of theire saide intended plantacion and habitacion there, are desirous to devide themselves into two severall colonies and companies, the one consisting of certaine Knightes, gentlemen, marchanntes and other adventurers of our cittie of London, and elsewhere, which are and from time to time shalbe joined unto them which doe desire to begin theire plantacions and habitacions in some fitt and conveniente place between fower and thirtie and one and fortie degrees of the said latitude all alongest the coaste of Virginia and coastes of America aforesaid and the other consisting of sondrie Knightes, gentlemen, merchanntes, and other adventurers of our citties of Bristoll and Exeter, and of our towne of Plymouthe, and of other places which doe joine themselves unto that colonie which doe desire to beginn theire plantacions and habitacions in some fitt and convenient place betweene eighte and thirtie degrees and five and fortie degrees of the saide latitude all alongst the saide coaste of Virginia and America as that coaste lieth;

Wee, greately commending and graciously accepting of theire desires to the furtherance of soe noble a worke which may, by the providence of Almightie God, hereafter tende to the glorie of His Divine Majestie in propagating of Christian religion to suche people as yet live in darkenesse and miserable ignorance of the true knoweledge and worshippe of God and may in tyme bring the infidels and salvages living in those parts to humane civilitie and to a setled and quiet govermente, doe by theise our lettres patents graciously accepte of and agree to theire humble and well intended desires;

And doe, therefore, for us, our heires and successors, grannte and agree that the saide Sir Thomas Gates, Sir George Sumers, Richarde Hackluit and Edwarde Maria Winghfeilde, adventurers of and for our cittie of London, and all suche others as are or shalbe joined unto them of that Colonie, shalbe called the Firste Colonie, and they shall and may beginne theire saide firste plantacion and seate of theire firste aboade and habitacion at anie place upon the saide coaste of Virginia or America where they shall thincke fitt and conveniente betweene the saide fower and thirtie and one and fortie degrees of the saide latitude; and that they shall have all the landes, woods, soile, groundes, havens, ports, rivers, mines, mineralls, marshes, waters, fishinges, commodities and hereditamentes whatsoever, from the said first seate of theire plantacion and habitacion by the space of fiftie miles of Englishe statute measure all alongest the saide coaste of Virginia and America towardes the weste and southe weste as the coaste lieth, with all the islandes within one hundred miles directlie over againste the same sea coaste; and alsoe all the landes, soile, groundes havens, ports, rivers, mines, mineralls, woods, marrishes [marshes], waters, fishinges, commodities and hereditamentes whatsoever, from the saide place of theire firste plantacion and habitacion for the space of fiftie like Englishe miles, all alongest the saide coaste of Virginia and America towardes the easte and northeaste [or toward the north] as the coaste lieth, together with all the islandes within one hundred miles directlie over againste the same sea coaste; and alsoe all the landes, woodes, soile, groundes, havens, portes, rivers, mines, mineralls, marrishes, waters, fishinges, commodities and hereditamentes whatsoever, from the same fiftie miles everie waie on the sea coaste directly into the maine lande by the space of one hundred like Englishe miles; and shall and may inhabit and remaine there; and shall and may alsoe builde and fortifie within anie the same for theire better safegarde and defence, according to theire best discrecions and the direction of the Counsell of that Colonie; and that noe other of our subjectes shalbe permitted or suffered to plante or inhabit behinde or on the backside of them towardes the maine lande, without the expresse licence or consente of the Counsell of that Colonie thereunto in writing firste had or obtained.

And wee doe likewise for us, our heires and successors, by theise presentes grannte and agree that the saide Thomas Hannam and Raleighe Gilberde, William Parker and George Popham, and all others of the towne of Plymouthe in the countie of Devon, or elsewhere, which are or shalbe joined unto them of that Colonie, shalbe called the Seconde Colonie; and that they shall and may beginne theire saide firste plantacion and seate of theire first aboade and habitacion at anie place upon the saide coaste of Virginia and America, where they shall thincke fitt and conveniente, betweene eighte and thirtie degrees of the saide latitude and five and fortie degrees of the same latitude; and that they shall have all the landes, soile, groundes, havens, ports, rivers, mines, mineralls, woods, marishes, waters, fishinges, commodities and hereditaments whatsoever, from the firste seate of theire plantacion and habitacion by the space of fiftie like Englishe miles, as is aforesaide, all alongeste the saide coaste of Virginia and America towardes the weste and southwest, or towardes the southe, as the coaste lieth, and all the islandes within one hundred miles directlie over againste the saide sea coaste; and alsoe all the landes, soile, groundes, havens, portes, rivers, mines, mineralls, woods, marishes, waters, fishinges, commodities and hereditamentes whatsoever, from the saide place of theire firste plantacion and habitacion for the space of fiftie like miles all alongest the saide coaste of Virginia and America towardes the easte and northeaste or towardes the northe, as the coaste liethe, and all the islandes alsoe within one hundred miles directly over againste the same sea coaste; and alsoe all the landes, soile, groundes, havens, ports, rivers, woodes, mines, mineralls, marishes, waters, fishings, commodities and hereditaments whatsoever, from the same fiftie miles everie waie on the sea coaste, directlie into the maine lande by the space of one hundred like Englishe miles; and shall and may inhabit and remaine there; and shall and may alsoe builde and fortifie within anie the same for theire better saufegarde according to theire beste discrecions and the direction of the Counsell of that Colonie; and that none of our subjectes shalbe permitted or suffered to plante or inhabit behinde or on the backe of them towardes the maine lande without the expresse licence or consente of the Counsell of that Colonie, in writing thereunto, firste had and obtained.

Provided alwaies, and our will and pleasure herein is, that the plantacion and habitacion of suche of the saide Colonies as shall laste plante themselves, as aforesaid, shall not be made within one hundred like Englishe miles of the other of them that firste beganne to make theire plantacion, as aforesaide.

And wee doe alsoe ordaine, establishe and agree for [us], our heires and successors, that eache of the saide Colonies shall have a Counsell which shall governe and order all matters and causes which shall arise, growe, or happen to or within the same severall Colonies, according to such lawes, ordinannces and instructions as shalbe in that behalfe, given and signed with our hande or signe manuell and passe under the Privie Seale of our realme of Englande; eache of which Counsells shall consist of thirteene parsons and to be ordained, made and removed from time to time according as shalbe directed and comprised in the same instructions; and shall have a severall seale for all matters that shall passe or concerne the same severall Counsells, eache of which seales shall have the Kinges armes engraven on the one side there of and his pourtraiture on the other; and that the seale for the Counsell of the saide Firste Colonie shall have engraven rounde about on the one side theise wordes: Sigillum Regis Magne Britanie, Francie [et] Hibernie; on the other side this inscripture rounde about: Pro Consillio Prime Colonie Virginie. And the seale for the Counsell of the saide Seconde Colonie shall alsoe have engraven rounde about the one side thereof the foresaide wordes: Sigillum Regis Magne Britanie, Francie [et] Hibernie; and on the other side: Pro Consilio Secunde Colonie Virginie.

And that alsoe ther shalbe a Counsell established here in Englande which shall in like manner consist of thirteen parsons to be, for that purpose, appointed by us, our heires and successors, which shalbe called our Counsell of Virginia; and shall from time to time have the superior managing and direction onelie of and for all matters that shall or may concerne the govermente, as well of the said severall Colonies as of and for anie other parte or place within the aforesaide precinctes of fower and thirtie and five and fortie degrees abovementioned; which Counsell shal in like manner have a seale for matters concerning the Counsell [or Colonies] with the like armes and purtraiture as aforesaide, with this inscription engraven rounde about the one side: Sigillum Regis Magne Britanie, Francie [et] Hibernie; and rounde about the other side: Pro Consilio Suo Virginie.

And more over wee doe grannte and agree for us, our heires and successors, that the saide severall Counsells of and for the saide severall Colonies shall and lawfully may by vertue hereof, from time to time, without interuption of us, our heires or successors, give and take order to digg, mine and searche for all manner of mines of goulde, silver and copper, as well within anie parte of theire saide severall Colonies as of the saide maine landes on the backside of the same Colonies; and to have and enjoy the goulde, silver and copper to be gotten there of to the use and behoofe of the same Colonies and the plantacions thereof; yeilding therefore yerelie to us, our heires and successors, the fifte parte onelie of all the same goulde and silver and the fifteenth parte of all the same copper soe to be gotten or had, as is aforesaid, and without anie other manner of profitt or accompte to be given or yeilded to us, our heires or successors, for or in respecte of the same.

And that they shall or lawfullie may establishe and cawse to be made a coine, to passe currant there betwene the people of those severall Colonies for the more ease of trafiique and bargaining betweene and amongest them and the natives there, of such mettall and in such manner and forme as the same severall Counsells there shall limitt and appointe. And wee doe likewise for us, our heires and successors, by theise presents give full power and auctoritie to the said Sir Thomas Gates, Sir George Sumers, Richarde Hackluit, Edwarde Maria Winghfeilde, Thomas Hannam, Raleighe Gilberde, William Parker and George Popham, and to everie of them, and to the saide severall Companies, plantacions and Colonies, that they and everie of them shall and may at all and everie time and times hereafter have, take and leade in the saide voyage, and for and towardes the saide severall plantacions and Colonies, and to travell thitherwarde and to abide and inhabit there in everie of the saide Colonies and plantacions, such and somanie of our subjectes as shall willinglie accompanie them, or anie of them, in the saide voyages and plantacions, with sufficiente shipping and furniture of armour, weapon, ordonnance, powder, victall, and all other thinges necessarie for the saide plantacions and for theire use and defence there: provided alwaies that none of the said parsons be such as hereafter shalbe speciallie restrained by us, our heires or successors.

Moreover, wee doe by theise presents, for us, our heires and successors, give and grannte licence unto the said Sir Thomas Gates, Sir George Sumers, Richarde Hackluite, Edwarde Maria Winghfeilde, Thomas Hannam, Raleighe Gilberde, William Parker and George Popham, and to everie of the said Colinies, that they and everie of them shall and may, from time to time and at all times for ever hereafter, for theire severall defences, incounter or expulse, repell and resist, aswell by sea as by lande, by all waies and meanes whatsoever, all and everie suche parson and parsons as without espiciall licence of the said severall Colonies and plantacions shall attempte to inhabit within the saide severall precincts and limitts of the saide severall Colonies and plantacions, or anie of them, or that shall enterprise or attempt at anie time hereafter the hurte, detrimente or annoyance of the saide severall Colonies or plantacions.

Giving and grannting by theise presents unto the saide Sir Thomas Gates, Sir George Somers, Richarde Hackluite, and Edwarde Maria Winghfeilde, and theire associates of the said Firste Colonie, and unto the said Thomas Hannam, Raleighe Gilberde, William Parker and George Popham, and theire associates of the saide Second Colonie, and to everie of them from time to time and at all times for ever hereafter, power and auctoritie to take and surprize by all waies and meanes whatsoever all and everie parson and parsons with theire shipps, vessels, goods and other furniture, which shalbe founde traffiqueing into anie harbor or harbors, creeke, creekes or place within the limitts or precincts of the saide severall Colonies and plantacions, not being of the same Colonie, untill such time as they, being of anie realmes or dominions under our obedience, shall paie or agree to paie to the handes of the Tresorer of the Colonie, within whose limitts and precincts theie shall soe traffique, twoe and a halfe upon anie hundred of anie thing soe by them traffiqued, boughte or soulde; and being strangers and not subjects under our obeysannce, untill they shall paie five upon everie hundred of suche wares and commoditie as theie shall traffique, buy or sell within the precincts of the saide severall Colonies wherein theie shall soe traffique, buy or sell, as aforesaide; which sommes of money or benefitt, as aforesaide, for and during the space of one and twentie yeres nexte ensuing the date hereof shalbe whollie imploied to the use, benefitt and behoofe of the saide severall plantacions where such trafficque shalbe made; and after the saide one and twentie yeres ended the same shalbe taken to the use of us, our heires and successors by such officer and minister as by us, our heires and successors shalbe thereunto assigned or appointed.

And wee doe further, by theise presentes, for us, our heires and successors, give and grannte unto the saide Sir Thomas Gates, Sir George Sumers, Richarde Hackluit, and Edwarde Maria Winghfeilde, and to theire associates of the saide Firste Colonie and plantacion, and to the saide Thomas Hannam, Raleighe Gilberde, William Parker and George Popham, and theire associates of the saide Seconde Colonie and plantacion, that theie and everie of them by theire deputies, ministers and factors may transport the goods, chattells, armor, munition and furniture, needfull to be used by them for theire saide apparrell, defence or otherwise in respecte of the saide plantacions, out of our realmes of Englande and Irelande and all other our dominions from time to time, for and during the time of seaven yeres nexte ensuing the date hereof for the better releife of the said severall Colonies and plantacions, without anie custome, subsidie or other dutie unto us, our heires or successors to be yeilded or paide for the same.

Alsoe wee doe, for us, our heires and successors, declare by theise presentes that all and everie the parsons being our subjects which shall dwell and inhabit within everie or anie of the saide severall Colonies and plantacions and everie of theire children which shall happen to be borne within the limitts and precincts of the said severall Colonies and plantacions shall have and enjoy all liberties, franchises and immunites within anie of our other dominions to all intents and purposes as if they had been abiding and borne within this our realme of Englande or anie other of our saide dominions.

Moreover our gracious will and pleasure is, and wee doe by theise presents, for us, our heires and successors, declare and sett forthe, that if anie parson or parsons which shalbe of anie of the said Colonies and plantacions or anie other, which shall trafficque to the saide Colonies and plantacions or anie of them, shall at anie time or times hereafter transporte anie wares, marchandize or commodities out of [any] our dominions with a pretence and purpose to lande, sell or otherwise dispose the same within anie the limitts and precincts of anie of the saide Colonies and plantacions, and yet nevertheles being at the sea or after he hath landed the same within anie of the said Colonies and plantacions, shall carrie the same into any other forraine countrie with a purpose there to sell or dispose of the same without the licence of us, our heires or successors in that behalfe first had or obtained, that then all the goods and chattels of the saide parson or parsons soe offending and transporting, together with the said shippe or vessell wherein suche transportacion was made, shall be forfeited to us, our heires and successors.

Provided alwaies, and our will and pleasure is and wee doe hereby declare to all Christian kinges, princes and estates, that if anie parson or parsons which shall hereafter be of anie of the said severall Colonies and plantacions, or anie other, by his, theire, or anie of theire licence or appointment, shall at anie time or times hereafter robb or spoile by sea or by lande or doe anie acte of unjust and unlawfull hostilitie to anie the subjects of us, our heires or successors, or anie of the subjects of anie king, prince, ruler, governor or state being then in league or amitie with us, our heires or successors, and that upon suche injurie or upon juste complainte of such prince, ruler, governor or state or their subjects, wee, our heires or successors, shall make open proclamation within anie the ports of our realme of Englande, commodious for that purpose, that the saide parson or parsons having committed anie such robberie or spoile shall, within the terme to be limitted by suche proclamations, make full restitucion or satisfaction of all suche injuries done, soe as the saide princes or others soe complained may houlde themselves fully satisfied and contented; and that if the saide parson or parsons having committed such robberie or spoile shall not make or cause to be made satisfaction accordingly with[in] such time soe to be limitted, that then it shalbe lawfull to us, our heires and successors to put the saide parson or parsons having committed such robberie or spoile and theire procurers, abbettors or comfortors out of our allegeannce and protection; and that it shalbe lawefull and free for all princes and others to pursue with hostilitie the saide offenders and everie of them and theire and everie of theire procurors, aiders, abbettors and comforters in that behalfe.

And finallie wee doe, for us, our heires and successors, grannte and agree, to and with the saide Sir Thomas Gates, Sir George Sumers, Richarde Hackluit and Edwarde Maria Winghfeilde, and all other of the saide Firste Colonie, that wee, our heires or successors, upon peticion in that behalfe to be made, shall, by lettres patents under the Greate [Seale] of Englande, give and grannte unto such parsons, theire heires and assignees, as the Counsell of that Colonie or the most part of them shall for that purpose nomminate and assigne, all the landes, tenements and hereditaments which shalbe within the precincts limitted for that Colonie, as is aforesaid, to be houlden of us, our heires and successors as of our mannor of Eastgreenwiche in the countie of Kente, in free and common soccage onelie and not in capite.

And doe, in like manner, grannte and agree, for us, our heires and successors, to and with the saide Thomas Hannam, Raleighe Gilberd, William Parker and George Popham, and all others of the saide Seconde Colonie, that wee, our heires [and] successors, upon petition in that behalfe to be made, shall, by lettres patentes under the Great Seale of Englande, give and grannte unto such parsons, theire heires and assignees, as the Counsell of that Colonie or the most parte of them shall for that purpose nomminate and assigne, all the landes, tenementes and hereditaments which shalbe within the precinctes limited for that Colonie as is afore said, to be houlden of us, our heires and successors as of our mannor of Eastgreenwich in the countie of Kente, in free and common soccage onelie and not in capite.

All which landes, tenements and hereditaments soe to be passed by the saide severall lettres patents, shalbe, by sufficient assurances from the same patentees, soe distributed and devided amongest the undertakers for the plantacion of the said severall Colonies, and such as shall make theire plantacion in either of the said severall Colonies, in such manner and forme and for such estates as shall [be] ordered and sett [downe] by the Counsell of the same Colonie, or the most part of them, respectively, within which the same lands, tenements and hereditaments shall ly or be. Althoughe expresse mencion [of the true yearly value or certainty of the premises, or any of them, or of any other gifts or grants, by us or any our progenitors or predecessors, to the aforesaid Sir Thomas Gates, Knt. Sir George Somers, Knt. Richard Hackluit, Edward-Maria Wingfield, Thomas Hanham, Ralegh Gilbert, William Parker, and George Popham, or any of them, heretofore made, in these presents, is not made; or any statute, act, ordnance, or provision, proclamation, or restraint, to the contrary hereof had, made, ordained, or any other thing, cause, or matter whatsoever, in any wise notwithstanding.] In witnesse wherof [we have caused these our letters to be made patents;] witnesse our selfe at Westminister the xth day of Aprill [1606, in the fourth year of our reign of England, France, and Ireland, and of Scotland the nine and thirtieth.]

[Lukin]
Exactum per breve de private sigillo [etc.]

Instructions for the Virginia Colony, 1606

Instructions Given by way of Advice by us whom it hath pleased the kings Maj[est]ie to appoint of the Counsel for the intended Voyage to Virginia to be Observed By those Captains and Company which are Sent at this [pre]sent to plant there—

As We Doubt not but you will have especial Care to Observe the Ordinances set Down by the King's Ma[jes]tie and Delivered unto you under the privy Seal So for your better Directions upon your first Landing we have thought Good to recommend unto your care these Instructions and articles following.

When it Shall please God to Send You on the Coast of Virginia you shall Do your best Endeavour to find out a Safe port in the Entrance of Some navigable River, making Choise of Such a One as runneth furthest into the Land. and if you happen to Discover Divers portable Rivers and amongst them any one that hath two main branches if the Difference be not Great make Choise of that which bendeth most towards the Northwest for that way you shall You soonest find the Other Sea.

When You have made Choice of the River on which you mean to Settle be not hasty in Landing Your Victual and Munitions but first Let Capt. [Christopher] Newport Discover how far that River may be found navigable that you may make Election of the Strongest most fertile and wholesome place for if You make many Removes besides the Loss of time You Shall Greatly Spoil your Victuals and Your Cask and with Great pain transport it in Small Boats.

But if You Choose your place so far up as A Bark of fifty tuns will float then you may Lay all Your provisions a Shore with Ease and the better Receive the trade of all the Countries about you in the Land and Such A place you may perchance find a hundred Miles from the Rivers mouth and the farther up the better for if you sit Down near the Entrance Except it be in Some Island that is Strong by nature An Enemy that may approach you on Even Ground may Easily pull You Out and if he be Driven to seek You a hundred miles within the Land in boats you shall from both Sides of your River where it is Narrowest So beat them with Your muskets as they shall never be Able to prevail Against You.

And to the end That You be not Surprised as the French were in Florida by Melindus and the Spaniard in the same place by the french you shall Do well to make this Double provision first Erect a Little Stoure at the mouth of the River that may Lodge Some ten men With Whom You Shall Leave a Light boat that when any fleet shall be in Sight they may Come with Speed to Give You Warning. Secondly you must in no Case Suffer any of the natural people of the Country to inhabit between You and the Sea Coast for you Cannot Carry Your Selves so towards them but they will Grow Discontented with Your habitation and be ready to Guide and Assist any Nation that Shall Come to invade You and if You neglect this You neglect Your Safety.—

When You have Discovered as far up the River as you mean to plant Your Selves and Landed your victuals and munitions to the End that Every man may know his Charge you Shall Do well to Divide your Six Score men into three parts whereof One party of them you may appoint to fortifie and build of which your first work must be your Storehouse for Victual so Others you may imploy in preparing your Ground, and Sowing your Corn and Roots the Other ten of these forty you must Leave as Centinel at the havens mouth The Other forty you may imploy for two Months in Discovery of the River above you And on the Contrary about you which Charge—Captain Newport and Captain Gosnold may undertake of these forty Discoverers when they Do Espie any high Lands or hills Capt. Gosnold may take 20. of the Company to Cross Over the Lands and Carrying half A Dozen pickaxes to try if they can find any mineral The Other twenty may Go on by River and pitch up boughs upon the Banks Side by which the Other boats Shall follow them by the same turnings You may also take with them a Wherry Such as is Used here in the Thames by Which You may Send back to the President for Supply of munition or any Other want that you not Drive in to Return for Every Small Defect—

You must Observe if you Can Whether the River on which You Plant Doth Spring out of Mountains or out of Lakes if it be out of any Lake the passage to the Other Sea will be the more Easy & it is Like Enough that Out of the same Lake you shall find Some Spring which run the Contrary way toward the East India Sea for the Great and famous River of Volga Tanis [Don River] & Dwina [Dvina River] have three heads near joyn'd and Yet the One falleth into the Caspian Sea the Other into the Euxine Sea [Black Sea] and the third into the Polonian Sea [Baltic Sea].

In All Your Passages you must have Great Care not to Offend the naturals if You Can Eschew it and imploy Some few of your Company to trade with them for Corn and all Other lasting Victuals if you have any and this you must

Do before that they perceive you mean to plant among them for not being Sure how your own Seed Corn will prosper the first Year to avoid the Danger of famine use and Endeavour to Store yourselves of the Country Corn.

Your Discoverers that passes Over Land with hired Guides must Look well to them that they Slip not from them and for more Assurance let them take a Compass with them and Write Down how far they Go upon Every point of the Compass for that Country having no way nor path if that Your Guides Run from You in the Great Woods or Deserts you Shall hardly Ever find A Passage back.

And how Weary Soever your Soldiers be Let them never trust the Country people with the Carriage of their Weapons for if they Run from You with Your Shott which they only fear they will Easily kill them all with their Arrows.

And whensoever any of Yours Shoots before them be sure they be Chosen out of your best Marksmen for if they See Your Learners miss What they aim at they will think the Weapon not So terrible and thereby Will be bould to Assault You.

Above all things Do not advertize the killing of any of your men that the Country people may know it if they Perceive they are but Common men and that with the Loss of many of theirs they may Deminish any part of Yours they will make many Adventures upon You if the Country be populous you Shall Do well Also not to Let them See or know of Your Sick men if You have any which may also Encourage them to many Enterprizes.

You must take Especial Care that You Choose a Seat for habitation that Shall not be over burthened with Woods near your town for all the men You have Shall not he able to Cleanse twenty Acres in a Year besides that it may Serve for a Covert for Your Enemies round about You neither must You plant in a low and moist place because it will prove unhealthfull You shall Judge of the Good Air by the People for Some part of that Coast where the Lands are Low have their people Clear Eyed and with Swollen bellies and Legs but if the naturals he Strong and Clean made it is a true sign of a wholesome Soil.

You must take Order to Draw up the Pinnace that is Left with You under your fort and take her Sails and Anchors A Shore all but a Small Ledge [kedge] to ride by Least Some ill Disposed Persons Slip away with her.

You must take Care that your Marriners that Go for wages Do not marr your trade for those that mind not to inhabite, for a Little Gain will Debase the Estimation of Exchange and hinder the trade for Ever after and therefore you Shall not admit or Suffer any person whatsoever other than Such as Shall be appointed by the president and Counsel there to buy any merchandizes or Other things Whatsoever.

It Were Necessary that all Your Carpenters and Other such like Workmen about building Do first build Your Storehouse and those Other Rooms of Publick and necessary Use before any house be Set up for any private person and though the Workman may belong to Any private persons yet Let them all Work together first for the Company and then for private men.

And Seeing order is at the same price with confusion it shall be adviseably done to Set your houses Even and by a line that You Streets may have a Good breadth & be carried Square about your market place and Every Streets End

Opening into it that from thence with a few feild peices you may Command Every street throughout which marketplace you may also fortify if you shall think it needfull.

You Shall do well to Send a perfect relation by Capt. Newport of all that is Done what height You are Seated how far into the Land what Comodities you find what Soil Woods and their Several Kinds and So of all Other things Else to advertise [per]ticularly and to Suffer no man to return but by pasport from the president and counsel nor to write any Letter of any thing that may Discourage others.

Lastly & Chiefly the way to prosper and to Obtain Good Success is to make your Selves all of one mind for the Good of Your Country & your Own and to Serve & fear God the Giver of all Goodness for Every plantation which our heavenly father hath not planted shall be rooted Out.

First Residents of Jamestown, 1607

On 13 May 1607, three English ships, the Susan Constant, *the* Godspeed, *and the* Discovery, *with approximately 144 settlers and sailors, landed in the New World, where they planted the first permanent English colony in North America. Established by the Virginia Company of London, this settlement would be called Jamestown, after King James I. On 15 June 1607, the fleet commander, Captain Christopher Newport, returned to England, leaving 104 settlers. Later, two supplies of settlers followed, consisting of approximately 120 and 70 persons, respectively. Although the names and numbers vary somewhat in the primary sources, the following contains the names of all known settlers.*

Original Settlers

Councell

Master Edward Maria Wingfield
Captaine John Smyth
Captaine John Martin
Captaine Bartholomew Gosnoll
Captaine John Ratliffe
Captaine George Kendall

Preacher

Master Robert Hunt

Gentlemen

Master George Percie
Captaine Gabriell Archer
Robert Fenton
William Bruster
Thomas Jacob
John Brookes
Thomas Sands
Anthony Gosnoll
George Flower
Robert Ford
Edward Harrington
Dru Pickhouse
Ellis Kingston
Benjamin Beast

John Robinson (Jehu Robinsonin)
Ustis Clovill (Eustace)
Kellam Throgmorton
Edward Morish
Edward Browne
John Penington
George Walker
Richard Crofts
Thomas Webbe
John Short
William Smethes
Richard Simons
Richard Dixon
George Martin
Anthony Gosnold
John Stevenson
Francis Midwinter
Thomas Mouton
Stephen Halthrop
Nathaniell Powell
Nathaniell Powell
Robert Behethland
Jeremy Alicock
Thomas Studley
Nicholas Houlgrave
John Waler (Waller)
William Tanker (Tankard)
Francis Snarsbrough
Edward Brookes
John Martin
Roger Cooke
Thomas Wotton, Surgeon
Thomas Gore
Richard Frith

Carpenters

William Laxon
Thomas Emry
Anas Todkill
Edward Pising
Robert Small
John Capper

Blacksmith

James Read

Sailer

Jonas Profit

Barber

Thomas Couper (Cowper)

Bricklayers

John Herd
William Garret

Mason

Edward Brinto

Taylor

William Love

Drum

Nicholas Skot (Scot)

Chirurgeon

William Wilkinson

Labourers

John Laydon
George Cassen
William Rods (Rodes)
Ould Edward (Old)
George Golding
William Johnson
William Wickinson, Surgeon
Samuell Collier
James Brumfield
William Cassen
Thomas Cassen
William White
Henry Tavin
John Dods
William Unger

Boyes

Nathaniel Peacock (Nathaniell Pecock)
Richard Mutton

With divers others (to the number of 100)

First Supply

Appointed to be of the Councell

Matthew Scrivner (Mathew Scrivener)

Gentlemen

Michaell Phetyplace (Phittiplace)
Ralfe Morton (Ralph)
Richard Wyffin (Wyffing)
Richard Fetherstone
George Pretty
John Taverner
Michaell Sickelmore
Thomas Coo (Coe)
Richard Killingbeck
William Causey
Richard Worley
William Bayley
Richard Molynex (Mullinax)
Jefrey Abots (Jeffrey Abbot)
Timothy Leds (Leeds)
George Forest
William Gryvill (Grivell)
William Phetyplace (Phittiplace)
William Cantrill (Cantrell)
Robert Barnes
George Hill
Nathaniell Causy
Robert Cutler
William Bentley
Peter Pory
William Spence
Doctor Russell
Richard Prodger
Francis Perkins (the elder)
Richard Pots
John Harper
Edward Gurganay (Gurgana)
John Nickoles (Nichols)

Jeweller

Daniell Stalling (Daniel Stallings)

Refiners

William Dawson
William Johnson
Abraham Ransacke (Abram Ransack)
Richard Belfield

A gunner

Peter Keffer

A Perfumer

Robert Alberton

Labourers

Raymond Goodyson (Goodison)
William Spence
William Simons
John Bouth
William Burket
Nicholas Ven
Francis Perkins (the elder)
William Bentley
Rowland Nelstrop (Rawland)
Thomas Salvage (Savage)
William May
Michaell
John Speareman (Spearman)
Richard Brislow (Bristow)
James Watkins
Christopher Rods
James Burre
William Perce
Francis Perkins (the younger)
Richard Gradon
Richard Salvage (Savage)
Richard Miler (Milmer)
Vere (Master)
Bishop Wyles

Tailers

John Powell
William Beckwith
Laurence Towtales
Thomas Hope
William Yonge (Yong)
William Ward

Apothecaries

Christopher Rodes (Rods)
Richard Fetherstone
Thomas Feld (Field)
James Watkings (Watkins)
James Burne (Burre)
John Harford

A Surgeon

Post Gittnat (Ginnat)

A Couper

John Lewes (Cooper)

A Tobacco-pipe-maker

Robert Cotton

A Blackesmith

Richard Dole

With divers others (to the number 120)

Second Supply

Were appointed to bee of the Councell

Captaine Peter Winne
Captaine Richard Waldo

Gentlemen

Master Francis West
Rawley Chroshaw
John Russell
William Russell
William Sambage
Henry Ley (Leigh)
Daniell Tucker (Daniel)
John Hoult
George Yarington
Henry Philpot
Michaell Lowicke (Michael Lowick)
Thomas Forest (Forrest)
John Dauxe
Thomas Graves
Gabriell Bedle (Gabriel Beadle)
John Bedle (Beadle)
John Gudderington (Cuderington)
Henry Collings (Collins)
Harmon Haryson (Harrison)
Hugh Wollystone (Wolleston)
Thomas Norton
George Burton
Thomas Maxes
Master Hunt
William Dowman
Thomas Abbey (Abbay)

Tradesmen

Thomas Phelps
John Clarke
Dionis Oconor
David ap Hugh
John Burras
Henry Bell
David Ellys (Ellis)
John Prat
Jefry Shortridge (Jeffrey)
Hugh Wynne (Winne)
Thomas Bradley
Thomas Lavander
Master Powell
Thomas Gipson (Gibson)

Laborers

Thomas Dowse (Dawse)
William Taler (Tayler)
Nicholas Hancock
Williams
Morrell (Morley, Morrell)
Scot
Thomas Mallard
Thomas Fox
Walker
Floud
Rose
Hardwin (Hardwyn)

Boys

Milman
Hellyard (Hilliard)

Mistresse Forrest, and Anne Burras her maide, eight Dutch men and poles, with some others (to the number of seventy persons, etc.)

Observations by Master George Percy, 1607

Observations gathered out of a Discourse of the Plantation of the Southerne Colonie in Virginia by the English, 1606. Written by that Honorable Gentleman, Master George Percy.

ON Saturday the twentieth of December in the yeere 1606. the fleet fell from London, and the fift of January we anchored in the Downes; but the winds continued contrarie for so long, that we were forced to stay there some time, where wee suffered great stormes, but by the skilfulnesse of the Captaine wee suffered no great losse or danger.

The twelfth day of February at night we saw a blazing Starre, and presently a storme.

The three and twentieth day we fell with the Iland of Mattanenio, in the West Indies. The foure and twentieth day we anchored at Dominico, within fourteene degrees of the Line, a very fair Iland, the Trees full of sweet and good smels, inhabited by many Savage Indians. They were at first very scrupulous to come aboord us. Wee learned of them afterwards that the Spaniards had given them a great overthrow on this Ile, but when they knew what we were, there came many to our ships with their Canoas, bringing us many kinds of sundry fruits, as Pines, Potatoes, Plantons, Tobacco, and other fruits, and Roane Cloth abundance, which they had gotten out of certaine Spanish ships that were cast away upon that Iland. We gave them Knives, Hatchets for exchange, which they esteeme much. Wee also gave them Beades, Copper Jewels which they hang through their nosthrils, eares, and lips, very strange to behold. Their bodies are all painted red to keepe away the biting of Muscetos. They goe all naked without covering. The haire of their head is a yard long, all of a length, pleated in three plats hanging downe to their wastes. They suffer no haire to grow on their faces. They cut their skinnes in divers workes. They are continually in warres, and will eate their enemies when they kill them, or any stranger if they take them. They will lap up mans spittle, whilst one spits in their mouthes, in a barbarous fashion like Dogges. These people and the rest of the Ilands in the West Indies, and Brasill, are called by the names of Canibals, that will eate mans flesh. These people doe poyson their Arrow heads, which are made of a fishes bone. They worship the Devill for their God, and have no other beliefe.

Whilest we remayned at this Iland we saw a Whale chased by a Thresher and a Sword-fish. They fought for the space of two houres. We might see the Thresher with his flayle lay on the monstrous blowes which was strange to behold. In the end these two fishes brought the Whale to her end.

The sixe and twentieth day we had sight of Marigalanta, and the next day, wee sailed with a slacke saile alongst the Ile of Guadalupa, where we went ashore, and found a Bath which was so hot, that no man was able to stand long by it. Our Admirall, Captaine Newport, caused a piece of Porke to be put in it; which boyled it so in the space of halfe, as no fire could mend it. Then we went aboord and sailed by many Ilands, as Mounserot and an Iland called Saint Christopher, both uninhabited. About two o'clocke in the afternoone wee anchored at the Ile of Mevis [Nevis]. There the Captaine landed all his men being well fitted with

Muskets and other convenient Armes; marched a mile into the Woods; being commanded to stand upon their guard, fearing the treacherie of the Indians, which is an ordinary use amongst them and all other Savages on this Ile. We came to a Bath standing in a Valley betwixt two Hils, where wee bathed our selves; and found it to be of the nature of the Bathes in England, some places hot and some colder: and men may refresh themselves as they please. Finding this place to be so convenient for our men to avoid diseases which will breed in so long a Voyage, wee incamped our selves on this Ile sixe dayes, and spent none of our ships victuall, by reason our men some went a hunting, some a fouling, and some a fishing, where we got great store of Conies, sundry kinds of fowles, and great plentie of fish. We kept Centinels and Courts de gard at every Captaines quarter, fearing wee should be assaulted by the Indians, that were on the other side of the Iland. Wee saw none, nor were molested by any; but some few we saw as we were a hunting on the Iand. They would not come to us by any meanes, but ranne swiftly through the Woods to the Mountaine tops; so we lost the sight of them; whereupon we made all the haste wee could to our quarter, thinking there had beene a great ambush of Indians there abouts. We past into the thickest of the Woods, where we had almost lost our selves. We had not gone above halfe a mile amongst the thicke, but we came into a most pleasant Garden, being a hundred paces square on every side, having many Cotton-trees growing in it with abundance of Cotton-wooll, and many *Guiacum* trees. Wee saw the goodliest tall trees growing so thicke about the Garden, as though they had beene set by Art, which made us marvell very much to see it.

The third day wee set saile from Mevis. The fourth day we sailed along by Castutia [St. Eustatius} and by Saba [Saba, Dutch Carribean Islands]. This day we anchored at the Ile of Virgines in an excellent Bay able to harbour a hundred Ships. If this Bay stood in England, it would be a great profit and commoditie to the Land. On this Iland wee caught great store of Fresh-fish, and abundance of Sea Tortoises, which served all our Fleet three daies, which were in number eight score persons. We also killed great store of wild Fowle. Wee cut the Barkes of certaine Trees which tasted much like Cinnamon, and very hot in the mouth. This Iland in some places hath very good ground, straight and tall Timber. But the greatest discommoditie that wee have seene on this Iland is that it hath no Fresh-water, which makes the place void of any Inhabitants.

Upon the sixt day, we set saile and passed by Becam and by Saint John de porto rico. The seventh day we arrived at Mona: where wee watered, which we stood in great need of, seeing that our water did smell so vildly that none of our men was able to indure it. Whilst some of the Saylers were a filling the Caskes with water, the Captaine and the rest of the Gentlemen, and other Soldiers, marched up in the Ile sixe myles, thinking to find some other provision to maintaine our victualling. As we marched we killed two wild Bores, and saw a huge wild Bull, his homes was an ell betweene the two tops. We also killed Guanas in fashion of a Serpent, and speckled like a Toade under the belly. These wayes that wee went, being so troublesome and vilde, going upon the sharpe Rockes, that many of our men fainted in the march, but by good fortune wee lost none but one Edward Brookes Gentleman, whose fat melted within him by the great heate and drought of the Countrey. We were not able to relieve him nor our selves, so he died in that great extreamitie.

The ninth day, in the afternoone, we went off with our Boat to the Ile of Moneta, some three leagues from Mona, where we had a terrible landing, and a troublesome getting up to the top of the Mountaine or Ile, being a high firme Rocke, ste[e]p, with many terrible sharpe stones. After wee got to the top of the Ile, we found it to bee a fertill and a plaine ground, full of goodly grasse, and abundance of Fowles of all kindes. They flew over our heads as thicke as drops of Hale; besides they made such a noise, that wee were not able to heare one another speake. Furthermore, wee were not able to set our feet on the ground, but either on Fowles or Egges which lay so thicke in the grasse. Wee laded two Boats full in the space of three houres, to our great refreshing.

The tenth day we set saile, and disimboged out of the West Indies, and bare oure course Northerly. The fourteenth day we passed the Tropicke of Cancer. The one and twentieth day, about five a clocke at night there began a vehement tempest, which lasted all the night, with winds, raine, and thunders, in a terrible manner. Wee were forced to lie at Hull that night, because we thought wee had beene neerer land then wee were. The next morning, being the two and twentieth day, wee sounded; and the three and twentieth, and foure and twenteth day; but we could find no ground. The five and twentieth day, we sounded, and had no ground at an hundred fathom. The six and twentieth day of Aprill, about foure a clocke in the morning, wee descried the Land of Virginia. The same day wee entred into the Bay of Chesupioc directly, without any let or hinderance. There wee landed and discovered a little way, but wee could find nothing worth the speaking of, but faire meddowes and goodly tall Trees, with such Fresh-waters running through the woods, as I was almost ravished at the first sight thereof.

At night, when wee were going aboard, there came the Savages creeping upon all foure, from the Hills, like Beares, with their Bowes in their mouthes, charged us very desperately in the faces, hurt Captaine Gabrill Archer in both his hands, and a sayler in two places of the body very dangerous. After they had spent their Arrowes, and felt the sharpnesse of our shot, they retired into the Woods with a great noise, and so left us.

The seven and twentieth day we began to build up our Shallop. The Gentlemen and Souldiers marched eight miles up into the land. We could not see a Savage in all that march. We came to a place where they had made a great fire, and had beene newly a resting Oysters. When they perceived our comming, they fled away to the mountaines, and left many of the Oysters in the fire. We eat some of the Oysters, which were very large and delicate in taste.

The eighteenth day we lanched our Shallop. The Captaine and some Gentlemen went in her, and discovered up the Bay. We found a River on the Southside running into the Maine; we entered it and found it very shoald water, not for any Boats to swim. Wee went further into the Bay, and saw a plaine plot of ground where we went on Land, and found the place five mile in compasse, without either Bush or Tree. We saw nothing there but a Cannow, which was made out of the whole tree, which was five and fortie foot long by the Rule. Upon this plot of ground we got good store of Mussels and Oysters, which lay on the ground as thicke as stones. Wee opened some, and found in many of them Pearles. Wee marched some three or foure miles further into the woods, where we saw great smoakes of fire. Wee marched to those smoakes and found that the Savages had beene there burning downe the grasse, as wee thought either to make their plantation there, or else to give signes to bring their forces together, and so to give us battell. We past through excellent ground full of Flowers of divers kinds and colours, and as goodly trees as I have seene, as Cedar, Cipresse, and other kindes. Going a little further we came into a little plat of ground full of fine and beautifull Strawberries, foure times bigger and better then ours in England. All this march we could neither see Savage nor Towne. When it grew to be towards night, we stood backe to our Ships, we sounded and found it shallow water for a great way, which put us out of all hopes for getting any higher with our Ships, which road at the mouth of the River. Wee rowed over to a point of Land, where wee found a channell, and sounded six, eight, ten, or twelve fathom: which put us in good comfort. Therefore wee named that point of Land, Cape Comfort.

The nine and twentieth day we set up a Crosse at Chesupioc Bay, and named that place Cape Henry. Thirtieth day, we came with our ships to Cape Comfort; where we saw five Savages running on the shoare. Presently the Captaine caused the shallop to be manned; so rowing to the shoare, the Captaine called to them in signe of friendship, but they were at first very timersome, until they saw the Captain lay his hand on his heart; upon that they laid downe their Bowes and Arrowes, and came very boldly to us, making signes to come a shoare to their Towne, which is called by the Savages Kecoughtan. Wee coasted to their Towne, rowing over a River running into the Maine, where these Savages swam over with their Bowes and Arrowes in their mouthes.

When we came over to the other side, there was a many of other Savages which directed us to their Towne, where we were entertained by them very kindly. When we came first a Land they made a dolefull noise, laying their faces to the ground, scratching the earth with their nailes. We did thinke they had beene at their Idolatry. When they had ended their Ceremonies, they went into their houses and brought out mats and laid upon the ground: the chiefest of them sate all in a rank; the meanest sort brought us such dainties as they had, and of their bread which they make of their Maiz or Gennea wheat. They would not suffer us to eat unlesse we sate down, which we did on a Mat right against them. After we were well satisfied they gave us of their Tabacco, which they tooke in a pipe made artifically of earth as ours are, but far bigger, with the bowle fashioned together with a piece of fine copper. After they had feasted us, they shewed us, in welcome, their manner of dancing, which was in this fashion. One of the Savages standing in the midst singing, beating one hand against another, all the rest dancing about him, shouting, howling, and stamping against the ground, with many Anticke tricks and faces, making noise like so many Wolves or Devils. One thing of them I observed; when they were in their dance they kept stroke with their feet just one with another, but with their hands, heads, faces and bodies, every one of them had a severall gesture: so they continued for the space of halfe an houre. When they had ended their dance, the Captaine gave them Beades and other trifling Jewells. They hang through their eares, Fowles legs; they shave the right side of their heads with a shell, the left side they weare of an ell long tied up with an artificiall knot, with a many of Foules feathers sticking in it. They goe altogether naked, but their privities are covered with Beasts skinnes beset commonly with little bones, or beasts teeth. Some paint their bodies blacke, some red, with artificiall knots of sundry lively colours, very beautiful and pleasing to the eye, in a braver fashion then they in the West Indies.

The fourth day of May we came to the King or Werowance of Paspihe: where they entertained us with much welcome. An old Savage made a long Oration, making a foule noise, uttering his speech with a vehement action, but we knew little what they meant. Whilst we were in company with the Paspihes, the Werowance of Rapahanna came from the other side of the River in his Cannoa. He seemed to take displeasure of our being with the Paspihes. He would faine have had us come to his Towne. The Captaine was unwilling. Seeing that the day was so far spent, he returned backe to his ships for that night.

The next day, being the fift of May, the Werowance of Rapahanna sent a Messenger to have us come to him. We entertained the said Messenger, and gave him trifles which pleased him. Wee manned our shallop with Muskets and Targatiers sufficiently: this said Messenger guided us where our determination was to goe. When wee landed, the Werowance of Rapahanna came downe to the water side with all his traine, as goodly men as any I have seene of Savages or Christians: the Werowance comming before them playing on a Flute made of a Reed, with a Crown of Deares haire colloured red, in fashion of a Rose fastened about his knot of haire, and a great Plate of Copper on the other side of his head, with two long Feathers in fashion of a paire of Homes placed in the midst of his Crowne. His body was painted all with Crimson, with a Chaine of Beads about his necke, his face painted blew, besprinkled with silver Ore as wee thought, his eares all behung with Braslets of Pearle, and in either eare a Birds Claw through it beset with fine Copper or Gold. He entertained us in so modest a proud fashion, as though he had beene a Prince of civill government, holding his countenance without laughter or any such ill behaviour. He caused his Mat to be spred on the ground, where hee sate downe with a great Majestie, taking a pipe of Tabacco: the rest of his company standing about him. After he had rested a while he rose, and made signes to us to come to his Towne. Hee went foremost, and all the rest of his people and our selves followed him up a steepe Hill where his Palace was settled. Wee passed through the Woods in fine paths, having most pleasant Springs which issued from the Mountaines. Wee also went through the goodliest Come fieldes that ever was seene in any Countrey. When wee came to Rapahannos Towne, hee entertained us in good humanitie.

The eight day of May we discovered up the River. We landed in the Countrey of Apamatica. At our landing, there came many stout and able Savages to resist us with their Bowes and Arrowes, in a most warlike manner, with the swords at their backes beset with sharpe stones, and pieces of yron able to cleave a man in sunder. Amongst the rest one of the chiefest, standing before them cross-legged, with his Arrow readie in his Bow in one hand, and taking a Pipe of Tobacco in the other, with a bold uttering of his speech, demanded of us our being there, willing us to bee gone. Wee made signes of peace, which they perceived in the end, and let us land in quietnesse.

The twelfth day we went backe to our ships, and discovered a point of Land, called Archers Hope, which was sufficient with a little labour to defend our selves against any Enemy. The soile was good and fruitfull, with excellent good

Timber. There are also great store of Vines in bignesse of a mans thigh, running up to the tops of the Trees in great abundance. We also did see many Squirels, Conies, Black Birds with crimson wings, and divers other Fowles and Birds of divers and sundrie collours of crimson, Watchet, Yellow, Greene, Murry, and of divers other hewes naturally without any art using.

We found store of Turkie nests and many Egges. If it had not beene disliked, because the ship could not ride neere the shoare, we had setled there to all the Collonies contentment.

The thirteenth day, we came to our seating place in Paspihas Countrey, some eight miles from the point of Land, which I made mention before: where our shippes doe lie so neere the shoare that they are moored to the Trees in six fathom water.

The fourteenth day, we landed all our men, which were set to worke about the fortification, and others some to watch and ward as it was convenient. The first night of our landing, about midnight, there came some Savages sayling close to our quarter. Presently there was an alarum given; upon that the Savages ran away, and we [were] not troubled any more by them that night. Not long after there came two Savages that seemed to be Commanders, bravely drest, with Crownes of coloured haire upon their heads, which came as Messengers from the Werowance of Paspihse, telling us that their Werowance was comming and would be merry with us with a fat Deare.

The eighteenth day, the Werowance of Paspihse came himselfe to our quarter, with one hundred Savages armed, which garded him in a very warlike manner with Bowes and Arrowes, thinking at that time to execute their villany. Paspihae made great signes to us to lay our Armes away. But we would not trust him so far. He seeing he could not have convenient time to worke his will, at length made signes that he would give us as much land as we would desire to take. As the Savages were in a throng in the Fort, one of them stole a Hatchet from one of our company, which spied him doing the deed: whereupon he tooke it from him by force, and also strooke him over the arme. Presently another Savage seeing that, came fiercely at our man with a wooden sword, thinking to beat out his braines. The Werowance of Paspiha saw us take to our Armes, went suddenly away with all his company in great anger.

The nineteenth day, my selfe and three or foure more walking into the Woods by chance wee espied a pathway like to an Irish pace: wee were desirous to knowe whither it would bring us. Wee traced along some foure miles, all the way as wee went, having the pleasantest Suckles, the ground all flowing over with faire flowers of sundry colours and kindes, as though it had been in any Garden or Orchard in England. There be many Strawberries, and other fruits unknowne. Wee saw the Woods full of Cedar and Cypresse trees, with other trees, which issues out sweet Gummes like to Balsam. Wee kept on our way in this Paradise. At length, wee came to a Savage Towne, where wee found but few people. They told us the rest were gone a hunting with the Werowance of Paspiha. We stayed there a while, and had of them Strawberries and other things. In the meane time one of the Savages came running out of his house with a Bowe and Arrowes and ranne mainly through the Woods. Then I beganne to mistrust some villanie, that he went to call some companie, and so betray us. Wee made all haste away wee could. One of the Savages brought us on the way to the Wood side, where there was a Garden of Tobacco and other fruits and herbes. He gathered Tobacco, and distributed to every one of us; so wee departed.

The twentieth day the Werowance of Paspiha sent fortie of his men with a Deere, to our quarter: but they came more in villanie than any love they bare us. They faine would have layne in our Fort all night, but wee would not suffer them for feare of their treachery. One of our Gentlemen having a Target which hee trusted in, thinking it would beare out a slight shot, hee set it up against a tree, willing one of the Savages to shoot; who tooke from his backe an Arrow of an elle long, drew it strongly in his Bowe, shoots the Target a foote thorow, or better: which was strange, being that a Pistoll could not pierce it. Wee seeing the force of his Bowe, afterwards set him up a steele Target; he shot again, and burst his arrow all to pieces. He presently pulled out another Arrow, and bit it in his teeth, and seemed to bee in a great rage; so hee went away in great anger. Their Bowes are made of tough Hasell, their strings of Leather, their Arrowes of Canes or Hasell, headed with very sharpe stones, and are made artificially like a broad Arrow: other some of their Arrowes are headed with the ends of Deeres homes, and are feathered very artificially. Pasphia was as good as his word; for hee sent Venison, but the Sawse came within a few dayes after.

At Port Cotage in our Voyage up the River, we saw a Savage Boy about the age of ten yeeres, which had a head of haire of a perfect yellow and a reasonable white skinne, which is a Miracle amongst all Savages.

This River which wee have discovered is one of the famousest Rivers that ever was found by any Christian. It ebbs and flowes a hundred and threescore miles, where ships of great burthen may harbour in safetie. Wheresoever we landed upon this River, wee saw the goodliest Woods as Beech, Oke, Cedar, Cypresse, Wal-nuts, Sassafras, and Vines in great abundance, which hang in great clusters on many Trees, and other Trees unknowne; and all the grounds bespred with many sweet and delicate flowres of divers colours and kindes. There are also many fruites as Strawberries, Mulberries, Rasberries, and Fruites unknowne. There are many branches of this River, which runne flowing through the Woods with great plentie of fish of all kindes; as for Sturgeon, all the World cannot be compared to it. In this Countrey I have seene many great and large Medowes having excellent good pasture for any Cattle. There is also great store of Deere both Red and Fallow. There are Beares, Foxes, Otters, Bevers, Muskats, and wild beasts unknowne.

The foure and twentieth day wee set up a Crosse at the head of this River, naming it Kings River, where we proclaimed James King of England to have the most right unto it. When wee had finished and set up our Crosse, we shipt our men and made for James Fort. By the way, wee came to Pohatans Towre, where the Captaine went on shore suffering none to goe with him. Hee presented the Commander of this place, with a Hatchet which hee tooke joyfully, and was well pleased.

But yet the Savages murmured at our planting in the Countrie, whereupon this Werowance made answere againe very wisely of a Savage, Why should you bee offended with them as long as they hurt you not, nor take any thing away by force. They take but a litle waste ground, which doth you nor any of us any good.

I saw Bread made by their women, which doe all their drugerie. The men takes their pleasure in hunting and their warres, which they are in continually, one Kingdome against another. The manner of baking of bread is thus. After they pound their wheat into flowre, with hote water they make it into paste, and worke it into round balls and Cakes, then they put it into a pot of seething water: when it is sod throughly, they lay it on a smooth stone, there they harden it as well as in an Oven.

There is notice to be taken to know married women from Maids. The Maids you shall alwayes see the fore part of their head and sides shaven close, the hinder part very long, which they tie in a pleate hanging downe to their hips. The married women weares their haire all of a length, and is tied of that fashion that the Maids are. The women kinde in this Countrey doth pounce and race their bodies, legges, thighes, armes and faces with a sharpe Iron, which makes a stampe in curious knots, and drawes the proportion of Fowles, Fish, or Beasts; then with paintings of sundry lively colours, they rub it into the stampe which will never be taken away, because it is dried into the flesh where it is sered.

The Savages beare their yeeres well, for when wee were at Pamonkies, wee saw a Savage by their report was above eight score yeeres of age. His eyes were sunke into his head, having never a tooth in his mouth, his haire all gray with a reasonable bigge beard, which was as white as any snow. It is a Miracle to see a Savage have any haire on their faces. I never saw, read, nor heard, any have the like before. This Savage was as lusty and went as fast as any of us, which was strange to behold.

The fifteenth of June we had built and finished our Fort, which was triangle wise, having three Bulwarkes, at every corner, like a halfe Moone, and foure or five pieces of Artillerie mounted in them. We had made our selves sufficiently strong for these Savages. We had also sowne most of our Come on two Mountaines. It sprang a mans height from the ground. This Countrey is a fruitfull soile, bearing many goodly and fruitfull Trees, as Mulberries, Cherries, Walnuts, Cedars, Cypresse, Sassafras, and Vines in great abundance.

Munday the two and twentieth of June, in the morning, Captaine Newport in the Admirall departed from James Port for England.

Captaine Newport being gone for England, leaving us (one hundred and foure persons) verie bare and scantie of victualls, furthermore in warres and in danger of the Savages, we hoped after a supply which Captaine Newport promised within twentie weekes. But if the beginners of this action doe carefully further us, the Country being so fruitfull, it would be as great a profit to the Realme of England, as the Indies to the King of Spaine. If this River which wee have found had been discovered in the time of warre with Spaine, it would have beene a commoditie to our Realme, and a great annoyance to our enemies.

The seven and twentieth of July the King of Rapahanna demanded a Canoa, which was restored, lifted up his hand to the Sunne (which they worship as their God), besides he laid his hand on his heart, that he would be our speciall friend. It is a generall rule of these people, when they swere by their God which is the Sunne, no Christian will keep their Oath better upon this promise. These people have a great reverence to the Sunne above all other things: at the rising and setting of the same, they sit downe lifting up their hands and eyes to the Sunne, making a round Circle on the ground with dried Tobacco; then they began to pray, making many Devillish gestures with a Hellish noise, foming at the mouth, staring with their eyes, wagging their heads and hands in such a fashion and deformitie as it was monstrous to behold.

The sixt of August there died John Asbie of the bloudie Flixe. The ninth day died George Flowre of the swelling. The tenth day died William Bruster Gentleman, of a wound given by the Savages, and was buried the eleventh day.

The fourteenth day, Jerome Alikock, Ancient, died of a wound, the same day, Francis Midwinter, Edward Moris Corporall died suddenly.

The fifteenth day, their died Edward Browne and Stephen Galthorpe. The sixteenth day, their died Thomas Gower Gentleman. The seventeenth day, their died Thomas Mounslic. The eighteenth day, there died Robert Pennington, and John Martine Gentleman. The nineteenth day, died Drue Piggase Gentleman. The two and twentieth day of August, there died Captaine Bartholomew Gosnold, one of our Councell: he was honourably buried, having all the Ordnance in the Fort shot off, with many vollies of small shot.

After Captaine Gosnols death, the Councell could hardly agree by the dissention of Captaine Kendall, which afterwards was committed about hainous matters which was proved against him.

The foure and twentieth day, died Edward Harington and George Walker, and were buried the same day. The six and twentieth day, died Kenelme Throgmortine. The seven and twentieth day died William Roods. The eight and twentieth day died Thomas Stoodie, Cape Merchant.

The fourth day of September died Thomas Jacob Sergeant. The fift day, there died Benjamin Beast. Our men were destroyed with cruell diseases, as Swellings, Flixes, Burning Fevers, and by warres, and some departed suddenly, but for the most part they died of meere famine. There were never Englishmen left in a forreigne Countrey in such miserie as wee were in this new discovered Virginia. Wee watched every three nights, lying on the bare cold ground, what weather soever came, [and] warded all the next day, which brought our men to bee most feeble wretches. Our food was but a small Can of Barlie sod in water, to five men a day, our drinke cold water taken out of the River, which was at a floud verie salt, at a low tide full of slime and filth, which was the destruction of many of our men. Thus we lived for the space of five moneths in this miserable distresse, not having five able men to man our Bulwarkes upon any occasion. If it had not pleased God to have put a terrour in the Savages hearts, we had all perished by those vild and cruell Pagans, being in that weake estate as we were; our men night and day groaning in every corner of the Fort most pittifull to heare. If there were any conscience in men, it would make their harts to bleed to heare the pitifull murmurings and out-cries of our sick men without reliefe, every night and day, for the space of sixe weekes, some departing out of the World, many times three or foure in a night; in the morning, their bodies trailed out of their Cabines like Dogges to be buried. In this sort did I see the mortalitie of divers of our people.

It pleased God, after a while, to send those people which were our mortall enemies to releeve us with victuals, as Bread, Come, Fish, and Flesh in great plentie, which was the setting up of our feeble men, otherwise wee had all perished. Also we were frequented by divers Kings in the Countrie, bringing us store of provision to our great comfort.

The eleventh day, there was certaine Articles laid against Master Wingfield which was then President; thereupon he was not only displaced out of his President ship, but also from being of the Councell. Afterwards Captaine John Ratcliffe was chosen President.

The eighteenth day, died one Ellis Kinistone, which was starved to death with cold. The same day at night, died one Richard Simmons. The nineteenth day, there died one Thomas Mouton.

William White (having lived with the Natives) reported to us of their customes. In the morning by breake of day, before they eate or drinke, both men, women, and children, that be above tenne yeares of age, runnes into the water, there washes themselves a good while till the Sunne riseth, then offer Sacrifice to it, strewing Tobacco on the water or Land, honouring the Sunne as their God. Likewise they doe at the setting of the Sunne.

Captain John Smith's Journey to the Pamunkey Indians, 1608

Captain John Smith's account of the 1608 expedition that he led to Werowocomico, Chief Powhatan's seat on the York River, about fifteen miles from Jamestown, is valuable for the detailed report it gives of the encounter between the colonists and the paramount chief of the native peoples of Virginia. How to best interpret the account, which is told only from the perspective of Smith, has been the subject of endless debate among scholars. Taken from the "Third Booke" of Smith's Generall Historie of Virginia, New England & The Summer Isles, *first published in London in 1624.*

Captaine Smiths Journey to Pamaunkee.

The twentie-nine of December he set forward for Werowocomoco: his Company

were these;

In the Discovery Barge himselfe.

Gent.

Robert Behethland.	Raleigh Chrashow.
Nathanael Graves.	Michael Sicklemore.
John Russell.	Richard Worley.

Souldiers.

Anas Todkill.	Jeffrey Shortridge.
William Love.	Edward Pising.
William Bentley.	William Ward.

In the Pinnace.

Lieutenant Percie, brother to the Earle of Northumberland.
Master Francis West, brother to the Lord La Warre.
William Phittiplace, Captaine of the Pinnace.
Jonas Profit, Master.
Robert Ford, Clarke of the Councell.

Gent.

Michael Phittiplace.	William Tankard.
Jeffrey Abbot, Serjeant.	George Yarington.

Souldiers.

James Browne.	Thomas Coe.
Edward Brinton.	John Dods.
George Burton.	Henry Powell.

Thomas Gipson, David Ellis, Nathanael Peacock, Saylers. John Prat, George Acrig, James Read, Nicholas Hancock, James Watkins, Thomas Lambert, foure Dutch-men, and Richard Salvage were sent by Land before to build the house for Powhatan against our Arrivall.

This company being victualled but for three or foure dayes, lodged the first night at Warraskoyack, where the President tooke sufficient provision. This kind King did his best to divert him from seeing Powhatan, but perceiving he could not prevaile, he advised in this manner. Captaine Smith, you shall find Powhatan to use you kindly, but trust him not, and be sure he have no oportunitie to seize on your Armes; for he hath sent for you onely to cut your throats. The Captaine thanking him for his good counsell: yet the better to try his love, desired guides to Chawwonock; for he would send a present to that King, to bind him his friend. To performe this journey was sent Mr. Sicklemore, a very valiant, honest, and a painefull Souldier: with him two guides, and directions how to seeke for the lost company of Sir Walter Raleighs, and silke Grasse. Then we departed thence, the President assuring the King perpetuall love; and left with him Samuel Collier his Page to learne the Language.

So this Kings deeds by sacred Oath adjur'd.
More wary proves, and circumspect by ods:
Fearing at least his double forfeiture;
To offend his friends, and sin against his Gods.

The next night being lodged at Kecoughtan; six or seaven dayes the extreame winde, rayne, frost and snow caused us to keepe Christmas among the Salvages, where we were never more merry, nor fed on more plentie of good Oysters, Fish, Flesh, Wild-foule, and good bread; nor never had better fires in England, then in the dry, smoaky houses of Kecoughtan: but departing thence, when we found no houses we were not curious in any weather to lye three or foure nights together under the trees by a fire, as formerly is sayd. An hundred fortie eight foules the President, Anthony Bagnall, and Serjeant Pising did kill at three shoots. At Kiskiack the frost & contrary winds forced us three or foure dayes also (to suppresse the insolency of those proud Salvages) to quarter in their houses, yet guard our Barge, and cause them give us what we wanted; though we were but twelve and himselfe, yet we never wanted shelter where we found any houses. The 12 of January we arrived at Werowocomoco, where the river was frozen neare halfe a myle from the shore; but to neglect no time, the President with his Barge so far had approached by breaking the ice, as the ebbe left him amongst those oasie shoules, yet rather then to lye there frozen to death, by his owne example he taught them to march neere middle deepe, a flight shot through this muddy frozen oase. When the Barge floated, he appoynted two or three to returne her aboord the Pinnace. Where for want of water in melting the ice, they made fresh water, for the river there was salt. But in this march Mr. Russell, (whom none could perswade to stay behinde) being somewhat ill, and exceeding heavie, so overtoyled himselfe as the rest had much adoe (ere he got ashore) to regaine life into his dead benummed spirits. Quartering in the next houses we found, we sent to Powhatan for provision, who sent us plentie of bread, Turkies, and Venison; the next day having feasted us after his ordinary manner, he began to aske us when we would be gone: fayning he sent not for us, neither had he any corne; and his people much lesse: yet for fortie swords he would procure us fortie Baskets. The President shewing him the men there present that brought him the message and conditions, asked Powhatan how it chanced he became so forgetfull; thereat the King concluded the matter with a merry laughter, asking for our Commodities, but none he liked without gunnes and swords, valuing a Basket of Corne more precious then a Basket of Copper; saying he could rate his Corne, but not the Copper.

Captaine Smith seeing the intent of this subtill Salvage began to deale with him after this manner. Powhatan, though I had many courses to have made my provision, yet beleeving your promises to supply my wants, I neglected all to satisfie your desire: and to testifie my love, I sent you my men for your building, neglecting mine owne. What your people had you have ingrossed, forbidding them our trade: and now you thinke by consuming the time, we shall consume for want, not having to fulfill your strange demands. As for swords and gunnes, I told you long agoe I had none to spare; and you must know those I have can keepe me from want: yet steale or wrong you I will not, nor dissolve that friendship we have mutually promised, except you constraine me by our bad usage.

The King having attentively listned to this Discourse, promised that both he and his Country would spare him what he could, the which within two dayes they should receive. Yet Captaine Smith, sayth the King, some doubt I have of your comming hither, that makes me not so kindly seeke to relieve you as I would: for many doe informe me, your comming hither is not for trade, but to invade my people, and possesse my Country, who dare not come to bring you Corne, seeing you thus armed with your men. To free us of this feare, leave aboord your weapons, for here they are needlesse, we being all friends, and for ever Powhatans.

With many such discourses they spent the day, quartering that night in the Kings houses. The next day he renewed his building, which hee little intended should proceede. For the Dutch-men finding his plentie, and knowing our want, and perceiving his preparations to surprise us, little thinking we could escape both him and famine; (to obtaine his favour) revealed to him so much as they knew of our estates and projects, and how to prevent them. One of them being of so great a spirit, judgement, and resolution, and a hireling that was certaine of his wages for his labour, and ever well used both he and his Countrymen; that the President knew not whom better to trust; and not knowing any fitter for that imployment, had sent him as a spy to discover Powhatans intent, then little doubting his honestie, nor could ever be certaine of his villany till neare halfe a yeare after.

Whilst we expected the comming in of the Country, we wrangled out of the King ten quarters of Corne for a copper Kettell, the which the President perceiving him much to affect, valued it at a much greater rate; but in regard of his scarcity he would accept it, provided we should have as much more the next yeare, or els the Country of Monacan. Wherewith each seemed well contented, and Powhatan began to expostulate the difference of Peace and Warre after this manner.

Captaine Smith, you may understand that I having seene the death of all my people thrice, and not any one living of these three generations but my selfe; I know the difference of Peace and Warre better then any in my Country. But now I am old and ere long must die, my brethren, namely Opitchapam, Opechancanough, and Kekataugh, my two sisters, and their two daughters, are distinctly each others successors. I wish their experience no lesse then mine, and your love to them no lesse then mine to you. But this bruit from Nandsamund, that you are come to destroy my Country, so much affrighteth all my people as they dare not visit you. What will it availe you to take that by force you may quickly have by love, or to destroy them that provide you food. What can you get by warre, when we can hide our provisions and fly to the woods? whereby you must famish by wronging us your friends. And why are you thus jealous of our loves seeing us unarmed, and both doe, and are willing still to feede you, with that you cannot get but by our labours? Thinke you I am so simple, not to know it is better to eate good meate, lye well, and sleepe quietly with my women and children, laugh and be merry with you, have copper, hatchets, or what I want being your friend: then be forced to flie from all, to lie cold in the woods, feede upon Acornes, rootes, and such trash, and be so hunted by you, that I can neither rest, eate, nor sleepe; but my tyred men must watch, and if a twig but breake, every one cryeth there commeth Captaine Smith: then must I fly I know not whether: and thus with miserable feare, end my miserable life, leaving my pleasures to such youths as you, which through your rash unadvisednesse may quickly as miserably end, for want of that, you never know where to finde. Let this therefore assure you of our loves, and every yeare our friendly trade shall furnish you with Corne; and now also, if you would come in friendly manner to see us, and not thus with your guns and swords as to invade your foes. To this subtill discourse, the President thus replyed.

Seeing you will not rightly conceive of our words, we strive to make you know our thoughts by our deeds; the vow I made you of my love, both my selfe and my men have kept. As for your promise I find it every day violated by some of your subjects: yet we finding your love and kindnesse, our custome is so far from being ungratefull, that for your sake onely, we have curbed our thirsting desire of revenge; els had they knowne as well the crueltie we use to our enemies, as our true love and courtesie to our friends. And I thinke your judgement sufficient to conceive, as well by the adventures we have undertaken, as by the advantage we have (by our Armes) of yours: that had we intended you any hurt, long ere this we could have effected it. Your people comming to James Towne are entertained with their Bowes and Arrowes without any exceptions; we esteeming it with you as it is with us, to weare our armes as our apparell. As for the danger of our enemies, in such warres consist our chiefest pleasure: for your riches we have no use: as for the hiding your provision, or by your flying to the woods, we shall not so unadvisedly starve as you conclude, your friendly care in that behalfe is needlesse, for we have a rule to finde beyond your knowledge.

Many other discourses they had, till at last they began to trade. But the King seeing his will would not be admitted as a law, our guard dispersed, nor our men disarmed, he (sighing) breathed his minde once more in this manner.

Captaine Smith, I never use any Werowance so kindely as your selfe, yet from you I receive the least kindnesse of any. Captaine Newport gave me swords, copper, cloathes, a bed, towels, or what I desired; ever taking what I offered him, and would send away his gunnes when I intreated him: none doth deny to lye at my feet, or refuse to doe what I desire, but onely you; of whom I can have nothing but what you regard not, and yet you will have whatsoever you demand. Captaine Newport you call father, and so you call me; but I see for all us both you will doe what you list, and we must both seeke to content you. But if you intend so friendly as you say, send hence your armes, that I may beleeve you; for you see the love I beare you, doth cause me thus nakedly to forget my selfe.

Smith seeing this Salvage but trifle the time to cut his throat, procured the salvages to breake the ice, that his Boate might come to fetch his corne and him: and gave order for more men to come on shore, to surprise the King, with whom also he but trifled the time till his men were landed: and to keepe him from suspicion, entertained the time with this reply.

Powhatan you must know, as I have but one God, I honour but one King; and I live not here as your subject, but as your friend to pleasure you with what I can. By the gifts you bestow on me, you gaine more then by trade: yet would you visit mee as I doe you, you should know it is not our custome, to sell our curtesies as a vendible commodity. Bring all your countrey with you for your guard, I will not dislike it as being over jealous. But to content you, to morrow I will leave my Armes, and trust to your promise. I call you father indeed, and as a father you shall see I will love you: but the small care you have of such a childe caused my men perswade me to looke to my selfe.

By this time Powhatan having knowledge his men were ready whilest the ice was a breaking, with his luggage women and children, fled. Yet to avoyd suspicion, left two or three of the women talking with the Captaine, whilest hee secretly ran away, and his men that secretly beset the house. Which being presently discovered to Captaine Smith, with his pistoll, sword, and target hee made such a passage among these naked Divels; that at his first shoot, they next him tumbled one over another, and the rest quickly fled some one way some another: so that without any hurt, onely accompanied with John Russell, hee obtained the corps du guard. When they perceived him so well escaped, and with his eighteene men (for he had no more with him a shore) to the uttermost of their skill they sought excuses to dissemble the matter: and Powhatan to excuse his flight and the sudden comming of this multitude, sent our Captaine a great bracelet and a chaine of pearle, by an ancient Oratour that bespoke us to this purpose, perceiving even then from our Pinnace, a Barge and men departing and comming unto us.

Captaine Smith, our Werowance is fled, fearing your gunnes, and knowing when the ice was broken there would come more men, sent these numbers but to guard his corne from stealing, that might happen without your knowledge: now though some bee hurt by your misprision, yet Powhatan is your friend and so will for ever continue. Now since the ice is open, he would have you send away your corne, and if you would have his company, send away also your gunnes, which so affrighteth his people, that they dare not come to you as hee promised they should.

Then having provided baskets for our men to carry our corne to the boats, they kindly offered their service to guard our Armes, that none should steale them. A great many they were of goodly well proportioned fellowes, as grim as Divels; yet the very sight of cocking our matches, and being to let fly, a few wordes caused them to leave their bowes and arrowes to our guard, and beare downe our corne on their backes; wee needed not importune them to make dispatch. But our Barges being left on the oase by the ebbe, caused us stay till the next high-water, so that wee returned againe to our old quarter. Powhatan and his Dutch-men bursting with desire to have the head of Captaine Smith, for if they could but kill him, they thought all was theirs, neglected not any oportunity to effect his purpose. The Indians with all the merry sports they could devise, spent the time till night: then they all returned to Powhatan, who all this time was making ready his forces to surprise the house and him at supper. Notwithstanding the eternall all-seeing God did prevent him, and by a strange meanes. For Pocahontas his dearest jewell and daughter, in that darke night came through the irksome woods, and told our Captaine great cheare should be sent us by and by: but Powhatan and all the power he could make, would after come kill us all, if they that brought it could not kill us with our owne weapons when we were at supper. Therefore if we would live shee wished us presently to bee gone. Such things as shee delighted in, he would have given her: but with the teares running downe her cheekes, shee said shee durst not be seene to have any: for if Powhatan should know it, she were but dead, and so shee ranne away by her selfe as she came. Within lesse then an hour came eight or ten lusty fellowes, with graat platters of venison and other victuall, very importunate to have us put out our matches (whose smoake made them sicke) and sit down to our victuall. But the Captaine made them taste every dish, which done hee sent some of them backe to Powhatan, to bid him make haste for hee was prepared for his comming. As for them hee knew they came to betray him at his supper: but hee would prevent them and all their other intended villanies: so that they might be gone. Not long after came more messengers, to see what newes; not long after them others. Thus wee spent the night as vigilantly as they, till it was high-water, yet seemed to the salvages as friendly as they to us: and that wee were so desirous to give Powhatan content, as hee requested, wee did leave him

Edward Brynton to kill him foule, and the Dutchmen to finish his house; thinking at our returne from Pamaunkee the frost would be gone, and then we might finde a better oportunity if necessity did occasion it, little dreaming yet of the Dutch-mens treachery, whose humor well suted this verse:

> Is any free, that may not live as freely as he list?
> Let us live so, then w'are as free, and bruitish as the best.

Second Virginia Charter, 23 May 1609

James, by the grace of God [King of England, Scotland, France and Ireland, defender of the faith, etc.] To all [to whom these presents shall come, greeting.]

Whereas, at the humble suite and request of sondrie oure lovinge and well disposed subjects intendinge to deduce a colonie and to make habitacion and plantacion of sondrie of oure people in that parte of America comonlie called Virginia, and other part and territories in America either apperteyninge unto us or which are not actually possessed of anie Christian prince or people within certaine bound and regions, wee have formerly, by oure lettres patents bearinge date the tenth of Aprill in the fourth yeare of oure raigne of England, Fraunce, and Ireland, and the nine and thirtieth of Scotland, graunted to Sir Thomas Gates, Sir George Somers and others, for the more speedie accomplishment of the said plantacion and habitacion, that they shoulde devide themselves into twoe colloniesthe one consistinge of divers Knights, gentlemen, merchaunts and others of our cittie of London, called the First Collonie; and the other of sondrie Knights, gentlemen and others of the citties of Bristoll, Exeter, the towne of Plymouth, and other places, called the Seccond Collonieand have yielded and graunted maine and sondrie priviledges and liberties to each Collonie for their quiet setlinge and good government therein, as by the said lettres patents more at large appeareth.

Nowe, forasmuch as divers and sondrie of oure lovinge subjects, as well adventurers as planters, of the said First Collonie (which have alreadie engaged them selves in furtheringe the businesse of the said plantacion and doe further intende by the assistance of Almightie God to prosecute the same to a happie ende) have of late ben humble suiters unto us that, in respect of their great chardeges and the adventure of manie of their lives which they have hazarded in the said discoverie and plantacion of the said countrie, wee woulde be pleased to graunt them a further enlargement and explanacion of the said graunte, priviledge and liberties, and that suche counsellors and other officers maie be appointed amonngest them to manage and direct their affaires [as] are willinge and readie to adventure with them; as also whose dwellings are not so farr remote from the cittye of London but that they maie at convenient tymes be readie at hande to give advice and assistance upon all occacions requisite.

We, greatlie affectinge the effectual prosecucion and happie successe of the said plantacion and comendinge their good desires theirin, for their further encouragement in accomplishinge so excellent a worke, much pleasinge to God and profitable to oure Kingdomes, doe, of oure speciall grace and certeine knowledge and meere motion, for us, oure heires and successors, give, graunt and confirme to oure trustie and welbeloved subjects,

Robert, Earle of Salisburie [Salisbury]
Thomas, Earle of Suffolke [Suffolk]
Henrie, Earle of Southampton
William. Earle of Pembroke [Henrie]
[Henrie] Earle of Lincolne [Lincoln]
Henrie, Earle of Dorsett [Dorset]
Thomas, Earle of Exeter
Phillipp, Earle of Mountgommery
Robert, Lord Vicount Lisle
Theophilus, Lord Howard of Walden
James Mountague, Lord Bishopp of Bathe and Wells
Edward, Lord Zouche
Thomas, Lord Lawarr
Wiliam, Lord Mounteagle
Raphe, Lord Ewre
Edmond, Lord Sheffeild [Sheffield]
Grey, Lord Shandis [Chandois]
[Grey], Lord Compton
John, Lord Petre
John, Lord Stanhope
George, Lord Carew
Sir Humfrey Welde, Lord Mayor of London [Weld]
George Pertie, Esquire [Percie]
Sir Edward Cecill, Knight [Cecil]
Sir George Wharton, Knight
Frauncis West, Esquire
Sir William Waade, Knight [Wade]
Sir Henrie Nevill, Knight [Nevil]
Sir Thomas Smithe, Knight [Smith]
Sir Oliver Cromwell, Knight
Sir Peter Manwood, Knight
Sir Dru Drurie, Knight [Drury]
Sir John Scott, Knight [Scot]
Sir Thomas Challouer, Knight [Challoner]
Sir Robert Drurie, Knight [Drury]
Sir Anthonye Cope, Knight
Sir Horatio Veere, Knight [Vere]
Sir Edward Conwaie, Knight [Conway]
Sir William Browne [Brown]
Sir Maurice Barkeley, Knight [Berkeley]
Sir Roberte Maunsell, Knight [Mansel]
Sir Amias Presou, Knight [Preston]
Sir Thomas Gates, Knight
Sir Anthonie Ashley, Knight [Ashly]
Sir Michaell Sandes, Knight [Sandys]

Sir Henrie Carew, Knight [Carey]
Sir Stephen Soame, Knight
Sir Calisthenes Brooke, Knight
Sir Edward Michelborne, Knight [Michelborn]
Sir John Racliffe, Knight [Ratcliffe]
Sir Charles Willmott, Knight [Wilmot]
Sir George Moore, Knight [Moor]
Sir Hugh Wirrall, Knight [Wirral]
Sir Thomas Dennys, Knight [Dennis]
Sir John Hollis, Knight [Holles]
Sir William Godolphin, Knight
Sir Thomas Monnson, Knight [Monson]
Sir Thomas Ridgwaie, Knight [Ridgwine]
Sir John Brooke, Knight
Sir Roberte Killigrew, Knight
Sir Henrie Peyton, Knight
Sir Richard Williamson, Knight
Sir Ferdinando Weynman, Knight
Sir William St. John, Knight
Sir Thomas Holcrofte, Knight [Holcroft]
Sir John Mallory, Knight
Sir Roger Ashton, Knight
Sir Walter Cope, Knight
Sir Richard Wigmore, Knight
Sir William Cooke, Knight [Coke]
Sir Herberte Crofte, Knight
Sir Henrie Faushawe, Knight [Fanshaw]
Sir John Smith, Knight
Sir Francis Wolley, Knight
Sir Edward Waterhouse, Knight
Sir Henrie Sekeford, Knight [Seekford]
Sir Edward Saudes, Knights [Edwin Sandys]
Sir Thomas Wayneman, Knight [Waynam]
Sir John Trevor, Knight
Sir Warrwick Heale, Knight [Heele]
Sir Robert Wroth, Knight
Sir John Townnesende, Knight [Townsend]
Sir Christopher Perkins, Knight
Sir Daniell Dun, Knight
Sir Henrie Hobarte, Knight [Hobart]
Sir Franncis Bacon, Knight
Sir Henrie Mountague, Knight [Montague]
Sir Georg Coppin, Knight
Sir Samuell Sandes, Knight [Sandys]
Sir Thomas Roe, Knight
Sir George Somers, Knight
Sir Thomas Freake, Knight
Sir Thomas Horwell, Knight [Harwell]
Sir Charles Kelke, Knight

Sir Baptist Hucks, Knight [Hicks]
Sir John Watts, Knight
Sir Roberte Carey, Knight
Sir William Romney, Knight
Sir Thomas Middleton, Knight
Sir Hatton Cheeke, Knight
Sir John Ogle, Knighte
Sir Cavallero Meycot, Knight
Sir Stephen Riddlesden, Knight [Riddleson]
Sir Thomas Bludder, Knight
Sir Anthonie Aucher, Knight
Sir Robert Johnson, Knight
Sir Thomas Panton, Knight
Sir Charles Morgan, Knight
Sir Stephen Powle, Knight [Pole]
Sir John Burlacie, Knight
Sir Christofer Cleane, Knight [Cleave]
Sir George Hayward, Knight
Sir Thomas Dane, Knight [Davis]
Sir Thomas Dutton, Knight [Sutton]
Sir Anthonie Forrest, Knight [Forest]
Sir Robert Payne, Knight
Sir John Digby, Knight
Sir Dudley Diggs, Knight [Digges]
Sir Rowland Cotton, Knight
Doctour Mathewe Rutcliffe [Sutcliffel
Doctor Meddowes [Meadows]
Doctor Tumer
Doctor Poe
Captaine Pagnam
Captaine Jeffrey Holcrofte
Captaine Raunne [Romney]
Captaine Henrie Spry
Captaine Shelpton [Shelton]
Captaine Spark [Sparks]
[Captain] Thomas Wyatt [Wyat]
Captaine Brinsley
Captaine William Courtney
Captaine Herbert
Captaine Clarke
Captaine Dewhurst
Captaine John Blundell
Captaine Frier [Fryer]
Captaine Lewis Orwell
Captaine Edward Lloyd [Loyd]
Captaine Slingesby
Captaine Huntley [Hawley]
Captaine Orme
Captaine Woodhouse

Captaine Mason
Captaine Thomas Holcroft
Captaine John Cooke [Coke]
Captaine Hollis [Holles]
Captaine William Proude
Captaine Henrie Woodhouse
Captaine Richard Lindeley [Lindesey]
Captaine Dexter
Captaine William Winter
Captaine Herle [Pearsel
Captain John Bingham
Captaine Burray
Captaine Thomas Conwey [Conway]
Captaine Rookwood
Captaine William Lovelace
Captaine John Ashley
Captaine Thomas Wynne
Captaine Thomas Mewtis
Captaine Edward Harwood
Captaine Michaell Evered [Everard]
Captaine Connoth [Comock]
Captaine Miles [Mills]
Captaine Pigott [Pigot]
Captaine Edward Maria Wingfeild [Wingfield]
Captaine ChristopherNewporte [Newport]
Captaine John Siclemore, alias Ratcliffe [Sicklemore]
Captaine John Smith
Captyn John Martyn [Martin]
Captaine Peter Wynne
Captaine Waldoe [Waldo]
Captyn Thomas Wood
Captaine Thomas Button
George Bolls, Esquire, Sheriffe of London
William Crashawe, [Clerk], Bachelor of Divinite
William Seabright, Esquire
Christopher Brook, Esquire
John Bingley, Esquire
Thomas Watson, Esquire
Richard Percivall, Esquire [Percival]
John Moore, Esquire
Hugh Brooker, Esquire
David Waterhouse, Esquire [Woodhouse]
Anthonie Auther, Esquier [Aucher]
Roberte Bowyer, Esquire [Boyer]
Raphe Ewens, Esquire
Zacharie Jones, Esquire
George Calvert, Esquire
William Dobson, Esquire
Henry Reynold, Esquire [Reynolds]

Thomas Walker, Esquire
Anthonie Barnars, Esquire
Thomas Sandes, Esquire [Sandys]
Henrie Sand, Esquire [Sandys]
Richard Sand [Sandys], Sonne of Sir Edwin Sandes [Sandys]
William Oxenbridge, Esquire
John Moore, Esquire
Thomas Wilson, Esquire
John Bullocke, Esquire [Bullock]
John Waller, [Esquire]
Thomas Webb
Jehughe Robinson
William Brewster
Robert Evelyn
Henrie Dabenie [Danby]
Richard Hacklewte, minister [Hackluit]
John Eldred, marchaunt [Eldrid]
William Russell, marchaunt
John Merrick, marchaunt
Richard Bannester, merchant [Banister]
Charles Anthonie, goldsmithe [Anthony]
John Banck [Banks]
William Evans
Richard Humble
Robert Chamberleyne, marchaunt [Richard Chamberlayne]
Thomas Barber, marchaunt
Richard Pevyrell, merchaunt [Pomet]
John Fletcher, merchant
Thomas Nicholls, merchant
John Stoak, merchaunt [Stoke]
Gabriell Archer
Franncis Covell [Covel]
William Bouham [Bonham]
Edward Harrison
John Wolstenholme
Nicholas Salter
Hugh Evans
William Barners [Barnes]
Otho Mawdett [Mawdet]
Richard Staper, marchant
John Elkin, marchaunt
William Cayse [Coyse]
Thomas Perkin, cooper
Humfrey Ramell, cooper [Humphrey James]
Henry Jackson
Roberte Shingleton [Singleton]
Christopher Nicholls
John Harper
Abraham Chamberlaine [Chamberlayne]

Thomas Shipton
Thomas Carpenter
Anthoine Crewe [Crew]
George Holman
Robert Hill
Cleophas Smithe [Smith]
Raphe Harrison
John Farmer
James Brearley
William Crosley [Crosby]
Richard Cocks [Cox]
John Gearinge [Gearing]
Richard Strough, iremonnger [Strongarm]
Thomas Langton
Griffith Hinton
Richard Ironside
Richard Deane [Dean]
Richard Turner
William Leveson, mercer [Lawson]
James Chatfeilde [Chatfield]
Edward Allen [Edward Allen Tedder]
Tedder Roberts
Heldebrand Sprinson [Robert Hildebrand Sprinson]
Arthur Mouse
John Gardener [Gardiner]
James Russell [Russel]
Richard Casewell [Caswell]
Richard Evanns [Evans]
John Hawkins
Richard Kerrill [Kerril]
Richard Brooke
Mathewe Scrivener, gentleman [Screvener]
William Stallendge, gentleman [Stallenge]
Arthure Venn, gentleman
Saund Webb, gentleman [Sandys Webbe]
Michaell Phettiplace, gentleman
William Phetiplace, gentleman [Phettiplace]
Ambrose Brusey, gentleman [Prusey]
John Taverner, gentleman
George Pretty, gentleman
Peter Latham, gentleman
Thomas Monnford, gentleman [Montford]
William Cautrell, gentleman [Cantrel]
Richard Wiffine, gentleman [Wilfin]
Raphe Mooreton, gentleman [Moreton]
John Cornellis [Comelius]
Martyn Freeman
Raphe Freeman
Andreau Moore

Thomas White
Edward Perkin
Robert Osey
Thomas Whitley
George Pitt [Pit]
Roberte Parkehurste [Parkhurst]
Thomas Morris
Peter Vaulore [Harloe]
Jeffrey Duppa
John Gilbert
William Hancock
Mathew Bromrigg [Brown]
Francis Tirrell [Tyrrel]
Randall Carter
Othowell Smithe [Smith]
Thomas Honnyman [Hamond]
Marten Bonde, haberdasher [Bond]
Joan Mousloe [John Moulsoe]
Roberte Johnson
William Younge [Young]
John Woddall [Woodal]
William Felgate
Humfrey Westwood
Richard Champion
Henrie Robinson
Franncis Mapes
William Sambatch [Sambach]
Rauley Crashawe [Ralegh Crashaw]
Daruel Lliacker
Thomas Grave
Hugh Willestone
Thomas Culpepper, of Wigsell, Esquire
John Culpepper, gentleman
Henrie Lee
Josias Kirton, gentleman [Kerton]
John Porie, gentleman [Pory]
Henrie Collins
George Burton
William Atkinson
Thomas Forrest [Forest]
John Russell [Russel]
John Houlte [Holt]
Harman Harrison
Gabriell Beedell [Beedel]
John Beedell [Beedel]
Henrie Dankes [Dawkes]
George Scott [Scot]
Edward Fleetewood, gentleman [Fleetwood]
Richard Rogers, gentleman

Arthure Robinson
Robert Robinson
John Huntley
John Grey [Gray]
William Payne
William Feilde [Field]
William Wattey
William Webster
John Dingley
Thomas Draper
Richard Glanvile [Glanvil]
Arnolde Lulls [Hulls]
Henrie Rowe [Roe]
William Moore [More]
Nicholas Grice [Gryce]
James Monnger [Monger]
Nicholas Andrewes [Andrews]
Jerome Haydon, iremonnger [Jeremy Haydon]
Phillipp Durrant [Philip Durette]
John Quales [Quarles]
John West
Madlew Springeham [Springham]
John Johnson
Christopher Hore
George Barkeley
Thomas Sued [Snead]
George Barkeley [Berkeley]
Ardhure Pett [Pet]
Thomas Careles
William Barkley [Berkley]
Thomas Johnson
Alexander Bent [Bents]
Captaine William Kinge [King]
George Sandes, gentleman [Sandys]
James White, gentleman
Edmond Wynn [Wynne]
Charles Towler
Richard Reynold
Edward Webb
Richard Maplesden
Thomas Levers [Lever]
David Bourne
Thomas Wood
Raphe Hamer
Edward Barnes, mercer
John Wright, mercer
Robert Middleton
Edward Litsfeild [Littlefield]
Katherine West

Thomas Webb [Web]
Raphe Kinge [King]
Roberte Coppine [Coppin]
James Askewe
Christopher Nicholls [Christopher Holt]
William Bardwell
Alexander Childe [Chiles]
Lewes Tate
Edward Ditchfeilde [Ditchfield]
James Swifte
Richard Widdowes, goldesmith
Edmonde Brundells [Brudenell]
John Hanford [Hansford]
Edward Wooller
William Palmer, haberdasher
John Badger
John Hodgson
Peter Monnsill [Mounsel]
Jahn Carrill [Carril]
John Busbridge [Bushridge]
William Dunn [Dun]
Thomas Johnson
Nicholas Benson
Thomas Shipton
Nathaniell Wade
Randoll Wettwood [Wetwood]
Mathew Dequester
Charles Hawkins
Hugh Hamersley
Abraham Cartwright
George Bennett [Bennet]
William Cattor [Cater]
Richard Goddart
Henrie Cromwell
Phinees Pett [Pet]
Roberte Cooper
Henrie Neite [Newce]
Edward Wilks [Wilkes]
Roberte Bateman
Nicholas Farrar
John Newhouse
John Cason
Thomas Harris, gentleman
George Etheridge, gentleman
Thomas Mayle, gentleman
Richard Stratford [Stafford]
Thomas
Richard Cooper
John Westrowe [Westrow]

Edward Welshe [Welch]
Thomas Brittanie [Britain]
Thomas Knowls [Knowles]
Octavian Thome
Edmonde Smyth [Smith]
John March
Edward Carew
Thomas Pleydall
Richard Lea [Let]
Miles Palmer
Henrie Price
John Josua, gentleman [Joshua]
William Clawday [Clauday]
Jerome Pearsye
John Bree, gentleman
William Hampson
Christopher Pickford
Thomas Hunt
Thomas Truston
Christopher Lanman [Salmon]
John Haward, clerke [Howard]
Richarde Partridge
Allen Cotton [Cassen]
Felix Wilson
Thomas Colethurst [Bathurst]
George Wilmer
Andrew Wilmer
Morrice Lewellin
Thomas Jedwin [Godwin]
Peter Burgoyne
Thomas Burgoyne
Roberte Burgoyne
Roberte Smithe, merchauntaylor [Smith]
Edward Cage, grocer
Thomas Canon, gentleman [Cannon]
William Welby, stacioner
Clement Wilmer, gentleman
John Clapham, gentleman
Giles Fraunces, gentleman [Francis]
George Walker, sadler
John Swinehowe, stacioner [Swinhow]
Edward Bushoppe, stacioner [Bishop]
Leonard White, gentleman
Christopher Barron [Baron]
Peter Benson
Richard Smyth [Smith]
George Prockter, minister [Proctor]
Millicent Ramesden, widowe [Ramsdent]
Joseph Soane

Thomas Hinshawe [Hinshaw]
John Baker
Robert Thorneton [Thomton]
John Davies [Davis]
Edward Facett [Facetl
George Nuce, gentleman [Newce]
John Robinson
Captaine Thomas Wood
William Browne, shoemaker [Brown]
Roberte Barker, shoemaker
Roberte Penington [Pennington]
Francis Burley, minister
William Quick, grocer
Edward Lewes, grocer [Lewis]
Laurence Campe, draper
Aden Perkins, grocer
Richard Shepparde, preacher [Shepherd]
William Sheckley, haberdasher [Sherley]
William Tayler, haberdasher [Taylor]
Edward Lukyn, gentleman [Edwin Lukin]
John Francklyn, haberdasher [Franklyn]
John Southicke [Southwick]
Peter Peate
George Johan, iremonnger
George Yardley, gentleman [Yeardley]
Henrie Shelly [Shelley]
John Pratt [Prat]
Thomas Church, draper
William Powell, gentleman [Powel]
Richard Frithe, gentleman [Frith]
Thomas Wheeler, draper
Franncis Hasilerigg, gentleman [Haselrig]
Hughe Shippley, gentleman [Shipley]
John Andrewes, thelder, [doctor], of Cambridge [Andrews]
Franncis Whistley, gentleman [Whistler]
John Vassall, gentleman
Richard Howle
Edward Barkeley, gentleman [Berkeley]
Richard Knerisborough, gentleman [Keneridgburg]
Nicholas Exton, draper
William Bennett, fishmonger [Bennet]
James Hawood, marchaunt [Haywood]
Nicholas Isaak, merchaunt [Isaac]
William Gibbs, merchannt
[William] Bushopp [Bishop]
Barnard Michell [Mitchel]
Isaake Michell [Isaac Mitchel]
John Streat [Streate]
Edward Gall

John Marten, gentleman [Martin]
Thomas Fox
Luke Lodge
John Woodleefe, gentleman [Woodliffel
Rice Webb [Piichard]
Vincent Lowe [Low]
Samuell Burnam [Burnham]
Edmonde Pears, haberdasher
Josua Goudge [John Googe]
John St. John
Edwarde Vaughan
William Dunn
Thomas Alcock [Alcocke]
John Andrewes, the younger, of Cambridge [Andrews]
Samuell Smithe [Smith]
Thomas Jerrard [Gerrard]
Thomas Whittingham
William Cannynge [Canning]
Paule Caminge [Canning]
George Chaudler [Chandler]
Henrye Vincent
Thomas Ketley
James Skelton
James Montain [Mountaine]
George Webb, gentleman
Josephe Newbroughesmith [Joseph Newbridge, smith]
Josias Mande [Mand]
Raphe Haman, the younger [Hamer]
Edward Brewster, the sonne of William Brewster
Leonard Harwood, mercer
Phillipp Druerdent
William Carpenter
Tristram Hill
Roberte Cock, grocer
Laurence Grene, grocer [Greene]
Daniell Winche, grocer [Samuel Winch]
Humfrey Stile, grocer
Averie Dransfeild, grocer [Dransfield]
Edwarde Hodges, grocer
Edward Beale, grocer
Raphe Busby, grocer
John Whittingham, grocer
John Hide, grocer
Mathew Shipperd, grocer [Shepherd]
Thomas Allen, grocer
Richard Hooker, grocer
Laurence Munckas, grocer [Munks]
John Tanner, grocer
Peter Gate, grocer

John Blunt, grocer
Roberte Berrisford, grocer
Thomas Wells, gentleman
John Ellis, grocer
Henrie Colthurst, grocer
John Cranage, grocer [Cavady]
Thomas Jenings, grocer [Jennings]
Edmond Peshall, grocer [Pashall]
Timothie Bathurst, grocer
Gyles Parslowe, grocer [Parslow]
Roberte Johnson, grocer [Richard]
William Janson, vintener [Johnson]
Ezechiell Smith
Richard Murrettone [Martin]
William Sharpe
Roberte Ritche [Rich]
William Stannerd, inholder [Stannard]
John Stocken
William Strachey, gentleman
George Farmer, gentleman
Thomas Gypes, clothworker
Abraham Dawes, gentleman [Davies]
Thomas Brockett, gentleman [Brocket]
George Bathe, fishmonger [Bache]
John Dike, fishmonger
Henrie Spranger
Richard Farringdon [Farrington]
Chistopher Vertue, vintener
Thomas Baley, vintener [Bayley]
George Robins, vintener
Tobias Hinson, grocer
Urian Spencer [Vrian]
Clement Chachelley [Chicheley]
John Searpe, gentleman [Scarpe]
James Cambell, iremonnger [Campbell]
Christopher Clitherowe, iremonnger [Clitheroe]
Phillipp Jacobson
Peter Jacobson, of Andwarpe
William Barckley [Berkeley]
Miles Banck, cutler [Banks]
Peter Highley, grocer [Higgons]
Henrie John, gentleman
John Stoakley, merchauntailor [Stokeley]
The companie of mercers
The companie of grocers
The companie of drapers
The company of fishmongers
The companie of gouldsmithes
The companie of skynners

The companie merchauntailors
The companie of haberdashers
The companie of salters
The companie of iremongers
The companie of vintners
The companie of clothworkers
The companie of dyers
The companie of bruers
The companie of lethersellers
The companie of pewterers
The companie of cutlers
The companie of whitebakers
The companie of waxchaundlers
The companie of tallowe chaundlers
The companie of armorers
The companie of girdlers
The companie of butchers
The companie of sadlers
The companie of carpenters
The companie of cordwayners
The companie of barbor chirurgions
The companie of painter stayners
The companie of curriers
The companie of masons
The companie of plumbers
The companie of inholders
The companie of founders
The companie of poulterers
The companie of cookes
The companie of coopers
The companie of tylers and bncklayers
The companie of bowyers
The companie of Retchers
The companie of blacksmithes
The companie of joyners
The companie of weavers
The companie of wollmen
The companie of wood monnvers [wood mongers]
The companie of scrivenors
The companie of fruterers
The companie of plasterers
The companie of brownebakers
The companie of stacioners
The companie of imbroderers
The companie of upholsters
The companie of musicions
The companie of turners
The companie of baskettmakers
The companie of glasiers

John Levett, merchaunt [Levet]
Thomas Nomicott, clothworker [Nomicot]
Richard Venn, haberdasher
Thomas Scott, gentleman [Scot]
Thomas Juxson, merchauntaylor [Juxon]
George Hankinson
Thomas Leeyer, gentleman [Seyer]
Mathew Cooper
Gorge Butler, gentleman
Thomas Lawson, gentleman
Edward Smith, haberdasher
Stephen Sparrowe
John Jones, merchaunt
[John] Reynold, brewer [Reynolds]
Thomas Plummer, merchaunt
James Duppa, bruer
Rowland Coytemore [Coitmore]
William Sotherne [Southerne]
Gorge Whittmoore, haberdasher [Whitmore]
Anthonie Gosoulde, the younger [Gosnold]
John Allen, fishemonger
John Kettlebye, gentleman [Kettleby]
Symonde Yeomans, fishmonger [Simon]
Richard Chene, gouldsmithe
Launcelot Davis, gentleman [Clene]
John Hopkins, an alderman of Bristoll
George Hooker, gentlernan
Roberte Shevinge, yeoman [Chening]

And to such and so manie as they doe or shall hereafter admitt to be joyned with them, in forme hereafter in theis presentes expressed, whether they goe in their persons to be planters there in the said plantacion, or whether they goe not, but doe adventure their monyes, goods or chattels, that they shalbe one bodie or communaltie perpetuall and shall have perpetual succession and one common seale to serve for the saide bodie or communaltie; and that they and their successors shalbe knowne, called and incorporated by the name of The Tresorer and Companie of Adventurers and Planters of the Citty of London for the Firste Collonie in Virginia.

And that they and their successors shalbe from hensforth, forever enabled to take, acquire and purchase, by the name aforesaid (licens for the same from us, oure heires or successors first had and obtained) anie manner of lands, tenements and hereditaments, goods and chattels, within oure realme of England and dominion of Wales; and that they and their successors shalbe likewise enabled, by the name aforesaid, to pleade and to be impleaded before anie of oure judges or justices, in anie oure courts, and in anie accions or suits whatsoever.

And wee doe also, of oure said speciall grace, certaine knowledge and mere mocion, give, grannte and confirme unto the said Tresorer and Companie, and their successors, under the reservacions, limittacions and declaracions hereafter expressed, all those lands, countries and territories scituat, lieinge and beinge in that place of America called Virginia, from the pointe of lande called Cape or Pointe Comfort all alonge the seacoste to the northward twoe hundred miles and from the said pointe of Cape Comfort all alonge the sea coast to the southward twoe hundred miles; and all that space and circuit of lande lieinge from the sea coaste of the precinct aforesaid upp unto the lande, throughoute, from sea to sea, west and northwest; and also all the island beinge within one hundred miles alonge the coaste of bothe seas of the precincte aforesaid; togeather with all the soiles, groundes, havens and portes, mynes, aswell royall mynes of golde and silver as other mineralls, pearles and precious stones, quarries, woods, rivers, waters, fishings, comodities, jurisdictions, royalties, priviledges, franchisies and preheminences within the said territorie and the precincts there of whatsoever; and thereto or there abouts, both by sea and lande, beinge or in anie sorte belonginge or appertayninge, and which wee by oure lettres patents maie or cann graunte; and in as ample manner and sorte as wee or anie oure noble progenitors have heretofore graunted to anie companie, bodie pollitique or corporate, or to anie adventurer or adventurers, undertaker or undertakers, of anie discoveries, plantacions or traffique of, in, or into anie forraine parts whatsoever; and in as large and ample manner as if the same were herin particulerly mentioned and expressed: to have, houlde, possesse and enjoye all and singuler the said landes, countries and territories with all and singuler other the premisses heretofore by theis [presents] graunted or mencioned to be grannted, to them, the said Tresorer and Companie, their successors and assignes, forever; to the sole and proper use of them, the said Tresorer and Companie, their successors and assignes [forever], to be holden of us, oure heires and successors, as of oure mannour of Estgreenewich, in free and common socage and not in capite; yeldinge and payinge, therefore, to us, oure heires and successors, the fifte parte onlie of all oare of gould and silver that from tvme to time, and at all times hereafter, shalbe there gotton, had and obtained, for all manner of service.

And, nevertheles, oure will and pleasure is, and wee doe by theis presentes chardge, commannde, warrant and auctorize, that the said Tresorer and Companie and their successors, or the major parte of them which shall be present and assembled for that purpose, shall from time to time under their common seale distribute, convey, assigne and set over such particuler porcions of lands, tenements and hereditaments, by theise presents formerly grannted, unto such oure lovinge subjects naturallie borne of denizens, or others, aswell adventurers as planters, as by the said Companie, upon a commission of survey and distribucion executed and retourned for that purpose, shalbe named, appointed and allowed, wherein oure will and pleasure is, that respect be had as well of the proporcion of the adventure[r] as to the speciall service, hazarde, exploite or meritt of anie person so as to be recompenced, advannced or rewarded.

And for as muche as the good and prosperous successe of the said plantacion cannot but cheiflie depende, next under the blessinge of God and the supporte of oure royall aucthoritie, upon the provident and good direccion of the whole enterprise by a carefull and understandinge Counsell, and that it is not convenient that all the adventurers shalbe so often drawne to meete and assemble as shalbe requisite for them to have metings and conference aboute theire affaires, therefore we doe ordaine, establishe and confirme that there shalbe perpetually one Counsell here resident, accordinge to the tenor of oure former lettres patents, which Counsell shall have a seale for the better governement and administracion of the said plantacion besides the legall seale of the Companie or Corporacion, as in oure former lettres patents is also expressed.

And further wee establishe and ordaine that

Henrie, Earl of Southampton
William, Earl of Pembrooke
Henrie, Earl of Lincoln
Thomas, Earl of Exeter
Roberte, Lord Viscounte Lisle
Lord Theophilus Howard
James, Lord Bishopp of Bathe and Wells
Edward, Lord Zouche
Thomas, Lord Laware
William, Lord Mounteagle
Edmunde, Lord Sheffeilde
Grey, Lord Shanndoys [Chandois]
John, Lord Stanhope
George, Lord Carew
Sir Humfrey Welde, Lord Mayor of London
Sir Edward Cecil
Sir William Waad [Wade]
Sir Henrie Nevill
Sir Thomas Smith
Sir Oliver Cromwell
Sir Peter Manwood
Sir Thomas Challoner
Sir Henrie Hovarte [Hobart]
Sir Franncis Bacon
Sir George Coppin
Sir John Scott
Sir Henrie Carey
Sir Roberte Drurie [Drury]
Sir Horatio Vere
Sir Eward Conwaye [Conway]
Sir Maurice Berkeley [Barkeley]
Sir Thomas Gates
Sir Michaele Sands [Sandys]
Sir Roberte Mansfeild [Mansel]
Sir John Trevor
Sir Amyas Preston
Sir William Godolphin
Sir Walter Cope
Sir Robert Killigrewe
Sir Henrie Faushawe [Fanshaw]
Sir Edwyn Sandes [Sandys]
Sir John Watts

Sir Henrie Montague
Sir William Romney
Sir Thomas Roe
Sir Baptiste Hicks
Sir Richard Williamson
Sir Stephen Powle [Poole]
Sir Dudley Diggs
Christopher Brooke, [Esq.]
John Eldred, and
John Wolstenholme

shalbe oure Counsell for the said Companie of Adventurers and Planters in Virginia.

And the said Sir Thomas Smith wee ordaine to be Tresorer of the said Companie, which Tresorer shall have aucthoritie to give order for the warninge of the Counsell and sommoninge the Companie to their courts and meetings.

And the said Counsell and Tresorer or anie of them shalbe from henceforth nominated, chosen, contynued, displaced, chaunged, altered and supplied, as death or other severall occasions shall require, out of the Companie of the said adventurers by the voice of the greater parte of the said Counsell and adventurers in their assemblie for that purpose; provided alwaies that everie Councellor so newlie elected shalbe presented to the Lord Channcellor of England, or to the Lord Highe Treasurer of England, or the Lord Chambleyne of the housholde of us, oure heires and successors, for the tyme beinge to take his oathe of a Counsellor to us, oure heires and successors, for the said Companie and Collonie in Virginia.

And wee doe by theis presents, of oure especiall grace, certaine knowledge and meere motion, for us, oure heires and successors, grannte unto the said Tresorer and Companie and their successors, that if it happen at anie time or times the Tresorer for the tyme beinge to be sick, or to have anie such cause of absente from the cittie of London as shalbe allowed by the said Counsell or the greater parte of them assembled, so as he cannot attende the affaires of that Companie, in everie such case it shall and maie be lawfull for such Tresorer for the tyme beinge to assigne, constitute and appointe one of the Counsell for Companie to be likewise allowed by the Counsell or the greater parte of them assembled to be the deputie Tresorer for the said Companie; which Deputie shall have power to doe and execute all things which belonge to the said Tresorer duringe such tyme as such Tresorer shalbe sick or otherwise absent, upon cause allowed of by the said Counsell or the major parte of them as aforesaid, so fullie and wholie and in as large and ample manner and forme and to all intents and purposes as the said Tresorer if he were present himselfe maie or might doe and execute the same.

And further of oure especiall grace, certaine knowledge and meere mocion, for us, oure heires and successors, wee doe by theis presents give and grannt full power and aucthoritie to oure said Counsell here resident aswell at this present tyme as hereafter, from time to time, to nominate, make, constitute, ordaine and confirme by such name or names, stile or stiles as to them shall seeme good, and likewise to revoke, dischardge, channge and alter aswell all and singuler governors, oficers and ministers which alreadie hath ben made, as also which hereafter shalbe by them thought fitt and meedefull to be made or used for the government of the said Colonie and plantacion.

And also to make, ordaine and establishe all manner of orders, lawes, directions, instructions, formes and ceremonies of government and magistracie, fitt and necessarie, for and concerninge the government of the said Colonie and plantacion; and the same att all tymes hereafter to abrogate, revoke or chaunge, not onely within the precincts of the said Colonie but also upon the seas in goeing and cominge to and from the said Collonie, as they in their good discrecions shall thinke to be fittest for [the] good of the adventurers and inhabiters there.

And we doe also declare that for divers reasons and consideracions us thereunto especiallie moving, oure will and pleasure is and wee doe hereby ordaine that imediatlie from and after such time as anie such governour or principall officer so to be nominated and appointed by oure said Counsell for the government of the said Colonie, as aforesaid, shall arive in Virginia and give notice unto the Collonie there resident of oure pleasure in this behalfe, the government, power and aucthority of the President and Counsell, heretofore by oure former lettres patents there established, and all lawes and constitucions by them formerlie made, shall utterly cease and be determined; and all officers, governours and ministers formerly constituted or appointed shalbe dischardged, anie thinge in oure said former lettres patents conserninge the said plantacion contayned in aniewise to the contrarie notwithstandinge; streightlie chardginge and commaundinge the President and Counsell nowe resident in the said Collonie upon their alleadgiance after knowledge given unto them of oure will and pleasure by theis presentes signified and declared, that they forth with be obedient to such governor or governers as by oure said Counsell here resident shalbe named and appointed as aforesaid; and to all direccions, orders and commandements which they shall receive from them, aswell in the present resigninge and giveinge upp of their aucthoritie, offices, chardg and places, as in all other attendannce as shalbe by them from time to time required.

And wee doe further by theis presentes ordaine and establishe that the said Tresorer and Counsell here resident, and their successors or anie fower of them assembled (the Tresorer beinge one), shall from time to time have full power and aucthoritie to admitt and receive anie other person into their companie, corporacion and freedome; and further, in a generall assemblie of the adventurers, with the consent of the greater parte upon good cause, to disfranchise and putt oute anie person or persons oute of the said fredome and Companie.

And wee doe also grannt and confirme for us, oure heires and successors that it shalbe lawfull for the said Tresorer and Companie and their successors, by direccion of the Governors there, to digg and to serche for all manner of mynes of goulde, silver, copper, iron, leade, tinne and other mineralls aswell within the precincts aforesaid as within anie parte of the maine lande not formerly graunted to anie other; and to have and enjoye the gould, silver, copper, iron, leade, and tinn, and all other mineralls to be gotten thereby, to the use and behoofe of the said Companie of Planters and Adventurers, yeldinge therefore and payinge yerelie unto us, oure heires and successors, as aforesaid.

And wee doe further of oure speciall grace, certaine knowledge and meere motion, for us, oure heires and successors, grannt, by theis presents to and withe the said Tresorer and Companie and their successors, that it shalbe lawfull and free for them and their assignes at all and everie time and times here after, oute of oure realme of England and oute of all other [our] dominions, to take and leade into the said voyage, and for and towards the said plantacion, and to travell thitherwards and to abide and inhabite therein the said Colonie and plantacion, all such and so manie of oure lovinge subjects, or anie other straungers that wilbecomme oure lovinge subjects and live under oure allegiance, as shall willinglie accompanie them in the said voyadge and plantation with sufficient shippinge armour, weapons, ordinannce, municion, powder, shott, victualls, and such merchaundize or wares as are esteemed by the wilde people in those parts, clothinge, implements, furnitures, catle, horses and mares, and all other thinges necessarie for the said plantation and for their use and defence and trade with the people there, and in passinge and retourninge to and from without yeldinge or payinge subsedie, custome, imposicion, or anie other taxe or duties to us, oure heires or successors, for the space of seaven yeares from the date of theis presents; provided, that none of the said persons be such as shalbe hereafter by speciall name restrained by us, oure heires or successors.

And for their further encouragement, of oure speciall grace and favour, wee doe by theis present for us, oure heires and successors, yeild and graunte to and with the said Tresorer and Companie and their successors and everie of them, their factors and assignes, that they and every of them shalbe free and quiett of all subsedies and customes in Virginia for the space of one and twentie yeres, and from all taxes and imposicions for ever, upon anie goods or merchaundizes at anie time or times hereafter, either upon importation thither or exportation from thence into oure realme of England or into anie other of oure [realms or] dominions, by the said Tresorer and Companie and their successors, their deputies, factors [or] assignes or anie of them, except onlie the five pound per centum due for custome upon all such good and merchanndizes as shalbe brought or imported into oure realme of England or anie other of theis oure dominions accordinge to the auncient trade of merchannts, which five poundes per centum onely beinge paid, it shalbe thensforth lawfull and free for the said Adventurers the same goods [and] merchaundizes to export and carrie oute of oure said dominions into forraine partes without anie custome, taxe or other duty to be paide to us oure heires or successors or to anie other oure officers or deputies; provided, that the saide goods and merchaundizes be shipped out within thirteene monethes after their first landinge within anie parte of those dominions.

And wee doe also confirme and grannt to the said Tresorer and Companie, and their successors, as also to all and everie such governer or other officers and ministers as by oure said Counsell shalbe appointed, to have power and aucthoritie of governement and commannd in or over the said Colonie or plantacion; that they and everie of them shall and lawfullie maie from tyme to tyme and at all tymes forever hereafter, for their severall defence and safetie, enconnter, expulse, repell and resist by force and armes, aswell by sea as by land, and all waies and meanes whatsoever, all and everie such person and persons whatsoever as without the speciall licens of the said Tresorer and Companie and their successors shall attempte to inhabite within the said severall precincts and lymitts of the said Colonie and plantacion; and also, all and everie such person and persons whatsoever as shall enterprise, or attempte at anie time hereafter, destruccion, invasion, hurte, detriment or annoyannce to the said Collonye and plantacion, as is likewise specified in the said former grannte.

And that it shalbe lawful for the said Tresorer and Companie, and their successors and everie of them, from time to time and at all times hereafter, and they shall have full power and aucthoritie, to take and surprise by all waies and meanes whatsoever all and everie person and persons whatsoever, with their shippes, goods and other furniture, traffiquinge in anie harbor, creeke or place within the limitts or precincts of the said Colonie and plantacion, [not] being allowed by the said Companie to be adventurers or planters of the said Colonie, untill such time as they beinge of anie realmes or dominions under oure obedience shall paie or agree to paie, to the hands of the Tresorer or [of] some other officer deputed by the said governors in Virginia (over and above such subsedie and custome as the said Companie is or here after shalbe to paie) five poundes per centum upon all goods and merchaundizes soe brought in thither, and also five per centum upon all goods by them shipped oute from thence; and being straungers and not under oure obedience untill they have payed (over and above such subsedie and custome as the same Tresorer and Companie and their successors is or hereafter shalbe to paie) tenn pounds per centum upon all such goods, likewise carried in and oute, any thinge in the former lettres patents to the contrarie not withstandinge; and the same sommes of monie and benefitt as aforesaid for and duringe the space of one and twentie yeares shalbe wholie imploied to the benefitt and behoof of the said Colonie and plantacion; and after the saide one and twentie yeares ended, the same shalbe taken to the use of us, oure heires or successors, by such officer and minister as by us, oure heires or successors, shalbe thereunto assigned and appointed, as is specified in the said former lettres patents.

Also wee doe, for us, oure heires and successors, declare by theis presents, that all and everie the persons beinge oure subjects which shall goe and inhabit within the said Colonye and plantacion, and everie of their children and posteritie which shall happen to be borne within [any] the lymitts thereof, shall have [and] enjoye all liberties, franchesies and immunities of free denizens and naturall subjects within anie of oure other dominions to all intents and purposes as if they had bine abidinge and borne within this oure kingdome of England or in anie other of oure dominions.

And forasmuch as it shalbe necessarie for all such our lovinge subjects as shall inhabitt within the said precincts of Virginia aforesaid to determine to live togither in the feare and true woorshipp of Almightie God, Christian peace and civill quietnes, each with other, whereby everie one maie with more safety, pleasure and profitt enjoye that where unto they shall attaine with great paine and perill, wee, for us, oure heires and successors, are likewise pleased and contented and by theis presents doe give and graunte unto the said Tresorer and Companie and their successors and to such governors, officers and ministers as shalbe, by oure said Councell, constituted and appointed, accordinge to the natures and lymitts of their offices and places respectively, that they shall and maie from time to time for ever hereafter, within the said precincts of Virginia or in the waie by the seas thither and from thence, have full and absolute power and aucthority to correct, punishe, pardon, governe and rule all such the subjects of us, oure heires and successors as shall from time to time adventure themselves in anie voiadge thither or that shall at anie tyme hereafter inhabitt in the precincts and territorie of the said Colonie as aforesaid, accordinge to such order, ordinaunces, constitution, directions and instruccions as by oure said Counsell, as aforesaid, shalbe established; and in defect thereof, in case of necessitie according to the good discretions of the said governours and officers respectively, aswell in cases capitall and criminall as civill, both marine and other, so alwaies as the said statuts, ordinannces and proceedinges as neere as convenientlie maie be, be agreable to the lawes, statutes, government and pollicie of this oure realme of England.

And we doe further of oure speciall grace, certeine knowledge and mere mocion, grant, declare and ordaine that such principall governour as from time to time shall dulie and lawfullie be aucthorised and appointed, in manner and forme in theis presents heretofore expressed, shall [have] full power and aucthoritie to use and exercise marshall lawe in cases of rebellion or mutiny in as large and ample manner as oure leiutenant in oure counties within oure realme of England have or ought to have by force of their comissions of lieutenancy. And furthermore, if anie person or persons, adventurers or planters, of the said Colonie, or anie other at anie time or times hereafter, shall transporte anie monyes, goods or marchaundizes oute of anie [of] oure kingdomes with a pretence or purpose to lande, sell or otherwise dispose the same within the lymitts and bounds of the said Collonie, and yet nevertheles beinge at sea or after he hath landed within anie part of the said Colonie shall carrie the same into anie other forraine Countrie, with a purpose there to sell and dispose there of that, then all the goods and chattels of the said person or persons so offendinge and transported, together with the shipp or vessell wherein such transportacion was made, shalbe forfeited to us, oure heires and successors.

And further, oure will and pleasure is, that in all questions and doubts that shall arrise upon anie difficultie of construccion or interpretacion of anie thinge contained either in this or in oure said former lettres patents, the same shalbe taken and interpreted in most ample and beneficiall manner for the said Tresorer and Companie and their successors and everie member there of.

And further, wee doe by theis presents ratifie and confirme unto the said Tresorer and Companie and their successors all privuleges, franchesies, liberties and immunties graunted in oure said former lettres patents and not in theis oure lettres patents revoked, altered, channged or abridged.

And finallie, oure will and pleasure is and wee doe further hereby for us, oure heires and successors grannte and agree, to and with the said Tresorer and Companie and their successors, that all and singuler person and persons which shall at anie time or times hereafter adventure anie somme or sommes of money in and towards the said plantacion of the said Colonie in Virginia and shalbe admitted by the said Counsell and Companie as adventurers of the said Colonie, in forme aforesaid, and shalbe enrolled in the booke or record of the adventurers of the said Companye, shall and maie be accompted, accepted, taken, helde and reputed Adventurers of the said Collonie and shall and maie enjoye all and singuler grannts, priviledges, liberties, benefitts, profitts, commodities [and immunities], advantages and emoluments whatsoever as fullie, largely, amplie and absolutely as if they and everie of them had ben precisely, plainely, singulerly and distinctly named and inserted in theis oure lettres patents.

And lastely, because the principall effect which wee cann desier or expect of this action is the conversion and reduccion of the people in those partes unto the true worshipp of God and Christian religion, in which respect wee would be lothe that anie person should be permitted to passe that wee suspected to affect the superstitions of the Churche of Rome, wee doe hereby declare that it is oure will and pleasure that none be permitted to passe in anie voiadge from time to time to be made into the saide countrie but such as firste shall have taken the oath of supremacie, for which purpose wee doe by theise presents give full power and aucthoritie to the Tresorer for the time beinge, and anie three of the Counsell, to tender and exhibite the said oath to all such persons as shall at anie time be sent and imploied in the said voiadge.

Although expresse mention [of the true yearly value or certainty of the premises, or any of them, or of any other gifts or grants, by us or any of our progenitors or predecessors, to the aforesaid Treasurer and Company heretofore made, in these presents is not made; or any act, statute, ordinance, provision, proclamation, or restraint, to the contrary hereof had, made, ordained, or provided, or any other thing, cause, or matter, whatsoever, in any wise notwithstanding.] In witnes whereof [we have caused these our letters to be made patent. Witness ourself at Westminster, the 23d day of May (1609) in the seventh year of our reign of England, France, and Ireland, and of Scotland the ****]

Per ipsum Regem exactum.

Winter of the Starving Time, 1609–1610

The terrible winter at Jamestown of 1609–1610, known as the Starving Time, saw the population of the colony reduced by four-fifths. When the survivors finally decided that it was completely hopeless to remain at Jamestown, they set sail for England. Before they got out of the Chesapeake Bay, however, they were turned back by a supply fleet commanded by Lord De La Warr. The following recounts that story and subsequent events at Jamestown under De La Warr's governorship. It was published in the "Fourth Booke" of Captain John Smith's Generall Historie of Virginia, New England & The Summer Isles, *first published in London in 1624.*

To make Plaine the True Proceedings of the Historie for 1609. we must follow the examinations of Doctor Simons, and two learned Orations published by the Companie; with the relation of the Right Honourable the Lord De la Ware.

What happened in the first government after the alteration in the time of Captaine George Piercie their Governour.

The day before Captaine Smith returned for England with the ships, Captaine Davis arrived in a small Pinace, with some sixteene proper men more: To these were added a company from James towne, under the command of Captaine John Sickelmore alias Ratliffe, to inhabit Point Comfort. Captaine Martin and Captaine West, having lost their boats and neere halfe their men among the Salvages, were returned to James towne; for the Salvages no sooner understood Smith was gone, but they all revolted, and did spoile and murther all they incountered. Now wee were all constrained to live onely on that Smith had onely for his owne Companie, for the rest had consumed their proportions, and now they had twentie Presidents with all their appurtenances: Master Piercie our new President, was so sicke hee could neither goe nor stand. But ere all was consumed, Captaine West and Captaine Sickelmore, each with a small ship and thirtie or fortie men well appointed, sought abroad to trade. Sickelmore upon the confidence of Powhatan, with about thirtie others as carelesse as himselfe, were all slaine, onely Jeffrey Shortridge escaped, and Pokahontas the Kings daughter saved a boy called Henry Spilman, that lived many yeeres after, by her meanes, amongst the Patawomekes. Powhatan still as he found meanes, cut off their Boats, denied them trade, so that Captaine West set saile for England. Now we all found the losse of Captaine Smith, yea his greatest maligners could now curse his losse: as for corne, provision and contribution from the Salvages, we had nothing but mortall wounds, with clubs and arrowes; as for our Hogs, Hens, Goats, Sheepe, Horse, or what lived, our commanders, officers & Salvages daily consumed them, some small proportions sometimes we tasted, till all was devoured; then swords, armes, pieces, or any thing, wee traded with the Salvages, whose cruell fingers were so oft imbrewed in our blouds, that what by their crueltie, our Governours indiscretion, and the losse of our ships, of five hundred within six moneths after Captaine Smiths departure, there remained not past sixtie men, women and children, most miserable and poore creatures; and those were preserved for the most part, by roots, herbes, acornes, walnuts, berries, now and then a little fish: they that had startch in these extremities, made no small use of it; yea, even the very skinnes of our horses. Nay, so great was our famine, that a Salvage we slew, and buried, the poorer sort tooke him up againe and eat him, and so did divers one another boyled and stewed with roots and herbs: And one amongst the rest did kill his wife, powdered her, and had eaten part of her before it was knowne, for which hee was executed, as hee well deserved; now whether shee was better roasted, boyled or carbonado'd, I know not, but of such a dish as powdered wife I never heard of. This was that time, which still to this day we called the starving time; it were too vile to say, and scarce to be beleeved, what we endured: but the occasion was our owne, for want of providence, industrie and government, and not the barrennesse and defect of the Countrie, as is generally supposed; for till then in three yeeres, for the numbers were landed us, we had never from England provision sufficient for six moneths, though it seemed by the bils of loading sufficient was sent us, such a glutton is the Sea, and such good fellowes the Mariners; we as little tasted of the great proportion sent us, as they of our want and miseries, yet notwithstanding they ever over-swayed and ruled the businesse, though we endured all that is said, and chiefly lived on what this good Countrie naturally afforded; yet had wee beene even in Paradice it selfe with these Governours, it would not have beene much better with us; yet there was amongst us, who had they had the government as Captaine Smith appointed, but that they could not maintaine it, would surely have kept us from those extremities of miseries. This in ten daies more, would have supplanted us all with death.

But God that would not this Countrie should be unplanted, sent and Sir Thomas Gates, and Sir George Sommers with one hundred and fiftie people most happily preserved by the Bermudas to preserve us: strange it is to say how miraculously they were preserved in a leaking ship, as at large you may reade in the insuing Historie of those Ilands.

The government resigned to Sir Thomas Gates, 1610.

When these two Noble Knights did see our miseries, being but strangers in that Countrie, and could understand no more of the cause, but by conjecture of our clamours and complaints, of accusing and excusing one another: They embarked us with themselves, with the best meanes they could, and abandoning James towne, set saile for England, whereby you may see the event of the government of the former Commanders left to themselves; although they had lived there many yeeres as formerly hath beene spoken (who hindred now their proceedings, Captaine Smith being gone.)

At noone they fell to the Ile of Hogs, and the next morning to Mulbery point, at what time they descried the Long-boat of the Lord la Ware, for God would not have it so abandoned. For this honourable Lord, then Governour of the Countrie, met them with three ships exceedingly well furnished with all necessaries fitting, who againe returned them to the abandoned James towne. Out of the observations of William Simmons Doctor of Divinitie.

The government devolved to the Lord la Ware.

His Lordship arrived the ninth of June 1610. accompanied with Sir Ferdinando Waynman, Captaine Houlcroft, Captaine Lawson, and divers other Gentlemen of sort; the tenth he came up with his fleet, went on shore, heard a Sermon, read his Commission, and entred into consultation for the good of the Colonie, in which secret counsell we will a little leave them, that we may duly observe the revealed counsell of God. Hee that shall but turne up his eie, and behold the spangled canopie of heaven, or shall but cast downe his eie, and consider the embroydered carpet of the earth, and withall shall marke how the heavens heare the earth, and the earth the Corne and Oile, and they relieve the necessities of man, that man will acknowledge Gods infinite providence: But hee that shall further observe, how God inclineth all casuall events to worke the necessary helpe of his Saints, must needs adore the Lords infinite goodnesse; never had any people more just cause, to cast themselves at the very foot-stoole of God, and to reverence his mercie, than this distressed Colonie; for if God had not sent Sir Thomas Gates from the Bermudas, within route daies they had almost beene famished; if God had not directed the heart of that noble Knight to save the Fort from fiering at their shipping, for many were very importunate to have burnt it, they had beene destitute of a present harbour and succour; if they had abandoned the Fort any longer time, and had not so soone returned, questionlesse the Indians would have destroied the Fort, which had beene the meanes of our safeties amongst them and a terror. If they had set saile sooner, and had lanched into the vast Ocean, who would have promised they should have incountered the Fleet of the Lord la Ware, especially when they made for New found land, as they intended, a course contrarie to our Navie approaching. If the Lord la Ware had not brought with him a yeeres provision, what comfort would those poore soules have received, to have beene relanded to a second distruction? This was the arme of the Lord of Hosts, who would have his people passe the red Sea and Wildernesse, and then to possesse the land of Canaan: It was divinely spoken of Heathen Socrates, If God for man be carefull, why should man bee over-distrustfull? for he hath so tempered the contrary qualities of the Elements,

That neither cold things want heat, nor moist things dry,
Nor sad things spirits, to quicken them thereby,
Yet make they musicall content of contrarietie,
Which conquer'd, knits them in such links together,
They doe produce even all this whatsoever.

The Lord Governour, after mature deliberation delivered some few words to the Companie, laying just blame upon them, for their haughtie vanities and sluggish idlenesse, earnestly intreating them to amend those desperate follies, lest hee should be compelled to draw the sword of Justice, and to cut off such delinquents, which he had rather draw, to the shedding of his vitall bloud, to protect them from injuries; heartning them with relation of that store hee had brought with him, constituting officers of all conditions, to rule over them, allotting every man his particular place, to watch vigilantly, and worke painfully: This Oration and direction being received with a generall applause, you might shortly behold the idle and restie diseases of a divided multitude, by the unitie and authoritie of this government to be substantially cured. Those that knew not the way to goodnesse before, but cherished singularitie and faction, can now chalke out the path of all respective dutie and service: every man endevoureth to outstrip other in diligence: the French preparing to plant the Vines, the English labouring in the Woods and grounds; every man knoweth his charge, and dischargeth the same with alacritie. Neither let any man be discouraged, by the relation of their daily labour (as though the sap of their bodies should bee spent for other mens profit) the setled times of working, to effect all themselves, or as the Adventurers need desire, required no more paines than from six of the clocke in the morning, untill ten, and from two in the afternoone, till foure, at both which times they are provided of spirituall and corporall reliefe. First, they enter into the Church, and make their praiers unto God, next they returne to their houses and receive their proportion of food. Nor should it bee conceived that this businesse excludeth Gentlemen, whose breeding never knew what a dales labour meant, for though they cannot digge, use the Spade, nor practice the Axe, yet may the staied spirits of any condition, finde how to imploy the force of knowledge, the exercise of counsell, the operation and power of their best breeding and qualities. The houses which are built, are as warme and defensive against wind and weather, as if they were tiled and slated, being covered above with strong boards, and some matted round with Indian mats. Our forces are now such as are able to tame the furie and trecherie of the Salvages: Our Forts assure the Inhabitants, and frustrate all assaylants. And to leave no discouragement in the heart of any, who personally shall enter into this great action, I will communicate a double comfort; first, Sir George Summers, that worthy Admirall hath undertaken a dangerous adventure for the good of the Colonie.

Upon the 15. of June, accompanied with Captaine Samuel Argall, hee returned in two Pinaces unto the Bermudas, promising (if by any meanes God will open a way to that Iland of Rocks) that he would soone returne with six moneths provision of flesh; with much crosse weather at last hee there safely arrived, but Captaine Argall was forced backe againe to James towne, whom the Lord De la Ware not long after sent to the River of Patawomeke, to trade for Corne; where finding an English boy, one Henry Spilman, a young Gentleman well descended, by those people preserved from the furie of Powhatan, by his acquaintance had such good usage of those kinde Salvages, that they fraughted his ship with Corne, wherewith he returned to James towne.

The other comfort is, that the Lord la Ware hath built two new Forts, the one called Fort Henry, the other Fort Charles, in honour of our most noble Prince, and his hopefull brother, upon a pleasant plaine, and neare a little Rivilet they call Southampton River; they stand in a wholsome aire, having plentie of Springs of sweet water, they command a great circuit of ground, containing Wood, Pasture and Marsh, with apt places for Vines, Corne and Gardens; in which Forts it is resolved, that all those that come out of England, shall be at their first landing quartered, that the wearisomnesse of the Sea, may bee refreshed in this pleasing part of the Countrie, and Sir Thomas Gates hee sent for England. But to correct some injuries of the Paspahegs, he sent Captaine Pearcie, Master Stacy, and fiftie or threescore shot, where the Salvages flying, they burnt their houses, tooke the Queene and her children prisoners, whom not long after they slew.

The fertilitie of the soile, the temperature of the climate, the forme of government, the condition of our people, their daily invocating of the Name of God being thus expressed; why should the successe, by the rules of mortall judgement, bee disparaged? why should not the rich harvest of our hopes be seasonably expected? I dare say, that the resolution of Ceasar in France, the designes of Alexander, the discoveries of Hernando Cortes in the West, and of Emanuel King of Portugal in the East, were not encouraged upon so firme grounds of state and possibilitie.

But his Lordship being at the fales [falls], the Salvages assaulted his troopes and slew three or foure of his men. Not long after, his Honour growing very sicke, he returned for England the 28. of March; in the ship were about five and fiftie men, but ere we arrived at Fyall, fortie of us were neare sicke to death, of the Scurvie, Callenture, and other diseases: the Governour being an Englishman, kindly used us, but small reliefe we could get, but Oranges, of which we had plenty, whereby within eight dales wee recovered, and all were well and strong by that they came into England. Written by William Box.

The Counsell of Virginia finding the smalnesse of that returne which they hoped should have defrayed the charge of a new supply, entred into a deep consultation, whether it were fit to enter into a new Contribution, or in time to send for them home, and give over the action, and therefore they adjured Sir Thomas Gates to deale plainly with them, who with a solemne and a sacred oath replyed, That all things before reported were true, and that all men know that wee stand at the devotion of politicke Princes and States, who for their proper utilitie, devise all courses to grind our Merchants, and by all pretences to confiscate their goods, and to draw from us all manner of gaine by their inquisitive inventions, when in Virginia, a few yeeres labour by planting and husbandry, will furnish all our defects with honour and securitie. Out of a Declaration published by the Counsell, 1610.

Third Virginia Charter, 12 March 1612

James, by the grace of God [King of England, Scotland, France and Ireland, Defender of the Faith;] to all to whom [these presents shall come,] greeting. Whereas at the humble suite of divers and sundry our lovinge subjects, aswell adventurers as planters of the First Colonie in Virginia, and for the propagacion of Christian religion and reclayminge of people barbarous to civilitie and humanitie, we have by our lettres patent bearing date at Westminster the three and twentieth daie of May in the seaventh yeare of our raigne of England, Frannce and Ireland, and the twoe and fortieth of Scotland, given and grannted unto them, that they and all suche and soe manie of our loving subjects as shold from time to time for ever after be joyned with them as planters or adventurers in the said plantacion, and their successors for ever, shold be one body politique incorporated by the name of The Treasorer and Planters of the Cittie of London for the First Colonie in Virginia;

And whereas allsoe for the greater good and benefitt of the said Companie and for the better furnishing and establishing of the said plantacion we did further [give], grannte and confirme by our said lettres patent unto the said Treasorer and Companie and their successors for ever, all those landes, contries and territories scituate, lyeing and being in that part of America called Virginia, from the point of land called Cape [or] Pointe Comfort all along the seacoste to the northward twoe hundred miles, and from the said point of Cape Comfort all along the seacoste to the sowthward twoe hundred miles, and all the space and circuit of land lying from the sea coste of the precinct aforesaid up or into the land throughout from sea to sea, west and northwest, and allso all the islandes lying within one hundred miles along the coast of both the seas of the precinct aforsaid, with diverse other grannts, liberties, franchises, preheminences, priviledges, profiitts, benefitts, and commodities, grannted in and by our said lettres patent to the said Tresorer and Companie, and their successors, for ever:

Now for asmuchas we are given to undestande that in these seas adjoyning to the said coast of Virginia and without the compasse of those twoe hundred miles by us soe grannted unto the said Treasurer and Companie as aforesaid, and yet not farr distant from the said Colony in Virginia, there are or may be divers islandes lying desolate and uninhabited, some of which are already made knowne and discovered by the industry, travell, and expences of the said Company, and others allsoe are supposed to be and remaine as yet unknowen and undiscovered, all and every of which itt maie importe the said Colony both in safety and pollecy of trade to populate and plant, in regard where of, aswell for the preventing of perill as for the better comodity and prosperity of the said Colony, they have bin humble suitors unto us that we wold be pleased to grannt unto them an inlardgement of our said former lettres patent, aswell for a more ample extent of their limitts and territories into the seas adjoyning to and uppon the coast of Virginia as allsoe for some other matters and articles concerning the better government of the said Company and Collony, in which point our said former lettres patents doe not extende soe farre as time and experience hath found to be needfull and convenient:

We, therefore, tendring the good and happy successe of the said plantacion both in respect of the generall weale of humane society as in respect of the good of our owne estate and kingedomes, and being willing to give furtherannt untoall good meanes that may advannce the benefitt of the said Company and which maie secure the safety of our loving subjects, planted in our said Colony under the favour and proteccion of God Almighty and of our royall power and authority, have therefore of our especiall grace, certein knowledge and mere mocion, given, grannted and confirmed, and for us, our heires and successors we doe by theis presents, give, grannt and confirme unto the said Treasurer and Company of Adventurers and Planters of the said Citty of London for the First Colony in Virginia, and to their heires and successors for ever, all and singuler the said iselandes [whatsoever] scituat and being in anie part of the said ocean bordering upon the coast of our said First Colony in Virginia and being within three hundred leagues of anie the partes hertofore grannted to the said Treasorer and Company in our said former lettres patents as aforesaid, and being within or betweene the one and fortie and thirty degrees of Northerly latitude, together with all and singuler [soils] landes, groundes, havens, ports, rivers, waters, fishinges, mines and mineralls, aswell royal mines of gold and silver as other mines and mineralls, perles, precious stones, quarries, and all and singuler other commodities, jurisdiccions, royalties, priviledges, franchises and preheminences, both within the said tract of lande uppon the maine and allso within the said iselandes and seas adjoyning, whatsoever, and thereunto or there abouts both by sea and land being or scituat; and which, by our lettres patents, we maie or cann grannt and in as ample manner and sort as we or anie our noble progenitors have heretofore grannted to anie person or persons or to anie Companie, bodie politique or corporate or to any adventurer or adventurers, undertaker or undertakers of anie discoveries, plantacions or traffique, of, in, or into anie foreigne parts whatsoever, and in as lardge and ample manner as if the same were herein particularly named, mencioned and expressed: provided allwaies that the said iselandes or anie the premisses herein mencioned and by theis presents intended and meant to be grannted be not already actually possessed or inhabited by anie other Christian prince or estate, nor be within the bounds, limitts or territories of the Northerne Colonie, hertofore by us grannted to be planted by divers of our loving subjects in the northpartes of Virginia. To have and to hold, possesse and injoie all and singuler the said iselandes in the said ocean seas soe lying and bordering uppon the coast or coasts of the territories of the said First Colony in Virginia as aforesaid, with all and singuler the said soiles, landes and groundes and all and singular other the premisses heretofore by theis presents grannted, or mencioned to be grannted, to them, the said Treasurer and Companie of Adventurers and Planters of the Cittie of London for the First Colonie in Virginia, and to their heires, successors and assignes for ever, to the sole and proper use and behoofe of them, the said Treasurer and Companie and their heires, successores and assignes for ever; to be holden of us, our heires and successors as of our mannor of Eastgreenwich, in free and common soccage and not in capite, yealding and paying therefore, to us, our heires and successors, the fifte part of the oare of all gold and silver which shalbe there gotten, had or obteined for all manner of services, whatsoever.

And further our will and pleasure is, and we doe by theis presents grannt and confirme for the good and welfare of the said plantacion, and that posterity maie hereafter knowe whoe have adventured and not bin sparing of their purses in such a noble and generous accion for the generall good of theire cuntrie, and at the request and with the consent of the Companie afore said, that our trusty and welbeloved subjects.

George, Lord Archbishopp of Canterbury
Gilbert, Earle of Shrewsberry
Mary, Countesse of Shrewes
Elizabeth, Countesse of Derby
Margarett, Countesse of Comberland
Henry, Earle of Huntingdon
Edward, Earle of Beddford
Lucy, Countesse of Bedford
Marie, Countesse of Pembroke
Richard, Earle of Clanrickard
Lady Elizabeth Graie
William, Lord Viscount Crambome
William, Lord Bishopp of Duresme
Henry, Lord Bishopp of Worceter
John, Lord Bishopp of Oxonford
William, Lord Pagett
Dudley, Lord North
Franncis, Lord Norries
William, Lord Knollis
John, Lord Harrington
Robert, Lord Spencer
Edward, Lord Denny
William, Lord Cavendishe
James, Lord Hay
Elianor, Lady Cave [Carre]
Maistres Elizabeth Scott, widdow
Edward Sackvill, Esquier
Sir Henry Nevill, of Aburgavenny, Knight
Sir Robert Riche, Knight
Sir John Harrington, Knight
Sir Raphe Wimwood, Knight
Sir John Graie, Knight
Sir Henry Riche, Knight
Sir Henry Wotton, Knight
Peregrine Berly, Esquier [Berty]
Sir Edward Phelipps, Knight, Maister of the Rolls
Sir Moile Finche, Knight

Sir Thomas Mansell, Knight
Sir John St. John, Knight
Sir Richard Spencer, Knight
Sir Franncis Barrington, Knight
Sir George Carie of Devonshire, Knight
Sir William Twisden, Knight
Sir John Leveson, Knight
Sir Thomas Walsingham, Knight
Sir Edward Care, Knight
Sir Arthure Manwaringe, Knight
Sir Thomas Jermyn, Knight
Sir Valentine Knightley, Knight
Sir John Dodderidge, Knight
Sir John Hungerford, Knight
Sir John Stradling, Knight
Sir John Bourchidd, Knight [Bourchier]
Sir John Bennett, Knight
Sir Samuel Leonard, Knight
Sir Franncis Goodwin, Knight
Sir Wareham St. Legier, Knight
Sir James Scudamore, Knight
Sir Thomas Mildmaie, Knight
Sir Percivall Harte, Knight
Sir Percivall Willoughby, Knight
Sir Franncis Leigh, Knight
Sir Henry Goodere, Knight
Sir John Cutt, Knight
Sir James Parrett, Knight
Sir William Craven, Knight
Sir John Sammes, Knight
Sir Carey Raleigh, Knight
Sir William Maynard, Knight
Sir Edmund Bowyer, Knight
Sir William Cornewallis, Knight
Sir Thomas Beomont, Knight
Sir Thomas Cunningsby, Knight
Sir Henry Beddingfeild, Knight
Sir David Murray, Knight
Sir William Poole, Knight
Sir William Throgmorton, Knight
Sir Thomas Grantham, Knight
Sir Thomas Stewkley, Knight
Sir Edward Heron, Knight
Sir Ralph Shelten, Knight
Sir Lewes Thesam, Knight
Sir Walter Aston, Knight
Sir Thomas Denton, Knight
Sir Ewstace Hart, Knight
Sir John Ogle, Knight

Sir Thomas Dale, Knight
Sir William Boulstrod, Knight
Sir William Fleetwood, Knight
Sir John Acland, Knight
Sir John Hanham, Knight
Sir Roberte Meller, Knight [Millor]
Sir Thomas Wilford, Knight
Sir William Lower, Knight
Sir Thomas Lerdes, Knight [Leedes]
Sir Franncis Barneham, Knight
Sir Walter Chate, Knight
Sir Thomas Tracy, Knight
Sir Marmaduke Darrell, Knight
Sir William Harrys, Knight
Sir Thomas Gerrand, Knight
Sir Peter Freetchvile, Knight
Sir Richard Trevor, Knight
Sir Amias Bamfeild
Sir William Smith of Essex, Knight
Sir Thomas Hewett, Knight
Sir Richard Smith, Knight
Sir John Heyward, Knight
Sir Christopher Harris, Knight
Sir John Pettus, Knight
Sir William Strode, Knight
Sir Thomas Harfleet, Knight
Sir Walter Vaughan, Knight
Sir William Herrick, Knight
Sir Samuell Saltonstall, Knight
Sir Richard Cooper, Knight
Sir Henry Fane, Knight
Sir Franncis Egiok, Knight
Sir Robert Edolph, Knight
Sir Arthure Harries, Knight
Sir George Huntley, Knight
Sir George Chute, Knight
Sir Robert Leigh, Knight
Sir Richard Lovelace, Knight
Sir William Lovelace, Knight
Sir Robert Yaxley, Knight
Sir Franncis Wortley, Knight
Sir Franncis Heiborne, Knight
Sir Guy Palme, Knight
Sir Richard Bingley, Knight
Sir Ambrose Turvill, Knight
Sir Nicholas Stoddard, Knight
Sir William Gree, Knight
Sir Walter Coverte, Knight
Sir Thomas Eversfeild, Knight

Sir Nicholas Parker, Knight
Sir Edward Culpeper, Knight
Sir William Ayliffe, Knight, and
Sir John Keile, Knight
Doctor George Mountaine, Dean of Westminster
Lawrence Bohan, Docktor in Phisick
Anthony Hinton, Doctor in Phisick
John Pawlett
Arthure Ingram
Anthony Irby
John Weld
John Walter
John Harris
Anthony Dyott
William Ravenscrofte
Thomas Warre
William Hackwill
Lawrence Hide
Nicholas Hide
Thomas Stevens
Franncis Tate
Thomas Coventry
John Hare
Robert Askwith
George Sanndys
Franncis Jones
Thomas Wentworth
Henry Cromewell
John Arundell
John Culpeper
John Hoskins
Walter Fitz Williams
Walter Kirkham
William Roscarrock
Richard Carmerdon
Edward Carne
Thomas Merry
Nicholas Lichfeild
John Middleton
John Smithe, and
Thomas Smith, the sonnes of Sir Thomas Smith
Peter Franke
George Gerrand
Gregory Sprynte
John Drake
Roger Puleston
Oliver Nicholas
Richard Nunnington [Monyngton]
John Vaughan

John Evelin
Lamorock Stradling
John Riddall
John Kettleby
Warren Townsend
Lionell Cranfeild
Edward Salter
William Litton
Humfrey May
George Thorpe
Henry Sandys, and
Edwin Sandys, the sonnes of Sir Edwin Sandys
Thomas Conway
Captaine Owen Gwinn
Captaine Giles Hawkridge
Edward Dyer
Richard Connock
Benjamin Brand
Richard Leigh, and
Thomas Pelham, Esquiers
Thomas Digges, and
John Digges, Esquiers, the sonnes of Sir Dudley Diggs,
Franncis Bradley
Richard Buckminster [Buck]
Franncis Burley
John Procter
Thomas Frake, thelder, and
Henry Freake, thelder, Ministers of God's word
The mayor and citizens of Chichester
The mayor and jurates of Dover
The bailiffs, burgesses and comonalty of Ipswich
The mayor and comunalty of Lyme Regis
The mayor and comonalty of Sandwich
The wardens, assistants and companie of the Trinity House
Thomas Martin
Franncis Smaleman
Augustine Steward
Richard Tomlins
Humfrey Jobson
John Legate
Robert Backley [Barkley]
John Crowe
Edward Backley [Barkley]
William Flett [Fleet]
Henry Wolstenholme
Edmund Alleyn
George Tucker
Franncis Glanville
Thomas Gouge

John Evelin
William Hall
John Smithe
George Samms
John Robinson
William Tucker
John Wolstenholme, and Henry Wolstenholme, sonnes of John Wolstenholme, Esquier
William Hodges
Jonathan Mattall [Nuttall]
Phinees Pett
Captaine John Kinge
Captaine William Beck
Giles Alington
Franncis Heiton, and
Samuell Holliland, gentleman
Richard Chamberlaine
George Chamberlaine
Hewett Staper
Humfrey Handford
Raph Freeman
George Twinhoe [Swinhoe]
Richard Pigott
Elias Roberts
Roger Harris
Devereux Wogan
Edward Baber
William Greenewell
Thomas Stilles
Nicholas Hooker
Robert Garsett
Thomas Cordell
William Bright
John Reynold
Peter Bartley
John Willett
Humfry Smithe
Roger Dye
Nicholas Leate
Thomas Wale
Lewes Tate
Humfrey Merrett
Roberte Peake
Powell Isaackson
Sebastian Viccars
Jarvis Mundes
Richard Wamer
Gresham Hogan Warner
Daniell Deruley

Andrew Troughton
William Barrett
Thomas Hodges
John Downes
Richard Harper
Thomas Foxall
William Haselden
James Harrison
William Burrell
John Hodsall
Richard Fisborne
John Miller
Edward Cooke
Richard Hall, marchaunt
Richard Hall, ankersmith
John Delbridge
Richard Francklin
Edmund Scott
John Britten
Robert Stratt
Edmund Pond
Edward James
Robert Bell
Richard Herne
William Ferrers
William Millett
Anthony Abdy
Roberte Gore
Benjamin Decrow
Henry Tunbedey [Timberly]
Humfrey Basse
Abraham Speckart
Richard Moorer
William Compton
Richard Poulsoune [Pontsonne]
William Wolaston
John Desmont, clothier [Beomont]
Alexannder Childe
William Fald, fishmonger
Franncis Baldwin
John Jones, marchant
Thomas Plomer
Edward Plomer, marchants
John Stoickden
Robert Tindall
Peter Erundell
Ruben Bourne
Thomas Hampton, and
Franncis Carter, citizens of London,

whoe since our said last lettres patent are become adventurers and have joined themselves with the former adventurers and planters of the said Companie and societie, shall from henceforth be reputed, deemed and taken to be and shalbe brethren and free members of the Companie and shall and maie, respectively, and according to the proportion and value of their severall adventures, have, hold and enjoie all suche interest, right, title, priviledges, preheminences, liberties, franchises, immunities, profitts and commodities whatsoever in as lardge, ample and beneficiall manner to all intents, construccions and purposes as anie other adventures nominated and expressed in anie our former lettres patent, or anie of them have or maie have by force and vertue of theis presents, or anie our former lettres patent whatsoever.

And we are further pleased and we doe by theis presents grannt and confirm that

Phillipp, Earle of Montgomery
William, Lord Paget
Sir John Harrington, Knight
Sir William Cavendish, Knight
Sir John Sammes, Knight
Sir Samuell Sandys, Knight
Sir Thomas Freke, Knight
Sir William St. John, Knight
Sir Richard Grobham, Knight
Sir Thomas Dale, Knight
Sir Cavalliero Maycott, Knight
Richard Martin, Esquier
John Bingley, Esquier
Thomas Watson, Esquier, and
Arthure Ingram, Esquier,

whome the said Treasurer and Companie have, since the said [last] lettres patent, nominated and sett downe as worthy and discreete persons fitt to serve us as Counsellors, to be of our Counsell for the said plantacion, shalbe reputed, deemed and taken as persons of our said Councell for the said First Colonie in such manner and sort to all intents and purposes as those whoe have bin formerly ellected and nominated as our Counsellors for that Colonie and whose names have bin or are incerted and expressed in our said former lettres patent.

And we doe hereby ordaine and grannt by theis presents that the said Treasurer and Companie of Adventurers and Planters, aforesaid, shall and maie, once everie weeke or oftener at their pleasure, hold and keepe a court and assembly for the better ordening [ordering] and government of the said plantacion and such thinges as shall concerne the same; and that anie five persons of the said Counsell for the said First Collonie in Virginia, for the time being, of which Companie the Treasurer or his deputie allwaies to be one, and the nomber of fifteene others at the least of the generality of the said Companie assembled together in such court or assembly in such manner as is and hath bin heretofore used and accustomed, shalbe said, taken, held and reputed to be and shalbe a full and sufficient court of the said Companie for the handling, ordring and dispatching of all such casuall and particuler occurrences and accidentall matters of lesse consequence and waight, as shall from time to time happen, touching and concerning the said plantacion.

And that, nevertheles, for the handling, ordring and disposing of matters and affaires of great waight and importance and such as shall or maie in anie sort concerne the weale publike and generall good of the said Companie and plantacion as namely, the manner of government from time to time to be used, the ordring and disposing of the said possessions and the setling and establishing of a trade there, or such like, there shalbe held and kept everie yeare uppon the last Wednesdaie save one of Hillary, Easter, Trinity and Michaelmas termes, for ever, one great, generall and solemne assembly, which fower severall assemblies shalbe stiled and called The Fower Great and Generall Courts of the Counsell and Companie of Adventurers for Virginia; in all and every of which said great and generall Courts soe assembled our will and pleasure is and we doe, for us, our heires and successors forever, give and grannt to the said Treasurer and Companie and their successors for ever by theis presents, that they, the said Treasurer and Companie or the greater nomber of them soe assembled, shall and maie have full power and authoritie from time to time and att all times hereafter to ellect and choose discreet persons to be of our [said] Counsell for the said First Colonie in Virginia and to nominate and appoint such officers as theie shall thinke fitt and requisit for the government, managing, ordring and dispatching of the affaires of the said Companie; and shall likewise have full power and authority to ordaine and make such lawes and ordinances for the good and wellfare of the said plantacion as to them from time to time shalbe thought requisite and meete: soe allwaies as the same be not contrary to the lawes and statutes of this our realme of England; and shall in like manner have power and authority to expulse, disfranchise and putt out of and from their said Companie and societie for ever all and everie such person and persons as having either promised or subscribed their names to become adventurers to the said plantacion of the said First Colonie in Virginia, or having bin nominated for adventurers in theis or anie our lettres patent or having bin otherwise admitted and nominated to be of the said Companie, have nevertheles either not putt in anie adventure [at] all for and towards the said plantacion or els have refused and neglected, or shall refuse and neglect, to bringe in his or their adventure by word or writing promised within sixe monthes after the same shalbe soe payable and due.

And wheras the failing and nonpaiment of such monies as have bin promised in adventure for the advanncement of the said plantacion hath bin often by experience found to be danngerous and prejudiciall to the same and much to have hindred the progresse and proceeding of the said plantacion; and for that itt seemeth to us a thing reasonable that such persons as by their handwriting have engaged themselves for the payment of their adventures, and afterwards neglecting their faith and promise, shold be compellable to make good and kepe the same; therefore our will and pleasure is that in anie suite or suites comenced or to be comenced in anie of our courts att Westminster, or elswhere, by the said Treasurer and Companie or otherwise against anie such persons, that our judges for the time being both in our Court of Channcerie and at the common lawe doe favour and further the said suits soe farre forth as law and equitie will in anie wise suffer and permitt.

And we doe, for us, our heires and successors, further give and grannt to the said Tresorer and Companie, and their successors for ever, that theie, the said

Tresorer and Companie or the greater part of them for the time being, so in a full and generall court assembled as aforesaid shall and maie, from time to time and att all times hereafter, for ever, ellect, choose and permitt into their Company and society anie person or persons, as well straungers and aliens borne in anie part beyond the seas wheresoever, being in amity with us, as our naturall liedge subjects borne in anie our realmes and dominions; and that all such persons soe elected, chosen and admitted to be of the said Companie as aforesaid shall thereuppon be taken, reputed and held and shalbe free members of the said Companie and shall have, hold and enjoie all and singuler freedoms, liberties, franchises, priviledges, immunities, benefitts, profitts and commodities, whatsoever, to the said Companie in anie sort belonging or apperteining as fully, freely [and] amplie as anie other adventurer or adventurers now being, or which hereafter att anie time shalbe, of the said Companie, hath, have, shall, maie, might or ought to have or enjoy the same to all intents and purposes whatsoever.

And we doe further of our speciall grace, certaine knowledge and mere mocion, for us, our heires and successors, give and grantt to the said Tresorer and Companie and their successors, for ever by theis present, that itt shalbe lawfull and free for them and their assignes att all and everie time and times hereafter, out of anie our realmes and dominions whatsoever, to take, lead, carry and transport in and into the said voyage and for and towards the said plantacion of our said First Collonie in Virginia, all such and soe manie of our loving subjects or anie other straungers that will become our loving subjects and live under our allegiance as shall willingly accompanie them in the said voyage and plantacion; with shipping, armour, weapons, ordinannce, munition, powder, shott, victualls, and all manner of merchandizes and wares, and all manner of clothing, implement, furniture, beasts, cattell, horses, mares, and all other thinges necessarie for the said plantacion and for their use and defence, and for trade with the people there and in passing and retourning to and froe, without paying or yealding anie subsedie, custome or imposicion, either inward or outward, or anie other dutie to us, our heires or successors, for the same, for the space of seven yeares from the date of theis present.

And we doe further, for us, our heires and successors, give and grannt to the said Treasurer and Companie and their successors for ever, by theis present, that the said Treasurer of the said Companie, or his deputie for the time being or anie twoe others of our said Counsell for the said First Colonie in Virginia for the time being, shall and maie att all times hereafter and from time to time, have full power and authoritie to minister and give the oath and oathes of supremacie and allegiannce, or either of them, to all and every person and persons which shall, at anie time and times hereafter, goe or passe to the said Colonie in Virginia:

And further, that itt shalbe likewise lawfull for the said Tresorer, or his deputy for the time, or anie twoe others of our said Counsell for the said First Colonie in Virginia, for the time being, from time to time and att all times hereafter, to minister such a formall oathe as by their discrescion shalbe reasonably devised, aswell unto anie person or persons imployed or to be imployed in, for, or touching the said plantacion for their honest, faithfull and just dischardge of their service in all such matters as shalbe committed unto them for the good and benefitt of the said Company, Colonie and plantacion; as alsoe unto such other person or persons as the said Treasurer or his deputie, with twoe others of the said Counsell, shall thinke meete for the examinacion or clearing of the truith in anie cause whatsoever concerninge the said plantacion or anie business from thence proceeding or there unto proceeding or thereunto belonging.

And, furthermore, whereas we have ben certefied that diverse lewde and ill disposed persons, both sailors, souldiers, artificers, husbandmen, laborers, and others, having received wages, apparrell or other entertainment from the said Company or having contracted and agreed with the said Companie to goe, to serve, or to be imployed in the said plantacion of the said First Colonie in Virginia, have afterwards either withdrawen, hid or concealed themselves, or have refused to goe thither after they have bin soe entertained and agreed withall; and that divers and sundry persons allso which have bin sent and imployed in the said plantacion of the said First Colonie in Virginia at and upon the chardge of the said Companie, and having there misbehaved themselves by mutinies, sedition, and other notorious misdemeanors, or having bin employed or sent abroad by the governor of Virginia or his deputie with some ship or pinnace for provisions for the said Colonie, or for some discoverie or other buisines and affaires concerning the same, have from thence most trecherouslie either come back againe and retorned into our realme of England by stelth or without licence of our Governor of our said Colonie in Virginia for the time being, or have bin sent hither as misdoers and offenders; and that manie allsoe of those persons after their retourne from thence, having bin questioned by our said Counsell here for such their misbehaviors and offences, by their insolent and contemptuous carriage in the presence of our said Counsaile, have shewed little respect and reverence, either to the place or authoritie in which we have placed and appointed them; and others, for the colouring of their lewdnes and misdemeanors committed in Virginia, have endeavored them by most vile and slanndrous reports made and divulged, aswell of the cuntrie of Virginia as alsoe of the government and estate of the said plantacion and Colonie, as much as in them laie, to bring the said voyage and plantacion into disgrace and contempt; by meanes where of not only the adventures and planters alreadie ingaged in the said plantacion have bin exceedingly abused and hindred, and a greate nomber of other our loving and welldisposed subjects otherwise well affected and inclyning to joine and adventure insoe noble, Christian and worthie an action have bin discouraged from the same, but allsoe the utter overthrow and ruine of the said enterprise hath bin greatlie indanngered which cannott miscarrie without some dishonor to us and our kingdome;

Now, for asmuch as it appeareth unto us that theis insolences, misdemeanors and abuses, not to be tollerated in anie civill government, have for the most part growne and proceeded inregard of our Counsaile have not anie direct power and authoritie by anie expresse wordes in our former lettres patent to correct and chastise such offenders, we therefore, for the more speedy reformacion of soe greate and enormous abuses and misdemeanors heretofore practised and committed, and for the preventing of the like hereafter, doe by theis present for us, our heires and successors, give and grannt to the said Treasurer and Companie, and their successors for ever, that itt shall and maie be lawfull for our said Councell for the said First Colonie in Virginia or anie twoe of them, whereof the said Tresorer or his deputie for the time being to be allwaies one by warrant under their handes to send for, or cause to be apprehended, all and every such person and persons who shalbe noted or accused or found, att anie time or times here after, to offend or misbehave themselves in anie the offences before mencioned and expressed; and uppon the examinacion of anie such offender or offendors and just proofe made by oath taken before the Counsaile of anie such notorious misdemeanors by them committed as aforesaid; and allsoe uppon anie insolent, contemptuous or unreverent carriage and misbehavior to or against our said Counsell shewed or used by anie such person or persons soe called, convented and apearing before them as aforesaid; that in all such cases theie, our said Counsell or anie twoe of them for the time being, shall and maie have full power and authoritie either here to binde them over with good suerties for their good behaviour and further therein to proceed to all intents and purposes, as itt is used in other like cases within our realme of England; or ells att their discrescion to remannd and send back the said offenders or anie of them unto the said Colonie in Virginia, there to be proceeded against and punished as the Governor, deputie and Counsell there for the time being shall thinke meete; or otherwise, according to such lawes and ordinannces as are or shalbe in use there for the well ordring and good governement of the said Colonie.

And, for the more effectuall advanncing of the said plantacion, we doe further, for us, our heires and successors, of our especiall grace and favour, by vertue of our prorogative royall and by the assent and consent of the Lordes and others of our Privie Counsalle, give and grannte unto the said Tresorer and Companie full power and authoritie, free leave, libertie and licence to sett forth, errect and publishe one or more lotterie or lotteries to have continuance and to [endure] and be held for the space of one whole yeare next after the opening of the same, and after the end and expiracion of the said terme the said lotterie or lotteries to continue and be further kept, during our will and pleasure onely and not otherwise. And yet, nevertheles, we are contented and pleased, for the good and wellfare of the said plantacion, that the said Tresorer and Companie shall, for the dispatch and finishing of the said lotterie or lotteries, have six months warninge after the said yeare ended before our will and pleasure shall, for and on that behalfe, be construed, deemed and adjudged to be in anie wise altered and determined.

And our further will and pleasure is that the said lottery or lottaries shall and maie be opened and held within our cittie of London or in anie other cittie or citties, or ellswheare within this our realme of England, with such prises, articles, condicions and limitacions as to them, the said Tresorer and Companie, in their discreascions shall seeme convenient.

And that itt shall and may be lawfull to and for the said Tresorer and Companie to ellect and choose receivors, auditors, surveyors, comissioners, or anie other officers whatsoever, att their will and pleasure for the better marshalling and guiding and governing of the said lottarie or lottaryes; and that itt shalbe likewise lawfull to and for the said Tresorer and anie twoe of the said Counsell to minister unto all and everie such persons soe ellected and chosen for officers as aforesaid one or more oathes for their good behaviour, just and true dealing in and about the lottarie or lottaries to the intent and purpose that none of our loving subjects, putting in their monies or otherwise adventuring in the said generall lotterie or lottaries, maie be in anie wise defrauded and deceived of their said monies or evill and indirectlie dealt withall in their said adventures.

And we further grannt in manner and forme aforesaid, that itt shall and maie be lawfull to and for the said Treasurer and Companie, under the seale of our Counsell for the plantacion, to publishe or to cause and procure to be published by proclamacion or otherwise, the said proclamacion to be made in their name by vertue of theise present, the said lottarie or lotteries in all citties, townes, boroughts, throughfaires and other places within our said realme of England; and we will and commande all mayors, justices of peace, sheriffs, bayliffs, constables and other our officers and loving subjects whatsoever, that in noe wise theie hinder or delaie the progresse and proceeding of the said lottarie or lottaries but be therein and, touching the premisses, aiding and assisting by all honest, good and lawfull meanes and endevours.

And further our will and pleasure is that in all questions and dobts that shall arise uppon anie difficultie of construccion or interpretacion of anie thing conteined in theis or anie other our former lettres patent the same shalbe taken and interpreted in most ample and beneficiall manner for the said Tresorer and Companie and their successors and everie member there of.

And lastly we doe by theis present retifie and confirme unto the said Treasorer and Companie, and their successors for ever, all and all manner of priviledges, franchises, liberties, immunities, preheminences, profitts and commodities whatsoever grannted unto them in anie our [former] lettres patent and not in theis present revoked, altered, channged or abridged. Although expresse mencion [of the true yearly value or certainty of the premises, or any of them, or of any other gift or grant, by us or any of our progenitors or predecessors, to the aforesaid Tresurer and Company heretofore made, in these Presents is not made; or any statute, act, ordinance, provisions, proclamation, or restraint, to the contrary thereof heretofore made, ordained, or provided, or any other matter, cause, or thing, whatsoever, to the contrary, in any wise, notwithstanding.]

In witnes whereof [we have caused these our letters to be made patents.] Wittnes our selfe att Westminster, the twelveth daie of March [1612] [in the ninth year of our reign of England, France, and Ireland, and of Scotland the five and fortieth.]

William Strachey's Description of the Natives of Virginia, 1612

The following description of the Indians encountered by the early settlers at colonial Jamestown was written by William Strachey and published in the First Book of the First Decade, Chapter 5, of his Historie of Travell Into Virginia Britania *(London, 1612). It is drawn mostly from personal observation, relying little on the published writings of Jamestown's most prolific chronicler, Captain John Smith.*

A true Description of the People; of their Collour, Constitution and Disposition; their Apparrell.

THEY are generally of a Coulour browne, or rather tawnye which the Mothers cast them into with a kynd of Arsenickstone (like redd Patise, or Orpement,) or rather with redd tempered oyntementes of earth, and the juyce of certayne scrused rootes, so sone as they ar borne, and this they doe (keeping themselves still so smudged and besmeered) either for the Custome of the Country, or the better to defend them (synce they goe most what naked) from the stinging of Muskeetoes, (kyndes of Flyes, or byting Gnatts, such as the Greeks called Scynipes, as yet in great swarmes within the Arches,) and which heere breed aboundantly, amongst the marish whorts, and fenburies; and of the same hue are their women, howbeit yt is supposed neither of them naturally borne so discoulored, for Captayne Smith (living sometyme amongest them) affirmeth, how they are from the woumb indifferent white, but as the men so doe the women, dye and disguise themselves, into this tawny coulour, esteeming yt the best beauty, to be neerest such a kynd of Murrey, as a sodden Quince is of, (to lyken yt to the neerest coulour I can) for which they daylie annoynt both face and bodyes all over, with such a kynd of fucus or unguent, as can cast them into that stayne, as is sayd of the Greek-women, how they colloured their faces all over with certayne rootes called Brenthyna; and as the *Britaynes* died themselves redd with woad: howbeit he, or shee, that hath obteyned the perfectest art in the tempering of this Coulour with any better kynd of earth, hearb, or roote, preserves yt not yet so secrett, and pretious unto her self, as doe our great Ladies their oyle of Talchum, or other Paynting white and redd, but they freindly comunicate the secrett, and teach yt one another: after their annoynting (which is dailye) they drie them in the Sun, and thereby make their skynnes (besyde the Coulour more black and spotted, which the Sun kissing oft, and hard, addes to their paynting) the more rough and rugged.

Their heades and showlders they paynt oftennest, and those red, with the roote Pochone, brayed to poulder mixed with oyle of the walnut, or Beares grease, this they hold in Summer doth check the heat, and in winter armes them (in some measure) against the Cold, many other formes of payntings they use; but he is the most gallant who is the most monstrous and ugly to behold.

Their hayre is black, grosse, longe and thick, the men have no beardes, their noses are broad flatt and full at the end, great bigge Lippes, and wyde mouthes, (yet nothing so unsightly as the Moores,) they are generally tall of stature, and streight, of comely proportion, and the women have handsome lymbes, slender armes, and pretty handes, and when they sing they have a delightful and pleasant tang in their voyces.

For their apparrell, they are sometymes covered with the skynns of wild beasts, which in winter are dressed with the haire, but in the Sommer without, the better sort use large mantells of divers skyns, not much differing from the Irish falinges; some ymbroydered with white Beads, some with copper, other paynted after their manner, but the Comon sort have scarse wherewithall to cover their nakednes, but stick long blades grasse, the leaves of Trees or such like under broad Baudricks of Leather which covers them behind and before.

The better sort of women cover them (for the most parte) all over with skyn mantells, fynely drest, shagged and frindged at the skirt, carved and coulored, with some pretty worke or the proportion of beasts, fowle, tortoyses, or other such like Imagery as shall best please or expresse the fancy of the wearer, their younger women goe not shadowed amongest their owne company untill they be nigh eleaven or twelve returnes of the Leafe old (for so they accompt and bring about the yeare) calling the fall of the leafe *Taquitock*) nor are they much ashamed thereof, and therefore would the before remembered *Pochohuntas,* a well featured but wanton young girle Powhatans daughter, sometymes resorting to our Fort, of the age then of 11. or 12. yeares, gett the boyes forth with her into the markett place and make them wheele, falling on their handes turning their heeles upwardes, whome she would follow, and wheele so her self naked as she was all the Fort over, but being past once 12. yeres they put on a kynd of semicinctum leathren apron (as doe our artificers or handicrafts men) before their bellies and are very shamefac'd to be seene bare: we have seene some use mantells, made both of Turkey feathers and other fowle so prettely wrought and woven with threeds that nothing could be discerned but the feathers, which were exceeding warme and very handsome: *Nuda mulier erat pulchra,* (saith Plautus) *quam purpurata pulchrior?* Indeed the ornament of that Sexe, who receave an addicion of delicacy, by their garments; true yt is sometymes in cold weather, or when they goe a hunting, or seeking the fruicts of the woodes, or gathering bents for their matts, both men and women, to defend them from the bushes) put on a kynd of leather breeches and stockings, all fastened togither, made of deere skynes, which they tye and wrappe about the loynes after the fashion of the Turkes or Irish Trouses.

They adorne themselves most with Copper beades and paynting, of the men there be some, who will paint their bodies black and some yellow, and being oyled over, they will stick therein the soft downe of sondry Coloured birdes, of blew birdes, white herneshews, and the feathers of the Carnation byrd, which they call *Ahshowcutteis,* as if so many variety of laces were stitched to their skyns, which makes a wonderous shew, the men being angry and prepared to fight paint and Crosse their foreheades, cheekes, and the right syde of their heades diversly, either with *terra-sigillata,* or with their root Pochone.

The women have their armes, breasts, thighes, showlders and faces, cunningly imbroydered with divers workes, for pouncing and searing their skyns with a kynd of Instrument (heated in the fire, they figure therein flowers and fruicts of sondry lively kyndes, as also Snakes, Serpents, Efts, etc., and this they doe by dropping upon the seared flesh, sondry Colours, which rub'd into the stampe will never be taken away agayne because yt will not only be dryed into the flesh, but grow therein.

The men shave their hayre on the right syde very Close keeping a ridge commonly on the toppe or Crowne like a Cox-comb; for their women with twoo shells will grate away the haire into any fashion they please; on the leaft syde they weare their haire at full length with a lock of an ell long, which they annoynt often with walnut oyle, whereby yt is very sleeke, and shynes like a Ravens wing: sometymes they tye up their lock with an arteficiall and well laboured knott (in the same fashion, as I have seene the *Carazzaies* of *Scio,* and *Pera:)* stuck with many coloured Gewgawes, as the cast head or Browantle of a deare, the hand of their Enemy dryed, Croisetts of bright and shyning Copper, like the new Moone, many weare the whole skyn of a hawke stuffed, with the winges abroad, and Buzzardes or other fowles whole wings, and to the feathers they will fasten a little Rattle about the bignes of the Chape of a rapier, which they take from the taile of a Snake, and sometymes divers kyndes of shells hanginge loose by smale purfleets or threedes, that, being shaken as they move, they will make a Certayne murmering or whistling noyse by gathering wynd, in which they seeme to take great iollety, and hold yt a kynd of bravery.

Their eares they boare with wyde holes comonly twoo or three, and in the same they doe hang chaynes of stayned perle, braceletts of white bone, or shredds of Copper, beaten thin and bright, and wound up hollow, and with a great pride certayne Fowles leggs, Eagles, Hawkes, Turkeys, etc., with Beasts Clawes, Beares, Arrahacounes, Squirrells, etc. the clawes thrust through, they lett hang upon the Cheeke to the full view; and some of their men there be, who will weare in these holes, a smale greene and yellow couloured live Snake neere half a yard in length, which Crawling and lapping himself about his neck oftentymes familiarly he suffers to kisse his lipps, others weare a dead ratt tyed by the Taile, and such like Conundrums.

The women are in themselves so modest, as in the tyme of their sicknes, they have great care to be seene abroad, at what tyme they goe apart, and keepe from the men in a severall roome, which they have for themselves as a kynd of Gynæceum, nor will the men at such a tyme presse into the nursery where they are.

The men are very strong of able bodies, and full of agility, accustoming themselves to endure hardnes, to lye in the woodes under a tree, by a smale fire in the worst of winter in Frost and Snow, or in the weedes and grasse, as in Ambuscado to accomplish their purposes in the Sommer.

They are inconstant in every thing, but what feare constrayneth them to keepe, Craftye tymerous, quick of apprehension, ingenious ynough in their owne workes, as may testefy the weeres, in which they take their Fish, which are certayne inclosures made of Reedes and framed in the fashion of a Labourinth or Maze, sett a fathome deepe in the water, with divers Chambers or bedds, out of which the entangled Fish cannot retourne or gett out being once in well may a great one by chaunce break the Reedes and so escape, otherwise he remaynes a pray to the Fisher-man the next low water, which they fish with a nett tyed at the end of a pole; as likewise may speake for them their Netts, their arteficiall dressing of Leather, their Cordage, which they make of their naturall hemp and flax togither with their Cunning dressing of that and preserving the whole yeare great Litches or bundells of the same to be used upon any occasion; and of their girdells, which they make of silke grasse, much like St. *Francis Cordon,* their Cloakes of feathers their bowes and Bowstrings, their Arrowes, their Crownetts, which their Weroances weare; and their Queenes *fasciae crinales,* Borders, or Frontalls, of white Beades Currall and Copper, especially their boates, which they call Quintans and are very shapefull, made of one piece of Tymber like the auncyent *Monoxylum Nauigium,* their Matts and all their howshold Implements and such like.

Some of them are of disposicion fearefull (as I said) and not easely wrought therefore to trust vs, or Come into our Forts, others agayne of them are so bould and audatious as they dare come unto our forts, truck and trade with vs and looke vs in the face, crying all freindes, when they have but new done vs a mischief, and when they intend presently againe, if yt lye in their power to doe the like, they are generally Covetous of our Cornodities, as Copper, white beades for their women, Hatchetts, of which we make them poore ones of Iron, Howes to pare their Corne grownd, knyves and such like.

They are soone moved to anger, and so malitious that they seldome forgett an Injury; they are very thievish, and will as closely as they can convey any thing away from vs, howbeit they seldome steale one from another, lest their Coniurers should reveale yt, and so they be pursued and punished: that they are thus feared yt is certayne; nor let any man doubt but that the devill cann reveale an offence actually committed.

William Strachey's Description of Chief Powhatan, 1612

The following description of Powhatan was written by William Strachey and published in the First Book of the First Decade, Chapter 4, of his Historie of Travell Into Virginia Britania *(London, 1612). It is, perhaps, the best single description of the great Weorance.*

The great Emperour at this tyme amongest them we Commonly call Powhatan for by that name true yt is, he was made known unto us, when we arryved in the Country first, and so indeed he was generally called when he was a young man, as taking his denomynacion from the Country Powhatan, wherein he was borne, which is above at the Falls as before mencioned, right over aneinst the Islands, at the head of our river, and which place or birth-right of his, he sold Anno 1609. about Sempemter, unto Captain Francis West, our Lord Generalls brother, who therefore erected there a Fort, calling yt Wests-Fort, and sate himself downe there with 120. English: the inhabitants themselves especially his frontier neighbour princes, call his still *Powhatan,* his owne people sometymes call his *Ottaniack,* sometymes *Mamanatowick,* which last signifyes great Kinge, but his proper right name which they salute him with (himself in presence) is *Wahunsenacawh.*

The greatness and bowndes of whose Empire by reason of his Powerfulnes, and ambition in his youth, hath lardger lymittes then ever had any of his Predicessors in former tymes: for he seemes to comaund South and North from the *Mangoags,* and *Chawonookes,* bordering upon *Roanoak* or South-Virginia, to *Tockwogh,* a towne pallisado'de, standign at the North-end of our Bay in 40. degrees or thereaboutes: South-west to *Anoeg* (not expressed in the Mappe) whose howses are buylt as ours, 10. dayes journye distant from us, from whence those inhabiting weroances sent unto him of their Commodityes, as Weionock (a servaunt in whom Powhatan reposed much trust) would tell our elder Planters, and could repeat many wordes of their language which he had learned amongest them, in his implоyment thither for his king, and whence he often retourned full of Presents to Powhatan; and west-ward, he Commaundes to *Monahassanugh,* which standes at the foot of the mountaynes, from *Chesapeak* or the mouth of our Bay 200. myles: Nor-west, to the bordures of *Massawomeck,* and *Bocootawwonough:* Nor-east and by east to *Accohanock, Accowmack,* and some other petty Nations, lying on the East syde of our Bay.

He hat divers seates or howses, his Chief when we came into the Country was upon Pamunky-River, on the North side which we call Pembrook-side, called *Werowocomaco,* which by interpretacion signifyes Kings-howse. howbeit not lyking to neighbour so neere us, that howse being within some 15. or 16. myles, where he saw we purposed to hold ourselves, and from whence in 6. or 7. howres we were able to visit him, he removed and ever synce hath most what kept, at a place in the desartes called *Orapaks,* at the top of the river *Chickahamania,* betweene *Youghtamund,* and *Powhatan.*

He is a goodly old-man, not yet shrincking, though well beaten with many cold and stormy wynters, in which he hath bene patient of many necessityes and attempts of his fortune, to make his name and famely great, he is supposed to be little lesse than 80. years old, (I dare not say how much more, others say he is). Of a tall stature, and cleane lymbes, of a sad aspect, rownd fat visag'd with gray haires, but playne and thyn hanging upon his broad showlders, some few haires upon his Chynne, and so on his upper lippe. He hath bene a strong and able salvadge, synowie, active, and of a daring spiritt, vigilant, ambitious, subtile to enlarge his dominions, for but the Countryes *Powhatan, Arrohateck, Appamatuck, Pamunky, Youghtamond,* and *Mattapanient* which are said to be come unto him by Inheritaunce, all the resto of the Territoryes before named and expressed in the Mappe, and which are all adioyning to that River, whereon we are seated, they report (as is likewise before mencioned) to have bene either by force subdued unto him, or through feare yeilded: Cruell he hath bene, and quarrellous, as well with his owne Weroances for triffles, and that to stryke a terrour and awe into them of his power and condicion, as also with his neighbours in his younger dayes, though now delighted in security, and pleasure, and therefore standes upon reasonable condicions of peace, with all the great and absolute Weroances about him, and is likewise more quietly setteled amongest his owne.

Watchful he is over us, and keeps good espiall upon our proceedings, Concerning which he hath his Sentinells, that at what tyme soever any of our boates, pinaces or shippes, come in, fall downe, or make up the River, give the Alarum, and take yt quickly the one from the other, untill yt reach and come even to the Court, or hunting howse, wheresoever he, and his *Cronoccoes,* I. Councellors, and Priests, are; and then he calls to advise, and gives out directions, what is to be done, as more fearing, then harmed at any tyme, with the danger and mischief, which he saith wee intend unto him, by taking away his land from him, and conspiring to surprize him, which we never yet ymagined nor attempted, and yet albeyt the Conceipt of as much strongly possesseth him, he doth often send unto us to temporize with us, awayting perhapps but a fitt opportunity (inflamed by his bloudy and furious priests) to offer us a tast of the same Cuppe which he made our poore Countrymen drinck off at *Roanoak* not yet seeming willing to hold any open quarrell or hostility with us, but in all advantages, which he sometymes takes against or credulous and beguyled people, he hath yt alwaies so carryed, as upon our Complaynt to him, yt is rather layd upon some of his worst and unruly people, of which he tells us even our King James, (comaunding so many divers men) must have some irreguler and unruly people, or ells upon some of his pettye Weroances, whome peradventure we have attempted (saith he) with offences of the like nature, then that yt is any act of his, or done by his commaund, or according to his will, often flattering us, that he will take order, thatyt shalbe no more so, but that the *Tassantasses,* that is the straungers, Kinge James his people, and his people, shalbe all one, brothers, and freindes, and thus he served us at what tyme he wrought the *Chickahamanias* (a Nationas we have learned, before the coming in of us, so far from being his subjectes, as they were ever his enemyes) into a hatred of us (being indeed a mighty people, and our neighbours, within some 10. or 12. myles of James-towne) and us into the suspicion of them, by telling us that they were naught, and not to he trusted by us, attending but opportunity to do us a mischief; and by urging them to betray such of our men as should come at any tyme to trade with them for corne, and true yt is, upon an advantage at such a tyme they slew three of our men without Cause or offence given, only put into this Jelousy of our faire dealing with them by Powhatan, and they had done as much for all the rest of ours at that tyme, with them in the Bardg, had not their owne feare and Cowardize more withheld them, then the readines of our people to stand upon their guard, and when this was complayn'd of unto Powhatan, he wholly lay'd the blame upon the unrulines, and force of so mightie a people, excusing himself to us by their nomber, and insolence; yea so far he will herein go sometyme, that when some of his people have done us wrong, (and by his provoaking too) he will not fayle underhand, after the fact, to tell us the Authors of our wronge, giving us leave, and bydding us revenge us upon them, of such subtile understanding and politique carriage is hee.

In all his ancient Inheritaunces, he hath howses built after their manner, and at every howse provision for his entertaynement, according to the tyme: about his person ordinarily attendeth a guard of 40. or 50. of the tallest men his Country doe affourd. every night upon the 4 quarters of his howse, are 4. Sentinells drawne forth, one from the *Corps du guard,* doth hollow, unto whome every Sentinell returns answere, rownd from his stand, yt any faile, an officer is presently sent forth, that beateth him extreamely.

The word Weroance, which wee call and conster for a king, is a Common word, whereby they call all Comaunders, for they have but few wordes in their language, and but few occasions to use any officers, more than one Commaunder, which comonly they call Weroance.

It is straung to see withwhat great feare and adoration all those people doe obey this Powhatan, for at his feet they present whatsoever he Commaundeth, and at the least frowne of his brow, the greatest will tremble, yt may be because he is very terryble, and inexorable in punishing such as offend him: for example, he caused certayne Malefactors (at what tyme Capt Smith was Prysoner with them, and to the sight whereof, Capt Smith for some purpose was brought) to be bound hand and foot, when certayne officers appointed thereunto, having from many fires gathered great store of burning Coales, raked the Coales rownd in forme of a Cockpit, and in the middst they cast the offenders to broyle to death: sometymes he causeth the heades of them that offend to be layd upon the Aulter or sacryficing stone, and one or twoo Clubbs beat out their braynes; when he would punish any notorious enemy or Trespasser, he causeth him to be tyed to a tree, and with muscle-shells or Reedes, the Executioner cutteth off his Joyntes one after another, ever casting what is cut off into the Fier, then doth he proceed with shells and reedes to case the skyn from his head and face, after which they rippe up his belly, teare out his bowells, and so burne him with the tree and all. Thus themselves reported, that they executed an englishman one George Cawson, whom the women enticed up from the barge unto their howses at a place called *Appocant.* Howebeit his ordinary correction is, to have an offendor whome he will only punish, and not put to death, to be beaten with Cudgells as the Turks doe, wee have seene a man kneeling on his knees, and at Powhatans comaund, twoo men have beat him on the bare skynn, till the skynne hat bene all bollen, and blistered, and all on a goare blood, and till he hath fallen senceles in a swound, and yet never cryed, complayned, nor seemed to aske pardon, for that they seldome doe.

Any sure yt is to be wondered at, how such a barbarous and uncivill Prynce, should take into him (adorned and set forth with no greater outward ornament and munificence) a forme and ostentacion of such Majestie as he expresseth, which oftentimes strykes awe and sufficient wonder into our people, presenting themselves before him, but such is (I believe) the Impression of the divine nature, and howsoever these (as other) heathens forsaken by the true light, have not that portion of the knowing blessed Christian-spirit, yet I am perswaded there is an infused kynd of divinenes, and extraordinary (appointed that it shallbe so by king of kings) to such who are his ymediate Instruments on earth (how wretched soever otherwise under the Course of misbelief and Infidelity, as it is in the Psalme. *Dixi vos sicut Dii estis,* to governe and dwell in the eyes and Countenaunces of Princes, somwhat may this Catagraph, or Portrayture following, serve to express the presentement of this great king Powhatan. [*blank half-page follows*]

According to the order and custome of sensuall Hethenisme in the Allowaunce of Poligamy, he may have as many women as he will, and hath (as is supposed) many more then one hundred, All which he doth not keepe, yet as the Turke in one Saraglia or howse, but hat an appointed number, which reside still in ever their severall places, amongest whome when he lyeth on his bedd, one sitteth at his head, and another at his feet, but when he sitteth at meat, or in presenting himself to any Straungers, one sitteth on his right hand, and another on his leaft, as is here expressed.

Of his women there are said to be about some dozen at this present, in whose Company he takes more delight then in the rest, being for the most parte very young women, and these Commonly remove with him from howse to howse, either in his tyme of hunting, or visitation of his severall howses; I obteyned their names from one *Kempes* an Indian, who died the last yeare of the Scurvye at James towne, after he had dwelt with us almost one whole yeare, much made of by our Lord Generall, and who could speake a pretty deale of English, and came orderly to Church every day to prayers, and observed with us the keeping of the Sabaoth, both by ceassing from Labour, and repayring to church, the names of the women I have not thought altogither amisse to set downe as he gave them unto me, and as they stood formost in his Kings affection, for they observe certayne degrees of greatness, according to the neerenes they stand in their Princes love, and amourous entertaynment.

Winganuske. *Attossocomiske.* *Ortoughnoiske.*
Ashetoiske. *Ponnoiske.* *Oweroughwough.*
Amopotoiske. *Appomosicut.* *Ottermiske.*
Ottopomtacke. *Appimmonoiske.* *Memeoughquiske.*

He was reported by the said Kemps, as also by the Indian Machumps, who was sometyme in England, and comes to and from amongest us, as he dares, and as Powhatan gives him leave, for yt is not otherwise safe for him, no more then yt was for one Amarice, who had his braynes knock't out for selling but a baskett of Corne, and lying in the English fort 2. or 3. daies with Powhatans leave, I say, they often reported unto us that Powhatan had then lyving twenty sonnes and ten daughters besydes a young one by *Winganuske,* Machumps his sister and a great Dearling of the kings, and besydes younge *Pocohunta* a daughter of his, using sometyme to our Fort in tymes past, now marryed to a pryvate Captayne called *Kocum* some 2. years synce.

As he is weary of his women, he bestowes them on those that best deserve them at his handes, when he dyneth or suppeth, one of his women before and after meat, bringeth him water in a wooden platter, to wash his handes, another wayting with a bunch of feathers to wipe them in steed of a towell, and the Feathers, when he hath wyped, are washed and dryed agayne.

A myle from *Oropaks* in a Thickett of wood he hath a principall howse, in which he keepeth his kind of Treasure, as Skins coper, Pearle, and Beads, which he storeth up against the tyme of his Death and buryall, here is also his store of redd paint for oyntment, and bowes and arrowes, this howse is 50. or 60. yards in length, frequented only by Priests, at the 4 corners of this howse stand 4 Imadges, not as Atlantes or Telamones, supportes ro beare up Pillers, Posts or somwhat ells in the stately building, nor as in the auncyent tymes, the Imadges and Pedegrees of the whole Stock or Famely were wont to be sett in Portches, or the first entraunce into howses, with a Porter of speciall trust, who had the Charge of keeping and looking unto them, called *Atrienses:* but these, are meerly sett, as carefull Sentinells (forsooth) to defend, and protect the howse: (for so they believe of them:) one is like a Dragon, another like a Beare, the third like a Leopard, and the fourth a Giant-Like man, all made evill favoured ynough, according to their best wormanshippe.

John Rolfe to Sir Thomas Dale, 1614

In the following letter, John Rolfe seeks permission from Governor Dale to marry the Indian princess, Pocahontas. Permission was granted by both Dale and Pocahontas's father, Chief Powhatan, whom Rolfe also approached, and the marriage took place on 5 April 1614. The transcript of the letter is taken from J. Franklin Jameson's Narratives of Early Virginia *(New York, 1907).*

The coppie of the Gentle-mans letters to Sir Thomas Dale, that after married Powhatans daughter, containing the reasons moving him thereunto.

Honourable Sir, and most worthy Governor:

When your leasure shall best serve you to peruse these lines, I trust in God, the beginning will not strike you into a greater admiration, then the end will give you good content. It is a matter of no small moment, concerning my own particular, which here I impart unto you, and which toucheth mee so neerely, as the tendernesse of my salvation. Howbeit I freely subject my selfe to your grave and mature judgement, deliberation, approbation, and determination; assuring my selfe of your zealous admonitions, and godly comforts, either perswading me to desist, or incouraging me to persist therin, with a religious and godly care, for which (from the very instant, that this began to roote it selfe within the secret bosome of my brest) my daily and earnest praiers have bin, still are, and ever shall be produced forth with as sincere a godly zeale as I possibly may to be directed, aided and governed in all my thoughts, words, and deedes, to the glory of God, and for my eternal consolation. To persevere wherein I never had more neede, nor (till now) could ever imagine to have bin moved with the like occasion.

But (my case standing as it doth) what better worldly refuge can I here seeke, then to shelter my selfe under the safety of your favourable protection? And did not my ease proceede from an unspotted conscience, I should not dare to offer to your view and approved judgement, these passions of my troubled soule, so full of feare and trembling in hypocrisie and dissimulation. But knowing my owne innocency and godly fervor, in the whole prosecution hereof, I doubt not of your benigne acceptance, and clement construction. As for malicious depravers, and turbulent spirits, to whom nothing is tastful but what pleaseth their unsavory paalat, I passe not for them being well assured in my perswasion (by the often trial and proving of my selfe, in my holiest meditations and praiers) that I am called hereunto by the spirit of God; and it shall be sufficient for me to be protected by your selfe in all vertuous and pious indevours. And for my more happie proceeding herein, my daily oblations shall ever be addressed to bring to passe so good effects, that your selfe, and all the world may truely say: This is the worke of God, and it is marvelous in our eies.

But to avoid tedious preambles, and to come neerer the matter: first suffer me with your patence, to sweepe and make cleane the way wherein I walke, from all suspicions and doubts, which may be covered therein, and faithfully to reveale unto you, what should move me hereunto.

Let therefore this my well advised protestation, which here I make betweene God and my own conscience, be a sufficient witnesse, at the dreadfull day of judgement (when the secret of all mens harts shall be opened) to condemne me herein, if my chiefest intent and purpose be not, to strive with all my power of body and minde, in the undertaking of so mightie a matter, no way led (so farre forth as mans weakenesse may permit) with the unbridled desire of carnall affection: but for the good of this plantation, for the honour of our countrie, for the glory of God, for my owne salvation, and for the converting to the true knowledge of God and Jesus Christ, an unbeleeving creature, namely Pokahuntas. To whom my hartie and best thoughts are, and have a long time bin so intagled, and inthralled in so intricate a laborinth, that I was even awearied to unwinde my selfe thereout. But almighty God, who never faileth his, that truly invocate his holy name hath opened the gate, and led me by the hand that I might plainely see and discerne the safe paths wherein to treade.

To you therefore (most noble Sir) the patron and Father of us in this countrey doe I utter the effects of this setled and long continued affection (which hath made a mightie warre in my mediations) and here I doe truely relate, to what issue this dangerous combate is come unto, wherein I have not onely examined, but throughly tried and pared my thoughts even to the quick, before I could Snde and fit wholesome and apt applications to cure so daungerous an ulcer. I never failed to offer my daily and faithfull praiers to God, for his sacred and holy assistance. I forgot not to set before mine eies the frailty of mankinde, his prones to evill, his indulgencie of wicked thoughts, with many other imperfections wherein man is daily insnared, and oftentimes overthrowne, and them compared to my present estate. Nor was I ignorant of the heavie displeasure which almightie God conceived against the sonnes of Levie and Israel for marrying strange wives, nor of the inconveniences which may thereby arise, with other the like good motions which made me looke about warily and with good circumspection, into the grounds and principall agitations, which thus should provoke me to be in love with one whose education hath bin rude, her manners barbarous, her generation accursed, and so discrepant in all nurtriture frome my selfe, that oftentimes with feare and trembling, I have ended my private controversie with this: surely these are wicked instigations, hatched by him who seeketh and delighteth in mans destruction; and so with fervent praiers to be ever preserved from such diabolical assaults (as I tooke those to be) I have taken some rest.

Thus-when I had thought I had obtained my peace and quitnesse, beholde another, but more gracious tentation hath made breaches into my holiest and strongest meditations; with which I have bin put to a new traill, in a straighter manner then the former: for besides the many passions and sufferings which I have daily, hourely, yea and in my sleepe indured, even awaking mee to astonishment, taxing mee with remisnesse, and carlesnesse, refusing and neglecting to performe the duetie of a good Christian, pulling me by the eare, and crying: why dost not thou indevour to make her a Christian? And these have happened to my greater wonder, even when she hath bin furthest seperated from me, which in common reason (were it not an undoubted worke of God) might breede forgetfulnesse of a farre more worthie creature. Besides, I say the holy spirit of God often demaunded of me, why I was created?

If not for transitory pleasures and worldly vanities, but to labour in the Lords vineyard, there to sow and plant, to nourish and increase the fruites thereof, daily adding witt the good husband in the Gospell, somewhat to the tallent, that in the end the fruites may be reaped, to the comfort of the laborer in this life, and his salvation in the world to come? And if this be, as undoubtedly this is, the service Jesus Christ requireth of his best servant: wo unto him that hath these instruments of pietie put into his hands and wilfillly despiseth to worke with them. Likewise, adding hereunto her great apparance of love to me, her desire to be taught and instructed in the knowledge of God, her capablenesse of understanding, her aptnesse and willingnesse to receive anie good impression, and also the spirituall, besides her owne incitements stirring me up hereunto.

What should I doe? Shall I be of so untoward a disposition, as to refuse to leade the blind into the right way? Shall I be so unnaturall, as not to give bread to the hungrie? or uncharitable, as not to cover the naked? Shall I despise to actuate these pious dueties of a Christian? Shall the base feare of displeasing the world, overpower and with holde mee from revealing unto man these spirituall workes of the Lord, which in my meditations and praiers, I have daily made knowne unto him? God forbid. I assuredly trust hee hath thus delt with me for my eternall felicitie, and for his glorie: and I hope so to be guided by his heavenly graice, that in the end by my faithfill paines, and christianlike labour, I shall attaine to that blessed promise, Pronounced by that holy Prophet Daniell unto the righteous that bring many unto the knowledge of God. Namely, that they shall shine like the starres forever and ever. A sweeter comfort cannot be to a true Christian, nor a greater incouragement for him to labour all the daies of his life, in the performance thereof, nor a greater gaine of consolation, to be desired at the hower of death, and in the day of judgement.

Againe by my reading, and conference with honest and religious persons, have I received no small encouragement, besides serena mea conscientia, the cleerenesse of my conscience, clean from the filth of impurity, quoe est instar muri ahenei, which is unto me, as a brasen wall. If I should set down at large, the perturbations and godly motions, which have striven within mee, I should but make a tedious and unnecessary volume. But I doubt not these shall be sufficient both to certifie you of my tru intents, in discharging of my dutie to God, and to your selfe, to whose gracious providence I humbly submit my selfe, for his glory, your honour, our Countreys good, the benefit of this Plantation, and for the converting of one unregenerate, to regeneration; which I beseech God to graunt, for his deere Sonne Christ Jesus his sake.

Now if the vulgar sort, who square all mens actions by the base rule of their owne filthinesse, shall taxe or taunt me in this my godly labour: let them know, it is not any hungry appetite, to gorge my selfe with incontinency; sure (if I would, and were so sensually inclined) I might satisfie such desire, though not without a seared conscience, yet with Christians more pleasing to the eie, and lesse fearefull in the offence unlawfully committed. Nor am I in so desperate an estate, that I regard not what becommeth of mee; nor am I out of hope but one day to see my Country, nor so void of friends, nor mean in birth, but there to obtain a mach to my great content: nor have I ignorantly passed over my hopes there, or regardlesly seek to loose the love of my friends, by taking this course: I know them all, and have not rashly overslipped any.

But shal it please God thus to dispose of me (which I earnestly desire to fulfill my ends before sette down) I will heartely accept of it as a godly taxe appointed me, and I will never cease, (God assisting me) untill I have accomplished, and brought to perfection so holy a worke, in which I will daily pray God to blesse me, to mine, and her eternall happines. And thus desiring no longer to live, to enjoy the blessings of God, then this my resolution doth tend to such godly ends, as are by me before declared: not doubting of your favourable acceptance, I take my leave, beseeching Almighty God to raine downe upon you, such plenitude of his heavenly graces, as your heart can wish and desire, and so I rest, At your command most willing to be disposed off

John Rolfe

Captain John Smith's Petition to Queen Anne on Behalf of Pocahontas, 1616

When Sir Thomas Dale returned to England in 1616, he took with him John Rolfe and his wife Pocahontas, who upon marriage was christened and given the Christian name Rebecca. Dale's ship arrived at Plymouth on 12 June, and Captain John Smith, hearing of their arrival, desired to express his gratitude to Pocahontas for saving his life. Smith was about to embark for New England, and fearing he should sail before Pocahontas got to London, he made the following petition on her behalf to Queen Anne. Taken from Robert Beverley, History and Present State of Virginia *(1705).*

Capt. Smith's petition to her Majesty, in behalf of Pocahontas, daughter to the Indian Emperor, Powhatan.

To the most high and virtuous princess, Queen Anne, of Great Britain:

Most admired madam—

The love I bear my God, my king, and country, hath so often emboldened me in the worst of extreme dangers, that now honestly doth constrain me to presume thus far beyond myself, to present your majesty this short discourse. If ingratitude be a deadly poison to all honest virtues, I must be guilty of that crime, if I should omit any means to be thankful.

So it was,

That about ten years ago, being in Virginia, and taken prisoner by the power of Powhatan, their chief king, I received from this great savage exceeding great courtesy, especially from his son, Nantaquaus; the manliest, comeliest, boldest spirit I ever saw in a savage; and his sister Pocahontas, the king's most dear and well-beloved daughter, being but a child of twelve or thirteen years of age, whose compassionate pitiful heart of my desperate estate gave me much cause to respect her. I being the first Christian this proud king and his grim attendants ever saw, and thus enthralled in their barbarous power; I cannot say I felt the least occasion of want, that was in the power of those my mortal foes to prevent, notwithstanding all their threats. After some six weeks fatting amongst those savage courtiers, at the minute of my execution, she hazarded the beating out of her own brains to save mine, and not only that, but so prevailed with her father, that I was safely conducted to Jamestown, where I found about eight and thirty miserable, poor and sick creatures, to keep possession for all those large territories of Virginia. Such was the weakness of this poor commonwealth, as had not the savages fed us, we directly had starved.

And this relief, most gracious queen, was commonly brought us by this lady Pocahontas, notwithstanding all these passages, when unconstant fortune turned our peace to war, this tender virgin would still not spare to dare to visit us; and by her our jars have been oft appeased, and our wants still supplied. Were it the policy of her father thus to employ her, or the ordinance of God thus to make her his instrument, or her extraordinary affection to our nation, I know not: but of this I am sure, when her father, with the utmost of his policy and power, sought to surprise me, having but eighteen with me, the dark night could not affright her from coming through the irksome woods, and, with watered eyes, give me intelligence, with her best advice to escape his fury, which had he known, he had surely slain her.

Jamestown, with her wild train, she as freely frequented as her fathers habitation; and during the time of two or three years, she, next under God, was still the instrument to preserve this colony from death, famine, and utter confusion, which if, in those times, had once been dissolved, Virginia might have lain, as it was at our first arrival, till this day. Since then, this business having been turned and varied by many accidents from what I left it, it is most certain, after a long and troublesome war, since my departure, betwixt her father and our colony, all which time she was not heard of, about two years after she herself was taken prisoner, being so detained near two years longer, the colony by that means was relieved, peace concluded, and at last, rejecting her barbarous condition, she was married to an English gentleman, with whom at this present she is in England. The first Christian ever of that nation; the first Virginian ever spake English, or had a child in marriage by an Englishman—a matter surely, if my meaning be truly considered and well understood, worthy a prince's information.

Thus, most gracious lady, I have related to your majesty, what at your best leisure, our approved histories will recount to you at large, as done in the time of your majesty's life; and however this might be presented you from a more worthy pen, it cannot from a more honest heart.

As yet, I never begged anything of the State; and it is my want of ability, and her exceeding desert; your birth, means, and authority; her birth, virtue, want and simplicity, doth make me thus bold, humbly to beseech your majesty to take this knowledge of her, though it be from one so unworthy to be the reporter as myself; her husband's estate not being able to make her fit to attend your majesty.

The most and least I can do, is to tell you this, and the rather because of her being of so great a spirit, however her stature. If she should not be well received, seeing this kingdom may rightly have a kingdom by her means; her present love to us and Christianity, might turn to such scorn and fury, as to divert all this good to the worst of evil. Where finding that so great a queen should do her more honor than she can imagine, for having been kind to her subjects and servants, 'twould so ravish her with content, as to endear her dearest blood, to effect that your majesty and all the king's honest subjects most earnestly desire. And so I humbly kiss your gracious hands, &c.

(Signed)
JOHN SMITH.
Dated June, 1616.

London Company Instructions to George Yeardley, 18 November 1618

The Treasurer and Companie of Adventurers and Planters of the City of London for the first Colony in Virginia. To Captain George Yeardly Elect Governor of Virginia and to the Council of State there being or to be Greeting.

Our former cares and Endeavours have been chiefly bent to the procuring and sending people to plant in Virginia so to prepare a way and to lay a foundation whereon A flourishing State might in process of time by the blessing of Almighty God be raised. Now our trust being that under the Government of you Captain Yeardly with the advice and Assistance of the said Council of State such public provisions of Corn and Cattle will again be raised as may draw on those Multitudes who in great Abundance from diverse parts of the Realm were preparing to remove thither if by the late decay of the said public Store their hopes had not been made frustrate and their minds thereby clene discouraged We have thought good to bend our present cares and Consultations according to the Authority granted unto us from his Majesty under his great Seal to the setling there of A laudable form of Government by Majestracy and just Laws for the happy guiding and governing of the people there inhabiting like as we have already done for the well ordering of our Courts here and of our Officers and accions for the behoof of that plantation And because our intent is to Ease all the Inhabitants of Virginia forever of all taxes and public burthens as much as may be and to take away all occasion of oppression and corruption we have thought fit to begin (according to the laudable Example of the most famous Common Wealthes both past and present) to alot and lay out A Convenient portion of public lands for the maintenance and support as well of Magistracy and officers as of other public charges both here and there from time to time arising We therefore the said treasurer and Company upon a solemn treaty and resolution and with the advice consent and assent of his Majesties Council here of Virginia being Assembled in A great and general Court of the Council and Company of Adventurers for Virginia require you the said Governor and Council of Estate to put in Execution with all convenient Speed a former order of Our Courts (which had been commended also to Captain Argal at his making Deputy Governor) for the laying and seting out by bounds and metes of three thousand Acres of land in the best and most convenient place of the territory of James town in Virginia and next adjoining to the said town to be the seat and land of the Governor of Virginia for the time being and his Successors and to be called by the name of the Governors Land which Governors Land shall be of the freed grounds by the common labor of the people sent thither at the Companies Charges And of the Lands formerly conquer'd or purchased of the Paspeheies and of other grounds next adjoining In like sort we require you to set and lay out by bounds and Metes other three thousand Acres of good land within the territory of James town which shall be convenient and in such place or places as in your discretions you shall find meet which latter three thousand Acres shall be and so called the Companies Land And we require you Captain Yeardley that immediately upon your arrival you take unto you the Guard assigned to Captain Argal at his going Deputy Governor or sithence by him assumed to be of your guard [for the better defence] of your Government and that as well the said guard as also fifty other persons now sent and transported with you you place as tennants on the said Governors land and that all other persons heretofore transported at the Common Charge of the Company since the coming away of Sr Thomas Dale Knight late Deputy Governor be placed as Tennants on the said Companies Lands And we will and ordain that all the said Tennants on the Governors and Companies Lands shall occupy the same to the half part of the profits of the said Lands so as the one half to be and belong to the said Tennants themselves and the other half respectively to the said Governor and to us the said Treasurer and Company and our Successors And we further will and ordain that of the half profits arising out of the said Companies Lands and belonging to us the said Treasurer and Company the one Moiety be imploied for the Entertainment of the said Councel of Estate there residing and of other public officers of the general Colony and plantation (besides the Governor) according to the proportion as hereafter we shall Express and in the mean time as you in your discretions shall think meet And the other moiety be carefully gathered kept and ship'd for England for the public use of us the said Treasurer and Company and our Successors And we will and ordain that out of the half profits of the said Companies Lands to us belonging one fifth part be deducted and alotted for the Wages of the Bailiffs and other Officers which shall have the oversight and Government of the said Tenants and Lands and the dividing gathering keeping or shiping of the particular moiety of the profits belonging Either to the said Council and Officer there or to us the said treasurer and Company and our Successors as aforesaid *Provided* alwaies that out of the said Companies Land A Sufficient part be exempted and reserved for the securing and Wintering of all sorts of Cattle which are or shall be the public Stock and Store of the said Company And forasmuch as our intent is to Establish one Equal [*blank of several lines*] Plantations, whereof we shall speak afterwards, be reduced into four Cities or Burroughs *Namely* the cheif City called James town Charles City Henrico and the Burrough of Kiccowtan And that in all these foresaid Cities or Burroughs the ancient Adventurers and Planters which [were] transported thither with intent to inhabit at their own costs and charges before the coming away of Sr Thomas Dale Knight and have so continued during the space of three years shall have upon a first division to be afterward by us augmented one hundred Acres of land for their personal Adventure and as much for every single share of twelve pound ten Shillings paid [for such share] allotted and set out to be held by them their heirs and assigns forever And that for all such Planters as were brought thither at the Companies Charge to inhabit there before the coming away of the said Sr Thomas Dale after the time of their Service to the Company on the common Land agreed shall be expired there be set out One hundred Acres of Land for each of their personal Adventurers to be held by them their heirs and Assigns for ever. paying for every fifty Acres the yearly free Rent of one Shilling to the said treasurer and Company and their Successors at one Entire payment on the feast day of St Michael the archangel for ever And in regard that by the singular industry and virtue of the said Sr Thomas Dale the former difficulties and dangers were in greatest part overcome to the great ease and security of such as have been since that time transported thither We do therefore hereby ordain that all such persons as sithence the coming away of the said Sr Thomas Dale have at their own charges been transported thither to inhabit and so continued as aforesaid there be allotted and set out upon a first division fifty acres of land to them and their heirs for ever for their personal Adventure paying a free rent of one Shilling yearly in manner aforesaid And that all persons which since the going away of the said Sr Thomas Dale have been transported thither at the Companies charges or which hereafter shall be so transported be placed as tenants on the Companies lands for term of seven years occupy the same to the half part of the profits as is abovesaid We therefore will and ordain that other three thousand Acres of Land be set out in the fields and territory of Charles City and other three thousand Acres of Land in the fields and territories of Henrico And other three thousand Acres of land in the fields and territory of Kiccowtan all which to be and be called the Companies lands and to be occupied by the Companies Tenants for half profits as afore said And that the profits belonging to the Company be disposed by their several moieties in the same manner as before set down touching the Companies lands in the territory of James town with like allowance to the Bailies and reservation of ground for the common Store of Cattle in those several places as is there set down And our will is that such of the Companies tenants as already inhabite in those several Cities or Burroughs be not removed to any other City or Burrough but placed on the Companies Lands belonging to those Cities or Burroughs where they now inhabite *Provided* alwaies that if any private person without fraud or injurious intent to the public at his own charges have freed any of the said Lands formerly appointed to the Governor he may continue and inhabite there till a valuable recompence be made him for his said Charges And we do hereby ordain that the Governors house in James town first built by Sr Thomas Gates Knight at the charges and by the Servants of the Company and since enlarged by others by the very same means be and continue for ever the Governors house any pretended undue Grant made by misinformation and not in a general and quarter Court to the contrary in anywise notwithstanding And to the intent that godly learned and painful Ministers may be placed there for the service of Almighty God & for the spiritual benefit and comfort of the people We further will and ordain that in every of those Cities or Burroughs the several quantity of one hundred Acres of Land be set out in quality of Glebe land toward the maintenance of the several Ministers of the parishes to be there limited and for a further supply of their maintenance there be raised a yearly standing and certain contribution out of the profits growing or renuing within the several farmes of the said parish and so as to make the living of every Minister two hundred pounds Sterling p annum or more as hereafter there shall be cause And for a further Ease to the Inhabitants of all taxes and Contributions for the Support and Entertainment of the particular magistrates and Officers and of other charges to the said Citys and Burroughs respectively belonging We likewise will and ordain that within the precincts or territories of the said Cities and Burroughs shall be set out and alotted the several Quantities of fifteen hundred Acres of Land to be the common Land of the said Citie Or Burrough for the uses aforesaid and to be known and called by the name of the Cities Or Burroughs Land *And Whereas* by a special Grant and licence from his Majesty a general Contribution over this Realm hath been made for the building and planting of a college for the training up of the Children of those Infidels in true Religion moral virtue and Civility and for other godly uses We do therefore according to a former Grant and order hereby ratifie confirm and ordain that a convenient place be chosen and set out for the planting of a University at the said Henrico in time to come and that in the mean time preparation be there made for the building of the said College for the Children of the Infidels according to such Instructions as we shall deliver And we will and ordain that ten thousand acres partly of the Lands they impaled and partly of other Land within the territory of the said Henrico be alotted and set out for the endowing of the said University and College with convenient possessions Whereas also we have heretofore by order of Court in consideration of the long good and faithful Service done by you Captain George Yeardley in our said Colony and plantation of Virginia and in reward thereof as also in regard of two single shares in money paid into our treasury granted unto you the said Captain Yeardley all that parcel of Marsh ground called Weynock and also one other peice and parcel of Land adjoining to the same Marsh called by the Natives *Konwan* one parcel whereof abutteth upon a Creek there called Mapscock towards the East and the other parcel thereof towards a creek there called Queens Creek on the West and extendeth in breadth to landward from the head of the said Creek called Mapscock up to the head of the said Creek called Queens Creek (which creek called Queens Creek is opposite to that point there which is now called the Tobacco point and abutteth south upon the River and North to the Landward) all which several Lands are or shall be henceforward accounted to be lying within the territory of the said Charles City and exceed not the quantity of two thousand and two hundred acres We therefore the said Treasurer and Company do hereby again grant ratifie and Confirm unto you the said Captain George Yeardley the said several Grounds and Lands to have and to hold the said Grounds and Lands to you the said Captain George Yeardley your heirs and Assigns for Ever And for the better Encouragement of all sorts of necessary and laudable trades to be set up and exercised within the said four Cities or Burroughs We do hereby ordain that if any artizans or tradesmen shall be desirous rather to follow his particular Art or trade then to be imploied in husbandry or other rural business It shall be lawful for you the said Governor and Councel to alot and set out within any of the precincts aforesaid One dwelling house with four Acres of Land adjoining and held in fee simple to every said tradsman his heirs and Assigns for ever upon condition that the said tradesman his heirs and Assigns do continue and exercise his trade in the said house paying only a free rent of four pence by the year to us the said Treasurer and Company and our Successors at the feast of St Michael the Archangel for ever And touching all other particular Plantations set out or like to be set out in convenient Multitudes either by divers of the ancient Adventurers Associating themselves together (as the Society of Smiths hundred and Martins hundred) or by some ancient Adventurer or Planter associating others unto him (as the plantation of Captain Samuel Argall and Captain John Martin and that by the late Lord La warre advanced) or by some new Adventurers joining themselves under one head (as the plantation of Christopher Lawne Gentleman and others now in providing) Our Intent being according to the Rules of Justice and good government to alot unto every one his due yet so as neither to breed Disturbance to the Right of others nor to interrupt the good form of Government intended for the benefit of the people and strength of the Colony We do therefore will and ordain that of the said particular plantations none be placed within five Miles of the said former Cities and Boroughs And that if any man out of his own presumption or pleasure without special direction from us hath heretofore done otherwise a convenient time be Assigned him and then by your Discretions to remove to Some farther place by themselves to be chosen with the Allowance and Assent of the Governor for the time being and the Council of Estate And that the Inhabitants of the said City or Burrough too near unto which he or they were placed make him and them a valuable recompense for their Charges and expence of time in freeing of Grounds and building within those precincts In like sort we ordain that no latter particular plantation shall at any time hereafter be seated within ten Miles of a former We also will and ordain that no particular plantation be or shall be placed straglingly in divers places to the weakening of them but be united together in one seat and territory that so also they may be incorporated by us into one body corporate and live under Equal and like Law and orders with the rest of the Colony We will and ordain also for the preventing of all fraud in abusing of our grants contrary to the intent and just meaning of them That all such person or persons as have procured or hereafter shall procure grants from us in general Words unto themselves and their Associates or to like Effect shall within one year after the date hereof deliver up to us in writing under their hands and seals as also unto you the said Governor and Councel what be or were the names of those their first Associates And if they be of the Adventurers of us the Company which have paid into our treasury money for their shares that then they express in that their writing for how many shares they join in the said particular Plantation to the End a Due proportion of Land may be set out unto them and we the said Treasurer and Company be not defrauded of Our due And if they be not of the Adventurers of the Company which have paid into our treasury money for their shares yet are gone to inhabit there and so continue for three years there be allotted and set out fifty Acres of Land for every such person paying a free rent of twelve pence the year in manner aforesaid and All such persons having been planted there since the coming away of Sr Thomas Dale And forasmuch as we understand that certain persons having procured such Grants in general Words to themselves and their Associates or to like Effect have corruptly of late endeavoured for gain and Worse respects to draw many of the ancient Planters of the said four Cities or Burroughs to take grants also of them and thereby to become associated unto them with intent also by Such means to over-strengthen their party And thereupon have adventured on divers Enormous Courses tending to the great hurt and hindrance of the Colony Yea and have also made Grants of like Association to Masters of Ships and Mariners never intending there to inhabit, thereby to defraud his Majesty of the Customs due unto him We to remedy and prevent such unlawful and greedy Courses tending also directly to faction and sedition Do hereby ordain that it shall not be lawful for the Grantees of such Grants to associate to any other unto them then such as were their Associates from the first time of the said grants without express licence of us the sd Treasurer and Company in a great General and Quarter Court under our seal obtained And that all such after or under Grants of Association made or to be made by the said Grantees shall be to all intents and purposes utterly void And for as much as we understand that divers particular persons (not members of our Company) with their Companies have provided or are in providing to remove into Virginia with intent (as appeareth) by way of Association to shroud themselves under the General Grants last aforesaid which may tend to the Great disorder of our Colony and hinderance of the good Government which we desire to Establish We do therefore hereby ordain that all such persons as of their own Voluntary Will and authority shall remove into Virginia without any Grant from us in a great general and Quarter Court in writing under our seal shall be deemed (as they are) to be occupiers of our Land that is to say of the Common Lands of us the said Treasurer and Company And shall yearly pay unto us for the said occupying of our Land one full fourth part of the profits thereof till such time as the same shall be granted unto them by us in manner aforesaid And touching all such as being Members of our Company and Adventurers by their monies paid into our Treasury shall either in their own person or by their agents Tennants or Servants set up in Virginia any such particular Plantation tho with the privity of us the said Treasurer and Company yet without any grant in Writing made in our said General Quarter Courts as is requisite We will and ordain that the said Adventurers or Planters shall within two year after the arrival of them or their Company in Virginia procure our grant in writing to be made, in Our General Quarter Court and under our seal, of the Lands by them possessed or occupied or from thenceforth shall be deemed only Occupiers of the Common Land As is aforesaid till such times as our said grant shall be obtained We also not more intending the reformation of the Errors of the said [ ] than for advancing of them into good Courses and therein to assist them by all good means We further hereby ordain that to all such of the said particular [ ] as shall truly fully observe the orders Afore and hereafter specified there be alotted and set out over and above Our former Grants One hundred Acres of glebe land for the Minister of every [ ] and fifteen hundred Acres of Burough Land for the public use of the said Plantation Not intending yet hereby either to abridge or enlarge such grant of glebe or common Land as shall be made in any of our grants in writing to any of the said particular plantations We also will and ordain that the like proportion of maintenance out of the [ ] and profits of the Earth be made for the several Ministers of the said particular Plantations as have been before set down for the Ministers of the said former Cities and burroughs We will and ordain that the Governor for the time being and the said Council of Estate do justly perform or cause to be performed all such grants Covenants and Articles as have or shall be in writing in Our great and general Quarter Courts to any of the said particular Plantations Declaring all other grants of Lands in Virginia not made in one of our great and general Quarter Courts by force of his Majesties Letters patents to be void And to the End aforesaid we will and ordain that all our grants in writing under our seal made in our great and general Quarter Courts be Entered into your records to be kept there in Virginia Yet directly forbiding that a Charter of Land granted to Captain Samuel Argal and his Associates bearing date the twentieth of March 1616 be entered in your Records or otherwise at all respected forasmuch as the same was obtained by slight and cunning And afterwards upon suffering him to go Governor of Virginia was by his own voluntary act left in our Custody to be cancelled upon Grant of a new Charter which [ ] We do also hereby declare that heretofore in one of our said general and Quarter Courts we have ordained and enacted and in this present Court have ratified and Confirmed these orders and laws following. That all Grants of Lands privileges and liberties in Virginia hereafter to be made be passed by Indenture A Counterpart whereof to be sealed by the Grantees and to be kept [ ] the Companies Evidences And that the Secretary of the Company have the Engrossing of all such Indentures That no patents or Indentures of Grants of Land in Virginia be made and sealed but in a full General and Quarter Court the same having been first thoroughly perused and Approved *under* the hands of A Select Committee for that purpose [ ] That all Grants of [ ] in Virginia to such Adventurers as have heretofore brought in their money here to the treasury for their several shares being of twelve pounds ten shillings the share be of one hundred Acres the share upon the first division and of as many more upon A Second Division when the land of the first division shall be Sufficiently peopled And for Every person which they shall transport thither within seven years after Midsummer Day One thousand six hundred and Eighteen if he continue there three years or dye in the mean time after he is Shiped it be of fifty Acres the person upon the first Division and fifty more upon a second Division the land of the first being Sufficiently peopled *without* paying any rent to the Company for the one or the Other And that in all such Grants the names of the said Adventurers and the several Number of Each of their Shares be Expressed *Provided* alwaies and it is ordained that if the said Adventurers or any of them do not truly and Effectually within One Year next after the Sealing of the said Grant pay and discharge all such Sums of money wherein by subscription (or otherwise upon notice thereof given from the Auditors) they stand indebted to the Company or if the said Adventurers or any of them having not lawful Right either by purchase from the Company or by Assignment from some other former Adventurers within one year after the said Grant or by Special Gift of the Company upon merit preceding in A full Quarter Court to so many shares as he or they pretend Do not within one year after the said Grant satisfie and pay to the said Treasurer and Company for every share so wanting after the rate of twelve pounds ten shillings the share That then the said Grant for so much as concerneth the [ ] part and all the shares of the said person so behind and not satisfying as aforesaid shall be utterly void *Provided* also and it is ordained that the Grantees shall from time to time during the said seven years make a true Certificate to the said Treasurer Councel and Company from the Chief Officer or Officers of the places respectively of the Number names ages sex trades and conditions of every such person so transported or shiped to be entered by the Secretary into a Register book for that purpose to be made That for all persons not comprised in the order next before which during the next seven years after Midsummer day 1618 shall go into Virginia with intent there to Inhabite If they continue there three years or dye after they are shiped there shall be a grant made of fifty acres for every person upon A first division and as many more upon a second division (the first being peopled) which grants to be made respectively to such persons and their heirs at whose charges the said persons going to Inhabite in Virginia shall be transported with reservation of twelve pence yearly Rent for every fifty acres to be answered to the said treasurer and Company and their Successors for ever after the first seven years of every such Grant In which Grants a provisoe to be inserted that the Grantees shall from time to time during the said Seven years make A true Certificate to the said Treasurer Councel and Company from the Chief Officer or Officers of places Respectively of the Number names ages sex trades and Conditions of every such person so transported or shiped to be entred by the Secretary into a Register book for that purpose to be made that all Grants as well of one sort as the other respectively be made with equal favours and grants of like Liberties and immunities as near as may be to the End that all

Complaint of partiality [*or*] differencie may be prevented All which said orders we hereby will and ordain to be firmly and unviolably kept and observed And that the Inhabitants of Virginia have notice of them for their use and benefit *Lastly* we do hereby require and Authorize you the said Captain George Yeardley and the said Council of Etats Associating with you such other as you shall there find meet to Survey or cause to be Survey'd all the Lands and territories in Virginia above mentioned and the same to set out by bounds and metes especially so as that the territories of the said Several Cities and Buroughs and other particular plantations may be conveniently divided and known the one from the other *Each* survey to be set down distinctly in writing and returned to us under your hands and seals *In Witness* whereof we have hereunto set our Common Seal *Given* in a great and general Court of the Council and Company of Adventurers of Virginia held the Eighteenth Day of November 1618 And in the years of the Reign of Our Soverain Lord *James* by the grace of God King of England Scotland France and Ireland Defender of the Faith &c Vizt of England France and Ireland the Sixteenth and of Scotland the two and fiftieth.

Novr 18. 1618.

Captain Anthony Chester's Description of a Sea Fight, 1620

The following dramatic account of two Spanish warships attempting to capture a small English vessel typifies the atmosphere of piracy that frequently occurred at the high seas from the fifteenth century through the eighteenth. The author, Captain Anthony Chester, commanded the English ship and appears as a matter-of-fact hero in the story. The account is taken from the "Fourth Booke" of Captain John Smith's Generall Historie of Virginia, New England & The Summer Isles, *first published in London in 1624.*

A desperat Sea-fight betwixt two Spanish men of warre, and a small English ship, at the Ile of Dominica going to Virginia, by Captaine Anthony Chester.

aving taken our journey towards Virginia in the beginning of February, a ship called the Margaret and John, of one hundred and sixty tuns, eight Iron Peeces and a Falcon, with eightie Passengers besides Sailers; After many tempests and foule weather, about the foureteenth of March we were in thirteene degrees and an halfe of Northerly latitude, where we descried a ship at hull; it being but a faire gale of wind, we edged towards her to see what she was, but she presently set saile, and ran us quickly out of sight: This made us keepe our course for Mettalina, and the next day passing Dominica, we came to an anchor at Guardalupo, to take in fresh water. Six French-men there cast away sixteene moneths agoe came aboord us; they told us a Spanish man of Warre but seven daies before was seeking his consort, and this was she we descried at hull. At Mevis we intended to refresh our selves, having beene eleven weeks pestered in this unwholsome ship; but there we found two tall ships with the Hollanders colours, but necessitie forcing us on shore, we anchored faire by them, and in friendly manner sent to hale them: but seeing they were Spaniards, retiring to our ship, they sent such a volley of shot after us, that shot the Boat, split the Oares, and some thorow the clothes, yet not a man hurt; and then followed with their great Ordnance, that many times over-racked our ship, which being so cumbred with the Passengers provisions, our Ordnance was not well fitted, nor any thing as it should have beene. But perceiving what they were, we fitted our selves the best we could to prevent a mischiefe, seeing them warp themselves to windward, we thought it not good to be boorded on both sides at an anchor, we intended to set saile, but that the Vice-Admirall battered so hard our star-boord side, that we fell to our businesse, and answered their unkindnesse with such faire shot from a Demiculvering, that shot her betweene wind and water, whereby she was glad to leave us and her Admirall together. Comming faire by our quarter, he tooke in his Holland flag, and put forth his Spanish colours, and so haled us.

We quietly and quickly answered him, both what wee were, and whither bound, relating the effect of our Commission, and the cause of our comming thither for water, and not to annoy any of the King of Spaines Subjects, nor any. She commanded us amaine for the King of Spaine, we replied with inlarging the particulars what friends both the Kings our Masters were, and as we would doe no wrong, we would take none. They commanded us aboord to shew our Commission, which we refused, but if they would send their Boat to us willingly they should see it. But for answer they made two great shot at us, with a volley of small shot, which caused us to leave the decks; then with many ill words they laid us aboord, which caused us to raise our maine saile, and give the word to our small shot which lay close and ready, that paid them in such sort, they quickly retired. The fight continued halfe an houre, as if we had beene invironed with fire and smoke, untill they discovered the waste of our ship naked, where they bravely boorded us loofe for loofe, hasting with pikes and swords to enter, but it pleased God so to direct our Captaine, and encourage our men with valour, that our pikes being formerly placed under our halfe deck, and certaine shot lying close for that purpose under the Port holes, encountred them so rudely, that their fury was not onely rebated, but their hastinesse intercepted, and their whole company beaten backe, many of our men were hurt, but I am sure they had two for one.

In the end they were violently repulsed, untill they were reinforced to charge againe by their commands, who standing upon their honors, thought it a great indignity to be so affronted, which caused a second charge, and that answered with a second beating backe: whereat the Captaine grew inraged, and constrained them to come on againe afresh, which they did so effectually, that question—lesse it had wrought an alteration, if the God that tosseth Monarchies, and teareth Mountaines, had not taught us to tosse our Pikes with prosperous events, and powred out a volley of small shot amongst them, whereby that valiant Commander was slaine, and many of his Souldiers dropped downe likewise on the top of the hatches. This we saw with our eies, and rejoyced with it at our hearts, so that we might perceive good successe comming on, our Captaine presently tooke advantage of their discomfiture, though with much comiseration of that resolute Captaine, and not onely plied them againe with our Ordnance, but had more shot under the Pikes, which was bestowed to good purpose, and amazed our enemies with the suddennesse.

Amongst the rest, one Lucas, our Carpenters Mate, must not be forgotten, who perceiving a way how to annoy them; As they were thus puzled and in a confusion, drew out a Minion under the halfe decke, and there bent it upon them in such a manner, that when it was fired, the cases of stones and peeces of Iron fell upon them so thick, as cleared the decke, and slew many, and in short time we saw few assailants, but such as crept from place to place covertly from the fury of our shot, which now was thicker than theirs: for although as far as we may commend our enemies, they had done something worthy of commendations; yet either wanting men, or being overtaken with the unlooked for valour of our men, they now began to shrinke, and give us leave to be wanton with our advantage. Yet we could onely use but foure peece of Ordnances, but they served the turne as well as all the rest: for she was shot so oft betweene wind and water, we saw they were willing to leave us, but by reason she was fast in the latch of our cable, which in haste of weighing our anchor hung aloofe, she could not cleare her selfe as she wrought to doe, till one cut the Cable with an axe, and was slaine by freeing us. Having beene aboord us two houres and an halfe, seeing her selfe cleere, all the shot wee had plaied on both sides, which lasted till we were out of shot, then we discovered the Vice-Admirall comming to her assistance, who began a farre off to ply us with their Ordnances, and put us in minde we had another worke in hand. Whereupon we separated the dead and hurt bodies, and manned the ship with the rest, and were so well incouraged wee waifed them a maine. The Admirall stood aloofe off, and the other would not come within Falcon shot, where she lay battering us till shee received another paiment from a Demiculvering, which made her beare with the shore for smooth water to mend her leakes. The next morning they both came up againe with us, as if they had determined to devour us at once, but it seemed it was but a bravado, though they forsooke not our quarter for a time within Musket shot; yet all the night onely, they kept us company, but made not a shot. During which time we had leasure to provide us better than before: but God bethanked they made onely but a shew of another assault, ere suddenly the Vice-admirall fell a starne, and the other lay shaking in the wind, and so they both left us. The fight continued six houres, and was the more unwelcome, because we were so ill provided, and had no intent to fight, nor give occasion to disturbe them. As for the losse of men, if Religion had not taught us what by the providence of God is brought to passe, yet daily experience might informe us, of the dangers of wars, and perils at sea, by stormes tempests, shipwracks, encounters with Pirats, meeting with enemies, crosse winds, long voiages, unknowne shores, barbarous Nations, and an hundred inconveniences, of which humane pollicies are not capable, nor mens conjectures apprehensive. We lost Doctor Bohun, a worthy valiant Gentleman, (a long time brought up amongst the most learned Surgeons, and Physitions in Netherlands, and this his second journey to Virginia:) and seven slaine out right, two died shortly of their wounds; sixteene was shot, whose limbs God be thanked was recovered without maime, and now setled in Virginia: how many they lost we know not, but we saw a great many lie on the decks, and their skuppers runne with bloud, they were about three hundred tunnes apeece, each sixteene or twentie Brasse-peeces. Captaine Chester, who in this fight had behaved himselfe like a most vigilant, resolute, and a couragious souldier, as also our honest and valiant master, did still so comfort and incourage us by all the meanes they could, at last to all our great contents we arrived in Virginia, and from thence returned safely to England.

Captain John Smith's Description of the Indian Massacre, 1622

Perhaps no English colonist was more astute in his observations of the Indians who inhabited Virginia at the time of English colonization of the New World than Captain John Smith, who had numerous encounters with the natives. Although he had been gone from Jamestown for a decade by the time Chief Opechancanough and his warriors made the devastating attack on Jamestown's outlying settlements on 22 March 1622, killing some 350 English colonists, Smith was greatly interested in the event and went to great lengths to gather as much information as he could. The following is the result, taken from the "Fourth Booke" of his Generall Historie of Virginia, New England & The Summer Isles, *first published in London in 1624.*

The massacre upon the two and twentieth of March.

The Prologue to this Tragedy, is supposed was occasioned by Nemattanow, otherwise called Jack of the Feather, because hee commonly was most strangely adorned with them; and for his courage and policy, was accounted amongst the Salvages their chiefe Captaine, and immortall from any hurt could bee done him by the English. This Captaine comming to one Morgans house, knowing he had many commodities that hee desired, perswaded Morgan to goe with him to Pamaunke to trucke, but the Salvage murdered him by the way; and after two or three daies returned againe to Morgans house, where he found two youths his Servants, who asked for their Master: Jack replied directly he was dead; the Boyes suspecting as it was, by seeing him weare his Cap, would have had him to Master Thorp: But Jack so moved their patience, they shot him, so he fell to the ground, put him in a Boat to have him before the Governor, then seven or eight miles from them. But by the way Jack finding the pangs of death upon him, desired of the Boyes two things; the one was, that they would not make it knowne hee was slaine with a bullet; the other, to bury him amongst the English. At the losse of this Salvage Opechankanough much grieved and repined, with great threats of revenge; but the English returned him such terrible answers, that he cunningly dissembled his intent, with the greatest signes he could of love and peace, yet within foureteene daies after he acted what followeth.

Sir Francis Wyat at his arrivall was advertised, he found the Countrey setled in such a firme peace, as most men there thought sure and unviolable, not onely in regard of their promises, but of a necessitie. The poore weake Salvages being every way bettered by us, and safely sheltred and defended, whereby wee might freely follow our businesse: and such was the conceit of this conceited peace, as that there was seldome or never a sword, and seldomer a peece, except for a Deere or Fowle, by which assurances the most plantations were placed straglingly and scatteringly, as a choice veine of rich ground invited them, and further from neighbours the better. Their houses generally open to the Salvages, who were alwaies friendly fed at their tables, and lodged in their bed-chambers, which made the way plaine to effect their intents, and the conversion of the Salvages as they supposed.

Having occasion to send to Opechankanough about the middle of March, hee used the Messenger well, and told him he held the peace so firme, the sky should fall or he dissolved it; yet such was the treachery of those people, when they had contrived our destruction, even but two daies before the massacre, they guided our men with much kindnesse thorow the woods, and one Browne that lived among them to learne the language, they sent home to his Master; yea, they borrowed our Boats to transport themselves over the River, to consult on the devillish murder that insued, and of our utter extirpation, which God of his mercy (by the meanes of one of themselves converted to Christianitie) prevented, and as well on the Friday morning that fatall day, being the two and twentieth of March, as also in the evening before, as at other times they came unarmed into our houses, with Deere, Turkies, Fish, Fruits, and other provisions to sell us, yea in some places sat downe at breakfast with our people, whom immediatly with their owne tooles they slew most barbarously, not sparing either age or sex, man woman or childe, so sudden in their execution, that few or none discerned the weapon or blow that brought them to destruction: In which manner also they slew many of our people at severall works in the fields, well knowing in what places and quarters each of our men were, in regard of their familiaritie with us, for the effecting that great master-peece of worke their conversion; and by this meanes fell that fatall morning under the bloudy and barbarous hands of that perfidious and inhumane people, three hundred forty seven men, women and children, most by their owne weapons, and not being content with their lives, they fell againe upon the dead bodies, making as well as they could a fresh murder, defacing, dragging, and mangling their dead carkases into many peeces, and carying some parts away in derision, with base and brutish triumph.

Neither yet did these beasts spare those amongst the rest well knowne unto them, from whom they had daily received many benefits, but spightfully also massacred them without any remorse or pitie; being in this more fell then Lions and Dragons, as Histories record, which have preserved their Benefactors; such is the force of good deeds, though done to cruell beasts, to take humanitie upon them, but these miscreants put on a more unnaturall brutishnesse then beasts, as by those instances may appeare.

That worthy religious Gentleman M. George Thorp, Deputie to the College lands, sometimes one of his Majesties Pensioners, & in command one of the principall in Virginia; did so truly affect their conversion, that whosoever under him did them the least displeasure, were punished severely. He thought nothing too deare for them, he never denied them any thing, in so much that when they complained that our Mastives did feare them, he to content them in all things, caused some of them to be killed in their presence, to the great displeasure of the owners, and would have had all the rest guelt to make them the milder, might he have had his will. The King dwelling but in a Cottage, he built him a faire house after the English fashion, in which he tooke such pleasure, especially in the locke and key, which he so admired, as locking and unlocking his doore a hundred times a day, he thought no device in the world comparable to it.

Thus insinuating himselfe into this Kings favour for his religious purpose, he conferred oft with him about Religion, as many other in this former Discourse had done, and this Pagan confessed to him as he did to them, our God was better then theirs, and seemed to be much pleased with that Discourse, and of his company, and to requite all those courtesies; yet this viperous brood did, as the sequell shewed, not onely murder him, but with such spight and scorne abused his dead corps as is unfitting to be heard with civill eares. One thing I cannot omit, that when this good Gentleman upon his fatall houre, was warned by his man, who perceiving some treachery intended by those hell-hounds, to looke to himselfe, and withall ran away for feare he should be apprehended, and so saved his owne life; yet his Master out of his good meaning was so void of suspition and full of confidence, they had slaine him, or he could or would beleeve they would hurt him. Captaine Nathaniel Powell one of the first Planters, a valiant Souldier, and not any in the Countrey better knowne amongst them; yet such was the error of an over-conceited power and prosperitie, and their simplicities, they not onely slew him and his family, but butcher-like hagled their bodies, and cut off his head, to expresse their uttermost height of cruelty. Another of the old company of Captaine Smith, called Nathaniel Causie, being cruelly wounded, and the Salvages about him, with an axe did cleave one of their heads, whereby the rest fled and he escaped: for they hurt not any that did either fight or stand upon their guard. In one place where there was but two men that had warning of it, they defended the house against 60. or more that assaulted it. M. Baldwin at Warraskoyack, his wife being so wounded, she lay for dead, yet by his oft discharging of his peece, saved her, his house, himselfe, & divers others. At the same time they came to one Master Harisons house, neere halfe a mile from Baldwines, where was Master Thomas Hamer with six men, and eighteene or nineteene women and children. Here the Salvages with many presents and faire perswasions, fained they came for Capt. Ralfe Hamer to go to their King, then hunting in the woods, presently they sent to him, but he not comming as they expected, set fire of a Tobacco-house, and then came to tell them in the dwelling house of it to quench it; all the men ran towards it, but Master Hamer not suspecting any thing, whom the Salvages pursued, shot them full of arrowes, then beat out their braines. Hamer having finished a letter hee was a writing, followed after to see what was the matter, but quickly they shot an arrow in his back, which caused him returne and barricado up the doores, whereupon the Salvages set fire on the house. Harisons Boy finding his Masters peece loaded, discharged it at randome, at which bare report the Salvages all fled, Baldwin still discharging his peece, and Mr. Hamer with two and twentie persons thereby got to his house, leaving their owne burning. In like manner, they had fired Lieutenant Basse his house, with all the rest there about, slaine the people, and so left that Plantation.

Captaine Hamer all this while not knowing any thing, comming to his Brother that had sent for him to go hunt with the King, meeting the Salvages chasing some, yet escaped, retired to his new house then a building, from whence he came; there onely with spades, axes, and brickbats, he defended himselfe and his Company till the Salvages departed. Not long after, the Master from the ship had sent six Musketiers, with which he recovered their Merchants store-house, where he armed ten more, and so with thirtie more unarmed workmen, found his Brother and the rest at Baldwins: Now seeing all they had was burnt and consumed, they repaired to James Towne with their best expedition; yet not far from Martins hundred, where seventy three were slaine, was a little house and a small family, that heard not of any of this till two daies after.

All those, and many others whom they have as maliciously murdered, sought the good of those poore brutes, that thus despising Gods mercies, must needs now as miscreants be corrected by Justice: to which leaving them, I will knit together the thred of this discourse. At the time of the massacre, there were three or foure ships in James River, and one in the next, and daily more to come in, as there did within foureteene daies after, one of which they indevoured to have surprised: yet were the hearts of the English ever stupid, and averted from beleeving any thing might weaken their hopes, to win them by kinde usage to Christianitie. But divers write from thence, that Almighty God hath his great worke in this Tragedy, and will thereout draw honor and glory to his name, and a more flourishing estate and safetie to themselves, and with more speed to convert the Salvage children to himselfe, since he so miraculously hath preserved the English; there being yet, God be praised, eleven parts of twelve remaining, whose carelesse neglect of their owne safeties, seemes to have beene the greatest cause of their destructions: yet you see, God by a converted Salvage that disclosed the plot, saved the rest, and the Pinnace then in Pamaunkes River, whereof (say they) though our sinnes made us unworthy of so glorious a conversion, yet his infinite wisdome can neverthelesse bring it to passe, and in good time, by such meanes as we thinke most unlikely: for in the delivery of them that survive, no mans particular carefulnesse saved one person, but the meere goodnesse of God himselfe, freely and miraculously preserving whom he pleased.

The Letters of Master George Sands, a worthy Gentleman, and many others besides them returned, brought us this unwelcome newes, that hath beene heard at large in publike Court, that the Indians and they lived as one Nation, yet by a generall combination in one day plotted to subvert the whole Colony, and at one instant, though our severall Plantations were one hundred and fortie miles up on River on both sides.

But for the better understanding of all things, you must remember these wilde naked natives live not in great numbers together, but dispersed, commonly in thirtie, fortie, fiftie, or sixtie in a company. Some places have two hundred, few places more, but many lesse; yet they had all warning given them one from another in all their habitations, though farre asunder, to meet at the day and houre appointed for our destruction at al our several Plantations; some directed to one place, some to another, all to be done at the time appointed, which they did accordingly: Some entring their houses under colour of trading, so tooke their advantage; others drawing us abroad under faire pretences, and the rest suddenly falling upon those that were at their labours.

Six of the counsell suffered under this treason, and the slaughter had beene universall, if God had not put it into the heart of an Indian, who lying in the house of one Pace, was urged by another Indian his Brother, that lay with him the night before to kill Pace, as he should doe Perry which was his friend, being so commanded from their King; telling him also how the next day the execution should be finished: Perrys Indian presently arose and reveales it to Pace, that used him as his sonne; and thus them that escaped was saved by this one converted Infidell. And though three hundred fortie seven were shine, yet thousands of ours were by the meanes of this alone thus preserved, for which Gods name be praised for ever and ever.

Pace upon this, securing his house, before day rowed to James Towne, and told the Governor of it, whereby they were prevented, and at such other Plantations as possibly intelligence could be given: and where they saw us upon our guard, at the sight of a peece they ranne away; but the rest were most slaine, their houses burnt, such Armes and Munition as they found they tooke away, and some cattell also they destroied. Since wee finde Opechankanough the last yeare had practised with a King on the Easterne shore, to furnish him with a kind of poison, which onely growes in his Country to poison us. But of this bloudy acte never griefe and shame possessed any people more then themselves, to be thus butchered by so naked and cowardly a people, who dare not stand the presenting of a staffe in manner of a peece, nor an uncharged peece in the hands of a woman. (But I must tell those Authors, though some might be thus cowardly, there were many of them had better spirits.)

Thus have you heard the particulars of this massacre, which in those respects some say will be good for the Plantation, because now we have just cause to destroy them by all meanes possible: but I thinke it had beene much better it had never happened; for they have given us an hundred times as just occasions long agoe to subject them, (and I wonder I can heare of none but Master Stockam and Master Whitaker of my opinion.) Moreover, where before we were troubled in cleering the ground of great Timber, which was to them of small use: now we may take their owne plaine fields and Habitations, which are the pleasantest places in the Countrey. Besides, the Deere, Turkies, and other Beasts and Fowles will exceedingly increase if we beat the Salvages out of the Countrey, for at all times of the yeare they never spare Male nor Female, old nor young, egges nor birds, fat nor leane, in season or out of season with them, all is one. The like they did in our Swine and Goats, for they have used to kill eight in tenne more then we, or else the wood would most plentifully abound with victuall; besides it is more easie to civilize them by conquest then faire meanes; for the one may be made at once, but their civilizing will require a long time and much industry. The manner how to suppresse them is so often related and approved, I omit it here: And you have twenty examples of the Spaniards how they got the West-Indies, and forced the treacherous and rebellious Infidels to doe all manner of drudgery worke and slavery for them, themselves living like Souldiers upon the fruits of their labours. This will make us more circumspect, and be an example to posteritie. (But I say, this might as well have beene put in practise sixteene yeares agoe as now.)

Thus upon this Anvill shall wee now beat our selves an Armour of proofe hereafter to defend us against such incursions, and ever hereafter make us more circumspect: but to helpe to repaire this losse, besides his Majesties bounty in Armes, he gave the Company out of the Tower, and divers other Honorable persons have renewed their adventures, we must not omit the Honorable Citie of London, to whose endlesse praise wee may speake it, are now setting forward one hundred persons, and divers others at their owne costs are a repairing, and all good men doe thinke never the worse of the businesse for all these disasters.

What growing state was there ever in the world which had not the like? Rome grew by oppression, and rose upon the backe of her enemies: and the Spaniards have had many of those counterbuffes, more than we. Columbus, upon his returne from the West-Indies into Spaine, having left his people with the Indies, in peace and promise of good usage amongst them, at his returne backe found not one of them living, but all treacherously slaine by the Salvages. After this againe, when the Spanish Colonies were increased to great numbers, the Indians from whom the Spaniards for trucking stuffe used to have all their corne, generally conspired together to plant no more at all, intending thereby to famish them; themselves living in the meane time upon Cassava, a root to make bread, onely then knowne to themselves. This plot of theirs by the Spaniards oversight, that foolishly depended upon strangers for their bread, tooke such effect, and brought them to such misery by the rage of famine, that they spared no uncleane nor loathsome beast, no not the poisonous and hideous Serpents, but eat them up also, devouring one death to save them from another; and by this meanes their whole Colony well-neere surfeted, sickned and died miserably, and when they had againe recovered this losse, by their incontinency an infinite number of them died on the Indian disease, we call the French Pox, which at first being a strange and an unknowne malady, was deadly upon whomsoever it lighted: then had they a little flea called Nigua, which got betweene the skinne and the flesh before they were aware, and there bred and multiplied, making swellings and putrifactions, to the decay and losse of many of their bodily members.

Againe, divers times they were neere undone by their ambition, faction, and malice of the Commanders. Columbus, to whom they were also much beholden, was sent with his Brother in chaines into Spaine; and some other great Commanders killed and murdered one another. Pizzaro was killed by Almagros sonne, and him Vasco beheaded, which Vasco was taken by Blasco, and Blasco was likewise taken by Pizzaros Brother: And thus by their covetous and spightfull quarrels, they were ever shaking the maine pillars of their Common-weale. These and many more mischiefes and calamities hapned them, more then ever did to us, and at one time being even at the last gaspe, had two ships not arrived with supplies as they did, they were so disheartned, they were a leaving the Countrey: yet we see for all those miseries they have attained to their ends at last, as is manifest to all the world, both with honour, power, and wealth: and whereas before few could be hired to goe to inhabit there, now with great sute they must obtaine it; but where there was no honesty, nor equity, nor sanctitie, nor veritie, nor pietie, nor good civilitie in such a Countrey, certainly there can bee no stabilitie.

Therefore let us not be discouraged, but rather animated by those conclusions, seeing we are so well assured of the goodnesse and commodities may bee had in Virginia, nor is it to be much doubted there is any want of Mines of most sorts, no not of the richest, as is well knowne to some yet living that can make it manifest when time shall serve: and yet to thinke that gold and silver Mines are in a country otherwise most rich and fruitfull, or the greatest wealth in a Plantation, is but a popular error, as is that opinion likewise, that the gold and silver is now the greatest wealth of the West Indies at this present. True it is indeed, that in the first conquest the Spaniards got great and mighty store of treasure from the Natives, which they in long space had heaped together, and in those times the Indians shewed them entire and rich Mines, which now by the relations of them that have beene there, are exceedingly wasted, so that now the charge of getting those Metals is growne excessive, besides the consuming the lives of many by their pestilent smoke and vapours in digging and refining them, so that all things considered, the cleere gaines of those metals, the Kings part defraied, to the Adventurers is but small, and nothing neere so much as vulgarly is imagined; and were it not for other rich Commodities there that inrich them, those of the Contraction house were never able to subsist by the Mines onely; for the greatest part of their Commodities are partly naturall, and partly transported from other parts of the world, and planted in the West-Indies, as in their mighty wealth of Sugarcanes, being first transported from the Canaries; and in Ginger and other things brought out of the East-Indies, in their Cochanele, Indicos, Cotton, and their infinite store of Hides, Quick-silver, Allum, Woad, Brasill woods, Dies, Paints, Tobacco, Gums, Balmes, Oiles, Medicinals and Perfumes, Sassaparilla and many other physicall drugs: These are the meanes whereby they raise that mighty charge of drawing out their gold and silver to the great & cleare revenue of their King. Now seeing the most of those commodities, or as usefull, may be had in Virginia by the same meanes, as I have formerly said; let us with all speed take the priority of time, where also may be had the priority of place, in chusing the best seats of the Country, which now by vanquishing the salvages, is like to offer a more faire and ample choice of fruitfull habitations, then hitherto our gentlenesse and faire comportments could attaine unto.

The numbers that were slaine in those severall Plantations.

1	At Captaine Berkleys Plantation, himselfe and 21. others, seated at the Falling-Crick, 66. miles from James City.	22
2	Master Thomas Sheffelds Plantation, some three miles from the Falling-Crick, himselfe and 12. others.	13
3	At Henrico Iland, about two miles from Sheffelds Plantation.	6
4	Slaine of the College people, twenty miles from Henrico.	17
5	At Charles City, and of Captaine Smiths men.	5
6	At the next adjoyning Plantation.	8
7	At William Farrars house.	19
8	At Brickley hundred, fifty miles from Charles City, Master Thorp and	10
9	At Westover, a mile from Brickley.	2
10	At Master John Wests Plantation.	2
11	At Captaine Nathaniel Wests Plantation.	2
12	At Lieutenant Gibs his Plantation.	12
13	At Richard Owens house, himselfe and	6
14	At Master Owen Macars house, himselfe and	3
15	At Martins hundred, seven miles from James City	73
16	At another place.	7
17	At Edward Bonits Plantation.	50
18	At Master Waters his house, himselfe and	4
19	At Apamatucks River, at Master Perce his Plantation, five miles from the College.	4
20	At Master Macocks Divident, Captaine Samuel Macock, and	4
21	At Flowerda hundred, Sir George Yearleys Plantation.	6
22	On the other side opposite to it.	7
23	At Master Swinhows house, himselfe and	7
24	At Master William Bickars house, himselfe and	4
25	At Weanock, of Sir George Yearleys people.	21

26	At Powel Brooke, Captaine Nathaniel Powel, and	12
27	At South-hampton hundred.	5
28	At Martin Brandons hundred.	7
29	At Captaine Henry Spilmans house.	2
30	At Ensigne Spences house.	5
31	At Master Thomas Perse his house by Mulbery Ile, himselfe and	4
The whole number		347

Men in this taking bettered with affliction,
Better attend, and mind, and marke Religion,
For then true voyces issue from their hearts,
Then speake they what they thinke in inmost parts,
The truth remaines, they cast off fained Arts.

This lamentable and so unexpected a disaster caused them all beleeve the opinion of Master Stockam, and drave them all to their wits end: it was twenty or thirty daies ere they could resolve what to doe, but at last it was concluded, all the petty Plantations should be abandoned, and drawne onely to make good five or six places, where all their labours now for the most part must redound to the Lords of those Lands where they were resident. Now for want of Boats, it was impossible upon such a sudden to bring also their cattle, and many other things, which with much time, charge and labour they had then in possession with them; all which for the most part at their departure was burnt, ruined and destroyed by the Salvages. Only Master Gookins at Nuportsnewes would not obey the Commanders command in that, though hee had scarce five and thirty of all sorts with him, yet he thought himselfe sufficient against what could happen, and so did to his great credit and the content of his Adventurers. Master Samuel Jorden gathered together but a few of the straglers about him at Beggersbush, where he fortified and lived in despight of the enemy. Nay, Mistresse Proctor, a proper, civill, modest Gentlewoman did the like, till perforce the English Officers forced her and all them with her to goe with them, or they would fire her house themselves, as the Salvages did when they were gone, in whose despight they had kept it, and what they had a moneth or three weekes after the Massacre; which was to their hearts a griefe beyond comparison, to lose all they had in that manner, onely to secure others pleasures. Now here in England it was thought, all those remainders might presently have beene reduced into fifties or hundreds in places most convenient with what they had, having such strong houses as they reported they had, which with small labour might have beene made invincible Castles against all the Salvages in the Land, and then presently raised a company, as a running Armie to torment the Barbarous and secure the rest, and so have had all that Country betwixt the Rivers of Powhatan and Pamaunke to range and sustaine them; especially all the territories of Kecoughtan, Chiskact and Paspahege, from Ozenies to that branch of Pamaunke, comming from Youghtanund, which strait of land is not past 4. or 5. miles, to have made a peninsula much bigger then the Summer Iles, invironed with the broadest parts of those two maine Rivers, which for plenty of such things as Virginia affords is not to be exceeded, and were it well manured, more then sufficient for ten thousand men. This, were it well understood, cannot but be thought better then to bring five or six hundred to lodge and live on that, which before would not well receive and maintaine a hundred, planting little or nothing, but spend that they have upon hopes out of England, one evill begetting another, till the disease is past cure: Therefore it is impossible but such courses must produce most fearefull miseries and extreme extremities; if it prove otherwise, I should be exceeding glad. I confesse I am somewhat too bold to censure other mens actions being not present, but they have done as much of me; yea many here in England that were never there, & also many there that knowes little more then their Plantations, but as they are informed; and this doth touch the glory of God, the honour of my Country, and the publike good so much, for which there hath beene so many faire pretences, that I hope none will be angry for speaking my opinion, seeing the old Proverbe doth allow losers leave to speake; and Du Bartas saith,

Even as the wind the angry Ocean moves,
Wave hunteth Wave, and Billow Billow shoves,
So doe all Nations justell each the other,
And so one people doe pursue another,
And scarce a second hath the first unhoused,
Before a third him thence againe have roused.

Richard Frethorne's Description of Indentured Service, 1623

The following letters from Richard Frethorne to his mother and father, written on 20 March and 2 and 3 April 1623, describe life in the Jamestown colony from the point of view of an indentured servant. The letters are printed in volume 4 of The Records of the Virginia Company of London, *edited by Susan Kingsbury (Washington, D.C., 1935).*

Loving and kind father and mother:

My most humble duty remembered to you, hoping in God of your good health, as I myself am at the making hereof. This is to let you understand that I your child am in a most heavy case by reason of the nature of the country, is such that it causeth much sickness, as the scurvy and the bloody flux and diverse other diseases, which maketh the body very poor and weak. And when we are sick there is nothing to comfort us; for since I came out of the ship I never ate anything but peas, and loblollie (that is, water gruel). As for deer or venison I never saw any since I came into this land. There is indeed some fowl, but we are not allowed to go and get it, but must work hard both early and late for a mess of water gruel and a mouthful of bread and beef. A mouthful of bread for a penny loaf must serve for four men which is most pitiful. If you did know as much as I, when people cry out day and night—Oh! that they were in England without their limbs—and would not care to lose any limb to be in England again, yea, though they beg from door to door. For we live in fear of the enemy every hour, yet we have had a combat with them on the Sunday before Shrovetide, and we took two alive and made slaves of them. But it was by policy, for we are in great danger; for our plantation is very weak by reason of the death and sickness of our company. For we came but twenty for the merchants, and they are half dead just; and we look every hour when two more should go. Yet there came four other men yet to live with us, of which there is but one alive; and our Lieutenant is dead, and his father and his brother. And there was some five or six of the last year's twenty, of which there is but three left, so that we are fain to get other men to plant with us; and yet we are but 32 to fight against 3000 if they should come. And the nighest help that we have is ten miles of us, and when the rogues overcame this place last they slew 80 persons. How then shall we do, for we lie even in their teeth? They may easily take us, but that God is merciful and can save with few as easily well as with many, as he showed to Gilead. And like Gilead's soldiers, if they lapped water, we drink water which is but weak.

And I have nothing to comfort me, nor is there nothing to be gotten here but sickness and death, except that one had money to lay out in some things for profit. But I have nothing at all—no, not a shirt to my back but two rags (2), nor no clothes but one poor suit, nor but one pair of shoes, but one pair of stockings, but one cap, but two bands. My cloak is stolen by one of my own fellows, and to his dying hour would not tell me what he did with it; but some of my fellows saw him have butter and beef out of a ship, which my cloak, I doubt, paid for. So that I have not a penny, nor a penny worth, to help me to either spice or sugar or strong waters, without the which one cannot live here only keeps life and soul together. But I am not half a quarter so strong as I was in England, and all is for want of victuals; for I do protest unto you that I have eaten more in day at home than I have allowed me here for a week. You have given more than my day's allowance to a beggar at the door; and if Mr. Jackson had not relieved me, I should be in a poor case. But he like a father and she like a loving mother doth still help me.

For when we go to Jamestown (that is 10 miles of us) there lie all the ships that come to land, and there they must deliver their goods. And when we went up to town, as it may be, on Monday at noon, and come there by night, then load the next day by noon, and go home in the afternoon, and unload, and then away again in the night, and would be up about midnight. Then if it rained or blowed never so hard, we must lie in the boat on the water and have nothing but a little bread. For when we go into the boat we stayed there two days, which is hard; and must lie all that while in the boat. But that Goodman Jackson pitied me and made me a cabin to lie in always when I come up, and he would give me some poor jacks home with me, which comforted me more than peas or water gruel. Oh they be very godly folks, and love me very well, and will do anything for me. And he much marvelled that you would send me a servant to the Company; he saith I had been better knocked on the head. And indeed so I find it now, to my great grief and misery; and saith that if you love me you will redeem me suddenly, for which I do entreat and beg. And if you cannot get the merchants to redeem me for some little money, then for God's sake get a gathering or entreat some good folks to lay out some little sum of money in meal and cheese and butter and beef. Any eating meat will yield great profit. Oil and vinegar is very good; but, father, there is great loss in leaking. But for God's sake send beef and cheese and butter, or the more of one sort and none of another. But if you send cheese, it must be very old cheese; and at the cheesemonger's you may buy very good cheese for twopence farthing or halfpenny, that will be liked very well. But if you send cheese, you must have a care how you pack it in barrels; and you must put cooper's chips between every cheese, or else the heat of the hold will rot them. And look whatsoever you send me—be it never so much—look, what I make of it, I will deal truly with you. I will send it over and beg the profit to redeem me; and if I die before it come, I have entreated Goodman Jackson to send you the worth of it, who hath promised he will. If you send, you must direct your letters to Goodman Jackson, at Jamestown, a gunsmith. (You must set down his freight, because there be more of his name there.) Good father, do not forget me, but have mercy and pity my miserable case. I know if you but see me, you would weep to see me; for I have but one suit. (But it is a strange one, it is very well guarded.) Wherefore, for God's sake, pity me. I pray you to remember my love to all my friends and kindred. I hope all my brothers and sisters are in good health, and as for my part I have set down my resolution that certainly will be; that is, that the answer of this letter will be life or death to me. Therefore, good father, send as soon as you can; and if you send me any thing let this be the mark.

ROT
Richard Frethorne,
Martin's Hundred

The names of them that be dead of the company came over with us to serve under our Lieutenants:

John Flower	George Goulding
John Thomas	Jos. Johnson
Thos. Howes	our lieutenant, his father and brother
John Butcher	Thos. Giblin
John Sanderford	George Banum
Rich. Smith	a little Dutchman
John Olive	one woman
Thos. Peirsman	one maid
William Cerrell	one child

All of these died out of my master's house, since I came; and we came in but at Christmas, and this is the 20th day of March. And the sailors say that there is two-thirds of the 150 dead already. And thus I end, praying to God to send me good success that I may be redeemed out of Egypt. So *vale in Christo.*

Loving father, I pray you to use this man very exceeding kindly, for he hath done much for me, both on my journey and since. I entreat you not to forget me, but by any means redeem me; for this day we hear that there is 26 of Englishmen slain by the Indians. And they have taken a pinnace of Mr. Pountis, and have gotten pieces, armor, swords, all things fit for war; so that it is too late—that they be upon us—and then there is no mercy. Therefore if you love or respect me as your child, release me, or let me be slain with infidels. Ask this man—he knoweth that all is true and just that I say here. If you do redeem me, the Company must send for me to my Mr. Harrod; for so is this Master's name. April, the second day.

Your loving son,
Richard Frethorne

Moreover, on the third day of April we heard that after these rogues had gotten the pinnace and had taken all furnitures as pieces, swords, armor, coats of mail, powder, shot and all the things that they had to trade withal, they killed the Captain and cut off his head. And rowing with the tail of the boat foremost, they set up a pole and put the Captain's head upon it, and so rowed home. Then the Devil set them on again, so that they furnished about 200 canoes with above 1000 Indians, and came, and thought to have taken the ship; but she was too quick for them—which thing was very much talked of, for they always feared a ship. But now the rogues grow very bold and can use pieces, some of them, as well or better than an Englishman; for an Indian did shoot with Mr. Charles, my master's kinsman, at a mark of white paper, and he hit it at the first, but Mr. Charles could not hit it. But see the envy of these slaves, for when they could not take the ship, then our men saw them threaten Accomack, that is the next plantation. And now there is no way but starving; for the Governor told us and Sir George that except the *Seaflower* come in or that we can fall foul of these rogues and get some corn from them, above half the land will surely be starved. For they had no crop last year by reason of these rogues, so that we have no corn but as ships do relieve us, nor we shall hardly have any crop this year; and we are as like to perish first as any plantaiton. For we have but two hogshead of meal left to serve us this two months, if the *Seaflower* do stay so long before she come in; and that meal is but three weeks bread for us, at a loaf for four about the bigness of a penny loaf in England—that is but a halfpennyloaf a day for a man. Is it not strange to me, think you? But what will it be when we shall go a month or two and never see a bit of bread, as my master doth say we must do? And he said he is not able to keep us all. Then we shall be turned up to the land and eat barks of trees or molds of the ground; therefore with weeping tears I beg of you to help me. Oh, that you did see my daily and hourly sighs, groans, and tears, and thumps that I afford mine own breast, and rue and curse the time of my birth, with holy Job. I thought no head had been able to hold so much water as hath and doth daily flow from mine eyes.

But this is certain: I never felt the want of father and mother till now; but now, dear friends, full well I know and rue it, although it were too late before I knew it.

I pray you talk with this honest man. He will tell you more than now in my haste I can set down.

Your loving son,
Richard Frethorne
Virginia, 3rd April, 1623

Captain John Smith on the Reformation of Virginia, 1623

Captain John Smith remained acutely interested in the fate of the Jamestown colony long after he made his last trip to Virginia, as evidenced by the document that follows. These are his answers to the royal commission charged with reforming the colony in the wake of serious financial setbacks in the London Company and the devastating

Indian raid in 1622. In the end, the commission recommended that the crown revoke the company's royal charter, which James I did in the spring of 1624. Taken from the "Fourth Booke" of Smith's Generall Historie of Virginia, New England & The Summer Isles, *first published in London in 1624.*

A briefe relation written by Captaine Smith to his Majesties Commissioners for the reformation of Virginia, concerning some aspersions against it.

Honourable Gentlemen, for so many faire and Navigable Rivers so neere adjoyning, and piercing thorow so faire a naturall Land, free from any inundations, or large Fenny unwholsome Marshes, I have not seene, read, nor heard of: And for the building of Cities, Townes, and Wharfage, if they will use the meanes, where there is no more ebbe nor floud, Nature in few places affoords any so convenient, for salt Marshes or Quagmires. In this tract of James Towne River I know very few; some small Marshes and Swamps there are, but more profitable then hurtfull: and I thinke there is more low Marsh ground betwixt Eriffe and Chelsey, then Kecoughton and the Falls, which is about one hundred and eighty miles by the course of the River.

Being enjoyned by our Commission not to unplant nor wrong the Salvages, because the channell was so neere the shore, where now is James Towne, then a thicke grove of trees; wee cut them downe, where the Salvages pretending as much kindnesse as could bee, they hurt and slew one and twenty of us in two houres: At this time our diet was for most part water and bran, and three ounces of little better stuffe in bread for five men a meale, and thus we lived neere three moneths: our lodgings under boughes of trees, the Salvages being our enemies, whom we neither knew nor understood; occasions I thinke sufficient to make men sicke and die.

Necessity thus did inforce me with eight or nine, to try conclusions amongst the Salvages, that we got provision which recovered the rest being most sicke. Six weeks I was led captive by those Barbarians, though some of my men were slaine, and the rest fled, yet it pleased God to make their great Kings daughter the means to returne me safe to James towne, and releeve our wants, and then our Common-wealth was in all eight and thirty, the remainder of one hundred and five.

Being supplied with one hundred and twenty, with twelve men in a boat of three tuns, I spent foureteene weeks in those large waters; the contents of the way of my boat protracted by the skale of proportion, was about three thousand miles, besides the River we dwell upon, where no Christian knowne ever was, and our diet for the most part what we could finde, yet but one died.

The Salvages being acquainted, that by command from England we durst not hurt them, were much imboldned; that famine and their insolencies did force me to breake our Commission and instructions, cause Powhatan fly his Countrey, and take the King of Pamaunke Prisoner; and also to keepe the King of Paspahegh in shackels, and put his men to double taskes in chaines, till nine and thirty of their Kings paied us contribution, and the offending Salvages sent to James towne to punish at our owne discretions: in the two last yeares I staied there, I had not a man slaine.

All those conclusions being not able to prevent the bad events of pride and idlenesse, having received another supply of seventie, we were about two hundred in all, but not twentie work-men: In following the strict directions from England to doe that was impossible at that time; So it hapned, that neither wee nor they had any thing to eat, but what the Countrey afforded naturally; yet of eightie who lived upon Oysters in June and July, with a pint of corne a week for a man lying under trees, and 120 for the most part living upon Sturgion, which was dried til we pounded it to powder for meale, yet in ten weeks but seven died.

It is true, we had of Tooles, Armes, & Munition sufficient, some Aquavitæ, Vineger, Meale, Pease, and Otemeale, but in two yeares and a halfe not sufficient for six moneths, though by the bils of loading the proportions sent us, would well have contented us, notwithstanding we sent home ample proofes of Pitch, Tar, Sope Ashes, Wainskot, Clapboord, Silke grasse, Iron Ore, some Sturgion and Glasse, Saxefras, Cedar, Cypris, and blacke Walnut, crowned Powhaton, sought the Monacans Countrey, according to the instructions sent us, but they caused us neglect more necessary workes: they had better have given for Pitch and Sope ashes one hundred pound a tun in Denmarke: Wee also maintained five or six severall Plantations.

James towne being burnt, wee rebuilt it and three Forts more, besides the Church and Store-house, we had about fortie or fiftie severall houses to keepe us warme and dry, invironed with a palizado of foureteene or fifteene foot, and each as much as three or foure men could carrie. We digged a faire Well of fresh water in the Fort, where wee had three Bulwarks, foure and twentie peece of Ordnance, of Culvering, Demiculvering, Sacar and Falcon, and most well mounted upon convenient platformes, planted one hundred acres of Corne. We had but six ships to transport and supply us, and but two hundred seventy seven men, boies, and women, by whose labours Virginia being brought to this kinde of perfection, the most difficulties past, and the foundation thus laid by this small meanes; yet because we had done no more, they called in our Commission, tooke a new in their owne names, and appointed us neere as many offices and Officers as I had Souldiers, that neither knew us nor wee them, without our consents or knowledge; since there have gone more then one hundred ships of other proportions, and eight or ten thousand people. Now if you please to compare what hath beene spent, sent, discovered and done this fifteene yeares, by that we did in the three first yeares, and every Governor that hath beene there since, give you but such an account as this, you may easily finde what hath beene the cause of those disasters in Virginia.

Then came in Captaine Argall, and Master Sedan, in a ship of Master Cornelius, to fish for Sturgion, who had such good provision, we contracted with them for it, whereby we were better furnished then ever.

Not long after came in seven ships, with about three hundred people; but rather to supplant us then supply us, their Admirall with their authoritie being cast away in the Bermudas, very angry they were we had made no better provision for them. Seven or eight weekes we withstood the inundations of these disorderly humors, till I was neere blowne to death with Gun-powder, which occasioned me to returne for England.

In the yeare 1609 about Michaelmas, I left the Countrey, as is formerly related, with three ships, seven Boats, Commodities to trade, harvest newly gathered, eight weeks provision of Corne and Meale, about five hundred persons, three hundred Muskets, shot, powder, and match, with armes for more men then we had. The Salvages their language and habitation, well knowne to two hundred expert Souldiers; Nets for fishing, tooles of all sorts, apparell to supply their wants: six Mares and a Horse, five or six hundred Swine, many more Powltry, what was brought or bred, but victuall there remained.

Having spent some five yeares, and more then five hundred pounds in procuring the Letters Patents and setting forward, and neere as much more about New England, &c. Thus these nineteene yeares I have here and there not spared any thing according to my abilitie, nor the best advice I could, to perswade how those strange miracles of misery might have beene prevented, which lamentable experience plainly taught me of necessity must insue, but few would beleeve me till now too deerely they have paid for it. Wherefore hitherto I have rather left all then undertake impossibilities, or any more such costly taskes at such chargeable rates: for in neither of those two Countries have I one foot of Land, nor the very house I builded, nor the ground I digged with my owne hands, nor ever any content or satistaction at all, and though I see ordinarily those two Countries shared before me by them that neither have them nor knowes them, but by my descriptions: Yet that doth not so much trouble me, as to heare and see those contentions and divisions which will hazard if not ruine the prosperitie of Virginia, if present remedy bee not found, as they have hindred many hundreds, who would have beene there ere now, and makes them yet that are willing to stand in a demurre.

For the Books and Maps I have made, I will thanke him that will shew me so much for so little recompence, and beare with their errors till I have done better. For the materials in them I cannot deny, but am ready to affirme them both there and here, upon such grounds as I have propounded, which is to have but fifteene hundred men to subdue againe the Salvages, fortifie the Countrey, discover that yet unknowne, and both defend & feed their Colony, which I most humbly refer to his Majesties most judiciall judgement, and the most honourable Lords of his Privy Councell, you his trusty and well-beloved Commissioners, and the Honourable company of Planters and well-willers to Virginia, New-England and Sommer-Ilands.

Out of these Observations it pleased his Majesties Commissioners for the reformation of Virginia, to desire my answer to these seven Questions.

Quest. 1. What conceive you is the cause the Plantation hath prospered no better since you left it in so good a forwardnesse?

Answ. Idlenesse and carelesnesse brought all I did in three yeeres in six moneths to nothing, and of five hundred I left, scarce threescore remained, and had Sir Thomas Gates not got from the Bermudas, I thinke they had beene all dead before they could be supplied.

Quest. 2. What conceive you should be the cause, though the Country be good, there comes nothing but Tobacco?

Answ. The oft altering of Governours it seemes causes every man make use of his time, and because Corne was stinted at two shillings six pence the bushell, and Tobacco at three shillings the pound, and they value a mans labour a yeere worth fifty or threescore pound, but in Corne not worth ten pound, presuming Tobacco will furnish them with all things; now make a mans labour in Corne worth threescore pound, and in Tobacco but ten pound a man, then shall they have Corne sufficient to entertaine all commers, and keepe their people in health to doe any thing, but till then, there will be little or nothing to any purpose.

Quest. 3. What conceive you to have beene the cause of the Massacre, and had the Salvages had the use of any peeces in your time, or when, or by whom they were taught?

Answ. The cause of the Massacre was the want of marshall discipline, and because they would have all the English had by destroying those they found so carelesly secure, that they were not provided to defend themselves against any enemy, being so dispersed as they were. In my time, though Captaine Nuport furnished them with swords by truck, and many fugitives did the like, and some Peeces they got accidentally, yet I got the most of them againe, and it was death to him that should shew a Salvage the use of a Peece. Since I understand they became so good shot, they were imployed for Fowlers and Huntsmen by the English.

Quest. 4. What charge thinke you would have setled the government both for defence and planting when you left it?

Answ. Twenty thousand pound would have hyred good labourers and mechanicall men, and have furnished them with cattle and all necessaries, and 100. of them would have done more then a thousand of those that went, though the Lord Laware, Sir Ferdinando Waynman, Sir Thomas Gates and Sir Thomas Dale were perswaded to the contrary, but when they had tried, they confessed their error.

Quest. 5. What conceive you would be the remedy and the charge?

Answ. The remedy is to send Souldiers and all sorts of labourers and necessaries for them, that they may be there by next Michaelmas, the which to doe well will stand you in five thousand pound, but if his Majesty would please to lend two of his Ships to transport them, lesse would serve, besides the benefit of his grace to the action would encourage all men.

Quest. 6. What thinke you are the defects of the government both here and there?

Answ. The multiplicity of opinions here, and Officers there, makes such delaies by questions and formalitie, that as much time is spent in complement as in action; besides, some are so desirous to imploy their ships, having six pounds for every Passenger, and three pounds for every tun of goods, at which rate a thousand ships may now better be procured then one at the first, when the common stocke defrayed all fraughts, wages, provisions and Magazines, whereby the Ships are so pestred, as occasions much sicknesse, diseases and mortality, for though all the Passengers die they are sure of their fraught; and then all must be satisfied with Orations, disputations, excuses and hopes. As for the letters of advice from hence, and their answers thence, they are so well written, men would beleeve there were no great doubt of the performance, and that all things were wel, to which error here they have beene ever much subject; and there not to beleeve, or not to releeve the true and poore estate of that Colony, whose fruits were commonly spent before they were ripe, and this losse is nothing to them here, whose great estates are not sensible of the losse of their adventures, and so they thinke, or will not take notice; but it is so with all men: but howsoever they thinke or dispose of all things at their pleasure, I am sure not my selfe onely, but a thousand others have not onely spent the most of their estates, but the most part have lost their lives and all, onely but to make way for the triall of more new conclusions, and he that now will adventure but twelve pounds ten shillings, shall have better respect and as much favour then he that sixteene yeere agoe adventured as much, except he have money as the other hath, but though he have adventured five hundred pound, and spent there never so much time, if hee have no more and not able to beg in a family of himselfe, all is lost by order of Court.

But in the beginning it was not so, all went then out of one purse, till those new devices have consumed both mony and purse; for at first there were but six Patentees, now more then a thousand, then but thirteene Counsailors, now not lesse then an hundred; I speake not of all, for there are some both honourable and honest, but of those Officers, which did they manage their owne estates no better then the affaires of Virginia, they would quickly fall to decay so well as it; but this is most evident, few Officers in England it hath caused to turne Banquerupts, nor for all their complaints would leave their places, neither yet any of their Officers there, nor few of the rest but they would be at home, but fewer Adventurers here will adventure any more till they see the businesse better established, although there be some so wilfully improvident they care for nothing but to get thither, and then if their friends be dead, or want themselves, they die or live but poorely for want of necessaries, and to thinke the old Planters can releeve them were too much simplicity; for who here in England is so charitable to feed two or three strangers, have they never so much; much lesse in Virginia where they want for themselves. Now the generall complaint saith, that pride, covetousnesse, extortion and oppression in a few that ingrosses all, then sell all againe to the comminalty at what rate they please, yea even men, women and children for who will give most, occasions no small mischiefe amongst the Planters.

As for the Company, or those that doe transport them, provided of necessaries, God forbid but they should receive their charges againe with advantage, or that masters there should not have the same privilege over their servants as here, but to sell him or her for forty, fifty, or threescore pounds, whom the Company hath sent over for eight or ten pounds at the most, without regard how they shall be maintained with apparell, meat, drinke and lodging, is odious, and their fruits sutable, therefore such merchants it were better they were made such merchandize themselves, then suffered any longer to use that trade, and those are defects sufficient to bring a well setled Common-wealth to misery, much more Virginia.

Quest. 7. How thinke you it may be rectified?

Answ. If his Majestie would please to intitle it to his Crowne, and yearely that both the Governours here and there may give their accounts to you, or some that are not ingaged in the businesse, that the common stocke bee not spent in maintaining one hundred men for the Governour, one hundred for two Deputies, fifty for the Treasurer, five and twenty for the Secretary, and more for the Marshall and other Officers who were never there nor adventured any thing, but onely preferred by favour to be Lords over them that broke the ice and beat the path, and must teach them what to doe, if any thing happen well, it is their glory; if ill, the fault of the old directors, that in all dangers must endure the worst, yet not five hundred of them have so much as one of the others; also that there bee some present course taken to maintaine a Garrison to suppresse the Salvages, till they be able to subsist, and that his Majesty would please to remit his custome, or it is to be feared they will lose custome and all, for this cannot be done by promises, hopes, counsels and countenances, but with sufficient workmen and meanes to maintaine them, not such delinquents as here cannot be ruled by all the lawes in England, yet when the foundation is laid, as I have said, and a common-wealth established, then such there may better be constrained to labour then here: but to rectifie a common-wealth with debaushed people is impossible, and no wise man would throw himselfe into such a society, that intends honestly, and knowes what he undertakes, for there is no Countrey to pillage as the Romans found: all you expect from thence must be by labour.

For the government I thinke there is as much adoe about it as the Kingdomes of Scotland and Ireland, men here conceiting Virginia as they are, erecting as many stately Offices as Officers with their attendants, as there are labourers in the Countrey, where a Constable were as good as twenty of their Captaines, and three hundred good Souldiers and labourers better then all the rest that goe onely to get the fruits of other mens labours by the title of an office. Thus they spend Michaelmas rent in Mid-summer Moone, and would gather their Harvest before they have planted their Corne.

As for the maintenance of the Officers, the first that went never demanded any, but adventured good summes, and it seemes strange to me, the fruits of all their labours, besides the expence of an hundred and fifty thousand pounds, and such multitudes of people, those collaterall Officers could not maintaine themselves so well as the old did, and having now such liberty to doe to the Salvages what they will, the others had not. I more then wonder they have not five hundred Salvages to worke for them towards their generall maintenance, and as many more to returne some content and satisfaction to the Adventurers, that for all their care, charge and diligence, can heare nor see nothing but miserable complaints; therefore under your correction to rectifie all, is with all expedition to passe the authority to them who will releeve them, lest all bee consumed ere the differences be determined. And except his Majestie undertake it, or by Act of Parliament some small tax may be granted throughout his Dominions, as a Penny upon every Poll, called a head-penny; two pence upon every Chimney, or some such collection might be raised, and that would be sufficient to give a good stocke, and many servants to sufficient men of any facultie, and transport them freely for paying onely homage to the Crowne of England, and such duties to the publike good as their estates increased reason should require. Were this put in practice, how many people of what quality you please, for all those disasters would yet gladly goe to spend their lives there, and by this meanes more good might be done in one yeere, then all those pety particular undertakings will effect in twenty.

For the Patent the King may, if he please, rather take it from them that have it, then from us who had it first, pretending to his Majesty what great matters they would doe, and how little we did, and for any thing I can conceive, had we remained still as at first, it is not likely we could have done much worse; but those oft altering of governments are not without much charge, hazard and losse. If I be too plaine, I humbly crave your pardon; but you requested me, therefore I doe but my duty. For the Nobility, who knowes not how freely both in their Purses and assistances many of them have beene to advance it, committing the managing of the businesse to inferiour persons, amongst whom questionlesse also many have done their utmost best, sincerely and truly according to their conceit, opinion and understanding; yet grosse errors have beene committed, but no man lives without his fault; for my owne part, I have so much adoe to amend my owne, I have no leisure to looke into any mans particular, but those in generall I conceive to be true. And so I humbly rest Yours to command,

J. S.

Thus those discords, not being to be compounded among themselves, nor yet by the extraordinary diligences, care and paines of the noble and right worthy Commissioners, Sir William Jones, Sir Nicholas Fortescue, Sir Francis Goston, Sir Richard Sutton, Sir Henry Bourgchier and Sir William Pit; a Corante was granted against Master Deputy Farrar, and 20. or 30. others of that party to plead their causes before the right Honourable, the Lords of his Majesties Privy Councell: now notwithstanding all the Relations, Examinations, and intercepting of all Letters whatsoever came from thence, yet it seemes they were so farre unsatisfied and desired to know the truth, as well for the preservation of the Colony, as to give content and doe all men right, they sent two Commissioners strictly to examine the true estate of the Colony. Upon whose returne after mature deliberation, it pleased his royall Majesty to suppresse the course of the Court at Deputy Farrars, and that for the present ordering the affaires of Virginia, untill he should make a more full settlement thereof, the Lord Viscount Mandevile, Lord President of his Majesties Privie Councell, and also other Privy Councellors, with many understanding Knights and Gentlemen, should every Thursday in the afternoone meet at Sir Thomas Smiths in Philpot lane, where all men whom it should concerne may repaire, to receive such directions and warrant for their better security, as more at large you may see in the Proclamation to that effect, under the great Seale of England, dated the 15. of July, 1624. But as for the relations last returned, what numbers they are, how many Cities, Corporations, townes, and houses, cattle and horse they have, what fortifications or discoveries they have made, or revenge upon the Salvages; who are their friends or foes, or what commodities they have more then Tobacco, & their present estate or what is presently to be put in execution, in that the Commissioners are not yet fully satisfied in the one, nor resolved in the other, at this present time when this went to the Presse, I must intreat you pardon me till I be better assured.

Thus far I have travelled in this Wildernesse of Virginia, not being ignorant for all my paines this discourse will be wrested, tossed and turned as many waies as there is leaves; that I have writ too much of some, too little of others, and many such like objections. To such I must answer, in the Companies name I was requested to doe it, if any have concealed their approved experiences from my knowledge, they must excuse me: as for every fatherles or stolne relation, or whole volumes of sofisticated rehearsals, I leave them to the charge of them that desire them. I thanke God I never undertooke any thing yet any could tax me of carelesnesse or dishonesty, and what is hee to whom I am indebted or troublesome? Ah! were these my accusers but to change cases and places with me but 2. yeeres, or till they had done but so much as I, it may be they would judge more charitably of my imperfections. But here I must leave all to the triall of time, both my selfe, Virginia's preparations, proceedings and good events, praying to that great God the protector of all goodnesse to send them as good successe as the goodnesse of the action and Country deserveth, and my heart desireth.

Captain John Smith's Description of the Plymouth Colony, 1624

The following passage is taken from the "Sixth Booke" of Captain John Smith's Generall Historie of Virginia, New England & The Summer Isles, *first published in London in 1624. From Smith's eyewitness account, it is apparent that England's second colony was off to a much better start than Jamestown had made during Smith's time there.*

The present estate of New-Plimoth.

At New-Plimoth there is about 180 persons, some cattell and goats, but many swine and poultry, 32 dwelling houses, whereof 7 were burnt the last winter, and the value of five hundred pounds in other goods; the Towne is impailed about halfe a mile compasse. In the towne upon a high Mount they have a Fort well built with wood, lome, and stone, where is planted their Ordnance: Also a faire Watch-tower, partly framed for the Sentinell, the place it seemes is healthfull, for in these last three yeeres, notwithstanding their great want of most necessaries, there hath not one died of the first planters, they have made a saltworke, and with that salt preserve the fish they take, and this yeare hath fraughted a ship of 180. tunnes. The Governour is one Mr. William Bradford, their Captaine Miles Standish, a bred Souldier in Holland; the chiefe men for their assistance is Master Isaak Alderton, and divers others as occasion serveth; their Preachers are Master William Bruster and Master John Layford.

The most of them live together as one family or houshold, yet every man followeth his trade and profession both by sea and land, and all for a generall stocke, out of which they have all their maintenance, untill there be a divident betwixt the Planters and the Adventurers. Those Planters are not servants to the Adventurers here, but have onely councells of directions from them, but no injunctions or command, and all the masters of families are partners in land or whatsoever, setting their labours against the stocke, till certaine yeeres be expired for the division: they have young men and boies for their Apprentises and servants, and some of them speciall families, as Ship-carpenters, Salt-makers, Fish-masters, yet as servants upon great wages. The Adventurers which raised the stocke to begin and supply this Plantation were about 70. some Gentlemen, some Merchants, some handy-crafts men, some adventuring great summes, some small, as their estates and affection served. The generall stocke already imploied is about 7000. l. by reason of which charge and many crosses, many of them would adventure no more, but others that knowes so great a designe cannot bee effected without both charge, losse and crosses, are resolved to goe forward with it to their powers; which deserve no small commendations and encouragement. These dwell most about London, they are not a corporation, but knit together by a voluntary combination in a society without constraint or penalty, aiming to doe good & to plant Religion; they have a President & Treasurer, every yeere newly chosen by the most voices, who ordereth the affaires of their Courts and meetings, and with the assent of the most of them, undertaketh all ordinary businesses, but in more weighty affaires, the assent of the whole Company is required. There hath beene a fishing this yeere upon the Coast about 50. English ships: and by Cape Anne, there is a Plantation a beginning by the Dorchester men, which they hold of those of New-Plimoth, who also by them have set up a fishing worke; some talke there is some other pretended Plantations, all whose good proceedings the eternal God protect and preserve. And these have beene the true proceedings and accidents in those Plantations.

Now to make a particular relation of all the acts and orders in the Courts belonging unto them, of the anihilating old Patents and procuring new; with the charge, paines and arguments, the reasons of such changes, all the treaties, consultations, orations, and dissentions about the sharing and dividing those large territories, confirming of Counsailers, electing all sorts of Officers, directions, Letters of advice, and their answers, disputations about the Magazines and Impositions, suters for Patents, positions for Freedomes, and confirmations with complaints of injuries here, and also the mutinies, examinations, arraignements, executions, and the cause of the so oft revolt of the Salvages at large, as many would have had, and it may be some doe expect it would make more quarrels then any of them would willingly answer, & such a volume as would the any wise man but to read the contents; for my owne part I rather feare the unpartiall Reader wil thinke this rather more tedious then necessary: but he that would be a practitioner in those affaires, I hope will allow them not only needfull but expedient: but how ever, if you please to beare with those errors I have committed, if God please I live, my care and paines shall endevour to be thankfull: if I die, accept my good will: If any desire to be further satisfied, what defect is found in this, they shall finde supplied in me, that thus freely have throwne my selfe with my mite into the Treasury of my Countries good, not doubting but God will stirre up some noble spirits to consider and examine if worthy Columbus could give the Spaniards any such certainties for his designe, when Queene Isabel of Spaine set him forth with 15. saile, and though I promise no Mines of gold, yet the warlike Hollanders let us imitate but not hate, whose wealth and strength are good testimonies of their treasury gotten by fishing; and New-England hath yeelded already by generall computation one hundred thousand pounds at the least. Therefore honourable and worthy Country men, let not the meannesse of the word fish distaste you, for it will afford as good gold as the Mines of Guiana or Potassie, with lesse hazard and charge, and more certainty and facility.

J.S.

Aftermath of Massacre, 1644

The 15–22 May 1645 issue of the anti-Royalist London weekly newspaper Mercurius Civicus *printed the following extracts of correspondence written in Virginia after the Indian insurrection in the colony in 1644.*

I doe not usually acquaint you with any forraine intelligence, conceiving the affaires at home to be more lookt after, yet haveing this weeke received some matters of importance in reference to this Kingdome in divers letters from Virginy, I shall for once give you a relation of their contents, which are thus:

We are still troubled with the Indians upon the frontier part of the Country, and therefore wee are now providing three forts in the middle of the Country being in the Kings Territories, which is not far from us, that so we may have a power amongst them able to destroy them and to deprive them of their livelihood. They lately in a treacherous manner cut off 400 of our people, they have not courage to doe it otherwise: we take this course now that so wee may follow our businesse in the summer. How ever the crops we make now cannot be so great as they have bin, and I think we shall be at the charge of halfe our labours to maintaine these forts, and the Souldiers at the middle plantation which is a narrow passage the Indians have into the Forrest, this is onely our charge that dwell on the Northside of *James* River, the people on the other side are to deale with the Indians there: This way though chargeable is thought most convenient to extirpate and subdue this people that doe much annoy us: they are so cowardly that ten of ours will make an hundred of them run away. We are at peace among our selves and have beene so ever since the massacre; Sir *William Barclay* [Governor Berkeley] went for Bristoll [England] and left Master [Richard] *Kempe* his Deputy and is not yet returned: It is my opinion that the massacre (though a judgement) did divert a great mischiefe that was growing among us by *Sir William Barclay's* courses; for divers of the most religious and honest inhabitants, were mark't out to be plundered and imprisoned for the refusall of an Oath that was imposed upon the people, in referrence to the King of England. It was tendered at mens houses, the people murmured, and most refused to take it: Those few that tooke it did it more for feare then affection; so that it is the opinion of judicious men that if the Indians had but forborne for a month longer, they had found us in such a combustion among our selves that they might with ease have cut of every man if once we had spent that little powder and shot that we had among our selves. I must not omit to give you notice of the governour of Mary-lands commissions lately brought hither in the Bristoll ship, though it may be you have already notice of in *England:* The governour of Mary-land [Leonnard Calvert] very tenderly discovered a commission that he had from His Majesty to take the *London* ships; to seize upon all debts due to *London* Merchants, to build custome-houses, and to receive the custome of Tobacco heere, and also to erect Castles and build Forts for the defence of the Country, and out of this revenue hee was to pay the governour of this Colony 2000 £. The Assembly seemed to comply with him and pretended the accomplishment of all his desires, and when they had gotten as much out of him as they could they seemed to commend the ingenious contrivance of the businesse, hee replied that was the only agent in the businesse himselfe, which they tooke good notice of, withdrew themselves, dissolved the Assembly, but published a Proclamation that all ships from *London,* and elsewhere should have free Trade, and so departed leaving him and his commissions.

Since the massacre because men should not be disabled to defend themselves, and their Plantations, it was thought fit to make a Law that no mans servant, his corne, or Ammunition should be taken in execution, but when it shall please God we shall suppresse our enemy, this Act will be repealed.

Certaine newes is brought hither by a credible person, That [Richard] *Ingle* hath taken and plundered all the Papists except the governour of Mary-land, and some few that are gone away among the Poluxant Indians for refuge, and that he hath sent 40 men by land, and 60 by water to fetch them by violence.

I should now leave the forraigne newes were it not that upon the day of the execution of the massacre upon the Christians by the Indians there hapned a great wonder (which to many may seeme incredible, and the rather for that it is related at so great a distance from this Kingdome; and indeed there are some people so criticall that they will believe no more then they see of the affaires of this Kingdome, and much lesse further of: yet for the satisfaction of such as are desirous, I shall onely set down the words of the Letter comming from an honest and knowne hand in that Plantation, to a person of good repute in this City, Gods goodnesse hath beene lately very eminent in delivering me and my family from the Indian massacre. Upon the first day of April my wife was washing a bucke of clothes, and of a sudden her clothes were all besprinkled with blood from the first beginning to the rincing of them, at last in such abundance as if an hand should invisibly take handfuls of gore blood and throw it upon the linnen. When it lay all of an heape in the washing-tub, she sent for me in, and I tooke up one gobbet of blood as big as my fingers end, and stirring it in my hand it did not staine my fingers nor the linnen: Upon this miraculous premonition and warning from God having some kinde of intimation of some designe of the Indians (though nothing appeared till that day) I provided for defence, and though we were but five men and mistrusted not any villany towards us before: yet we secured our selves against 20 savages which were three houres that day about my house. Blessed be the name of God.

List of Those Executed for Bacon's Rebellion, 1676

The following, "A List of Those That Have Been Executed for the Late Rebellion in Virginia," was prepared by Sir William Berkeley, governor of the Jamestown colony. It was printed by Peter Force in volume one of his Tracts and Other Papers, Relating Principally to the Origin, Settlement, and Progress of the Colonies in North America, from the Discovery of the Country to the Year 1776 *(Washington, D.C., 1835).*

A LIST OF THOSE THAT HAVE BEEN EXECUTED FOR Ye LATE REBELLION IN VIRGINIA.

1.—One Johnson, a stirer up of the people to sedition but no fighter.
2.—One Barlow, one of Cromwell's soldiers, very active in this rebellion, and taken with forty men coming to surprise me at Accomack.
3.—One Carver, a valiant man, and stout seaman, taken miraculously, who came with Bland, with equall com'n and 200 men to take me and some other gentlemen that assisted me, with the help of 200 soldiers; miraculously delivered into my hand.
4.—One Wilford, an interpreter, that frighted the Queen of Pamunkey from ye lands she had granted her by the Assembly, a month after peace was concluded with her.
5.—One Hartford, a valiant stout man, and a most resolved rebel.

All these at Accomack.

AT YORK WHILST I LAY THERE.

1.—One Young, commissionated by Genl. Monck long before he declared for ye King.
2.—One Page, a carpenter, formerly my servant, but for his violence used against the Royal Party, made a Colonel.
3.—One Harris, that shot to death a valiant loyalist prisoner.
4.—One Hall, a Clerk of a County but more useful to the rebels than 40 army men—that dyed very penitent confessing his rebellion against his King and his ingratitude to me.

AT THE MIDDLE PLANTATION.

One Drummond, a Scotchman that we all suppose was the originall cause of the whole rebellion, with a common Frenchman, that had been very bloody.

CONDEMNED AT MY HOUSE, AND EXECUTED WHEN BACON LAY BEFORE JAMESTOWN.

1.—One Coll'l Crewe, Bacon's parasyte, that continually went about ye country, extolling all Bacon's actions, and (justifying) his rebellion.
2.—One Cookson, taken in rebellion.
3.—One Darby, from a servant made a Captain.

WILLM. BERKELEY.

An Account of Our Late Troubles in Virginia, 1676

The following account of Bacon's Rebellion was written by Ann Dunbar Cotton, the wife of John Cotton of Queen's Creek in York County, Virginia. The Cottons' passage to the New World apparently had been paid for by William Drummond, the first governor of North Carolina and Bacon's chief supporter in the insurrection against Governor Berkeley. The account was first printed from the original manuscript in the 12 September 1804 issue of the Richmond Enquirer *and reprinted by Peter Force in vol-*

ume one of his Tracts and Other Papers, Relating Principally to the Origin, Settlement, and Progress of the Colonies in North America, from the Discovery of the Country to the Year 1776 *(Washington, D.C., 1835). Speculation has it that Ann Cotton also was the author of an elegiac poem honoring Bacon.*

To Mr. C. H. at Yardly in Northamptonshire.

Sr. I haveing seene yours directed to —— and considering that you cannot have your desires satisfied that way, for the forementioned reasons, I have by his permition, adventured to send you this briefe acount, of those affaires, so far as I have bin informed.

The Susquehanians and Marylanders of friendes being ingaged enimyes (as hath by former letter bin hinted to you) and that the Indians being ressalutely bent not to forsake there forte; it came to this pointe, yt the Marylanders were obliged (findeing themselves too weake to do the worke themselves) to suplycate (too soone granted) aide of the Verginians, put under the conduct of one Collonel Washingto[n] (him whom you have sometimes seen at your howse) who being joyned with the Marylanders, invests the Indians in there forte, with a neglegent siege; upon which the enimye made severall salleys, with as many losses to the beseegers; and at last gave them the opertunity to disart the Fort, after that the English had (contrary to ye law of arms) beate out the Braines of 6 grate men sent out to treate a peace: an action of ill consequence, as it proved after. For the Indians having in the darke, slipt through the Legure, and in there passage knock'd 10 of the beseigers on the head, which they found fast a-sleep, leaving the rest to prosecute the Seige, (as Scoging's Wife brooding the Eggs which the Fox had suck'd) they resolved to imploy there liberty in avenging there Commissionres blood, which they speedily effected in the death of sixty inosscent soules, and then send in there Remonstrance to the Governour, in justification of the fact, with this expostulation annext: Demanding what it was moved him to take up arms against them, his professed friends, in the behalfe of the Marylanders, there avowed enimyes. Declaring there sorow to see the Verginians, of friends to becom such violent enimies as to persue the Chase in to anothers dominions. Complanes that there messingers sent out for peace were not only knock'd on the head but the fact countenanc'd by the governour; for which (finding no other way to be satisfied) they had revenged themselves, by killing ten for one of the English; such being the disperportion between there men murthered, and those by them slane, theres being persons of quallety, the other of inferiour Ranke: Professing that if they may have a valluable satisfaction, for the damage they had sustained by the English, and that the Verginians would with-draw there aides from the Marylanders quarrill; that then they would renew the league with Sr W. B. otherways they would prossecute ye war to the last man; and the hardest fend of.

This was faire play, from fowle gamesters. But the perposealls not to be alowed of as being contrary to the honour of the English, the Indians proceede, and having drawn the neighboring Indians into there ade, in a short time, they commit abundance of ungarded and unrevenged murthers; by which meanes a grate many of the outward plantations were disarted; the doeing whereof did not onely terefye the wholl collony, but subplanted those esteemes the people had formerly for Sr. W. B. whom they judged too remiss in applying meanes to stop the fewrye of the Heathen; and to settle there affections, and expectations, upon one Esqr. Bacon, newly come into the Countrey, one of the Councell, and nearly related to your late wives father-in-law, whom they desired might be commissionated Generall, for the Indian war; Which Sr. William (for some reasons best knowne unto himself) denying, the Gent: man (without any scruple) accepts of a commission from the peoples affections, signed by the emergences of affaires and the Countreys danger; and so forthwith advanceth with a small party (composed of such that owne his Authorety) against the Indians; on whom, it is saide he did signall execution: In his absence hee and those with him, were declared Rebells to the State, May 29, and forces raised to reduce him to his obedience; at the head of which the Governour advanceth, some 30 or 40 miles to find Bakon out, but not knowing which way he was gon, he dismisseth his army, retireing himself and councell, to James Towne, there to be redy for the assembly, which was now upon the point of meeting: Whiter Bacon, some few days after his return hom from his Indian march, repared to render an account of his servis; for which himself and most of those with him in the expedition, were imprisoned; from whence they were freed by a judgment in court upon Bacon's tryall, himself readmited into the councell and promised a commission the Monday following (this was on the Saturday) against the Indians; with which deluded, he smothers his resentments, and beggs leave to visit his Lady (now sick, as he pretended) which granted, hee returnes to Towne at the head of 4 or 5 hundred men, well Arm'd: reassumes his demands for a commission. Which, after som howers strugling with the Governour, being obtained, according to his desire, hee takes order for the countreyes security, against the attemps of sculking Indians; fills up his numbers and provissiones, according to the gage of his commission; and so once more advanceth against the Indians, who heareing of his approaches, calls in there Runers and scouts, be taking themselves to be there subterfuges and lurking holes. The General (for so he was now denominated) had not reach'd the head of York River, but that a Post overtakes him, and informes, that Sr. W. B. was a raiseing the Traine-bands in Glocester, with an intent, eather to fall into his reare, or otherways to cutt him off when he should return wery and spent from his Indian servis. This strange newes put him, and those with him, shrodly to there Trumps, beleiveing that a few such Deales or shufles (call them what you will) might quickly ring both cards and game out of his hands. He saw that there was an abselute necessety of destroying the Indians, and that there was som care to be taken for his owne and Armys safety, other-ways the worke might happen to be rechedly done, where the laberours were made criples, and be compeld (insteade of a sword) to make use of a cruch. It vext him to the heart (as he said) to thinke, that while he was a hunting Wolves, tigers and bears, which daly destroyd our harmless and innosscent Lambs, that hee, and those with him, should be persewed in the reare with a full cry, as more savage beasts. He perceved like the corne, he was light between those stones which might grinde him to pouder; if he did not looke the better about him. For the preventing of which, after a short consult with his officers, he countermarcheth his Army (about 500 in all) downe to the midle Plantation: of which the Governour being informed, ships himself and adhearers, for Accomack (for the Gloster men refused to owne his quarill against the Generall) after he had caused Bacon, in these parts to be proclamed a Rebell once more, July 29.

Bacon being sate down with his Army at the midle Plantation, sends out an invitation unto all the prime Gent: men in these parts, to give him a meeting in his quarters, there to consult how the Indians were to be proceeded against, and himself and Army protected against the desines of Sr. W. B. aganst whose Papers, of the 29 of May, and his Proclameation since, he puts forth his Replication and those papers upon these Dellama's.

First, whether persons wholy devoted to the King and countrey, haters of sinester and by-respects, adventering there lives and fortunes, to kill and destroy all in Arms, against King and countrey; that never ploted, contrived, or indeviou red the destruction, detryement or wrong of any of his Majesties subjects, there lives, fortunes, or estates can desurve the names of Rebells and Traters: secondly he cites his owne and soulders peaceable behaviour, calling the wholl countrey to witness against him if they can; hee upbrades som in authorety with the meaneness of there parts, others now rich with the meaneness of there estates, when they came into the countrey, and questions by what just ways they have obtained there welth; whether they have not bin the spunges that hath suck'd up the publick tresury: Questions what arts, sciences, schools of Learning, or manufactorys, have bin promoted in authorety: Justefyes his adverssion, in generall against the Indians; upbrades the Governour for manetaneing there quarill, though never so unjust, aganest the Christians rights; his refuseing to admit an English mans oath against an Indian, when that Indians bare word should be accepted of against an Englishman: sath sumthing against ye Governour concerning the Beaver trade, as not in his power to dispose of to his owne proffit, it being a Monopeley of the crowne; Questions whether the Traders at the heads of the Rivers being his Facters, do not buy and sell the blood of there bretheren and country men, by furnishing the Indians with Pouder, shott and Fire Arms, contrary to the Laws of the Collony: He araignes one Collonell Cowells asscertion, for saying that the English are bound to protect the Indians, to the hassard of there blood. And so concludes with an Appeale to the King and Parliament, where he doubts not but that his and the Peoples cause will be impartially heard.

To comply with the Generalls Invetation, hinted in my former Letter, there was a grate convention of the people met him in his quarters; the result of whose meeting was an Ingagement, for the people (of what qullety soever, excepting servants) to subscribe to consisting of 3 heads. First to be aideing, with there lives and estates, the Generall, in the Indian war: secondly, to opose Sr. Williams designes, if hee had any, to hinder the same: and lastly, to protect the Generall, Army and all that should subscribe this Ingagement, against any power that should be sent out of England, till it should be granted that the countreys complaint might be heard, against Sr. William before the King and Parliament. These 3 heads being methodized, and put in to form, by the Clarke of ye Assembly, who happened to be at this meeting, and redd unto the people, held a despute, from allmost noone, till midnight, pro and con, whether the same might, in the last Article especially, be with out danger taken. The Generall, and som others of the cheife men was Resalute in the affirmative, asserting its innosscency, and protesting, without it, he would surrender up his commission to the Assembly, and lett them finde other servants, to do the countreys worke: this, and the newse, that the Indians were fallen downe in to Gloster county, and had kill'd som people a bout Carters Creeke; made the people willing to take the Ingagement. The cheife men that subscribed it at this meeting, were coll. Swan, coll. Beale, coll. Ballard, Esq. Bray, (all foure of the councell) coll. Jordan, coll. Smith, of Purton, coll. Scarsbrook, coll. Miller, coll. Lawrane, and Mr. Drommond, late Governour of Carolina; all persons, with whom you have bin formerly acquainted.

This worke being over, and orders taken for an Assemblye to sitt downe the 4 of September (the writs being issued out in his majestyes name, and signed by 4 of the Councell, before named) the Generall once more sitts out to finde the Indians: of which Sr. William have gained intelligence, to prevent Bacons designes by the Assembley, returns from Accomack, with a bout 1000 soulders, and others, in 5 shipps and 10 sloops to James towne; in which was som 900 Baconians (for soe now they began to be called, for a marke of destinction) under the command of coll. Hansford, who was commissionated by Bacon, to raise Forces (if need were) in his absence, for the safety of the countrey. Unto these Sr. William sends in a summons for a Rendition of ye place, with a pardon to all that would decline Bacons and entertaine his cause. What was returned to this sommons I know not; but in the night the Baconians forsake the Towne, by the advice of Drummond and Lawrance (who were both excepted, in the Governours sommons, out of mercy) every one returning to there owne aboades, excepting Drommond, Hansford, Lawrence, and some few others, who goes to finde out the Generall, now returned to the head of York River, haveing spent his provisions in following the Indians on whom he did sum execution, and sent them packing a grate way from the Borders.

Before that Drommond and those with him had reached the Generall, he had dismist his Army, to there respective habitations, to gather strength against the next intended expedition; eccepting som frew resarved for his Gard, and persons liveing in these parts; unto whom, those that came with Hansford being joyned, made about 150 in all: With these Bacon, by a swift march, before any newes was heard of his return from the Indians, in these parts, comes to Towne, to ye consternation of all in it, and there blocks the Governour up; which he easily effected by this unheard of project. He was no sooner arived at Towne, but by several small partyes of Horse (2 or 3 in a party, for more he could not spare) he fetcheth into his little League, all the prime mens wives, whose Husbands were with the Governour, (as coll. Bacons Lady, Madm. Bray, Madm. Page, Madm. Ballard, and others) which the next morning he presents to the view of there husbands and ffriends in towne, upon the top of the smalle worke hee had cast up in the night; where he caused them to tarey till hee had finished his defence against his enemies shott, it being the onely place (as you do know well enough) for those in towne to make a salley at. Which when compleated, and the Governour understanding that the Gentle women were withdrawne in to a place of safety, he sends out some 6 or 700 hundred of his soulders, to beate Bacon out of his Trench: But it seems that those works, which were protected by such charms (when a raiseing) that plug'd up the enimys shot in there gains, could not now be storm'd by a vertue less powerfull (when finished) then the sight of a few white Aprons: otherways the servis had bin more honourable and the damage less, several of those who made the salley being slaine and wounded, without one drop of Blood drawne from the enimy. With in too or three days after this disaster, the Governour reships himself, soulders, and all the inhabitants of the towne, and there goods: and so to Accomack a gane; leaving Bacon to enter the place at his pleasure, which he did the next morning before day, and the night following burns it downe to the ground to prevent a futer seege, as hee saide. Which Flagrant, and Flagitious Act performed, he draws his men out of town, and marcheth them over York River, at Tindells point, to finde out collnell Brent, who was advancing fast upon him, from Potomack, at the head of 1200 men, (as he was informed) with a designe to raise Bacons seige, from before the towne, or other ways to fight him, as he saw cause. But, Brents shoulders no sooner heard that Bacon was got on the north-side Yorke River, with an intent to fight them, and that he had beate the Governour out of the towne, and fearing, if he met with them, that he might beate them out of there lives they basely forsake there colours, the greater part adheareing to Bacons cause; resolveing with the Perssians to go and worship the rising sun, now approaching nere there Horisson: of which Bacon being informed, he stops his proceedings that way, and begins to provide for a nother expedition a gainst the Indian, of whom he had heard no news since his last March, a gainst them: which while he was a contriveing, Death summons him to more urgent affairs in to whose hands (after a short seige) he surrenders his life, leaving his commition in the custody of his Leif't Generall, one Ingram, newly comin to the countrey.

Sr. William no sooner had news that Bacon was Dead but he sends over a party, in a sloope to Yorke who snap'd Collonell Hansford, and others with him, that kep a negilegent Gard at coll. Reades howse under his command: When Hansford came to Acomack, he had the honour to be the first Verginian born that ever was hang'd; the soulders (about 20 in all) that were taken with him, were commited to Prisson. Capt. Carver, Capt. Wilford, Capt. Farloe, with 5 or 6 others of less note, taken at other places, ending there days as Hansford did; Major Cheesman bein apointed (but it seems not destinated to the like end, which he prevented by dying in prisson through ill usage, as it is said.

This execution being over (which the Baconians termed crewilty in the abstract) Sr. William ships himself and soulder for York River, casting Anchor at Tindells point; from whence he sends up a hundred and 20 men to surprise a Gard, of about, 30 men and boys, kept at coll. Bacons howse under the command of Major Whaly; who being fore-warn'd by Hansford fate, prevented the designed conflict with the death of the commander in cheife, and the taking som prisoners: Major Lawrence Smith, with 600 men, meeting with the like fate at coll. Pates howse, in Gloster, a gainst Ingram, (the Baconian Generall) onely Smith saved himself, by leaving his men in the lurtch, being all made prissoners; whom Ingram dismist to their owne homes; Ingram himself, and all under his command, with in a few days after, being reduced to his duty, by the well contrivance of Capt. Grantham, who was now lately arived in York River: which put a period to the war, and brought the Governour a shoare at coll. Bacons, where he was presented with Mr. Drumond; taken the day before in Cheekanonimy swomp, half famished, as him self related to my Husband. From coll. Bacons, the next day, he was convayed, in Irons to Mr. Brays (whither the Governour was removed) to his Tryall, where he was condemn'd with in halfe an hower after his coming to Esqr. Brays, to be hanged at the midle Plantation, within 4 howers after condemnation; where he was accordingly, executed, with a pitifull French man. Which don, the Governour removes to his owne howse, to settle his and the countryes repose, after his many troubles; which he effected by the advice of his councel and an Assembly convein'd at the Greene Spring; where severall were condemned to be executed, prime actors in ye Rebellion; as Esqr. Bland, coll. Cruse, and som other hanged at Bacons Trench; Capt. Yong, of Cheekahominy, Mr. Hall, clarke of New-Kent court, James Wilson (once your servant) and one Leift. Collonell Page, (one that my Husband bought of Mr. Lee, when he kep store at your howse) all four executed at coll. Reads, over against Tindells point; and Anthony Arnell (the same that did live at your howse) hanged in chanes at West point, besides severall others executed on the other side James River: enough (they say in all) to out number those slane in the wholl war; on both sides: it being observable that the sword was more favourable then the Halter, as there was a grater liberty taken to run from the sharpness of the one, then would be alowed to shun the dull imbraces of the other: the Hangman being more dredfull to the Baconians, then there Generall was to the Indians: as it is counted more honourable, and less terable, to dye like a soulder, then to be hang'd like a dogg.

Thus Sr. have I rendered you an account of our late troubles in Verginia, which I have performed too wordishly; but I did not know how to help it; Ignorance in som cases is a prevalent ovatour in pleading for pardon, I hope mine may have the fortune to prove soe in the behalfe of Sr. Yor. ffriend and servant,

AN. COTTON.
From Q. Creeke.

Eulogy of the Dead Rebel, 1676

The American intellectual historian Moses Coit Tyler (1835–1900) speculated that the unknown author of the following ode was Ann Cotton of Queen's Creek, who left a letter describing the events surrounding Bacon's Rebellion. Tyler likened the poem to "the commemorative verse of Ben Jonson" and printed it in his A History of American Literature *(New York, 1879).*

Death, why so cruel? What! no other way
To manifest thy spleen, but thus to slay
Our hopes of safety, liberty, our all,
Which, through thy tyranny, with him must fall
To its late chaos? Had thy rigid force
Been dealt by retail, and not thus in gross,
Grief had been silent. Now, we must complain,
Since thou in him hast more than thousands slain;
Whose lives and safeties did so much depend
On him their life, with him their lives must end.
If 't be a sin to think Death bribed can be,

We must be guilty; say't was bribery
Guided the fatal shaft. Virginia's foes,
To whom for secret crimes just, vengeance owes
Deserved plagues, dreading their just desert,
Corrupted Death by Paracelsian art
Him to destroy; whose well-tried courage such,
Their heartless hearts, nor arms, nor strength could touch.
Who now must heal those wounds, or stop that blood
The heathen made, and drew into a flood?
Who is 't must plead our cause? Nor trump, nor drum,
Nor deputations; these, alas, are dumb,
And cannot speak. Our arms—though ne'er so strong—
Will want the aid of his commanding tongue,
Which conquered more than Cæsar: he o'erthrew
Only the outward frame; this could subdue
The rugged works of nature. Souls replete
With dull chill cold, he'd animate with heat
Drawn forth of reason's lymbic.
In a word Mars and Minerva both in him concurred
For arts, for arms, whose pen and sword alike,
As Cato's did, may admiration strike
Into his foes; while they confess withal,
It was their guilt styled him a criminal.
Only this difference doth from truth proceed,
They in the guilt, he in the name, must bleed;
While none shall dare his obsequies to sing
In deserved measures, until Time shall bring
Truth crowned with freedom, and from danger free;
To sound his praises to posterity.
Here let him rest; while we this truth report,
He's gone from hence unto a higher court,
To plead his cause, where he by this doth know
Whether to Cæsar he was friend or foe.

Charles II's Patent Appointing Thomas, Lord Culpeper, Governor of Virginia, 1680

In the following document, King Charles II of England grants to Thomas, Lord Culpeper, Second Baron of Thoresway, the office of lieutenant and governor of Virginia, for life. Culpeper took the oath of office immediately after news of Governor William Berkeley's death reached England, and the recording of this patent was Culpeper's first act as governor upon arriving in Virginia. Culpeper was the sole proprietor of the Northern Neck, a Virginia land grant of more than 5 million acres. The document is taken from Hening, The Statutes at Large *(New York, 1823), vol. 2:565–67.*

---

10 May 1680

Patent appointing Thomas Lord Culpeper, baron of Thorsway, governor of Virginia.

CHARLES the Second by the grace of God King of England Scotland ffrance and Ireland King Defender of the Faith &c. To all to whom these presents shall come Greeting. Know yee that wee for and in consideration of the many good faithfull and acceptable services done and rendered unto us from time to time, as well in forraigne parts as within our dominions by our right trusty and well beloved Thomas Lord Culpeper baron Thorsway eldest son and heir of our late right trusty and well beloved Councellor John Lord Culpeper deceased of whose memory and services we alsoe retain a gracious and favourable sence and for divers other good causes and considerations us thereunto esspecially moving of our esspecial certaine knowledge and meer motion, have given and granted and by these presents for us our heirs and successors doe give and grant unto the said Thomas Lord Culpeper the office of our Lieut. and Governor General of all that our colony and dominion of Virginia in America with all the rights members and appertenances whatsoever, and him the said Thomas Lord Culpeper our Lieut. and Governor General of all our said colony and dominion of Virginia in America and of all the rights members and appertenances whatsoever we for us our heirs and successors do make ordaine constitute and appoint by these presents, To have hold occupie possesse and enjoy the said office of our Lieut. and Governor General above mentioned with all and singular the rights authorities preheminences jurisdictions proffits sallaries and appertenances whatsoever thereunto belonging and appertaining unto him the said Thomas Lord Culpeper to be executed by himselfe or in his absence by such deputy or deputies as we our heirs and successors shall and will commission thereunto from time to time from and imediately after the death surrender fforfieture or other avoidance of Sir Wm. Berkeley our present Govr. there for and during the natural life of him the said Thomas Lord Culpeper. And for the better support of the dignity of the said office wee do for us our heirs and successors give and grant unto the said Lord Culpeper the yearly fee and salary of one thousand of one thousand pounds of lawfull money of England during his natural life which for us our heirs and successors wee do appoint to be paid from time to time to the said Lord Culpeper and his assigns during his natural live aforesaid out of the first revenews and monies which are or shall be from time to time raised there for the support of the Government and payment of our officers of our said colony and dominion by quarterly payments upon the feast day of St. John the Baptist St. Michal the Archangel the nativity of our Lord God and the annunciation of the Blessed Virgin Mary by equal portions. The first payment thereof to begin and be made upon the first of the said feast days which shall next immediately ensue the death surrender fforfeture and other avoidance of Sir Wm. Berkeley and also all such other fees sallaries allowances profitts perquisites powers authorities priviledges preheminences and jurisdictions whatsoever civill and military as to the said office of our Lieut. and Governor General do and ought to appertaine and in as large and ample manner to all intents and purposes whatsoever as the said Sr. Wm. Berkeley or any other persons hath do or ought to execute and enjoy the same. And lastly we hereby strictly charge and command all our officers ministers and subjects whatsoever in or about the said collony or dominion of Virginia to bee at all and on all occasions obedient aydeing and assisting to the said Thomas Lord Culpeper and such deputy or deputies as shall bee commissioned by us our heirs or successors from time to time as aforesaid touching the due execution of the said office and employment and all the matters and things herein specified according to the tenor purport and intent of these presents any former grants commissions instructions or any other matter or thing whatsoever to the country notwithstanding. Although express mention of the true yearely value or certainty of the premisses or any of them or of any other gifts or grants by us or any of our progenetors or predecessors heretofore made to the aforesaid Thomas Lord Culpeper in these presents is not made or any statute act ordenance provision proclamation or restriction heretofore had made published ordeyned, or provided or any other thing cause or matter whatsoever to the contrary thereof in any wise notwithstanding. In witness whereof wee have caused these our letters to be made pattent. Witness ourselves at Westminster the eight day of July in the seaven and twentieth yeare of our reigne.

Per Breevi privato Sigillo—duplex.

James City May the 10th 1680.
This commission publickly read in Court
and Recorded in the Secretarys office.
Teste HEN. HARTWELL, Cl. Ct.

Of the Waters, 1688

The following description of the rivers and springs of Virginia was written in a letter from the Reverend John Clayton to the Royal Society, 12 May 1688, following Clayton's return to England after a two-year residence in Virginia. It is the most succinct description of the waters of Virginia made by a seventeenth-century observer.

'TWixt the two Capes, the Southern, called *Cape Henry,* the more Northerly, called *Cape Charles,* there runs up a great Bay, called the Bay of *Cheesepeak;* nine Leagues over in some places; in most seven, which lying West, Nore and South, divides *Virginia* into two unequal Parts. On the East Side of this Bay there lies a narrow Neck of Land, which makes the Counties of *Northampton* and *Accomack.* On the West Side of the Bay there branch forth four great Rivers, *James River, York River, Rapahanack* and *Potomack,* that rise from a Ridge of Mountains, whereof more in the Sequel. These Rivers plentifully water all the other Parts of *Virginia,* emptying themselves into the great Bay. The Mouth of *James River,* which is the most Southerly of them, and the Mouth of *Potomack,* which is the most Northerly, may be a hundred Miles Distance: but as I have been credibly inform'd that the Falls of *James River* are not past thirty Miles from *Potomack,* which is a vast large River nine Miles over in many Places. I have been told it was navigable nigh two hundred Miles, much higher than any of the other Rivers: Whence I conclude, in future Times, it will be the most considerable for Trade when the Country comes to be inhabited further up into the main Land. The other Rivers are much about three Miles over-a-piece. And *James River* is navigable at least eighty Miles. Within four or five Miles of *James Town, James River* and *York River* are not past four or five Miles asunder. Yea, Sloops of considerable Carriage may sail up the Branches of the two Rivers, till they come within a Mile the one of the other; for I take it to be no more from Collonel Bollard's to Major Troop's Landing, and I believe they may come much about as near again as Collonel Cole's, and several other Places. *York River* is distant from *Rapahanack* in some places not past ten or twelve Miles, *Rapahanack* from *Potomack* not past seven Miles in one Place, tho' it may be sixty in others. The Heads of the Branches of the Rivers interfere and lock one within another, which I think is best expressed after the Manner that an *Indian* explained himself once to me, when I enquired how nigh the Rivers of *Carolina, Virginia,* and *Maryland* arose out of the Mountains, from those that ran Westerly on the other Side of the Mountains, he clapt the Fingers of one Hand 'twixt those of the other, crying, they meet thus; the Branches of different Rivers rising not past a hundred Paces distant one from another: So that no Country in the World can be more curiously watered. But this Conveniency, that in future Times may make her like the *Netherlands,* the richest Place in all *America,* at the present I look on the greatest Impediment to the Advance of the Country, as it is the greatest Obstacle to Trade and Commerce. For the great Number of Rivers, and the Thinness of the Inhabitants, distract and disperse a Trade. So that all Ships in general gather each their Loading up and down an hundred Miles distant; and the best of Trade that can be driven is only a Sort of *Scotch* Peddling; for they must carry all Sorts of Truck that trade thither, having one Commodity to pass off another. This (*i.e.*) the Number of Rivers, is one of the chief Reasons why they have no Towns: for every one being more sollicitous for a private Interest and Conveniency, than for a publick, they will either be for making forty Towns at once, that is, two in every Country, or none at all, which is the Country's Ruin. But to return, the Tides in these Rivers regularly ebb and flow about two Foot perpendicular at *James Town;* there is there, as they call it, a Tide and half Tide; that is, it flows near two Hours along by the Shore, after that it is ebb in the Channel; and again, it ebbs near two Hours by the Shore, after that it is Flood in the Channel. This is great Advantage to the Boats passing up and down the River, I suppose this is caused by many Creeks and Branches of the Rivers, which being considerable many, tho' only three or four Miles long, yet as broad as the *Thames* at *London,* others ten Miles long, some above twenty, that have little fresh Water which they carry of their own, but their Current primarily depending upon the Flux and Re-flux of the Sea. So that after the Tide is made in the Channel, it flows by the Shore a considerable Time afterwards, being that those Creeks are still to fill, and therefore as it were draws up a Source upwards by the Shore; and likewise when the Tide returns in the Channel, the Creeks that could not so readily disburse their Water, being still to empty themselves, they make an Ebbing by the Shore a considerable Time after that it is Flood, as I say, in the Channel. So far as the salt Waters reach the Country is deemed less healthy. In the Freshes they more rarely are troubled with the Seasonings, and those endemical Distempers about *September* and *October.* This being very remarkable, I refer the Reason to the more piercing Genius of those most judicious Members of the Society: And it might perhaps be worthy the Disquisition of the most Learned to give an Account of the various Alterations and fatal Effects that the Air has on humane Bodies, especially when impregnated with a marine Salt; more peculiarly when such an Air becomes stagnant: This might perhaps make several beneficial Discoveries, not only in Relation to those Distempers in *America,* but perhaps take in your *Kentish* Agues, and many other remarkable enough in our own Nation. I lately was making some Observations of this Nature, on a Lady of a delicate Constitution, who living in a clear Air, and removing towards the Sea-Coast, was lamentably afflicted therewith, which both my self and others attributed to this Cause, she having formerly upon her going to the same, been seized in the same Manner. But to return: There is one thing more in reference to this very thing very remarkable in *Virginia:* generally twice in the Year, Spring and Fall, at certain Spring-Tides, the most of the Cattle will set on gadding, and run, tho' it be twenty or thirty Miles, to the River to drink the salt Water, at which Time there's scarce any stopping of them, which the People know so well, that if about those Times their Herds are strayed from their Plantations, without more Sollicitation they go directly to the Rivers to fetch them home again. As for the Waters in the Springs in general, they are, I think, somewhat more eager than those in *England.* In that I have observed, they require some Quantity more of Malt to make strong Beer than our *English* Waters, and will not bear Soap. I have try'd several by infusing of Galls, and found little difference in the Colours, turning much what the Colour of common Sack in Taverns. I tried two Wells at Collonel Bird's by the Falls of *James River,* several Wells near *James Town,* some Springs in the *Isle of Wight County:* There's a Spring in the *Isle of Wight,* or *Nanzamond County,* vents the greatest Source of Water I ever saw, excepting *Holy-Well* in *Wales,* but I had not Opportunity to make Experiments thereof. I tried likewise some Springs on the Banks of *York River,* in *New Kent* and *Glocester County,* but found them vary very little as to Colour. I could not try any thing as to their specifick Gravity, having neither Aquapoise, nor those other Glasses I had contrived peculiary for making such Experiments, they being all lost with my other things. I had Glasses blown would hold about five Ounces, others about ten Ounces, with Necks so small, that a Drop would make a considerable Variation; with these I could make much more critical and satisfactory Observations as to the specifical Gravity of Liquors, having critical Scales, than by any other Way yet by me tried. I used this Method to weigh Urines; which Practice I would recommend to the inquisitive and critical Physicians. I had made many Observations hereof, but all Notes were likewise lost with my other things. Yet I have begun afresh; for there are more signal Variations in the Weights of Urines than one would at first imagine; and when the Eye can discover little, but judge two Urines to be alike, they may be found to differ very much as to Weight. By Weight I find Observations may be made of Affections in the Head, which rarely make any visible Alterations in the Urine. I have found two Urines not much unlike differ two and twenty Grains in the Quantity of about four or five Ounces: But let them that make these Essays weigh all their Urines when cold, lest they be thereby deceiv'd. But to return to the Spring Waters in *Virginia.* There's a Spring at my Lady Berkley's, called *Green-Spring,* whereof I have been often told, so very cold, that 'tis dangerous drinking thereof in Summer-time, it having proved of fatal Consequence to several. I never tried any thing of what Nature it is of.

There be many petrifying Waters; and indeed I believe few of the Waters but participate of a petrifying Quality, tho' there be few Pebbles or paving Stones to be found in all the Country. But I have found many Sticks with crusty Congelations round them in the Ruins of Springs, and Stones figured like Honey-Combs, with many little Stars as it were shot in the Holes. And nothing is more common than petrify'd Shells, unless you would determine that they are Parts of natural Rock shot in those Figures, which indeed I rather think; but thereof hereafter. Mr. Secretary Spencer has told me of some Waters participating much of *Alome* or *Vitriol* towards *Potomack.* Up beyond the Falls of *Rapahanack* I have heard of poisonous Waters. But these I only mention as a Hint to further Enquiry of some others, for I can say nothing of them my self.

When you make the Capes of *Virginia,* you may observe it low Land, so that at some Distance the Trees appear as if they grew in the Water; and as you approach nigher to emerge thence. For a hundred Miles up into the Country, there are few Stones to be found, only in some Places, Rocks of Iron Oar appear, which made me expect to have found many Waters turn Purple with Galls, but never met with any. Providence has supplied the common Use of Stones, by making the Roads very good: So that they ride their Horses without shoeing them; which yet are more rarely beaten on their Feet, than ours are in *England,* the Country and Clime being dry, their Hoofs are much harder; for I observed, that take a Horse out of the wet Marshes, and Swamps, as they there call them, and ride him immediately, and he'll quickly be tender-footed. In some Places, for several Miles together, the Earth is so intermix'd with Oyster-shells, that there may seem as many Shells as Earth; and how deep they lie thus intermingled, I think, is not yet known: For at broken Banks they discover themselves to be continued many Yards perpendicular. In several Places these Shells are much closer, and being petrified, seem to make a Vein of a Rock. I have seen in several Places, Veins of these Rocky Shells, three or four Yards thick, at the foot of a Hill, whose Precipice might be twenty Yards perpendicular, whose Delf, I suppose, shot under the Hill; pieces of these Rocks broken off, lie there, which, I suppose, may weigh twenty or thirty Tuns a-piece, and are as difficult to be broken as our Free-stone. Of these Rocks of Oyster-shells that are not so much petrified, they burn and make all their Lime; whereof they have that store, that no Generation will consume. Whether these were formerly Oysters, which left by the subsiding Seas, (as some suppose, that all that Tract of Land, now high Ground, was once overflowed by the Sea) were since petrified, or truly Stones, *sui Generis,* I leave to the honourable Society to determin. But when I consider the constant and distinct Shooting of several Salts, Nature's Curiosity, in every thing, so far exceeding that of Art, that the most ingenious, when referr'd thereto, seem only endued with an apish Fondness, I cannot think any thing too difficult or wonderful for Nature; and indeed I do not apprehend, why it may not be as feasible to suppose them to have been Rocks, at first shot into those Figures, as to conceive the Sea to have amass'd such a vast Number of Oyster-shells one upon another, and afterwards subsiding, should leave them cover'd with such Mountains of Earth, under which they should petrify: But not to launch forth too far into those Disputes, since I must modestly remember to whom I write. Often, in the looser Banks of Shells and Earth, are found perfect Teeth petrified, some whereof I have seen, could not be less than two or three

Inches long, and above an Inch broad: Tho' they were not maxillary Teeth, the Part that one might suppose grew out of the Jaw, was polished, and black, almost as Jett; the Part which had been fasten'd in the Jaw and Gums, was brown, and not so shiningly polished, or smooth; if they were, as they seemed to be, really Teeth, I suppose, they must have been of Fishes. The Back-bone of a Whale, and as I remember, they told me of some of the Ribs, were digg'd out of the Side of a Hill, several Yards deep in the Ground, about four Miles distant from *James Town,* and the River. Mr. Banister, a Gentleman pretty curious in those things, shew'd me likewise the Joynt of a Whale's Back-bone, and several Teeth, some whereof, he said, were found in Hills beyond the Falls of *James River,* at least, a hundred and fifty Miles up into the Country.

The Reverend John Clayton's Description of Tobacco Cultivation in Virginia, 1688

The Reverend John Clayton (1665–1737) resided in Virginia between April 1684 and May 1686, during which time he made a series of remarkable observations about Virginia and its countryside and inhabitants. The follow excerpt is from Clayton's letter to the Royal Society, 17 August 1688, one of several valuable letters of Clayton describing the Virginia countryside and its inhabitants.

The Soil in general is sandy: I had designed, and I think it might be worth a critical Remark, to observe, the difference of Soils seem appropriated to the several Sorts of Tobacco: For there is not only the two distinct Sorts of sweet-scented, and Aranoko Tobacco, but of each of these be several Sorts much different, the Seeds whereof are known by distinct Names, they having given them the Names of those Gentlemen most famed for such Sort of Tobacco, as of *Prior* Seed, *&c.* Nay, the same Sort of Seed in different Earths, will produce Tobacco much different, as to Goodness. The richer the Ground, the better it is for Aranoko Tobacco, whose Scent is not much minded, their only Aim being to have it specious, large, and to procure it a bright Kite's Foot Colour. Had not my Microscopes, *&c.* Tools to grind Glasses, been cast away, with my other things, I had made some critical Enquiries into their several Natures, I would have examined what Proportions of Salts, all the Sorts of Earths had afforded, and how Water impregnated with their Salts, would have changed with infusing Galls, how with the Syrup of Violets, and how they would have precipitated Mercury, or the like, and so far forth as I had been able, examined them by the several Tryals of Fire. I conceive Tobacco to be a Plant abounding with nitro-sulphureous Particles; for the Planters try the Goodness of their Seed, by casting a little thereof into the Fire; if it be good, it will sparkle after the Manner of Gun-powder: So will the Stalks of Tobacco-leaves, and perhaps has something analagous to the narcotick Sulphur of *Venus,* which the Chymists so industriously labour after. The World knows little of the Efficacy of its Oil, which has wonderful Effects in the curing of old inveterate Sores, and scrophulous Swellings, and some, otherwise applied and qualified. The Goodness of Tobacco I look on primarily consists in the Volatility of its Nitre: And hence the sandy Grounds that are most impregnated therewith, and whose nitrous Salt is most volatile, for such Grounds are quickliest spent, yield Tobacco's that have the richest Scent and that shortly become a pleasant Smoak; whereas, in Tobacco that grows on stiff Ground, the Salts seem more fix'd, and locked up in the Oyl, so that whilst new, 'tis very heady and strong, and requires some time for its Salts to free themselves, and become volatile; which it manifests, by its having an urinous Smell. The same Reason satisfies, why Tobacco that grows on low Lands as far as the Salts, tho' the Plant be never overflowed with salt Water, yet the Ground that feeds the Plant being impregnated with salt Water, that Tobacco smoaks not pleasantly, and will scarcely keep Fire; but do all that a Man can, will oft go out, and gives much trouble in frequent lighting the Pipe, 'till after it has been kept some considerable Time: Which may be assign'd to the more fixt saline Particles of the marine Salt in these Plants; which require more time ere they be rendered volatile. Here it might be worthy of an Enquiry into the nature of Filtration of Plants, since we may hence gather, Particles of the marine Salt are carried along with the *Succus Nutritius* of the Plant; concerning which, if it were not too much to deviate from the Matter in hand, I should offer some Reflections of my own, which the learned Society might perhaps improve: For I think thence might be made many happy Conjectures as to the Virtues of Plants. So where we see Plants, or Trees of an open Pore growing low, we shall find their Juice has subtile Parts; So have all Vines, whether the grape Vine, or briony, or a smilax, or the like. If a gummous Plant or Tree, that grows low, and close pored, it abounds with acid Spirits, as *Lignum Vitae,* &c. if it grow tall, and be open pored, it abounds with a subtile volatile Spirit, as your Firs, and the Turpentine Tree. But to insist no further herein, than as this may be applicable to the present Discourse: For I have observed, that that which is called Pine-wood Land, tho' it be a sandy Soil, even the sweet-scented Tobacco that grows thereon, is large and porous, agreeable to Aranoko Tobacco, and smokes as coarsely as Aranoko: Wherefore 'tis, that I believe the Microscope might make notable Discoveries towards the Knowledge of good Tobacco: For the closer the Composition of the Leaf, the better the Tobacco; and therefore the Planters and Merchants brag of the Substance of their Tobacco; which Word, did they always take it in a true Sense, for the Solidness, and not mistake it for the Thickness, it would be more consonant to a true Observation: For as I said of the Pine-wood Tobacco, some of it is thick and not solid, and differs from the best tobacco, as Buff does from tanned Leather; so that if the Tobacco be sound and not rotten, you may give a great guess at the Goodness of Tobacco, when you weigh the Hogsheads, before you see them: For if an equal Care be taken in the packing of them, the best Tobacco will weigh the heaviest, and pack the closest. Now I said, that the sweet-scented Tobacco most in vogue, which was most famed for its Scent, was that which grew on sandy Land; which is true, if you would smoak it whilst new, or whilst only two or three Years old; but if you keep the stiff Land Tobacco, which is generally a Tobacco of great Substance five or six Years, it will much excel: for tho' the sandy Land Tobacco abounds with a volatile Nitre at first, yet the stiff Land Tobacco abounds with a greater Quantity of Nitre, only that it is locked up in its Oyl at first, and requires more time to extricate it self, and become volatile; but the Pine-wood Land having little of the Nitro-sulphureous Particles, neither is, nor ever will make any thing of a rich Smoak. Discoursing hereof some Days since, to a Gentleman of good Observation, that has been versed with maulting, he assured me, to back this my Supposition, or Hypothesis, he had observed, that Barley that grew on stiff Ground, required more time considerably to mellow, and come to Perfection, than that which grew on light Land. Having proceeded thus far to speak of Tobacco, I shall add one or two things more. The Planters differ in their Judgments about the time of planting, or pitching their Crops: Some are for pitching their Crops very early, others late, without any Distinction of the nature of the Soils; and 'tis from the different Effects that they find, in that, sometimes early, sometimes the late planting succeeds: But they have not the reason to judge of the Cause, to consider the Accidents of the Year, and the difference of the Soils. In sandy Grounds they need not strive so much for early Planting, the Looseness of the Earth, and the kind natur'd Soil, yielding all that it can, easily and speedily, and Sand retaining the Heat, makes the Plants grow faster. But in stiff Soils, if the Crops be not early pitched so that during the Season of Rains it have got considerable Roots, and shot them some depth, if early Droughts come, it so binds the Land, that the Roots never spread or shoot deeper, or futher than the Hill that they are planted in: For they plant them as we do Cabbages, raising Hills to set every Plant in, about the bigness of a common Mole-hill: observing this on the Plantation where I lived, that it was stiff Ground, I advised them to plant their Crops as early as possible; and in order thereunto, I tried several ways to further the Plants; but not to trouble you with the several Experiments that I made, in reference thereto: What I found most advantageous was, by taking an Infusion of Horsedung, and putting thereon Soot, and then my Seeds; this I kept forty eight Hours in an ordinary digestive Heat, I had two Beds left me to sow, in the midst of those the People sowed, and the quantity of Seed that they generally allotted to the same Quantity of Ground; when I sowed, I mix'd Ashes with the Seed, having decanted the Liquor, that the Seed might sow the evener: The effect was, that my Plants came up much sooner, grew swifter, and I had five Plants for one more than any of the other Beds bore; I left the Country shortly after, and so no certainty of the final Result. There are various Accidents and Distempers, whereunto Tobacco is liable, as the Worm, the Fly, firing to turn, as they call them, Frenchmen, and the like. I proposed several ways to kill the Worm and Fly, as by Sulphur and the like; but had no Opportunity to experiment it: I shall set down that I had most hopes of, which perhaps may give a Hint to others to try or improve. Tobacco-seed is very small, and by consequence so is the young Plant at first, that if gloomy Weather happen at that time, it breeds a small Fly, which consumes the Plume of the Plant; now it being early in the Year when they sow the Seed, *viz.* about the fourteenth of *January,* they cover the Ground, to secure, as well as they can, their tender Plants, from the niping Frosts, that may happen in the Nights; they cover them only with a few Oak-leaves, or the like; for Straw they find apt to harbour and breed this Fly: I therefore would advise them to smoak Straw with Brimstone, once in two or three Nights, and so they might cover them securely, with that which would preserve them infinitely beyond the Covering with Oak-boughs; indeed, I would advise them to keep peculiarly so much of their *Indian* Corn-blades, which they gather for their Fodder, for this very purpose, being, as I conceive, much the best, there being no Chaff to foul their Beds, and prejudice them when they should weed them. What they call firing is this: when Plants are of small Substance, as when there has been a very wet and cold Season, and very hot Weather suddenly ensues, the Leaves turn brown, and dry to Dust: The Cause I conceive to be hence: The Plant being feeble, and having a small quantity of Oyl, which makes the more solid part of the Plant, the Earth being suddainly heated by the Sun's fiercer Beams, the Roots are rather scorched and dried up in the Earth, than nourished; so that the Plant consisting only of watry parts, is consumed, as it were by Fire: sometimes hopeful Plants, when by a sudden Gust some Master Veins are broken; if suddain Heat ensues, they likewise fire: for being not come to Maturity, and being deprived of the Supports of Life and Vegetation they likewise perish, are dried up, and fall to Dust. *French*-men they call those Plants, whose Leaves do not spread and grow large, but rather spire upwards, and grow tall; these Plants they don't tend, being not worthy their Labour. Were they so critical, I believe, they might have great guess what Plants were most likely to turn *French*-men, by observing whether the Roots of the Plants run downwards, as those whose Branches are aptest to spire upwards: For tho' I have not made positive Proof thereof, I have something more than bare Fancy for my Conjecture; I have pulled up some of these *French*-men, and compared them with the Roots of some other Plants, and found them much longer than others; and 'tis observable, loose Soils, and sandy Ground are more subject thereto than the stiff Land. The Country of it self is one entire Wood, consisting of large Timber Trees of several sorts, free from Thickets or Under-Wood, the small Shrubs growing only on Lands that have been clear'd, or in Swamps; and thus it is for several hundreds of Miles, even as far as has yet been discovered.

Robert Beverley's Description of the Beaver in Virginia, 1705

The admirable economy of the beavers deserves to be particularly remembered. They cohabit in one house, are incorporated in a regular form of government, something like monarchy, and have over them a superintendent, which the Indians call pericu. He leads them out to their several employments, which consist in felling of trees, biting off the branches, and cutting them into certain lengths, suitable to the business they design them for, all which they perform with their teeth. When this is done, the pericu orders several of his subjects to join together, and take up one of those logs, which they must carry to their house or dam, as occasion requires. He walks in state by them all the while, and sees that every one bears his equal share of the burden; while he bites with his teeth, and lashes with his tail, those that lag behind, and do not lend all their strength; their way of carriage is upon their tail. They commonly build their houses in swamps, and then to raise the water to a convenient height, they make a dam with logs, and a binding fort of clay, so firm, that though the water runs continually over, it cannot wash it away. Within these dams they'll inclose water enough to make a pool like a mill pond; and if a mill happen to be built on the same stream, below their dam, the miller, in a dry season, finds it worth his while to cut it, to supply his mill with water. Upon which disaster the beavers are so expert at their work, that in one or two nights' time they will repair the breach, and make it perfectly whole again. Sometimes they build their houses in abroad marsh, where the tide ebbs and flows, and then they make no dam at all. The doors into their houses are under water. I have been at the demolishing of one of these houses, that was found in a marsh, and was surprised to find it fortified with logs, that were six feet long, and ten inches through, and had been carried at least one hundred and fifty yards. This house was three stories high, and contained five rooms, that is to say, two in the lower, two in the middle story, and but one at the top. These creatures have a great deal of policy, and know how to defeat all the subtlety and stratagems of the hunter, who seldom can meet with them, tho' they are in great numbers all over the country.

—*Robert Beverley,* History and Present State of Virginia *(London, 1705)*

Appendix One

Jamestown Colony Chronology

1497–1498	John Cabot and sons explore coastline of North America and lay claim for England.
1501–1504	Anglo-Portuguese voyages from Bristol, England, to Newfoundland.
1509–1570s	English fishermen visit North American coastline.
1553	London Company of Merchant Adventurers of England for the Discovery of Regions Unknown is organized, a model for future Virginia Company of London.
1558–1603	Reign of Queen Elizabeth I.
1561	Spanish ships under command of Pedro Menendez Aviles land near future site of Jamestown settlement while foraging for supplies.
1562	Jean Ribault settles ill-fated Huguenot colony (Charles Fort), at Port Royal in South Carolina.
	John Hawkins makes first voyage to West Indies.
1563	Charles Fort abandoned.
1564	Rene de Laudonniere settles second Huguenot colony, at St. John's River in Florida.
	John Hawkins makes second voyage to West Indies.
1565	Spain settles St. Augustine.
1567	John Hawkins embarks on third voyage to West Indies.
1568	John Hawkins fight Spaniards at Battle of Vera Cruz, loses three of six ships.

	English assist Low Countries (the Netherlands) in their break with King Philip II of Spain.
1576	Martin Frobisher makes first voyage in search of Northwest Passage.
1577	Martin Frobisher makes second voyage.
1577–1580	Francis Drake circumnavigates the earth.
1578	Martin Frobisher makes third voyage.
	Sir Humphrey Gilbert receives letters patent to settle Newfoundland.
1583	Sir Humphrey Gilbert makes voyage to Newfoundland and claims land for England, but is lost at sea on return voyage.
1584	Walter Raleigh obtains patent of his half brother, Sir Humphrey Gilbert.
	Walter Raleigh sends voyage under Captains Philip Amadas and Arthur Barlowe to Roanoke Island in North Carolina.
	Captain Barlowe encounters Algonquin Indians and returns to England with two natives, Manteo and Wanchese.
1585	Elizabeth I assumes control of Protestant Netherlands.
	Walter Raleigh knighted by Queen Elizabeth, who makes him governor of lands discovered by Captains Amadas and Barlowe.
	Sir Walter Raleigh claims North American coast for English crown and names it "Virginia" in honor of virgin Queen Elizabeth.
	Sir Walter Raleigh sends fleet commanded by Richard Grenville and Ralph Lane to settle Roanoke Island with 108 men, as well as Manteo and Wanchese, who are returning home.
	Philip II of Spain retaliates against England for its support of the Dutch by ordering the seizure of all English ships in Spanish ports, opening Elizabethan War between England and Spain (1585–1604), and making resupply of Roanoke Island almost impossible.
	Roanoke Island settlers under Ralph Lane attack Indian village Dasemunkepeuc.
1586	Elizabeth I executes Mary Queen of Scots, the Catholic heir to the English throne.
	Sir Francis Drake arrives at Roanoke Island and carries Ralph Lane and other colonists back to England.
	Sir Richard Grenville returns with supply ship and more colonists to Roanoke Island, where he finds only three men left behind by Drake.

1587 Sir Walter Raleigh sends artist John White and 150 settlers to settle colony at Roanoke Island.

John White returns to England for supplies.

1588 Spanish Armada defeated off English coast.

1590 Captain Christopher Newport commands voyage carrying John White back to Roanoke Island, where they find the colony deserted—the Lost Colony.

1592 Christopher Newport makes voyage to West Indies.

Elizabeth I imprisons Sir Walter Raleigh for his secret marriage to one of her ladies-in-waiting.

1595 Birth of Pocahontas (Matoaka).

1596 Captains Amias Preston and George Somers make voyage to West Indies.

1602 Sir Walter Raleigh sends Samuel Mace on fruitless voyage to search for Lost Colony.

Captains Bartholomew Gosnold, Bartholomew Gilbert, Gabriel Archer, and others make voyage to New England coast.

English traders make voyage to Nova Scotia.

1603 Queen Elizabeth I dies.

James VI of Scotland ascends throne as James I of England.

Captain Martin Pring makes voyage to New England coast for Bristol merchants.

Captain Bartholomew Gilbert makes voyage to the Chesapeake Bay and explores Eastern Shore, where he and four others are killed by Indians.

Sir Walter Raleigh tried and convicted in connection with the Main Plot, in November.

1604 Treaty of London ends Anglo-Spanish War.

James I anonymously publishes an anti-tobacco tract, *A Counter-Blaste to Tobacco,* in London.

1605 Gunpowder Plot to assassinate James I discovered, resulting in arrest of Catholic conspirators.

England claims Barbados as part of Virginia.

Captain Christopher Newport makes voyage of discovery along the North American coast in search of a passage to South Sea (Pacific Ocean).

1606 Gunpowder Plot conspirators, including Guy Fawkes, executed.

James I grants Virginia Company of London a royal charter to plant a colony in America.

Three ships, *Susan Constant, Godspeed,* and *Discovery,* sail from England for the New World under the command of Captain Christopher Newport, with 120 colonists and supplies.

1607 Captain John Smith imprisoned en route to Virginia.

Captain Christopher Newport explores West Indies and the Chesapeake Bay while en route to Virginia.

Three ships under Captain Christopher Newport enter Chesapeake Bay, on 26 April.

English welcomed by Kecoughtan Indians at Cape Comfort, on 30 April.

English enter Powhatan River, which Captain Christopher Newport renames in honor of James I, on 13 May.

First landing on Jamestown Island, at which time Captain Newport opens Virginia Company's sealed instructions, to discover thirteen people named to a ruling council, including prisoner Captain John Smith, on 14 May.

Reverend Robert Hunt holds outdoor church and communion service, on 14 May.

English settlers begin construction of James Fort, on 14 May.

Captains Christopher Newport, John Smith, George Percy, Gabriel Archer, and others explore the James River up to the falls, where they encounter Indian Chief Powhatan at his village, 14–19 May.

200 Powhatan Indians attack Jamestown colonists for first time, killing 1 and wounding 11, on 26 May.

Jamestown colonists begin month-long process of palisading fort, on 28 May.

Paspahegh Indians, assisted by warriors from other tribes, attack James Fort, on 8 June.

Captain John Smith arrested at Jamestown, then released and sworn in as council member, on 10 June.

Settlers plant first crop corn, at Jamestown, in June.

The *Susan Constant* and the *Godspeed,* under Captain Christopher Newport, set sail on the return voyage to England, laden with mineral samples, on 22 June.

Meeting of stockholders of the Virginia Company, to consider Captain Christopher Newport's report of his voyage and the state of the colony, on 17 August.

George Kendall is imprisoned after being accused of sowing discord among the colonists, on 28 August.

Jamestown President Edward-Maria Wingfield deposed and John Ratcliffe elected, 10 September.

Captain Christopher Newport sets sail for Jamestown with two supply ships and 100 new colonists, on 8 October.

Captain John Smith captured by Opechancanough while on a trading expedition and carried to Chief Powhatan at Werowocomoco, where he is saved from execution by Pocahontas, early December.

1608 Captain Christopher Newport arrives with First Supply, to find settlers abandoning the colony, 2 January.

Chief Powhatan releases Captain John Smith, in January.

Jamestown almost completely destroyed by fire, 7 January.

Captain Christopher Newport, John Smith, Thomas Savage, and others sail up the York River to exchanger prisoners with Chief Powhatan, in February.

Captain Christopher Newport sets sail for England on the *John and Francis,* 10 April.

Captain Francis Nelson arrives at Jamestown with the *Phoenix,* a supply separated from Captain Newport's fleet, on 20 April.

Pocahontas visits Jamestown, where she meets Captain John Smith and teaches him Powhatan language.

The *Phoenix* sets sail for England with a load of cedar, on 2 June.

Captain Christopher Newport sails from England for Jamestown, in August.

Samuel de Champlain makes voyages to St. Lawrence River for France and founds colony of Quebec.

Captain John Smith succeeds John Ratcliffe, who was killed by Indians, as president on 10 September.

Captain Christopher Newport arrives with Second Supply, bringing 70 more colonists, including two women, Mrs. Forrest and her maid Ann Burras, and eight glassworkers, October.

Captain John Smith publishes his *True Relation of Virginia* in London.

1609 Construction takes place at James Fort.

James I grants Second Charter, placing control in the Virginia Company.

	Virginia Company transfers authority of the Council to the governor, on 23 May.
	Pocahontas goes to live with the Patawomeke Indian tribe.
	Powhatan orders massacre of colonists visiting Werowocomoco.
	Fleet of nine ships scattered and *Sea Venture* wrecked in Bermuda.
	First ships of scattered fleet arrived in Virginia, in August.
	Captain George Percy succeeds Captain John Smith as president, on 10 September.
	Captain Christopher Newport sets sail for England with a cargo of pitch, tar, glass, and other goods, carrying with him Captain John Smith, who has been injured, in October.
	First marriage at Jamestown when Anne Burras marries John Layden, in November.
1609–1610	Starving Time.
1610	The *Sea Venture* arrives at Jamestown from Bermuda, on 23 May.
	Sir Thomas Gates serves as acting governor, on 23 May.
	Sir Thomas Gates issues *The Divine, Moral, and Martial Laws,* 24 May.
	Sir Thomas Gates and settlers abandon Jamestown, on 7 June.
	Settlers turn back to Jamestown after meeting Governor Lord De La Warr at Mulberry Island, on 8 June.
	Governor Lord De La Warr and his supply ships, with 150 planters, along with the settlers with Sir Thomas Gates, arrive at Jamestown, on 10 June.
	Reverend Richard Buck comes to serve as minister at Jamestown.
	Glassworks begun at Jamestown.
	English attack Paspahegh Indian village and executes Queen and her children, on 9 August.
1611	Governor Lord De La Warr, very ill, sails for England with Sir Thomas Gates, leaving Sir George Percy in charge as deputy governor, on 28 March.
	Lieutenant Governor Sir Thomas Dale arrives at Point Comfort with supplies and 300 people, on 12 May.
	Sir Thomas Dale assumes power from Sir George Percy, in late May.

	Sir Thomas Dale enforces *The Divine, Moral, and Martial Laws.*
	Sir Thomas Gates returns to Jamestown with another 280 settlers and reassumes power as lieutenant governor, on 2 August.
	Sir Thomas Dale begins building Henricus, with 350 men, in September.
	William Strachey leaves Jamestown for England.
	John Rolfe imports tobacco seeds from Trinidad, which he uses to experiment with hybrid plants.
	King James Bible (Authorized Version) printed in England.
1612	Sir Thomas Dale reinforces palisaded fortifications.
	James I grants Third Charter to Virginia Company, giving more self-governance, on 12 March.
	James I authorizes use of lotteries to raise money for the Virginia Company.
	English colonize Bermuda, from Virginia.
	John Rolfe exports first small crop of hybrid tobacco.
1613–1614	Reverend Alexander Whitaker instructs Pocahontas in Christianity, resulting in her conversion, baptism, and adoption of the Christian name, Rebecca.
	Virginia colonists destroy French colony at Port Royal, Nova Scotia, and stop French attempts to settle Maryland.
1613	Pocahontas captured and held hostage at Jamestown, in April.
	Sir Thomas Gates sails for England, in February.
	Sir Thomas Dale returns to power as deputy governor, in February.
	John Rolfe and Robert Sparkes take Pocahontas up the Pamunkey River to negotiate a truce with Chief Powhatan, in March.
	Reverend Richard Buck performs the marriage ceremony of Pocahontas and John Rolfe, cementing peace between the English and the Powhatan Indians, on 5 April.
	Captain Samuel Argall negotiates a treaty with the Chickahominy Indians.
	Captain Samuel Argall and Ralph Hamor sail for England, with first shipment of John Rolfe's improved tobacco, on 28 June.
	Colonists move into the interior, bringing number of settlements to four.

1615	Thomas Rolfe born to John Rolfe and Pocahontas, on 30 January.
	Ralph Hamor publishes *A True Discourse of the Present Estate of Virginia* in London.
	James I issues charter for the Bermuda Company.
1616	Sir Thomas Dale sails for London with John Rolfe and Pocahontas, and their child Thomas, in May.
	George Yeardley assumes command in stead of Sir Thomas Dale, in May.
	Sir Thomas Dale arrives at Plymouth, on 12 June.
	Pocahontas meets Captain John Smith, who thanks her for saving his life.
	Deputy Governor George Yeardley attacks and kills 20–40 Chickahominy Indians.
	Captain Samuel Argall returns to Virginia and replaces George Yeardley.
	Sir Walter Raleigh released from the Tower of London.
	Sir Thomas Dale publishes *A True Relation of the State of Virginia, Left by Sir Thomas Dale, Knight, in May last, 1616.*
	London Company creates a subsidiary joint-stock company known as the Magazine, which operates independently and has a monopoly on supplying the Jamestown colony.
1617	Lord De La Warr dies en route to Virginia.
	Pocahontas dies and is buried in Gravesend, England, on 21 March.
	John Rolfe returns to Jamestown, leaving his son Thomas to be raised by relatives.
	Powhatan abdicates power to his second brother, Opitchapam.
1618	Nathaniel Powell exercises power until Governor George Yeardley arrives.
	Powhatan dies.
	Sir Edwin Sandys becomes treasurer of the London Company.
	George Yeardley becomes governor of Jamestown.
	The Great Migration begins, bringing 4,500 hundred new settlers to Virginia over the next five years.
	James I issues anti-Puritan *Book of Sports.*
	Sir Walter Raleigh executed for treason.
	London Company declares tobacco as medium of exchange.

General Assembly establishes system of headrights, on 18 November 1618.

1619 Opechancanough becomes chief of Powhatan Indians.

Samuel Argall tried for neglect of duty while serving as governor, in April.

General Assembly convenes for first time, on 30 July.

John Rolfe gets married again, to Captain William Pierce's daughter, Jane.

First Africans brought to Jamestown in Dutch vessel commanded by Captain Jope, in August.

London Company recruits 100 young women for Jamestown, in November.

Captain John Woodleefe, commanding the *Margaret,* arrives at Jamestown with 36 new settlers, on 4 December.

Sir Edwin Sandys issues patent under which Pilgrims sail to Plymouth.

Governor George Yeardley begins erecting New Towne.

1620 90 young women arrive at Jamestown.

London Company dissolves the Magazine, ending company's trade monopoly.

Sir George Yeardley's term as governor expires.

First public library organized in colony with books supplied by English landowners.

1621 Sir Francis Wyatt replaces Sir George Yeardley as governor.

Governor Sir Francis Wyatt establishes quarterly sessions of courts.

Sir Edwin Sandys replaced as treasurer of the Virginia Company by his staunch supporter, the Earl of Southampton.

Virginia Company issues positive report of its activities, *A Declaration of the State of the Colony and Affairs in Virginia,* on 22 July.

Nemattanow, known as Jack-of-the-Feather to the English, kills several colonists.

James I abolishes use of lotteries by the Virginia Company.

Mayflower arrives at Cape Cod on the New England coast, on 11 November.

1622 Nemattanow, known as Jack-of-the-Feather to the English, is executed, in early March.

	Pamunkey Indian boy Chanco warns of impending Indian attack, on 21 March.
	Powhatan Indians under Chief Opechancanough kills 350 settlers, on 22 March.
	Martin's Hundred, which by patent is independent of the London Company and the General Assembly, is relinquished by Captain John Martin in exchange for new land, in April.
	Governor Sir Francis Wyatt institutes stricter punishments for various offenses, on 21 June.
	Settlers retaliate against Powhatan Indians, in August.
	Virginia and Bermuda given monopoly on tobacco trade.
	Epidemic caused by diseases brought in ship *Abigail* kills hundreds, in December.
	Starving Time, in winter.
1623	London Company reports on colony's affairs to crown, on 12 April.
	Bermuda Governor Captain Nathaniel Butler presents unfavorable report of the colony to Privy Council, "Unmasked Face of Our Colony in Virginia as it Was in the Winter of the Year 1622," on 23 April.
	Powhatan Indians kill 20 colonists in search of food when bargaining goes awry, in April.
	James I creates commission to examine the London Company's finances, on 9 May.
1624	General Assembly establishes monthly courts.
	Royal commission, including future Virginia governor Sir John Harvey, visits Jamestown.
	James I revokes charter of London Company and places colony under royal control, in May.
1625	Palisade built across peninsula from James River to the York River.
	King James I dies, on 27 March.
	Charles I, son of James I, succeeds father as king of England.
	Charles I proclaims the Bermudas, Virginia, and New England royal colonies, on 13 May.
	Sir Francis Wyatt named as royal governor.
	Charles I denies General Assembly's petition to legislate.
1626	Governor Sir Francis Wyatt leaves colony for England.

Charles I names Sir George Yeardley to succeed Sir Francis Wyatt as governor.

Dutch establish colony of New Amsterdam (later New York).

1627 Governor Sir George Yeardley dies.

Virginia Council of State sets precedent of senior councilor serving as acting governor when it chooses Councilor Francis West to act as governor following the death of Sir George Yeardley.

Charles I appoints Sir John Harvey governor.

A slave ship from Angola is captured, and Negroes are bartered for tobacco.

1628 Charles I authorizes General Assembly to meet, in March.

Governor Francis West returns to England and is replaced by Dr. John Pott.

English set up colony at St. Nevis in Caribbean Islands.

1629 Council has four members, and the House of Burgesses has forty-six.

Charles I grants charter to Massachusetts Bay Company.

Charles I dissolves Parliament.

Lord Baltimore arrives in Virginia from New Foundland.

1630 Sir John Harvey arrives in colony.

Sir John Harvey commissions Nathaniel Basse to recruit New Englanders for Virginia.

London Company dissolved.

England and Spain sign peace treaty, on 5 November.

1631 Henry Fleet takes Indian corn to New England.

Charles I creates commission to govern Virginia.

Dutch Indian Company sets up colony at Delaware River.

England colonizes St. Kitts.

Captain John Smith dies in England.

Powhatan Indians war with colonists.

1632 Charles I grants charter giving Maryland to Lord Baltimore, out of Virginia land.

General Assembly meets at Middle Plantation (later Williamsburg).

General Assembly revises statute law for first time.

General Assembly sets up quarterly court system.

	Jamestown declared port of call for all ships trading in colony.
	Colonists make temporary peace with Powhatan Indians.
	Dutch set up colony in Connecticut.
1634	Virginia colony is carved into eight counties (Accomack, Charles City, Charles River, Elizabeth City, Henrico, James City, Warwick River, and Warrosquyoake (Isle of Wight), of which Jamestown is one.
	Charles I creates Board of Commissions for Foreign Plantations to govern Virginia in place of royal commission of 1631.
	Virginia settlers send corn to assist colonists in New England.
	Virginia Council of State expels Governor Sir John Harvey.
	General Assembly appoints John West to govern in Sir John Harvey's stead.
1635	Twenty-one ships laden with tobacco sail for London.
1636	New Norfolk is carved out of Elizabeth City County.
	Sir John Harvey resumes governorship and sends mutineers to London for trial.
1637	New Norfolk splits into Upper and Lower Norfolk.
	Charles I gives approval for Virginia General Assembly to meet.
	Charles I restricts English emigration to American colonies.
1638	Governor Sir John Harvey recalled to England.
	Charles I appoints Sir Francis Wyatt governor.
	First public auctions of slaves in colony.
	Colony of New Haven in Connecticut established.
1639	Charles I authorizes annual sessions of General Assembly, in January.
	Sir John Harvey returns to England.
	Construction begins on fourth church building at Jamestown, first one of brick.
	First Bishop's War in Scotland.
1640	Conflict between Charles I and Parliament.
	Short and Long Parliaments meet.
	Second Bishop's War, resulting in defeat of Charles I.
	Virginia General Assembly codifies in statute law servitude status of indentured whites and enslaved blacks.
1641	Sir William Berkeley appointed governor of Virginia.

1642	Sir William Berkeley arrives in Virginia.
	Civil War begins in England.
	General Assembly revises statute law for second time.
	Northampton created out of Accomack.
	King's army defeated at Marston Moor.
1644	Powhatan Chief Opechancanough attacks colony, killing 500 colonists, in April.
	County lieutenants muster all able-bodied men between the ages of 16 and 60 with arms and ammunitions to retaliate against Indians.
	Opechancanough captured and carried to Jamestown, where he is murdered, in October.
	William Claiborne attacks Leonard Calvert in Maryland with force raised in Virginia.
1645	General Assembly creates Northumberland County out of Indian land.
	General Assembly treats for peace with Necatowance, the Powhatan successor to Opechancanough.
	Oliver Cromwell's New Model Army defeats Charles I at the Battle of Naseby.
1646	Powhatan Indians cede most Tidewater lands to colony.
	England occupies the Bahamas.
1647	Charles I arrested and imprisoned.
	Virginia remains loyal to the crown.
1648	Presbyterian Church replaces Anglican as state church of England.
1649	Trial of Charles I on charges of treason begins, on 1 January.
	Charles I beheaded in London, on 30 January.
	Parliament abolishes monarchy and declares England a Commonwealth on, 6 February.
	Cromwell invades Catholic Ireland.
	Governor Sir William Berkeley and General Assembly recognizes Charles II as king.
	Puritans exiled from Virginia.
	Maryland passes Toleration Act to accept religious refugees from Virginia.
	Scotland proclaims Charles II king.

1650	Long Parliament forbids trade with Virginia.
	England and Dutch set North American borders.
	Colonists attack Powhatan Indians.
1651	Gloucester County carved out of York and Lancaster County carved out of Northumberland.
	General Assembly approves Articles of Surrender to the Commonwealth of England.
	Parliament enacts first Navigation Act, restricting transportation of goods from colony to English ships.
	Charles II invades England but is defeated at Battle of Worcester.
1652	Richard Bennett is elected governor by the General Assembly.
	General Assembly revises statute law for third time.
	Parliamentary commission arrives at Jamestown.
	England and Dutch go to war over England's Navigation Act of 1651, in July.
1653	Westmoreland County carved out of Northumberland.
	Parliament makes Oliver Cromwell lord protector of English Commonwealth.
1654	New Kent County carved out of York.
	General Assembly elects Edward Diggs as governor.
1655	Governor Edward Diggs leaves for England.
	General Assembly elects Samuel Mathews as governor.
	Anglican Church services prohibited in England.
	England takes Jamaica.
1656	Rappahannock County carved out of Lancaster.
	General Assembly attempts to subsidize an alternative crop to tobacco.
1657	Governor Samuel Matthews and Council fails in an attempt to dissolve the House of Burgesses.
	Oliver Cromwell rejects offer of crown.
1658	Oliver Cromwell dissolves Second Protectorate Parliament, 4 February.
	Oliver Cromwell dies, on 3 September.
	Richard Cromwell succeeds his father as lord protector on, 3 September.
	Governor Samuel Matthews announces to colony Oliver Cromwell's death, on 7 March.

1659 Richard Cromwell dissolves the Protectorate and reinstates Rump Parliament, in January 1659

Parliament enacts second Navigation Act, reinforcing first England's trade monopoly with colonies.

Richard Cromwell resigns as lord protector, on 25 May.

Privy Council enforces Navigation Acts in American colonies through the lords of trade.

1660 Governor Samuel Mathews dies, in January.

General Assembly recalls Sir William Berkeley as governor on, 13 March.

Charles II restored to throne on his birthday, 29 May.

Charles II appoints Sir William Berkeley governor, on 31 July.

Parliament enacts first Restoration-era Navigation Act.

1661 General Assembly revises statute law for fourth time.

General Assembly recognizes slavery in statutory law.

Governor Sir William Berkeley sails for England to lobby for more autonomy for colony.

Francis Moryson serves as acting governor in absence of Sir William Berkeley.

John Eliot completes translation of Bible into Algonquian language.

1662 Governor Sir William Berkeley returns to colony.

General Assembly revises statute law for fifth time.

Jamestown loses monopoly as port of call for all ships trading in colony.

Accomack County carved out of Northampton.

Tobacco prices drop to all-time low.

1663 Stafford County carved out of Westmoreland.

1664 England claims land of New Netherlands, between the Connecticut and Delaware Rivers.

Parliament enacts First Conventicle Act, restricting meetings of Puritans.

England claims New Amsterdam and renames it New York.

Charles II gives New York to his brother, James, Duke of York.

1665 General Assembly unsuccessfully attempts to curtail tobacco production; and tobacco prices drop even further.

English settlers colonize New Jersey.

1666	Dutch warships burn 6 ships in James River.
	Great Fire of London.
	English privateers take Tobago.
1667	Tobacco crops destroyed by wet summer and hurricane, temporarily driving prices back up.
	Dutch warships capture 13 ships laden with tobacco in Chesapeake Bay.
	Middlesex County carved out of Lancaster.
	James Fort rebuilt.
	Parliament discusses death rate in Virginia.
1668	General Assembly codifies in statute law the legal inequality of free blacks.
	Virginia General Assembly codifies in statute law the servitude status of indentured whites and enslaved blacks.
	Almost no tobacco is planted in Virginia, in an effort to drive prices up.
1669	German John Lederer explores the Shenandoah Valley.
	Governor Sir William Berkeley enforces conformity to King's Northern Neck Land Grant.
1670	Party sent by Abraham Wood explores the Shenandoah Valley.
1671	Parliament enacts Second Conventicle Act.
	England settles colony in Charlestown, South Carolina.
1672	General Assembly opposes royal land grants to Culpeper and Arlington.
1673	Relations with Indians deteriorate, prompting plan for war with Indians.
	Parliament enacts Test Act, excluding Catholics from holding public office.
	Anglican Church creates commissaries to substitute for bishops in the colony.
1674	England and Dutch sign treaty ending a decade of hostilities, on 9 February.
1675–1676	King Philip's War.
1675	Doeg Indians attack colonists in Stafford County.
1676	Nathaniel Bacon and 500 armed settlers retaliate against Indians, in April.

Governor Sir William Berkeley declares Nathaniel Bacon a rebel, on 10 May.

Governor Sir William Berkeley reconvenes General Assembly after many years, in June.

Nathaniel Bacon captured and carried to Jamestown.

Governor Sir William Berkeley pardons Nathaniel Bacon, on 7 June.

Nathaniel Bacon takes seat in council, on 10 June.

Nathaniel Bacon demands of Governor Sir William Berkeley a commission to lead an armed force against the Indians, on 23 June.

Governor Sir William Berkeley grants commission to Nathaniel Bacon, on 29 July.

Governor Sir William Berkeley revokes Nathaniel Bacon's commission and declares Bacon a rebel once again.

Nathaniel Bacon and armed settlers rendezvous at Middle Plantation.

Governor Sir William Berkeley flees Jamestown.

Nathaniel Bacon and armed settlers enter and burn Jamestown, on 19 September.

Nathaniel Bacon dies, on 26 October.

1677 Colonists sign treaty with Powhatan Indians.

Third Anglo-Dutch war.

Dutch warships raid in James River.

Governor Sir William Berkeley executes rebels at Green Spring.

Royal commission arrives in colony to investigate insurrection led by Nathaniel Bacon.

Sir William Berkeley replaced by one of the royal commissioners, Herbert Jeffreys, and sails to England.

20-year period of reconstruction in Jamestown begins, with rebuilding of state house.

1678 Herbert Jeffreys dies.

Henry Chicheley succeeds Herbert Jeffreys.

Charles II grants new charter to colony limiting authority of General Assembly, on 10 October.

1680 Governor Lord Thomas Culpeper comes to colony.

	General Assembly meets in unfinished church building, on 25 April.
	Parliament's Act for Ports seriously burdens colony's tobacco growers and shippers.
1681	Tobacco growers destroy crops because of low prices.
1682	Governor Lord Thomas Culpeper returns to England.
	Nicholas Spencer serves as deputy governor.
1683	Lord Howard of Effingham named to replace Lord Thomas Culpeper as governor.
1684	Lord Howard of Effingham arrives in Virginia, in February.
1685	Charles II dies, 6 February.
	James II, Catholic brother of Charles II, ascends to throne.
	Bermudas become royal colony.
	General Assembly dissolved by Lords of Trade on basis of complaint by Governor Lord Howard of Effingham.
1687	General Assembly petitions James II for redress of grievances.
1688	Lord Howard of Effingham returns to England, leaving Nathaniel Bacon, the Elder, as acting governor.
	Glorious Revolution.
	James II abdicates.
	James II flees England, on 11 December.
	English lords invite William, Duke of Orange, and his wife Mary, both Protestants, to rule as King William III and Queen Mary II.
	William and Mary land in England, December.
1689	William and Mary crowned, February.
	Declaration of Rights establishes constitutional monarchy in England.
	William and Mary recognize charters of American colonies.
	Jamestown celebrates ascension of William and Mary.
	Lieutenant Governor Francis Nicholson replaces Nathaniel Bacon, the Elder.
1690	General Assembly petition Governor Francis Nicholson to assist in establishing a college.
1691	King and Queen County carved out of New Kent.
	Norfolk and Princess Counties replace Lower Norfolk.
	Governor Francis Nicholson leaves colony for Maryland.

	Edmund Andros becomes governor, in late September.
1692	General Assembly and Governor Edmund Andros petition crown to establish a college.
	Jamestown holds Olympic Games on St. George's Day, 23 April.
	Essex and Richmond Counties replace Old Rappahannock.
	James Blair arrives in colony with charter for the College of William and Mary.
1693	General Assembly and Governor Edmund Andros quarrel, resulting in Andros dissolving the General Assembly.
1694	Foundation stone of College of William and Mary laid at Middle Plantation.
	Queen Mary II dies.
1697	Francis Nicholson returns to colony and replaces Edmund Andros as governor.
1698	Fire destroys State House and surrounding parts of Jamestown, 31 October.
	General Assembly meets at Jamestown and then adjourns to Middle Plantation.
	Parliament opens slave trade to English merchants, resulting in increase of slaves imported into the colony.
1699	Governor Francis Nicholson proclaims the Act of Toleration.
	General Assembly and Governor Francis Nicholson formally move capital to Middle Plantation, renamed Williamsburg.
	General Assembly meets at the College of William and Mary.
	Jamestown reverts to private ownership and becomes farm land.
1702	William III dies.
	Anne I, Protestant daughter of James II, becomes queen.
1707	Act of Union, creating Great Britain.
1750s	Ownership of Jamestown consolidated into Travis and Ambler families.
1781	French troops land at Jamestown as part of Yorktown Campaign.
1807	Bicentennial of the founding of Jamestown celebrated in Virginia at Williamsburg, Norfolk, Portsmouth, and Petersburg.
1831	Jamestown purchased from Travis and Ambler families by David Bullock.

1857	250th anniversary of the founding of Jamestown celebrated at ceremonies attended by 6,000 people.
1861	Confederate army constructs earthworks on Jamestown Island.
1892	Jamestown purchased by Mr. and Mrs. Edward Barney.
1893	Mr. and Mrs. Edward Barney convey title of 22.5 acres of Jamestown to the Association for the Preservation of Virginia Antiquities.
1897	Association for the Preservation of Virginia Antiquities excavates foundations of brick church building at Jamestown.
1901–1902	Colonel Samuel H. Yonge of the U.S. Army Corps of Engineers excavates brick church building and cemetery at Jamestown.
1903	Colonel Samuel H. Yonge continues excavations at Jamestown.
1907	Tercentenary of the founding of Jamestown.
	Brick church building at Jamestown reconstructed on original foundations.
	Tercentenary Monument erected on Jamestown Island.
1934–1936	National Park Service acquires remaining 1,500 acres of Jamestown Island.
	John T. Zaharov, H. Summerfield, Alonzo W. Pond, and W. J. Winter conduct excavations at Jamestown for Civilian Conservation Corps.
1936–1941	J. C. Harrington conducts excavations at Jamestown.
1948–1949	J. C. Harrington excavates site of Glass House.
1954–1956	John L. Cotter conducts excavations at Jamestown.
	Louis Caywood excavates Green Spring.
1957	350th Anniversary Festival commemorates founding of Jamestown.
1976–1983	Ivor Noël Hume and Audrey Noël Hume conduct excavations at Martin's Hundred uncovering seventeenth-century Wolstenholme Town.
1992–1996	Archaeological assessment of Jamestown Island in preparation for quadricentenary of the founding of Jamestown.
1994–present	Jamestown Rediscovery under the direction of William M. Kelso conducts extensive excavations at Jamestown, discovering original fort site and 700,000 artifacts.
2007	Jamestown Quadricentenary.

Appendix Two

Tribes of the Powhatan Confederacy

The following list of Algonquian-speaking groups of Native Americans living in Virginia's coastal plain at the time of the founding of Jamestown in 1607 is adapted from Helen C. Rountree's The Powhatan Indians of Virginia: Their Traditional Culture *(Norman, OK, and London, 1989). Rountree, who derived her list from written accounts of English settlers, notes that some groups "refused to become Powhatan's subjects"—the Chickahominies, the Chesapeakes, and the Nansemonds. The estimates of the number of men in each group, where given, were gathered from the accounts of Captain John Smith and the colony's secretary, William Strachey. In addition to the Algonquian tribes, three Iroquoian and one-half dozen Siouan tribes lived in Virginia at the time of the Englishment settlement.*

Accomac — Northampton County — 80 men

Appamattuck (Appomattox) — Chesterfield County — 60–100 men

Arrohateck — Henrico County — 30–60 men

Chesapeake — City of Chesapeake — 100 men

Chickahominy — Counties of James City, Charles City, and New Kent — 200–300 men

Chiskiack (Kiskiack) — York County — 40–50 men

Cuttatawomen — King George County — 20 men

Cuttawomen (Corrotoman) — Lancaster County — 30 men

Kecoughtan — City of Hampton — 20–30 men

Mattapanient (Mattaponi) — Counties of King William or King and Queen — 30–140 men

Moraughtacund (Morattico) — Richmond County — 80 men

Nandtaughtacund (Nanzatico) — Caroline County — 150 men

Nansemond — City of Suffolk — 200 men

Occohannock (Accohannock) — Accomac County — 40 men

Onawmanient (Nomini) — Northumberland County — 100 men

Ospiscopank (Opiscatumek, Piscataway) — Middlesex County

Pamunkey — Counties of King William and New Kent — 300 men

Paspahegh — James City County — 40 men

Patawomeck (Potomac) — Stafford County — 200 men

Piankatank (Payankatank, Peanketank) — Middlesex County — 40–60 men

Pissaseck — Westmoreland County

Powhatan — City of Richmond — 40–50 men

Quiyoughcohannock — Surry County — 25–60 men

Rappahannock (Toppahannock) — Counties of Richmond and Essex — 100 men

Sekakawon (Secacawoni, Chickacone, Coan) — Northumberland County — 100 men

Warraskoyack — Isle of Wight County — 40–60 men

Werowocomoco — Gloucester County — 40 men

Weyanock (Weyanoke) — Counties of Charles City and Price George — 150 men

Wiccocomico (Wicomico) — Northumberland County — 130 men

Youghtanund — Counties of King William or New Kent — 60–70 men

Appendix Three

Villages of the Powhatan Confederacy

The following names and locations of the villages or towns that are known to have existed in Powhatan's empire during the period of the English settlement of the Jamestown colony are adapted from John R. Swanton's The Indian Tribes of North America *(Washington, D.C., 1952).*

Accohannock — Accomac and Northampton Counties on the Accohannock River

Accomac — Northampton County at Cheriton on Cherrystone Inlet

Acconoc — New Kent County between the Chickahominy and Pamunkey Rivers

Accoqueck — Caroline County above Secobec on the Rappahannock River

Accossuwinck — King William County on the Pamunkey River

Acquack — Caroline County on the north bank of the Rappahannock River

Appamattoc — Prince George County at Bermuda Hundred

Appocant — New Kent County on the north bank of the Chickahominy River

Arrohattoc — Henrico County about twelve miles below the falls of the James River

Askakep — New Kent County on the Pamunkey River

Assaomeck — at Alexandria

Assuweska — King George County on the north bank of the Rappahannock River

Attamtuck — New Kent County between the Chickahominy and Pamunkey Rivers

Aubomesk — Richmond County on the north bank of the Rappahannock River

Aureuapeugh — Essex County on the Rappahannock River

Cantaunkack — Gloucester County on the York River

Capahowasic — Gloucester County at Cappahosic

Cattachiptico — King William County on the Pamunkey River

Chawopo — Surry County at the mouth of Chipoak Creek

Cawwontoll — Richmond County on the north bank of the Rappahannock River

Checopissowo — Caroline County on the Rappahannock River above Tobacco Creek

Chesakawon — Lancaster County at the mouth of the Corotoman River

Chesapeake — Princess Anne County on a Lynnhaven River stream flowing north to the Chesapeake Bay

Chiconessex — Accomac County at Wiseville

Chincoteague — Accomac County at Chincoteague Inlet

Chiskiac — on the south side of the York River about ten miles below the fork of the Mattapony and Pamunkey Rivers

Cinquack — Northumberland County near Smiths Point on the Potomac River

Cinquoteck — King William County at the fork of the Mattapony and Pamunkey Rivers

Cuttatawomen — Lancaster County on the Rappahannock River at the Corotoman River and King George County on the Rappahannock River at Lamb Creek

Gangasco — Northampton County at Eastville

Kapawnich — Lancaster County on the north bank of the Rappahannock River at Corotoman River

Kerahocak — King George County on the north bank of the Rappahannock River

Kiequotank — Accomac County north of Metomkin Inlet

Kupkipcock — King William County on the Pamunkey River

Machapunga — Northampton County and on the Potomac River

Mamanahunt — Charles City County on the Chickahominy River

Mamanassy — King and Queen County at the fork of the Pamunkey and Mattapony Rivers

Mangoraca — Richmond County on the north bank of the Rappahannock River

Mantoughquemec — Nansemond County on the Nansemond River

Martoughquaunk — Caroline County on the Mattapony River

Massawoteck — King George County on the north bank of the Rappahannock River

Matchopick — Richmond County on the north bank of the Rappahannock River

Matchut — New Kent County on the Pamunkey River

Mathomauk — Isle of Wight County on the west bank of the James River

Matomkin — Accomac County at Metomkin Inlet

Mattacock — Gloucester County on the north bank of the York River

Mattacunt — King George County on the south side of the Potomac River

Mattanock — Nansemond County on the west side of the mouth of the Nansemond River

Maysonec — New Kent County on the north bank of the Chickahominy River

Menacupunt — King William County on the Pamunkey River

Menaskunt — Richmond County on the north bank of the Rappahannock River

Meyascosic — Charles City County on the north side of the James River

Mohominge — Richmond County near the falls of the James River

Mokete — Isle of Wight County on Warrasqueoc Creek

Moraughtacund — Richmond County near the mouth of the Moratico River

Mouanast — King George County on the north bank of the Rappahannock River

Mutchut — King and Queen County on the north bank of the Mattapony River

Muttamussinsack — Caroline County on the north bank of the Rappahannock River

Myghtuckpassu — King William County on the south bank of the Mattapony River

Namassingakent — Fairfax County on the south bank of the Potomac River

Nameroughquena — Alexandria County on the south bank of the Potomac River across from Washington

Nansemond — Nansemond County at Chuckatuck

Nantapoyac — Surry County on the south bank of the James River

Nantaughtacund — Essex County and Caroline County on the south side of the Rappahannock River

Nawacaten — Richmond County on the north bank of the Rappahannock River

Nawnautough — Richmond County on the north bank of the Rappahannock River

Nechanicok — Henrico County on the south bank of the Chickahominy River

Nepawtacum — Lancaster County on the north bank of the Rappahannock River

Onancock — Accomac County at Onancock

Onawmanient — Westmoreland County on Nominy Bay

Opiscopank — Middlesex County on the south bank of the Rappahannock River

Oquomock — Richmond County on the north bank of the Rappahannock River

Orapaks — New Kent County between the Chickahominy and Pamunkey Rivers

Ottachugh — Lancaster County on the north bank of the Rappahannock River

Ozatawomen — King George County on the south bank of the Potomac River

Ozenic — New Kent County on the Chickahominy River

Pamawauk — perhaps the Pamunkey

Pamuncoroy — New Kent County on the south bank of the Pamunkey River

Pamunkey — King William County at West Point

Papiscone — King George County on the north bank of the Rappahannock River

Pasaugtacock — King and Queen County on the north bank of the York River

Paspahegh — Charles City County on the south bank of the Chickahominy River and the north bank of the James River

Passaunkack — King William County on the south bank of the Mattapony River

Pastanza — Stafford County on the Potomac River at Aquia Creek

Pawcocomac — Lancaster County on the north bank of the Rappahannock River at the mouth of the Corotoman River

Peccarecamek — settlement on the southern Virginia border

Pemacocack — Prince William County on the west bank of the Potomac River about thirty miles below Alexandria

Piankatank — Middlesex County on the Piankatank River

Pissacoac — Westmoreland County on the north bank of the Rappahannock River at Leedstown

Poruptanck — Gloucester County on the north bank of the York River

Potaucac — New Kent County between the Chickahominy and Pamunkey Rivers

Potomac — Stafford County between the Potomac River and the Potomac Creek about fifty-five miles from the Chesapeake Bay

Powcomonet — Richmond County on the north bank of the Rappahannock River

Powhatan — Richmond city on the north bank of the James River at the falls

Poyektauk — Richmond County on the north bank of the Rappahannock River

Poykemkack — Richmond County on the north bank of the Rappahannock River

Pungoteque — Accomack County at Metomkin Inlet

Quackcohowaon — King William County on the south bank of the Mattapony River

Quioucohanock — Surry County on Upper Chipoak Creek at Wharf Bluff

Quiyough — Stafford County on the south bank of Aquia Creek at its mouth

Rappahannock — Richmond County on the Rappahannock River

Rickahake — Norfolk County

Righkahauk — New Kent County on the west bank of the Chickahominy River

Ritanoe — apparently Powhatan, Virginia, or North Carolina

Roscows — Elizabeth City County

Secacawoni — Northumberland County on the south bank of the Potomac River at the mouth of Coan Creek

Secobeck — Caroline County on the south bank of the Rappahannock River

Shamapa — on the Pamunkey River or the York River

Sockobeck — King George County on the north bank of the Rappahannock River

Tantucquask — Richmond County on the Rappahannock River

Tauxenent — Fairfax County on the Potomac River at Mount Vernon

Teracosick — Nansemond County on the west bank of the Nansemond River

Utenstank — Caroline County on the north bank of the Mattapony River

Uttamussac — King William County on the north bank of the Pamunkey River

Uttamussamacoma — Westmoreland County on the south bank of the Potomac River

Waconiask — King George County on the north bank of the Rappahannock River

Warrasqueoc — Isle of Wight County on the south bank of the James River at the mouth of Warrasqueoc Creek

Weanoc — Prince George County below the mouth of the Appomattox River at Weyanoke

Wecuppom — Richmond County on the north bank of the Rappahannock River

Werawahon — New Kent County on the north bank of the Chickahominy River

Werowacomoco — Gloucester County on the north bank of the York River at the mouth of Queen Creek

Wicocomoco — Northumberland County at the mouth of Wicomico River

Winsack — Richmond County on the north bank of the Rappahannock River

Appendix Four

List of Indian Words and Phrases

Captain John Smith included the following list of Algonquian-language words and phrases spoken by the Powhatan Indians in his A Map of Virginia. With a Description of the Countrey, The Commodities, People, Government and Religion *(London, 1612). It was not the most comprehensive list compiled—William Strachey collected more words than anyone at the time and included them in his* Historie of Travaile into Virginia Britannia *(London, 1612)—but Smith's list was circulated more widely. The language of the Powhatans did not survive English colonization.*

Because many doe desire to knowe the maner of their language, I have inserted these few words.

Ka ka torawincs yowo. What call you this.

Nemarough. a man.

Crenepo. a woman.

Marowanchesso. a boy.

Yehawkans. Houses.

Matchcores. Skins, or garments.

Mockasins. Shooes.

Tussan. Beds.

Pokatawer. Fire.

Attawp. A bowe.

Attonce. Arrowes.

Monacookes. Swords.

Aumoughhowgh. A Target.

Pawcussacks. Gunnes.

Tomahacks. Axes.

Tockahacks. Pickaxes.

Pamesacks. Knives.

Accowprets. Sheares.

Pawpecones. Pipes.

Mattassin. Copper.

Ussawassin. Iron, Brasse, Silver, or any white metal.

Musses. Woods.

Attasskuss. Leaves, weeds, or grasse.

Chepsin. Land.

Shacquohocan. A stone.

Wepenter. a cookold. [cuckold]

Suckahanna. Water.

Noughmass. Fish.

Copotone. Sturgion.

Weghshaughes. Flesh.

Sawwehone. Bloud.

Netoppew. Friends.

Marrapough. Enimies.

Maskapow. The worst of the enimies.

Mawchick chammay. The best of friends.

Casacunnakack, peya quagh acquintan uttasantasough. In how many daies will there come hether any more English ships?

Their Numbers.

Necut. 1.

Ningh. 2.

Nuss. 3.

Yowgh. 4.

Paranske. 5.

Comotinch. 6.

Toppawoss. 7.

Nusswash. 8.

Kekatawgh. 9.

Kaskeke. [10.]

They count no more but by tennes as followeth.

Case, how many.

Ninghsapooeksku. 20.

Nussapooeksku. 30.

Yowghapooeksku. 40.

Parankestassapooeksku. 50.

Comatinchtassapooeksku. 60.

Nussswashtassapooeksku. 80.

Toppawousstassapooeksku. 70.

Kekataughtassapooeksku. 90.

Necuttoughtysinough. 100.

Necuttweunquaough. 1000.

Rawcosowghs. Daies.

Keskowghes. Sunnes.

Toppquough. Nights.

Nepawweshowghs. Moones.

Pawpaxsoughes. Yeares.

Pummahumps Starres.

Osies. Heavens.

Okes. Gods.

Quiyoughcosucks. Pettie Gods, and their affinities.

Righcomoughes. Deaths.

Kekughes. Lives.

Mowchick woyawgh tawgh noeragh kaquere mecher. I am verie hungrie? What shall I eate?

Tawnor nehiegh Powhatan. where dwels Powwhatan.

Mache, nehiegh yowrowgh, orapaks. Now he dwels a great way hence at orapaks.

Uttapitchewayne anpechitchs nehawper werowacomoco. You lie, he staide ever at werowocomoco.

Kator nehiegh mattagh neer uttapitchewayne. Truely he is there I doe not lie.

Spaughtynere keragh werowance mawmarinough kekaten wawgh peyaquaugh. Run you then to the king mawmarynough and bid him come hither.

Utteke, e peya weyack wighwhip. Get you gone, and come againe quickly.

Kekaten pokahontas patiaquagh niugh tanks manotyens neer mowchick rawrenock audowgh. Bid Pokahontas bring hither two little Baskets, and I wil give her white beads to make her a chaine.

FINIS.

Appendix Five

Members of the First General Assembly

Thirty men made up the first General Assembly in America, which convened at Jamestown on 30 July 1619. Following are their names, and, if known, their fate.

Governor Sir George Yeardley, Governor (died in Virginia, 12 November 1627)

John Pory, Speaker (died in Lincolnshire, England, 1635)

Samuel Maycock, Councilor (killed in the Indian Massacre of 1622)

Nathaniel Powell, Councilor (killed with his wife in the Indian Massacre of 1622)

John Rolfe, Councilor (probably killed in the Indian Massacre of 1622)

Daniel Tucker, Councilor (died in Bermuda in February 1624)

William Wickham, Councilor (unknown)

Thomas Pierce, Sergeant at Arms (killed in the Indian Massacre of 1622)

John Twine, Clerk (unknown)

Burgesses

William Powell, James City (killed by Indians in 1623)

William Spence, James City (killed in the Indian Massacre of 1622)

Samuel Sharp, Charles City (unknown)

Samuel Jordan, Charles City (died 1623)

Thomas Dowse, Henricus (probably killed in the Indian Massacre of 1622)

John Polentine, Henricus (died c.1627)

William Tucker, Kecoughtan (apparently went to Ireland)

William Capp, Kecoughtan (unknown)

Thomas Davis, Martin's Brandon (unknown)

Robert Stacy, Martin's Brandon (unknown)

Thomas Graves, Smythe's Hundred (died during Assembly, 1 August 1619)

John Boys, Martin's Hundred (killed in the Indian Massacre of 1622)

John Jackson, Martin's Hundred (probably killed in the Indian Massacre of 1622)

Thomas Pawlett, Argall's Gift (unknown)

Edward Gourgainy, Argall's Gift (died c.1620)

Ensign Rossingham, Flowerdieu Hundred (unknown)

John Jefferson, Flowerdieu Hundred (apparently went to West Indies)

Christopher Lawne, Lawne's Plantation (died in Charles City, November 1620)

Ensign Washer, Lawne's Plantation (unknown)

Captain Ward, Ward's Plantation (unknown)

Lieutenant Gibbs, Ward's Plantation (unknown)

Appendix Six

Virginia's Chief Executives, 1607–1699

Virginia's seventeenth-century governors and lieutenant-governors held commissions issued by either the Virginia Company or the Crown, whereas acting or deputy-governors served at the pleasure of a governor or lieutenant-governor, usually to act in his stead. When the official chief executive was absent from Jamestown, the president of the Council of State acted as governor. During the Interregnum, the House of Burgesses elected the governors. The following list is adapted from W. W. Abbot, A Virginia Chronology, 1585–1783 *(Williamsburg, Virginia, 1957).*

Presidents of the Council in Virginia

Edward-Maria Wingfield, 1607

John Ratcliffe, 1607–1608

Captain John Smith, 1608–1609

George Percy, 1609–1610

Virginia Company Governors

Thomas West, Third Lord De La Warr, 1610–1618

Sir Thomas Gates (lieutenant-governor), 1610

George Percy (deputy-governor), 1611

Sir Thomas Dale (deputy-governor), 1611

Sir Thomas Gates (lieutenant-governor), 1611–1614

Sir Thomas Dale (deputy-governor), 1614–1616

George Yeardley (deputy-governor), 1616–1617

Samuel Argall (acting governor), 1617–1619
Nathaniel Powell (deputy-governor), 1619
Sir George Yeardley, 1619–1621
Sir Francis Wyatt, 1621–1625

Royal Governors

Sir Francis Wyatt, 1625–1626
Sir George Yeardley, 1626–1627
Francis West (council president), 1627–1629
Dr. John Pott (council president), 1629–1630
Sir John Harvey, 1630–1635
John West (council president), 1635–1637
Sir John Harvey, 1637–1639
Sir Francis Wyatt, 1639–1642
Sir William Berkeley, 1642–1652
Richard Kemp (deputy-governor), 1644–1645

Commonwealth Governors

Richard Bennett, 1652–1655
Edward Digges, 1655–1656
Samuel Mathews, II, 1656–1660
Sir William Berkeley, 1660

Royal Governors

Sir William Berkeley, 1660–1677
Francis Moryson (deputy-governor), 1661–1662
Sir Henry Chicheley (deputy-governor), 1674–1682
Sir Herbert Jeffreys, 1677–1678
Thomas, Lord Culpeper, Second Baron of Thoresway, 1677–1683
Nicholas Spencer (deputy-governor), 1683–1684
Francis, Lord Howard, Fifth Baron of Effingham, 1683–1692
Nathaniel Bacon, Sr. (deputy-governor), 1684–1690
Francis Nicholson (lieutenant-governor), 1690–1692
Sir Edmund Andros, 1692–1698
Ralph Wormeley, II (deputy-governor), 1693
Francis Nicholson, 1698–1705

Bibliography

W. W. Abbott. 1957. *A Virginia Chronology, 1585–1783.* Williamsburg, VA: 350th Anniversary Celebration Corp.

Charles M. Andrews, ed. 1915. *Narratives of the Insurrections, 1675–1690.* New York: Charles Scribner's Sons.

"APVA Preservation Virginia Fact Sheet." 2003. Richmond, VA: Association for the Preservation of Virginia Antiquities.

Edward Arber, ed. 1910. *Travels and Works of Captain John Smith* (parts 1, 2). Edinburgh, Scotland: J. Grant.

James Axtell. 1995. *The Rise and Fall of the Powhatan Empire: Indians in Seventeenth-Century Virginia.* Williamsburg, VA: Colonial Williamsburg Foundation.

Philip L. Barbour. 1962. "Captain George Kendall, Mutineer or Intelligencer?" (*Virginia Magazine of History and Biography,* vol. 70).

——. 1964. "The Identity of the First Poles in America" (*William and Mary Quarterly,* vol. 21).

——. 1964. *The Three Worlds of Captain John Smith.* Boston: Houghton Mifflin.

——. 1969. *The Jamestown Voyages Under the First Charter: 1606–1609* (vol. 1). Cambridge, England: Cambridge University Press.

——. 1969. *Pocahontas and her World.* Boston: Houghton Mifflin.

——, ed. 1986. *The Complete Works of Captain John Smith (1580–1631).* 4 vols. Chapel Hill and London: University of North Carolina Press.

Michael R. Bauer. 2001. "Collaborative Environmental Decisionmaking: A Power Sharing Process that Achieves Results through Dialogue" (Ph.D. thesis). Blacksburg: Virginia Polytechnic Institute and State University

William Berkeley. 1663. *A Discourse and View of Virginia.* London.

Robert Beverley. 1705. *The History and Present State of Virginia.* London.

——. 1855. *The History of Virginia, in Four Parts.* Richmond, VA.

Warren M. Billings. 1991. "The Law of Servants and Slaves in Seventeenth-Century Virginia" (*Virginia Magazine of History and Biography,* vol. 99).

——. 1994. "Imagining Green Spring House" (*Virginia Cavalcade,* vol. 44).

——. 2004. *A Little Parliament: The Virginia General Assembly in the Seventeenth Century.* Richmond: Library of Virginia.

——. 2004. *Sir William Berkeley and the Forging of Colonial Virginia.* Baton Rouge: Louisiana State University Press.

Jeffrey P. Brain. 1998. "Fort St. George on the Kennebec" (*Bermuda Journal of Archaeology and Maritime History,* vol. 10).

——. 2003. "The Popham Colony: An Historical and Archaeological Brief" (*Maine Archaeological Society Bulletin,* vol. 43).

T. H. Breen. 1973. "A Changing Labor Force and Race Relations in Virginia, 1660–1710" (*Journal of Social History,* vol. 7).

Rick Britton. 1999. "The Lost Culture of the Monacans: People of the River Banks" (*Albemarle,* vol. 11).

Alexander Brown. 1890. *The Genesis of the United States.* 2 vols. Boston: Houghton Mifflin.

——. 1898. *The First Republic in America.* Boston: Houghton Mifflin.

Philip Alexander Bruce. 1896. *Economic History of Virginia in the Seventeenth Century: An Inquiry into the Material Condition of the People, Based on Original and Contemporaneous Records.* New York: Macmillan.

Henry S. Burrage, ed. 1932. *Early English and French Voyages: Chiefly from Hakluyt: 1534–1608.* New York: Charles Scribner's Sons.

David I. Bushnell, Jr. 1930. *The Five Monacan Towns in Virginia, 1607.* Washington, DC: Smithsonian Institution.

——. 1935. *The Manahoac Tribes in Virginia, 1608.* Washington, DC: Smithsonian Institution.

Jane Carson. 1951. "Sir William Berkeley, Governor of Virginia: A Study in Colonial Policy" (Ph.D. thesis). Charlottesville: University of Virginia.

Louis R. Caywood. 1957. "Green Spring Plantation" (*Virginia Magazine of History and Biography,* vol. 65).

E. Clowes Chorley. 1930. "The Planting of the Church in Virginia" (*William and Mary Quarterly,* 2d ser., vol. 10).

John Herbert Claiborne. 1917. *William Claiborne of Virginia, with Some Account of His Pedigree.* New York and London: G. P. Putnam's Sons.

Samuel R. Cook. 2000. *Monacans and Miners: Native American and Coal Mining Communities in Appalachia.* Lincoln: University of Nebraska Press.

Wesley Frank Craven. 1957. *The Virginia Company of London, 1606–1624.* Charlottesville: University Press of Virginia.

——. 1971. *White, Red, and Black: The Seventeenth-Century Virginian.* Charlottesville: University Press of Virginia.

S. G. Culliford. 1965. *William Strachey, 1572–1621.* Charlottesville: University Press of Virginia.

Donald A. D'Amato. 1992. *Warwick's 350-Year Heritage: A Pictorial History.* Virginia Beach, VA: Donning.

Richard Beale Davis. 1955. *George Sandys: Poet-Adventurer: A Study in Anglo-American Culture in the Seventeenth Century.* New York and London: Columbia University Press.

Charles Deane, ed. 1860. *"A Discourse of Virginia," by Edward-Maria Wingfield . . . now First Printed from the Original Manuscripts in the Lambeth Library.* Boston: J. Wilson and Son.

Jesse Dimmick. 1929. "Green Spring" (*William and Mary Quarterly,* 2d ser., vol. 9).

Elizabeth River Project's Watershed Action Team and Stakeholder Review Team. 2002. *Elizabeth River Restoration and Conservation: A Watershed Action Plan,* rev. 2nd ed. Portsmouth, VA: Elizabeth River Project.

James Ellison. 2002. *George Sandys: Travel, Colonialism and Tolerance in the Seventeenth Century.* Woodbridge, Suffolk, UK, and Rochester, NY: Boydell and Brewer.

James Taylor Ellyson. 1908. *The London Company of Virginia: A Brief Account of its Transactions in Colonizing Virginia with Photogravures of the More Prominent Leaders. . . .* New York and London: De Vinne Press.

Joseph Ewan and Nesta Ewan. 1970. *John Banister and his Natural History of Virginia, 1678–1696.* Urbana: Illinois University Press.

Michael J. Focazio and Robert E. Cooper. 1995. *Selected Characteristics of Stormflow and Base Flow Affected by Land Use and Cover in the Chickahominy River Basin, Virginia, 1989–91.* Richmond, VA: U.S. Department of the Interior, U.S. Geological Survey.

Lucian F. Fosdick. 1906. *The French Blood in America.* New York: F. H. Revell.

A. J. Foster. 1965. *Early James River History in and Around Hopewell, Virginia.* Falls Church, VA: Falcon.

Martin D. Gallivan. 2003. *James River Chiefdoms: The Rise of Social Inequality in the Chesapeake.* Lincoln and London: University of Nebraska Press.

Eric Gethyn-Jones. 1982. *George Thorpe and the Berkeley Company: A Gloucestershire Enterprise in Virginia.* Gloucester, England: Alan Sutton Publishing.

Frederic W. Gleach. 1997. *Powhatan's World and Colonial Virginia: A Conflict of Cultures.* Lincoln and London: University of Nebraska Press.

Michael Golay and John S. Bowman. 2003. *North American Exploration.* Hoboken, NJ: John Wiley.

Warner F. Gookin and Philip L. Barbour. 1963. *Bartholomew Gosnold: Discoverer and Planter, New England—1602, Virginia—1607.* Hamden, CT, and London: Archon Books.

Gary C. Grassl. 1997. *First Germans at Jamestown.* Washington, DC: German Heritage Society of Greater Washington.

Edward Wright Haile, ed. 2001. *Jamestown Narratives: Eyewitness Accounts of the Virginia Colony: The First Decade: 1607–1617.* Champlain, VA: Round House.

Nathaniel C. Hale. 1951. *Virginia Venturer: A Historical Biography of William Claiborne, 1600–1677.* Richmond, VA: Dietz Press.

——. 1959. *Pelts and Palisades: The Story of Fur and the Rivalry for Pelts in Early America.* Richmond, VA: Dietz Press.

Paul E. J. Hammer. 1998. "A Welshman Abroad: Captain Peter Wynn of Jamestown." (*Parergon: Journal of the Australian and New Zealand Association for Medieval and Early Modern Studies,* vol. 16, July).

Ralph Hamor. 1615. *A True Discourse of the Present State of Virginia.* London.

Oscar Handlin and Mary F. Handlin. 1950. "Origins of the Southern Labor System" (*William and Mary Quarterly,* 3d series, vol 7).

Jeffrey L. Hantman. 1990. "Between Powhatan and Quirank: Reconstructing Monacan Culture and History in the Context of Jamestown" (*American Anthropologist,* vol. 92).

Jean Carl Harrington. 1952. *Glassmaking at Jamestown, America's First Industry.* Richmond, VA: Dietz Press.

Malcolm H. Harris. 1977. *Old New Kent County: Some Account of the Planters, Plantations, and Places in King William County, St. John's Parish.* West Point, VA: M. H. Harris.

Fairfax Harrison. 1926. *The Proprietors of the Northern Neck: Chapters of Culpeper Genealogy.* Richmond, VA: Old Dominion Press.

Charles E. Hatch, Jr. 1941. "Glassmaking in Virginia, 1607–1625" (*William and Mary Quarterly,* 2d ser., vol. 21).

——. 1952. *Jamestown, Virginia: The Town Site and Its Story.* Washington, DC: National Park Service.

——. 1957. "Archer's Hope and the Glebe" (*Virginia Magazine of History and Biography,* vol. 65).

——. 1995. *The First Seventeen Years: Virginia, 1607–1624.* Charlottesville: University Press of Virginia.

Charles E. Hatch, Jr., and Thurlow Gates Gregory. 1962. "The First American Blast Furnace, 1619–1622: The Birth of a Mighty Industry on Falling Creek in Virginia" (*Virginia Magazine of History and Biography,* vol. 70).

Jonathan Haynes. 1986. *The Humanist as Traveler: George Sandys's Relation of a Journey begun An. Dom. 1610.* Cranbury, NJ, and London: Associated University Presses, for Fairleigh Dickinson University Press.

Burton J. Hendrick. 1935. *The Lees of Virginia: Biography of a Family.* Boston: Little, Brown.

William Waller Hening. 1823. *The Statutes at Large, being a Collection of All the Laws of Virginia from the First Session of the Legislature, in the Year 1619* (vols. 1–2). New York: R. & W. & G. Bartow.

——. 1823. *The Statutes at Large, being a Collection of All the Laws of Virginia from the First Session of the Legislature, in the Year 1619* (vol. 3). Philadelphia: Thomas Desilver.

Richard Hooker. 1593–1604. *Of the Lawes of the Ecclesiasticall Politie.* London: John Windet.

James Horn. 2005. *A Land as God Made It: Jamestown and the Birth of America.* New York: Basic Books.

J. Paul Hudson. 1962. *Glassmaking at Jamestown, 1608–09 and 1621–24: One of the First English Industries in the New World.* Jamestown, VA: Jamestown Foundation.

——. 1970. *Jamestown Church.* Jamestown, VA: Jamestown Foundation.

——. 1970. *Plantation, Refuge, Prison, Statehouse: This Was Green Spring.* Jamestown, VA: Jamestown Foundation.

James I. 1604. *A Counter-Blaste to Tobacco.* London.

Jamestown-Yorktown Foundation. c.1985. *Sailing into History: The Story of the Godspeed.* Williamsburg, VA: Jamestown-Yorktown Foundation.

Thomas Jefferson. 1787. *Notes on the State of Virginia.* London.

Robert C. Johnson, ed. 1963. "The Indian Massacre of 1622: Some Correspondence of the Reverend Joseph Mead" (*Virginia Magazine of History and Biography,* vol. 71).

William M. Kelso. 1984. *Kingsmill Plantations: Archaeology of Country Life in Colonial Virginia.* San Diego, CA: Academic Press.

——. 1997. *Archaeology at Monticello: Artifacts of Everyday Life in the Plantation Community.* Charlottesville, VA: University Press of Virginia.

William M. Kelso et al. 1995–2001. *Jamestown Rediscovery.* 7 vols. Richmond, VA: Association for the Preservation of Virginia Antiquities.

William M. Kelso with Beverly Straube. 2004. *Jamestown Rediscovery, 1994–2004.* Richmond, VA: Association for the Preservation of Virginia Antiquities.

Susan Myra Kingsbury, ed. 1933, 1935. *The Records of The Virginia Company of London* (vols. 3, 4). Washington, DC: Government Printing Office.

Karen Ordahl Kupperman. 1984. *Roanoke: The Abandoned Colony.* Totowa, NJ: Rowman & Littlefield.

——, ed. 1988. *Captain John Smith: A Select Edition of His Writings.* Chapel Hill and London: University of North Carolina Press.

——. 2000. *Indians & English: Facing Off in Early America.* Ithaca, NY: Cornell University Press.

Robert Hunt Land. 1938. "Henrico and Its College" (*William and Mary Quarterly,* 2d ser., vol. 18).

Johannes Leo. 1600. Reprint, 1969. *A Geographical Historie of Africa, Written in Arabicke and Italian.* Amsterdam and New York: Theatrum Orbis Terrarum and Da Capo Press.

David W. Lewes, et al. 2003. *Windows into the Past: Archaeological Assessment of Three City Point Lots, City of Hopewell, Virginia.* Williamsburg, VA: William and Mary Center for Archaeological Research.

Clifford M. Lewis and Albert J. Loomie. 1953. *The Spanish Jesuit Mission in Virginia: 1570–1572.* Chapel Hill: University of North Carolina Press for the Virginia Historical Society.

Nicholas M. Lucketti, Mary Ellen N. Hodges, and Charles T. Hodges, eds. 1994. *Paspahegh Archaeology: Data Recovery Investigations of Site 44JC308 at the Governor's Land at Two Rivers, James City County, Virginia.* Williamsburg, VA: Colonial Williamsburg Foundation.

R. H. Major, ed. 1849. *The Historie of Travaile into Virginia Britannia; Expressing the Cosmographie and Comodities of the Country, Together with the Manners and Customes of the People. Gathered and Observed as Well by Those Who Went First Thither as Collected by William Strachey, Gent., the first Secretary of the Colony.* London: Hakluyt Society.

Seth W. Mallios. 1999. *Archaeological Excavations at 44JC568, The Reverend Richard Buck Site.* Richmond, VA: Association for the Preservation of Virginia Antiquities.

——. 2000. *At the Edge of the Precipice: Frontier Ventures, Jamestown's Hinterland, and the Archaeology of 44JC802.* Richmond, VA: Association for the Preservation of Virginia Antiquities.

Pierre Marambaud. 1973. "William Byrd I: A Young Virginia Planter in the 1670's" (*Virginia Magazine of History and Biography,* vol. 81).

Lee Miller. 2002. *Roanoke: Solving the Mystery of the Lost Colony.* New York: Penguin Books.

Mary R. Miller. 1983. *Place-Names of the Northern Neck of Virginia: From John Smith's 1606 Map to the Present.* Richmond: Virginia State Library.

Sally Mills. 1997. *The York River Watershed Fact Sheet.* Waterton, VA: Friends of the York River.

Giles Milton. 2000. *Big Chief Elizabeth: How England's Adventurers Gambled and Won the New World.* London: Hodder and Stoughton.

John W. Moore. 1879. *School History of North Carolina, from 1584 to the Present Time.* Raleigh, NC: Alfred Williams.

Edmund S. Morgan. 1975. *American Slavery, American Freedom: The Ordeal of Colonial Virginia.* New York: W. W. Norton.

Philip D. Morgan. 1998. *Slave Counterpoint: Black Culture in the Eighteenth-Century Chesapeake and Lowcountry.* Chapel Hill: University of North Carolina Press for the Omohundro Institute of Early American History and Culture.

Samuel Eliot Morison. 1971. *The European Discovery of America: The Northern Voyages A.D. 500–1600.* New York: Oxford University Press.

Paul C. Nagel. 1990. *The Lees of Virginia: Seven Generations of an American Family.* New York and Oxford, England: Oxford University Press.

Edward D. Neill. 1869. *History of the Virginia Company of London, with Letters to and from the First Colony Never Before Printed.* Albany, NY: Joel Munsell.

——. 1871. *The English Colonization of America: During the Seventeenth Century.* London: Strahan.

Ivor Noël Hume. 1982. *Martin's Hundred.* New York: Alfred A. Knopf.

——. 1994. *The Virginia Adventure: Roanoke to James Towne: An Archaeological and Historical Odyssey.* New York: Alfred A. Knopf.

Ivor Noël Hume and Audrey Noël Hume. 2001. *The Archaeology of Martin's Hundred.* 2 vols. Philadelphia and Williamsburg, VA: University of Pennsylvania Museum of Archaeology and Anthropology.

Milan Novak, Martyn E. Obbard, James G. Jones, Robert Newman, Annie Booth, Andrew J. Satterthwaite, and Greg Linscombe. 1987. *Furbearer Harvests in North America, 1600–1984.* Ontario, Canada: Ministry of Natural Resources.

Herbert L. Osgood. 1904. *The American Colonies in the Seventeenth Century* (vol. 3). New York: Columbia University Press.

George Percy. 1922. "'A Trewe Relacyon'—Virginia from 1609 to 1612" *(Tyler's Quarterly Historical and Genealogical Magazine,* vol. 4).

John Pory. 1915. *A Report of the Manner of Proceeding in the General Assembly Convented at James Citty in Virginia, July 30, 1619.* (H. R. McIlwaine, ed., *Journals of the House of Burgesses of Virginia, 1619–1658/59.* vol. 6.) Richmond: Virginia State Library.

David A. Price. 2003. *Love and Hate in Jamestown: John Smith, Pocahontas, and the Heart of a New Nation.* New York: Alfred A. Knopf.

William S. Powell. 1977. *John Pory, 1572–1636: The Life and Letters of a Man of Many Parts.* Chapel Hill: University of North Carolina Press.

Stevan C. Pullins and Dennis B. Blanton. 2000. "Prehistoric Settlement on Jamestown Island: Archaeological Data Recovery at Site 44JC895 on Black Point, Jamestown Island, James City County, Virginia." Yorktown, VA: National Park Service.

David Beers Quinn, ed. 1967. *Observations Gathered Out of "A discourse on the Plantation of the Southern Colony in Virginia by the English, 1606," Written by that Honorable Gentleman, Master George Percy.* Charlottesville: University Press of Virginia.

——. 1971. *North American Discovery: Circa 1000–1612.* Columbia: University of South Carolina Press.

——. 1974. *England and the Discovery of America, 1481–1620.* New York: Alfred A. Knopf.

——. 1977. *North America from Earliest Discovery to First Settlements: The Norse Voyages to 1612.* New York: Harper & Row.

——, ed. 1979. *New American World: A Documentary History of North America to 1612* (vol. 2). New York: Arno Press and Hector Bye.

——. 1985. *Set Faire for Roanoke: Voyages and Colonies, 1584–1606.* Chapel Hill and London: University of North Carolina Press.

R. I. 1612. *The New Life of Virginea: Declaring the Former Success and Present Estate of that Plantation. Being the Second Part of Nova Britannia.* London.

Theodore K. Rabb. 1998. *Jacobean Gentleman: Sir Edwin Sandys, 1561–1629.* Princeton, NJ: Princeton University Press.

Theodore R. Reinhart, ed. 1984. *The Archaeology of Shirley Plantation.* Charlottesville, VA: University Press of Virginia.

Edward M. Riley and Charles E. Hatch, Jr., eds. 1946. *James Towne In the Words of Contemporaries.* Washington, DC: National Park Service.

Norma Elizabeth Roberts and Bruce Roberts. 2001. *Cape Henry: First Landing, First United States Lighthouse.* Morehead City, NC: Outer Banks Lighthouse Society.

Helen C. Rountree. 1989. *The Powhatan Indians of Virginia: Their Traditional Culture.* Norman and London: University of Oklahoma Press.

——. 1990. *Pocahontas's People: The Powhatan Indians of Virginia Through Four Centuries.* Norman: University of Oklahoma Press.

——. 1993. *Powhatan Foreign Relations: 1500–1722.* Charlottesville: University Press of Virginia.

——. 2005. *Pocahontas, Powhatan, Opechancanough: Three Indian Lives Changed by Jamestown.* Charlottesville: University Press of Virginia.

Conway Whittle Sams. 1929. *The Conquest of Virginia: The Second Attempt: An Account, Based on Original Documents, of the Attempt, Under the King's Form of Government, to Found Virginia at Jamestown, 1606–1610.* Norfolk, VA: Keyser-Doherty.

Sir Edwin Sandys. 1605. *A Relation of the State of Religion, and With What Hopes and Pollicies it Hath Beene Framed, and is Maintained in the Severall States of These Westerne Partes of the World.* London: Printed by Val. Sims for Simon Waterson.

——. 1615. *Sacred Hymns, Consisting of Fifti Select Psalms of David and Others, Paraphrastically Turned into English Verse.* London: Thomas Snodham, by the assignment of the Company of Stationers.

D. Dewey Scarboro. 2005. *The Establisher: The Story of Sir Thomas Dale.* Fayetteville, NC: Old Mountain Press.

Arthur M. Schlesinger, Jr., ed. 1993. *The Almanac of American History.* New York: Charles Scribner's Sons.

E. Thomson Shields, Jr., and Charles R. Ewen, eds. 2003. *Searching for the Roanoke Colonies: An Interdisciplinary Collection.* Raleigh: North Carolina Office of Archives and History.

Captain John Smith. 1608. *A True Relation of Such Occurrences and Accidents of Noate as Hath Hapned in Virginia Since the First Planting of that Colony, which is now Resident in the South Part Thereof, till the Last Returne from Thence.* London: Printed by Edward Alde for John Tappe, and are to bee solde at the Greyhound in Paules-Church-yard, by W. W.

——. 1612. *A Map of Virginia. With a Description of the Countrey, The Commodieis, People, Government and Religion.* London: S.I.

——. 1630. *The True Travels, Adventures and Observations of Captain John Smith in Europe, Asia, Africa and America.* 2 vols. London: John Haviland for Thomas Slater.

——. 1907. *The Generall Historie of Virginia, New England & The Summer Isles Together with The True Travels, Adventures and Observations, and A Sea Grammar.* 2 vols. Glasgow, Scotland: MacLehose and Sons.

Frank G. Speck. 1926. *The Rappahannock Indians of Virginia.* New York: Charles Scribner's Sons.

Mary Newton Standard. 1907. *The Story of Bacon's Rebellion.* New York: Neale.

Mary A. Stephenson. 1964. *Carter's Grove Plantation: A History.* Williamsburg, VA: Colonial Williamsburg Foundation.

David Stick. 1983. *Roanoke Island: The Beginnings of English America.* Chapel Hill: University of North Carolina Press.

William Strachey. 1953. *The Historie of Travell into Virginia Britania (1612)* (Louis B. Wright and Virginia Freund, eds.) London: Hakluyt Society.

John R. Swanton. 1952. *The Indian Tribes of North America.* Washington, DC: Government Printing Office.

William Talbot, trans. 1672. *The Discoveries of John Lederer, In Three Several Marches from Virginia, to the West of Carolina, And Other Parts of the Continent: Begun in March 1669, and Ended in September 1670. Together with A General Map of the Whole Territory which He Traversed.* London: J.C. for Samuel Heyrick.

Marion Tinling, ed. 1977. *The Correspondence of The Three William Byrds of Westover, Virginia, 1684–1776* (vol. 1). Charlottesville: University Press of Virginia.

Lyon Gardiner Tyler. 1904. *England in America, 1580–1652.* New York: Harper and Brothers.

——. 1906. *The Cradle of the Republic: Jamestown and James River.* Richmond, VA: Hermitage Press.

——, ed. 1907. *Narratives of Early Virginia: 1606–1625.* New York: Charles Scribner's Sons.

U.S. Environmental Protection Agency, Chesapeake Bay Program. 2001. *Virginia's Tributary Strategies: A Customized Approach to Reduce Nutrient Pollution in the Rivers Flowing into the Chesapeake Bay, The York River.* Richmond: Virginia Department of Environmental Quality.

U.S. Senate, 109th Congress. 2005. *Thomasina E. Jordan Indian Tribes of Virginia Federal Recognition Act of 2005.* Washington, DC: Government Printing Office.

William J. Van Schreeven and George H. Reese, eds. 1969. *Proceedings of the General Assembly of Virginia, July 30–August 4, 1619. Written & Sent from Virginia to England by Mr. John Pory.* Jamestown, VA: Jamestown Foundation.

Alden T. Vaughn. 1972. "Blacks in Virginia: A Note on the First Decade" (*William and Mary Quarterly,* 3d series, vol. 29).

——. 1975. *American Genesis: Captain John Smith and the Founding of Virginia.* Boston: Little, Brown.

George Southall Vest. 1947. "William Claiborne" (M.A. thesis). Charlottesville: University of Virginia.

Willard Mosher Wallace. 1940. "Sir Edwin Sandys and the First Parliament of James I" (Ph.D. thesis). Philadelphia: University of Pennsylvania.

Lorena S. Walsh. 1989. "Plantation Management in the Chesapeake, 1620–1820" (*Journal of Economic History*, vol 49).

Charles Dudley Warner. 1881. *Captain John Smith.* New York: Henry Holt.

Wilcomb E. Washburn. 1957. *The Governor and the Rebel.* Chapel Hill: University of North Carolina Press for the Institute of Early American Culture.

Sandra F. Waugaman and Danielle Moretti-Langholtz. 2000. *We're Still Here: Contemporary Virginia Indians Tell Their Stories.* Richmond, VA: Palari.

Thomas Jefferson Wertenbaker. 1914. *Virginia Under the Stuarts: 1607–1688.* Princeton, NJ: Princeton University Press.

C. A. Weslager. 1959. *The Accomac and Accohannock Indians from Early Relations.* Onancock, VA: Eastern Shore of Virginia Historical Society.

Susan Westbury. 1985. "Slaves of Colonial Virginia: Where They Came From" (*William and Mary Quarterly*, 3d series, vol. 42).

———. 2004. "Theatre and Power in Bacon's Rebellion: Virginia, 1676–77." (*The Seventeenth Century*, vol. 19).

John C. Wilson. 1984, 2003. *Virginia's Northern Neck: A Pictorial History.* Virginia Beach, VA: Donning.

Jocelyn R. Wingfield. 1993. *Virginia's True Founder: Edward-Maria Wingfield and His Times, 1550–c.1614.* Athens, GA: Wingfield Family Society.

Karenne Wood and Diane Shields. 1999. *The Monacan Indians: Our Story.* Madison Heights, VA: Office of Historical Research, Monacan Indian Nation.

Grace Steele Woodward. 1969. *Pocahontas.* Norman: University of Oklahoma Press.

Samuel H. Yonge. 1904. *The Site of Old "James Towne" 1607–1698.* Richmond, VA: Hermitage Press.

Index

Note: Page locators in boldface type refer to main encyclopedia entries; page locators in italics reference sidebars in the text.

About the Authors

Frank E. Grizzard, Jr. is director of the Lee Family Digital Archive, an online repository of the collected papers of the historic Lee Family of Virginia located at Washington and Lee University in Lexington, Virginia. His published works include ABC-CLIO's *George Washington: A Biographical Companion.*

D. Boyd Smith was born and grew up in the Jamestown, Virginia area and has spent most of his career in the information technology field. He works as an archaeologist on both prehistoric and historic sites in Virginia, including the Jamestown Colony site.